The Book Named The Governor V1

Thomas Elyot

In the interest of creating a more extensive selection of rare historical book reprints, we have chosen to reproduce this title even though it may possibly have occasional imperfections such as missing and blurred pages, missing text, poor pictures, markings, dark backgrounds and other reproduction issues beyond our control. Because this work is culturally important, we have made it available as a part of our commitment to protecting, preserving and promoting the world's literature. Thank you for your understanding.

THE BOKE
NAMED THE GOUERNOUR

DEUISED BY SIR THOMAS ELYOT, KNIGHT

EDITED FROM THE FIRST EDITION OF 1531

BY

HENRY HERBERT STEPHEN CROFT, M.A.

BARRISTER-AT-LAW

With Portraits of Sir Thomas and Lady Elyot

Copied by permission of Her Majesty from Holbein's Original Drawings at Windsor Castle

IN TWO VOLUMES

VOL. I.

LONDON
C. KEGAN PAUL & CO., 1 PATERNOSTER SQUARE
1880

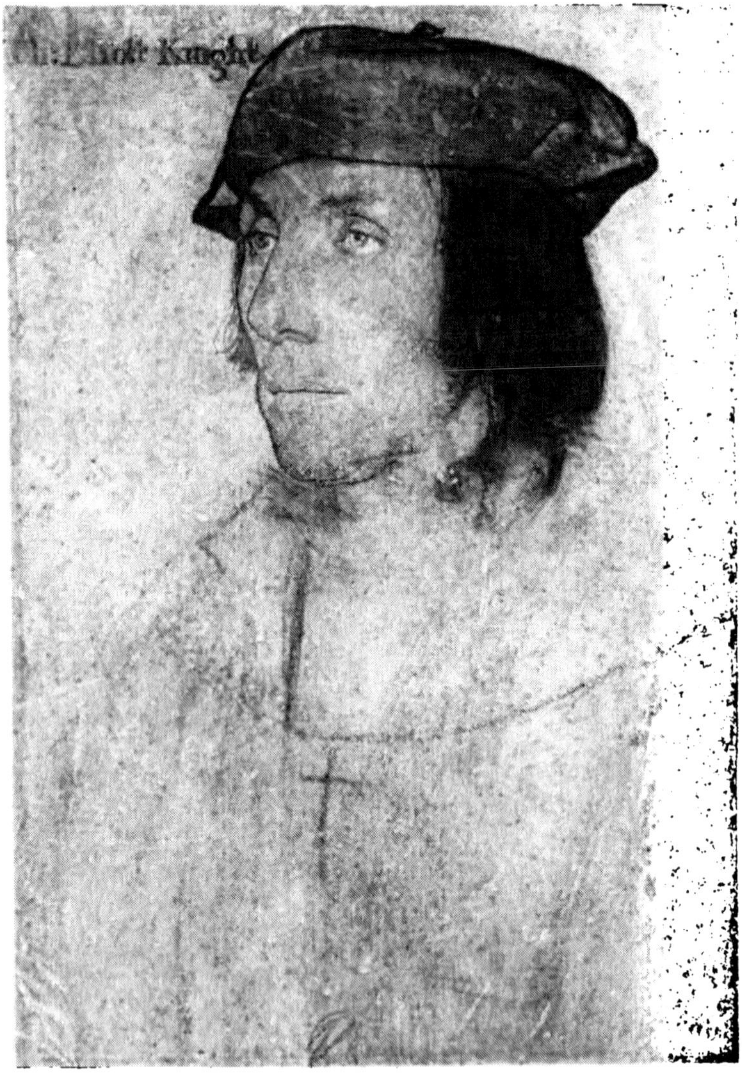

Knight

THE EDITOR'S PREFACE.

MANY readers will be surprised to learn that the present is in reality the tenth edition of a once popular book. This undoubted fact must, however, be qualified by the admission that no complete reproduction of the original text of 1531 has ever appeared before. It will be seen presently that several passages were expunged in the subsequent editions of the sixteenth century some of which were probably not in harmony with the religious views prevailing at the respective periods of publication. These suppressed passages will be easily detected in the present edition, being either pointed out by a footnote or placed within brackets; the latter device, which seemed preferable, having been uniformly adopted throughout the second volume in which the omissions are more frequent.

The Governour does not appear to have been reprinted either in the seventeenth or the eighteenth century. In 1834, however, a new edition, professing to be based upon one of 1564 (though it seems doubtful whether this date should not be 1546), was published by Mr. Arthur Turberville Eliot, Scholar of Catherine Hall, Cambridge. Of this work, for which the editor had prudently solicited subscriptions beforehand (to judge from a list containing more than ninety names printed at the end of the volume), perhaps the less said the better. But Mr. Eliot's claim to 'have bestowed both considerable labour and attention upon this new edition,' invites criticism from one who desires that justice should be done to his author. After premising that he has 'adhered as closely as possible to the original text, occasionally "mutatis mutandis, exceptis excipiendis,"' Mr. Eliot informs his readers that he does not hold himself 'responsible either for the apparent quaintness or obscurity of style in *The Governour*,' and that where he 'could in any degree with propriety simplify the composition of the original work,' he has 'never failed to do so.'

It is easy to predict the kind of work which would be likely to be produced under such circumstances and by an editor who regarded his duty in such a light, and when we compare Mr. Eliot's 'emendations' with the text of his author, the result seems hardly satisfactory. In the following instances, taken at random, it cannot be said that Mr. Eliot's design 'to simplify the composition of the original,' has been skilfully executed. For 'abrayded' (Vol. II. p. 72) Mr. Eliot prefers to read 'prayed,' for 'adumbrations' (Vol. II. p. 403) 'adjurations,' for 'prease' (Vol. II. p. 48) 'praise,' for 'bayne' (Vol. II. p. 282) 'vain,' for 'craftes man' (Vol. II. p.

320) 'crafts of men,' for 'embrayde' (Vol. II. p. 421) 'embraced,' for 'verbe' (Vol. II. p. 385) 'herb;' whilst he converts 'singular aduaile' (Vol. II. p. 99) into 'individual advantage,' 'taken with the maynure' (Vol. II. p. 75) into 'seized with the mania,' and 'shaking his here' (Vol. I. p. 47) into 'slacking his ear;' on the other hand 'timorous royle' (Vol. I. p. 178) should be read according to Mr. Eliot 'timorous rule,' 'sely bestis' (Vol. II. p. 5) 'self beasts;' in the same chapter 'fame' is altered into 'same,' 'comelynesse of nobilitie' (Vol. II. p. 43) into 'comeliness of no utility, 'nobles' (Vol. II. p. 36) into 'metals,' and 'jurates' (Vol. II. p. 256) into 'curates.' The enumeration of similar errors might be prolonged much further, were it not for the fear of wearying the reader who will probably be of opinion that sufficient evidence has already been adduced of the want of taste, not to employ a harsher term, exhibited by Mr. Eliot.

Nor can this gentleman be said to have performed what may be called the more mechanical part of his editorial duty, with the accuracy which we have a right to expect from one who boasts of having 'bestowed both time and labour' upon it. Long paragraphs, in some cases extending to whole chapters, of the original text are frequently omitted, the absence of which though occasionally denoted by the suggestive phrase 'hiatus valde deflendus,' can generally be discovered only by comparison with the black letter edition; nor is this loss compensated by any elucidation of the many obscure

THE EDITOR'S PREFACE.

allusions in the text, or by any new information furnished to us with regard to the author's history. Mr. Eliot indeed claims to 'have enriched the whole with various and instructive notes' which he trusts 'will be deemed both valuable and important.' But we look in vain, in Mr. Eliot's edition, for a single footnote; though the numerous quotations and obsolete phrases which we continually encounter in the original afford abundant scope for illustration and explanation, and the only information with regard to the life of Sir Thomas Elyot himself, which can be considered either valuable or important, is contained in copious extracts from Strype, arranged however in such a confused manner as to make it difficult for the reader to understand how much is due to Mr. Eliot and how much to Strype.

But perhaps the best proof of the perfunctory way in which Mr. Eliot has discharged his editorial duty is furnished by his own view of the scope of *The Governour*. The latter, he tells us, 'may justly be said to be an able treatise on the interesting and important science of political economy.' This description, however, of a work which regards essentially the ethics of morals was apparently no sooner enunciated than it was seen to be somewhat inaccurate, for Mr. Eliot adds apologetically: 'The propriety of applying this name to *The Governour* may on a primâ facie view appear *somewhat questionable*, but I feel assured that the *discerning reader* will readily allow its propriety in the more strict and comprehensive meaning of the term Political Economy.'

Mr. Eliot, to judge by his own statement, had a twofold object in view, and seems to have thought that to 'have rescued this valuable work from its present comparative obscurity' would be a less honourable distinction than if he 'could at any time discover that the republication of this famous treatise had in any degree suppressed the visionary schemes of political enthusiasts who broach in the present day doctrines which cannot be reconciled with religion, justice, or with reason.' A work undertaken with this singular intention, and executed in the way we have described, was hardly calculated to fulfil the ambitious anticipations of its editor.

After what has been said, the reader will not be unprepared to hear that the booksellers have appraised the value of Mr. Eliot's edition of a work in which he claimed to have an hereditary interest at a very moderate figure. Within the last few years a copy was offered for sale at the price of half-a-crown, although at the same time it was stated that copies of this particular edition were very seldom in the market. It would appear, therefore, that 'the discerning reader,' to whom Mr. Eliot appealed, has exhibited his discernment in a manner not contemplated by that gentleman, and has abstained altogether from inquiring for a book from which he could hope to derive so little ' benefit, amusement, or instruction.'

With regard, however, to one defect in Mr. Eliot's work, it must in fairness be said that the materials from which alone a life of the author can be compiled were less accessible half a century ago. The documents which have since been sorted and arranged, and of which calendars are now printed under the direction of the Master of the Rolls, were known to exist, but the labour involved in their investigation must necessarily have been much greater. And though a new edition of a work like *The Governour* may justly be considered imperfect without some introductory notice of the author, such notice must after all depend for its completeness upon the accessibility of the materials available for the purpose. On the other hand, it is simply inexcusable that one who claims to 'have bestowed both considerable labour and attention' upon a new edition should make no attempt either to verify the numerous quotations from ancient authors or to explain the obsolete phrases with which a work like *The Governour* is replete.

It seems curious that no new edition of *The Governour* should have been brought out since 1834. It may be that the fate of Mr. Eliot's book acted as a deterrent, a fate which was perhaps attributed to a wrong cause—to the indifference of the public with regard to the author and subject of the original work rather than to the intrinsic worthlessness of the modern edition. It may be that the prospect of the labour in store for an editor, and from which there can be no escape, if a book like *The Governour* is to be edited conscientiously, proved too repulsive. To whatever cause the omission be attributable, the fact remains that a work, which may truly be said to be of no ordinary interest to Englishmen, has been so entirely neglected that from 1834 down to the present day no one has attempted to make it more generally known. In saying this, however, we must not forget to take into account one fact of great importance—the extreme scarcity of the *Editio princeps* of *The Governour*, that, viz., of 1531. From a letter printed by Mr. Eliot, it would seem that his 'friend and relative,' Col. William Granville Eliot, possessed a copy of the original edition which he had bought 'at Mr. Dudley North's sale,' and which he flattered himself was almost an unique copy. In this respect, however, Col. Eliot was mistaken, for several others are known to be still in existence. Of these one copy (said to be imperfect) is in the Grenville Library; Mr. Henry Pyne, of 18 Kent Terrace, Regent's Park, possesses, we believe, another; while a third was bought by Mr. Quaritch, at the sale of Dr. Laing's famous library in December, 1879. The fact, however, that Mr. Quaritch admitted to the present Editor that he had never previously had a copy of the first edition for sale, proves that Col. Eliot was at least fortunate in possessing a rare volume. The copy which has been used for the purpose of the present edition has remained in the possession of the same family during a period of at least a hundred years. It is in the original sixteenth-century binding, which is in excellent preservation, and measures $6\frac{5}{8}$ inches in height by $4\frac{1}{2}$ inches in breadth. In the centre of each of the sides the royal arms are stamped in relief and surrounded by a square border containing the motto ' Deus det nobis suam pacem et post mortem vitam æternam. Amen;' with four compartments containing respectively a rose, fleur de lys, castle, and pomegranate. It is well known that in all the subsequent black letter editions the size was diminished. A copy in Dr. Garrod's possession, which bears the date 1565 and which is also in the original binding, measures only $5\frac{7}{8}$ inches × 4 inches.

A book like *The Governour* may be edited in one of two ways. The text may be collated carefully with that of every other known edition of the same work, and then reproduced in modern type, preserving the antique spelling, pointing, etc.; with only such annotations as are necessary to indicate the various verbal alterations, but without any attempt by verifying quotations or explaining allusions to elucidate the text. Another, and, as most persons will probably think, a far more satisfactory method, is to explain by means of footnotes every allusion and obscure phrase in the text which seems to require explanation, and above all to verify the author's quotations by reference to the original authorities.

It is not pretended that the text of the present edition is the result of a careful collation of the

texts of the various editions of *The Governour*.
All that the Editor can lay claim to in this direction
is to have transcribed the text of the first edition,
and wherever a passage was found to have been
omitted in subsequent editions, the fact has been duly
noted, but no particular attention has been paid to
merely verbal alterations. On the other hand the
greatest possible care has been taken to verify the
author's quotations. In this respect, as the reader can
see at a glance, *The Governour* presents very considerable difficulty to a conscientious editor. Although
the whole book abounds to a surprising extent in
passages translated from ancient and sometimes very
little known authors, Sir Thomas Elyot, except in
rare instances, did not deem it necessary to give
his readers the benefit of exact references to his
authorities. Consequently the labour involved in
merely verifying these authorities has been out of all
proportion to the size of the work. In some cases, as
for instance the story of Hiero (Vol. I. p. 216), the
quotation from Plotinus (Vol. II. p. 326), the saying
of Cato, erroneously attributed by Sir T. Elyot to
Plato (Vol. II. p. 313), the story of Belinger Baldasine (Vol. II. p. 439), the apophthegm of the Stoics
(Vol. II. p. 303), and the saying attributed to S.
Chrysostom (Vol. II. p 321), it was only after the
most laborious researches, extending over many
months, and involving the consultation of a multitude
of volumes, that the Editor was enabled to trace the

quotation to its primitive source. Fortunately in a very few instances only was the Editor finally unsuccessful, and compelled to acknowledge that one or two passages, more stubborn than the rest, resisted the most pertinacious efforts to ascertain their parentage.

It may perhaps be objected that to give more than a mere reference to the original authorities, was to incumber the work unnecessarily; but when we consider the wide range over which these extend, it is obvious that no ordinary library would enable the reader to consult them. Even were this not the case, the mere mechanical labour involved in turning over the pages of such a great number of volumes in order to compare the translation with the original would be so irksome that the Editor decided at the risk of largely increasing the bulk of his volumes to print *in extenso*, in the notes, the passages translated more or less literally in the text by Sir Thomas Elyot. It is these translations which render *The Governour* such an extremely interesting and valuable book, for by them we are enabled to gauge the state of classical learning, or, to speak more correctly, the knowledge possessed by at least one learned man, in the early part of the sixteenth century. It seemed important that the reader should have at hand the means of forming for himself an opinion as to the accuracy of Sir Thomas Elyot's translations by comparing the latter with the originals. On this ground alone, therefore, the method adopted in these volumes may probably be justified. The

Editor ventures to think that the same excuse may be pleaded for the insertion in the notes of quotations from modern writers of acknowledged ability on matters treated of by Sir Thomas Elyot. It is at least an interesting study to compare the condition of the critical faculty, as it existed in the sixteenth century, with its more complete development in the nineteenth.

One fact connected with *The Governour* ought alone to redeem it from obscurity, and must ever entitle it to rank as an exceptionally interesting specimen of early English literature. It is very seldom remembered that Sir Thomas Elyot is our earliest and, as the reader will hereafter see, practically our only authority for the statement that Henry the Fifth, when Prince of Wales, was committed to prison for a gross contempt of court committed *in facie curiæ*. The reasons which have led the Editor to the conclusion that this statement is inaccurate are so fully stated elsewhere, that it is unnecessary to do more than allude to them here. Whether the reader be led to the same conclusion or not, at least he cannot fail to regard *The Governour* with feelings akin to reverence as containing the details of a story which from boyhood he has probably been led to regard as one of the established facts of English history.

The style in which *The Governour* is written is peculiar: whilst many words and phrases are employed which were even then gradually going out of use, and were destined soon to become obsolete; on the other hand many words are introduced which were then avowedly new importations, but which in most cases still retain their places in the language. From a linguistic point of view *The Governour* may be regarded almost as a connecting link between the English of the time of Chaucer and the English of the time of Sir Francis Bacon. A glossary, therefore, seemed indispensable. In this particular branch of English literature there is an extraordinary and deplorable deficiency. The best glossaries, those for example of Nares and Halliwell, fall very far short indeed of what we have a right to expect. In this respect the French are a very long way ahead of us. The splendid Dictionary of M. Littré is as much superior to that of Richardson as the best modern Latin-English Dictionary is to that of Sir T. Elyot. The Editor is glad to take this opportunity of acknowledging the very great assistance he has derived from M. Littré's valuable work in compiling his glossary, without which, he does not hesitate to say, the latter must necessarily have been far less complete. It would add immensely to the chances of obtaining a really good glossary of old English if all editors of our early authors would adopt the plan pursued by Mr. Morris in the Aldine edition of Chaucer, and append to their editions a full index of words with exact references to their place in the text. The absence of such an index in the Aldine edition of Spenser, which forms one of the same series, greatly detracts from the value of this edition for the purposes of reference as compared with the corresponding edition of Chaucer.

With regard to Elyot himself, it is unfortunate that we are left in the most tantalising uncertainty with respect to many important points in his history about which we have positively no information. His public career is surrounded by a certain air of mystery. For some reason which at present we are totally at a loss to explain, very few of his letters have been preserved and literally none on strictly official business. Yet it is certain from the position which he occupied in the service of the State that his correspondence on official matters must have been considerable and of an unusually interesting character. It is a singular fact too that Sir Thomas Elyot is seldom mentioned by his own contemporaries, though he was undoubtedly well known to all the eminent men of that time. His name, for instance, does not occur once in the whole of the eleven volumes forming the series known as the *State Papers*.

It is a source of regret to the Editor that the Calendars of State Papers of the reign of Henry VIII. have not at present advanced beyond 1530, and consequently he has been unable to avail himself of the assistance which they might be expected to afford in throwing light upon some parts of Elyot's career which are at present involved in obscurity. It is to be hoped that the Government may be induced to provide the means for accelerating the progress of calendaring these important documents. At the same time the Editor is happy to acknowledge the kindly interest in this edition exhibited by J. Gairdner, Esq., of the Public Record Office, who so ably carries on the work commenced by the late Rev. J. S. Brewer, and to him and to his colleague, C. Trice Martin, Esq., it is only due to say that the Life of Elyot has been rendered far more complete than it could have been without such assistance. To Walford D. Selby, Esq., of the same office, to Richard Garnett, Esq., the Superintendent of the Reading Room at the British Museum, to the Rev. Ponsonby A. Lyons, of whose great knowledge of bibliography he has very frequently availed himself, and to the many other gentlemen to whom, in the course of this work he has had occasion to apply for information, the Editor begs to tender his most grateful thanks.

In conclusion it should be stated that the Editor obtained permission to reproduce, by means of photography applied to the engraver's art, the valuable portraits of Sir Thomas and Lady Elyot from the originals, painted by Holbein, in the possession of Her Majesty the Queen at Windsor.

11 KING'S BENCH WALK
  TEMPLE:
    August 1880.

LIFE OF ELYOT.

IT would hardly be an exaggeration to say that no man of equal eminence has suffered as much from the neglect of posterity as the subject of the present Memoir. The name of Eliot (adopting for the moment the modern orthography, although we prefer to retain his own way of spelling it, in speaking of our author and his family) must always possess a peculiar interest for Englishmen. The services rendered by Sir John Eliot to the cause of constitutional liberty, and the fact that he endured a long and painful imprisonment which death alone terminated rather than yield what has ever since been justly considered the most cherished privilege of Parliament, will always secure for his memory the respect and admiration of his grateful countrymen. The story of his life, his sufferings, and his death is so inseparably connected with the history of Parliamentary Government in England that every schoolboy is familiar with the name of Sir John Eliot as one of the greatest statesmen whom the seventeenth century produced. How few are there, on the other hand, even among those professing an extensive acquaintance with English literature who have ever heard of the man bearing the same family name to whom this country had already been indebted, a full century previous, for services, of a less

heroic kind, it is true, but still not lightly to be forgotten.
It would seem, indeed, as if the very halo of glory encircling
the later Eliot had had the effect of obscuring and confusing
to some extent the memory of his earlier namesake.[*]

It cannot be said, however, that Englishmen as a rule are
either indifferent or ungrateful to those who have helped to
form the national character. Now we may fairly reckon Sir
Thomas Elyot among the earliest advocates of that system of
education under which, with certain modifications introduced
from time to time to suit the habits of the age, English gentlemen have been trained during the last three centuries and a
quarter. It seems probable, therefore, that the ignorance
undoubtedly prevailing with respect to him has arisen from a
combination of circumstances peculiarly unfavourable to the
perpetuation of his memory. Let us see what those circumstances are. In the first place we must recollect that
although Sir Thomas Elyot was employed in the public
service of his country, and, in the capacity of ambassador
conducting most delicate negotiations, occupied a conspicuous
place in the eyes of his own contemporaries, yet his claims to
the remembrance of posterity rest principally, if not entirely,
upon his services to literature. The productions of his pen,
as we shall endeavour to show in the course of this sketch,
were not only highly creditable performances in point of
scholarship, but were fully appreciated by the learned men of
his own and the next succeeding generation.

At a time when classical learning was struggling into
existence in England and when the ability to interpret the
works of ancient authors was as yet confined to an extremely

---

[*] The reader will find, for instance, that the author of *The Governour* has been styled by modern writers, and even by one so cautious as Hallam, Sir *John* Elyot. See *Lit. of Eur.* vol. i. p. 254, note, 4th edn.

small band of labourers in that virgin soil, it was natural that the translations which Elyot published for English readers in their own native tongue should not only meet with a ready sale, but should be reprinted again and again. When, however, in the progress of time the rising wave of educational development bursting the barriers of national ignorance and enlarging the area of general knowledge poured from the press a vast flood of literature over the land, it was equally natural that the rivulets which had given the first direction and impetus to the torrent should gradually disappear and finally be lost sight of altogether. Hence it happened that the tiny volumes which had been well thumbed and circulated from hand to hand by the subjects of the Tudors and the Stuarts were hardly at all in request in the reign of Queen Anne, and in the nineteenth century have become so scarce as to be regarded only as literary curiosities. Another and possibly a yet more potent reason for the strange indifference with which Elyot's merits have been requited may be traced to the fact which, at first sight, seems certainly remarkable that no details with regard to him have been furnished by his own family. This omission however is capable of explanation. Elyot died childless, and though his widow married a very eminent lawyer, the copious *Reports* of Sir James Dyer would lead us to suppose that their author, even if he had had the inclination to become the biographer of his wife's first husband, could have had little time to devote to such a purpose. It happened also that of the families with which Elyot was most intimately allied several, by a singular coincidence, experienced a common fate and became altogether extinct. Of the Beselles, the Fyndernes, and the Fetiplaces, with each and all of whom Elyot, as we shall see presently, was closely connected, the two former during at least three centuries, and the last during many generations, have had no living representatives.

The combined effect of these various causes is shown in the fact that in an age which has witnessed the reproduction of the works of many writers of the sixteenth century, by no means superior in point of merit to Elyot, the latter has been completely ignored.

On the other hand, those who from time to time have assumed to speak with authority about him have apparently neglected the most obvious precautions to insure the accuracy of their information. A whole series of writers, including such names as Pits, Anthony à Wood, Fuller, and Chalmers, and numerous works of reference, including the *Biographia Britannica* and the *Nouvelle Biographie Générale*, have uniformly represented Elyot as having been born in Suffolk. For this blunder Bale, who was himself a contemporary of Elyot, and therefore ought to have been better informed, is clearly responsible. Bale, however, was himself a Suffolk man, and, as was recently pointed out by a writer in the *Quarterly Review*,[a] his knowledge of topography seems to have been confined to the limits of his own county. Bale's statement is that Elyot 'in Sudovolciae comitatu (ut à fide dignis accepi) primam duxit originem.'[b] Now Bale's book was published in 1548, when Elyot had been dead only two years, and it seems hardly credible that Bale should have been misinformed with regard to such an important fact as this, at a time when without much trouble it might have been easily verified. But Bale, unfortunately, has not the reputation of a very careful writer, and he seems to have accepted a

---

[a] See an article on *The Founder of Norwich Cathedral* in the *Quarterly Review*, No. 296, p. 412.
[b] *Scriptores Britanniae*, fo. 228 b, ed. 1548.

good deal of merely hearsay evidence on at least questionable authority. Perhaps too his natural inclination might dispose him to claim such a distinguished member of the fraternity of letters as a fellow-countryman of his own.

Strange, therefore, as it appears to us, it is certain that, when only two years had elapsed since Elyot's death, one of the simplest facts concerning him could not be ascertained with accuracy by one who professed to be his biographer.

If such were the case then, the reader will be able to form some idea of the difficulty of discovering now the exact place of Elyot's birth, after the lapse of more than three hundred years.

Nor is this assertion of Bale's the only error with respect to Elyot's early life with which we have to deal; for Wood, with even greater recklessness than Bale, boldly declared that Elyot was 'educated in academical learning in the hall of St. Mary the Virgin' at Oxford.[a] The evidence upon which Wood relied for this statement was an entry which he found on the rolls of the University, under the date 1518, of one Thomas Elyot who seems to have been admitted in that year 'ad lecturam alicujus libri facultatis Artium Logices Aristotelis.' This, says Wood, is the admission to the degree of Bachelor of Arts. He further tells us that 'the said Tho. Elyot was in the beginning of Aug. an. 1524 admitted "ad lecturam alicujus libri Institutionum," that is to the degree of bachelor of the civil law.' Yet at the very time at which, according to Wood, Elyot was taking his B. C. L. degree we are able to prove by the evidence of a silent but unimpeachable witness, namely the Patent Roll still preserved in the Public Record Office that he was going the Western

[a] *Athen. Oxon.* vol. i. col. 150.

xxiv *LIFE OF ELYOT.*

circuit in company with Sir John Fitzjames and Robert Norwich.

Wood himself, indeed, appears to have felt that the identification he proposed was not altogether satisfactory, for he adds immediately afterwards: 'Now if we could find that Sir Tho. Elyot was about fifty years of age when he died, then we may certainly conclude that Elyot the bach. of arts and of the civil law might be the same with him, otherwise we cannot well do it.'[a] If Wood had but turned to Elyot's own *Dictionary* (a copy of which was actually in the Bodleian Library) he would have found that the author's statement in the Preface completely negatived this theory, and might have spared himself the trouble of searching the Register of the University.

To make matters worse, and as if purposely to create a fresh source of confusion, Wood quoted from a MS. in his possession the following note which had been written by Miles Windsor, a member of Corpus Christi Coll.: 'Parker in his *Select. Cantab.* makes this Sir Tho. Elyot to have been bred in Jesus College, Cambridge.'[a] The work here referred to (the title of which it will be observed is misprinted by Wood) is of course the *Sceletos Cantabrigiensis* of Richard Parker. This has been printed by Hearne and will be found in the fifth volume of Leland's *Collectanea*. Probably Wood himself did not attach any great importance to a suggestion emanating from one of whom he speaks in another place in terms of great disparagement. It seems that a volume of Windsor's MSS. had come into Wood's hands, and the latter tells us that he found there 'many vain and credulous matters (not at all to be relied upon) committed to writing.'[b]

[a] *Ubi supra.*   [b] *Athenæ Oxon.* vol. ii. col. 359, ed. 1815.

After such testimony to the general character of these collections, the reader will hardly be surprised to hear that there is nothing whatever in Parker's account of Jesus College, Cambridge, to warrant Windsor's statement.

These unfounded assumptions of Bale and Wood respecting Sir Thomas Elyot's place of birth and education have been adopted by subsequent writers, unfortunately without any attempt to investigate their correctness. Thus even Mr. C. H. Cooper, although he has evidently taken considerable pains to render his brief notice of Elyot in his *Athenæ Cantabrigienses* as trustworthy as possible, has adopted without hesitation the notion that he received an university education. His remark that Elyot 'was more probably a native of Wiltshire' than of Suffolk might, as we shall see presently, be more easily justified. We may embrace this opportunity to observe that Mr. Cooper has appended to his article a list of references to almost all the authorities throwing any light upon Elyot's career from which we have derived considerable assistance.

One more example may be adduced to exhibit the evil result of trusting too implicitly to such authorities as Bale and Wood. The writer of the article on Elyot in the most recent (the ninth) edition of the *Encyclopædia Britannica*, after referring to Wood's conjecture that he studied at Saint Mary's Hall, Oxford, adds with judicial impartiality, 'but according to Parker and others he belonged to Jesus College Cambridge.' Without attempting to untie the knot caused by such a direct variance of opinion the writer merely contents himself with drawing the inevitable conclusion that Elyot 'evidently received a university education.'

Mr. Cooper, as it appears, was the first to cast doubts upon the statement which had hitherto been generally accepted, that

Suffolk was the county of Elyot's origin, by hinting that it was more probably Wiltshire. Although he assigns no reason for this opinion in the *Athenæ Cantabrigienses*, we gather from a communication made by him to *Notes and Queries*[a] in September 1853, that he had discovered an inquisition post mortem of the time of Henry VIII. from which it appeared that Sir Thomas Elyot's father had been in receipt of the profits arising from the Manor of Wanborough in the county of Wilts. This circumstance, to which we shall allude more fully hereafter, seemed for the first time to supply a reason for discrediting Bale's idea that Elyot was born in Suffolk.

We must frankly acknowledge that we are not able to say with certainty in what place, nor even in what county, Sir Thomas Elyot was born. But on the other hand, we are fortunately able for the first time to trace his descent with precision. This we are enabled to do by means of his father's will still existing in an excellent state of preservation among the archives of the Court of Probate at Somerset House. This document, although somewhat voluminous, appeared to be of such intrinsic interest, not merely from a legal or genealogical point of view but from the insight which it affords into the habits and sentiments of that age, that the Editor determined to print it *in extenso*, the fact that it had never, so far as can be ascertained, been published before appearing to counterbalance the obvious objection arising from its great length. Although referred to by Browne Willis,[b] Sir Egerton Brydges,[c] Lysons[d] and Foss,[e] it is a singular fact that not one of these writers has made any use

---

[a] See vol. viii. p. 276.   [b] *Notitia Parliament.* vol. ii. p. 145.
[c] *Collins's Peerage*, vol. viii. p. 3.   [d] *Hist. of Berkshire*, p. 360.
[e] *The Judges of England*, vol. v. p. 158.

of the excellent materials which it supplies for filling up the gaps in the pedigree of the family, and for establishing beyond doubt what has hitherto been merely matter of conjecture.

On this ground alone, therefore, the reader will probably be disposed to regard the insertion of such a valuable piece of evidence in the Appendix to the present edition as neither irrelevant nor superfluous.

From the document in question we learn that Sir Thomas Elyot's great-grandfather on the father's side was one Michell Elyot, who was probably of Coker, a village about two miles from Yeovil on the borders of Somersetshire and Dorsetshire. We say 'probably' because although his place of residence is not expressly mentioned, one of his grandsons is described in the will as of Coker, and presuming that this description applies to an elder son, it seems not unnatural to suppose that the family had been seated at the same place during at least two generations. Michell Elyot had two sons, Philip and Simon. Of the former all that we know is that he had a son living in 1522, who is designated in his cousin's will as 'John Michell otherwise called Elyot of Coker,' from which fact we may perhaps infer that Philip was the eldest son of his father. Simon the brother of Philip married Joan, a daughter of John Bryce otherwise called Basset. The fruit of this marriage was a son, Richard, the future judge, destined to derive still greater lustre from the light reflected upon him by his son, the accomplished author of *The Governour*. Richard Elyot must have been born about the middle of the fifteenth century. Adopting the profession of the law, he seems to have practised as an advocate as early as the eighth year of Henry the Seventh.[*] Six years later he obtained an official ap-

[*] See the *Year Books*.

pointment in Wiltshire. The manor of Wanborough near Swindon formed part of the vast estates of Francis Lord Lovell, and came into the possession of the Crown on the attainder of that nobleman in 1485. Sir John Cheyne, one of the king's most trusted councillors, had been placed in possession of this manor immediately after its forfeiture, and had continued to receive the rents and profits until his death, which occurred in 1498. From that date down to July 1511, when it was granted to Sir Edward Darrell, a neighbouring landowner, Richard Elyot was connected with this estate as Receiver for the Crown, and accounted in that capacity for the revenues which accrued during the period of his occupation. It is clear from the terms of an inquisition taken at Amesbury in 1514, and printed in the Appendix to this volume, that Richard Elyot's tenure of the manor of Wanborough was on the footing of a trustee for the Crown rather than of a beneficiary. It seems the more necessary that this should be explained because the contrary has evidently been assumed by some writers. The Rev. J. E. Jackson, for instance, in his valuable edition of *Aubrey's Wiltshire* says, in reference to Wanborough: 'Between that year (*i.e.* 1487) and 1515 the Manor "late Viscount Lovels" was *enjoyed* by John Cheyne, Knight, then by Sir Richard Elyot, father of Sir Thomas, the diplomatist, and lastly by Sir Edward Darell of Littlecote, who died owner, 1549.'[*] It would appear from the expression which we have italicised, that Mr. Jackson regarded all three occupants as being on the same footing as beneficial owners or grantees. The fact, however, seems to be that the last occupant alone had a grant of the Manor, Cheyne's title being unknown. Elyot on the other hand, so far from 'enjoying' the profits accruing

[*] P. 195.

during his occupation, is expressly stated to have received them 'ad usum Domini Regis,' and to have paid them over to the proper officer appointed by the Crown, not only during the reign of Henry VII. but also after the accession of his son.

It was, no doubt, in consequence of the official position which Elyot occupied at Wanborough, that in 1503, he was appointed a commissioner for the county of Wilts to collect the 'aids' required by the King to defray the expenses of knighting the Prince of Wales and of marrying the Princess Margaret to the King of Scotland.[a] In Michaelmas term of this year he was made a serjeant at-law; Lewis Pollard, with whom he was afterwards so frequently associated as justice of Assize on the Western circuit, and Guy Palmes, being invested with the coif at the same time. An interesting account of the ceremonies observed on this occasion is given by Dugdale (who, however, by a strange oversight, gives Elyot the Christian name of Edward instead of Richard) from a MS. which is still in the possession of the Benchers of the Middle Temple.[b] We may remark by the way that though new patents were made out and delivered to Elyot and Pollard within a week after the accession of the new sovereign in accordance with the usual custom, Guy Palmes, the junior serjeant, does not appear to have received his new patent till four years afterwards, although he continued not only to practise as a serjeant but to act as a justice of Assize in the interval.

Richard Elyot must have stood high in the royal favour, for in the same year in which he was created a serjeant he held the appointment of Attorney-General to the Queen

[a] *Rot. Parl.* vol. vi. p. 535.   [b] *Origines*, p. 113.

Consort.[a] The office seems to have been a lucrative one, and those who are curious in such matters may compare the fee of ten pounds paid 'to Richard Elyot the Qüenes Attourney,' with the smaller amount of xxvi*s*. viii*d*. paid in the same month (March 1503) 'to James Hobert the Kings Attourney,' and may speculate on the nature of the professional services for which these sums were the respective remuneration.

That Richard Elyot must have married many years before he was created a serjeant we can have little doubt; for only eight years after that event, viz. in 1511, we find his son Thomas accompanying him on the Western circuit in the capacity of Clerk of Assize. Now as it is in the highest degree improbable that an office of such importance would be conferred upon a minor, even though he were the son of a judge, we are justified in assuming that Thomas Elyot was born certainly not later than 1490. In any case his birth must have preceded his father's occupation of Wanborough. Two questions then arise, when and whom did Richard Elyot marry? And here, unfortunately, we are confronted by the difficulty to which we referred above when speaking of our author's birth-place. The time of which we are speaking may be described as the pre-registration period, and we can hope for no assistance from parish registers. A clue, indeed, to the solution of one of the above questions is supplied by Sir Thomas Elyot himself in a letter written, after his father's death, to his old friend Thomas Cromwell, afterwards Secretary of State. He there speaks of 'my cosen Sir William Fynderne, whoes fader was my mothers unkle.'[b] Sir William Fynderne was the son of Sir Thomas Fynderne, who, for the support

---

[a] *P. P. Exp. of Elizabeth of York*, p. 100.
[b] Ellis, *Orig. Let.* vol. ii. p. 115, 1st series.

he gave to the house of Lancaster, was attainted of high treason and forfeited both his life and estates in 1461.[a]

We might infer, then, from Sir Thomas Elyot's own statement, that his father, Sir Richard Elyot, had married the daughter of a brother or a sister of Sir Thomas Fynderne. Moreover, the surrounding circumstances all tend to corroborate this inference. The Fyndernes, who derived their name from a village in Derbyshire, where they had a mansion dating from the time of Edward I., were people of considerable importance in the fifteenth and sixteenth centuries. The hamlet of Findern, about five miles from Derby, still exists and serves to perpetuate the memory of the ancient lords of the soil. But the manor-house in which they lived, and the church in which they were buried, with the splendid monuments erected over their tombs, have alike been destroyed. Sir Bernard Burke narrates with some pathos that when he visited the spot in 1850 the sole surviving traces of the former occupants were some little flowers, called *Findernes flowers*, which, according to the tradition of the simple villagers, had been 'brought by Sir Geoffrey from the Holy Land,' and they added, 'do what we will they will never die.'[b] Alas! even this frail link connecting the present with the past has at length been finally severed. A still more recent visitor informs us that the last tiny flower which had for ages preserved a name and a memory which the elaborate works of man's hand had failed to rescue from oblivion, has been ruthlessly uprooted from the soil.[c] In course of time members of this influential Derbyshire family intermarried with the

---

[a] *Lett. and Pap. Hen. VI.* vol. ii. pt. 2, pp. 778, 782.
[b] *Vicissitudes of Families*, vol. i. p. 26, ed. 1869.
[c] See an article on *Findern and the Fyndernes* in *The Reliquary*, vol. iii. p. 198.

gentry of other counties. Thus it happened that a William Fynderne in the fifteenth century married a Berkshire lady, the widow of Sir John Kingstone. She was an heiress, the daughter of Sir Thomas de Chelrey, lord of the manor of Frethornes, in the parish of Childrey, near Wantage. This manor she brought to her husband as her marriage portion. The village of Childrey is not more than ten or twelve miles from the borders of Wiltshire, and an old Roman road, known as Icknield Street, may be traced almost in a straight line from Childrey to Wanborough. Another manor in the same parish, called the manor of Rampanes, belonged, at the time of which we are now speaking, to the family of Fetiplace, and remained in their possession down to the middle of the eighteenth century, when the Fetiplaces, like the Fyndernes, became extinct.[a] Richard Fetiplace, a brother of the owner of Rampanes, was the owner of two estates in the county, viz., East-Shefford and Besselsleigh near Abingdon, and one of his daughters married the son and heir of Sir John Kingstone. Young Kingstone died in 1514, having previously conveyed his estate of South Fawley, near Childrey, to Richard Elyot, William Fetiplace, his wife's uncle, John Fetiplace, his wife's brother, and Charles Bulkeley, their heirs and assigns, as trustees to hold to the use of himself, his wife, and his heirs.[b] This John Kingstone the younger was buried in the church at Childrey, where a monument to his memory may still be seen.[c] His widow, who survived her husband many years, seems to have retired from the world and devoted herself to a religious life, for she is described as a 'vowess' on a monumental brass in the church of Shalstone in Bucking-

---

[a] Lysons' *Berkshire*, p. 260.
[b] *Lett. and Pap. temp. Hen. VIII.* vol. i. p. 940.
[c] See Clarke's *Par. Top. of Wanting*, p. 76.

hamshire, where it is also stated that she died on September 23, 1540.[a] It was to this lady, whom he styles 'my ryghte worshypfull suster dame Susan Kyngestone,' that Sir Thomas Elyot dedicated one of his books, a translation of a sermon of Saint Cyprian. It is, perhaps, due to the fact of her having become a *religieuse*, and so in the eye of the law civilly dead, that her name is omitted in the family pedigree.

The insertion of Richard Elyot's name in the deed of conveyance of the manor of Fawley becomes intelligible when we find that he married for his second wife the widow of Richard Fetiplace, and thus stood in the relation of stepfather to the younger Kingstone's wife. The circumstances above mentioned make it highly probable that Richard Elyot's appointment to Wanborough may have been the result of his previous acquaintance with some of the principal landowners in that part of the country; and, as soon as we learn that he selected for his second wife a member of a family closely connected with Childrey, the suggestion that his first wife might have come from the same neighbourhood seems quite natural. All doubt, however, on the matter is dispelled by reference to the will of Sir William Fynderne, dated May 5, 1516. There we find that, in the event of Sir William's grandson Thomas dying without issue, his estates are bequeathed to 'the said Richard Elyot and my cosyn Alice his wife and the heirs of their two bodies lawfully begotten.'[b] Hence we may infer that Richard Elyot married for his first wife Alice Fynderne, a niece of that Sir Thomas Fynderne who suffered the extreme penalty of the law for treason in

---

[a] We may mention on the authority of the Rev. W. C. Risley, the present Rector of Shalstone, that this interesting memorial, of which an engraving is given in Lipscombe's *Hist. of Bucks*, is still in excellent preservation.

[b] Chan. Inq. p. m. 16 Hen. VIII. No. 164.

1460, and a granddaughter of the Sir William Fynderne who died in 1444, and whose tomb, with an inscription recording the date of his death, may still be seen in the chancel of the church at Childrey.[a] In the absence of any evidence as to the exact period of Richard Elyot's first marriage we can only conjecture that it must have taken place in the last quarter of the fifteenth century. Two children only were the result of this union, a son, Thomas, the subject of this Memoir, and a daughter, Margery, who subsequently married Robert Puttenham, the son of Sir George Puttenham of Sherfield near Basingstoke.[b]

We do not know where Richard Elyot resided during the first years of his married life. It is obvious, however, that a great portion of his time must have been passed in London in the active exercise of his profession. He certainly occupied chambers in one of the Inns of Court, for various articles of furniture appertaining to them are mentioned in his will. That his connection with Wiltshire was not limited to that northern portion of the county in which Wanborough is situated appears from the significant fact that he possessed property at Chalk and also at Winterslow within a few miles of Salisbury. This latter circumstance renders it probable that he spent a good deal of his time in the immediate vicinity of the cathedral city. The peculiar regard which he entertained for the latter is evidenced by the directions contained in his will. His son also was apparently well acquainted with this part of the county, and probably accompanied his father in many excursions in the neighbourhood. An incident which occurred in the course of one such ramble is related by Sir Thomas Elyot in his *Dictionary*. It appears

[a] Clarke's *Paroch. Topog.* p. 76.
[b] Berry's *Hampshire Geneal.* p. 288.

from this narrative that whilst Richard Elyot and his son were visiting the monastery at Ivy Church, a short distance from Salisbury, some workmen who were engaged in digging stone happened to turn up some human bones, which when put together formed a gigantic skeleton measuring no less than 14 feet 10 inches in length.[a] We are enabled to fix with tolerable accuracy the date of this occurrence. Sir Thomas Elyot himself speaks of it as having taken place 'about xxx years passed.' The passage in which he mentions the event was extracted by Leland from a copy of the first edition of Elyot's *Dictionary*, which appears even at that time to have been so scarce that Leland knew of no other impressions of it. ' Nec Bibliothecæ ejus impressiones primæ ubivis occurrunt.'[b] The date of what is generally called the first edition, and of which a copy is in the British Museum Library, is 1538, but this does not contain the passage in question. In the Preface, however, Sir Thomas Elyot mentions the fact that he had begun a Dictionary ' about a yere passed,' but that, for certain reasons which he gives, he had ' caused the printer to cesse,' when the work was only half finished. Now it is possible that Leland may have copied the story from this incomplete edition, the date of which, therefore, on the author's own showing, would be 1537. On this hypothesis the visit to Ivy Church must have taken place about 1507, that is to say, at the time when Richard Elyot was still holding for the Crown the manor of Wanborough. Camden evidently alludes to the same incident, though he gives a somewhat different version of it. ' Heereby is Iuy Church,' he says, speaking through his translator, Philemon Holland, ' sometime a small Priory, where, as a tradition runneth, in our grandfathers remembrance was

[a] Leland, *Collect.* vol. iv. p. 141.   [b] Leland, *ubi supra*.

found a grave and therein a corps of twelve foote and not farre of a stocke of wood hollowed and the concaue lined with lead with a booke therein of very thicke parchment all written with capitall Romane letters. But it had lien so long that when the leaues were touched they fouldred to dust. Sir Thomas Elyot, who saw it, iudged it to be an Historie.'[a] Another fact also mentioned by Camden, in speaking of Stonehenge, points to our author's familiarity with this part of Wiltshire. 'I haue heard that in the time of King Henrie the Eight there was found neere this place a table of mettall as it had been tinne and lead commixt, inscribed with many letters but in so strange a character that neither Sir Thomas Elyot nor Master Lilye, Schoole-maister of Paules, could read it, and therefore neglected it. Had it been preserved, somewhat happily might have been discovered as concerning Stoneheng which now lieth obscured.'[b]

The elder Elyot's connection with the West of England is indicated by the fact that almost immediately after the confirmation of his patent as Serjeant-at-law by Henry VIII. he received a commission to act as Justice of Assize on the Western circuit,[c] and from that time till his death he always went the same circuit. In July, 1509, we find his name and that of his brother-serjeant, Lewis Pollard, who was a Devonshire man, included in the commission of the peace for the county of Cornwall.[d]

Meanwhile the Serjeant's son was growing up to man's estate and imbibing under his father's roof and in the society of his father's friends copious draughts of classical learning. It was doubtless no small advantage to Thomas Elyot that he reckoned amongst his acquaintance nearly all the most

[a] *Britain*, p. 251, ed. 1610.
[c] *Lett. and Pap. Hen. VIII.* vol. i. p. 12.
[b] *Ibid.* p. 254, ed. 1610.
[d] *Ibid.* p. 43.

learned men of the day. The zeal with which he pursued his studies and the wide range which he gave to his researches would assuredly make him a welcome addition to the little band of devoted scholars, such men for example as Colet, Linacre, Lupset, Croke, Lilly, Latimer, and a few others whom More delighted to gather round him at Chelsea.[a]

Although the question has been much controverted, it is certain, as we have already stated, that he was not a student either at Oxford or Cambridge. The decline of both Universities had been so marked during the reign of Edward IV.[b] that it is not difficult to conceive the reasons which would be likely to operate upon the mind of a man in Richard Elyot's station when called upon to decide with regard to his son's education. In view of his own professional advancement and with the prospect of being able to assist his son through the influence which he would probably be in a position to exert, it seems natural that Thomas Elyot's father should prefer to secure for him a legal rather than an academical training. Many years after the time of which we are now speaking the author of *The Governour* gave a sketch of his early life, and inasmuch as his own account precludes all doubt in a matter which has been much disputed we shall quote the passage in his own words. It occurs in a Latin 'Address to the Readers' prefixed to the first edition of his *Dictionary*, when, after apologising for any defects that may be found in the latter, he proceeds as follows:—' Id breviter à vobis impetrare cupio, ut meam voluntatem in hâc re æqui bonique consulatis cogitetisque apud vos ipsos id operis jam cœptum ab equite britanno, barbarissimo scilicet, utpote in paternis tantùm ædibus educato, nec ab anno ætatis duodecimo

---

[a] See the *Life of Sir T. More* in Wordsworth's *Eccles. Biog.* vol. ii. p. 96.
[b] See Hallam, *Lit. of Eur.* vol. i. pp. 107, 163 note, 185, 4th ed.

ab altero quopiam preceptore literis instructo sibi ipsi nimirum duce tam in scientiis liberalibus quàm in utrâque philosophiâ.' Notwithstanding, therefore, what has been said by Antony Wood and Mr. Cooper to the contrary, each of whom claims Elyot as an alumnus of his respective University, the reader will probably consider the passage just quoted as conclusively disproving the assertions of both. Inasmuch, however, as Mr. Cooper had stated that 'there is good evidence that Sir Thomas Elyot was really educated in Jesus College in this University (*i.e.* Cambridge) and here proceeded M.A., 1507,'[*] it seemed incumbent upon the Editor to clear up any lingering doubts that might remain in the mind of the reader so long as the accuracy of such an apparently authoritative statement remained untested. Accordingly application was made to the authorities of Jesus College Cambridge for information on the subject, the result proving that Mr. Cooper's statement would not bear the test of close examination.

Mr. Arthur Gray, a Fellow of the College, in a letter to the Editor dated July 16, 1879, writes as follows:—

'I find that the earliest entry contained in our book of College entries does not go beyond 1618, and the College possesses no record of entries of an earlier date. Traditionally Sir Thomas Elyot has, I believe, been reckoned among the College worthies, but I cannot say on what authority. If he proceeded M.A. in 1507, he must have entered very soon after the foundation of the College in 1496.'

So far, therefore, as Mr. Cooper's statement is concerned, this letter appeared almost to decide the matter. There remained, however, one other possible source of information, the University List of Degrees and Admissions. The Registrary of the University, the Rev. H. R. Luard, most kindly

[*] *Athena Cantab.* vol. i. p. 89.

undertook to search this list, and communicated the result of his investigation in the following note, dated October 2, 1879. 'Our matriculation registers only begin in 1544, consequently if Sir T. Elyot were here we should have no record of his admission. He certainly, as far as our books show, took no degree. My belief is that his statement in the preface to his *Dictionary* is absolutely conclusive that he had no university education.'

But if, on the one hand, we are compelled to relinquish the picture of Elyot studying at the University, we need not, on the other, draw entirely upon our imagination to fill up the blank during the corresponding period of his career. He himself tells us what works he read whilst yet quite a young man, and we are thus enabled to form some conception of the wide range of his studies, which appears the more astonishing when we remember that he could derive no assistance from lexicons or dictionaries, now considered the indispensable handmaids to learning. 'Before that I was xx yeres olde,' he says, 'a worshipfull phisition and one of the moste renoumed at that tyme in England perceyuyng me by nature inclined to knowledge rad unto me the workes of Galene of temperamentes, natural faculties, the Introduction of Johannicius, with some of the Aphorismes of Hippocrates. And afterwarde by mine owne study I radde ouer in order the more parte of the warkes of Hippocrates, Galenus, Oribasius, Paulus Celius, Alexander Trallianus, Celsus, Plinius the one and the other, with Dioscorydes. Nor I dyd ommit to reade the longe Canones of Auicena, the Commentaries of Auerrois, the practisis of Isake Halyabbas, Rasys, Mesue and also of the more part of them which were their aggregatours and folowers.'[a] The 'wor-

[a] Preface to *The Castel of Healthe.*

shipful physician' here alluded to was doubtless Linacre, the head of the College of Physicians, and one of the best Greek scholars in England. His translation of Galen, according to Hallam, is 'one of the few in that age that escape censure for inelegance or incorrectness.'[a] He probably inspired Elyot with some of his own enthusiam for the study of Greek, and we may trace the influence of his early guidance in the pages of *The Castel of Health*.

In the summer of 1511 Serjeant Elyot obtained for his son, probably from the Chancellor Warham, or from Sir John Fineux, the Chief Justice of the King's Bench, the appointment of Clerk of Assize of the Western Circuit. The salary attached to this office, as the holder of it himself tells us, was 'worth yearly one hundred marcs.'[b] Reckoning the value of a mark at thirteen shillings and fourpence, and adopting Mr. Froude's estimate of the penny as being equivalent in purchasing power to the present shilling,[c] this would represent an income at the present day of about 800*l.* per annum. In the month of June of this year we find Thomas Elyot for the first time accompanying his father and Serjeant Pollard, his father's colleague, in the capacity, to use his own phrase, of 'Clerk of the Assises Westward.'[d] The fact that his name, in accordance with the immemorial practice, is included in the same commission as that by which the Justices of Assize are appointed, has misled some writers into the belief that the younger Elyot was himself at this time exercising judicial functions. Thus, in an article on Elyot in the last (the ninth) edition of the *Encyclopædia Britannica*, we find it stated that 'his name begins to appear in the list of Justices of Assize for the Western Circuit about 1511.' The mistake, however,

[a] *Lit. of Eur.* vol. i. p. 271.   [b] Ellis, *Orig. Lett.* vol. ii. p. 116, 1st series.
[c] *Hist. of Eng.* vol. i. p. 23.   [d] Ellis, *ubi supra*.

is no doubt attributable to the writer having consulted Mr. Brewer's *Letters and Papers of the Reign of Henry VIII*, in which the commissions are given without any explanation that the Clerks of Assize are included in those documents as well as the Justices of Assize.

In the autumn of this year Richard Fetiplace, the father-in-law of John Kingstone, died. His death must have occurred between June 1511 and February 1512, for his name, which appears in the commission of the peace for Berkshire in the former month, is omitted in the latter. He resided at East or Little-Shefford, a hamlet situated near the point where the high road from Wantage to Hungerford bisects that from Lambourne to Newbury, and well known to hunting men as a meet of the Craven hounds. The manor-house which he rebuilt has long been in ruins, and is at present, we believe, used as a barn; but the monument of one of his sons, John, who died in 1524, and who is mentioned in the will of Sir Richard Elyot printed in the Appendix, is still preserved in the church.

Richard Fetiplace had married Elizabeth, the only daughter and heiress of William Besilles, and had had by her a large family. His brother William lived, as we have already seen, at Childrey, where he founded an almshouse and free school, which are still kept up, and a chantry, which was abolished at the Reformation. Nothing, therefore, was more natural than that Serjeant Elyot, through his connection with the Fynderne family, who possessed a manor in Childrey, should become intimately acquainted with Richard Fetiplace and his wife.

We do not know in what year Richard Elyot's first wife Alice died. We are enabled, however, approximately to fix the time of his second marriage. It is a somewhat significant fact that his official tenure of the forfeited estate at Wanborough terminated in the same year in which Richard Fetiplace died. The manor, as already stated, was granted on July 5, 1511, to Sir Edward Darrell of Littlecote near Hungerford. Eighteen months later, namely in Hilary term 1513, William Grevile, one of the judges of the Common Pleas, died, and on April 26 in that year Serjeant Elyot was appointed to fill the vacant seat on the bench.[a] Only ten days before this event[b] his name had been inserted in the deed already mentioned by which John Kingstone assigned his estate of South Fawley to trustees to the use of himself and his wife, the daughter of Richard Fetiplace. It seems a legitimate inference from this fact to suppose that Richard Elyot was already at this time connected by marriage with the family of Fetiplace. Probably, therefore, we shall not be far wrong in assigning 1512-13 as the period at which the elder Elyot, himself a widower, married for his second wife the widow of the lord of East Shefford.

Besides this manor, which his wife brought him as her marriage portion, he acquired a farm at Petwick in the parish of Letcombe-Regis, close to Childrey. Being now therefore a landed proprietor in Berkshire, his name appears in June, 1514, for the first time in the commission of the peace for that county.[c] Two years later, by the death of his wife's father, William Besilles, the owner of Besselsleigh near Oxford, he came into possession not only of that estate but of some property in his own native county, comprising the manor of Brompton Regis near Dulverton in Somersetshire, of which his father-in-law had died seised, and which consequently

[a] *Lett. and Pap. Hen. VIII.* vol. i. p. 547.   [b] *Ibid.* vol. i. p. 940.
[c] *Ibid.* vol. i. p. 826.

devolved upon Elyot in right of his wife.[a] We may mention here by the way that the celebrated group of Sir Thomas More's family, attributed to Holbein, and which is now at Burford Priory, was formerly in the old manor-house at Besselsleigh,[b] and, when we consider the intimacy which subsisted between More and Thomas Elyot, it seems not at all unlikely that this picture may have been originally in the possession of the latter.

In July 1517 we find the new judge of the Common Pleas styled for the first time Sir Richard Elyot. He is so designated in the commission appointing him a Justice of Assize on the Western Circuit.[c] It would appear from this circumstance that the honour of knighthood was not conferred upon him immediately upon his elevation to the bench. It is certain, however, that he had not been knighted whilst he was a Serjeant, for Dugdale expressly tells us 'that none of that degree were knights before the 26th of Hen. VIII.'[d] Moreover in the writs of summons to Parliament which were directed to him in the first, third, and sixth years of the king's reign, he is described as Richard Elyot simply without the addition of the title *Miles*.[e] It is noticeable also that in this same month of July his colleague, who had been raised to the bench the year after Elyot, is styled for the first time Sir Lewis Pollard in the commission of the peace for Devonshire, from which we may infer that these old friends and constant companions were knighted together.

One important case in which the judge was concerned about this time was an award made by Wolsey as arbitrator in a long-pending suit between the Mayor and Corporation of

[a] Collinson's *Hist. of Somerset*, vol. iii. p. 504.   [b] Lysons' *Berkshire*, p. 240.
[c] Brewer, *Lett. and Pap.* vol. ii. pt. 2, p. 1104.   [d] *Origines*, p. 137.
[e] Dugdale, *Summons to Parl.* p 487-490.

Norwich and the Prior and Convent of Christchurch in that city, with reference to some waste land called *Tomblands*. Richard Elyot's name is appended to the final award amongst a number of other signatures headed by Wolsey. According to Mr. Brewer the award was made in August 1520,[a] but Mr. Blomefield postpones it to the year 1524.[b] Inasmuch, however, as Richard Elyot would in that case have been in his grave for about two years, we can scarcely hesitate to adopt the former as the true date. A still more important event in connection with Sir Richard Elyot's professional career was the trial of Edward Stafford, Duke of Buckingham, Lord High Constable of England, for high treason. The duke, as is well known, was arrested in London and conveyed to the Tower on Thursday April 16, 1521. But as Stowe tells us, 'after the apprehension of the duke, inquisitions were taken in diuers shires of him, so that by the knights and gentlemen he was indicted of high treason.'[c] This statement is fully borne out by records still existing, for we find from the latter that on Monday the Feast of Saint John Port-Latin (May 6), Sir Richard Elyot and his old associate, Sir Lewis Pollard, with two laymen Sir William Compton and Sir William Kingston, held a special commission of Oyer and Terminer at Bedminster, near Bristol, for the county of Somerset, at which a true bill was found by a jury composed of gentlemen and yeomen, of whom Sir William Courtney was foreman.[d] The following day a similar court was held at Bristol Castle for the county of Gloucester, by the same commissioners, and another true bill returned by a jury of twenty, Sir John Hungerford being the foreman. It does not appear, however, that Sir Richard took any further

[a] *Lett. and Pap.* vol. iii. pt. 2, p. 1566. [b] *Hist. of Norfolk*, vol. iii. p. 195.
[c] *Annales of Egland*, p. 511. [d] Brewer, *Lett. and Pap.* vol. iii. pt. 1, p. 493.

part in the actual trial, which was held the following week before the Duke of Norfolk, as Lord High Steward, at Westminster.

Sir Richard Elyot went the Western Circuit for the last time in February 1522.[a] He must have died either actually on circuit or very soon after his return from it, for his will, made two years previously, was proved at Lambeth by his son on May 26. Unfortunately we have no means of ascertaining whether his request that he might be buried in the Cathedral at Salisbury 'in the place there prepared for him and his wife' was really carried out. We must presume, however, that it was, and it is probably due to the too faithful compliance of his executor with the testator's direction that no tomb should be made over his grave, that we are left at the present day in total ignorance of the exact spot where the judge's remains were interred. All traces of the 'flat stone with convenient writing' indicating to the stranger that beneath was the grave of 'Sir Richard Elyot, knight, one of the King's Justices of his Common Bench' have long ago disappeared. For a few short years no doubt 'placebo, dirige, and mass' were duly said and sung for the repose of the soul of the departed judge. But when the final blow was struck at the religious establishments, and property bestowed upon them by liberal benefactors for pious uses was transferred by a stroke of the pen to the rapacious hands of the laity, we can have little doubt that 'the lands in Chalk,' bequeathed for the express purpose of providing that masses should be said for the soul of the judge and his 'frendes soules and all christen soules' did not escape the general confiscation.[b]

[a] Brewer, *Lett. and Pap.* vol. iii. pt. 2, p. 889.
[b] Both the clerk to the Dean and Chapter of Salisbury, F. Macdonald, Esq.,

For some years after the death of his father, Thomas Elyot continued to go the Western Circuit and to retain his old office of Clerk of Assize. In 1523, however, through the premature decease of his cousin Thomas Fynderne, he came into possession of some estates in Cambridgeshire comprising the manors of Carlton Parva and Weston Colville, not far from Newmarket. This piece of good fortune fell to him 'not moche loked for' to use his own expression.[a] The circumstances in which Elyot became entitled to this property were as follows. Under the limitations contained in the will of Sir William Fynderne already mentioned, in the event of his grandson Thomas Fynderne dying without issue, his Cambridgeshire estates would devolve upon the heirs of Sir Richard Elyot, whose first wife Alice was the testator's cousin. Thomas Fynderne outlived the judge by one year only, dying at the early age of seventeen. Although so young he had been married to Bridget, the daughter of Sir William Waldegrave,[b] but having no issue the contingency provided for by his grandfather's will occurred, and the devise in favour of Richard Elyot's heir took effect. Unluckily for the latter, and as if 'to temper that sodayne joye,' which he had felt on first hearing the news of his good fortune he 'was furthwith assaultid with trouble by them which made title withoute ryght or goode consyderation.'[c]

As already stated, Sir William Fynderne's family was an offshoot from the main stock which had been seated in Derby-

and the town clerk of that city, R. Marsh Lee, Esq., informed the Editor that after making a careful search they were unable to discover any trace of the 'indenture tripartite,' mentioned in the will of Sir Richard Elyot, although a duplicate of the original must have formerly existed among the municipal as well as the ecclesiastical muniments.

[a] Ellis, *Orig. Lett.* vol. ii. p. 114, 1st series.
[b] Morant's *Hist. of Essex*, vol. ii. p. 235.
[c] Ellis, *Orig. Lett.* vol. ii. p. 115, 1st series.

shire for nine generations.[a] Upon the death of young Thomas Fynderne, the branch of which he was the last male heir became extinct. The Derbyshire line was then represented by another Thomas Fynderne, whose son George had married Elizabeth, daughter of John Port of Etwall,[b] then a Serjeant-at-law, but afterwards better known as Sir John Port, one of the judges of the King's Bench.

The elder Fynderne disputed Elyot's right to the succession. Legal proceedings were commenced, and advantage was taken of the new connection with Serjeant Port to enlist his services in the cause. Elyot was thus put to great expense in defending his title. 'By the meanes of Mr. Porte the justice, whoes daughter myn adversaries sone hadd maried, I was constrayned to retayne so many lernyd men, and so to applie my busyness, that the saide sute contynuyng one yere and an half stoode me above one hundred pounds.'[c] The cause came on for hearing before Wolsey as Chancellor, who seems from the first to have entertained an opinion in favour of our author. 'My lorde Cardinall, whome God pardone, knowing my title to be perfect and suer as having it enrollid bifore him and at the first beginning hiering him self the mutuall covenaunts bytwene my fader and my cosen Sir William Fynderne, whoes fader was my mothers unkle, by his goode justice gave me good comfort.'[d]

The suit terminated in Elyot's favour, and when we call to mind the complaints of 'the law's delay,' that have been raised in much more recent times particularly with regard to chancery proceedings, it would appear that our author had rather reason to congratulate himself upon this comparatively speedy termination of a troublesome litigation.

[a] Lysons' *Derbyshire*, p. cxxvii.
[b] Egerton, MSS. 996, fo. 15. Harl. MSS. 1486, fo. 27 b, and 1093, fo. 72.
[c] Ellis, *Orig. Lett.* vol. ii. p. 115, 1st series.   [d] Ellis, *ubi supra*.

The estate at East Shefford of course remained with the Fetiplaces, and John Fetiplace, Sir Richard Elyot's eldest step-son, to whom the household furniture was bequeathed continued to reside there, but the property did not long remain in the family. The absence of a resident squire at the present day may explain, but cannot excuse, the neglected state of the parish. When the British Archæological Association visited East Shefford in September, 1859 'the melancholy appearance of the church' standing 'as it were submerged,' the river being much above the level of the floor, produced a painful impression upon the members.[a] This is the more to be regretted from the fact that the church contains a most interesting fifteenth century monument of Thomas Fetiplace, the grandfather of Richard Fetiplace, and his wife Beatrice, long supposed to be the natural daughter of John, the first King of Portugal.[b] It has now, it is true, been 'clearly demonstrated that Beatrice, the illegitimate daughter of John, King of Portugal, who was first Countess of Arundel and then Countess of Huntingdon, was a perfectly distinct personage from Beatrice, Lady Talbot, afterwards wife of Thomas Fetiplace, Esq., of East Shefford, Berkshire.'[c] But it is not the less certain that the latter lady was also by birth a Portuguese, for 'immediately after Lord Talbot's decease a writ was issued to the escheator of Shropshire, stating that Beatrix, the widow of Lord Talbot, was born in Portugal.'[d] Engravings of the seals of both ladies are given in the *Collectanea*, and whilst the shield of the latter exhibits in the first and second quarters ' the arms

---

[a] *Journal of the Arch. Assoc.* vol. xvi. p. 245.
[b] An engraving of this tomb is given in the *Journal of the Archæolog. Association*, vol. xvi. p. 154.
[c] *Ubi supra*, p. 146.   [d] *Collectanea Topog. et Gen.* vol. i. p. 87.

of Portugal as borne by some of the sovereigns of that country previous to the reign of Alphonso III., A.D. 1248, viz., *argent*, five escutcheons in saltire *asure*, each charged with as many plates in saltire also,'[a] the shield of the former is surrounded with a bordure *gules* charged with nine castles *or* which Alphonso is reported to have added to the royal arms 'in commemoration, according to Portuguese heralds, of his acquisition of the kingdom of the Algarves, A.D. 1267.'

Now it is somewhat remarkable that Sir Thomas Elyot's coat of arms contains three *castles* in two quarters of the shield, and it seems just possible that these may have been an addition consequent upon his father's marriage with a member of the Fetiplace family. We may observe here that the pedigrees of this family are in great confusion, and present the strangest discrepancies, the one printed by Ashmole[c] not agreeing with that given by Clarke,[d] whilst the copy in the *Bibliotheca Topographica Britannica*[e] is not only very imperfect, but differs materially from both the preceding. The difficulty of unravelling this tangled skein has been much increased by the statements of some writers. Thus, according to Lysons, 'Edmund Fetiplace, the *grandson* of Thomas above-mentioned (i.e. the husband of Beatrice) quitted Shefford for Besils Legh.'[f] In fact, however, the former was the great-great-grandson of the latter. Again, the inscription on the tomb of Sir John Fetiplace, who died in 1580 and was buried at Appleton, as given by Ashmole,[g] differs altogether from the genealogy given by Clarke.[h]

No notice is taken in any of these pedigrees of the

---

[a] *Journ. Arch. Assoc.* vol. xvi. p. 150.   [b] *Ibid.*
[c] *Antiq. of Berkshire*, vol. iii. p. 306.   [d] *Paroch. Topog. of Wanting.* p. 68.
[e] Vol. iv. p. 84.   [f] *Berkshire*, p. 360.
[g] *Antiq. of Berkshire*, vol. i. p. 109.   [h] *Paroch. Top. of Wanting,* p. 68.

marriage of Richard Fetiplace's widow with Sir R. Elyot, and we are unable to fix the date of her death. She was probably buried at Salisbury, as indicated in her second husband's will. The estate of the Fetiplaces at Shefford was eventually purchased by the Winchcombes,[a] and that at Besselsleigh by William Lenthall, speaker of the Long Parliament,[b] and the family became finally extinct in 1743.[c]

By his father's death Thomas Elyot had come into possession of an estate at Combe, now called Long Combe, near Woodstock, and his name appears for the first time in the commission of the peace for Oxfordshire in July 1522. Thus, by a curious coincidence, although he had not studied at either Cambridge or Oxford, he became connected by the ties of property with both the counties in which those two ancient seats of learning are situated.

Soon after the termination of his law-suit, and therefore some time in the course of the year 1523, he was promoted by Wolsey to the office of Clerk of the Council. Apparently the appointment was unsolicited by Elyot himself. 'Afterward my saide lorde Cardinall, for some goode oppynion that he conceyvyd of me withoute my merites, advauncid me (as he supposid) to be Clerk of the Counsayle withoute my sute or desyre.'[d] There can be little doubt, indeed, that his learning and ability had attracted the notice of Wolsey, and that the latter was anxious to avail himself of the services of one who had already obtained the reputation of an accomplished scholar. The office of Clerk to the Council had been held successively by Robert Rydon, who combined a curious variety of qualifications in his own person, for in 1490 he was sent on a commission to Spain, and is described as a

---

[a] Lyson's *Berkshire*, p. 360. [b] *Ibid*, p. 240. [c] *Ibid*. p. 288.
[d] Ellis, *Orig. Lett.* vol. ii. p. 115, 1st series.

Bachelor of Laws and Vice-Admiral;[a] by John Meautys, or Mewtys, French Secretary to Henry VIII., and appointed by the latter to fill the vacancy created by Rydon's death in 1509;[b] and finally by Richard Eden, a clergyman who succeeded Meautys in 1512.[c] Eden seems to have been a pluralist, for he was afterwards Archdeacon of Middlesex and Clerk of the Star Chamber, with an annual salary for the latter office of 26*l*. 13*s*. 4*d*.[d]

We learn from Sir Harris Nicolas that 'very few of the acts of Henry the Eighth's Privy Council before the year 1540, when the register commences, are now extant.'[e] We know consequently very little of the transactions of that body during the period of Elyot's connection with it. In January 1526, when regulations were made for the better government of the Royal Household, the Privy Council consisted of twenty members. As many of these, however, must of necessity be frequently absent on other business, it was ordered by the King that a select committee, consisting of the Lord Chamberlain, the Bishop of Bath, the Treasurer and Comptroller of the King's Household, the Secretary, the Chancellor of the Duchy of Lancaster, the Dean of the King's Chapel, the Vice-Chamberlain, the Captain of the Guard, 'and for ordering of poor men's complaints and causes Dr. Wolman,' should 'give their continual attendance in the causes of his said Council unto what place soever his Highness shall resort.'[f]

About this time Wolsey largely increased the jurisdiction of the Court of Star Chamber, although it did not incur under his presidency the odium to which it was so justly

---

[a] Rymer, *Fœd.* vol. xii. p. 429.   [b] *Lett. and Pap. Hen. VIII.* vol. i. p. 83.
[c] *Ibid.* p. 428.   [d] *Ibid.* vol. iv. pt. 1, p. 869.
[e] *Proc. and Ord. Priv. Council,* vol. vii. p. ii.   [f] *Ibid.* p. vi.

obnoxious at a later period. 'This Court,' says Sir Thomas Smyth, 'began long before, but tooke great augmentation and authoritie at that time that Cardinall Wolsey, Archebishop of Yorke, was Chauncellor of Englande, who of some was thought to haue first deuised the Court, because that he, after some intermission by negligence of time, augmented the authoritie of it.'[a] The reason of this extension of the powers of the Star Chamber was, we are told, in order 'to represse the insolencie of the noble men and gentlemen of the north partes of Englande, who being farre from the King and the eate of justice, made almost, as it were, an ordinarie warre among themselues, and made their force their lawe.'[b] This statement of Sir Thomas Smyth's is to some extent corroborated by a letter from Lord Dacre, the Warden of the Marches, written in December 1518, in answer to one from the King, desiring to be informed of the truth of certain alleged riots in Northumberland, and unlawful assemblies in Tyndale and Riddesdale.[c] In this letter the Warden encloses a list of the names of 'the maintainers,' and recommends that they should be summoned before the Star Chamber and fined.

We have seen that by the regulations for the Royal Household one member of the Council, Dr. Wolman, a clergyman, who was Archdeacon of Sudbury and afterwards Dean of Wells, was specially assigned 'for the ordering of poor men's complaints and causes.' In 1519 we find that certain members of the Council, consisting of the Abbot of Westminster, the Dean of St. Paul's, the Abbot of St. John's, Sir Thomas Nevyle, Sir Andrew Windesore, Sir Richard Weston, Dr. Clerc, and Mr. Rooper had been ap-

[a] *De. Rep. Angl.* p. 96, ed. 1584.   [b] *Ibid.*
Lett and Pap. Hen. VIII. vol. ii. pt. 2, p. 1433.

pointed by Wolsey and the Council 'to hear the causes of poor men depending in the Sterred Chambre,' and they were directed to sit 'in the White Hall in Westminster, where the said suitors shall resort.'[a] It was part of Elyot's duty as Clerk of the Council to settle the fees to be paid by these poor suitors, and he takes credit to himself for doing this in a way which was no doubt more satisfactory to the suitors than to his own subordinates. 'Those few (causes),' he says, 'that remayned, were for the more parte the complaynts of beggars, which shortly perceyving, I, my clerks repugning, did sett such a rate in fees ordinary, as neither any man shold be excessifly grievyd, nor that I shold be seene to pike oute substance oute of other mennys povertie.'[b] One decree of the Star Chamber, made in 1528, during the time that Elyot was Clerk to the Council, was subsequently incorporated in an Act of Parliament (21 Hen. VIII. cap. 16). This decree, which is set out at length in the Statute Book, was made at the instance of certain artificers and handicraftsmen of London, to restrain the excessive number of foreign apprentices, and in the 'exemplificacion,' of which the formal commencement is here subjoined, the writ, it will be seen, is directed to Elyot. 'Henricus Octavus Dei gratiâ Angliæ et Franciæ Rex fidei Defensor et Dominus Hiberniæ Omnibus ad quos præsentes literæ pervenerint salutem. Inspeximus quoddam breve nostrum de certiorando Thome Elyot Clerico Consilii nostri directum, et in filaciis Cancellarie nostre resydens in hec verba:—Dilecto sibi Thome Elyot, Armigero, Clerico Consilii nostri salutem. Volentes cunctis de causis certiorari super tenore cujusdam finalis Decreti coram nobis et Consilio nostro habiti de et super execucione quorundam Statutorum et

[a] *Lett. and Pap. Hen. VIII.* vol. iii. pt. 1, p. 196.
[b] Ellis, *Orig. Lett.* vol. ii. p. 115, 1st series.

liv *LIFE OF ELYOT.*

Ordinacionum contra Alienigenas exercentes artes et artificia manualia inhabitantes infra regnum nostrum Angliæ editorum et provisorum ; tibi præcipimus quod tenorem finalis Decreti prædicti cum omnibus eam tangentibus nobis in Cancellariam nostram sub sigillo tuo distincte et apte sine dilatione mittas et hoc breve. Teste me ipso apud Westmonasterium xiv. die Aprilis anno regni nostri vicesimo.'

In November 1527, Elyot was pricked for Sheriff of Oxfordshire and Berkshire,[a] the two counties being then united for this purpose by an arrangement which continued until the reign of Elizabeth.[b] It was during this year that the strange and fatal pestilence popularly known as 'the sweating sickness,' raged in this country smiting high and low with rigid impartiality. 'By reason of this sicknes,' says Hall, 'the terme was adiorned and the circuites of Assise also.'[c] There would therefore have been no occupation for the Clerk of Assize of the Western circuit had he not been called upon to serve his country in the more exalted office.

The following letter from Elyot to Cromwell must undoubtedly be referred to this period, and gives us the first indication of the friendship subsisting between these two celebrated contemporaries, a friendship which the untimely death of one of them alone dissolved.

'Mr. Crumwell, Yn my moste harty manner I recommend me unto you. And touching my good Lordes busynes, I will to the utterest of my power endeuour me to the satisfieng of his pleasure and the accomplisshment thereof. I now do send to myn undershrif that he semblably with all expedition do cause such personages to appier bifore the Exchetour

---
[a] *Lett. and Pap. Hen. VIII.* vol. iv. pt. 2, p. 1610.
[b] Fuller's *Worthies*, p. 344.   [c] *Chron.* (*Hen. VIII.*) fo. clxxvi b.

as yn this case shall be lawfull and expedyent, and I dought not but he will so doo, and as my lordes grace shall be well servyd. Right gladly wold I see you yn my pour house if you make long abode yn thes parties. All be it I can not make you suche chere as you have yn Oxford, but onely hartily welcom.

'At Combe, the xxv. day of March.

'Your lovyng companyon,

'TH. ELYOT.' [a]

Although the year is not given, we may certainly assign March 25, 1528, as the date of this letter. We know from independent evidence that Cromwell was in Oxfordshire at this very time. A letter is still in existence written by Stephen Vaughan (to whom we shall allude more at length presently) from London on 'Passion even' and addressed 'to his right worshipful master Mr. Cromwell be this yoven at Oxford.'[b] Now in 1528, Easter Sunday fell on April 12, consequently Vaughan's letter must have been written on March 28. Secondly we have a letter from Cromwell himself to Wolsey, dated 'Oxford, April 2,' in which he speaks of having been to the monastery at Wallingford and found all the church and household implements conveyed away except the evidences which he had given to the dean of Wolsey's college at Oxford.[c] It will be observed too that Elyot addresses Cromwell as Wolsey's solicitor. Now this is exactly the expression used by Fox, who says, 'It happened that in this meane season as Cromwell was placed in this office to be sollicitour to the cardinall, the said cardinall had then in

[a] MS. P.R.O. *Cromwell Corresp.* vol. x. No. 56. The letter is addressed 'To the right wurshipful and my very frende Mr. Crumwell, Solicitor to my lord Legates grace.'

[b] *Lett. and Pap. Hen. VIII.* vol. iv. pt. 2. p. 1813.

[c] *Ibid.* vol. iv. pt. 2, p. 1829.

hand the building of certaine colleges, namely his college in Oxford, called then Frideswide, now Christ's Church.'[a]

In March 1528, according to a letter still preserved in the British Museum, the Abbot of Bruerne in Oxfordshire was indicted for a riot. It is possible that it was with reference to this that John Knolles writing from Calais to Sir Edward Chamberlain on June 7, the same year, says that he 'understands that Mr. Ellyat has made a riot of the business beside Woodstock, when Chamberlain met him hunting, and has almost undone the poor men of Woodstock by summoning them to London at their own cost.' And then he adds, 'My lord Cardinal has made him Clerk of the Council.'[b]

Up to this time Elyot had continued to act in the capacity of Clerk of Assize whilst performing the more important duties of his new office. But he was now induced to resign the former appointment. 'By the solicitation of some men which yet doo lyve, my sayde lorde bearing me on hand that I was and sholde be so necessary to be continually attendant on the Counsayle that it shold be expedient for me to leve the office of the Assises, (promysing moreover that by his meanes the King shold otherwise shortly promote me bothe to more worship and proffite) finally willed me to resigne my said office takyng onely for it CCli., which after longe resistence finally I meist folow his pleasure to keepe him my goode Lorde.'[c] The office which Elyot resigned was bestowed upon Robert Dacres the nephew of Dr. John Tayler the Master of the Rolls.[d]

The reader will doubtless have observed in the account

[a] Wordsworth's *Eccles. Biog.* vol. ii. p. 231.
[b] *Lett. and Pap. Hen. VIII.* vol. iv. pt. 3, p. 3156.
[c] Ellis, *Orig. Lett.* vol. ii. p. 116, 1st series.
[d] *Lett. and Pap. Hen. VIII.* vol. iv. pt. 3, p. 3129.

above quoted from Elyot's own letter of the manner of his appointment by Wolsey a somewhat singular expression. 'The Cardinal,' he says, 'advauncid me (as he supposid) to be Clerk of the Counsayle.' The words in parenthesis have a special significance of their own and were not added without good reason. Although Elyot not only discharged the duties of Clerk of the Council, but had even resigned another lucrative office at the express request of Wolsey, the salary which was due to him as Clerk of the Council continued to be withheld. We naturally inquire the reason of this manifest injustice and Elyot himself supplies the answer. 'Whan the yere was finisshid,' he says, 'I suyd to him (*i.e.* the Cardinal) to optayne a patent for the office in the Counsayle, which his Grace didd as I herd say, but I could never com by it: Doctor Cleyburgh and other keping it from me. After I suyd for the fee, which as I herd saye was fourti marcs by the yere, wherof I hadd promyse, but I never receyvid it. So by the space of six yeres and an half I servyd the King not in the Sterre Chamber onely, but in some things pertayning to the Clerk of the Croune, some to the Secretaries, and other travailes which I will not now reherce lest ye sholde deeme me longe in praising my self, and all this time without fee, withoute reward more than the ordinare: and that which more grevith me, withoute thank of the King which I deservyd as it wold appier if his Grace hadd ben truely infourmed of me, and my drawghtes seene which I devisid and made to my sayde Lorde. In this unthankfull travayle I no thing gate but the colike and the stone, debilitating of nature, and all moste contynuell destillations or rewmes, ministres to abbreviate my lif; which though it be of no grete importance, yet some wayes it mought be necessary. Finally, after the deth of my sayde Lorde, there was a former patente founde of the sayde office and myn was callid in and cancelled.'[a]

The literal truth of this last statement is most strikingly confirmed by a document still preserved in the Public Record Office, and now printed for the first time in the Appendix to this volume. It purports to be a grant of letters patent conferring the office of Clerk of the Council upon Elyot. The pen has been drawn obliquely across the original record and in the margin is a note stating why the grant was cancelled. This latter course was adopted apparently for the following reason. A patent was made out for Elyot in 1528, on the express condition that Richard Eden, the then holder of the office, would surrender the letters patent granted to him on October 21, 1512. Eden, who as we have already said was a pluralist, and is indeed actually stated in this document to be incapable of properly performing the duties of the office because *diversis negociis suis implicitus*, omitted or refused to surrender the grant, but no doubt continued to draw the salary. This condition precedent therefore not having been performed, the grant to Elyot was held to be legally void and inoperative. The Doctor Cleyburgh, mentioned above, was one of the Masters in Chancery[b] whose duty it probably was to enrol the letters patent.

The temptation to recoup himself for the loss of his salary by indirect means must have been very great, and probably in that age would have overcome the scruples of most men placed in a similar position. But Elyot resisted the temptation; conscientiously 'refusing fees, to thintent in servyng the Kyng I wold lyve out of all suspicion.'[c] His

---

[a] Ellis, *Orig. Lett.* vol. ii. pp. 116, 117, 1st series.
[b] *Lett. and Pap. Henry VIII.* vol. iv. pt. 3, p. 2717.
[c] Ellis, *Orig. Lett.* vol. ii. p. 117, 1st series.

punctilious honesty in this respect stands out in pleasing relief against the dark background of corruption in which many public men at this period were involved, and none more than the Cardinal himself. What evidently affected Elyot more than the loss of his salary to which he was justly entitled, was the fact that his services were not only not recognised as they deserved, but were actually concealed from the King. The 'drawghtes,' to which he alludes, were in all probability minutes of the proceedings of the Privy Council. The register, as we have already said, is missing for this period, and does not commence until August 10, 1540, from which date it has been regularly continued down to the present day.

The foregoing circumstances considered, we can scarcely be surprised at Elyot's forcible denunciation of ingratitude, as in his opinion 'the most damnable vice and most against justice.' If, however, he failed to get the due reward of his labour, he made a bargain with the King about this time, which may possibly have compensated him in some measure for the loss of his salary. The royal wardships, that is, the right of the sovereign as lord paramount to dispose of the estates of his wards during minority, an incident of the feudal system, formed a considerable part of the revenues of the Crown. In May 1528, Elyot bought from the King for the sum of 80*l.*, the wardship of Erasmus Pym, the infant son and heir of Reginald Pym, together with the custody of the manor of Cannington near Bridgewater, and a third part of the manor of Exton and Hawkridge near Dulverton in Somersetshire.[a] It is interesting to us to know that this young Pym was the father of the famous John Pym, celebrated for all time as

---

[a] *Lett. and Pap. Hen. VIII.* vol. iv. pt. 2, p. 1897, and pt. 3, p. 2433.

one of the 'five members' impeached by Charles I.[a] Thus, if it be true, as stated by Browne Willis,[b] that our author was allied to the family of Sir John Eliot, the two famous champions of the seventeenth century, who represent respectively the earlier and the later struggle for Parliamentary liberty, were actually connected by an hereditary bond of union hitherto unsuspected.

In June 1530 the Archdeacon of Middlesex obtained a new grant of letters patent of the office of Clerk of the Council to himself and Thomas Eden (probably his son) in survivorship.[c] Elyot's services were accordingly no longer required. To quote his own words, he was 'discharged without any recompence, rewarded only with the order of Knighthode, honorable and onerouse, having moche lasse to lyve on than bifore.'[d] Knighthood in the sixteenth century was conferred not so much for the purpose of doing honour to the recipients as of replenishing the royal exchequer. Hence Elyot regarded this new dignity much as the gift of a white elephant. To make matters worse, he had lately been compelled to pay 348*l*., a large sum in those days, and certainly more than ten times the amount now represented by those figures, to Sir William Fynderne's executor. 'To minish my poure astate, I hadd a little before payid to doctor Naturess, executor to Syr William Fynderne, to redeeme certayne yeres, duryng the which he claymed to take the profits of my land for the execution of a wille, thre hundred and xlviii pounds.'[e] This Doctor Naturess or Natares, was Master of Clare College, Cambridge, in 1513, and subsequently Vice-Chancellor of the University. He was Rector of Weston Colville, in which

[a] Collinson, *Hist. Somersetshire*, vol. i. p. 234.
[b] *Notitia Parliament.* vol. ii. p. 145.
[c] *Lett. and Pap. Hen. VIII.* vol. iv. pt. 3, p. 2917.
[d] Ellis, *Orig. Lett.* vol. ii. p. 117, 1st series.   [e] Ellis, *ubi supra*.

parish Sir William Fynderne had a manor, and it was very natural therefore that the latter should appoint him his executor.

In June 1530 we find Elyot's name (he was now Sir Thomas) in the Commissions of Gaol Delivery for both Cambridge Castle and Oxford Castle.[a] In the following month he was one of five Commissioners appointed to inquire concerning the possessions held by Wolsey in Cambridgeshire on December 2, 1523, the Cardinal's attainder having relation back to that date. Elyot's colleagues were Sir Robert Payton, Giles Alyngton, Thomas Lucas, and Philip Parys.[b] The fact of Elyot's name appearing on this Commission is relied upon by Mr. Cooper as a proof of his 'having been a time-server.'[c] Such an inference, however, seems hardly a fair one. The duty of making this inquiry, which was not instituted until long after Wolsey had pleaded guilty to the *præmunire*, was imposed upon Elyot in common with hundreds of other gentlemen throughout England, for no other reason than that he happened to be one of the principal landed proprietors in this particular county. With quite as much reason might Mr. Cooper accuse Sir Richard Lister, the Chief Baron of the Exchequer, or Sir Christopher Hales, the Attorney-General, of being time-servers, for both sat on the same Commission, and both probably owed their advancement to the same patron, the late Chancellor. Moreover, the duty which Elyot in common with all the other Commissioners had to perform was a purely formal one, viz., to take evidence on oath. It is therefore, difficult to see how the charge which Mr. Cooper brings against him can be sustained, when we consider that his appointment by the Government to take part in an

[a] *Lett. and Pap. Hen. VIII.* vol. iv. pt. 3, pp. 2918, 2919.
[b] Rymer, *Fœdera*, vol. xiv. p. 403.   [c] *Athen. Cantab.* vol. i. p. 89.

inquiry, for the institution of which he was in no degree responsible, was due solely to the fact of his being a gentleman of position, and perhaps specially qualified from his previous employment in the public service.

We do not know in what year Thomas Elyot married. That event, however, probably took place after his father's death, and before the period in his career at which we have now arrived. His wife was Margaret, daughter of John Abarrow, of North Charford, a parish in Hampshire, about six miles from Salisbury.[a] Her family, therefore, must have been well known to Elyot, for they had been close neighbours. Her literary tastes had perhaps influenced his choice, and would certainly cement the bond of sympathy between them. She, as well as her husband, was a frequent student in that famous school of Sir Thomas More,[b] which, we are told, was 'rather an universitie than a private schole,' and 'was liked and praysed of great and learned both at home and abroade.'[c] A portrait of her painted by Holbein, is now in the possession of Her Majesty at Windsor.

Elyot's official occupations had evidently not absorbed the whole of his time or thoughts, and he must have employed whatever intervals of leisure fell to his lot to exceedingly good purpose. In 1530–31 he published his first, and, as the verdict of posterity has pronounced it to be, his most celebrated work, *The Governour*, dedicating it to the King as the first-fruits of his study. His principal object in writing this book was, as he has himself told us, 'to instruct men in such vertues as shall be expedient for them

---

[a] Berry, *Hampshire Geneal.* p. 265.

[b] 'Thomam Eliottum scriptorem inter Anglos clarum, cujus etiam uxor in scholâ Mori (de quâ postea) operam literis dedit.'—Stapleton, *Vita Thomæ Mori*, p. 59, ed. 1588.

[c] Wordsworth's *Eccles. Biog.* vol. ii. p. 122, ed. 1853.

whiche shall haue auctoritee in a weale publike.'[a] In 'the Proheme,' or Preface, he explains his choice of the title, which as a combination of terseness and vagueness, may perhaps be compared most appropriately with the titles not unfrequently adopted by novelists of the present day.

The Governour may very fairly be described as the earliest treatise on moral philosophy in the English language. 'By moral philosophy,' says Hallam, 'we are to understand not only systems of ethics and exhortations to virtue, but that survey of the nature or customs of mankind which men of reflecting minds are apt to take, and by which they become qualified to guide and advise their fellows. The influence of such men through the popularity of their writings, is not the same in all periods of society; it has sensibly abated in modern times, and is chiefly exercised through fiction, or at least a more amusing style than was found sufficient for our forefathers; and from this change of fashion, as well as from the advance of real knowledge and the greater precision of language, many books once famous, have scarcely retained a place in our libraries, and never lie on our tables.'[b] These remarks are especially applicable to *The Governour*. For one person at the present day who has heard of the existence of such a book, one hundred might probably have been counted in the sixteenth century who had almost got it by heart.

The moral and social duties of princes, a topic which in the middle ages had frequently exercised the pens of the schoolmen and theologians, acquired still greater prominence in the fifteenth century, in consequence probably of the steady progress towards absolute monarchy, and formed the subject of numerous treatises, especially in Italy. To

---

[a] See Preface to *The Image of Governance*.
[b] *Lit. of Europe*, vol. i. p. 395, 4th ed.

John of Salisbury belongs the credit of being one of the earliest, if not the first, in mediæval times, to point out how a prince owing obedience to the law is superior to an irresponsible despot.[a] In the following century Thomas Aquinas commenced, and his disciple, Bartholomæus of Lucca, is reputed to have completed,[b] the famous treatise, *De Regimine Principum,* which has been imitated and plagiarised by so many subsequent writers. Ægidio Colonna, a member of the celebrated Neapolitan family, but better known by his French *sobriquet,* Gilles de Rome, was the next deserving of notice who directed attention to this subject. His treatise, of which not merely the idea, but the title, was borrowed from that of the great Dominican, was written early in the fourteenth century, although it did not appear in print till 1473. Our own countryman Occleve, the contemporary of Chaucer, was guilty of a similar plagiarism, and adopted the same title for his own poem. He did not, however, stoop to conceal the source of his inspiration. 'Of Gyles of Regement of Prynces plotmele thynke I to translate.'[c]

In the fifteenth century two celebrated Italian writers, Giovanni Pontano and Philip Beroaldo, composed treatises on the same subject but with different titles, that of the former being entitled *De Principe,* whilst that of the latter was styled *De Optimo Statu et Principe.*

In the same century and in the same country there appeared a more elaborate work, following the plan of Valerius Maximus, which acquired a still greater reputation than either of the preceding. This was the *De Regno et Regis Institutione* of Francesco Patrizi, which has an especial interest for us from the fact that Sir Thomas

[a] See *Polycraticus,* lib. iv.   [b] Quetif, *Script. Ord. Prædic.* tom. i. p. 543.
[c] *De Reg. Prin.* p. 74. Roxburghe Club.

Elyot borrowed largely from its pages. It appears, indeed, as if the author of *The Governour* had taken it for his model. Francesco Patrizi, has often been confounded with his namesake, a philosophical writer in the succeeding century, whose best known works are two treatises on Roman antiquities, called respectively *Della Milizia Romana* and *Paralleli Militari*. The elder Patrizi, a native of Sienna, from which city he appears to have been banished about 1457, was raised by Pius II., the patron of all the learned men of his time, to the episcopal throne of Gaieta in 1460, over which diocese he presided during the long period of thirty-four years.[a] His *De Regno et Regis Institutione* remained unpublished for many years after his death, and was printed for the first time at Paris in 1518 by Jean de Savigny from a MS. which Jean Prévost, Councillor of State, had brought with him from Italy.[b] The great number of editions through which Patrizi's work subsequently passed, affords tolerably good evidence of the estimation in which it was held by the learned in the sixteenth century. When, moreover, we find that it was translated into the vernacular in two countries, we need scarcely seek further for a proof of its general popularity. Italian versions appeared in 1545 and 1547, and French in 1520, 1550, and again in 1577.

On comparing the *De Regno et Regis Institutione* with *The Governour*, it will be seen at once that there is a very remarkable similarity in the plan of the respective works. But independently of this general resemblance, the identity of some particular passages is now so clearly established,[c] that we may fairly conclude that Elyot had made himself well

---

[a] Niceron, *Hom. Ill.* tom. xxxvi. pp. 15-20.
[b] Chevillier, *L'Orig. de l'Imprim.* p. 187.
[c] See the passages referred to in the Appendix to this volume.

acquainted with the contents of Patrizi's book, published, as we have seen, about twelve years earlier, and of which he probably possessed a copy. It is curious, however, that whilst on the one hand he refers in express terms to the *Institutio Principis Christiani* of Erasmus, which supplied him, amongst other things, with materials for his 'Seven Articles,'[a] and on the other acknowledges his obligation to Pontano, from whom also he borrowed largely, Elyot makes no allusion whatever to Patrizi.

The English author, however, had another object in view beyond that of writing an ethical treatise according to the approved pattern, and in this respect his book, when compared with those which preceded it, may undoubtedly claim the merit of originality. Elyot was very conscious of the poverty of the Anglo-Saxon as compared with other languages, and he desired above all things to augment its vocabulary. Like other reformers, he had to encounter the contemptuous opposition of those who hated all innovation. 'Diuers men rather scornyng my benefite than receyuing it thankfully, doo shewe them selfes offended (as they say) with my strange termes.'[b] But the King, who was himself a good linguist, showed a higher appreciation of Elyot's efforts than these cavillers. 'His Highnesse benignely receyuynge my boke, whiche I named *The Gouernour*, in the redynge therof sone perceyued that I intended to augment our Englyshe tongue wherby men shulde as well expresse more abundantly the thynge that they conceyued in theyr hartis (wherfore language was ordeyned), hauynge wordes apte for the pourpose, as also interprete out of greke, latyn, or any other tonge into Englysshe, as sufficiently as

---

[a] See Vol. II. p. 2.
[b] See Preface to *The Knowledge whiche maketh a wise man*, ed. 1533.

out of any one of the said tongues into an other. His Graec also perceyued that through out the boke there was no terme new made by me of a latine or frenche worde, but it is there declared so playnly by one mene or other to a diligent reder, that no sentence is therby made derke or harde to be understande.'

In another respect, too, the King exhibited a degree of tolerance hardly to be expected from a man of his high spirit. Elyot had foreseen the possibility of an indignant outcry being raised, as soon as his book appeared, by some of those in authority, who might consider themselves aggrieved by his censure of the vices of noblemen, and had anticipated the coming storm by protesting that his remarks must be taken as capable only of a general, and not a particular application. These apprehensions were not altogether groundless. For writing two years after the publication of *The Governour*, he tells us that some men, 'finding in my bokis the thing dispreysed whiche they do commende in usynge it, lyke a galde horse abidynge no playsters, be alwaye gnappynge and kyckynge at suche examples and sentences as they do feele sharpe or do byte them; accomptyng to be in me no lyttel presumption that I wyll in notynge other mens vices correct Magnificat, sens other moche wyser men and better lerned than I doo forbeare to wryte anythynge. And whiche is warse than all this, some wyll maliciously diuine or coniecte that I wryte to the intent to rebuke some particular persone, couaytinge to brynge my warkes and afterward me into the indignation of some man in auctorytie.'[a] But the man who was highest of all in authority took a far wider and nobler view of the author's design. 'Ne the sharpe and quycke sentences or the rounde and playne examples set out

[a] Preface to *The Knowledge whiche maketh a wise man*.

in the versis of Claudiane the poete, in the seconde boke, or in the chapiters of Affabilitie, Beneuolence, Beneficence, and of the diuersitie of flaterers, and in dyuers other places in any parte offended his Hyghnes, but (as hit was by credible persones reported unto me) his Grace not onely toke hit in the better parte, but also with princely wordes full of maiestie, commended my diligence, simplicite, and corage, in that I spared none astate in the rebukynge of vice.'[a]

However cold a reception *The Governour* may have met with in some quarters, the King at all events seems to have regarded its author as deserving of favour at his hands. There can be little doubt that Elyot's appointment as Ambassador to the Emperor in the Low Countries was not unconnected with the publication of a book which at once stamped its author not merely as one of the foremost scholars of the day, but as a staunch adherent to the monarchical form of government.

It has been suggested by an eminent writer that Elyot 'did not venture to handle the political part of his subject as he wished to do.'[b] It may be admitted that the reader will look in vain in *The Governour* for the admirable ingenuity of the *Utopia* or the cynical boldness of *The Prince* of Machiavel. But we must remember that Elyot's object was neither to construct an ideal form of government nor to teach rulers the arts of state-craft. He designed in the first place to call attention to one of the chief necessities of the age, a better system of education for the sons of noblemen and gentlemen who were afterwards to take part in public affairs, those 'that hereafter may be deemed worthy to be gouernours.' In the second place he designed to instil into the minds of such persons, when they should arrive at the age of maturity, and be called to the

---

[a] Preface to *The Knowledge whiche maketh a wise man*, ed. 1533.
[b] Hallam, *Lit. of Eur.* vol. i. p. 401, 4th edn.

government of the State, those principles of morality which should regulate their conduct and enable them to be of service to their country, 'for the which purpose only they be called to be gouernours.' These two principal designs are the guiding stars which from first to last Elyot keeps steadily in view in the pages of *The Governour*. That in carrying out his intention he has, whether consciously or unconsciously, imitated the plan of the Italian writer does not at all diminish the credit which is due to himself. But *The Governour* is very far indeed from being merely a servile copy of Patrizi's work. Certainly in knowledge of the world, acquired by personal observation of men and manners, if not in mere book-learning, the Italian would have to yield the palm to the English writer.

The success of *The Governour* from a literary point of view, notwithstanding 'the malignity' of the time, 'all disposed,' as its author tells us, 'to malicious detraction,' was soon completely established. Its popularity eclipsed that of any other book of the same period, not excepting even the *Utopia*. So great was the demand in fact that the printer could scarcely supply copies fast enough. *The Governour* was reprinted three times, under the personal supervision of its author. In the space of fifty years no less than eight editions of this work were published, the last being dated 1580.[a] Of these five at least were put forth from the same press, that of Thomas Berthelet, who printed the first edition. Of the remainder one was printed by Thomas Marsh, another (the last) by East, whilst an edition published in 1557 has no printer's name or place appended. 'The price and convenience of books,' says Hallam, 'are evidently not unconnected with their size.'[b] The shape in

---

[a] Hazlitt, *Collect. and Notes*, p. 143. Mr. Henry Pyne, of 18 Kent Terrace, Regent's Park, is, we believe, in possession of a copy of each of the editions which are mentioned by Hazlitt.

[b] *Lit. of Eur.* vol. i. p. 246, 4th ed.

which *The Governour* appeared, as a small octavo volume, capable of being easily carried in the pocket (after the first edition the size was still further reduced), would be well calculated to render it attractive in the eyes of men, whose libraries hitherto had consisted chiefly if not entirely of ponderous folios or quartos.

The interest which *The Governour* excited among men of letters is attested not merely by its rapid and extensive sale, but by the subsequent appearance of numerous imitations. Without going so far as to suggest that the work which Budæus wrote and dedicated to Francis I. in 1547, entitled *De l'Institution du Prince*, might have been inspired by a perusal of Elyot's book, we may remark that the points of resemblance between them seem almost too close to be entirely accidental. The same observation would apply to John Sturm's treatise *De educandis erudiendisque Principum liberis*, published in 1570, and dedicated to Duke William, brother of Anne of Cleves. Indeed, it is by no means improbable that Sturm had become acquainted with *The Governour*, if not with its author. His treatment of the subject of education is at any rate similar in many respects to that of Elyot. But not to look further than our own country. In 1555 a book, bearing the title of *The Institucion of a Gentleman*, was published anonymously, and dedicated 'to the Lorde Fitzwater,' son and heir of the Earl of Sussex. In 1606 Ludovick Bryskett, the friend of the poet Spenser, wrote *A Discourse of Civill Life, containing the Ethike part of Morall Philosophie fit for the instructing of a Gentleman in the course of a vertuous life*. In 1622 *The Compleat Gentleman*, by Henry Peacham, appeared, and was so well received that it was several times reprinted. In each and all of the above-mentioned works we see that the main idea of

The Governour has been borrowed and adapted according to the taste of the writer. A more careful search would doubtless enable us to discover many other works bearing traces of the influence exercised by *The Governour* upon the minds of men in the sixteenth century. Ascham's *Schoolmaster* and Locke's *Thoughts concerning Education*, works of an analogous character, though far removed from each other in point of time, may be regarded as still further developing ideas to which Elyot was the first to give expression. And as we have alluded to Ascham, we may observe that Hallam considers Elyot 'worthy upon the whole, on account of the solidity of his reflections, to hold a higher place' than the author of *The Schoolmaster*, 'to whom in some respects he bears a good deal of resemblance.'[a] On such a point the reader will probably be content to accept Hallam's verdict as conclusive.

In the autumn of the year in which *The Governour* was published Sir Thomas Elyot received his commission as the accredited envoy of Henry to Charles V. On Sept. 4, 1531, Chapuys, the Imperial Ambassador at the English Court, wrote word to the Emperor that being lately with the King to ask a reply to his letter touching the chapter of the *Toison D'Or*, the King ordered him to say that in ten days he would despatch a new Ambassador with the requisite instructions. And a week later he writes, 'The Ambassador to be sent to your Majesty is Master Vuylliot (Elyot), a gentleman of 700 or 800 ducats of rent, formerly in the Cardinal's service, now in that of the lady (Anne Boleyn), who has promoted him to this charge. When he starts, the Master of the Rolls (Dr. Tayler), who is an old ecclesiastical doctor, goes with him to France as successor to Brian.'[b]

[a] *Lit. of Eur.* vol. i. p. 401, 4th ed.   [b] MS. Public Record Office.

In this latter statement Chapuys appears to have been mistaken. Sir Francis Brian was not superseded. On the contrary, he remained in France for several years after this date.

We are fortunately enabled to lay before the reader the instructions as to the object of his embassy which Sir Thomas Elyot received from the King on this occasion, from a MS. preserved among the Cottonian collection in the British Museum. This interesting document, which from the style of the handwriting is evidently a modern copy, has already been printed by Mr. Pocock.[*] That gentleman has, however, assigned to it the date October 7, 1532, but the Editor came to the conclusion, after consulting Mr. J. Gairdner, that an error of a whole year had been made, and that the true date is October 7, 1531. The following are the instructions referred to:

'Trusty and right well beloved, we greet you well; and thinking it expedient to fish out and know in what opinion the Emperor is of us, and whether, despairing of our old friendship towards him, or fearing other our new communication with France he seeketh ways and means that might be to our detriment or no, we have thought it right convenient that ye, knowing our mind and purpose in this behalf, should at the first repair to the Emperor, after such words of salutation as be comprised in your instructions, say unto the same Emperor on our behalf that whereas we by our Ambassadors at Rome complaining to the Pope of the misintreating of us, and the manifest injuries done to us by his deputies in calling us to Rome, there by ourself or our Proctor to make answer, the which the universities of Paris and Orleans the Chauncelor of France and our good brother's the French

[*] See *Rec. of Ref.* vol. ii. p. 329, ed. 1870.

King's Councillors and Presidents of the Court of Parliament in Paris affirm to be notorious wrong against all laws, and that all other learned men for the most part elsewhere confirm the same; forasmuch as answer hath been made by the Pope that the Emperor written unto by him will not otherwise agree, but saith (as the Pope voucheth) that he will have the cause examined in none other place but at Rome, we have thought good to signify the premisses unto the said Emperor by you in your first access to the same, and to say on our behalf that we, remembering what words the Emperor hath heretofore spoken concerning our great cause between us and the Queen, how he would not meddle otherwise than according to justice, with that considering how little cause he hath to do us wrong, or to be author or favourer of any injustice to be done unto us, we having always deserved favour, pleasure, and kindness on our part, we be induced to believe rather that the said Emperor is wrongfully reported by the Pope, and that they would for the extension of their authority use the said Emperor for a visage than otherwise. And yet on the other side the Pope so often repeating the same unto us, and brought to a point to stay to use for a refuge, to say the Emperor will not, that hath compelled us by you to open this matter unto the said Emperor, who we doubt not, if he hath so encouraged the Pope upon ignorance to do us wrong, he will himself reform it, and also knowing by you what the Universities of Paris and Orleans, and also the Chauncelor of France, being a Cardinal and learned in the Pope's law, with other the French King's Councillors, our learned men, and them also in Italy affirm the same, he will rather believe this public asseveration, and especially of the Council of France being friends indifferent, than any private information made to him to the contrary, or else in case the said Emperor hath not so

far meddled as the Pope saith nor answered . . . .
. . . . to us he will declare himself accordingly. And if the Emperor, desirous to have the matter more opened, shall ask what the Pope doth wherein we think ourself wronged, ye may say, in calling and citing us to Rome, there to appear by us or our Proctor, which is contrary to all laws, as all lawyers affirm, and especially they in France, as friends indifferent, and answering only for the testification of the truth, against whom can be alleged no cause of affection which should move them to swarve from the truth. And if the Emperor shall reply to know what the Universities affirm, and what the Chauncellor and other the Presidents of the Court of Parliament of Paris do say, ye may answer how they say that we may not be cited to Rome, there to appear by us or our Proctor, and that such a citation is not only nought, and all their process thereupon following, but also manifest injuries and wrong, which trust ye may say the Emperor of his honour will not maintain. And if the Emperor shall say that he is not learned, and understandeth not these matters, but will do that Justice will, and that further he cannot skill ne will meddle, ye may reply that forasmuch as he is not learned he may be the sooner abused, and whether he hath answered to the Pope, as is affirmed, or no, he knoweth ne yet requireth any learning. Wherefore if he have so done, perceiving that intending only justice he hath been in this point moved to advance injustice, we doubt not but like a prince of honor he will reform himself, and rather desist from doing or procuring his friend wrong, than to proceed any further in the same. And for this purpose we have willed you to declare the premisses unto him on our behalf, whereunto you shall desire him to make his answer to be signified unto us accordingly, willing you to note his answer to the particularities,

and how he taketh the determination of the French King's Council, and what he saith to you therein, and by all the means you can to ensearch whether there is any meeting intended.'[a]

Stephen Vaughan was at this time the English Resident at Antwerp, and had been instructed to watch Tyndale's movements, who was known to be in that city. Vaughan was suspected by Henry of being favourably disposed towards the great Reformer, and had thereby caused great embarrassment to Cromwell, his friend and patron. Advantage was therefore taken of Elyot's mission to the Emperor to adopt a more vigorous course of action. The new envoy was ordered, before he returned to England, to search for and if possible to apprehend Tyndale.

By the end of November Elyot had reached Tournai, and had placed himself in communication with Vaughan. For the latter writing to Cromwell, Dec. 9, says, 'Master Elyot, the King's Ambassador, this day sent me a letter from Tournay with another enclosed to you, wherein I think he desires you to be a solicitor to the King's Majesty and to his honourable Council for him, that he may from time to time have answer of his letters, and be made thereby more able to do the King honour in these parts. It is not well done that he should be so long without letters, considering his little experience in these parts, who in short time, in mine opinion, would do right well if he were a little holpen.'[b]

This extract from Vaughan's letter is interesting for two reasons. It shows us that Elyot was kept without instructions from home, and with his own letters unacknowledged, and further that Vaughan had evidently conceived a favourable

[a] Cotton MSS. Vitell. B. XXI. fo. 56.
[b] Cotton MSS. Galba B. X. fo. 21. See Demaus, *Life of Tyndale*, p. 337.

opinion of the new Ambassador. The good understanding which evidently subsisted between these two envoys, Vaughan and Elyot, is worthy of notice when we remember that ultimately the latter was no more successful in arresting Tyndale than the former had been in persuading the Reformer to come to England. Taking this fact in connection with Elyot's protest to Cromwell, to be mentioned presently, it seems not unlikely that Elyot himself incurred a somewhat similar suspicion to that under which Vaughan laboured. Be this as it may, the circumstance that Vaughan entertained a good feeling for Elyot, and spoke of him in a way which he would hardly have done if he had regarded him as personally a bitter enemy of Tyndale, has been entirely ignored by the author of the *Biography of William Tyndale*. Mr. Demaus has nothing but praise for Vaughan, acknowledging 'a deep debt of gratitude to the official whose kindness comforted the noble heart of the martyr in his exile, and whose writings have preserved for posterity such genuine and picturesque glimpses of the personal history of the Reformer.'[a] On the other hand, he seems to regard Sir Thomas Elyot with special aversion, and as deserving of the utmost contempt, merely for endeavouring faithfully to discharge his duty to his sovereign. This unfair view of Elyot's conduct can only be compared with the charge brought against him by Mr. Cooper of ingratitude to Wolsey, with which we have already dealt. The Rev. H. Waller, the editor of Tyndale's works, affords a similar example of the length to which prejudice can be carried. This gentleman informs us that Elyot 'consented to be employed in the mean work of trepanning Tyndale to gratify the King's evil passions.'[b] Statements like these are

[a] Page 340.   [b] *Doctrinal Treatises*, p. li. ed. Park. Soc.

apt to impose upon the reader, until he remembers that Elyot could have had no option at all in the matter.

In March, 1532, Elyot reached Ratisbon, and on the 14th of that month he writes the following most interesting letter to his friend the Duke of Norfolk:

'My duetie remembrid with moste humble thankes unto your Grace [that it] pleasid you so benevolently to remembre me unto the Kinges High[ness] concerning my retorne into England. All be it the King willeth me by his Graces lettres to remayne at Bruxelles some space of time for the apprehension of Tyndall, which somewhat minisshith my hope of soone re[torning], consydering that like as he is in witt moveable semblably so is his person uncertayne to come by; and as ferre as I can perceyve, hering of the Kinges diligence in thapprehention of him, he withdrawith him into such places where he thinkith to be ferthist oute of daunger. In me there shall lakk none endevor. Finally, as I am all the Kinges, except my soule, so shall I endure all that shall be his pleasure, employing my poure lif gladly in that which may be to his honor or welth of his Realm. Pleasith it your Grace, according as I have writen to the Kinges Highness, the Emperor, being yet sore grievyd with a fall from his horse, kepith himself so close that Mr. Cranmer and I can have none accesse to his Maiestie, which allmoste grievith me as moche as the Emperors fall grievith him. I have promysid to the King to write to your Grace the ordre of things in the towne of Nurenberg, specially concerning the fayth. But first I will reherce some other townes as they laye in oure waye. The citie of Wormes, for the more part and allmoste the hole, is possessid with Lutherians and Jewes, the residue is indifferent to be shortly the one or the other; trouthe it is that the Busshop kepith well his name of Episcopus, which is in Englissh an overseer, and is in the case that overseers of testamentes be in England, for he shall have leve to looke so that he meddle not. Yet some tyme men callyth him overseene, that is drunke, whan he neither knowith what he doeth, nor what he owght to doo. The Citie of Spire, as I here saye, kepith yet their faith well, except some saye there be many do err in taking to largely this article *Sanctorum Communionem*, which hath inducid more charitie than may stonde with honestie. One thing I markid, suche as were lovers, divers of them hadd theire paramors sitting with theim in a draye which was drawen with a horse trapped with bells, and the lovers, whipping theim, causid theim to trott and to draw theim thurghoute everie strete, making a grete noyse with their bells; the women sate with theire heddes discoverid, saving a chaplet or crounet wrought with nedil wark. I hadd forgoten to tell that there were grete hornes sett on the horsis heddis. I suppose it was the tryumphe of Venus, or of the Devil, or of bothe. All townes ensuing be rather wars than better. But I passe theim over at this time. Touching Nurenberg, it is the moste propre towne and best ordred publike weale that ever I beheld. There is in it so moche people that I mervaylid how the towne mowght contayne them, beside theim which folowid the Emperor.[a] And notwithstanding, there was of all vitaile more abundance than I could see in any place, all thoughe the contray adjoyning of his nature is very barrayn. I appoyntid to lodge in an Inne, but Sir Laurence Staber the Kinges servaunt came to me desyring me to take his house, whereunto I browght with me the Frenche Ambassador,[b] where we were well entertayned,

---

[a] M. Henne tells us that Charles V. was escorted by '150 hommes d'armes des bandes d'ordonnances qui l'accompagnèrent jusqu'à Ratisbonne.'—*Hist. du Règne de Charles V. en Belgique*, tom. vi. p. 13.

[b] Claude Dodieu otherwise known as Le Sieur de Velly. See *Papiers d'État du Card. de Granvelle*, tom. i. p. 549.

and that night the Senate sent to us thirty galons of wyne, twenty pikes, thirty carpes, a hundrid dasis, with sondry confectiones; the residue of oure chier I will kepe in store untill I speke with your Grace, which I pray God may be shortly. Allthough fish was sent to us, yet universally and openly thurghout the towne men did eate flessh. Allthowgh I hadd a chapleyne, yet could not I be suffrid to have him to sing Mass, but was constrayned to here their Mass which is but one in a Churche, and that is celebrate in forme folowing. The Preest in vestmentes after oure manner singith everi thing in Latine as we use, omitting suffrages. The Epistel he readith in Latin. In the meane time the sub Deacon goeth into the pulpite and readeth to the people the Epistle in their vulgare; after thei peruse other thinges as our prestes doo. Than the Preeste redith softly the Gospell in Latine. In the meane space the Deacon goeth into the pulpite and readith aloude the Gospell in the Almaigne tung. Mr. Cranmere sayith it was shewid to him that in the Epistles and Gospels thei kept not the ordre that we doo, but doo peruse every daye one chapitre of the New Testament. Afterwards the prest and the quere doo sing the *Credo* as we doo; the secretes and preface they omitt, and the preest singith with a high voyce the wordes of the consecration; and after the Levation the Deacon torneth to the people, telling to them in Almaigne tung a longe process how thei shold prepare theim selfes to the communion of the flessh and blode of Christ; and than may every man come that listith, withoute going to any Confession. But I, lest I sholde be partner of their Communyon, departid than; and the Ambassador of Fraunce followed, which causid all the people in the Churche to wonder at us, [as though] we hadd ben gretter heretikes than thei. One thing liked me well (to shew your Grace freely my hart). All the preestes hadd wyves ; and thei were the fayrist women of the towne, &c. To saye the trouth, all women of this contray be gentill of spirit, as men report. The day after our coming the Senate sent gentilmen to shew us their provision of harneis, ordinance, and corne. I suppose there was in our sight thre thousand pieces of complete harneys for horsemen; the residue we saw not for spending of time ; of gunnes grete and small it required half a daye to numbre them ; arkbusshes and crossebowes, I thowght theim innumerable. The provision of grayn I am aferd to reherse it for jeoperding my credence. I saw twelve houses of grete length, every house having twelve floures, on every one corne thurghoute, the thickness of three feete. Some of the Senate shewed me that thei hadd sufficient to kepe fifty thousand men abundantly for one yere. Moche of it have layen long and yet is it goode as it shall appier by an example that I have now sent to your Grace of rye, which was layde in there 19 yeres passid, whereof there remaynith yet above vc quarters. I doubtid moche to report this to your Grace, but that I trustid your Grace wold take it in stede of tidinges, and not suppose me to be the author. Considering that moche strange report may bring me in suspicion of lying with some men, which hath conceyvid wrong oppinion of me. Newes there be none worth the writing ; thei doe looke every day here for King Ferdinandoes wif,[*] who men doo suppose will somewhat doo in persuading the princes of Germany ; bringing with her all hir children, which is a high poynte of Rhetorike and of moche efficacie, as old writars supposid. And here an ende of my poure lettre, which I besieche your Grace to take in goode part with my harty service. And our Lord mayntayne you

[*] Anne of Bohemia, who married in 1521, Ferdinand, the brother of Charles V.

in honor with long lif. Writen at Regenspurg the xivth day of Marche.

'If it shall please your [Grace] ... Baynton to know some of theis stories I wo ...'[a]

Elyot must have left Ratisbon very soon after this despatch, for early in the following month Augustine, who had formerly been physician to Wolsey, and was now in the service of the Emperor, writing from that city to Cromwell, speaks of Elyot as having been there a little while before.

The following extract from Augustine's letter exhibits very clearly not only the friendship which subsisted between these two men of letters of different nationalities, but the esteem in which the English Ambassador was held by the members of the Emperor's court:

'Ceterum quia necessitas omnes vias tentare cogit ac omnem movere lapidem, cum mihi tam multos annos cum sub recolendæ memoriæ Reverendo Domino Winton tum sub felicis recordationis Reverendissimo Domino Cardinali non vulgaris intercesserit amicicia inter me ac Dominum Thomam Elioth, paulo ante hac[b] oratorem vestrum, propter virtutes illius, quas semper amavi et amplexatus sum, sicuti e contra ille propter forsan aliquam de me conceptam virtutis opinionem, cumque crescor [in his][c] magis ac magis ob mutuam conver sationem, in quâ cum sæpius de calami[tatibus meis][c] incideret sermo, non potuit vir ille optimus, eum ad id impellente bonitate m[entis][c] suæ et familiaritate nostrâ, non sæpius

---

[a] Addressed 'To my Lord of Norfolkes Grace.' Cotton, MSS. Vitell. B. XXI. fo. 54 orig. This letter has been printed by Ellis in *Orig. Lett.* vol. ii p. 189, 3rd Series, as an anonymous letter; and also by Mr. Pocock in *Rec. of Ref.* vol. ii. p. 228, who erroneously attributes it to Augustine; but though the original signature is wanting, the writer is identified by the indorsement.

[b] The word *olim*, which had been first written, is struck out in the original.

[c] The words in brackets are supplied by conjecture, the original being nearly undecipherable on account of the ink having faded, but Mr. Pocock's

ærumnas meas non indolere et congemiscere, [atque ut]* est ferventis spiritûs in piis causis, omnem operam suam mihi pollicitus est, ac tecum, [in]* quo omnem spem meam positam post Deum illi frequenter solitus sum prædicare, omnia communicaturum, necnon tuo consilio in meâ [causâ]* à te velle et cupere dirigi, si inde forte aliquid fructûs possit provenire. Id etiam postremum cum hinc discederet efficacissimè promisit maximo certe sui omnium ordinum immo totius hujus Aulæ relicto desyderio, adeo quod omnium judicio hoc ausim dicere, quòd nemo ex eo inclyto regno jam multis annis exierit rebus gerundis aptior, principibus gratior, ac tam diversis nationibus accommodatior. Atque in eo certè verificatum est illud sapientis dictum, Magistratus scilicet virum ostendit. Hunc igitur, præstantissime Cromwell, tui non parum amantem et ingenii tui admiratorem in hâc meâ causâ foveas, dirigas, et adjuves velim, si forte tuo consilio ingenio et industriâ ambo conjunctis viribus mihi aliquid boni acquirere valeatis. In te tamen unico et potissimo præsidio omnis spes mea posita est, ut tu qui incepisti hanc provinciam eam etiam læto successu perficias. Ne igitur quæso moleste feras si per eum tanquam subministratorem tuum tento causæ meæ expeditionem, aut si per alios tentavero, nam id ago (ita me Deus amet) non quia tibi diffidam, in cujus manibus vitam meam ponere velim, sed ut magis sis animatus ad negocium meum perficiendum, et ut junctis studiis opibusque tandem res ista mea aliquem consequatur eventum.' [b]

Elyot returned to England in the spring of 1532. On

reading 'cresco in diem,' must be wrong, the letter r after o, and the letter h and not d being plainly visible.

* These words are supplied by conjecture, the MS. being here mutilated by fire.

[b] Cotton MSS. Vitell. B. XXI. fo. 83 orig. See also Pocock's *Records of Ref.* vol. ii. p. 249, where the letter is assigned to the beginning of April, presumably rom the internal evidence.

LIFE OF ELYOT. lxxxiii

June 5 of that year Chapuys, the Imperial Ambassador in London, gives the following account of an interview he had had with him two days previously: 'The day before yesterday Master Thomas Elyot, on his return from your Majesty's court, where he has been residing as Ambassador, came to visit me, and told me a great deal about his conversation with this King, which he said had been greatly to the benefit of your Majesty, of the Queen your Aunt,[a] and principally of the King his master, who he said knowing about it still showed great desire to hear all the particulars of his mission. But whatever may be Master Elyot's assertions, I have strong doubts of his report having produced as good effect as he says on the King, for whatever remonstrances have been addressed to him by different parties have hitherto been disregarded, and a smile or tear from the Lady[b] has been enough to undo any good that might have been done in that quarter. The said Ambassador Elyot, as he tells me, has put down in writing the whole of his conversation with this King, and addressed it to Senor Don Fernando de la Puebla,[c] according to your Majesty's wishes, in the very cypher which that gentleman gave him for the purpose, and therefore I will forbear saying anything more about it. I am daily expecting to hear what the Italian gentleman whom Camillo Orsino left behind him here is really about, and likewise the return of the spy I sent after him. As soon as I am in possession of reliable information I will not fail to acquaint Your Majesty, and will also try to sound the Ambassador Elyot, and pay him as much court as possible for the better success of the Queen's case.'[d]

[a] Catharine of Aragon.   [b] Anne Boleyn.
[c] This was the nephew of the Doctor de Puebla who was the Imperial Ambassador in England *temp.* Hen. VII. See *State Pap.* vol. vii. p. 161.
[d] K. u. K. Haus- Hof u. Staats Arch. Wien. Rep. P. Fasc. c. 227, No. 27.

This letter, taken in connection with the one written by Chapuys some months earlier in which he hints that Elyot's appointment as Ambassador to the Emperor was due to the influence of Anne Boleyn, throws a strong light upon a pitfall to which the statesmen of Henry VIII. often found themselves exposed. The obedience due to the sovereign, and which was felt to be of paramount importance for the preservation of the public weal, not unfrequently conflicted with what must have been felt to be duties of at least moral obligation and the inward promptings of conscience. If Chapuys' information were correct, the selection of Elyot for this special mission was probably made because it was supposed that he would prove to be, as Augustine's letter shows us that he was, *persona grata* to the Emperor. There can be little doubt indeed that his real sympathy, like that of all high-minded men, was enlisted on the side of the injured Catharine, and that his own feelings with respect to the question of divorce could not be effectually concealed from the Court to which he was attached. It is evident too from this letter of Chapuys that Elyot was not deficient in moral courage, and did not hesitate to present in plainer language perhaps than Henry was accustomed to, the view which Charles V. took of the latter's conduct.

Elyot's mission, as we shall see presently, proved ruinously expensive to him, and he spent far more than his allowance in endeavouring to maintain an establishment suitable to his rank as Ambassador to 'the second King in Christendom.' In this respect, however, he seems to have fared no worse than his contemporaries. The inadequacy of the pay and the irregularity with which it was remitted were frequent causes of complaint by the English agents on the Continent.* Nor

---

* See for instance a letter from Sir John Hackett, *State Pap.* vol. vii. p. 211, and one from Dr. Richard Croke, *ibid.* p. 244.

was this their only grievance. If we may believe Dr. Nicholas Hawkins, whilst the Ambassadors of other countries, 'as well small as great,' had their dinner services of silver, he and Cranmer when at Bologna, were obliged to be content with tin or pewter. 'To buy myself I am not able,' he says, 'and I were, I would, for the King's honour.'[a] Elyot's own case was no different; he had returned to England enriched indeed with a large stock of experience and knowledge of men and manners, but sadly impoverished in purse. To make matters worse, he was this year nominated Sheriff of Cambridgeshire, which would necessarily involve him in still further expenditure. He wrote therefore to his friend Cromwell begging him to exert his influence to have him excused from serving the office. The date of this letter is fixed beyond all doubt by the allusion to the King's return from his interview with Francis I. at Calais. According to Hall, Henry landed at Dover on Wednesday, November 14, 1532.[b] The following letter therefore was written four days after the King's arrival: 'Mr. Cromwell, I moste hartily commend me unto you. Assuring you that heering of the honorable and saulf retorne of the Kinges Highness, I am more joyfull than for any thing that ever hapned unto me. As contrary wise, whan I first herd that his Grace intendid to passe the sees, feare of the greate aventure of his moste Royall person so attachid my harte, that sens unto this daye it hath bireft me the more parte of my slepe, whiche I pray godd may be redubbed with theise comfortable tidinges of his Graces saulfe retorne. And that I speake without flatery Allmyghti godd is my juge, unto whome I have more often and more hartily prayid for the Kinges goode speede than ever I didd for myself in any

[a] *State Pap.* vol. vii. p. 407, and see *ibid.* p. 453.
[b] *Chron. (Hen. VIII.)* fo. ccix. b, ed. 1548.

necessitie. Moreover, Sir, I doo not rejoyce a litle that in well using your excellent witt ye dayly augment the Kinges goode opinion and favour toward you, to the comfort of your frendes, of the which numbre thowgh I be one of the leste in substance, yet in benevolence and syncere love toward you I will compare with any, onely movid thereto for the wisedom and aptness that I see in you to be a necessary Counsaylour unto my master, whereby I hope the right oppinion of vertue shall ones be revyved, and false detraction tried oute and putt to silence, by whome some true and paynefull service have ben frustrate and kept from suche knowlege as hadd ben expedient. For my part godd and my conscience knowith that whan the Kinges highness commaundid me to serve him as his graces Ambassadour, knowing my disshabilitie bothe in inward and exterior substaunce, I was lothe to go, the King not offendid; but whan I perceyvid his graces determination, I, conformyng me unto his graces pleasure, didd deliberate with myself to extend not onely my poure witt, but allso my powar above my powar in his graces service, intending to serve his grace no lasse to his honour than any bachelor Knight his Ambassadour hadd doone of late dayes. Wherfor besydes the furniture of myselfe and my servauntes, at my commyng to Bruxelles I shewid myself according as it beseemyd to the King of Englondes Ambassadour, that is to saye, the seconde Kinge in Christendom, bothe at my table and other entertaynement of straungers, thereby fisshing oute [*] some knowlege that doing otherwise I sholde have lakkid. How I usid me in myn accesse unto the Emperour godd is my juge that in my replications I have seene him chaunge countenance, which, as they know

[*] The reader will observe that the very same phrase was used by the King in his Instructions to Elyot as to the object of his mission. See *ante* p. lxxii.

that have been with him, is no litle thinge. All be it
by suche raisons as I made to serve my master, awayting
oportunity and using such a prince with silken wordes,
as was the counsayls of King Darius mother, I attayned
with him suche familiaritie in communication, that he usid
with me more abundance of wordes than (as some of his
Counsaile confessid) any Ambassadour byfore me hadd founde
in him, which I markid diligently and provyded the better to
serve my master according to his expectation, as moche as
mowght be doone with suche a prince as with long travayle
in counsaile is becom (if I shall not lye falsely) of a mervay-
lous deepe and assurid witt. Finally, that journay is nowe
moche grievouse unto me, as well for that I have browght
myself thereby in grete dett, spending therein allmoste six
hundred marcs above the Kinges alowance, and thereby am
constrayned to putt away many of my servauntes whome I
loved well. As allso that I perceyve the Kinges opynion
mynisshid toward me by that that I perceyve other men
avauncid openly to the place of Counsaylours which neither
in the importaunce of service neither in chargis have servyd
the King as I have doone, and I being ommittid had in
lass estimation than I was in whan I servid the King first in
his Counsayle. Which I speke not for any ambition, but that
onely I desyre that my true hart should not cause me to lyve
bothe in povertie and oute of estimation, for God juge my
soule as I desyre more to lyve oute of dett and in quyete study
than to have as moche as a Kinge may give me. Now know
you my misery, which I pray you helpe as you may. I borowed
of the Kinge a hundred marcs, which I wold fayne paye if
myn other creditours wer not more importune on me than
frendes shold be. Sir, for as moche as the Kinge alowid me
but xxs. the day and I spent xls. the day, and oftentymes

four marcs, and moreover I receyvyng the Kinges money in angells, I lost in every angell xivd. sterling. So that I lakkid moche of the Kinges alowance. And allso I gave many rewardes, partly to the Emperours servauntes to gete knowlege, partly to suche as by whoes meanes I trustid to apprehend Tyndall, according to the Kinges commaundment. Which thinges consyderid may it like you, goode Mr. Cromwell, to move the Kinge to be my goode lorde either to forgyve to me my dett, or els to alow to me that I lost by myn exchange and my said rewardes, and to graunt me some lenger tyme to pay the residue. I heresaye that I am named in the bill of Sheriffs for Cambrige Shyre. If the King should appoynt me, than am I more undone, and shall never be able to serve him nor to kepe my house; consydering that no man eskapith oute of that office withoute the losse of one hundred marcs, and as for my practise in office for my profite ye somewhat doo know. If Godd sent me not other lyving I were likely to begg. If ye here me named, I pray you shewe to me that kyndness that by your meanes I may be dischargid. For besides that which I have spoken, by my fayth I knowe yet no part of the contray above thre myles from my house, and have very litle acquayntance to serve the Kinge as he owght to be.

'My long lettres have made ye lese tyme, but nede have constrayned me to be lenger than wisedom wold. But for your paynes ye shall have my prayer to godd to encrease you in worship with longe lif.

'Writen at Carlestowne the xviii day of Novembre,
  'By him that loveth you,
    'TH. ELYOT, Kt.' *

Apparently Cromwell was unable to procure for our

* MS. P. R. O. The letter is addressed 'To the right wurshipfull Mr. Cromwell, one of the Kinges most honorable Counsayle.

author the exemption he so earnestly desired; for within a month we find Elyot again renewing his application, and repeating the same arguments *ad misericordiam*, to induce his friend to make intercession on his behalf. Some portions of this letter, in which Sir Thomas Elyot reminded Cromwell of his claim to consideration on the ground of his public services, have already been given in sketching his previous career, and may therefore be omitted in this place.

'Right worshipfull, I recommend me unto you; and hartily thanke you for your gentill and wyse advertisements and counsayles gyven unto me in your lettres which I receyvyd of my lovyng frende Mr. Raynsford.* All be it, Sir, whan ye shall knowe all the occasions of my discomforte ye will not so moche blame me as pitie me, if your olde gentill nature be not chaunged. Mr. Cromwell, I know well howe moche my duetie is to serve my soveraign lorde truely and diligently, which godd is my juge I have doone to my powar with as goode a wille and as gladly as any man could ymagine to doo, neither for myne obedience onely nor for hope of promocion, but for very harty love that I bare and doo bere to the Kinges Highnesse, besydes myn aleageance, thereto moved by the incomparable goode qualities bothe of his persone and witte, which I have long wondred at and lovid, as is my nature to doo in private persones, moche more in Princes, moste of all in the chief Governor of this Roialm and my soveraigne Lorde and Master. But whan I consyder myn infelicitie and losse of tyme in unprofitable study, will I or no, I am inforced to be cruciate in my poure mynde, which I confesse to be for lak of wisedom, but I have ben to little a tyme studious in philosophy. I suppose ye, being wery of my longe bablyng, tary to here the infelicitie that I com-

* One of the Gentlemen Ushers to Henry VIII.

playne me of. I pray you than take some pacience to here some part of my grief.' [Elyot then gives the details of his lawsuit and of his appointment as Clerk to the Council quoted above.] 'So withoute any ferme, withoute stokk of catell except foure hundred shepe to compasse the lands of my tenaunts, I have hitherto kept a pour house, equall with any knight in the contrayes wher I dwell, and not withoute indignation of them which have moche more to lyve on. Nowe althowgh very unmeete and unhabile, I have servyd the King in his Graces message, how our Lord knoweth, suer I am truely and faithfully. Therein employed I fyve hundred and fourty marks above all the Kinges alowance, which I nothing repent me of, trusting that his Grace is pleased with my service; but now that I trusted to lyve quietely, and by little and little to repay my creditors and to reconsile myself to myn olde studies and pray for the King (for other promotion I lokid not for), I wote not by what malice of fortune I am constrayned to be in that office wherunto is, as it were appendant, losse of money and good name. Of the one I am certayne; the other is hard to eskape, all sharpnesse and diligence in Justice now a dayes being every where odiouse. As godd helpe me, sens my commyng over I have dischargid oute of my service fyve honest and tall personages, constraynid of necessitie, untill I mowght recover myself oute of dett, and now am I compelled to augment my household eftsones, or ells shold I serve the Kinge sklenderly. Ye here myn occasions. I pray you than blame me not, thowgh I have my mynde somewhat inquieted; not that I imbrayde the King with my service, but that I sorow that his Grace hath not ben so informed of me as my service requyred, and moreover that I am not of powar to serve his Grace according to his expectation and as my pour hart desyreth. And goode Mr. Cromwell I thank you that ye will lese so moche tyme to reade this longe lettre, praying you to bear part of it in your remembrance, that as oportunitie servith ye may truely aunswere for your frend, who hartily desyreth the increase of your worship. And I pray you continue your favor towards Mr. Raynsford, whom ye shall fynde as honest and faithfull as any that ever ye were acquaynted with. And I beseche Godd send you longe lif and well to doo.

'Writen at Carleton the viii day of Decembre,
   'By yours assured,

        'TH. ELYOT, Kt.'[a]

These two letters, written in November and December 1532, in both of which Elyot complains of the losses he had incurred through his embassy to the Emperor of Germany, render it clear that he was not sent on a mission to Rome in September 1532. Yet such has hitherto been supposed to have been the case by all our historians, including Strype, Burnet, and Rapin. The error is probably due to the fact that on the margin of a MS. in the Cottonian Collection,[b] headed 'Instruckecion given to Sir Thomas Elliotte being sente to the Pope towchinge the devorce,' the date 1532, September, is written in a later hand. Now this is the very MS. which is referred to by Burnet as his authority for the statement that 'Sir Thomas Elyot was sent to Rome with answer to a message the Pope had sent to the King.'[c] There are two other copies of these 'Instructions' in the British Museum. One in the Harleian Collection, (No. 283, fo. 102 b orig.) is apparently a duplicate of the Cotton MS., and probably

---

[a] Addressed 'To the right worshipfull and myne assuryd frende Mr. Cromwell.' Cotton MSS. Titus B. I. fo. 371, orig. printed in Ellis, *Orig. Lett.* vol. ii. p. 113, 1st Series.
[b] Vitell. B. XIII. fo. 228. [c] *Hist. of Ref.* part i. p. 125, ed. 1679.

earlier in date. The other, in Rymer's Collection (Add. MSS 4,622, fo. 91), is headed simply, 'A minute of a letter sent by the King to his Embassadour at Rome,' but varies considerably from the two former, and is much fuller. Amongst the archives of the Public Record Office is the original draft of these 'Instructions,' with numerous corrections and additions in the King's own hand. This document bears the following indorsement, in a later hand than the body of the draft, 'A Minute of a lettre sent by the King to his Embassadour at Rome,' but there is no date, and nothing on the face of the document itself to indicate to whom it was sent. Now the Rymer MS. is either a copy of this draft, with the additions and alterations, or of a fair copy of an original, embodying the emendations. On the other hand, both the Cottonian and Harleian MSS. are evidently transcripts of the draft as it originally stood before it was corrected and altered by the King. How Elyot's name came to be introduced is a mystery which the Editor frankly admits he is quite unable to solve. One thing, however, is abundantly clear. Burnet made use of both the Cotton and the Rymer MSS. to illustrate two different periods of his history without discovering that they were copies of one and the same document. Thus he makes Elyot go to Rome armed with these Instructions in 1532,[a] whilst he quotes the very same Instructions as the contents of a letter sent by the King 'to his Ambassadors at Rome,' subsequent to November 1533.[b] There can be no doubt on this point, because he prints the Rymer MS. *in extenso* amongst his Collection of Records[c] as his authority for the latter statement. Thus the same document is really made to serve a double purpose. Burnet's positive assertion that Elyot

[a] *Hist. of Ref.* part i. p. 125, ed. 1679. [b] *Ibid.* part iii. p. 86.
[c] *Ibid.* part iii. (Coll. of Rec.) p. 47.

LIFE OF ELYOT.

was sent to Rome in the autumn of 1532, was adopted without hesitation by Rapin,[a] and apparently without any independent investigation. Strype, the contemporary of Burnet, may have had no better authority for saying that Elyot was 'in the year 1532 the King's Ambassador to Rome.'[b] Indeed the modern heading for which no authority has yet been discovered to the 'Instructions' in the Cottonian and Harleian MSS. seems after all to be the sole foundation for alleging as a fact that which can be proved *aliunde* to be most improbable. For in the first place it is hardly likely that a man who was called upon to serve the important office of sheriff, and who prayed in vain to be excused from serving, should be sent out of the country in another capacity during his term of office. Now we know that Elyot's shrievalty extended from November 1532 to November 1533; for in the accounts of the treasurers of the town of Cambridge for the year ending Michaelmas 1533, we find among other charges the following: 'Paid to Sir Thomas Elyot, Knt., Sheriff, for his friendship, liii.s. iv.d.'[c] Again, we have letters from Elyot himself, written in England in April and May of this year, making no allusion whatever to any such embassy, and Chapuys mentions a conversation he had had with him in the latter month. Moreover, if Elyot had gone as Ambassador to Rome we should expect to find some reference to him in the letters of Bonner or Gregory de Cassalis, yet no mention is made of him in this capacity until nearly a century and a half after the date of his supposed mission. Hence it appears certain that this so-called historical fact rests upon no surer foundation than the heading given by an unknown copyist to these 'Instructions' many years after they were issued.

[a] *Hist. of Eng.* vol. i. p. 796, ed. 1732.
[b] *Eccles. Mem.* vol. i. pt. i. p. 341.
[c] Cooper, *Annals of Cambridge*, vol. i. p. 361.

The following letter from Elyot to Sir John Hackett, the English Ambassador in the Low Countries, although the year is not given, must from internal evidence be referred to 1533, Cranmer having been consecrated Archbishop only a few days previously:[a]

'Mr. Hakett, I hartily commend me unto you, and thanke you for your gentill lettre that ye sent to me by Mr. Raynsford. I wold that I hadd some comfortable newes to send you oute of theise partes, but the world is all otherwise. I beseche oure lord amend it. We have hanging over us a grete kloude, which is likely to be a grete storme whan it fallith. The Kinges highness, thankid be godd, is in goode helth. I beseche godd contynue it, and send his comfort of spirite unto him, and that truthe may be freely and thankfully herd. For my part I am finally determined to lyve and dye therin, neither myn importable expences unrecompencid shall so moche feare me, nor the advauncement of my successor,[b] the busshop of Caunterbury, so much alure me, that I shall ever deklyne from trouthe or abuse my soveraigne lorde, unto whome I am sworne, for I am sure that I and you allso shall ones dye, and I know that ther is a godd, and he is all trouthe, and therefor he will grievousely punissh all fallshode, and that everlastingly. Ye shall here er it be longe some straunge thinges of the spiritualitie, for betwene theim selfes is no perfect agrement. Some do saye that thei diggid the diche that thei be now fallen in, which causith manye goode men the lass to pitie theim. All other thinges be in the state that

---

[a] According to Strype he was consecrated March 30, 1533. See *Mem. of Cranmer*, vol. i. p. 26.

[b] According to Fox, Cranmer went to the Emperor from Rome after the Earl of Wiltshire, &c. had returned to England in 1530, but according to Strype his commission bore date Jan. 24, 1531; this, however, was O.S. and should be 1532. He was succeeded by Hawkins in Oct. 1532. See *State Pap.* vol. vii. p. 386.

ye left theim. If ye doo send to me any newes I will recompence you. Oure lord sende you moche honor. And I pray you have me hartily commended to my lord of Palermo,[a] the Duke of Soers[b] good grace, my lord of Berghes,[c] and my lord Molynbayse,[d] and all my goode lordes, and allsoe to gentill Master Adrian[e] and his goode bedfelowe Mastres Philip, whoes honestie, pacience, and moste gentill entretaynement I cese not to advaunce amonge oure women, as she is worthy.

'Writen at London the vi. day of April,
    'Your son and assurid frend,
        'TH. ELYOT, Kt.'[f]

A week later Anne Boleyn was publicly acknowledged as Queen. In 1533 Easter day fell on April 13; and Hall tells us that 'On Easter eue she went to her closet openly as Quene, with all solempnitie; and then the Kyng appoynted the daie of her Coronacion to bee kept on Whitson Sundaie[g] next folowyng; and writynges wer sent to al Shriues to certifie the names of menne of fourtie pounde to receiue the Ordre of

---

[a] This was Jean de Carondelet, who in 1520 had been made Archbishop of Palermo and Primate of Sicily, and on April 15, 1522, President of the Council of the Low Countries. See Henne, *Hist. du règne de Chas. V. en Belgique*, tom. ii. p. 242, ed. 1858.

[b] Philippe de Croy, Duc de Soria, Marquis d'Aerschot, was appointed successively Chamberain, Chancellor of the Exchequer, and Captain-General of Hainault by Chas. V. Henne, *ubi supra*, tom. ii. p. 346, note.

[c] Antoine de Berghes, created Count of Walhain in April 1533, and Marquis de Berghes in May of the same year. Henne, *ubi supra*, tom. vi. p. 83, note 7.

[d] Philippe de Lannoy, Seigneur de Molembais, Grand Master of Artillery under Charles V., died Sept. 22, 1543. Henne, *ubi supra*, tom. iii. p. 148.

[e] Possibly Adrien de Croy, created Comte de Rœulx, Feb. 24, 1530. See Henne, *ubi supra*, tom. v. p. 117.

[f] Addressed 'A Monsr. Sr Jehan Haket, Ambassador de le Roy.' MS. P. R. O. *Cromwell Corresp.* vol. x. No. 102.

[g] June 1st.

knighthod or els to make a fine, the assessement of whiche fines were appoynted to Thomas Cromwell, Master of the Kynges Juell house and counsailer to the kyng, and newly in his high fauour, whiche so pollitikely handeled the matter that he raised of that sessyng of fines a greate somme of money to the Kynges use.'[a] The following letter from Elyot to Cromwell evidently refers to this measure, and was therefore written either in April or May of this year:

'May it like you, Sir. Uppon the Kinges writt deliverid me with your lettres for the summonyng of suche as were able to receyue thordre of Knyghthode, I sent doune into the contray myn undersherif for the more sure expedition thereof; who afterward browght unto me a bill of names, wherein was named one Wawton, whoes substance I knewe not, and unneth his personage. Finally, according to myn office I retorned him among other into the Chauncery; sens the which tyme diuerse wurshipfull men knowing the saide Wawton and his substance have to me affirmid precisely on theire faith that he hath not landes in his possession to the yerely value of fourty poundes by a grete porcion lakking. Notwithstanding with his industry in provision for his householde, withoute ferme, grasing of catell, or regrating, he kepith an honest port, and findeth many sones to skoole, which by his education be very towardly. And moreover he hath many dowghters for to sett furth in mariage, which, as ye well know, be grete corrosives of a litle substance. And therefor it was well provyded therein by the Statute of Knyghtes.[b] Wherfor, in as moche as the gentillman is poure and abasshfull, but right wise, and having sondry goode qualities, and accordingly bringith upp many his children,

[a] *Chron.* (*Hen. VIII.*) fo. ccx. ed. 1548.
[b] Stat. de Militibus, 1 Ed. II.

may it please you, after speaking with him at your goode leisour, to shew your gentill hart toward him in declaring how moche ye tendre the necessitie of poure gentillmen. Whereby ye shall not onely bynde him to pray for you, but allso gratifie to many wurshipfull men withoute hindraunce in any part to the Kinges Highness. I am thus bolde to write to the intent that I wold not with my presence interrupt your travaile aboute grett affaires.

'Your pourest frende,

'TH. ELYOT, Kt.'[a]

The gentleman referred to in this letter may possibly be the same Mr. Wharton 'a justice of peace in Suffolk,' who according to Strype was afterwards employed by Cromwell 'as his visitor about Suffolk and those parts.'[b]

It is evident from this and the preceding letter that Elyot was in London in the spring of this year. He had, therefore, an opportunity of seeing Chapuys, the Imperial Ambassador, and of discussing with him the political outlook. Writing to the Emperor on May 10, 1533, Chapuys says, 'The love and affection which the English in general bear your Majesty and the Queen is so very great, that no violence is to be apprehended unless the King's ministers themselves, by false representations, stir the people on to disorder, and find an excuse to arm against your Majesty, thereby depriving the English of all hope of that goodwill towards them at which, as I have understood from Ambassador Elyot, they are nowadays aiming.'[c]

One object of Elyot's residence in London at this time

[a] MS. P. R. O. *Cromwell Corresp.* vol. x. no. 57. There is no address to this letter, but it is indorsed 'Sir Thomas Eliott.'
[b] See *Eccles. Mem.* vol. i. pt. i. p. 539, and vol. iii. pt. i. p. 175.
[c] MS. P. R. O.

was probably to be near his printer, Berthelet. For in this year he published two more works, *Pasquil the Playne*, and *Of the Knowledge which Maketh a Wise Man*. The former, which is in the form of a dialogue between Pasquil, Gnatho, and Harpocrates, may have been suggested by a little brochure which had appeared, not long before, in Rome, entitled *Dialogus Marphorii et Pasquilli*.[a] This tract had been sent by Bonner to Cromwell a few months previously. For the former, writing from Bologna on December 24, 1532, says, 'This dialoge bytwen Marforius and Pasquillus, which of late cam to my handes, I doo send to your Maystership to laughe, not havyng a better thing as I moche desired. Your Maystership dothe, I knowe, well remember that great statua lyeng benethe the Capitole whiche is called Marforius; and as for Mr. Pasquillus ye knowe, I know well.'[b] According to Castelvetro, a writer of the sixteenth century, 'Maestro Pasquino' was a tailor in Rome, who, whilst at work, used to amuse himself by making caustic remarks about the Pope, the cardinals, priests, &c. Hence any scurrilous or ludicrous saying was, after a time, attributed to Pasquino.[c] When the latter died, the torso of an ancient statue was dug up, and placed near Pasquino's shop, and lampoons, in the shape of ridiculous questions, were affixed to it, the answers to which were suspended in a similar manner from a colossal statue called Marforio. The word *pasquinade* owes its origin to this custom.

According to Mr. Payne Collier, *Pasquil the Playne* is a 'semi-serious argument on the subject of loquacity and silence. . . . The question discussed is, when men

[a] See *Pasquillorum Tomi duo*, p. 296, ed. 1544.
[b] *State Papers*, vol. vii. p. 397.
[c] *Ragioni d alcune cose segnate nella Canzone di Messer Annibal Caro*, fo. 141, ed. 1560.

ought, and when they ought not to speak, Gnatho beginning with a quotation on the point from Æschylus. . . . Gnatho is the advocate of talking, and Harpocrates of silence, while Pasquil agrees with neither, and throughout is very plain-spoken in his severe remarks; in fact, in some places the dialogue assumes the character of a prose satire.'[a] There is no copy of this curious little book in the British Museum Library, and we are, therefore, compelled to rely upon works of bibliography for this meagre account of it. It is styled by Ames 'a work of considerable interest as well as rarity,'[b] but although both he and Mr. Collier give extracts from the book itself, neither of them has thought proper to preserve 'the prefatory epistle,' from which we should probably have gained more insight into the author's intention in writing this squib than from half-a-dozen passages selected at random from the body of the work. It was reprinted by Berthelet in 1540, and copies of this last edition are said to have been in the possession of Sir Charles Frederick[c] and of Mr. Heber.[d]

With the other work, published by Elyot in 1533, we are fortunately better acquainted. He tells us in the preface how he came to write it, and to designate it *Of the Knowledge which Maketh a Wise Man*. 'Touchynge the title of my boke,' he says, 'I considered that wisedome is spoken of moch more than used. For wherin it resteth fewe menne be sure. The commune opinion is into thre partis deuided. One sayeth it is in moche lernynge and knowledge. An other affirmeth that they whiche do conducte the affayres of greatte princis or countrayes be onely

[a] *Bibliograph. Catalogue*, vol. i. p. 254, ed. 1865.
[b] *Typ. Ant.*, vol. iii. p. 283.
[c] Surveyor of the Ordnance in 1750.
[d] Ames, *Typ. Ant.*, vol. iii. p. 307, ed. 1816.

wyse men. Nay, saythe the thyrde, he is wysest that leste dothe meddle and can sytte quietly at home and tourne a crabbe and looke onely unto his owne busynesse. Nowe, they whiche be of the fyrste oppinion be alwaye at varyance. For somme doo chiefly extoll the study of holy scripture (as it is rayson), but while they do wrest it to agree with theyr willes, ambition, or vayne glory, of the mooste noble and deuoute lernyuge they doo endeuor them to make hit seruile and full of contention. Some do preferre the studie of the lawes of this realme, callynge it the onely studye of the publyke weale. But a great noumbre of persones whiche haue consumed in sute more thanne the value of that that they sued for in theyr angre do cal it a commune detriment. All thoughe, undoubtedly, the verye selfe lawe trewely practised passeth the lawes of all other countrayes.'

We can well imagine that this passage reflects Elyot's own sentiments, and that whilst smarting from the effects of the Chancery suit in which he had been involved with the Fyndernes, he must have been sorely tempted to denounce the expensive process, by which alone he had maintained his rights, as a 'common detriment.'

'In thinkynge on these sondrye opynyons,' he continues, 'I happened for my recreacyon to reede in the booke of Laertius[*] the lyfe of Plato, and beholdynge the aunswere that he made to king Dyonyse, at the fyrste syghte it semed to me to be very dissolute and lackyng the modestie that belonged to a philosopher, but whan I had better examined it, therein appered that whiche is best worthy to be called wysedome. Wherefore to exercyse my wytte and to auoyde idelnes, I toke my penne and

---

[*] Diogenes Laertius was the author of a History of Philosophy. The first complete edition of the Greek text was printed at Basle in this very year, 1533.

assayde howe, in expressyng my conceyte, I mought profyte to them whiche without disdayne or enuye wolde often tymes reade it. If any man wyll thinke the boke to be very longe let hym consyder that knowlege of wysedome can not be shortly declared. All be hit, of them whiche be well wyllinge it is soone lerned, in good faythe sooner thanne Primero or Gleeke.[a] Suche is the straunge propretie of that excellent counnynge that it is sooner lerned than taught, and better by a mannes rayson than by an instructour.

'Finally, if the reders of my warkis by the noble example of our mooste dere soueraygne lorde do iustly and louyngely interprete my labours, I durynge the residue of my lyfe wyll nowe and than sette forthe suche frutes of my study, profitable (as I trust) unto this my countray. And leuynge malycious reders with their incurable fury I wyll say unto god the wordes of the Catholike Churche in the boke of Sapience: To knowe the good lorde is perfecte Justice, and to knowe thy Justyce and vertue is the very roote of Immortalite;[b] and therin is the knowlege that is very wysedome.'

The book takes the form of a dialogue between Plato and Aristippus, who discuss wisdom, the soul, knowledge, ignorance, kings, tyrants, &c., it being supposed that Plato had been sent for by King Dionysus that the latter might be instructed in philosophy. But the tyrant, proving ungrateful, instead of giving the philosopher thanks was greatly displeased with him. Elyot evidently foresaw that this dialogue, as well as that of *Pasquil*, might not be taken in good part by some who would suppose that his remarks were addressed to themselves. For he disclaims

[a] These were games of cards played by three and four persons respectively.
[b] Wisdom, xv. 3.

the notion of intending to allude to any particular person. If the cap fitted, he could not help it. 'For my parte,' he says, 'I eftesones do protest that in no boke of mi making I haue intended to touche more one manne than an nother. For there be Gnathos in Spayne as wel as in Grece, Pasquilles in Englande as welle as in Rome, Dionises in Germanye as welle as in Sicile, Harpocrates in France as wel as in Ægipt, Aristippus in Scotlande as well as in Cyrena. Platos be fewe, and them I doubte where to fynde. And if men wyll seke for them in Englande whiche I sette in other places I can nat lette them. I knowe well ynowghe dyuers do delyte to have theyr garmentes of the facion of other countreyes, and that whiche is mooste playne is unplesant, but yet it doth happen sometyme that one man beynge in auctorytie or fauour of his prince beinge sene to weare somme thing of the old facion, for the straungenes therof it is taken up ageine with many good felowes. What I doo meane euery wyse man perceyuethe.'

At the end of 1533 we have the following letter from Elyot to the Lady Lisle, who had accompanied her husband to Calais in June of this year:—

'My syngulere goode lady, in moste humble manner I recommend me unto your goode ladisship. And where, by the reporte of your servaunt, Thomas Raynsforde, I perceyve that he hathe founden you allway his speciall goode lady, I, in the numbre of his frendes, doo moste hartily thank you. And for the experience that I have hitherto founde in him and all his bretherne concerning theire loyaltie and assurid honestie, I am movid to desyre your ladiship hartily to continue his goode lady, according as I doubt not but that ye shall finde his merites in doing his service and duetie unto my goode lorde and your ladishipp. All be it for as moche as I consydere that he hath to moche delyted in dysing, whereby he hath ben an ill husbonde in provyding for that which mowght now honestly fournissh him in serving my lorde and you, and as it seemith he now moche repentith with other losse of tyme, recounting to me how moche he is bounden to your ladisship for your honorable and moste gentill advertisementes, I, as one of his poure frendes, and allso in the name and at the request of his bretherne, specially Mr. Raynsford, gentillman huissher, my longe approved frende, doo humbly desyre youre ladisship to poursue your honorable and moste charitable favour toward your sayde servaunt. And in doing his diligent and true service to my lord and you, on my parte, I beseche your ladisship to recommend him unto my lordes good remembraunce for his advauncement. And, as your ladisship have doone, whan ye shall perceyve any lakk in him touching his service or excess in gamyng, of your goodness and wisedom withdraw him with your sharpe admonicion and commaundment, which I perceyve he doeth moche esteme and dreade. And so doing, besydes that his father and bretherne shall be bounden to pray for you, I shall on my behalf moste humbly thank you with my poure service. Our Lorde sende my goode lorde and you longe life in moche honour.

'Writen at London, the iii[d] day of Decembre.

'At your commaundment,

'TH. ELYOT, Kt.'[a]

The lady to whom the above letter was addressed was Honor, the second wife of Arthur Plantagenet, a natural son of Edward IV., who was created Viscount Lisle, by letters

[a] MS. P.R.O. *Chapter House Lisle Papers*, vol. x. no. 96. The letter is addressed "To the right honorable and my singuler goode lady My lady Lisles goode Ladisshipp."

patent, dated April 25, 1523,[a] and had quite recently been appointed Deputy of Calais, in succession to Lord Berners.[b] Lady Lisle, who was the daughter of Sir Thomas Granville, had been previously married to Sir John Basset,[c] of Umberleigh, near Barnstaple, and may, therefore, by her first marriage have been connected with the family of Elyot.

Our author seems now to have occupied himself entirely with that 'quiet study' which he had told his friend Cromwell he desired more than anything a king could give him. In 1534, no less than three separate treatises from his pen were published by Berthelet, in addition to a reprint of his last work. These consisted of a translation of a sermon of Saint Cyprian, another of an oration of Isocrates, and a medical treatise of still greater importance, entitled *The Castel of Helth.* With the first of these, of which the full title is *A swete and devoute Sermon of Holy saynt Ciprian of Mortalitie of Man,* the author joined *The Rules of a Christian lyfe made by Picus erle of Mirandula.* The sermon on mortality had been originally written by the Bishop of Carthage for the consolation of the faithful during a frightful pestilence which devastated Africa in the third century. Sir Thomas Elyot had probably perused this sermon in the folio edition of the works of the father lately published at Basle, by Erasmus. John Picus, of Mirandola, whose famous challenge to the world in 1486 to dispute his nine-hundred propositions had rendered him one of the most remarkable men of the age, during the few last years of his short life had devoted himself entirely to the study of the Scriptures. Amongst many other more elaborate works he composed

[a] *Lett. and Pap. Hen. VIII.*, vol. iii. pt. ii. p. 1259.
[b] Rymer, *Fœd.*, vol. xiv. p. 452.
[c] Collins, *Peerage,* vol. viii. p. 503, ed. 1812.

some short rules for the guidance of those who would lead a spiritual life, which in the original Latin are styled *Regulæ duodecim partim excitantes partim dirigentes hominem in pugnâ spirituali*.[a] It was an English version of these Rules which Sir Thomas Elyot appended to his translation of the sermon of Saint Cyprian. The two together forming a tiny volume of 64 pages, exclusive of the preface, were published on July 1, 1534. This work Elyot dedicated to the lady who has been already mentioned, the widow of John Kingstone the younger, and who, as the inscription on her monument informs us, had become a 'vowess.' Whilst telling her that he sends it as a token 'that ye shall perceyue that I doo not forgeat you, and that I doo unfaynedly loue you, not onely for our allyaunce, but also moche more for your perseuerance in vertu and warkes of true faith,' he prays her 'to communicate it with our two susters religiouse Dorothe and Alianour.' Of these last Dorothy was the daughter of Sir John Danvers, and widow of young John Fetiplace,[b] of East Shefford, who died in 1524, and is buried in the church there,[c] whilst 'Alianour' was, no doubt, the 'daughter-in-law' Eleanor, daughter of Richard Fetiplace, mentioned in the will of Sir Richard Elyot, and to whom he left a legacy of an annual sum 'till she be professed in religion.'

The full title of the other translation published by Elyot this year is *The Doctrinal of Princes made by the noble oratour Isocrates, and translated out of Greke in to Englishe by Syr Thomas Elyot, knight*. This is an English version of the oration to Nicocles, of which several foreign editions had already been published. The Greek text of all the orations had been

[a] Niceron, *Hom. Ill.* tom. xxxiv. p. 142.
[b] Clarke, *Par. Top. of Wanting*, p. 68.
[c] Lysons, *Berkshire*, p. 360.

published for the first time at Milan, in 1493, but the orations to Demonicus and Nicocles were published separately at Paris in 1508, at Strasbourg in 1515, at Louvain in 1522, and at Paris again in 1529. In the Preface Elyot informs his readers that he had translated the oration out of Greek 'not presumyng to contende with theim whiche haue doone the same in latine, but to thintent onely that I wolde assaie if our Englisshe tunge mought receive the quicke and propre sentences pronounced by the greekes. And in this experience I have founde (if I be not muche deceiued) that the forme of speakyng used of the Greekes, called in greeke and also in latine *Phrasis*, muche nere approcheth to that whiche at this daie we use than the order of the latine tunge, I meane in the sentences and not in the wordes: whiche I doubte not shall be affirmed by them who sufficiently instructed in all the saide three tunges shall with a good iudgement read this worke.' He then proceeds to tell us his object in publishing this translation, which was 'to the intent that thei which do not understande greeke nor latine shoulde not lacke the commoditee and pleasure whiche maie be taken in readyng therof.' And he announces his intention to devote the rest of his life to literary work if the reception accorded to the present volume should encourage him to do so. 'If I shall perceiue you to take this myne enterprise thankefully, I shall that little porcion of life whiche remeineth, (God sendyng me quietnesse of minde), bestowe in preparing for you such bookes in the readyng wherof ye shall finde bothe honest passe tyme and also profitable counsaile and lernyng.'

The last of the three new works published by Elyot in 1534, was *The Castel of Helth.* No copy of this edition is to be found in the Library of the British Museum,

LIFE OF ELYOT. cvii

and we may, therefore, not unreasonably presume that copies of this year are extremely scarce. According to Ames, who must have seen one, the dedication was to 'Thomas, Lord Cromwell.'[a] Now, as Cromwell was not created a baron before July 10, 1536,[b] there must be some error in Ames's description. For we cannot agree with Dibdin, that 'the date must be a mistake,' nor with Herbert that 'such date is to be considered only as an appendage to the wood-cut border of the title.'[c] It is true, no doubt, that in many cases the title-pages to the later editions were printed from old wood blocks, and that where a double date is given that which appears in the space contained within the printed border must be assumed to indicate the date of publication of that particular edition. But where only one date is given, and that *on* the ornamental border itself, as in this case, there seems to be no adequate reason for supposing that this does not really indicate the true date. It is, at any rate, easier to suppose that Ames himself was mistaken, or that the copy which he saw and described really belonged to an edition of 1536, than to assume that the date 1534 does not in fact indicate the date of first publication. At any rate, it is rather strange that in a copy of this work in the Grenville Library the same date, 1534, appears on the border of an edition which was certainly published in 1541, the latter date having been added to the title; whilst in another copy, in the British Museum, in which the same date has been added to the title, the space usually occupied by the date on the ornamental border is left blank. One can hardly suppose that unless the date on the ornamental border really indicated the year of *first* publication

---

[a] *Typog. Ant.*, p. 168, ed. 1749. [b] Stow, *Annales*, p. 572.
[c] Ames, *Typog. Ant.* vol. iii. p. 288, ed. 1816.

of the work the printer would be so careless as to employ the same wood block for a later edition without erasing the misleading figures.

The Castel of Helth, as its name implies, is a medical treatise. We have already seen that Elyot, partly, perhaps, from natural inclination, and still more, probably, from his intimacy with Linacre, whilst yet quite a young man, had turned his attention to the study of medicine, and had perused the voluminous tomes, not only of the Greek but of the Oriental writers on the art of healing. In England the practise of that art had hitherto been confined, for the most part, to ecclesiastics, who substituted superstition for science, and empiricism for observation. With the revival of classical learning it was at once seen by men like Linacre and Elyot, that the knowledge of Greek would rescue medicine from the hands of the ignorant, and restore it to the dignity of a science. The establishment of the College of Physicians is no less a monument to the enlightened views of its Royal founder than to the sagacity of its first President. In writing a medical treatise Elyot evidently designed to impart, so far as he was able, a knowledge of this hitherto occult science to the laity. His object, as in all his other works, was a purely disinterested one, not the hope of temporal reward, but as he himself tells us 'only for the feruent affection whiche I have euer borne toward the publike weale of my countrie.' Having himself suffered, as he has already told us,[*] from various disorders, he was moved with pity for the thousands of helpless patients whom he saw around him on every side. 'The intent of my labour,' he tells us, 'was that men and women readyng this worke and obseruyng the counsayles therin should adapte therby their bodies

[*] See *ante* p. lvii.

to receiue more sure remedie by the medicines prepared by good physicions in dangerous sicknesses, thei kepyng good diete, and infourmyng diligently the same physicions of the maner of their affectes, passions, and sensible tokens. And so shall the noble and moste necessarie science of phisicke, with the ministers therof, escape the sclaunder whiche they haue of long tyme susteyned.'·[a]

The book, as already stated, appears to have been dedicated to Cromwell, and the following letter no doubt accompanied a presentation copy.

'After moste harty recomendations. Sir, I have sent to you by the bringer hereof a litle treatise, which in exchuyng idleness, for the comfort of my self and other of equall debilitie, I late made. Wherin if ye finding sufficient leisour (as it will be hard for you to doo) and will spende a fewe houres I doubt not but that your goode witt shall finde more frute than ye wolde have looking for of any thinge that sholde have passid from my folissh hedd. But (as the olde greeke proverbe is) it is sometyme goode to here the pour gardyner.[b] In this warke I have done no thing but onely browght to mennes re membraunce that which naturall raison hath towght theim ; and that withoute desyre of reward or glory. For according to your voise and frendely aunswere unto me I can not compelle men to esteme me as I wolde that thei sholde, that is (as I saye) benevolent unto my contraye and faithfull unto him that will trust me. For no thinge els goode is there in me. Yet myne indevor shall be never the lasse to sett furth in some wise that litle portion of knowlege which I have receyved of godd by the meane of study and some experience, which I suppose mowght be profitable to them which will reade or

[a] *The Castell of Helth*, fo. 90, ed. 1541.
[b] Probably Sir T. Elyot refers to the following proverb Ἀγροίκου μὴ καταφρό-νει ῥήτορος. See Gaisford's *Parœmiog.* p. 231, ed. 1836.

heere it. The mater contayned in this booke is of suche importance that it requireth a quyete lesson and a pregnant iugement with allso a stable remembrance; to the help wherof I have of pourpose usid often repetitions, whereby the matere seemyth the lenger; but being radd diligently and well concoct to theim in whome is any aptness to receyue goode counsayle it will not seeme very tediouse. As it is I pray you take it in goode part, and after your olde gentill manere defend your frende in his true meaning agayne theim whoes myndes have suche a fever contynuall that every goode counsaile is in theire taste unsavery and bitter. And if it shall please you to recommend one of theise bookes unto the Kinges highness when ye shall fynde thereunto oportunitie, I conforme me to your pleasure, sens this is the last Englissh booke which I pourpose ever to make, onelass the desyre of some speciall frende doo compelle me. Notwithstanding if I may in this povertie be suffrid to lyve in quyeteness I trust to be so occupyed as neither godd nor honest man shall have cause to blame me for consumyng my tyme. Our lorde send you longe life with moche worship.

'Yours to my litle powar,

'TH. ELYOT, Kt.'[a]

We are enabled to fix the year of this letter by the address, in which Cromwell is designated as 'Treasurer of the King's Jewels.' He is so described in a letter from Sir William Paget, dated Hamburgh, Feb. 22, 1534.[b]

It was perhaps natural that the medical profession should resent the publication of a book which threatened not only to

---

[a] Harleian MSS., 6989, no. 21. The letter is addressed 'To my specially assurid frende Mr. Cromewell, treasorer of the Kinges Jewelles.'

[b] See *State Papers*, vol. vii. p. 542. He must have held this office two years, for his patent of appointment is dated April 14, 1532. See Foss, *Judges of England*, vol. v. p. 148.

expose the ignorance of those who assumed to be in exclusive possession of the secrets of the art of healing but to destroy the monopoly which they had hitherto enjoyed. 'A worthy matter,' said one of these indignant professors, ' Syr Thomas Elyot is become a phisicion and writeth in phisicke, whiche besemeth not a knight; he mought have ben muche better occupied.' But in a later edition Elyot gave a most complete answer to his opponents, beating them with their own weapons. 'Truely,' he said, 'if they wyll call hym a phisicion whiche is studiouse about the weale of his countrey, I wytsaufe[a] thei so name me, for duryng my life I wyll in that affection alwaie continue. And why, I pray you, should men haue in disdaine or small reputacion the science of phisike? Which beyng well understand, truely experienced, and discretely ordred, doth conserue helth, without the whiche all pleasures be peynefull, rychesse unprofitable, company annoyance, strength turned to febleness, beauty to lothsomnes, sences are dispersed, eloquence interrupted, remembraunce confounded. . . . It seemeth that physicke in this realme hath been well esteemed, sens the hole studie of Salern at the request of a kyng of England wrate and set foorthe a compendious and profitable treatise called The Gouernance of health, in latine, Regimen Sanitatis.[b] And I trust in almightie God that our soueraigne lorde the Kynges maiestee, who daiely prepareth to stablisshe among us true and uncorrupted doctrines, will shortly examine also this part of studie in suche

[a] *I.e.* vouchsafe, of which the word in the text is the primitive form.

[b] This was a poem in Latin hexameters composed for Robert Duke of Normandy, the eldest son of William the Conqueror, at the end of the eleventh century, by the celebrated School of Medicine at Salerno. It was so popular that it is said above 160 editions were published. English translations of a prose commentary by Arnaldus de Villa Nova were printed by Berthelet in August 1528, February 1530, and 1535, and it is curious that the wood block used for the titlepage is the same as that for Elyot's book.

wyse as thynges apt for medicine growyng in this realme by conference with most noble authors may be so knowen that we shal haue lesse nede of thynges brought out of farre countreis, by the corrupcion wherof innumerable people haue perished without blame to be geuen to the physicions, sauyng onely that some of them not diligent inough in beholdyng their drugges or ingredience at all tymes dispensed and tried. . . . This well considered I take it for no shame to studie that science, or to set foorth any bokes of the same, beyng thereto prouoked by the moste noble and vertuous exaumple of my moste noble maister Kyng Henrie the VIII. whose helth I hertily pray god as long to preserue as god hath constitute mans life to continue, for his highnesse hath not disdeined to be the chiefe author and setter foorth of an Introduction into grammer for the children of his louyng subiectes, whereby hauyng good maysters thei shall most easily and in short time apprehend the understandyng and forme of speakyng of true and eloquent latine.* O roiall hert full of very

---

* This evidently refers to a book entitled *An Introduction of the eyght partes of speche and the construction of the same, compiled and sette forthe by the commaundement of our most gracious souerayne lorde the King*, A.D. 1542. This date seems to be confirmed by the Address 'to the Reder,' which ends as follows, 'Let noble prynce Edwarde encourage your tender hartes, a prynce of greate towardnes, a prynce in whome god hath powred his graces abundantly, a prynce framed of suche perfectnes of nature that he is lyke, by the grace of God, to ensue the steppes of his fathers wysedome, lernynge and vertue, and is nowe almost in a redynesse to rounne in the same rase of lernyng with you. For whom ye haue great cause to praye that he may be the soonne of a longe lyuyng father.' Now the Prince of Wales was not born till Oct. 12, 1537, and therefore was five years old at the time of this edition. The copy in the British Museum is printed on vellum and illuminated, and is evidently the same as that mentioned by Ames, who, however, is mistaken in saying that the date is 1543. It is obvious, however, that the publication preceded that of the edition of the *Castell of Helth* from which we are quoting, viz. 1541. There may therefore have been a previous edition. It is curious that Ames mentions *The Instruction of a christen man by order of King Hen. VIII.* as printed in 1537, and Herbert, '*Certain brief Rules of the regiment or construction of the eight parts of speche in English and Latin*, in the same year, and

nobilitee. O noble breast settyng foorth vertuous doctrine and laudable studie. But yet one thyng muche greueth me, that notwithstandyng I haue euer honoured and specially fauoured the reuerend colledge of approued phisicions, yet some of them heryng me spoken of haue saied in derision, that although I were pretily seen in hystories, yet beyng not lerned in physicke I haue put in my booke diuers errours in presumyng to write of herbes and medicines. First as concernyng hystories as I haue planted them in my workes, beyng wel understand they be not so light of importance as they dooe esteme them, but may more surely cure mens affections then diuers physicions do cure maladies. Nor whan I wrate first this boke I was not all ignoraunt in physicke. And although I haue neuer been at Mountpellier, Padua, nor Salern, yet haue I found some thyng in phisicke wherby I haue taken no littell profite concernyng myne owne helth. Moreouer I wote not why Physicions should be angrie with me, sens I wrate and did set forth the *Castell of Helth* for their commoditee, that the uncertayne tokens of urines and other excrementes should not deceiue them, but that by the true informacion of the sicke man by me instructed they might be the more sure to prepare medicines conuenient for the diseases. Also to the intent that men, obseruyng a good order in diete and preuentyng the great causes of sicknesse, they should of those maladies the soner be cured. But if physicions be angry that I haue written physicke in englishe, let them remember that the grekes wrate in greke, the Romains in latin, Auicenna and the other in Arabike, whiche were their

one or both of these may be an earlier edition of *The Introduction*. The copy in the B. M. is followed by 'Institutio Compendiaria totius grammaticæ quam et eruditissimus atque idem illustrissimus Rex noster hoc nomine evulgari jussit, ut non alia quàm hæc una per totam Angliam pueris prælegeretur. Londini, A.D. 1542.'

own proper and maternall tongues. And if thei had been as muche attached with enuie and couetise as some nowe seeme to be, they would haue deuised some particuler language with a strange cypher or forme of letters wherin they wold haue written their scyence, whiche language or letters no manne should haue knowen that had not professed and practised physicke. But those, although they were Paynims and Jewes, in this part of charitee they farre surmounted us christians, that they would not haue so necessarie a knowlage as physicke is to be hidde from theim whiche would be studiouse about it. Finally God is my iudge I write neyther for glorie, rewarde nor promocion, onely I desire men to deeme well mine intent, sens I dare assure them that all that I haue written in this boke I haue gathered of the most principall writers in physicke. Whiche beyng throughly studied and wel remembred shall be profitable (I doubt not) unto the reader, and nothyng noyouse to honest physicions that dooe measure their studie with moderate liuyng and christen charitee.'

The Castel of Helth soon became a very popular book, notwithstanding the depreciatory remarks of the faculty. According to Lowndes, it was reprinted no less than ten times, the last edition being that of 1595, and there were probably two other editions without date.

In addition to these three new productions of Elyot's pen, another edition of *The Governour* was issued by Berthelet in 1534.[*] It is extremely difficult to ascertain precisely in what years these various editions came from the press, on account of the practice adopted by Berthelet of employing the old woodblocks for title-pages. There are two copies, for instance, of *The Castel of Helth* in the British Museum Library, varying

---

[*] Ames, *Typog. Ant.*, vol. iii. p. 289, note, ed. 1816.

in size and type but both bearing the same date, viz. 1541.[a] It is probable, however, that the larger of these two is really a re-issue of the first edition.

It may be doubted whether even this list exhausts the whole number of the works which Elyot gave to the world in this year. For it seems extremely probable that *The Bankette of Sapience* was published for the first time in 1534. According to Lowndes, an edition of 1542 is 'the earliest known edition,' but in this he is clearly mistaken, for in the British Museum there is a copy printed by Berthelet in 1539, that being the date given in the colophon. The date on the ornamental border of the title-page, however, which is precisely the same as that of the smaller copy of *The Castel of Helth* (1541) is 1534, and for the reasons given above it seems fair to assume that the latter date refers to the year in which *The Bankette of Sapience* was first published. This work consists of a collection of moral sayings or sentences from various authors but chiefly from the fathers. It was dedicated to the King, and appears from 'the prologue; to have been published in the spring of the year. It was reprinted in 1542, and 1545, and again after the author's death in 1557 and 1563.

On October 8, 1534, Thomas Cromwell was appointed Master of the Rolls, being the first layman who had ever been advanced to that office.[b] His immediate predecessor was Dr. John Taylor, a clergyman whose nephew, as already stated, had succeeded Elyot as Clerk of Assize. The following summer Cromwell commenced his visitation of the religious houses. 'The last year,' says Strype, 'the Parliament had, for the augmentation of the King's royal estate,

[a] See Ames, *ubi supra*, p. 316.
See Foss, *Judges of England*, vol. v. p. 146.

given him the first-fruits of all spiritual livings throughout the realm and the tenths.[a] For the better execution of this Act the King sent abroad his Commissioners to take the true value of the benefices through the whole land ; several Commissioners for each county. There was also a certain number of auditors joined with them. . . . When the valuations were made and taken by the Commissioners they were all returned to Crumwel now Master of the Rolls.'[b] From the following letter it is evident that Sir Thomas Elyot was employed on this Commission :—

'With most humble recomendations. Sir, wher it likid you at my last being with you at the Rolles to ministre unto me moste gentill wordes to my grete comfort, I have often tymes sens revolved theim in my remembraunce setting in you onely all my hole confidence and so doo persist. Where late I have travaylid aboute the survaying of certayne monasteries by the Kinges commaundment, wher in my paynes shold appiere not unthankfull if opportunitie mowght happen for me to declare it. If now, Sir, it mought like you in approvyng your benevolent mynde toward me, wherein I doo specially trust, to sett furth with your gentill report unto the Kinges highness my true hart and diligent indevour in his graces service, to my importable charges and unrecuperable decay of my lyving, onlas his highness relieve me with his abundaunt and graciouse liberalitie; and therwith it mowght please you to devise with his highness for my convenient recompence toward my sayde charges either by landes now suppressid or pencion, I shall not onely take comfort of your approved fidelitie and the same advaunce unto your honour, but allso in suche wise ordre me toward you as ye shall deeme me not

---

[a] By 26 Hen. VIII. cap. 3.
[b] *Eccles. Mem.*, vol. i. pt. i. p. 325.

unworthy your gentill remembraunce and benefite; putting you in this assuraunce that never may have founden or shall fynde me ingrate or unthankfull. I wold awaytid on you as my duetie hadd ben, but that I dradd to fynde you occupied with grete affayres, which of late hath causid me to make many vayne journayes whan I have ben right desyrouse to see [you], not for my necessitie onely but to have communicate with you some tokens of harty frendship. If it be your pleasure that I shall attend on you at the Court to revyve your gentill remembraunce, I, that knowing, shall folow your commaundment and counsaile, godd willing, who send to you his grace with long contynuance in honour.

'Yours with true affection,

'TH. ELYOT, Kt.'[a]

This letter was probably written in the autumn of 1534 or the spring of 1535. It must certainly have been written prior to the month of July in the latter year. Sir Thomas More was executed on July 6, 1535. And we know that Elyot was out of England when that event happened. The tradition that the news was communicated to him for the first time by the Emperor himself rests on too high an authority to be rejected. On his return from the siege of Tunis, Charles landed in Sicily, August 22, 1535, and after staying some time at Palermo made his entry into Messina on October 21. He arrived in Naples on November 25, and remained there about four months.[b] It was perhaps whilst the Emperor was resident in this city that the following incident occurred. 'Soone after Mores death came intelligence thereof to the Emperor

---

[a] MS. P.R.O. *Cromwell Corresp.*, vol. x. no. 58. The letter is addressed 'To the right honorable Mr Secretary.'

[b] See *Pap. d'État du Card. de Granvelle*, tom. ii. p. 387 note, and p. 413 note.

Charles, whereuppon he sent for Sir Thomas Eliott, our Eenglish Embassodor and sayd unto him, "My Lord Embassodor, wee understand that the Kinge your Master hath putt his faythfull servaunt and grave wise Councellor Sir Thomas Moore to death." Whereunto Sir Thomas Eliott aunsweared that hee understood nothinge thereof. "Well," sayd the Emperor, "it is verye true, and this will we saye, that if wee had bine Mr. of such a servaunt, of whose doinges our selves have had these many yeares noe small experience, wee would rather have lost the best Cittie of our dominiones then have lost such a worthie Councellor.' Now this story is related by William Roper, Sir Thomas More's own son-in-law, who adds:—'Which matter was bye Sir Thomas Eliott to my selfe, to my wife, to Mr. Clement and his wife, to Mr. John Haywood and his wife, and divers others of his frends accordingely reported.' [a]

Stapleton, who was born in the very year that More died, had evidently heard the same account probably from some member of the family, for he says, 'Illud postremo loco ponam, quod à fide dignis accepi, nobilissimum in hâc causâ et sempiternâ memoriâ dignum testimonium. Carolus V. Imperator, princeps non minus judicio acer quàm bello fortis et felix, auditâ Roffensis et Mori nece, Thomæ Elioto tunc Henrici apud eum legato hæc verba dixit. "Ego, si in meis regnis duo hujusmodi lumina haberem, quamlibet munitissimam civitatem potius periclitari sinerem, quàm me illis privari, nedum injustę tolli permitterem." Hæc ille. Præstantissimi Principis præclarum elogium fuit.'[b] Substantially the same version is also given by the writer (supposed to be Nicholas Harpsfield) of another Life of More which still re-

---

[a] Roper, *Vita Mori*, p. 58, ed. Hearne 1716.
[b] *Tres Thomæ*, p. 359, ed. 1588.

LIFE OF ELYOT.   cxix

mains in MS. in the Lambeth Library,[a] by the anonymous author of the Life printed by Dr. Wordsworth,[b] and by Thomas More, the great grandson of the Chancellor, in a work which Wood describes as 'incomparably well written.'[c] It is obvious, however, that none of these except, perhaps, the last mentioned can pretend to so much authority as the two from which we have quoted.

It appears at first sight remarkable that no allusion is made by Elyot himself to this incident, neither in any work published after this date nor in any letter at present discovered. And in fact but for Roper's statement there would, so far as the Editor has been able to ascertain, be no ground for asserting positively that Elyot was employed as Ambassador or even absent from England at this period. Roper's statement, however, which in itself is too precise to be disputed, is indirectly confirmed by the following circumstances.

We have seen already that Elyot, when employed as Ambassador in the Low Countries, had complained to Vaughan that his letters remained unanswered and that he was left without instructions from England, a complaint which Vaughan had forwarded to Cromwell. It would seem that Elyot experienced similar treatment on this second mission and was left to hear the news of More's death, not from the King or Cromwell, but from the Emperor to whose Court he was accredited. Now, curiously enough, we have a letter from the latter to his Ambassador in France,[d] written from Naples in January, 1536, in which occurs the following pas-

[a] See Wordsworth, *Eccles. Biog.*, vol. ii. p. 45.
[b] *Ibid.* p. 179.
[c] See Wood's *Ath. Oxon.* vol. i. col. 87, ed. 1813.
[d] Jean Hannaert, Vicomte de Lombeke. See Henne, *Hist. du règne de Chas. V.* tom. v. p. 118.

sage, showing that the English Ambassador (presumably Elyot) was then placed in such a predicament. 'Depuis ce que dessus, nous avons receu voz lectres des xv et xvi de ce mois, et nous desplaît extrêmement des nouvelles du trespas de la royne d'Angleterre, nostre tante,[a] dont pour ce que n'en avons encoires la certitude de nostre ambassadeur estant audit Angleterre, et que celluy dudit Angleterre résident devers nous n'en a nulles lectres de son maistre, ne l'avons voulsu tenir pour certain, comme chose que créons mal voluntiers et de très-grand déplésir.'[b] We have also the fact to be referred to more at length presently that Elyot himself alludes in a work published some years after this period to his having borrowed a book from 'a gentleman of Naples.' Now this may very well have taken place at the time when he was himself resident at Naples, in the autumn of 1535, as the accredited Ambassador to the Emperor. As for the absence of any written or printed account by Elyot himself of his conversation with the Emperor, it is easier to understand the omission when we read the instructions given by Cromwell to the English Ambassador at the Court of France,[c] and remember that Henry 'was greatly nettled' when informed of the conversation between Francis and Sir John Wallop under circumstances precisely similar to those detailed by Roper with regard to Elyot and Charles.[d]

But conceding the truth of Roper's story, the question remains yet to be answered, *Where* was Elyot if he was not in England in July 1535? Charles sailed from Barcelona on his African expedition on May 30. He certainly had an English Ambassador in his suite, for in a letter written by the Em-

---
[a] Catharine of Aragon died on Jan. 8, 1536.
[b] *Pap. d'état du Card. de Granvelle*, tom. ii. p. 429, ed. 1841.
See Strype, *Eccles Mem.*, vol. i. pt. 2. p. 247.
[d] *Ibid.* vol. 1, pt. 1, p. 360.

peror as he was on the point of sailing, he says, 'Ledit Ambassadeur de France a parsisté de nous suyvir en ce voyage, après qu'il eust tenu propos de soy retirer, et que aultre venoit en son lieu ; et pour ce ne luy avoit esté pourveu de galères, supposant que luy et aultres ambassadeurs suyvans nostre court yroient en naves ; et sur ce qu'il a parsisté à ladite galère, en avons ordonné une pour luy et l'ambassadeur d'Angleterre et celluy du marquis de Saluces,[a] avec aucungs gentilshommes de nostre maison, pour gaigner place, selon le grand nombre de gens que menons.'[b] The French Ambassador was the Sieur de Vély who, as we have already seen, was in Elyot's company at Ratisbon in 1532. Now whoever the English Ambassador may have been, it is certain that he and de Vély were thrown a great deal together and were on the best possible terms during the voyage and subsequent operations. This is clearly shown by the following passage in the Emperor's letter, written from Messina to his Ambassador in France, in the following October. 'En oultre, nous avons veu ce qu'avez escript au Sr de Granvelle touchant ce que ledit Sr de Vély, ambassadeur dudit S^r roy, a escript par delà, de la naviere en laquelle il est allé durant nostre voiage de Thunes, et mesmes touchant ce que luy fut dit lorsque étions au camp devant la Goulette, et de la compaignie que luy fut baillée en ladite naviere de l'escuyer Vandenesse et Anthoine de Bedia, que nous sembla estre pour le mieulx, pour les considérations que le Sr de Granvelle dit de nostre part audit Sr de Vély, non pas pour le tenir estroitement, comme il dit, mais pour sa plus grande commodité, et aussi afin qu'il ne luy advint quelque inconvénient, et davantaige que, à la vérité, ledit ambassadeur se démonstroit par trop curieulx d'assentir

[a] Francois, Marquis de Saluces, or Saluzzo, a town in the Vaudois.
[b] *Pap. d'état du Card. de Granvelle*, tom. ii. p. 359.

et enquérir nouvelles, et alloient aucungs de ses gens par le camp, voire armez, et se trouvoient souvent aucungs d'eulx en nostre tente et à l'encontre d'icelle et d'aultres de nostredit conseil, suspectement et à mensongières occasions. Et si avons entendu que ledit ambassadeur a escript plusieurs nouvelles non vrayes, que sont esté publiées au cousté d'Angleterre et aillieurs : et entre aultres choses a esté trop curieulx à luy, et aussi au Sr de Vaugy, d'avoir faict faire et pourter par delà la platte-forme de la fortisfication de ladite Goulette, comme l'escripvez. Toutesfois, n'est besoing que en faictes semblant, et souffit qu'en soiez adverty pour, s'il survenoit quelques aultres advertissemens que ledit ambassadeur pourroit faire ; et que ledit ambassadeur et son cousin sont extrêmement curieulx de veoir, sçavoir et entendre tout ce que passe en ceste court, et fort véhémentement ; et au regard d'avoir tenu à ses gaiges ladite naviere, ledit ambassadeur s'est de ce advancé, car elle a tousjours esté à nostre soulde, et ce nonobstant, au commandement dudit ambassadeur ; et est bien vray que jusques au désembarquement en ladite Goulette, y eust quelques gens de guerre beaulcoup plus que en d'aultres, mais au retour n'y en a point eu, et a esté ledit ambassadeur très-bien traicté, et mieulx que nul des autres, tant de galères que de batteaulx, et en a eu très-grand contentement, et l'a mercié souvent l'ambassadeur d'Angleterre, que tousjours a esté avec ledit Sr de Vély.'[*] It seems from this that de Vély had proved rather troublesome on account of his inquisitiveness, and had been the means of disseminating false information about the Emperor which had been published in England and elsewhere. He seems also to have acknowledged his obligations to the English Ambassador, who was on board the same ship and appears to

[*] *Pap. d'état du Card. de Granvelle*, tom. ii. p. 393.

have helped to make things pleasant for his French colleague.

Now it is curious that the name of the English ambassador is not only not given by the Emperor, or by Sandoval, or other foreign writers who have left us accounts of the expedition to Tunis, but the fact that a representative of England was present is totally ignored by Mr. Thomas in his *Historical Notes*, and, so far as we have been able to ascertain, by every other English writer. We may observe here that M. Henne, who has devoted ten octavo volumes to the reign of Charles V., dismisses the subject of what he calls 'this glorious expedition' in a couple of pages, but this may probably be because the services of the Belgians who took part in it have not been recorded.[a] A list of the ambassadors present at the capture of Tunis is supplied by M. Chotin, who has followed Sandoval's account. They represented respectively England, France, Portugal, Milan, Florence, Venice, Ferrara, Saluce, Genoa, Sienne, Mantua, and Naples.[b] Their names, however, except in the case of de Vély, are not given. Now, starting with the fact that Elyot was not in England in July, and that he heard the news of More's death not direct from England but from the Emperor, it seems not at all unlikely that he had left this country in May to embark with the Emperor at Barcelona, or perhaps had joined the contingent from the Low Countries at Antwerp.[c] If he had merely gone to Naples to meet the Emperor on his return from Tunis, he would hardly have left

---

[a] 'Les historiens se sont tus sur la part prise par les Belges à cette glorieuse expédition ; pourtant là, comme partout, ils soutinrent noblement leur réputation de vaillance.'—*Hist. du règne de Chas. V.*, tom. vi. p. 89, ed. 1859.

[b] *Hist. des exped. marit. de Chas. V.*, p. 164, ed. 1849.

[c] 'Il est constant qu'une grande partie de la flotte avait été fournie par les Pays-Bas.'—Henne, *ubi supra*, tom. vi. p. 90.

England so early as July, and, in any case, could not fail to have heard the news of More's death on passing through Rome. If, on the other hand, he actually took part in the expedition, it is easy to understand that he might be without intelligence from England, whilst other means of information would doubtless be open to the Emperor. Moreover the fact that Elyot had been previously acquainted with de Vély makes it highly probable that he would be ready to exert his influence with the Emperor to make matters smooth for his colleague, the representative of a power of whom Charles had some present ground of complaint.[a]

All things considered, then, it seems not unlikely that Elyot was really present as a spectator of the Spanish operations in Africa, notwithstanding the absence of any positive evidence as to the fact. We can only deplore here, as at other points in Elyot's career, the strange fate which has deprived us of the greatest part of a correspondence which must surely have been voluminous and could not fail to be most interesting.

In 1536 a Royal Proclamation was issued 'For callyng in diuers writings and bokes, and specially one boke imprinted, comprising a sermon made by John Fysher, late Bishop of Rochester: and also against light persons called pardoners and sellers of indulgences.'[b] It is unfortunate that we are obliged to rely for our knowledge of this Order upon a mere bibliographical catalogue, but no collection of the

---

[a] Francesco Contarini, Venetian Ambassador with the King of the Romans, in a letter to the Signory dated July 23, 1535, says, 'I understand that the Emperor complains greatly of the most Christian King, saying that the cannon balls fired at the Imperial forces are stamped with the lily.' –*Cal. State Pap.* (*Venetian*), vol. v. p. 30, the Rolls ed.

[b] See Ames, *Typog. Ant.* vol. iii. p. 292, ed. 1816.

proclamations of this reign has ever been made, which is much to be regretted, for, as Mr. Herbert has pointed out 'they would afford much light to our historians.' The short notice of the one mentioned above is given by Ames without comment, but is said to be taken 'from Mr. T. Baker's interleaved copy of Maunsell's catalogue.' This last was one of the volumes bequeathed to the Cambridge University Library by the will of Mr. Thomas Baker, formerly fellow of St. John's Coll. dated Oct. 15, 1739.[a] Mr. Herbert inquires, 'which of the Bishop's sermons it was that came under this lash?' and supposes it 'to have been rather a treatise in answer to a book printed in 1530, concerning the King's marriage.' It seems however much more probable that it referred to the sermon preached by Fisher at the funeral, or rather at the 'months mind' of the Lady Margaret, mother of Henry VII., who died June 29, 1509. This was afterwards printed by Wynkyn de Worde, and is decidedly of a Popish tendency.[b] In consequence of this Proclamation it appears that Elyot thought it necessary to write the following letter to Cromwell.

'Mr. Secretary, in my right humble maner I have me recommended unto you. Sir, all beit that it were my duetie to awayte on you desyring to be perfeitly instructed in the effectuall understanding of the Kinges most graciouse pleasure contayned in his graces proclamation concerning sediciouse bookes. Now for as moche as I have ben very sikk and yet am not entierly recovered, I am constrayned to importune you with theise my homely lettres, which consydering my necessitie and syncere meaning, I trust will not be fastidiouse unto you whome I have allway accompted one

[a] See *Bishop Fisher's Sermon*, p. 274, ed. Hymers, 1840.
[b] See Baker's Preface to the Sermon, p. 58, ed. 1840.

of my chosen frendes for the similitude of our studies which undoubtidly is the moste perfeict fundacion of amitie. Sir, as ye knowe, I have ben ever desyrouse to reade many bookes specially concerning humanitie and morall philosophy, and therefore of suche studies I have a competent numbre. But concerning holy scripture I have very fewe, for in questionistes I never delyted, unsavery gloses and commentes I ever abhorred, the bostars and advauntars of the pompouse authoritie of the Busshop of Rome I never esteemyd. But after that, by moche and seriouse reading, I had apprehendid a jugement or estimacion of thinges, I didd anon smell oute theire corrupt affections and beheelde with sorowful eyes the sondry abusions of theire authorities adorned with a licenciouse and dissolute forme of lyving; of the which, as well in theim as in the universall state of the clergy, I have oftentymes wisshed a necessary reformacion. Whereof hath happed no litle contencion betwixt me and suche persones as ye have thought that I have specially favored, even as ye allso didd, for some laudable qualities which we supposid to be in theim. But neither they mowght persuade me to approve that which both faith and my raison condemned, nor I mowght dissuade theim from the excusing of that which all the worlde abhorred. Which obstinacy of bothe partes relentid the grete affection betwene us and withdrue oure familiar repayre. As touching suche bookes as be now prohibited contayning the Busshop of Romes authoritie, some indeede I have joyned with diverse other workes in one grete volume or twoo at the moste, which I never found laysor to reade. Notwithstanding if it be the Kinges pleasure and yours that I shall bringe or send theim I will do it right gladly. As for the warkes of John Fisshar, I never hadd any of theim to my knowlege except one litle sermone, which aboute eight or nyne yeres passid was translatid into Latine by Mr. Pace, and for that cause I bowght it more than for the author or mater, but where it is I am not sure, for in goode faithe I never redd it but ones sens I bowght it. Finally, if your pleasure be to have that and the other, for as moche as my bookes be in sondry houses of myne own, and farre asonder, I hartily pray you that I may have convenient respeyte to repayre thither after my present recovery, and as I wold that godd sholde helpe me I will make diligent serche, and suche as I shall finde savering any thinge agaynst the Kinges pleasure I will putt theim in redyness either to be browght to you or to be cut oute of the volume wherein they be ioyned with other, as ye shall advyse me, after that I have certified to you the titles of theim. Wherefore, Sir, I hartily besieche you for the syncere love that I have towardes you to advertyse me playnly (ye lakking laisor to write) either by Mr. Petre Vanes or Mr. Augustine, thei writing what your counsaile and advise is herein, which to my power I will folow. And goode Mr. Secretary, consvder that from the tyme of our first acquayntance, which began of a mutual benevolence, ye never knew in me froward opynion or dissimulacion, perchaunce naturall symplicitie not discretely ordred mowght cause men suspect that I favored hypocrysy, supersticion, and vanitie. Notwithstanding, if ye mowght see my thowghtes as godd doeth, ye shold finde a reformar of those thynges, and not a favorar, if I mowght that I wold, and that I desire no lass that my Soveraigne Lord sholde prosper and be exaltid in honor than any servaunt that he hath, as Christe knowith, who send to you abundaunce of his grace with longe lif. Writen at Combe on the Vigil of Saint Thomas.

'Yours unfaynedly,
'TH. ELYOT, Kt.'[a]

[a] Cotton MSS. Cleop. E. VI. fo. 248, orig. printed in *Archæologia*, vol. xxxiii. p. 352, and Strype's *Eccles. Mem.* vol. i. pt. 2, p. 228.

Upon this letter Strype has founded a theory of his own which really seems quite unnecessary. He tells us that Cromwell, 'where he saw occasion, directed his letters to particular persons to bring in their books of this nature upon their peril. And though Sir Thomas Elyot, the learned knight, and in the year 1532 the King's Ambassador to Rome, was his old friend and very well known to him, yet he, suspecting him to be favourable to the old religion, and knowing him to be a great acquaintance of Sir Thomas More, writ to him, warning him to send in any popish books that he had. Whereat Elyot wrote to the said Crumwel a letter, wherein he declared to him his judgment of the need of a reformation of the Clergy, and concerning Papists and popish books, to clear himself of any surmise the King or the Secretary might have of him.'[*] Now, there is really no evidence whatever to support Strype's assertion that Cromwell himself wrote to particular persons, &c. On the contrary, we may fairly infer from the tenor of Elyot's letter, 1st. that the first intimation he received of the prohibition of the books in question was from the Royal Proclamation itself; 2nd. that Elyot took the initiative in writing to Cromwell to plead his state of health as an excuse for not calling upon the latter to receive his instructions; and 3rd. that his letter was not in answer to a previous one addressed to him by Cromwell. We have already dealt with the question of the accuracy of Strype's statement that Elyot was sent on a mission to Rome in 1532, and therefore need not further discuss it. We note here, however, another, though a much more venial error, on the part of this writer in making Elyot date his letter from 'Cambridge' instead of from Combe.

According to Lowndes, the sermon of Fisher, which Pace

[*] *Eccles. Mem.* vol. i. pt. 1, p. 341.

translated into Latin, was on the text John XV. 26, and was printed at Cambridge in 1521.[a] If this be, as it probably is, the same which Elyot alludes to, the latter either did not make sufficient allowance for the lapse of time, or he reckoned only the years which had passed since he himself purchased the book. The Mr. Peter Vannes mentioned by Elyot was the King's secretary for the Latin tongue, who had been sent to Marseilles in 1533, and the following year was made Archdeacon of Worcester in succession to Dr. Clayburgh,[b] who, as we have already seen, was one of the Masters in Chancery.

On July 2, 1536, Thomas Cromwell was appointed Lord Privy Seal, an office which was rendered vacant by the resignation of Sir Thomas Boleyn.[c] It was probably in the autumn of this year, the smaller monasteries having been suppressed in the spring, that Elyot, who had not yet succeeded in obtaining compensation for the losses he had suffered in the King's service, wrote the following letter to his old friend, to whom the King had shown so much more favour than to Elyot himself.

'My moste speciall goode Lorde. Whereas by your contynuell exercise in waighty affayres, allso frequent access of sutars unto your goode lordship, I could not fynde oportunity to gyve to your lordship due and convenyent thankes for your honourable and gentill report to the Kinges maiesty on Wenysday last passid in my favor, I am now constrayned to supply with my penne my sayde duety. Offryng unto your lordship all harty love and servyce that a poure man may owe and beare to his goode lorde and approved frende, which, allthowgh hability lakking in me I can not expresse by any

---

[a] *Bibliographer's Manual*, vol. ii. p. 718, ed. 1834.
[b] Le Neve, *Fasti Ecc. Ang.* vol. iii. p. 75.
[c] Rymer. *Fœd.* vol. xiv. p. 571.

benefyte, your wisedom, notwithstanding, (which I have allway honoured and trustid) will I doubt not accept my goode intent, being I thank godd ever syncere and without flatery or ill dissimulacion. I wisshing unto your lordship the honorable desyres of your hart with the contynuall favor of godd and of your Prynce. My lorde, for as moche as I suppose that the Kinges moste gentill communicacion with me and allso his moste comfortable report unto the lordes of me proceded of your afore remembred recommendacions, I am animate to importune your good lordship with moste harty desyres to contynue my goode lorde in augmenting the Kinges goode estimacion of me, whereof I promise you before godd your lordship shall never have cause to repent. And where I perceyve that ye suspect that I favour not truely holy Scripture, I wold godd that the King and you mowght see the moste secrete thowghtes of my hart, surely ye shold than perceyve that, the ordre of charity savyd, I have in as moche detestation as any man lyving all vayne supersticions, superfluouse ceremonyes, sklaunderouse ionglynges, countrefaite mirakles, arrogant usurpacions of men callid Spirituall, and masking religious, and all other abusions of Christes holy doctrine and lawes. And as moche I inioy at the Kinges godly proceding to the due reformacion of the sayde enormyties as any his graces poure subiect lyving. I therefor beseche your goode lordship now to lay apart the remembraunce of the amity betwene me and sir Thomas More, which was but *usque ad aras*, as is the proverb, consydering that I was never so moche addict unto hym as I was unto truthe and fidelity toward my soveraigne lorde as godd is my juge. And where my speciall trust and onely expectation is to be holpen by the meanes of your lordship, and naturall shamefastness more raigneth in me than is necessary, so that I wold not prese to the Kinges maiesty withoute your lordshippes assistence unto whome I have sondry tymes declarid myn indigence, and whereof it hath hapned, I therefor moste humbly desyre you, my speciall goode lorde, so to bryng me into the Kinges most noble remembrance that of his moste bounteouse liberality it may like his highnesse to reward me with some convenyent porcion of his suppressid landes whereby I may be able to contynue my life according to that honest degree whereunto his grace hath callid me. And that your lordship forgete not that neither of his grace, nor of any other persone I have fee, office, pencion, or ferme, nor have any maner of lucre or advauntage besydes the revenues of my poure land which are but small and no more than I may therewith mayntayne my poure house. And if by your lordshippes meanes I may achieve goode effect of my sute your lordship shall not fynde me ingrate. And whatsoever porcion of land that I shall attayne by the Kinges gift, I promyse to give to your lordship the first yeres frutes with myn assured and faithfull hart and servyce. This lettre I have writen bycause that I herd that your lordship went to the Court. And as for my first sute, I shall at your lordshippes better laysour recontynue it, trusting allso in your lordshippes favor therein. Writen at my house by Smythfeld this Moneday.

'Yours moste bounden,
'TH. ELYOT, Kt.'[a]

This letter shows us pretty plainly that Elyot's friendship and intimacy with Sir Thomas More had, as we might naturally expect, caused him to be looked upon with some

[a] Addressed 'To my speciall goode lorde my lorde Pryvy Seale.' Cotton MSS. Cleop. E. IV. fo. 220, orig. printed in *Archæologia*, vol. xxxiii. p. 353, and also in Wright's *Lett. relating to Suppress. of Monast.* p. 140.

suspicion not only by the King but by Cromwell. It is only in this way that we can account for the apparent neglect with which Elyot, after a long and useful career in the public service of his country, found himself treated. The repeated requests contained in the letters we have quoted for some substantial recognition of his services afford unmistakable proof that for some reason hitherto not quite intelligible, but which the allusion to More in this last letter helps to explain, those services important though they were, had remained unrequited. But it is quite unnecessary to assume that Elyot intended to disown his friendship for More, or to charge him as Mr. Cooper has thought fit to do with 'meanly apologising for an intimacy of which he might well have been proud.'[a] Such an imputation could not have been made if Elyot's meaning had been properly understood. Now, in order to do this we must first understand the meaning of the proverb to which he alludes. This in its expanded form is *usque ad aram amicus sum* a translation of the Greek μέχρι τοῦ βωμοῦ φίλος εἰμί, the answer attributed by Plutarch[b] to Pericles when asked by a friend to give false testimony on his behalf. The interpretation put upon this proverb by Erasmus is as follows: 'Admonet proverbium nonnunquam quo consulamus amicorum commodis, eorumque voluntati morem geramus, fas videri paululum à recto deflectere, verum eatenus, ne propter hominem amicum numinis reverentiam violemus.'[c] And we can have little doubt that Elyot understood and quoted the apophthegm in this sense. What he meant by saying that his friendship with More was only *usque ad aras* was not to deny the fact, but to assure Cromwell that he had never allowed his feeling of regard and affection for More in a

[a] *Athenæ Cantab.* vol. i. p. 89.   [b] *De Vitioso Pudore*, cap. 6.
[c] *Adagia*, p. 490, ed. 1517.

private capacity to interfere with the performance of his own duty to the King, or to detract from the full measure of his allegiance. If we read Elyot's letter by this light we shall have no occasion to impute to him the meanness of intending to disavow a life-long friendship.

A third edition of *The Governour* was published in 1537, but the great work which now occupied the attention of its author was the preparation of a Latin-English Dictionary. Up to this time a correct knowledge of Latin, as written not by mediæval diplomatists and lawyers but by the best classical authors, had been acquired by a slow and painful process involving immense industry and under the serious disadvantage arising from the absence of any complete and accurate dictionary of that language. Ludovicus Vives who had visited England some years previously and been introduced to all the most eminent men of the day, including without doubt Sir Thomas Elyot, had already called attention in his treatise *De tradendis disciplinis*, printed in 1531, to the necessity for a comprehensive work of this kind, considering the imperfect character of those then in use.[a] In England nothing of the kind existed 'beyond the mere vocabularies of school-boys;'[b] for the *Promptorium Parvulorum* printed by Pynson in 1499, and the *Ortus Vocabulorum* by Wynkyn de Worde in 1500, do not deserve, and indeed do not aspire to be designated by a higher title. Elyot in the interest of his own countrymen adopted the suggestion thus thrown out by

---

[a] 'Ex quibus universis confletur dictionarium Latinæ linguæ, quòd nullum est plenum satis et justum. . . . Expediet in quâque etiam vulgari linguâ geminum pueris tradi, unum quo Latina verba reddantur vulgaribus, alterum quo vice versâ vulgaria Latinis : quod in nostro sermone Antonius Nebrissensis fecit, opus non satis exactum, tyronibus magis quàm provectioribus utile.'—*Opera*, vol. i. p. 475, ed. 1555.

[b] Hallam, *Lit. of Europe*, vol. i. p. 344, 4th ed.

Vives, and in 1536-7 commenced to lay the foundation of the first work entitled to be called a Dictionary printed in England. A report of his design was quickly carried to the King, who was graciously pleased to signify his approbation, not by mere words of courtesy, but by the more substantial favour of a loan of books from the Royal Library. Elyot's own account of this act of royal condescension, which exhibits Henry in his most pleasing aspect is as follows: 'About a yere passed,' he says (he is writing in 1538), 'I beganne a Dictionarie declaryng latine by englishe, wherin I used lyttell study, beinge than occupied about my necessarye busynes, whiche letted me from the exacte labour and study requisyte to the makynge of a perfyte Dictionarie. But whyles it was in printyng and uneth the half deale performed your hyghnes being informed therof by the reportes of gentyll maister Antony Denny, for his wysedome and diligence worthily callyd by your highnesse into your priuie Chamber, and of Wyllyam Tildisley, keper of your gracis Lybrarie, and after mooste specially by the recommendation of the most honourable lorde Crumwell, lorde priuie seale, fauourer of honestie, and next to your highnesse chiefe patron of vertue and cunnyng, conceyued of my labours a good expectation, and declaryng your moste noble and beneuolent nature in fauouryng them that wyll be well occupied, your hyghnesse in the presence of dyuers your noble men commendynge myne enterprise affirmed that if I wolde ernestely trauayle therin, your highnes, as well with your excellent counsaile as with suche bokes as your grace had and I lacked, wold therin ayde me.' The encouragement he thus received induced Elyot to re-cast his work and to take still greater pains to render it worthy of such high patronage. His criticisms on the works of his predecessors, and his account of the state in which he found this department of literature are well worth quoting in his own words. 'I well perceyued that all though dictionaries had ben gathered one of an other, yet nethelesse in eche of them ar omitted some latin wordes interpreted in the bokes whiche in order preceded. For Festus[a] hath manye whiche are not in Varros Analogi:[b] Nonius[c] hath some whiche Festus lacketh: Nestor[d] toke nat all that he founde in them bothe. Tortellius[e] is not so abundant as he is diligent: Laurentius Valla[f] wrate only of words which are called elegancies, wherin he is undoubtedly excellent; Perottus[g] in Cornucopie dyd omitte

[a] Sextus Pompeius Festus, *temp. incert.* A portion only of the MS. of this work was transferred by Pomponius Lætus, a celebrated scholar of the fifteenth century, to Manilius Rallus, in whose hands they were seen in 1485 by Politian. The portion which remained in the custody of Lætus was repeatedly transcribed, but it is known that the archetype was lost before 1581, when Ursinus published his edition. The original codex written upon parchment, probably in the eleventh or twelfth century, appears to have consisted, when entire, of 128 leaves, or 256 pages, each page containing two columns; but at the period when it was first examined by the learned, 58 leaves at the beginning were wanting, comprehending all the letters before M. See Smith's *Dict. of Biog.* It is rather a remarkable coincidence that Elyot had proceeded in the first instance only as far as the same letter. Is it possible that he could have had in his possession this missing portion of the ancient MS. ?
[b] M. Terentius Varro, B.C. 116-28. His treatise, *De Linguâ Latinâ*, was printed at Rome by Pomponius Lætus in 1471.
[c] Nonius Marcellus, *temp. incert.* The editio princeps of his work was printed at Rome in 1471.
[d] Dionysius Nestor, of Novara, in Italy, compiled *Onomasticon*, or Latin Dictionary, which was published at Milan in 1488, and at Paris in 1496. See Fabric. *Biblioth. Latina*, tom. v. p. 97, ed. 1754, and Wadding, *Script. Ord. Min.* p. 179.
[e] An Italian grammarian who was born at Arezzo about A.D. 1400, and died before 1466. His *Comment. de Orthographiâ dictionum è Græcis tractatum opus* appeared at Venice and Rome in 1471.
[f] Laurentius Valla was born at Rome in 1406, and died at Naples in 1457. His *De Elegantiâ Latinæ linguæ* was published simultaneously at Rome, Venice, and Paris, in 1471.
[g] Nicolas Perotti, Bishop of Siponto or Manfredonia, on the east coast of Italy, was born in 1430 and died in 1480. His chief work was *Cornucopia sive linguæ*

almost none that before him were written, but in wordis compounde he is to compendiouse; Fryere Calepine [a] (but where he is augmented by other) nothyng amended but rather appaired that which Perottus had studiousely gathered. Nebressensis [b] was both well lerned and diligent, as it appereth in some wordes which he declareth in latin; but bicause in his dictionarie wordes are expounde in the spainyshe tunge whiche I do nat understand, I can nat of hym shewe myn opinion: Budeus [c] in the exact triall of the natiue sence of wordes, as well greke as latine, is assuredly right commendable, but he is moste occupied in the conference of phrasis of bothe the tunges whiche in comparison are but in a fewe wordes. Dyuers other men haue written sondry annotations and commentaries on olde latine authors, among whom also is discorde in their expositions.' Elyot tells us that when he considered the difficulty of the undertaking in which he had embarked, he began to despair of executing the work satisfactorily, but the

Latinæ commentarii, the first edition of which was published in 1489. See Hallam, *Hist. of Lit.* vol. i. p. 192.

[a] Ambroise Calepino was born at Bergamo in 1435, and died in 1511. The first edition of his Dictionary, which, though far better than one or two obscure books that preceded it, and enriched by plundering the stores of Valla and Perotti, was very defective, appeared at Reggio in 1502. See Hallam, *ubi supra*, p. 253.

[b] Ælius Antony de Lebrixa, who turned his name into Nebrissensis in Latin, was born in 1444 at Lebrixa, a village on the Guadalquivir, in Spain. He read lectures for some years at the Universities of Seville and Salamanca, and wrote an infinite number of books about grammar. In 1513 he forsook the University of Salamanca, and addicted himself entirely to the service of Cardinal Ximenes, who gave him the government of his own University of Complutum or Alcala d'Enarez, where Nebrissensis died in 1522, aged 77 years. See Dupin, *Eccl. Writers*, vol. iii. p. 79, ed. 1724.

[c] Budé, or, as he is generally called by the Latinised form of his name, Budæus, was born at Paris in 1467, and died in 1540. 'He raised himself to a pinnacle of philological glory,' says Hallam, 'by his *Commentarii Linguæ Græcæ*, Paris, 1529. . . . In this large and celebrated treatise Budæus has established the interpretation of a great part of the language. . . . His Commentaries stand not only far above anything else in Greek literature before the middle of the sixteenth century, but are alone in their class.'—*Ubi supra*, pp. 328.

favour extended to him by the King induced him to persevere. He then explains in what respects his Dictionary surpassed any that had preceded it in England. 'Whan I consydred all this I was attached with an horrible feare, remembryng my dangerous enterprise (I being of so smal reputation in lernyng in comparison of them whom I haue rehersed) as well for the difficultie in the true expressynge the lyuely sence of the latine wordes as also the importable labours in serching, expending and discussing the sentences of ancient writers. This premeditation abated my courage, and desperation was euen at hand to rent al in pieces that I had written had nat the beames of your royal maiestie entred into my harte by remembraunce of the comforte whiche I of your grace had lately receyued, wherwith my spirite was reuyued and hath set up the sayle of good courage, and under your graces gouernance, your highnesse being myn onely mayster and styrer[*] of the shyppe of all my good fortune, I am entred the goulfe of disdaynous enuie, hauynge fynished for this tyme this symple Dictionarie, wherin I dare affirme may be founde a thousande mo latine wordes than were togither in any one Dictionarie publyshed in this royalme, at the tyme whan I fyrste began to write this commentarie, which is almost two yeres passed. For beside the conference of phrases or fourmes of speakynge latin and englishe, I haue also added proper termes belongynge to lawe and phisike, the names of diuers herbes knowen among us, also a good number of fishes founden as wel in our occean as in our riuers; moreouer sondrie poysis, coyne, and measures sometymes used among the aunciēt Romaynes, Grekes, and Hebrues. Whiche knowlege to the reders not only of histories and orations of Tullie, but also of holy scripture, and the bokes of auncient

[*] *I.e.* steerer.

phisitions shall be founde pleasant and also commodiouse. Nor I haue omitted prouerbes callyd Adagia, or other quicke sentences whiche I thought necessarie to be had in remembraunce. All be it for as moche as partely by negligence at the begynnynge, partly by untrue information of them whom I trusted, also by to moche trust had in Calepine, some fautes may be founden by dilygent redynge, I therfore most humbly beseche your excellent maiestie, that where your hyghnesse shall happen to doubte of any one worde in the fyrste parte of this warke, or perchance do lacke any worde whiche your maiestie shall happen to rede in any good author, that it may lyke your grace to repayre incontinente unto the seconde parte, whiche is myn addition, sekyng there for the same worde in the letter wherwith he begynneth, trustynge veryly that your highnes there shall be satisfied. And for as moche as by haste made in printyng some letters may happen to lacke, some to be sette in wronge places or the ortography nat to be truely obserued, I therfore haue put all those fautes in a table folowing this preface, wherby they may be easily corrected; and that done, I truste in god no manne shall fynde cause to reiect this boke, but rather thankefully to take my good wyll and labours, gyuynge to your maiestie mooste hartye thankes as to the chiefe author therof, by whose gracious meanes menne beinge studious may understande better the latine tunge in syxe monethes than they mought haue doone afore in thre yeres withoute perfyte instructours, whyche are not many, and suche as be are not easy to come by : the cause, I nede not to reherse, sens I ones declared it in my booke called *The Gouernour*, whiche about viii yeres passed I dydde dedicate unto your hyghnesse. And for my parte I render most humble thankes unto your maiestie for the good estimation that your grace retayneth of my poore lerning and honestie, promysynge therfore to your highnes that duryng my lyfe naturall I shall faythfully employe all the powers of my wytte and body to serue truely your maiestie in euery thynge wherto your mooste excellent iudgement shall thynke my seruyce conuenient and necessary. In the meane tyme and alway, as your bounden seruant, I shal hartily pray unto god to prospere your hyghenes in all your vertuouse procedynges, grauntynge also that your maiestie may longe raigne ouer us, to the incomparable comforte and ioye of all your naturall and louynge subiectes. Amen.'

This, the most ambitious of Elyot's works, whether we consider the age in which it was produced, or compare it with similar philological works of the same or even a later period in England, certainly deserves to be spoken of in more respectful terms than it is by Hallam, who styles it 'but a meagre performance.'[a] Such at any rate was not the opinion of Fuller, who calls it 'an excellent Dictionary of Latine and English, if not the first, the best of that kind in that age.'[b] Thomas Cooper, the subsequent editor, whilst greatly enlarging it, and thereby adding immensely to its utility, paid a just tribute to the learning and industry of the author. He changed the original title of *Bibliotheca* to *Thesaurus*, being unwilling, as he tells us, to deprive Elyot of the credit of his share in the production of the work, and as a mark of gratitude for the assistance he had derived from the labours of his predecessor. Elyot presented a copy of his work to his friend and patron Cromwell with a complimentary letter inscribed *propriâ manu* on the fly leaf. This identical copy is now in the Library of the British Museum, but in 1748, when Tanner published his great bibliographical work, it was in the King's

[a] *Hist. of Lit.* vol. i. p. 344, 4th ed.
[b] *Worthies of England*, p. 168, ed. 1662.

Library at Westminster.[a] As the letter to Cromwell has never been printed, and is an interesting specimen of Elyot's skill in Latin composition, and as moreover it concludes the correspondence, so far as we have been able to discover, between these two eminent contemporaries, we make no apology for inserting it *verbatim*.

'Nobili Baroni[b] D. T. Cromoello, virtutis et scientiarum patrono, T. Eliota Anglobritannus Eques S.D.

Fateor equidem, vir clarissime, te rebus maxumis esse natum, nec tam Fortunæ beneficio quàm Dei Opt. Max ergaque gentem nostram benevolentis perpetuâ voluntate ad hunc dignitatis gradum fæliciter pervenisse. Quandoquidem Regi longè sapientissimo (fatis applaudentibus) additus es Minister ac Consiliarius, ut summâ industriâ summâque prudentiâ cum multa tum ampla negotia, illo imperante, conficeres. Macte igitur ingenti animo hosque vulgares hominum affectus te quidem indignos existimes, tum succensere scilicet, deque eo gravius existimare qui statim non applaudat his quæ abs te primum ac merito fortassis comprobantur. Quod si feceris, me multum amplexabere, quòd leges amicitiæ retinuerim, habebisque magnam gratiam mihi, quòd iis profecto consiliis pepererim tibi tum gratam omnibus tum solidam ac diuturnam fælicitatem famamque mirificam apud posteros, quòd, quum sis in dignitatis fastigio positus, tam charus habeare bonis viris quàm jure metuendus sceleratis atque nefariis. Hæc valde liberè sed ab amico quo neminem habiturus es fide ac voluntate erga te prestantiorem. Quod non mentior tute judicaveris primi congressûs nostri memor, à quo hic

[a] *Bibliotheca Britannico-Hibernica*, p. 259, ed. 1748.
[b] According to Stow, Thomas Cromwell was made Lord Cromwell July 10, 1536 (See *Annales*, p. 572, ed. 1615); but according to Strype not till April 18, 1539 (*Eccles. Mem.* vol. i. pt. 1, p. 561); the latter date however is obviously incorrect.

quidem annus est undevigesimus, quòd maxumam erga te concœptam benevolentiam non tantidem relaxarim ut non optarim semper ex animo dignam tuo ingenio fortunam augeri longoque ævo perpetuam fieri. Si tamen istæc non satis tibi persuadeant me tuis tantum favere fortunis quàm qui maxume, revoca quàm sæpe fassus es in privatis colloquiis me bonum virum esse, quàm confidenter in publicis me doctum compellasti, quæ vis, quæ necessitas, quod meum beneficium (quum nusquam egregium fuerit) te tantum virum adigere potuit ut hæc de me vel assentando diceres, vel aliud prædicares quàm tu te experiundo noveris? Scio nimirum quòd magis tuâ prædicatione quàm re ipse bonus aut doctus sim. Nempe quòd ad alterum nunquam aspirare, alterum optare magis quàm assequi potuissem. Sed ne videar tuis beneficiis obluctari, perge me bonum virum existimare, vel quod tollerabilius est, minimè malum, minimèque magnis in artibus amplissimisve consiliis secordem aut improbum. Possitne (si diis placet) inesse tali viro malum aliquod? Et ego cum Cicerone fateor nullum esse magnum malum preter culpam. At nulla culpa gravior (meâ quidem sententiâ) quàm fidem fallere, amicique de se pleraque benè meriti vel famam imminuere vel periclitantem non tueri, si possit. Ita Deum habeam propitium, ut semper vehementer optarim dicta factaque tua optumis quibusque probari. Nam omnibus satisfacere ne quidem in votis esset, nedum superis unquam licuit. Cæterum post hac omni submotâ suspitione confirmes me ejusmodi virum esse qualem existimare debes tuâ dignum amicitiâ, provocatum non tam insigni quopiam beneficio vel ambitione quâpiam quàm rarissimâ ingenii tui fœcunditate studiorumque similitudine.

'Vive fælix amicorum Præses.

'Tuus quantus sum et extra fucum,

'T. ELIOTA.'

This letter seems completely to dispose of Dean Hook's suggestion that 'it is more than doubtful whether Cromwell ever understood Latin at all.'[a]

The *Bibliotheca* was reprinted at least once in the lifetime of its author, viz. in 1545.[b] It is evident indeed that Elyot at the time when the first edition was published, contemplated making further improvements in it, for in the preface to *The Image of Governance* he says: 'My Dictionary declarynge latyne by englishe, by that tyme that I haue performed it shall not only serue for children as men haue excepted it, but also shall be commodiouse for them which perchaunce be well lerned.' After Elyot's death it was corrected and augmented, as already mentioned, by Cooper, afterwards Bishop of Lincoln, who brought out a new edition in 1550,[c] and a second in 1552,[d] and it was no doubt a copy of this last which was presented to Edward the Sixth in 1553.[e]

In 1540 a new edition of *Pasquyll the Playne* was brought out by Berthelet, and in the previous year one of *The Castel of Helth*, the latter being dedicated 'To the ryght honourable Thomas lorde Crumwell, lorde priuye seale.'[f] *The Education or bringinge up of children, translated oute of Plutarche*, probably belongs to an earlier date, but was certainly written before 1540, as it is mentioned in the preface to *The Image of Governance*. It is dedicated 'to his only

---

[a] *Lives of the Archbishops of Canterbury*, vol. vi. p. 120, ed. 1868.
[b] See Ames *Typog. Ant.* vol. iii. p. 331. A copy of this edition was formerly in the Harleian Library, as we learn from the sale catalogue of that collection, where there is the following curious note, exhibiting the strange ignorance which has prevailed with regard to Elyot. 'Eliota jurisconsultus secundum ni fallor Dict. Lat. Angl. concinnavit tempore Henrici Septimi.'—*Catal. Bibl. Harl.* vol. ii. p. 987, ed. 1743.
[c] See *Catalog. Bibl. Harleiana*, vol. ii. p. 987.
[d] See Ames, *Typog. Ant.* vol. iii. p. 337.
[e] Strype, *Eccles. Mem.* vol. ii. pt. , p. 124.
[f] See Ames, *Typog. Ant.* vol. iii. p. 307.

entierly beloued syster, Margery Puttenham,' and was obviously written some time after her marriage, for the author expresses a hope that she will 'folowe the intent of Plutarche in brynginge and inducynge my litell neuewes into the trayne and rule of vertue.' Elyot also probably about this time carried out his intention, expressed in *The Governour*, to write a book for ladies, by publishing *The Defence of good Women*, which afforded Fuller an opportunity to make the facetious but ungallant remark that 'such are hardly found and easily defended.'[a] This book, like *Pasquyll* and *The knowledge which maketh a wise man*, is in the form of a dialogue between three imaginary interlocutors, the purport of which may be best gathered from 'the Argument.' According to the latter, 'A contencion' is supposed to arise ' betwene two gentill men, the one named Caninius, the other Candidus. Caninius, like a curre, at womens condicions is alway barkyng, but Candidus, whiche maie be interpreted benigne or gentill, iudgeth euer well and reproueth but seldom. Betwene them two the estimacion of womankinde cometh in question. After long disputacion wherin Candidus (as reason is) hath the preheminence, at the last, for a perfect conclusion, Queene Zenobia (which liued aboute the yere after the incarnacion of Christe, 274, the noble Aureliane being emperour of Rome) by the example of hir life confirmeth his argumentes and also vanquissheth the obstinate mynd of froward Caninius, and so endeth the matier.' The following concise description of this treatise, given by the author himself, expresses his own opinion of its object. 'My little boke called the defence of good women not onely confoundeth villainous

[a] *Worthies of England*, p. 168, ed. 1662.

reporte, but also teacheth good wyues to know well theyr dueties.'[a] It was reprinted five years afterwards.[b]

On Saturday, January 3, 1540, Anne of Cleves was received at Blackheath with all the pomp befitting the welcome of a royal bride, and with all the pageantry which Henry loved and knew so well how to display. To do honour to so momentous an occasion, the nobility and principal gentry of the realm were required to give their attendance. A roll is still extant containing the names of all the noble men and gentlemen who were ordered 'to receive the Ladie Anne Cleave and waite on the Kinge.'[c] In this document we find Sir Thomas Elyot's name included in the great company of knights and esquires who formed part of the royal train at Shooter's Hill. The Lord Privy Seal, now Lord Cromwell, was also present as one of the High Officers of State, and this may have been the last occasion which brought together these two eminent spectators of the scene, friends at this time of more than twenty years standing, and for one of whom, ere many months should elapse, the same fatal axe, which had spared neither Fisher nor More nor even the bridegroom's late consort, was to be sharpened.

Among the many distinguished men of letters with whom Elyot must have been brought into contact at the court of Charles the Fifth was one who obtained an extraordinary reputation in Europe by a treatise so utterly forgotten at present that, if we may believe Hallam, Bouterwek has even omitted his name.[d] This was Antonio de Guevara, a Biscayan by birth, who in 1528 became a Franciscan monk, but who 'enjoying the favour of the Emperor, seems to have been

[a] Preface to *The Image of Gouernaunce*.
[b] See Ames, *Typog. Ant.* vol. iii. p. 329.
[c] *Chron. of Calais*, p. 177, ed. 1846, Camden Soc.
[d] *Lit. of Europe*, vol. i. p. 396, 4th ed.

transformed into a thorough courtier, accompanying his master during his journeys and residences in Italy and other parts of Europe, and rising successively by the royal patronage to be court preacher, imperial historiographer, Bishop of Guadix, and Bishop of Mondoñedo.'[a] His 'Dial for Princes, or Marcus Aurelius,' more commonly known as *The Golden Book* was first published in 1529. 'It was continually reprinted in different languages for more than a century; scarce any book except the Bible, says Casaubon, has been so much translated or so frequently printed.'[b] According to the author of the *History of Spanish Literature*, 'it is a kind of romance, founded on the life and character of Marcus Aurelius, and resembles in some points the Cyropædia of Xenophon; its purpose being to place before the Emperor Charles the Fifth the model of a prince more perfect for wisdom and virtue than any other of antiquity.'[c] This book was afterwards censured as a literary forgery, but 'more severely,' says Hallam, 'than is quite reasonable.'

In 1540, Berthelet printed *The Image of Governance, compiled of the actes and sentences notable of the moste noble Emperour Alexander Seuerus, late translated out of Greke into Englyshe by syr Thomas Elyot, knight, in the fauour of nobylitie.* By the critics of a later age Elyot has been roughly handled for writing this book. Bayle did not scruple to denounce him as an impostor, to characterise the work as a fraud, and to suggest that the success which had attended the publication of the *Libro Aureo* and made the name of Guevara famous, had probably induced Elyot to perpetrate a similar deception. About the same time Dr. William Wotton, a writer ridiculed by Swift in his famous *Battle of the Books*, endeavoured in a

[a] Ticknor, *Hist. of Span. Lit.* vol. ii. p. 16, ed. 1872.
[b] Hallam, *Lit. of Eur.* vol. i. p. 396, 4th. ed.   [c] *Ubi supra.*

learned note, appended to his *History of Rome,* to demonstrate the spurious character of *The Image of Governance.* Wotton adduced no less than nineteen categorical 'Reasons,' based upon as many different extracts from the book itself, to prove not only that Encolpius* never wrote the original, but that Elyot had not translated from the Greek. What strikes a modern reader as most curious in reading Wotton's argument is that a man of his undoubted ability should not at a glance have discerned the true character of Elyot's work, and acquitted its author of any fraudulent intention. But on the contrary, after making an elaborate investigation, during which passage after passage was separately considered and its accuracy carefully tested, this pedantic critic, ignoring alike Elyot's own admissions in the preface and the internal evidence afforded by the work itself, condemned the latter as a forgery.

It is difficult to reconcile such intellectual obliquity with a really lavish display of erudition. But the very excess of Wotton's learning perhaps caused him to overstep the bounds of common sense, and to lose sight of the most obvious landmarks. If he had done Elyot the justice to give credit to the statements contained in the preface to *The Image of Governance,* it is impossible to suppose that he could seriously have brought forward a charge of imposture. After exhausting every argument to destroy Elyot's reputation for honesty he seems at last to have had a slight perception of the true state of the case, for he admits that when the book first appeared it 'deceived nobody,' and remembering Bale's description of the work as an original composition, he thinks it 'very probable that the public believed the book to be spurious at that

---

* We may observe that whilst the name appears as Encolpius in Lampridius, it is uniformly spelt Eucolpius in *The Image of Governance.*

time, and *composed*, not *translated*, by Sir T. Elyot.' After which he complacently concludes that 'this argument is perhaps as good a one' to prove his point 'as any of those that have been urged already.'[a]

The charge brought against Elyot of palming off upon the public a composition of his own under the guise of a translation of an original work by Encolpius seems altogether so preposterous that it is scarcely credible that it should have remained unanswered down to the present day had not Wotton's apparently plausible arguments imposed upon subsequent writers, who accepted his conclusions without verifying his premisses.[b] The very title of the work, which purports to be a compilation, ought at the outset to have precluded the suggestion that it pretended to the character of a continuous translation. Let us see, however, what account Elyot himself gives of his own work. He tells us in the preface that in searching among his books to find something wherewith to 'recreate' his spirits, 'beinge almoste fatigate with the longe study aboute the correctinge and ampliatinge of my *Dictionary* of Latine and Englishe,' he 'hapned to fynde certeyne quaires of paper' which he 'had writen about ix. yeres passed.' These papers 'contayned the actes and sentences notable of the moste noble Emperour Alexander, for his wysedome and grauity callid Seuerus.' Now as Elyot's *Dictionary* was published, as we have seen, in 1538, these papers must have been written about 1529-30, which would be just the time when he was engaged in preparing *The Governour* for the press. It is not unreasonable to assume, therefore, that they may have formed a portion of the materials which Elyot

[a] *Hist. of Rome*, p. 540, ed. 1701.
[b] See for example a note in Hallam's *Lit. of Eur.* vol. i. p. 398, 4th ed., and the article *Encolpius* in Smith's *Dict. of Class. Biog*

had collected to assist him in the composition of the latter work. Without laying too great stress upon this argument, we may call attention to what appears like an indirect confirmation of it, in the fact that a superfluous paragraph had by some means crept into the text of the first edition of *The Governour*, which might with more propriety have been inserted in *The Image of Governance*.[a] The mistake was detected by the author himself in time to allow of its correction in the list of Errata. But if we suppose the impertinent paragraph to have been taken by mistake from 'the quaires of paper' mentioned above, its relevancy to *The Image of Governance* becomes at once apparent. For it is not difficult to imagine that from the mass of translations and notes which must have accumulated during the composition of *The Governour*, one might by accident get intermixed with the 'copy' which from time to time was transmitted to the printer.

The 'Acts and Sentences,' which Elyot himself says, were contained in these 'quaires of paper,' formed part of a translation of a Greek book, which he tells us, 'by good chaunce was lente unto me by a gentille man of Naples called Pudericus.' This statement was rejected by Wotton as altogether unworthy of belief, and as having been 'told only to give his book the more authority among the nobility and gentry of England to whom it is inscribed.'[b] If such was the opinion deliberately pronounced of so learned a man as Wotton, it is necessary for us before contradicting it to examine very carefully for ourselves the credibility of Elyot's own statement. Two questions present themselves at the outset of this inquiry which, if answered in the negative, would tend strongly to corroborate the view taken by Wotton. We require to know, 1st,

---

[a] See Vol. II. p. 184, note *, where for chapter xx. read chapter xv.
[b] *Hist. of Rome*, p. 533.

whether the name Pudericus was real or fictitious? 2nd. If it was a real name, whether it was borne by any gentleman of Naples who was contemporary with Sir Thomas Elyot? Fortunately for the latter's credit we are in a position to answer both these questions in the affirmative. Upon the authority of the biographer of noble Neapolitan families we are able to assert as a positive fact that a family bearing the surname of Poderico, the Latinised form of which was Pudericus, had been connected with Naples from very early times. John Maria, one of the most distinguished members of this house, was installed as Archbishop of Nazareth, by Innocent VIII. in 1491, and was translated to the see of Tarentum in 1510. He was a member of the Royal Council, and chaplain to the Emperor (presumably Charles the Fifth,) and died in 1525, as appears from his monument in the Church of St. Laurence at Naples.[a] John Antony Poderico, a brother of the prelate, is mentioned as having held several important offices of state under Ferdinand I. and II., and received estates at St. Mauro and Cannella in 1498, in recognition of his services. Many other members of the same family who lived in the sixteenth century are recorded, whose claims to special notice are less conspicuous. Even had we been without any direct evidence of the fact, we could scarcely doubt that a man who held such important preferment as the Archbishop would be distinguished as a scholar, but we are not left in any uncertainty upon this point, because Toppi has enrolled him among the learned men of his time at Naples and deemed him worthy of the significant epithet 'molto dotto.'[b] This writer, whom we may presume to be accurate in such matters, designates the Archbishop as 'Cavaliere

---

[a] Carlo de Lellis, *Discorsi delle Famiglie nobili del regno di Napoli*, vol. iii. p. 142, ed. 1671.
[b] *Biblioteca Napoletana*, p. 148, ed. 1678.

Napolitano,' of which the nearest English equivalent would seem to be 'a gentleman of Naples.'

John Maria Poderico, or, as he is styled in the Latin inscription on his monument in the church of St. Laurence at Naples, Joannes Maria Pudericus,[*] was thus certainly contemporary with Elyot. It is therefore possible that the latter may have been indebted, if not to the Archbishop himself, perhaps to some member of his family for the loan of the book above referred to. Be this however as it may we have at any rate produced perfectly independent testimony to prove that there existed a family at Naples in the sixteenth century bearing the very name mentioned by Elyot. The latter's statement, therefore, that he obtained a book from 'a gentleman of Naples called Pudericus,' is evidently not so antecedently improbable that we are bound to treat it as a fiction.

The book in question, Sir Thomas Elyot tells us, 'was first writen in the greke tung.' Now *The Image of Governance* contains internal evidence to some extent confirming the view that the author had translated part of a Greek book or MS. In Chapter XXV. which contains a translation of a letter alleged to have been written by Alexander Severus to Alexander, Bishop of Alexandria, the Greek phrase εὖ πράττειν is printed in the margin, whilst the word Eucolpius, placed in a similar position on the preceding leaf, seems intended to indicate to the reader the fact that the authority for the statements respecting the Emperor, contained in this particular chapter, was the 'boke first writen in the greke tung by his secretary named Eucolpius,' to which Elyot had already alluded in the Preface.

It was this letter from the Emperor to his namesake,

---

[*] See Cesare d'Engenio, *Napoli Sacra*, p. 113, ed. 1623, and De Lellis, *Discorsi delle Famiglie Nobili*, tom. iii. p. 143, ed. 1671.

the Bishop, which attracted the attention of Selden, who alludes to it in his *Commentary on Eutychius*. The great jurist's unrivalled acquaintance with Oriental literature enabled him at once to detect an anachronism. No Bishop of Alexandria, bearing the name Alexander, had ever been contemporary with the Emperor Alexander Severus. 'Sed nullus tunc temporis planè Episcopus Alexandriæ Alexander dictus est, nec ullus ante Constantinum.'[a] It is a fact now well ascertained that the first patriarch of that name was the famous opponent of Arius in the fourth century. But although Selden saw that the letter itself was a forgery, and must have been composed at a much later period, this did not appear to him a sufficient reason for disbelieving Elyot's assertion, that *The Image of Governance* was in part translated from a Greek MS.: 'Neque aliud quàm Græculi alicujus recentioris commentum libellum illum fuisse dubito, utcunque sanè Lampridio subinde satis concordem.'[b] In the face of this criticism, Wotton was obliged to admit that he could not call Selden as a witness in support of his indictment against Elyot. 'Mr. Selden,' he says, 'thought the imposture lay at another door, and believed that Sir T. E. really translated a Greek MS.'[c] But not disconcerted by the adverse opinion of a much more competent judge than himself, Wotton endeavoured to bolster up his own theory by suggesting that 'it was no wonder if the maker of the *Image* made it agree with the original from which he copied it.'

The French historian of the Roman Emperors, whose great work had been published a few years before Wotton wrote, had said in reference to the real Encolpius, 'On a

[a] *Eutychii Orig. Comment.* p. 175, ed. 1642.
[b] *Ubi supra.*
[c] *Hist. of Rome*, p. 539.

imprimé autrefois en anglois un livre traduit du grec, qu'on pretendoit estre de cet Encolpe, sous le titre d'*Image du Gouvernement*, et il s'accordoit assez souvent avec Lampride. Il parloit fort d'un entretien d'Alexandre avec Origene. Mais il y mettoit des circonstances qui ne conviennent pas avec l'histoire. De sorte qu'on juge que c'est quelque fiction des nouveaux Grecs.'[a] Selden's treatise was doubtless designed for the learned of all countries, and was therefore written in Latin. It may indeed be doubtful whether Tillemont was himself acquainted with *The Image of Governance*, but it is certain that he had read the remarks made upon it by Selden in his commentary upon Eutychius, for he refers expressly to the latter work. Wotton at once saw that the arguments he sought to controvert would gain additional publicity when presented in the more popular form adopted by the French historian. He endeavoured therefore to counteract the increased weight which Tillemont's name might be expected to lend to that of Selden by suggesting that 'Mr. Selden's authority imposed upon M. de Tillemont, who probably understood no English, and had never seen the book itself.'[b] Selden and Tillemont were both dead when the *History of Rome* appeared in 1701, but Wotton was well aware that a far higher degree of respect would be accorded to their opinions than to his own. 'The names of those two learned men,' he says, 'have made it necessary that this book should be examined with care and that the public should be warned of it, that no man hereafter may be imposed upon by the authority of this mock-Encolpius.'[b]

To the careful reader of *The Image of Governance* it would appear that there never was the slightest necessity for

[a] Tillemont, *Hist. des Empereurs*, tom. iii. p. 211, ed. 1720.
[b] *Hist. of Rome*, p. 539.

this solemn warning, and Wotton's elaborate 'Reasons' will only inspire a feeling of regret that so much superfluous erudition should have been displayed to so little purpose. For, after all, the most conclusive answer to the charge of forgery brought by Wotton against Elyot is afforded by Elyot himself. In the preface to *The Image of Governance* the author admits us to his confidence, and relates with every appearance of candour the circumstances under which the book came to be written. Having told us that he obtained the loan of the Greek MS. in the way already described, he goes on to say, 'In reading wherof, I was maruaylousely rauished, and as it hath ben euer myn appetite, I wisshed that it had ben published in such a tunge as mo men mought understande it.' Accordingly he set about translating it into English, but before he had completed his task 'the owner importunately called for his boke.' What was to be done? Elyot was not one of those who, having discovered hidden treasure are reluctant to admit others to share their good fortune. On the contrary, his chief anxiety seems to have been lest the *Acts and Sentences*, a mine of wisdom as it doubtless appeared to him, should be lost to his fellow-countrymen, or at most known only to himself and perhaps a few other scholars. The same generous impulse had prompted him, as we have already seen, to translate *The Doctrinal of Princes*. Another and still stronger motive induced him to undertake the present work. He desired to fulfil the promise made to his readers in the pages of *The Governour* ten years previously. 'Hauing this boke' (*i.e.* the one lent to him by the gentleman of Naples) in my hande, I remembred that in my boke named *The Gouernour* I promised to write a boke of the forme of good gouernance.* And for as moch as in this

---

* He alludes probably to his statement in Vol. I. p. 24.

boke (*i.e.* the one lent to him) was expressed of gouernance so perfite an ymage, I supposed that I shuld sufficiently discharge my selfe of my promise if I dyd nowe publishe this boke, whiche (except I be moche deceyued) shall minister to the wyse readars both pleasure and profite.' Inasmuch however as the translation of the Greek MS. was incomplete and insufficient to form a volume by itself, Elyot determined to supply what was needed from other sources. 'I was constrained to leue some part of the wark untranslated; which I made up, as welle as I coulde, with somme other Autours as wel latines as grekis.' Can anything be more ingenuous than this admission? So far from claiming for his book the merit of being a continuous and complete translation (as Wotton assumes that he did), the author informs his readers at the outset in as plain language as possible that it is 'made up,' in other words, that it has no pretensions to any other character than that of a compilation. Moreover, at a still earlier stage, viz. in the title-page, he had called attention to the fact that it was 'compiled.' That after reading the simple narrative in the Preface, Wotton should have deemed it necessary to warn the reader against the imposition which he supposed Elyot to have attempted is indeed surprising. But the singular obtuseness which prevented the author of the *History of Rome* from comprehending the true state of the case, and the misdirected energy he exhibited in combating a fallacy created by his own too fertile imagination, excite our astonishment almost in an equal degree.

To us it seems that even apart from Elyot's own statement, than which nothing can be more explicit, the internal evidence of the book itself is conclusive as to its real character. This evidence may be conveniently arranged under the following heads: 1st. The marginal references. 2nd. The translated passages.   3rd. The style and scope of the whole work.

And first, as to the references in the margin to original authorities. In Chapter III. the reader is referred to Herodian, cap. 5. In Chapter V. the words '*Ave, Alexander,*' in the margin clearly indicate, that the phrase ' Be glad, Alexander,' in the text was a literal translation of that used by Lampridius.[a] In Chapter VII. the quotation 'Quem metuunt oderunt, et quem odiunt perisse expetunt,' referred to Ennius, was obviously borrowed by Elyot from Cicero,[b] who attributes the verse 'Quem metuunt, oderunt ; quem quisque odit, periisse expetit,' to that ancient poet. In Chapter XI. there is a marginal reference to Lampridius. In Chapter XXIV. the Latin word *mulsum* is given in the margin as the equivalent of the word 'methe' used in the text. On the other hand, when Elyot is translating from an original Greek document his marginal reference is in the Greek character, and hence the phrase εὖ πράττειν already mentioned denotes that it is the exact equivalent of the phrase 'well to doo' in the text. In Chapter XXIX. there are two more marginal references to Lampridius.

Secondly, as to the translated passages. In Chapter XVI. ' The publyke weale giueth to you right harty thankes ' is obviously a literal translation of *Gratias tibi agit Respublica,* the phrase attributed to the Emperor by Lampridius.[c] Again, ' With fume shal he dy that fumes hath sold,' in Chapter XIV. represents the Latin *Fumo punitur qui vendidit fumum.*[d] On the other hand, the ' sentences ' quoted in Chapter XXV. might very well be translations from the Greek and savour too much of orthodoxy to have been written by a pagan. Part of a speech put into the mouth of the Emperor may be taken as

---

[a] *Hist. August,* tom. 1, p. 907, ed. 1671.
[c] See *Hist. Aug.* tom. i. p. 936.
[b] *De Off.* lib. ii. cap. 7.
[d] *Ubi supra,* p. 949.

an example of what we mean. 'That he was moche lasse than his maister Chryste, whiche rode but one daye in his lyfe, and that was on a sely asse mare. Wherfore he wold not ryde except he were sycke or decrepite, so that his leggis mought not serue him to go.' So also the following: 'Eucolpius wryteth that on a tyme he sayd to him and to Philip his bondeman, I perceyue ye do wonder at the lernynge of Origene, wherby ye be induced to imbrace the christiane profession. Trewely the humilitie and charytie of the chrysten people whiche I haue herde of and do dayly beholde doo moche more stere me to beleue that theyr Chryste is god than the residue of all his perswasion. And on a tyme whan two chrysten men contended proudely together and they accused eche other of spekynge reprochefull wordes of the Emperour, he called them before hym and prohibited them to name themselfes christen men, saying, Your pryde and malyce do declare that ye be not the folowers of hym whome ye professe. Wherfore, thoughe ye fynde lacke in me, the whiche I wyll gladly amende, yet wyll I not lette you agaynste iustyce reproue by your actes hym whose lyfe and doctrine ye all doo affirme to be uncorrupted and without any lacke. Whiche wordes being ones sprad amonge the christen men in the citie of Rome, it made them all afterwarde more circumspecte, and in humilitie and charitie to be the more constante.' Now it is quite conceivable that these and other similar passages may have been translated by Elyot from a Greek MS. fabricated by some early Christian writer, at the time possibly when the Arian controversy was agitating the schools of Alexandria. Again, in Chapter XXVI. the author, speaking of Alexander's wife, says, 'Eucolpius wyll not be knowen that he had any moo wyues, but Lampridius useth the authoritie of one Desippus, who sayth that Alexander had an nother wyfe, who was doughter of oone Martianus. But whan it was founde that he wolde haue slayne themperour by treason, he was put to deth, and his doughter separate from the Emperour.' Now this is almost a literal translation of the following passage in Lampridius: 'Dexippus dixit uxorem eum cujusdam Martiani filiam duxisse, eundemque ab eo Cæsarem nuncupatum. Verum quum vellet insidiis occidere Alexandrum Martianus, detectâ factione, et ipsum interemptum, et uxorem abjectam.'[a] It is easy to understand that the author of the Greek MS., presumably a convert to Christianity, would not allow that 'the good' Alexander had more than one wife. Elyot goes on to say, 'Herodianus affyrmeth that all that was done by the malyce of Mammea, the emperours mother, without other cause, only bycause she coulde not susteyne hir sonnes wyfe to be called Augusta, and therfore she caused her to be exyled into Affrica, and all the landes and goodes of her father Mammea toke and conuerted unto hir owne profite.' Now let us compare this with Herodian's own language: Ἠγάγετο δ' αὐτῷ καὶ γυναῖκα τῶν εὐπατριδῶν, ἣν συνοικοῦσαν καὶ ἀγαπωμένην μετὰ ταῦτα τῶν βασιλείων ἐδίωξεν· ἐνυβρίζουσά τε καὶ βασίλισσα εἶναι θέλουσα μόνη, φθονοῦσά τε τῆς προσηγορίας ἐκείνῃ, εἰς τοσοῦτον προεχώρησεν ὕβρεως ὡς τὸν πατέρα τῆς κόρης, καίτοι ὑπ' Ἀλεξάνδρου γαμβροῦ ὄντος πάνυ τιμώμενον, μὴ φέροντα τὴν Μαμμαίαν ἐνυβρίζουσαν αὐτῷ τε καὶ τῇ θυγατρὶ αὐτοῦ, φυγεῖν εἰς τὸ στρατόπεδον, τῷ μὲν Ἀλεξάνδρῳ χάριν εἰδότα ἐφ' οἷς ἐτιμᾶτο, τὴν δὲ Μαμμαίαν αἰτιώμενον ἐφ' οἷς ὑβρίζετο. ἐκείνη δὲ ἀγανακτήσασα αὐτόν τε ἀναιρεθῆναι ἐκέλευσε, καὶ τὴν κόρην ἐκβληθεῖσαν τῶν βασιλείων εἰς Λιβύην ἐφυγάδευσε.[b]

Thus we see that in both the above instances Elyot has not merely given the substance of the authors, to whom he refers,

[a] *Hist. Aug.* tom. i. p. 1002.   [b] *Hist.* lib. vi. cap. 1. ed. Bekker, 1826.

but has adhered more or less closely to the text of the originals. Why then may we not give him equal credit when he refers to the unknown writer whom he calls Eucolpius?

Thirdly, *The Image of Governance* resembles Elyot's other works, but more particularly *The Governour* in this remarkable feature, viz. that although it abounds in translations from ancient authors, it is singularly deficient in exact references to the original authorities. Some phrases, and even some passages, which had already appeared in *The Governour* are reproduced in *The Image of Governance*, as for instance Cicero's definition of faith as the foundation of justice, the story of the self-devotion of Codrus, and many others. This similarity helps to confirm the view already suggested of the way in which certain passages in the earlier work had got misplaced, and is more easily accounted for when we find that some of the materials employed were common to both.

Within a very few years after Wotton's critical analysis of *The Image of Governance*, the authenticity of the latter was discussed by a still more formidable opponent, Dr. Humphrey Hody, Regius Professor of Greek in the University of Oxford. This eminent scholar, in his treatise on the Septuagint, combated the notion that the Greek version was undertaken at the command of Ptolemy Philadelphus, King of Egypt. This tradition, which had been handed down from the earliest times by various patristic authorities, such as Tertullian,[a] Eusebius,[b] Epiphanius,[c] Clemens of Alexandria,[d] Cyril,[e] and Josephus,[f] is thus referred to by Elyot. 'Who euer kept his countrey in suche a quietnesse and made it so ryche as dyd Salomon kynge of the Hebrewes? Whyche as

[a] *Apolog.* cap. xviii.
[b] *Præpar. Evang.* lib. viii. cap. 2.
[c] *Liber de Mens. et Pond.* cap. xi.
[d] *Stromatum*, lib. i. cap. 22.
[e] *Contra Julian.* lib. i.
[f] *Antiq. Jud* lib. xii. cap. 2.

LIFE OF ELYOT. clix

it is founden in their hystories translated into greke by the commaundement of Ptholome called Philadelphus, kyng of Egypte, was soo great a philosopher that he dysputed of all thynges naturall and supernaturall, and for his wonderfulle knowlege there came to here hym out of all partes of the worlde men and women, beynge at that tyme in moste reputation of lernynge.' The passage we have quoted occurs in a chapter (XXXIV.), which is headed, 'The moste noble aunswere of Alexander made to Alphenus concernynge the disablynge of Sextilius Rufus in his absence.' Now it is evident that the whole of this chapter is 'made up,' for at the very commencement there is a marginal reference to Lampridius. Hody, however, like Wotton, chose to disregard the author's own explanation, and to assume that Elyot had represented the whole speech as resting on the authority of Encolpius. 'Non omiserim hoc loco,' says Hody, 'Alexandrum Severum Romanorum Imp. in oratione quâdam apud Encolpii historiam illius vitæ testimonium suum perhibere Ptolemæi Philadelphi jussu confectam fuisse versionem. At quis Encolpius iste apud quem oratio hæc extat? Historia ejus quam citamus prorsus ignota est viris literatis, neque multis inter nostrates, quorum lingua sola habetur, nota, forsan uni tantum aut alteri. Ex Græco vero in sermonem Anglicanum translata est (si ipsi titulo fides) à Thoma Elyoto *Medico*, et edita anno 1549.'[a] In these remarks Hody unconsciously affords a capital proof of the absolute ignorance with respect to Elyot's life and services which prevailed even among the most distinguished men of letters in the eighteenth century. The Regius Professor was ready to believe that Elyot had intended wilfully to mislead the public. It was not a subject for regret therefore that an acquaintance with

[a] *De Bibliorum textibus*, p. 108, ed. 1705.

this fiction would be confined to English readers. 'Sed non est cur doleant viri eruditi linguâ solum Anglicanâ historiam istam extare. Quamvis enim ex Lampridio appareat extitisse olim historiam vitæ Alexandri Severi ab Encolpio scriptam, tamen fidem dederim non illius hanc esse, sed ab aliquo Christiano ejus nomini suppositam. Neque orationes quæ in eâ multæ habentur ex codice Græco conversæ sunt, sed ab ipso (crede mihi) Elyoto compositæ. Scio ego hominis ingenium et orationes confingendi morem ex aliis ejus scriptis.' And yet, notwithstanding this last admission, Hody could describe the author of *The Governour* as a *Doctor*, and persuade himself that the man whose whole life had been devoted to the service of the public weal was capable of perpetrating a deliberate fraud. 'Imo totum librum ab ipso Elyoto compositum fuisse mihi ego facile persuadeo, quamvis prætendat a nobili quodam Neapolitano exemplar Græcum se mutuo accepisse.' In arriving at the conclusion that *The Image of Governance* was Elyot's own composition Dr. Hody had been anticipated by Bale 150 years previously, for the latter, dividing Elyot's works into two classes, compositions and translations, had included it among the former. It by no means follows, however, that Bale had anticipated Hody's opinion as to the author's statement about the loan of the Greek book. Considering that Bale was by no means unduly biassed in favour of Elyot, regarding him as 'veteri excæcatus pappismo,' he would hardly have failed to stigmatise this as a falsehood if it had appeared so to him. Nor, on the other hand, is it 'very probable,' as Wotton has suggested, ' that the public believed the book to be spurious at that time,' *i.e.* when it first appeared. On the contrary, although in common with all Elyot's other works *The Image of Governance* no doubt enjoyed much greater popularity in the sixteenth than in the succeeding century, it does not seem to have occurred to any one to throw suspicion upon it until Wotton himself did so in 1701. It is now nearly 200 years since the author of the *History of Rome* first assailed a reputation, which up to that time had remained unsullied. During the period which has thus elapsed no one has thought fit to re-open the question. We have however found ourselves compelled to do so, and have endeavoured to the best of our ability to vindicate Elyot's character for truthfulness and honesty. If we have succeeded in doing so, we may hope that no one will again be found to say of one of the earliest and most indefatigable of English scholars that 'he justly passes for an impostor.'

In connection with our present subject it may not be out of place to call attention to the fact that Lipenius, in his catalogue of works on jurisprudence, mentions one entitled, *Aur. Alex. Severi Imperatoris Axiomata politica et ethica item rescripta commentario Alex. Chassanæi illustrata*, published at Paris in 1635.[a] It would be interesting to compare this with the *Acts and Sentences*, but unfortunately it appears to be even a greater bibliographical rarity than the latter, and is not noticed even by Brunet or Quérard. Of the commentator Alexandre Chasseneux or Chassanæus we know nothing more than that he was a French jurisconsult and philologer, and for this scanty information we are indebted, not to his own countrymen, but to the researches of two Germans, Saxius,[b] and Jöcher.[c]

Having disposed of the charge made against Elyot of having falsely pretended that *The Image of Governance* was one entire translation of an original work in Greek, we

---

[a] *Bibliotheca Juridica*, tom. i. p. 103, ed. 1757.
[b] *Onomast. Liter.* pars iv. p. 229, ed. 1782.
[c] *Gelehrten-Lexicon*, theil i. col. 1850, ed. 1750.

may observe that to readers of the present day the great interest of the work is really concentrated in the Preface, in which the author gives the titles of all the books previously written by him with a short descriptive notice of each. We learn also that Elyot, anticipating the fate of too many men of letters since his day, had not found his publications remunerative. 'Yet am I not ignoraunt,' he says, 'that diuerse there be which do not thankfully esteme my labours, dispraysinge my studies as vayne and unprofitable, sayinge in derision that I haue nothing wonne therby, but the name onely of a maker of bokes, and that I sette the trees but the printer eateth the fruites. In dede al though disdaine and enuy do cause them to speke it, yet will I not deny but that they saye truly. For yf I wold haue employed my study about the increace of my priuate commodity which I haue spent in wrytinge of bokes for others necessity, few men doubt (I suppose) that do knowe me, but that I shuld haue attayned or this tyme to haue ben moche more welthy and in respect of the worlde in a more estimation. But to excuse me of foly, I will professe without arrogaunce that whan I consydered that kunninge contynueth whan fortune flytteth, hauinge also rynginge alway in myn eare the terrible checke that the good maister in the gospell gaue to his ydel seruaunte for hidinge his money in a clowte and not disposinge it for his maisters aduantage, those two wordes, *Serve nequam*, so sterid my spirites that it caused me to take more regarde to my last rekning than to any riches or worldly promotion. And all thoughe I do neither dyspute nor expounde holy scripture yet in suche warkes as I haue and intend to sette forth, my poore talent shall be, God willinge, in such wise bestowed that no mannes conscience shalbe therwith offended. . . . . And in none of these warkes I dare undertake a man shall finde any sentence against the commandmentes of god, the trewe catholyke faythe, or occasion to stere men to wanton deuises. Wherfore I trust unto god myn accompt shall of hym be fauorably accepted, all though some ingrate persons with ille reporte or mockes requite yl my labours.' Elyot then alludes to a saying, that 'the greatest clerks are not the wisest men,' with which scholars were at that time frequently taunted, in order to demonstrate its absurdity. 'First the said prouerb semeth by him which lacked lerninge to be deuised, sens that he preferrith ignorance before kunninge, whiche arrogance declared hym to be a very foole and unwitty, consideringe that by knowlege most chiefly a man excelleth al other mortall creatures and therby is moste like unto god. And lerninge is none other thinge but an aggregation of many mens sentences and actes to the augmentation of knowlege. And if som lerned men do neglect their temporal commodities it is for one of these causes, eyther by cause they haue ben so desirouse of knowlege, and in respect therof estemed so lytle all other pleasures that they thought the tyme all to lytle which they dyd spend in it, holdinge themselfes with that which serued for natures necessitie right wel contented . . . . And for the confutation of that pestiferous opinion that gret lerned men be unapt to the ministration of thinges of waighty importaunce, this shalbe sufficient. First, as I late said, lerning is the augmentation of knowlege, which the more that it is the more maye be perceiued what shalbe most necessary in thinges which happen in consultation, and the more that it is perceyued, the better and more aptly may it be ministred and executed. Examples we haue of Moyses, who beinge excellently lerned in the most dyffuse doctrines of the Egyptians and Ethiopians was by almighty god chosen to guide and rule his people which were innumerable and moste froward of nature; and with what wonderfull wisedome and pacience dyd he gouerne them by the space of xl yeres, beinge without any cities, townes, or any certain possessions. Who were better leders of armies than great Alexander, Scipio, Lucullus, and Cesar, whiche were men al of great lerning? Who better handled matters of waighty importaunce than Octauian called Augustus, Hadrian, Marcus Antoninus, Alexander Seuerus, and of late yeres Carolus Magnus, al emperours of Rome and men very studiouse in all noble sciences? Whan was there a better consul than Tully, or a better senator than Cato called Uticensis? And to retourne home to our owne countray, and wherof we our selfes may be witnesses, howe moche hath it profited unto this realme that it nowe hath a kynge, our souerayne lorde kyng Henry theyght, exactly well lerned? Hath not he therby onely sifted out detestable heresies late mingled amonge the corne of his faythfull subiectes and caused moche of the chaffe to be throwen in the fyre? Also hipocrisy and vayne superstition to be cleane banysshed? Wherof I doubt not but that there shalbe, or it be longe, a more ample remembrance, to his most noble and immortal renome. This well considered, let men ceasse their sayde foolishe opinion and holde them content with their owne ignorance. And for my part, say what they liste, I wil during my life be in this wise occupied in bestowing my talent, beinge satisfied with the contentynge of suche men as ye be,* adourned with vertue, the most preciouse garment of very nobylitie.'

The Image of Governance was reprinted twice by Berthelet, viz. in 1544 and 1549, and by William Seres in 1556.

About this time Elyot acquired some more property in Cambridgeshire, viz. the manors of Carleton and Willingham

* *I.e.* the nobility of England.

near Newmarket, which had formerly belonged to his old friend Thomas Cromwell from whom he had purchased them. In consequence of Cromwell's attainder it had been impossible for Elyot to get seisin of these manors, for though the indenture of bargain and sale was dated March 14, 1540, the treasons with which Cromwell was charged were alleged to have been committed in the preceding year. The attainder therefore having a retrospective effect, the property sold to Elyot passed with Cromwell's other possessions into the hands of the Crown, and it therefore became necessary for Elyot to obtain a re-grant from the latter. This was accordingly effected by letters patent dated August 4, 1540. It is curious that though Fuller enumerates Cromwell amongst the Sheriffs of Cambridgeshire he professes himself 'at a perfect loss' to understand why his name should be on the Roll. 'No Cromwell Thomas' he says, 'can I find at this time in this county, and can hardly suspect him to be the Cromwell of that age, because only additioned *Armiger*.... besides the improbability that he would condescend to such an office, having no interest I ever met with in Cambridgeshire, though (which may signifie somewhat) he was at this time Chancellor of the University of Cambridge.'[a] It is certain however that in 1535 Cromwell was High Steward of the University;[b] and several letters which passed between him and the Corporation have been printed by Mr. Cooper. It is possible therefore that in the following year he may have been nominated Sheriff, and this is rendered more probable by the fact that he undoubtedly possessed property in the county.

There is a translation from Plutarch, entitled *Howe one may take profite of his enmyes*, the date of which is un-

[a] *Worthies of England*, p. 168, ed. 1662.
[b] *Annals of Cambridge*, vol. i. p. 371.

certain. No author's name appears in the copy in the British Museum Library, but it has always been attributed to Elyot.[a] With this treatise is joined another of *The Maner to chose and cherysshe a frende*. The reason for this addition is thus stated by the author 'To fylle up the padges that els wold haue ben voide, I thought it shuld nother hurt nor displese to adde hereunto a fewe sayenges, howe a man shulde chose and cherysshe a frende.' The 'sayings' are chiefly taken from various classical authors. These two short pieces are not mentioned by Elyot when enumerating the various works he had already written in the preface to *The Image of Governance*. They were subsequently reprinted by Berthelet in a tiny volume, together with *The Table of Cebes*, which was a translation made by Sir Francis, the brother of Sir Anthony Pointz.

In 1542 Sir Thomas Elyot was elected M.P. for the borough of Cambridge, his colleague being Mr. Robert Chapman. For this information we are indebted to Browne Willis, who gives Elyot's name in his list of the Members of the Parliament held at Westminster 32 Hen. VIII.[b] In the Return, however, of the names of all Members of Parliament from the earliest times, recently printed by order of the House of Commons, the Return for the borough of Cambridge for the year above mentioned is left blank. Unless therefore the record itself has disappeared since the publication of *Notitia Parliamentaria*, we must conclude that the author of that work had access to some other source of information which is now unknown.

In November 1544 Elyot was for the second time called upon to serve the office of Sheriff of the combined counties

---

[a] Ames, *Typ. Ant.* vol. iii. p. 347, note, ed. 1816.
[b] *Not. Parl.* vol. i. p. 190.

of Cambridgeshire and Huntingdonshire.[a] It was during his tenure of office that he wrote a little treatise called *A Preservative agaynste Deth*. The title seems peculiarly appropriate when we consider that this was the last book which Elyot ever wrote. It is easy to imagine that the author's thoughts were at this time wholly turned in one direction, the approaching end of his own labours, for which his advancing years must have prepared him.

Elyot dedicated this book which was published on July 2, 1545, 'to his worshypfull frende syr Edwarde North, knight, chancellour of the court of the augmentacions of the reuenues of the kinges croune.' The Court of Augmentations had been erected some ten years previously by 27 Hen. VIII. cap. 27, for the purpose of collecting and administering the revenues of the suppressed monasteries. It consisted of a chancellor, a treasurer, an attorney and solicitor, ten auditors, seventeen receivers, a clerk, an usher, and a messenger. Sir Edward North was treasurer, and afterwards chancellor of the new court,[b] and was himself apparently one of the first to derive advantage from the arbitrary proceedings which were adopted. Strype tells us that when the Charter House was dissolved, 'the house was given to Sir Edward North, who there built himself a fair dwelling, and made a parlour of the church; pulling down most of the cloisters.'[c] He received other marks of royal favour, for his name appears in the list of 'aiders' to the executors of the King's will.[d] He was one of the Council of Edward VI.[e] and was subsequently raised to the peerage by the title of Lord

[a] Fuller, *Worthies of England*, p. 166, ed. 1662.
[b] Collins, *Peerage*, vol. iv. p. 455, ed. 1812.
[c] *Eccles. Mem.* vol. i. pt. 1, p. 428, ed. 1822.
[d] *Ibid.* vol. ii. pt. 1, p. 19.
[e] *Ibid.* vol. ii. pt. 2, p. 160.

North of Kirtling.[a] Catlage, Carteleigh, or Kirtling, as it is now called, is a parish in Cambridgeshire, about five miles south of Newmarket, and a short distance only from Carleton. The Manor of Kirtling had been purchased (probably of the Warwick family) by Sir Edward North,[b] who was therefore a near neighbour of Sir Thomas Elyot. Moreover he was at one time actually in possession of the Manor of Carleton Magna, which Elyot subsequently acquired by purchase from Cromwell as already mentioned.[c] Elyot, having himself been employed in the survey of the monasteries, would naturally have been brought in contact with the principal officer of the court which had special jurisdiction in such matters; but inasmuch as Sir Edward North was M.P. for the county in the same year (1542) that Sir Thomas Elyot represented the town of Cambridge,[d] and that these two knights were adjoining landowners, we can easily imagine that they were very intimately acquainted.

Elyot's reasons for writing *The Preservative agaynste Deth*, and for dedicating it to his friend may be gathered from the Preface. 'The lyttel boke whyche I sent to you at the begynnynge of lent last passed, a smal requitall of your gentyll benefites, I haue caused nowe to be printed, as well for a testimonie of the herty loue whiche I doo beare toward you, and that beinge printed it maie the lengar endure with you and others, as also that my priuate gyft maie be beneficiall to many men whiche without disdaine or enuy will oftentymes reade it. I knowe well some men will thinke and saie also perchaunce, that I spende my witte vainely, for

---

[a] Strype, *Eccles. Mem.* vol. iii. pt. 2, p. 159, where he is styled 'baron of Carteleigh.' Fuller, on the other hand, calls it Catlidge.
[b] Lyson's *Cambridgeshire*, p. 224.
[c] *Ibid.* p. 159.
[d] Willis, *Not. Parl.* vol. i. p. 190, and vol. iii. pt. 2, p. 4.

it is the office of priestes for to preache, and that it dothe not perteine to a knyght, muche lesse to a sheriffe, to write, specially of suche holy mattiers. Also that in wrytyng to you, whiche are continually occupied about the kynges maiesties busynesse, I lose all my labour. Considering that beside the tymes of meale and of slepe (whiche also be littell and scarse, as I well haue perceyued) there remaineth with you none oportunitie to reade any bokes of englyshe or latin. Truely I confesse that priestes ought to preache, and that it is their propre office. And yet no christen man is excluded to gyue good counsaile in that whiche pertayneth to the lawes and commandementes of almighty god. And he that can do it, and will not (though he be no priest), I dout not but he shall make a straite reknyng for hydynge his talent. A knyght hath receiued that honour not onely to defende with the swerde Christis faithe and his propre countrey agaynst them whiche impugneth the one or inuadeth the other, but also, and that most chiefly by the meane of his dignitie (if that be imploied where it shuld be, and estemed as it ought to be), he shuld more effectually with his learnyng and witte assayle vice and errour, moste pernicious ennemies to christen men, hauinge therunto for his sworde and speare his tunge and his penne. And where for the more reuerence due to the order of priesthode it is most congruent and fittyng that preaching in commune assembles be reserued onely to that ministracion, yet where a knyght or other man, not being of a lite estimacion, hath lernyng ioyned with moderate discrecion, yf he, being zelouse of vertue and meued only by charitie, wolde fayne haue other men to remember their state and condicion, and according to their dueties to loue god and to feare his terrible sentence, what lawe or raison should lette hym with an humble spirite and uncorrupted intent to set furth in

writing or print that whiche shalbe commodious to many
men? And if he be a knight or in other authoritie (for the
rarenesse of learnynge founden in suche men), the warke shal
be muche the better imbraced, and of the moo men desyred.
Also, for asmuche as I am a sheriffe, I think my selfe the more
bounden to bee thus occupied. For sens it pertaineth to
myn office, and also the lawes of this realme doo compell me,
to punishe transgressours, howe muche more is it my duetie
to doo the best that I can by all studye and meanes to withdrawe men from transgressing the lawes and commaundementes
of god, whiche beinge diligently and truely obserued, the
occasions of transgressyng of temporall lawes should be
clerely excluded? Moreouer, as often as I doo consyder the
temporall punyshementes and doo abhorre the sharpenesse
of theim, I do reuolue in my mynde what horrible peynes
are prepared for theim whome the sonne of god shall con-
demne at his generall iugement, to the whiche temporall
tormentes being compared doo seme but a shadow. Here
begynne I to feare, not for my selfe onely, but alsoo for other,
which either in transgressing goddis lawes or neglectynge
our dueties do prouoke his wrath daily by displesyng hym.
Wherfore aswel for myn owne erudicion as for the remembrance of other men I haue gathered togither out of holy
scripture this litle treatise, whiche often tymes radde and kept
in remembraunce shall be a preseruatiue against death euer-
lasting. And as touching your oportunitie in the receiuyng
it, althoughe your ministracion be necessary, yet remembre
the wordes whiche our sauiour Christ spake unto Martha.
What I meane therby, by redyng and digestyng that place
whiche is in the tenthe chapitre of Luke, ye shal easily perceiue without an expositour. At the least waie, either by
day or by night, Martha shall finde oportunitie to sitte downe

by her sister, if not, she shall find but litle thanke for all her good housewyfery. If Martha ministrynge unto Christ temporally had no more thanke for hir labor, what thanke shal we loke fore whiche alwaie bee occupied about thynges that be worldly? thereby seekyng onely our temporall commoditie. But yet in our dayly exercise we maie oftentymes ioyne the two systers togither, as well by secrete thankes gyuen to god for his sundry benefittes as by frequent meditacion of our laste daie. Wherunto we shall fynde occasion, as often as we do here the bell ryng at the death or terrement of any man, or here reported of pestilence or warre, thynkyng theim than to be the trumpettes of death whiche do call us to reknyng. And as touchynge the readyng of this litle woorke, if ye do rede it in the masse while, for lacke of tyme more conuenient, I dare undertake god will bee therwith nothyng offended; but ye being therwith stered the more deuoutly to serue hym, he shall receyue it of you as a good praier, sens that meditacion and praier be but one thing in their nature. And yet meditacion is the more constant. For in praier the mynde is oftentimes wandring and thinketh least on that whiche by the tunge is expressed. In this wise dooinge, ye shall not lacke oportunitie to reade ouer this boke, whiche shall not seme longe unto suche as I thinke that ye be, that is to saie, in whome witte ouerfloweth not grace but giueth place to her. Finally by readyng therof I trust unto god we bothe shall receyue eche comforte of other, as well in this present worlde as in the worlde to come, whiche is the perfection of amitie, whiche many mo men haue writen of than haue truely used as they should doo. Thus I committe you to god, whom I moste hertily praie to keepe you alwaie in his fauour long to continue.'

This little book, which consists chiefly of a collection of passages from Scripture and the Fathers, is not mentioned by

Ames and is therefore presumably very scarce, but a copy in excellent preservation is in the British Museum Library. Bale does not include it in his list of Elyot's works, in the edition of the *Scriptores Britanniæ* published in 1557. On the other hand, that list includes some which have not come down to us, or at least have not been attributed to Elyot. Among these Bale enumerates one entitled *De rebus Angliæ memorabilibus*. That Elyot contemplated publishing such a work is beyond all doubt. For Ascham in his *Toxophilus* says: 'Now, sir, by my iudgement the artillarie of England farre excedeth all other realmes; but yet one thing I doubt, and longe haue surely in that point doubted, when or by whom shotyng was first brought in to Englande, and for the same purpose, as I was ones in companye with syr Thomas Eliot, knight, which surelie for his lerning in all kynde of knowlege bringeth much worshyp to all the nobilite of Englande, I was so bould to aske hym yf he at any tyme had marked any thing as concernynge the bryngynge in of shootynge in to Englande; he aunswered me gentlye agayne that he had a worcke in hand which he nameth *De rebus memorabilibus Angliæ*, which I trust we shal se in print shortlye, and for the accomplyshmente of that boke he had read and perused ouer many olde monumentes of Englande, and in sekyng for that purpose he marked this of shootynge in an excedyng olde cronicle, the which had no name, that what tyme as the Saxons came first into this realme in kyng Vortigers dayes, when they had bene here a whyle, and at last began to faull out with the Brittons, they troubled and subdewed the Brittons wyth nothynge so much as with theyr bowe and shaftes, whiche wepon beynge straunge and not sene here before was wonderfull terrible unto them, and this beginninge I can thynke verie wel to be true.'[*]

[*] *Toxophilus*, fo. 39, ed. 1545.

LIFE OF ELYOT.

Now it appears from this that when Ascham wrote, Elyot's book was then in hand, and Ascham hoped to see it printed shortly. We know that the *Toxophilus* was in the press in the summer of 1544, and that Ascham expected that it would be published before the King started on his expedition to Boulogne. For in a letter to Sir William Paget, he says: 'Scripsi etiam librum ad Regiam Majestatem, *qui nunc sub prælo est,* de re Sagittariâ . . . . . Hic libellus, ut spero, cum apparebit in lucem, *quod fiet, Deo volente, ante Regis profectionem,* nec obscurum amoris mei in patriam signum nec mediocris meæ eruditionis mediocre testimonium erit.'[a] The King started from Dover, and 'toke shippinge towards Calleys,' on July 14, 1544.[b] Ascham's letter was therefore probably written in the month of June preceding.

We may take it as a fact, then, that in the spring of 1544, Elyot had almost completed writing a book, the title of which he had communicated to Ascham, and which the latter was expecting shortly to see in print. Here a most important question arises, Was this book ever published? At first sight Ascham's evidence seems to be confirmed by that of Bale, but when we consider that no such work is mentioned in the first edition of the *Scriptores Britanniæ* published in 1548, it is at least an open question whether Bale did not insert the title in his second edition on the authority of the *Toxophilus.* It is however, curious that he mentions immediately afterwards 'Opus aliud imperfectum,' and does not include in his list the *Preservative agaynst Deth.* Although Pits attributes to Elyot a work with the same title, *De rebus Angliæ memorabilibus,* we cannot fairly attach any additional weight to this circumstance, inasmuch as Pits undoubtedly copied from Bale. After what

[a] Elstob, *Aschami Epistolæ,* p. 97, ed. 1703.
[b] Rymer, *Fœd.* vol. xv. p. 52.

has been stated, the reader will hardly be surprised to learn that no work of Elyot's bearing this title has come down to us. Are we, however, justified in assuming that no such book was ever printed? From Ascham's description of the work it would seem to have been just such a one as Elyot might have been expected to write, inasmuch as his employment in the survey of monasteries must have afforded him unusual facilities for making himself acquainted with the contents of their libraries, consisting chiefly of old chronicles. We have further Ascham's positive assertion, founded upon Elyot's own statement, that the latter had such a work actually 'in hand' in 1544. Now when we consider the nature of the work, and the physical condition of the author, we can have little difficulty in imagining that the former might occupy a longer time than was originally anticipated, and that the delay and ultimate postponement of the publication, were due solely to the mortal sickness of the latter.

In the eighteenth century the actual publication of this book seems to have been assumed. The Bishop of Carlisle tells us that Elyot 'left behind him a learned and judicious Commentary *de rebus memorabilibus Angliæ.*'[*] When however he goes on to inform us that 'this work gain'd him the repute of a most accomplish'd antiquary in the opinion of J. Leland, who is almost immoderate in his praises,' we are not without a suspicion that the worthy Bishop was labouring under some misapprehension, and confounding Ascham with Leland. The passage referred to as his authority for this statement, viz., the verses addressed to Elyot by Leland in his *Encomia illustrium virorum*, does not in any way support Dr. Nicolson's assertion.

The fate of Elyot's contribution to the history of England

[*] Nicolson, *Engl. Hist. Lib.* p. 3, ed. 1736.

is at present a mystery. If it was nearly finished in 1544, it seems impossible to say that it could not have been published in the author's lifetime, when we remember that the *Preservative agaynst Deth* was written in the spring of 1545, and published in the summer of that year. On the other hand it might very well be that, though Elyot was in 1544-45 capable of composing a short treatise on a devotional subject, his state of health would not permit him to prosecute the laborious researches necessary for the completion of such a work as that mentioned by Ascham. What, however, seems most probable is that the book remained still in MS. at Elyot's death, and that some antiquary obtained possession of it, and perhaps incorporated it in some work of his own.[*] Whether this long-lost treatise will ever be recovered is a speculative question which is not without interest to men of letters, though its discovery would probably not throw any very new light upon the early history of this country. One thing, however, is certain; we could better have spared some other productions of the same period which have come down to us

---

[*] It seems not at all unlikely that in the compilation of the *Description of Britain and England*, prefixed to Holinshed's *Chronicle*, Elyot's MSS. may have been employed. As some confirmation, however slight, of the theory advanced above, we may remark that in a MS. belonging to G. F. Wilbraham, Esq., of Delamere House, co. Chester, examined by the Historical MSS. Commissioners, one of the authors cited is 'Sir Thomas Elyot, his chronicle of the description of Brittaine' (*Report*, vol. iv. p. 416). This of course may be an inaccurate citation, or it may, on the other hand, refer to the unknown *De rebus memorabilibus Angliæ*, under another name. The *Chronologie* of William Harrison, the author of the *Description of Britain*, which had been supposed to be lost, was at length discovered in Ireland, together with 'a curious and terribly-corrected MS. of an English work on Weights and Measures, Hebrew, Greek, English, &c.,' which Mr. Furnivall assumed to be Harrison's also. But possibly this last may have been the MS. of Elyot's table of Greek, Hebrew, &c., weights and measures which is printed at the end of the copy of his *Dictionary*, 1538, now in the British Museum. See Harrison's *Descript. of England*, p. v. ed. 1877, printed for the New Shakespeare Society.

uninjured, but whose value, except as relics of the age, is very slight.

It has been said that Elyot wrote many other works, besides those which we have enumerated.[a] If he did, they have either altogether perished, or are so exceedingly scarce, that they have escaped the notice of the most acute bibliographers. This, however, we must at least admit, that some passages in his extant works indicate an intention on the part of the author to treat of other subjects than those with which his name is now associated.[b]

With the publication of *A Preservative agaynste Deth* Sir Thomas Elyot's career as a writer may be said to have closed. On the assumption that he was born about 1490, and it is hardly possible that we can assign a later period for his birth, he would now have reached his fifty-fifth year. It is probable, however, that he was at least ten years older. His constitution had at no time been robust. We have already noticed his own account of his sufferings, brought on by his assiduous labours in the public service. In the *Castel of Helth* he gives us a still more graphic picture of himself in the character of an invalid. 'I my selfe,' he says, 'was by the space of foure yeres continually in this discrasy,' (he is speaking of cold in the head), ' and was counsayled by dyvers phisitions to kepe my hed warme and to use *diatrion piperion* and such other hot thinges as I haue rehersed ; at the last, felynge my selfe very feeble and lackinge appetite and slepe, as I hapned to reade the boke of Galene *De temperamentis* whiche treatith *de in-*

---

[a] Bale, for instance, after giving a list of his published works which corresponds with one or two exceptions only with those given by modern bibliographers, says, '*Aliaque fecit multa.*' While Pits, whose catalogue is identical with Bale's, adds, *Et alia multa partim scripsit, partim transtulit.*'

[b] See, for example, some passages in this book, and *The Castel of Helth*, lib. iv. fo. 80 b, ed. 1541.

æquali temperaturâ, and afterwarde the vi boke *De tuendâ Sanitate* I perceyued that I had ben longe in an errour. Wherfore first I dyd throwe away my quylted cappe and my other close bonettes, and onely dyd lye in a thynne coyfe, whiche I haue euer sens used both wynter and somer, and ware a light bonet of veluet only. Than made I oxymel after the doctrine of Galen, sauynge that I boyled in the vynegar rootes of persely and fenell with endyue, cichory, and betayne, and after that I hadde taken it thre dayes continually, euery day thre sponesful in the mornynge warme, than toke I of the same oxymell, wherein I had infused or steapid one dramme of Agaryke and halfe a dramme of fyne Reubarbe, the space of iii dayes and iii nyghtes. Whyche I receyued in the mornynge, eatynge noo meate vi houres after, and that but a lyttel brothe of a boyled henne, wherof ensuyd viii stoles abundant of choler and fleume. Soone after I slepte soundly and had good appetite to eate. After supper I wolde eyther eate a fewe colyander sedes prepared, or swalowe downe a litel fyne mastyx, and forbeare wyne and dranke only ale, and that but lytell and stale and also warmed. And sometyme in the morninge woulde take a perfume of *Storax Calamitæ*, and now and than I wolde put in to my nosethrilles eyther a leafe of grene laurell or betaine, or water of maiorame bruised, which caused the humour to distill by my nosethrilles. And if I lacked storax, I toke for a perfume the ryndes of olde rosemary and burned them, and held my mouth ouer the fume closynge myne eyes; afterwarde to comfort my stomake and make it strong, sometyme I wold eate with my meat a litel white pepper grosse bruysed, sometyme Galens electuary made of the iuice of quinces called *Diacytonites*, somtyme marmalade of quynces or a quynce rosted. And by this diete I thanke almighty god, unto whome onely be gyuen all glory, I was reduced to a better state in my stomacke and head than I was xvi yeres before, as it maye appere unto them whiche haue longe knowen me.'[a]

This improvement in health, however, had taken place a good many years before the period of his life at which we have now arrived.

But to the predisposition to disease arising from a naturally 'cholerike humour' was now superadded the infirmity of age. The pen that had once been so busily employed was now laid aside for ever. On March 26,[b] 1546, he who had wielded it so long and to such good purpose was called away, not unprepared we may feel quite sure for the summons, nor yet fearing the sound of the terrible trumpet.'

If not as fortunate in life as the two friends whom he had seen raised to highest honour in the State, Elyot was far happier in his end. To him it had been a melancholy retrospect to 'consider daily how many men he had known, being of years lusty, strong, and couragious, abounding in the gifts of nature and fortune, how suddenly, above men's expectation and also their own, they had been attacked with death either natural or violent, that is to say being either slain or put to execution by laws.'[c] For himself no such terrible fate was reserved. He had lived through troublous times, and had experienced without doubt many bitter pangs as he had seen his friends summoned to take that fatal journey 'before that they looked for death.' But the same 'pure and constant faith,' which had already enabled him to 'bear up against all worldly vexations and troubles, called the toys of fortune or the cranks of the world,' would, we may feel assured, sustain him 'as well

---

[a] *The Castel of Health*, fol. 79, ed. 1541.
[b] According to Bale, who is followed by Pits, Wood, and others, he was buried on March 25, but this must be a mistake.
[c] *A Preservative agaynste deth*.

LIFE OF ELYOT. clxxix

agaynste the mooste certayne sikenes and fynall dyssolution of nature.'[a]

Sir Thomas Elyot was buried in the church of Carleton, the parish where he died and in which he had spent the latter years of his life. Wood informs us that a monument was soon after put over his grave.[b] This was still to be seen a hundred years afterwards. For Layer, whose collections for Cambridgeshire were written about 1632, gives the following account of it. 'In Ecclesiâ de Carleton. Upon a large brasse is seene the portratures of Sr . . . Elliott knight and his wife, with these armes quarterlie: 1 and 4, a Fesse int. two Barres gules wavie; 2 and 3, a chevron int. three Castles triple towered, paled with two swordes in Saltire, points in cheife, int. four flower de luces.'[c] This monument is not now in existence, and there seems good reason to suppose that its destruction is attributable to the indefatigable iconoclast William Dowsing, in which case it must have disappeared about ten years after Layer had seen and described it. Dowsing's journal for Cambridgeshire has never been published,[d] but Mr. Cole must have seen it, for writing of Carleton, on April 30, 1750, he says: 'Dowsing, in 1643 visiting this church, makes the following entry in his journal: "Carleton cum Willingham, March 22. A crosse on the steeple promised to be taken downe, and we brake diverse superstitious pictures."[e] The exact spot in the little Cambridgeshire church where Sir Thomas Elyot's remains were interred has long been

---

[a] Preface to *A swete & sermon of Saynt Ciprian.*
[b] *Athen. Oxon.* vol. i. col. 152, ed. 1813. Oldys says, 'having a handsome monument over his grave.' *Brit. Lib.* p. 261, ed. 1738.
[c] Cole's MSS. No. 5819, fo. 62.
[d] Only Dowsing's journal for Suffolk has as yet been printed, but that for Cambridgeshire would be no less interesting.
[e] Cole's MSS. No. 5820, fo. 87.

forgotten.[a] Thus by a singular coincidence, the same fate overtook three different generations, and the last resting-places of the three men who successively contributed to render the name of Eliot famous are unknown to their descendants.

But though no inscription in brass or marble has survived to show us where Sir Thomas Elyot lies, it might not unreasonably have been supposed that his works would have furnished *monumentum ære perennius*. So far, however, is this from being the case that, as we have already had occasion to point out, comparatively few persons are acquainted with the writings of one whom Strype called 'one of the learnedest and wisest men of this time.'[b] We should, however, expect that the memory of the author of *The Governour*, the friend of Wolsey, of More, and of Cromwell, would at least be cherished by the inhabitants of the parish with which he was so long connected. But the indifference to which we have already alluded is strikingly exemplified in the statement of the present Rector of Carleton, whose family have possessed property in the parish for many years, and who informed the Editor, in answer to some inquiries, that 'Sir Thomas Elyot's name is not known here.'

Elyot died intestate; having no children[c] he probably thought it unnecessary to make a will. His widow, who had been joint-tenant with her husband of the Cambridgeshire estates, now enjoyed the whole as the survivor. She did not, however, long retain the garb of widowhood, but married for her second husband another Somersetshire man, Serjeant

---

[a] In Hamilton's *National Gazetteer*, published in 1868, in the description of the parish of Carlton cum Willingham, it is stated that 'the church *contains* a monument to Sir Thomas Elyot.' An error which has been allowed to remain uncorrected.

[b] *Eccles. Mem.* vol. i. pt. 1, p. 342, ed. 1822.

[c] There is no evidence whatever to support Wood's statement that Sir Thomas Elyot had three sons. See *Athen. Oxon.* vol. i. col. 481, ed. 1813.

James Dyer, who was M.P. for the county of Cambridge during the whole of the short reign of Edward the Sixth. Dyer was appointed a Judge of the Common Pleas in 1557,[a] and three years afterwards his wife Lady Dyer, formerly Lady Elyot, died and was buried at Great Staughton, in Huntingdonshire, August 26, 1560.[b]

With the death of his widow, we might fairly bring our notice of Elyot to a close; but it happens that a most interesting question involving the identity of the author of one of the most celebrated books published in the reign of Elizabeth arises in connection with the devolution of his property, upon which it seems almost incumbent upon us to make some further remarks.

Upon Elyot's death an inquisition post mortem (printed in the Appendix) was taken at Newmarket, in September 1546, by which it was ascertained that Richard Puttenham, the eldest son of Elyot's sister Margery, was his next heir, and that this young man was then twenty-six years of age. The family of Puttenham, who probably derived their name from the place where they lived, possessed the manors of Puttenham and Long Marston, on the borders of Hertfordshire and Buckinghamshire. Richard Puttenham had an only brother George,[c] and a sister Margery, married to Sir John Throckmorton, of Feckenham, in Worcestershire.[d]

In 1550, Sir Thomas Elyot's heir purchased from Richard Hardy, citizen and merchant tailor of London, an estate at Sherfield upon Loddon, in Hants,[e] and two years later he

[a] Foss. *Judges of England*, vol. v. p. 482.
[b] Wood, *Athen. Oxon.* vol. i. col. 482, ed. 1813. Another instance of Wood's inaccuracy may be noticed in the fact that on the same page he assigns three different dates for Dyer's burial and two for that of his wife.
[c] Chan. Proceed. Eliz. PP. 11, No. 49, P.R.O.
[d] Nash, *Hist. Worcest.* vol. i. p. 440.
[e] Close Roll, 4 Ed. VI. No. 467, P.R.O.

sold to one Hugh Stewkeley his reversion to his uncle's estates in Carleton and Willingham, for the sum of 250*l.*[a]

Richard Puttenham married Mary, the only daughter and heiress of Sir William Warham, of Malshanger, near Basingstoke,[b] and had one child, a daughter, Anne, who married previous to 1567 Francis Morris, of Coxwell, in Berkshire.[c] George Puttenham, the brother, married Elizabeth, the widow of William, second Lord Windsor, of Bradenham, in Bucks,[d] who according to Strype was 'buried very splendidly according to his quality,'[e] on August 29, 1558. Lady Windsor, who was the daughter and heiress of Peter Coudray, of Herriard, near Basingstoke, had been previously married to Richard Paulet.[f]

Both the brothers seem to have made unhappy marriages, and both were involved in perpetual litigation of a most disastrous character. With their domestic troubles, however, though these alone would furnish materials for a volume, we are not concerned except as they help to elucidate one important question.

The Arte of English Poesie, first published in 1589, has, at least in modern times, been generally attributed to George Puttenham. Was this the brother of Richard, or did Richard himself write it, or had each of the brothers, or neither of them, a hand in its composition? It will appear that the solution of all these questions is involved in the answer to the inquiry who was the real author of *The Arte of English Poesie?* It must not be forgotten that even the printer,

[a] Close Roll, 6 Ed. VI. No. 481, P.R.O.
[b] Chan. Proceed. Eliz. PP. 11, No. 49, P.R.O.
[c] Close Roll, 9 Eliz. No. 743, P.R.O.
[d] State Pap. Dom. Eliz. vol. 157, No. 75, P.R.O.
[e] *Eccles. Mem.* vol. iii. pt. 2, p. 117.
[f] Collins, *Peerage*, vol. iii. p. 672, ed. 1812.

Richard Field, was ignorant of the author's name, that Sir John Harrington, only two years after its publication, was unable to ascertain who had written it, and that the first person to connect it with the name of Puttenham was Edmund Bolton, in his *Hypercritica*, written probably in the first quarter of the seventeenth century, but not published till 1722. Even Bolton was ignorant of the author's Christian name, and had merely heard a rumour that this now celebrated book was the work of one of Queen Elizabeth's gentlemen-pensioners.[a] Wood adopted Bolton's statement, being unable himself to supply any fresh details with regard to the author.[b] Ames, writing in 1749, says 'the supposed author of this book is Webster Puttenham,'[c] an impossible combination which Ritson not only did not criticise but sanctioned.[d] Mr. Haslewood appears to have been the first who unhesitatingly affirmed that 'the Christian name of our author was certainly George.'[e] It must be confessed, however, that the reasons he gives for coming to this conclusion are not altogether satisfactory. Having found the will of a George Puttenham, dated September 1, 1590, and a MS. in the Harleian Collection purporting to be written by George Puttenham as an Apology or Defence of Queen Elizabeth's conduct in her treatment of the Queen of Scots, Mr. Haslewood considered that these wholly unconnected facts justified him in converting a plausible hypothesis into a positive certainty.

Modern readers will hardly be content to accept a conclusion based upon such flimsy premisses. A careful examination of documents preserved in the Public Record

[a] Haslewood, *Essays*, vol. ii. p. 250.
[b] *Athen. Oxon.* vol. i. col. 741, ed. 1813.
[c] *Bibliograph. Ant.* p. 418, ed. 1749.
[d] *Bibliographia Poetica*, p. 303, ed. 1802.
[e] *Essays*, vol. i. p. vi. ed. 1811.

Office, and of the internal evidence afforded by *The Arte of English Poesie* itself, suggests the notion that this celebrated book was written not by George, but by his elder brother Richard. It may perhaps be objected that there is but slight evidence that it was written by either of the brothers. With regard to this, however, we have first the fact, stated by Bolton within a quarter of a century of the publication of the work in question, that current rumour attributed the authorship to some person of the name of Puttenham. Secondly, there are at least two passages in the book itself which tend to confirm this view. At p. 226 a story is told of the offence given to the Emperor Charles V. by an ambassador of Henry VIII., 'whom,' says the author, 'I could name but will not, for the great opinion the world had of his wisdome and sufficiency in that behalfe.' The point of the story turns upon the Englishman's ignorance of the Spanish phrase appropriate to the occasion. Now we know by Sir Thomas Elyot's own admission that he did not know Spanish, and his nephew would naturally be reluctant to betray his uncle, for whom he no doubt entertained a high respect, by connecting his name with a story redounding somewhat to his discredit. Secondly, at p. 149 the author mentions the fact that he had composed an epitaph 'to the honourable memorie of a deere friend, Sir John Throgmorton, knight, Justice of Chester, and a man of many commendable vertues.' When we remember that the latter had married Margery Puttenham, there seems little difficulty in attributing the passage in question to the pen of a near relative. There is therefore a high degree of probability that 'fame' was correct in assigning the authorship of *The Arte of English Poesie* to one of the two Puttenhams. The important question yet remains, to which of the two brothers ought it to be assigned? Here arises the preliminary inquiry whether either of the brothers held the appointment, mentioned by Bolton, of gentleman-pensioner to Queen Elizabeth. Mr. Selby, of the Public Record Office, who at the request of the Editor kindly undertook to search the roll of the gentlemen-pensioners for the whole reign of Elizabeth, has informed him that they contain no entry of the name of Puttenham. Apart, however, from this positive contradiction of Bolton's description, a passage in the work itself would seem to negative the suggestion that the author had occupied such a position. At p. 253, speaking of 'the courtiers of forraine countreyes,' the writer says that he had 'very well obserued their maner of life and conuersation,' but immediately adds that, with regard to those of his own country, he had 'not made so great experience.' Such a statement could surely never have been made by one who if he held the appointment mentioned by Bolton must have enjoyed frequent opportunities for such observation. Bolton therefore was so far misinformed, that neither of the Puttenhams would have satisfied his description of the author. In order to determine to which of the two brothers the authorship may with the greater probability be assigned, let us see in what respect the internal evidence of the book is applicable to the one rather than to the other. And first it is evident that the author, whoever he was, spent a considerable portion of his life on the continent. Moreover, two passages enable us to fix approximately the period of his absence from England. At p. 227 the author mentions a circumstance which occurred at a banquet given by the Duchess of Parma, the Regent of the Low Countries, in honour of the Earl of Arundel, and of which the author himself was an eye-witness. Now we know from Lord Burghley's journal, that the Earl 'went over seas' in March 1565.[a] From a decree of the Court of Requests, made February 7, 1566, we learn that Richard Puttenham was at that date absent from England, and had been so absent at least from February 1563.[b] Again at p. 233 the author tells us that 'in the time of Charles the ninth French King,' he happened to be at Spa when 'a Marshall of Fraunce, called Monsieur de Sipier,' who was also there for his health, received from the king 'a letters patents of six thousand crownes yearely pension during his life.' Now François de Scepeaux, better known as de Vieilleville, received the appointment of Maréchal de France on December 21, 1562, and he died November 30, 1571.[c] His biographer tells us that in 1569 'sa majesté luy faisoit present de dix mille escus en or pour commencer à le rembourser de la despence infinie qu'il avoit faicte depuis cinq ou six ans pour son service.'[d] By records still existing we know that Richard Puttenham obtained a special pardon from the Queen in 1570, for having been absent from the realm without licence.[e] It may be presumed therefore that he had returned not long before. George Puttenham was certainly in England during the time that his brother was abroad, for he is ordered by the decree mentioned above to contribute to the support of his brother's wife 'until such time as the said Richard her husband shall make his return into this realm of England.' The passages above quoted from *The Arte of Poesie* are therefore certainly more consistent with the view that Richard was the author, than with the hitherto received opinion which attributes it to George. On the other

[a] Murdin, *Burghley State Pap.* p. 761, ed. 1759.
[b] Court of Requests (Orders and Dec.) vol. xi. fo. 590, P.R.O.
[c] Pinard, *Chronol. Hist. Milit.* tom. ii. p. 289, ed. 1760.
[d] *Mém. sur Vieilleville*, p. 799, ed. P. L.
[e] Pat. Roll, 12 Eliz. P.R.O.

LIFE OF ELYOT. clxxxvii

hand it must be admitted that there is one piece of evidence which at first sight strongly militates against this view. At p. 141 the author refers to 'our Eglogue intituled *Elpine*, which we made, being but eightene yeares old, to King Edward the sixt, a Prince of great hope.' Now inasmuch as Richard Puttenham is stated to have been twenty-six years old some months previous to the accession of Edward VI., it would seem impossible to reconcile these conflicting statements. But it appears to have been not unusual to address Edward as the Sixth, while his father was still living;[a] and allowance must be made for some slight inaccuracy on the part of the author, due to the length of time which had elapsed and to the pardonable disposition observable in old age to exaggerate the exploits of youth. Finally there is the curious and most important fact that *The Arte of English Poesie* was not only published anonymously, but that even the printer was unacquainted with the writer. 'This booke,' says the former, in his address to Lord Burghley, 'comming to my handes with his bare title without any authours name.' Such is the statement made by Richard Field on May 28, 1589. But on referring to the Register of the Stationers' Company we find that a licence to print the same book had been granted six months earlier to Thomas Orwin, viz., on November 9, 1588.[b] Now it is not a little singular that ten days previous to this latter date Richard Puttenham was in prison. Of this important fact there is absolutely conclusive evidence. Among the archives of the Public Record Office there is preserved a document purporting to be a petition to the Lords of the Privy Council from Richard Puttenham, who therein describes himself as 'prisoner the second time,

[a] See ex. gr. Hallam. *Lit. of Eur.* vol. i. p. 344, note b, 4th ed.
[b] *The Stationers' Registers*, vol. ii. p. 506, ed. 1875.

and complains bitterly of the harsh treatment he had received from Mr. Seckford, Master of Requests. This petition concludes with an urgent appeal to their lordships 'to appoint him counsel to speak for him before ye, and *in formâ pauperis*, for otherwise he is not able to pay them their fees nor to retain any.'[*] It is impossible to give here the chain of evidence by which the Editor satisfied himself that this humble suppliant was undoubtedly Sir Thomas Elyot's nephew and heir. The reader, however, may take it for granted that there are abundant materials existing in the Public Record Office to justify this startling conclusion. Happily we are enabled to trace the course of this petition, though the tale which it unfolds is one of treachery and heartlessness which conveys a very unfavourable impression of the parties concerned. Along with the petition there is preserved a letter from the Lord Mayor of London, one Wolstan Dixie, dated October 30, 1588, and addressed 'to the right worshipful Mr. Seckford, one of the Masters of her Ma[ties] Court of Requests.' In this letter the Lord Mayor informs Mr. Seckford that 'this afternoon there was brought unto me by a constable and one other with him the supplication here inclosed,' and finding whom it concerned, he had 'thought good to send the same unto you, referring the matter therein contained unto your grave consideration.' Of the result of the petition we have no positive evidence, but the reader will probably infer that it was at any rate not favourable to the suppliant, when he is informed that there is still to be found at Somerset House the will of 'Richard Puttenham, Esq., nowe prisoner in her Majesties Bench,' bearing date April 22, 1597. Looking to the fact that Richard Puttenham was a prisoner in very distressed circumstances at the end of October

[*] State Pap. Dom. Eliz. vol. 183, No. 66, P.R.O.

1588, and that a few days afterwards a licence was obtained by Orwin to print the book in question, no author's name being given, and that only a few months later it was published, not by Orwin but by Field, in the manner above described, it must be admitted that a very fair foundation of probability is laid for connecting with its authorship the name of Richard Puttenham. We shall scarcely be assuming too much if we suppose that the unfortunate prisoner, in his anxiety to raise the necessary funds to enable him to prosecute his appeal to the Privy Council, or to procure his release, parted with the MS. of his work under circumstances which precluded the revelation of his name to the printer. It was impossible, however, that a work of this kind, in which, according to a competent judge, 'we find an approach to the higher province of philosophical criticism'[a] should not attract attention in that or indeed in any age. Inquiries would inevitably be made as to its authorship, and presently 'fame,' flitting like a bee from one name to another, would at last settle upon that which by general consent seemed the most probable, and thus would enable posterity to detect in the anonymous author of *The Arte of English Poesie* him who, together with the possessions, had inherited no inconsiderable portion of the genius of Sir Thomas Elyot.

[a] Hallam, *Lit. of Eur.* vol. ii. p. 210, 4th ed.

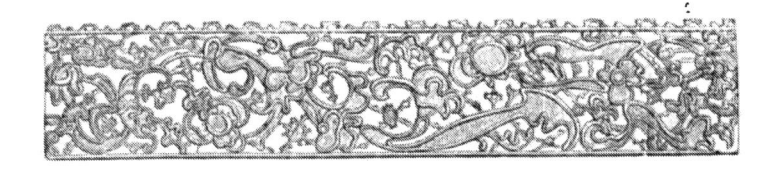

The Proheme.

The proheme of Thomas Elyot, knyghte, unto the most noble and victorious prince kinge Henry the eyght, kyng of Englande and Fraunce, defender of the true faythe, and lorde of Irelande.[a]

LATE consideringe (moste excellent prince and myne onely redoughted soueraigne lorde) my duetie that I owe to my naturall contray with my faythe also of aliegeaunce and othe, wherewith I am double bounden unto your maiestie, more ouer thaccompt that I haue to rendre for that one litle talent deliuered to me to employe (as I suppose) to the increase of vertue, I am (as god iuge me) violently stered[b] to deuulgate or sette fourth some part of my studie, trustynge therby tacquite me of my dueties to god, your hyghnesse, and this my contray. Wherfore takinge comfort and boldenesse, partly of your graces moste beneuolent inclination towarde the uniuersall weale of your subiectes, partly inflamed with

---

[a] In the edition of 1546 and all the subsequent editions the royal style i altered, and runs thus: 'By the grace of god kyng of Englande, Fraunce, ands Irelande, defender of the faith, and in erth of the Churche of England and also of Ireland supreme head.' The change of style was rendered necessary by the Act 35 Hen. VIII. cap. 3, which was passed in 1543.

[b] *I.e.* stirred.

zele, I haue nowe enterprised to describe in our vulgare tunge the fourme of a iuste publike weale : whiche mater I haue gathered as well of the sayenges of moste noble autours (grekes and latynes) as by myne owne experience, I beinge continually trayned in some dayly affaires of the publike weale of this your moste noble realme all mooste from my chylhode.[a] Whiche attemptate is nat of presumption to teache any persone, I my selfe hauinge moste nede of teachinge : but onely to the intent that men which wil be studious about the weale publike may fynde the thinge therto expedient compendiously writen. And for as moch as this present boke treateth of the education of them that hereafter may be demed worthy to be gouernours of the publike weale under your hyghnesse (whiche Plato[b] affirmeth to be the firste and chiefe parte of a publyke weale; Salomon[c] sayenge also where gouernours be nat the people shall falle in to ruyne), I therfore haue named it *The Gouernour*, and do nowe dedicate it unto your hyghnesse as the fyrste frutes of my studye, verely trustynge that your moste excellent wysedome wyll therein esteme my loyall harte and diligent endeuour by the

---

[a] See *Life of Sir Thomas Elyot*, p. xxx, ante.

[b] See *ex. gr.* Plato, *Rep.* lib. iv. 423 E. Οὗτοι, ἦν δ' ἐγώ, ὦ 'γαθὲ 'Αδείμαντε, ὦ δόξειεν ἄν τις, ταῦτα πολλὰ καὶ μεγάλα αὐτοῖς προστάττομεν, ἀλλὰ πάντα φαῦλα, ἐὰν τὸ λεγόμενον ἓν μέγα φυλάττωσι, μᾶλλον δὲ ἀντὶ μεγάλου ἱκανόν. Τί τοῦτο; ἔφη. Τὴν παιδείαν, ἦν δ' ἐγώ, καὶ τροφήν..... τροφὴ γὰρ καὶ παίδευσις χρηστὴ σωζομένη φύσεις ἀγαθὰς ἐμποιεῖ, καὶ αὖ φύσεις χρησταὶ τοιαύτης παιδείας ἀντιλαμβανόμεναι ἔτι βελτίους τῶν προτέρων φύονται. Compare also *Legg.* lib. vii. 804: ἀλλὰ τὸ λεγόμενον πάντ' ἄνδρα καὶ παῖδα κατὰ τὸ δυνατὸν, ὡς τῆς πόλεως μᾶλλον ἢ τῶν γεννητόρων ὄντας, παιδευτέον ἐξ ἀνάγκης.

[c] See Prov. xi. 14.

The Table.

THE TABLE OF THE FIRSTE BOKE OF THE GOUERNOUR.

CHAPTER I.

The significacion of a publike weale, and why it is called in latyne Respublica 1

CHAPTER II.

That one soueraigne gouernour ought to be in a publike weale, and what damage hath hapned by lackyng one soueraygne gouernour . 8

CHAPTER III.

That in a publyke weale oughte to be inferior gouernours called magistratis 24

CHAPTER IV.

The education or fourme of bryngynge up the chylde of a gentilman, which is to haue auctorite in the publike weale 28

CHAPTER V.

The ordre of lernynge before the child cometh to thage of vii *yeres* . 31

CHAPTER VI.

Whan a Tutour shulde be prouided, and what shall appertaine to his office 35

CHAPTER VII.
In what wyse musike may be to a noble man necessary . . . 38

CHAPTER VIII.
That it is commendable in a gentilman to paynte or karue exactely, if nature do therto induce hym 43

CHAPTER IX.
What exacte diligence shulde be in chosinge of maisters . . . 50

CHAPTER X.
What order shulde be in lerninge and whiche autours shulde be first radde 53

CHAPTER XI.
The mooste necessarie studies succedynge the lesson of Poetes . . 72

CHAPTER XII.
Why gentyllmen in this present time be nat equall in doctrine to the auncient noble men 98

CHAPTER XIII.
The seconde and thirde decaye of lerninge 113

CHAPTER XIV.
Howe the studentes in the lawes of this realme may take excellent commoditie by the lessons of sondry doctrines 133

CHAPTER XV.
The causes why in Englande be fewe perfecte schole maisters . . 163

example of Artaxerxes, the noble kynge of Persia, who reiected nat the pore husbondman whiche offred to hym his homely handes full of clene water, but mooste graciously receyued it with thankes, estemynge the present nat after the value but rather to the wyll of the gyuer.[a] Semblably kynge Alexander retayned with hym the poete Cherilus honorably for writing his historie, all though that the poete was but of a small estimation.[b] Whiche that prynce dyd not for lacke of iugement, he beynge of excellent lernynge as disciple to Aristotell,[c] but to thentent that his liberalite emploied on Cherilus shulde animate or gyue courage to others moche better lerned to contende with hym in a semblable enterpryse.

And if, moste vertuous prince, I may perceyue your hyghnes to be herewith pleased, I shall sone after (god giuing me quietenes) present your grace with the

[a] This incident is related by Pluturch: Ἐπεὶ δὲ, ἄλλων ἄλλα προσφερόντων καθ' ὁδὸν, αὐτουργὸς ἄνθρωπος οὐδὲν ἐπὶ καιροῦ φθάσας εὑρεῖν τῷ ποταμῷ προσέδραμε καὶ ταῖν χεροῖν ὑπολαβὼν τοῦ ὕδατος προσήνεγκεν, ἡσθεὶς ὁ Ἀρτοξέρξες φιάλην ἔπεμψεν αὐτῷ χρυσῆν καὶ χιλίους δαρεικούς.—Plut. *Artoxerxes*, cap. 5.

[b] 'Gratus Alexandro regi Magno fuit ille
Chærilus, incultis qui versibus et male natis,
Rettulit acceptos, regale nomisma, Philippos.'—Hor. *Ep.* ii.1, 232.

Curtius says: 'Agis quidam Argivus, *pessimorum carminum post Chærilum conditor*, et ex Siciliâ Cleo (hic quidem non ingenii solum sed etiam nationis vitio adulator) et cætera urbium suarum purgamenta, quæ propinquis etiam maximorumque exercituum ducibus à rege præferebantur.'—Lib. viii. cap. 5.

[c] Plutarch is the authority for this fact: Ἦν δὲ καὶ φύσει φιλόλογος καὶ φιλαναγνώστης. Καὶ τὴν μὲν Ἰλιάδα τῆς πολεμικῆς ἀρετῆς ἐφόδιον καὶ νομίζων καὶ ὀνομάζων ἔλαβε μὲν Ἀριστοτέλους διορθώσαντος, ἣν ἐκ τοῦ νάρθηκος καλοῦσιν, εἶχε δὲ ἀεὶ μετὰ τοῦ ἐγχειριδίου κειμένην ὑπὸ τὸ προσκεφάλαιον ὡς Ὀνησίκριτος ἱστόρηκε.—Plut. *Alex.* cap. 8. Aristotle dedicated his treatise, Περὶ Κόσμου, to his illustrious pupil.

residue of my studie and labours,[a] wherein your hyghnes shal well perceiue that I nothing esteme so moche in this worlde as youre royall astate, (my most dere soueraigne lorde), and the publike weale of my contray. Protestinge unto your excellent maiestie that where I commende herin any one vertue or dispraise any one vice I meane the generall description of thone and thother without any other particuler meanynge to the reproche of any one persone. To the whiche protestation I am nowe dryuen throughe the malignite of this present tyme all disposed to malicious detraction.[b] Wherfore I mooste humbly beseche your hyghnes to dayne to be patrone and defendour of this litle warke agayne the assaultes of maligne interpretours whiche fayle nat to rente and deface the renoume of wryters, they them selfes beinge in nothinge to the publike weale profitable. Whiche is by no man sooner perceyued than by your highnes, being bothe in wysedome and very nobilitie equall to the most excellent princes, whome, I beseche god, ye may surmount in longe life and perfect felicitie. Amen.

[a] See the *Life of Sir Thomas Elyot*, p. ci, ante.   [b] *Ibid.* p. cxi.

CHAPTER XVI.

Of sondrye fourmes of exercise necessarye for a gentilman . . 169

CHAPTER XVII.

Exercises whereof cometh both recreation and profite . . . 173

CHAPTER XVIII.

The auncient huntyng of Greekes Romanes and Persianes . . . 186

CHAPTER XIX.

That all daunsinge is nat to be reproued 203

CHAPTER XX.

The fyrst begynnyng of daunsyng and the olde estimation therof. . 213

CHAPTER XXI.

Wherefore in the good ordre of daunsynge a man and a woman do daunse together 233

CHAPTER XXII.

How daunsing may be an introduction into the fyrst morall vertue, called Prudence 238

CHAPTER XXIII.

Of Prouidence and industrie 246

CHAPTER XXIV.

Of Circumspection 253

CHAPTER XXV.

Of election, experience, and modestie 262

CHAPTER XXVI.

Of other exercyses whiche, moderately used, be to euery astate of man expedient 269

CHAPTER XXVII.

That shotyng in a longe bowe is principall of all other exercises . 286

Finis tabule.

Consydering that in settynge the letters to print there can nat be alway so exacte diligence used but that some thing may happe to eskape worthy correction all though Argus were the artificer, I therfore wyll desyre the gentill reders of this warke that or they seriously rede it they will amende the defautes in printynge accordinge to the instructions immediately followynge.

THE FAUTES.

Vol. I. p. 104, line 3 *for* That   *rede* that
,,   146, ,, 1 ,, af   ,, of
,,   169, ,, 20 ,, as moche the   ,, as moche as the
,,   170, ,, 6 ,, densed   ,, clensed
Vol. II. p. 174, last line ,, vnethe   ,, unethe
,,   222, line 9 ,, That   ,, that

THE GOVERNOUR.

The firste Boke.

CHAPTER I.

The significacion of a Publike Weale, and why it is called in Latin Respublica.

A PUBLIKE weale is in sondry wyse defined by philosophers, but knowyng by experience that the often repetition of anything of graue or sad importance wyll be tedious to the reders of this warke, who perchance for the more parte haue nat ben trayned in lernyng contaynynge semblable matter, I haue compiled one definition out of many in as compendious fourme as my poure witte can deuise, trustyng that in those fewe wordes the trewe signification of a publike weale shall euidently appere to them whom reason can satisfie. *Publyke Weale.* A publike weale is a body lyuyng, compacte or made of sondry astates and degrees of men, whiche is disposed by the ordre of equite and gouerned by the rule and moderation of reason. In the latin tonge it is called *Respublica*, of the whiche the worde *Res* hath diuers significations, and dothe nat only betoken that, that is called a thynge, whiche is distincte from a persone, but also signifieth astate, condition, substance, and profite. In our olde vulgare, profite is called weale. And it is called *Profytte.*[*]

---

[*] The word *Plebs* is inserted here in the margin of the original, but has evi-

a welthy contraye wherin is all thyng that is profitable. And he is a welthy man that is riche in money and substance. Publike (as Varro[a] saith) is diriuied of people, whiche in latin is called *Populus*, wherfore hit semeth that men haue ben longe abused in calling *Rempublicam* a commune weale. And they which do suppose it so to be called for that, that euery thinge shulde be to all men in commune, without discrepance of any astate or condition, be thereto moued more by sensualite than by any good reason or inclination to humanite. And that shall sone appere unto them that wyll be satisfied either with autorite or with naturall ordre and example.

Publyke.[b]

Fyrst, the propre and trewe signification of the wordes[c] publike and commune, whiche be borowed of the latin tonge for the insufficiencie of our owne langage, shal sufficiently declare the blyndenes of them whiche haue hitherto holden and maynteyned the sayde opinions. As I haue sayde, publike toke his begynnyng of people: whiche in latin is *Populus*, in whiche worde is conteyned all the inhabitantes of a realme or citie, of what astate or condition so euer they be. *Plebs* in englisshe is called the communaltie, which signifieth only the multitude, wherin be contayned the base and vulgare inhabitantes not auanced to any honour or dignite, whiche is also used in our dayly communication; for in the citie of London and other cities they that be none aldermen or sheriffes be called communers.[d] And in the countrey, at a cessions

Populus.

Plebs.

---

dently been transposed from its proper place at the top of folio 2, p. 2 of the present edition. The word Profit is inserted here in the margin in all the subsequent editions.

[a] (À populus) et publicus (ut quidam existimant) quasi populicus quod non privatim alicujus sed populi sit.—*Cornucopiæ*, p. 313, ed. 1527.

[b] The word *Publyke* is not inserted here in the margin of the original, but has evidently been misplaced by the printer, and transferred *per incuriam* to the opposite page, folio 1*b*; it now appears in its proper place in the present edition.

[c] The erroneous reading 'workes' has crept into the later editions.

[d] This definition, however, is not quite accurate, for under certain circumstances both aldermen and sheriffs might be included in the general term 'common-

or other assembly, if no gentyl men be there at, the sayenge is that there was none but the communalte, whiche proueth in myn oppinion that *Plebs* in latine is in englisshe communaltie and *Plebeii* be communers. And consequently there may appere lyke diuersitie to be in englisshe betwene a publike weale and a commune weale, as shulde be in latin betwene *Res publica* and *Res plebeia*, And after that signification, if there shuld be a commune weale, either the communers only must be welthy, and the gentil and noble men nedy and miserable, orels[a] excluding gentilite, al men must be of one degre and sort, and a new name prouided. For as moche as *Plebs* in latin, and comminers in englisshe, be wordes only made for the discrepance of degrees, wherof procedeth ordre: whiche in thinges as wel naturall as supernaturall hath euer had suche a preeminence, that therby the incomprehensible maiestie of god, as it were by a bright leme[a] of a torche or candel, is declared to the blynde inhabitantes of this worlde. More ouer take away ordre from all thynges what shulde than remayne? Certes nothynge finally, except some man wolde imagine eftsones[a] *Chaos*: whiche of some is expounde a confuse mixture. Also where there is any lacke of ordre nedes must be perpetuall conflicte: and in thynges subiecte to Nature nothynge of hym selfe onely may be norisshed; but whan he hath distroyed that where with he dothe participate

Publike and Commune.

Ordre.

Chaos.

---

alty,' thus we find, e.g., that in some of the ancient charters of the City of London preserved in the *Liber Custumarum*, now printed under the direction of the Master of the Rolls, grants were sometimes made 'majori et communæ Londoniarum;' at other times 'le Maire et la communalte de tote la cite de Londres' entered into an agreement, e.g. with the merchants of Amyas, Corbie, and Nesle. 21 Henry III. Again, as illustrating the legal distinction, we find that Communitas civitatis Londoniarum summonita fuit ad respondendum Domino Regi quo warranto Major Aldermanni et Vicecomites in Hustingo civitatis prædictæ corrigunt judicia in curiis Regis coram Vicecomitibus civitatis prædictæ, etc., et communitas venit.' Writs on the other hand were usually issued, 'Majori et Vicecomitibus Londoniarum.'

[a] See the Glossary.

by the ordre of his creation, he hym selfe of necessite muste than perisshe, wherof ensuethe uniuersall dissolution.

But nowe to proue, by example of those thynges that be within the compasse of mannes knowlege, of what estimation ordre is, nat onely amonge men but also with god, all be it his wisedome, bounte, and magnificence can be with no tonge or penne sufficiently expressed. Hath nat he set degrees and astates in all his glorious warkes?

Fyrst in his heuenly ministres, whom, as the churche affirmeth, he hath constituted to be in diuers degrees called hierarches.[a]

Also Christe saithe by his euangelist that in the house of his father (which is god) be many mansions.[b] But to treate of that whiche by naturall understandyng may be comprehended.

Elements. Beholde the foure elementes wherof the body of man is compacte, howe they be set in their places called spheris, higher or lower, accordynge to the soueraintie of theyr natures, that is to saye, the fyer as the most pure element, hauyng in it nothing that is corruptible, in his place is higheste and aboue other elementes. The ayer, whiche next to the fyre is most pure in substance, is in the seconde sphere or place. The water, whiche is somewhat consolidate, and approcheth to corruption, is next unto the erthe. The erthe, whiche is of substance grosse and ponderous, is set of all elementes most lowest.

Beholde also the ordre that god hath put generally in al his creatures, begynnyng at the moste inferiour or base, and assendynge upwarde: he made not only herbes to garnisshe the

---

[a] Thus Thomas Aquinas, citing as his authority a work which was erroneously ascribed to Dionysius the Areopagite, says: 'Sic igitur et in quâlibet hierarchiâ angelicâ ordines distinguuntur secundum diversos actus et officia, et omnis ista diversitas ad tria reducitur, scilicet ad summum, medium, et infimum; et propter hoc in quâlibet hierarchiâ Dionysius (*Cælest. hier.*, cap. vi. § 2), ponit tres ordines nempe Seraphim, Cherubim, et thronorum, in primâ; dominationum, virtutum, et potestatum, in secundâ; principatuum, archangelorum, et angelorum, in tertiâ.'— *Summ. Theolog.* pt. I. quæst. cviii.

[b] See S. John, chap. xiv. 2.

erthe, but also trees of a more eminent stature than herbes, and yet in the one and the other be degrees of qualitees; some pleasant to beholde, some delicate or good in taste, other holsome and medicinable, some commodious and necessary. Semblably in byrdes, bestis, and fisshes, some be good for the sustinance of man, some beare thynges profitable to sondry uses, other be apte to occupation and labour; in diuerse is strength and fiersenes only; in many is both strength and commoditie; some other serue for pleasure; none of them hath all these qualities; fewe haue the more part or many, specially beautie, strength, and profite. But where any is founde that hath many of the said propreties, he is more set by than all the other, and by that estimation the ordre of his place and degree euidentlye apperethe; so that euery kynde of trees, herbes, birdes, beastis, and fisshes, besyde theyr diuersitie of fourmes, haue (as who sayth) a peculier disposition appropered unto them by god theyr creatour: so that in euery thyng is ordre, and without ordre may be nothing stable or permanent; and it may nat be called ordre, excepte it do contayne in it degrees, high and base, accordynge to the merite or estimation of the thyng that is ordred.

Nowe to retourne to the astate of man kynde, for whose use all the sayd creatures were ordayned of god, and also excelleth them all by prerogatife of knowlege and wisedome, hit semeth that in hym shulde be no lasse prouidence of god declared than in the inferiour creatures; but rather with a more perfecte ordre and dissposition. And therfore hit appereth that god gyueth nat to euery man like gyftes of grace, or of nature, but to some more, some lesse, as it liketh his diuine maiestie.

Ne they be nat in commune, (as fantasticall foles wolde haue all thyngs), nor one man hath nat al vertues and good qualities. Nat withstandyng for as moche as under- *Understandyng is the most excellent gyfte that man can standynge.* receiue in his creation, wherby he doth approche most nyghe unto the similitute of god; whiche understandynge is the principall parte of the soule : it is therfore congruent, and accordynge that as one excelleth an other in that influence, as therby beinge next to the similitude of his maker, so shulde the astate of his persone be auanced in degree or place where understandynge may profite : whiche is also distributed in to sondry uses, faculties, and offices, necessary for the lyuing and gouernance of mankynde. And like as the angels whiche be most feruent in contemplation be highest exalted in glorie, (after the opinion of holy doctours[a]), and also the fire whiche is the most pure of elementes, and also doth clarifie the other inferiour elementes, is deputed to the highest sphere or place ; so in this worlde, they whiche excelle other in this influence of understandynge, and do imploye it to the detaynyng of other within the boundes of reason, and shewe them howe to prouyde for theyr necessarye lyuynge ; suche oughte to be set in a more highe place than the residue where they may se and also be sene ; that by the beames of theyr excellent witte, shewed throughe the glasse of auctorite, other of inferiour understandynge may be directed to the way of vertue and commodious liuynge. And unto men of suche vertue by very equitie appertaineth honour, as theyr iuste rewarde and duetie, whiche by other mennes labours must also be mainteined according to their merites. For as moche as the saide persones, excelling in knowlege wherby other be gouerned, be ministers for the only profite and commoditie of them whiche haue nat equall understandyng : where they whiche do exercise artificiall science or corporall labour, do nat trauayle for theyr superiours onely, but also for theyr owne necessitie. So the husbande man fedethe hym selfe and the clothe maker : the clothe maker apparayleth hym selfe and the husbande : they both socour other artificers : other artificers them : they and other artificers them that be gouernours. But they that be gouernours (as I before sayde)

Honour.

---

[a] 'In coelesti enim hierarchiâ tota ratio ordinis est ex propinquitate ad Deum ; et ideo illi, qui sunt Deo propinquiores, sunt et gradu sublimiores et scientiâ clariores.'—Aquinas, *Summ. Theolog.* pars I. quæst. cvi.

nothinge do acquire by the sayde influence of knowlege for theyr owne necessities, but do imploye all the powers of theyr wittes, and theyr diligence, to the only preseruation of other theyr inferiours: amonge whiche inferiours also behoueth to be a disposition and ordre accordynge to reason, that is to saye, that the slouthfull or idell persone do nat participate with hym that is industrious and taketh payne: wherby the frutes of his labours shulde be diminisshed: wherin shulde be none equalite, but therof shulde procede discourage, and finally disolution for lacke of prouision. Wherfore it can none other wyse stande with reason, but that the astate of the persone in preeminence of lyuynge shulde be estemed with his understandyng, labour, and policie: where unto muste be added an augmentation of honour and substaunce; whiche nat onely impressethe a reuerence, wherof procedethe due obedience amonge subiectes, but also inflameth men naturally inclined to idelnes or sensuall appetite to coueyte lyke fortune, and for that cause to dispose them to studie or occupation. Nowe to conclude my fyrst assertion or argument, where all thynge is commune, there lacketh ordre; and where ordre lacketh, there all thynge is odiouse and uncomly. And that haue we in dayly experience; for the pannes and pottes garnissheth wel the ketchyn, and yet shulde they be to the chambre none ornament. Also the beddes, testars, and pillowes besemeth nat the halle, no more than the carpettes and kusshyns becometh the stable. Semblably the potter and tynker, only perfecte in theyr crafte, shall littell do in the ministration of iustice. A ploughman or carter shall make but a feble answere to an ambassadour. Also a wayuer* or fuller shulde be an unmete capitaine of an armie, or in any other office of a governour. Wherfore to conclude, it is onely a publike weale, where, like as god hath disposed the saide influence of understandyng, is also appoynted degrees and places accordynge to the excellencie therof; and therto also wold be substance conuenient and necessarye for the orna-

* *I.e.* weaver.

ment of the same, whiche also impresseth a reuerence and due obedience to the vulgare people or communaltie; and with out that, it can be no more said that there is a publike weale, than it may be affirmed that a house, without his propre and necessarye ornamentes, is well and sufficiently furnisshed.

CHAPTER II.

That one soueraigne gouernour ought to be in a publike weale. And what damage hath happened where a multitude hath had equal authorite without any soueraygne.

LYKE as to a castell or fortresse suffisethe one owner or souerayne, and where any mo[a] be of like power and authoritie seldome cometh the warke to perfection; or beinge all redy made, where the one diligently ouerseeth and the other neglecteth, in that 'contention all is subuerted and commeth to ruyne. In semblable wyse dothe a publike weale that hath mo chiefe gouernours than one. Example we may take of the grekes, amonge whom in diuers cities weare diuers fourmes of publyke weales gouerned by multitudes: wherin one was most tollerable where the gouernance and rule was alway permitted to them whiche excelled in vertue,[b] and was in the greke tonge called *Aris-*

---

[a] See the Glossary.

[b] Thucydides, however, shows us that even in the opinion of Phrynicus, himself one of the chief organizers of the oligarchical movement, the rule of the so-called 'good and virtuous' men hardly merited this description: τούς τε καλοὺς κἀγαθοὺς ὀνομαζομένους οὐκ ἐλάσσω αὐτοὺς νομίζειν σφίσι πράγματα παρέξειν τοῦ δήμου, ποριστὰς ὄντας καὶ ἐσηγητὰς τῶν κακῶν τῷ δήμῳ, ἐξ ὧν τὰ πλείω αὐτοὺς ὠφελεῖσθαι· καὶ τὸ μὲν ἐπ' ἐκείνοις εἶναι, καὶ ἄκριτοι ἂν καὶ βιαιότερον ἀποθνήσκειν, τὸν τε δῆμον σφῶν τε καταφυγὴν εἶναι καὶ ἐκείνων σωφρονιστήν. καὶ ταῦτα παρ' αὐτῶν τῶν ἔργων ἐπισταμένας τὰς πόλεις σαφῶς αὐτὸς εἰδέναι, ὅτι οὕτω νομίζουσι. Lib. viii. cap. 48. Mr. Grote says: 'In taking the comparison between oligarchy and democracy in Greece there is hardly any evidence more important than this passage : a testimony to the comparative merit of democracy, pronounced by an oligarchical

tocratia, in latin *Optimorum Potentia*, in englisshe the rule of men of beste disposition, which the Thebanes of longe tyme obserued.[a]   *Aristocraties.*

An other publique weale was amonge the Atheniensis, where equalitie was of astate amonge the people, and only by theyr holle consent theyr citie and dominions were gouerned:[b] whiche moughte well be called a monstre with many heedes: nor neuer it was certeyne nor stable:[c] and often tymes they

conspirator and sanctioned by an historian himself unfriendly to the democracy.'— *Hist. of Greece*, vol. v. p. 363, note.

[a] Xenophon, speaking of the Bœotian cities which were favourable to Thebes, says: ἐν πάσαις γὰρ ταῖς πόλεσι δυναστεῖαι καθειστήκεσαν, ὥσπερ ἐν Θήβαις.—*Hellen.* lib. v. cap. 4. 'These words,' says Mr. Grote, 'allude to the "factio optimatium" at Thebes, of whom Leontiadês was the chief, who betrayed the Kadmeia (the citadel of Thebes) to the Lacedæmonian troops under Phœbidas, B.C. 382; and who remained masters of Thebes, subservient to Sparta and upheld by a standing Lacedæmonian garrison in the Kadmeia, until they were overthrown by the memorable conspiracy of Pelopidas and Mellon B.C. 379. It is to this oligarchy under Leontiadês at Thebes, devoted to Spartan interests and resting on Spartan support, that Xenophon compares the governments planted by Sparta after the peace of Antalkidas in each of the Bœotian cities. What he says of the government of Leontiadês and his colleagues at Thebes is: "that they deliberately introduced the Lacedæmonians and enslaved Thebes to them, in order that they might themselves exercise a despotism."'—*Hist. of Greece*, vol. vii. p. 25, note.

[b] 'Kleisthenês abolished the four Ionic tribes, and created in their place ten new tribes founded upon a different principle, independent of the gentes and phratries. Each of his new tribes comprised a certain number of demes or cantons, with the enrolled proprietors and residents in each of them. The demes taken altogether included the entire surface of Attica, so that the Kleisthenean constitution admitted to the political franchise all the free native Athenians; and not merely these, but also many metics, and even some of the superior order of slaves. Putting out of sight the general body of slaves, and regarding only the free inhabitants, it was, in point of fact, a scheme approaching to *universal suffrage*, both political and judicial.'—Grote, *Hist. of Greece*, vol. iii. p. 109.

[c] Mr. Grote vindicates the Athenian democracy from the charges of inconstancy and ingratitude especially with regard to the treatment of Miltiades. 'It is a well known fact,' he says, 'that feelings, or opinions, or modes of judging which have once obtained footing among a large number of people, are more lasting and unchangeable than those which belong only to one or a few; insomuch that the judgments and actions of the many admit of being more clearly understood as to the past, and more certainly predicted as to the future. If we are to predicate any attribute of the multitude it will rather be that of undue tenacity than undue fickleness. There will occur nothing in the course of this

banyssed or slewe the beste citezins, whiche by their vertue and wisedome had moste profited to the publike weale.* [This maner of gouernaunce was called in greke *Democratia*, in latin *Popularis potentia*, in englisshe the rule of the comminaltie.] Of these two gouernances none of them may be sufficient. For in the fyrste, whiche consisteth of good men, vertue is nat so constant in a multitude, but that some, beinge ones in authoritie, be incensed with glorie: some with ambition: other with coueitise and desire of treasure or possessions: wherby they falle in to contention: and finallye, where any achiuethe the superioritie, the holle gouernance is reduced unto a fewe in nombre, whiche fearinge the multitude and their mutabilitie, to the intent to kepe them in drede to rebelle, ruleth by terrour and crueltie, thinking therby to kepe them selfe in suertie: nat withstanding, rancour coarcted and longe detained in a narowe roume, at the last brasteth out with intollerable violence, and bryngeth al to confusion. For the power that is practized to the hurte of many can nat continue. The populare astate, if it any thing do varie from equalitie of substance or estimation, or that the multitude of

Demo-cratia.

history to prove that the Athenian people changed their opinions on insufficient grounds more frequently than an unresponsible One or Few would have changed.' —*Hist. of Greece*, vol. iii. p. 321.

* Sir Thomas Elyot of course alludes to the ostracism of Aristides and Miltiades, &c., but Mr. Grote shows that so far from the system of ostracism being employed as an engine of oppression or caprice, it was an indispensable adjunct to the democratical form of government. 'Plutarch,' says Mr. Grote, ' has affirmed that the ostracism arose from the envy and jealousy inherent in a democracy, and not from justifiable fears,—an observation often repeated, yet not the less demonstrably untrue. Not merely because ostracism so worked as often to increase the influence of that political leader whose rival it removed, but still more because if the fact had been as Plutarch says, this institution would have continued as long as the democracy; whereas it finished with the banishment of Hyperbolus, at a period when the government was more decisively democratical than it had been in the time of Kleisthenês. It was, in truth, a product altogether of fear and insecurity on the part both of the democracy and its best friends —fear perfectly well grounded, and only appearing needless because the precautions taken prevented attack. As soon as the diffusion of a constitutional morality had placed the mass of the citizens above all serious fear of an aggressive usurper, the ostracism was discontinued.'—*Hist. of Greece*, vol. iii. pp. 137, 138.

people haue ouer moche liberte, of necessite one of these inconueniences muste happen: either tiranny, where he that is to moche in fauour wolde be elevate and suffre none equalite, orels in to the rage of a communaltie, whiche of all rules is moste to be feared. For lyke as the communes, if they fele some seueritie, they do humbly serue and obaye, so where they imbracinge a licence refuse to be brydled, they flynge and plunge: and if they ones throwe downe theyr gouernour, they ordre euery thynge without iustice, only with vengeance and crueltie: and with incomparable difficultie and unneth [a] by any wysedome be pacified and brought agayne in to ordre. Wherfore undoubtedly the best and most sure gouernance is by one kynge or prince, whiche ruleth onely for the weale of his people to hym subiecte: [b] and that maner of gouernaunce is beste approued, and hath longest continued, and is moste auncient.[c] For who can denie but that all thynge in heuen and

[a] See the Glossary.

[b] The words 'to hym subiecte' are omitted in the subsequent editions.

[c] The above passage exhibits very clearly the bias of the author's own mind, for the sentiment there expressed could scarcely have been inspired by a perusal of classical writers. Herodotus, for example, says: κῶς δ' ἂν εἴη χρῆμα κατηρτημένον μουναρχίη, τῇ ἔξεστι ἀνευθύνῳ ποιέειν τὰ βούλεται; καὶ γὰρ ἂν τὸν ἄριστον ἀνδρῶν πάντων στάντα ἐς ταύτην τὴν ἀρχὴν ἐκτὸς τῶν ἐωθότων νοημάτων στήσειε . . . . . Πλῆθος δὲ ἄρχον πρῶτα μὲν οὔνομα πάντων κάλλιστον ἔχει ἰσονομίην. δεύτερα δέ, τούτων τῶν ὁ μούναρχος ποιέει οὐδέν. Πάλῳ μὲν ἀρχὰς ἄρχει, ὑπεύθυνον δὲ ἀρχὴν ἔχει, βουλεύματα δὲ πάντα ἐς τὸ κοινὸν ἀναφέρει. Τίθεμαι ὦν γνώμην μετέντας ἡμέας μουναρχίην, τὸ πλῆθος ἀέξειν. ἐν γὰρ τῷ πολλῷ ἔνι τὰ πάντα.—Lib. iii. cap. 80. Again, Aristotle says: 'Ἀλλ' ἐκ τῶν εἰρημένων γε φανερὸν ὡς ἐν μὲν τοῖς ὁμοίοις καὶ ἴσοις οὔτε συμφέρον ἐστὶν οὔτε δίκαιον ἕνα κύριον εἶναι πάντων, οὔτε μὴ νόμων ὄντων, ἀλλ' αὐτὸν ὡς ὄντα νόμον, οὔτε νόμων ὄντων, οὔτε ἀγαθὸν ἀγαθῶν, οὔτε μὴ ἀγαθῶν μὴ ἀγαθον οὐδ' ἂν κατ' ἀρετὴν ἀμείνων ᾖ, εἰ μὴ τρόπον τινά.—Polit., lib. iii. cap. 17. Mr. Grote contrasts very clearly the ancient and modern ideas with regard to monarchy, and shows how impossible it was even for Aristotle, 'the wisest as well as the most cautious of ancient theorists,' to form any conception of a constitutional king, as we understand the term. 'It has been found,' he says, 'in practice possible to combine regal government with fixity of administration, equal law impartially executed, security to person and property and freedom of discussion under representative forms, in a degree which the wisest ancient Greek would have deemed hopeless. Such an improvement in the practical working of this species of government, speaking always comparatively, with the kings of ancient times in Syria, Egypt, Judæa, the Grecian cities, and Rome, coupled with the increased force

erthe is gouerned by one god, by one perpetuall ordre, by one prouidence? One Sonne ruleth ouer the day, and one Moone ouer the nyghte; and to descende downe to the erthe, in a litell beest, whiche of all other is moste to be maruayled at, I meane the Bee, is lefte to man by nature, as it semeth, a perpetuall figure of a iuste gouernaunce or rule: who hath amonge them one principall Bee for theyr gouernour, who excelleth all other in greatnes, yet hath he no pricke or stinge, but in hym is more knowlege than in the residue.[a] For if the day folowyng shall be fayre and drye, and that the bees may issue out of theyr stalles[b] without peryll of rayne or vehement wynde, in the mornyng erely he calleth them, makyng a noyse as it were the sowne of a horne or a trumpet; and with that all the residue prepare them to labour, and fleeth abrode, gatheryng nothing but that shall be swete and profitable, all though they sitte often tymes on herbes and other thinges that be venomous and stynkinge.

The capitayne hym selfe laboureth nat for his sustinance, but all the other for hym; he onely seeth that if any drane[c]

of all established routine and the greater durability of all institutions and creeds which have once obtained footing throughout any wide extent of territory and people, has caused the monarchical sentiment to remain predominant in the European mind (though not without vigorous occasional dissent) throughout the increased knowledge and the enlarged political experience of the last two centuries.'
—*Hist. of Greece*, vol. ii. pp. 228, 229.

[a] Chaucer uses the same metaphor as a 'sign of gentleness' in the Persone's Tale. 'Wherfore, as seith Senek, ther is nothing more covenable to a man of heigh estate than debonairté and pité; and therfore thise flies than men clepen bees, whan thay make here king, thay chesen oon that hath no pricke wherwith he may stynge.'—*Poetical Works*, vol. iii. p. 301, ed. 1866.

[b] The author's use of the word 'stall' is justified by the authority of Virgil, who employs the word 'stabulum' in the same sense in the fourth Georgic, and the context indicates that Sir T. Elyot had Virgil's description in his mind at the time of writing the above:—

'Nec vero à stabulis pluviâ impendente recedunt
Longius, aut credunt cœlo adventantibus Euris.'

Georg. iv. 191.

[c] *I.e.* drone. Compare Virgil's

'Ignavum fucos pecus à præsepibus arcent.'

Georg. iv. 168.

or other unprofitable bee entreth in to the hyue, and consumethe the hony, gathered by other, that he be immediately expelled from that company. And when there is an other nombre of bees encreased, they semblably haue also a capitayne, whiche be nat suffered to continue with the other. Wherfore this newe company gathered in to a swarme, hauyng their capitayne amonge them, and enuironynge hym to preserue hym from harme, they issue forthe sekyng a newe habitation, whiche they fynde in some tree, except with some pleasant noyse they be alured and conuayed unto an other hyue. I suppose who seriously beholdeth this example, and hath any commendable witte, shall therof gather moche matter to the fourmynge of a publike weale. |But bicause I may nat be longe therin, consideryinge my purpose, I wolde that if the reder herof be lerned, that he shulde repayre to the Georgikes of Virgile, or to Plini, or Collumella, where he shall fynde the example more ample and better declared.| And if any desireth to haue the gouernance of one persone proued by histories, let hym fyrste resorte to the holy scripture: where he shall fynde that almyghty god commanded Moses only, to brynge his elected people out of captiuite, gyuynge onely to hym that authoritie, without *Moses.* appoyntynge to hym any other assistence of equall power or dignitie, excepte in the message to kynge Pharo, wherin Aaron, rather as a ministre than a companyon, *Aaron.* wente with Moses.[a] But onely Moses conducted the people through the redde see; he onely gouerned them fourtie yeres in deserte. And bicause Dathan and Abiron dis- *Dathan* dayned his rule, and coueyted to be equall with hym, *and* the erthe opened, and fyre issued out, and swalowed *Abiron.* them in, with all their holle familie and confederates, to the nombre of 14,700.[b]

[a] See Exodus iv. 14-16.
[b] This is manifestly incorrect—the author having confused the results of the earthquake, the fire, and the plague. See Numbers xvi. 32, 35, 49.

THE GOVERNOUR.

The counsayle of Hietro.
And all thoughe Hietro,[a] Moses' father in lawe, counsailed hym to departe his importable labours, in continual iugementes, unto the wise men that were in his company, he nat withstandynge styll retayned the soueraintie by goddis commandement, untyll, a litle before he dyed, he resigned it to Josue, assigned by god to be ruler after hym.[b]

Josue successour to Moises.
Semblably after the deth of Josue, by the space of 246[c] yeres, succeded, from tyme to tyme, one ruler amonge the Jewes, whiche was chosen for his excellencie in vertue and speciallye iustice, wherfore he was called the iuge, untill the Israelites desired of almightye god to let them haue a kynge as other people had:[d] who appointed to them Saul to be their kynge, who exceded all other in stature.[e]

Saul.

And so successiuely one kynge gouerned all the people of Israell unto the time of Roboaz,[f] sonne of the noble kynge Salomon, who, beinge unlike to his father in wisedome, practised tyranny[g] amonge his people, wherfore ix partes of them which they called Tribus forsoke hym, and elected Hieroboaz,[h] late seruant to Salomon, to be theyr kynge, onely the x parte remaynynge with Roboaz.[i]

Roboas.

And so in that realme were continually two kynges, untill the kynge of Mede had depopulate the countrey, and brought the people in captiuite to the citie of Babylon;[k] so that durynge the tyme that two kinges rayned ouer the iewes was euer continuall bataile amonge them selfes: where if one kynge had alway rayned lyke to Dauid or Solomon of lykelyhode

---

[a] *I.e.* Jethro. See Exodus xviii. 17–26.
[b] See Numbers xxvii. 18.
[c] This does not agree with the Authorised Version of Acts xiii. 20, but Doctor Wordsworth says that the true reading of the oldest MSS. gives 450 years as the period which elapsed between the birth of Isaac, A.M. 2046 and A.M. 2493, when the land began to be cultivated by the Israelites, so that the calculation in the text is not necessarily irreconcilable with that of S. Paul.—*Nov. Test. in loc. cit.*
[d] See 1 Sam. viii. 5.
[e] See 1 Sam. ix. 2.
[f] *I.e.* Rehoboam.
[g] See 1 Kings xii. 14.
[h] *I.e.* Jeroboam.
[i] See 1 Kings xii. 20.
[k] See 2 Kings xxiv. 14–16.

the countrey shuld nat so sone haue ben brought in captiuite.

Also in the tyme of the Machabeis, as longe as they had but one busshop whiche was their ruler, and was in the stede of a prince at that dayes, they valiantly resisted the gentils: and as well the Romanes, then great lordes of the worlde, as Persians and diuers other realmes desired to haue with them amitie and aliaunce: and all the inhabitantes of that countrey liued in great weale and quietnes. But after that by symony and ambition there happened to be two bisshops whiche deuided their authorities, and also the Romanes had deuided the realme of Judea to foure princes called *tetrarchas*, and also constituted a Romane capitayne or president ouer them: among the heddes there neuer cessed to be sedition and perpetuall discorde: wherby at the last the people was distroyed, and the contray brought to desolation and horrible barrennes.*

The Grekes, which were assembled to reuenge the reproche of Menelaus, that he toke of the Troians by the rauisshing of

---

* 'After the death of Esdras and Nehemiah the Jews were governed by their High Priest; in subjection, however, to the Persian kings, to whom they paid tribute. At the same time, this subjection to the Persian kings left them in the full enjoyment of their religious liberties: whilst it could be hardly said to have interfered with their civil freedom. Nearly three centuries of uninterrupted prosperity ensued. The privileges granted by the Persian kings being continued by Alexander the Great, and the various Grecian monarchs, his successors, to whom the Jews were subject. Then came the reign of Antiochus Epiphanes, king of Syria, by whom they were most cruelly oppressed and compelled to take up arms in their own defence. Owing to the valiant conduct of Judas Machabeus and his brothers the Jews sustained a vigorous struggle for twenty-six years against five successive kings of Syria; and at length succeeded in establishing their independence. From this period down, for the space of more than one hundred years, the family of the Machabees gave rulers to the Jewish nation, who united in their own persons the regal and pontifical dignity. The downfall of the Machabean princes had its beginning in family disputes—Hyrcanus the Second having been opposed by his brother Aristobulus. Then the Romans under Pompey interfered; defeated Aristobulus; captured Jerusalem; and reduced Judea to a tributary province of the Republic.'—Dixon's *Introduction to the Scriptures*, vol. ii. p. 46. Sir Thomas Elyot's own knowledge of the history of the Machabees was in all probability derived from the pages of Josephus.

Helene, his wyfe, dyd nat they by one assent electe Agamemnon to be their emperour or capitain: obeinge him as theyr soueraine duryng the siege of Troy? All though that they had diuers excellent princes, nat onely equall to hym, but also excelling hym:[a] as in prowes, Achilles, and Aiax Thelemonius: in wisedome, Nestor and Ulisses, and his oune brother Menelaus, to whom they mought haue giuen equall authoritie with Agamemnon,: but those wise princes considered that, without a generall capitayne, so many persones as were there of diuers realmes gathered together, shulde be by no meanes well gouerned: wherfore Homere calleth Agamemnon the shepeherde of people.[b] They rather were contented to be under one mannes obedience, than seuerally to use theyr authorities or to ioyne in one power and dignite; wherby at the last shuld have sourded[c] discention amonge the people, they beinge seperately enclined towarde theyr naturall souerayne lorde, as it appered in the particuler contention that was betwene Achilles and Agamemnon for theyr concubines, where Achilles, renouncynge the obedience that he with all other princes had before promised, at the bataile fyrst enterprised agaynst the Troians. For at that tyme no litell murmur and sedition was meued[d]

Prynces of Grece.

Agamemnon.

---

[a] Thucydides, however, says: Ἀγαμέμνων τέ μοι δοκεῖ τῶν τότε δυνάμει προύχων, καὶ οὐ τοσοῦτον τοῖς Τυνδάρεω ὅρκοις κατειλημμένους τοὺς Ἑλένης μνηστῆρας ἄγων, τὸν στόλον ἀγεῖραι. . . . . ἅ μοι δοκεῖ Ἀγαμέμνων παραλαβὼν, καὶ ναυτικῷ τε ἅμα ἐπὶ πλέον τῶν ἄλλων ἰσχύσας, τὴν στρατείαν οὐ χάριτι τὸ πλεῖον ἢ φόβῳ ξυναγαγόν ποιήσασθαι.—Lib. i. cap. 9. Mr. Gladstone, in his *Studies on Homer*, thinks that 'the statements of Homer respecting the position of Agamemnon and the motives of the war fall short of, but are not wholly at variance with the opinion which has been expressed by Thucydides;' and 'comes to the conclusion that 'a combination of hope, sympathy, respect, and fear, but certainly a very strong personal feeling, whatever its precise ingredients may have been, towards the Pelopid house, must have operated largely in the matter.'—Vol. iii. pp. 64, 65.

[b] ποιμὴν λαῶν.—*Il.* ii. 85, and passim. Mr. Gladstone says, 'I find it on the whole impossible to detect in this phrase anything of a definite character, except that it expresses political rule at large, and expresses it under the form of a figure adapted to the early and patriarchal state of society.'—*Studies on Homer*, vol. i. p. 449.

[c] See the Glossary.   [d] See the Glossary.

in the hoste of the grekes, whiche nat withstandyng was wonderfully pacified, and the armie unscatered by the maiestie of Agamemnon, ioynynge to hym counsailours Nestor and the witty Ulisses.[a]   *Maiestie.* *Nestor.* *Ulisses.*

But to retourne agayne. Athenes and other cities of Grece, whan they had abandoned kynges,[b] and concluded to

[a] Obviously referring to *Iliad* ii. 402:

Αὐτὰρ ὁ βοῦν ἱέρευσεν ἄναξ ἀνδρῶν Ἀγαμέμνων. . . .
Κίκλησκεν δὲ γέροντας ἀριστῆας παναχαιῶν·
Νέστορα μὲν πρώτιστα, καὶ Ἰδομενῆα ἄνακτα,
Αὐτὰρ ἔπειτ' Αἴαντε δύω, καὶ Τυδέος υἱόν·
Ἕκτον δ' αὖτ' Ὀδυσῆα, Διὶ μῆτιν ἀτάλαντον.

[b] Instead of 'kings' we should read 'tyrants' or 'despots,' because the context shows that the author intended to contrast the government of Athens, as it existed down to the expulsion of the Peisistratids, (which, curiously enough, coincided with the regifuge at Rome) with the democratical constitution of which Kleisthenês was the founder. According to Sir Thomas Elyot's reading of history, the balance of advantage inclined decidedly in favour of the former *régime*; but modern writers, with better means of judging, have been enabled to restore the Athenian democracy to its true position. Mr. Grote, in discussing the fate of Miltiadês, says, 'To speak ill of the people, as Machiavel has long ago observed, is a strain in which everyone at all times, even under a democratical government, indulges with impunity, and without provoking any opponent to reply. In this instance the hard fate of Miltiadês has been imputed to the vices of the Athenians and their democracy—it has been cited in proof partly of their fickleness, partly of their ingratitude. . . . . Of the despots who gained power in Greece, a considerable proportion began by popular conduct and by rendering good service to their fellow-citizens; having first earned public gratitude, they abused it for purposes of their own ambition. There was far greater danger, in a Grecian community, of dangerous excess of gratitude towards a victorious soldier, than of deficiency in that sentiment. The person thus exalted acquired a position such that the community found it difficult afterwards to shake him off. Now there is a disposition almost universal among writers and readers to side with an individual, especially an eminent individual, against the multitude. Accordingly, those who, under such circumstances, suspect the probable abuse of an exalted position, are denounced as if they harboured an unworthy jealousy of superior abilities; but the truth is that the largest analogies of the Grecian character justified that suspicion, and required the community to take precautions against the corrupting effects of their own enthusiasm. There is no feature which more largely pervades the impressible Grecian character than a liability to be intoxicated and demoralised by success; there was no fault from which so few eminent Greeks were free; there was hardly any danger against which it was at once so necessary and so difficult for the Grecian governments to take security, especially the demo-

lyue as it were in a communaltie, whiche abusifly they called equalitie, howe longe tyme dyd any of them continue in peace? yea what vacation had they from the warres? or what noble man had they whiche auanced the honour and weale of theyr citie, whom they dyd not banisshe or slee in prison? Surely it shall appiere to them that wyll rede Plutarche, or Emilius probus, in the lyues of Milciades, Cimon, Themistocles, Aristides, and diuers other noble and valiant capitaynes: which is to longe here to reherce.

Kyngs in Rome. In lyke wyse the Romanes, durynge the tyme that they were under kynges, which was by the space of 144 yeres,[a] were well gouerned, nor neuer was amonge them discorde or sedition. But after that by the persua-*Lucretia.* tion of Brutus and Colatinus, whose wyfe (Lucretia) was rauysshed by Aruncius, sonne of Tarquine, kynge of Romanes, nat only the saide Tarquine and al his posterite were exiled out of Rome for euer, but also it was finally determined amonge the people, that neuer after they wolde haue a kinge reigne ouer them.[b]

---

cracies, where the manifestations of enthusiasm were always the loudest. Such is the real explanation of those charges which have been urged against the Grecian democracies, that they came to hate and ill-treat previous benefactors. The history of Miltiadês illustrates it in a manner no less pointed than painful.'— *Hist. of Greece,* vol. iii. pp. 316-321.

[a] 'Dionysius gives 244 years as the length of the regal period (lib. i. cap. 75). Livy (lib. i. 60) and other writers agree as to the sum. Cic. de Rep. ii. 30, gives it in round numbers at 240 years. Eutropius has 243 years.'—*Credibility of Early Roman History,* vol. i. p. 528. Niebuhr says that the discovery of the books on the Republic has established the fact on the authority of the pontiffs, 'for their table was adopted by Polybius for his Roman chronology, and he is the authority followed by Cicero in fixing the years of the Roman kings.'—*Hist. of Rome,* vol. i. p. 242. As these books were not discovered until A.D. 1826, Sir Thomas Elyot had no reason to prefer the computation of Polybius. It seems probable, however, that there is an error in the figures in the text, and that the number intended is that given by Dionysius.

[b] Sir George Cornewall Lewis says: 'The idea that a king was an absolute monarch, which prevailed throughout the later ages of Rome, was probably in part derived from the belief respecting the character of the last Tarquin's rule, though it is inconsistent with their own history of their other kings.'—*Credibility of Early Roman History,* vol. i. p. 107.

Consequently the communaltie more and more encroched a licence, and at the last compelled the Senate to suffre them to chose yerely amonge them gouernours of theyr owne astate and condition, whom they called Tribunes:[a] under whom they resceyued suche audacitie and power that they finally optained the higheste authoritie in the publike weale, in so moche that often tymes they dyd repele the actes of the Senate, and to those Tribunes mought a man appele from the Senate or any other office or dignite.[b]

Tribunes.

But what came therof in conclusion? Surely whan there was any difficulte warre immynent, than were they constrained to electe one soueraine and chiefe of all other, whom they named *Dictator*, as it were commander, from whom it was not laufull for any man to appele.[c] But bicause there appered to be in hym the pristinate authorite and mai-

Dictator.

[a] Dr. Liddell says: 'The tribunes were not properly magistrates or officers, for they had no express functions or official duties to discharge. They were simply Representatives and Protectors of the Plebs.'—*Hist. of Rome*, vol. i. p. 105.

[b] 'Since the time of the Gracchi,' says Dr. Liddell, 'the Tribunes and the Tribes had learnt their strength, and had gradually absorbed more and more, not only of the Legislative, but also of the Executive power. Sylla struck a determined blow at this democratic power. He ordained that candidates for the Tribunate should necessarily be members of the Senate; that no one who had been Tribune should be capable of holding any curule office; that no Tribune should have power to propose a law to the Tribes; and lastly, that the right of Intercession should be limited to its original purpose—that is, that it should not be available to stop Decrees of the Senate or Laws brought before the Senate, but only to protect the personal liberty of citizens from the arbitrary power of the Higher Magistrates. The Tribunes were thus effectually shackled, and their power returned to the low condition in which it had been during the earlier period of its existence.'—*Hist. of Rome*, vol. ii. p. 345.

[c] Sir George Cornewall Lewis says: 'Dr. Arnold appears to me to be mistaken in supposing that the dictator was "liable, like the consuls, to be arraigned *after the expiration of his office* for any acts of tyranny which he might have committed during its continuance." The power of the dictator was originally absolute and not subject to appeal; and such (notwithstanding the passage of Festus, *Optim. Lex*, p. 198) it probably always remained. Considering the shortness of the term of office, this irresponsibility would have been nugatory, if it had not been continuous. The security to the public was derived from the limited duration of the office; not from any subsequent legal remedy against the officer.'—*Credibility of Early Roman History*, vol. ii. p. 48, note.

estie of a kyng,[a] they wolde no longer suffre hym to continue in that dignite than by the space of vi. monethes, excepte he then resigned it,[b] and by the consente of the people eftsones dyd resume it. Finally, untill Octauius Augustus had distroyed Anthony, and also Brutus, and finisshed all the Ciuile Warres, (that were so called by cause they were betwene the same selfe Romane citezins,) the cite of Rome was neuer longe quiete from factions or seditions amonge the people. And if the nobles of Rome had nat ben men of excellent lernynge, wisedome, and prowesse, and that the Senate, the moste noble counsaile in all the worlde, whiche was fyrste ordayned by Romulus, and encreased by Tullus hostilius, the thyrde kynge of Romanes, had nat continued and with great difficultie retayned theyr authorite, I suppose verily that the citie of Rome had ben utterly desolate sone after the expellyng of Tarquine: and if it had bene eftsones renewed it shulde haue bene twentye tymes distroyed before the tyme that Augustus raigned: so moche discorde was euer in the citie for lacke of one gouernour.[c]

Warres Civile.

[a] Dionysius of Halicarnassus, speaking of the institution of the dictatorship, says: Ἦν δ' ἄρα ἡ κρείττων ἀρχὴ τῆς κατὰ νόμους τυραννίς.—*Antiq. Rom.*, lib. v. cap. 70. And again, Οὗτος πρῶτος ἐν Ῥώμῃ μόναρχος ἀπεδείχθη, πολέμου τε καὶ εἰρήνης καὶ πάντος ἄλλου πράγματος αὐτοκράτωρ .... τὸ γὲ τῆς ἐξουσίας μέγεθος, ἧς ὁ δικτάτωρ ἔχει, ἥκιστα δηλοῦται ὑπὸ τοῦ ὀνόματος, ἐστὶ γὰρ αἱρέτη τυραννίς ἡ δικτατορία.—*Ibid.*, lib. v. cap. 73. Eutropius says: 'Neque quicquam similius potest dici quam dictatura antiqua huic imperii potestati quam nunc Tranquillitas vestra (*i.e.* the Emperor Valens) habet.'—Lib. i. cap. 12.

[b] 'That a dictator appointed for formal and ceremonial purposes should have abdicated as soon as his special functions were performed is not extraordinary; but that so many dictators should have spontaneously laid down absolute power, even at the moment of victory, and often before their term of office was expired, is a remarkable proof of the empire of law over the minds of the Romans, and of their fixed constitutional habits even in early times.'—*Credibility of Early Roman History*, vol. ii. p. 48.

[c] Dr. Liddell has traced very carefully the rise and progress of Roman despotism to its supreme assumption by Octavian. 'The Roman world had long been preparing for it. At no time had such authority been altogether alien from the mind of the people of Rome. Dictatorships were frequent in their earlier history. In later times the consuls were, by the will of the senate, raised to dictatorial power to meet emergencies, military or civil. The despotic commands

But what nede we to serche so ferre from us, sens we haue sufficient examples nere unto us? Beholde the astate *Florence* of Florence[a] and Gene,[b] noble cites of Italy, what *and Gene.*

conferred upon Sylla and Pompey, the powers seized first by Cæsar and after him by the Triumvirate, were all of the same form as the authority conferred upon Octavian—that is, all were in form at least temporary and provisional. The disorders of the State required the intervention of one or more persons endued with absolute authority. And whether power was vested in a Dictator, such as Sylla and Cæsar; in a sole Consul, such as Pompey; in a commission of Three, such as the Triumvirate of Antony, Octavian, and Lepidus; or in an Imperator, such as Octavian alone, the constitutional principle was the same. These despotic powers were in every case, except in the cases of Sylla and Cæsar, granted for a definite term; even in Cæsar's case all his Dictatorships, save the last, were conferred for limited periods. The Triumvirate was renewed at intervals of five years, the imperial rule of Octavian at intervals of ten. In theory these powers were conferred exceptionally for a temporary purpose; and when the purpose was served the exception was to yield to the rule. Even in the reign of Octavian there were some persons credulous enough to expect a restoration of the Republic. It belongs not to our present purpose to examine in detail the arts of government by which a power formally provisional and temporary was converted by the adroitness of the new ruler into the substance and reality of a despotic monarchy. This belongs to the History of the Empire.'—*Hist. of Rome*, vol. ii. p. 518. 12th ed.

[a] 'Throughout all the vicissitudes of party Florence had never yet lost sight of republican institutions. Not that she had never accommodated herself to temporary circumstances by naming a signior. Charles of Anjou had been invested with that dignity for the term of ten years; Robert, king of Naples, for five; and his son, the Duke of Calabria, was at his death, Signior of Florence. These princes named the podestà, if not the priors; and were certainly pretty absolute in their executive powers, though bound by oath not to alter the statutes of the city. But their office had always been temporary. Like the dictatorship of Rome it was a confessed unavoidable evil; a suspension but not extinguishment of rights. Like that, too; it was a dangerous precedent, through which crafty ambition and popular rashness might ultimately subvert the republic.'—Hallam, *Middle Ages*, vol. i. p. 426. 12th ed.

[b] *I.e.* Genoa. 'The annals of one of the few surviving republics, that of Genoa, present to us, during the fifteenth as well as the preceding century, an increasing series of revolutions, the shortest enumeration of which would occupy several pages. Torn by the factions of Adorni and Fregosi, equal and eternal rivals, to whom the whole patrician families of Doria and Fieschi were content to become secondary, sometimes sinking, from weariness of civil tumult, into the grasp of Milan or France, and again, from impatience of foreign subjection, starting back from servitude to anarchy, the Genoa of those ages exhibits a singular contrast to the calm and regular aristocracy of the next three centuries.'—Hallam *Middle Ages*, vol. i. p. 494.

22   THE GOVERNOUR.

calamite haue they both sustained by their owne factions, for lacke of a continuall gouernour. Ferrare[a] and the moste excellent citie of Venise, the one hauyng a duke,[b] the other an erle, seldome suffreth damage excepte it happen by outwarde hostilitie. We have also an example domisticall, whiche is moste necessary to be noted. After that the Saxons by treason had expelled out of Englande the Britons, whiche were the auncient inhabitantes, this realme was deuyded in to sondry regions or kyngdomes. O what mysery was the people than in.[c] O howe this most noble Isle of the worlde was decerpt and rent in pieces : the people pursued and hunted lyke wolfes or other beastes sauage : none industrie auayled, no strength defended, no riches profited. Who wolde than haue desired to haue ben rather a man than a dogge : whan men either with sworde or with hungre perisshed, hauynge no profit or sustinance of their owne corne[d] or catell, whiche by mutuall

Ferraria.

Englande deuided.

---

[a] 'In 1208 the people of Ferrara set the fatal example of sacrificing their freedom *for tranquillity*, by electing Azzo VII., Marquis of Este, as their lord or sovereign.—Hallam, *Middle Ages*, vol. i. p. 382. 12th ed.

[b] 'An hereditary prince could never have remained quiet in such trammels as were imposed upon the Doge of Venice. But early prejudice accustoms men to consider restraint, even upon themselves, as advantageous ; and the limitations of ducal power appeared to every Venetian as fundamental as the great laws of the English constitution do to ourselves. Many Doges of Venice, especially in the middle ages, were considerable men ; but they were content with the functions assigned to them, which, if they would avoid the tantalizing comparison of sovereign princes, were enough for the ambition of republicans. . . . *Compared with the Tuscan republics, the tranquillity of Venice is truly striking.*'—Hallam, *Middle Ages*, vol. i. pp. 458, 459.

[c] 'About the end of the eighth century the northern pirates began to ravage the coast of England. By their command of the sea it was easy for them to harass every part of an island presenting such an extent of coast as Britain ; the Saxons, after a brave resistance, gradually gave way, and were on the brink of the same servitude or extermination which their own arms had already brought upon the ancient possessors.'—Hallam, *Middle Ages*, vol. ii. p. 269.

[d] A passage in Baker's *Chronicle*, describing the state of the country in the time of King Ethelred is probably quite as applicable to an earlier period : 'the land was emptied of all coin, and the English were brought so low that they were fain to till and ear the ground whilst the Danes sate idle and eat the fruit of their labours.' —p. 13, ed. 1730.

warre was continually distroyed? yet the dogges, either takynge that that men coulde nat quietly come by, or fedynge on the deed bodies, whiche on euery parte laye scatered plenteously, dyd satisfie theyr hunger.[a]

Where finde ye any good lawes that at that tyme were made and used, or any commendable monument of any science or crafte in this realme occupied? suche iniquitie semeth to be than, that by the multitude of soueraigne gouernours all things had ben brought to confusion, if the noble kynge Edgar had nat reduced the monarch to his pristinate astate and figure:[b] whiche brought to passe, reason was reuiued, and people came to conformitie, and the realme began to take comforte and to shewe some visage of a publike weale : and so (lauded be god) haue continued : but nat beinge alway in like astate or condition. All be it it is nat to be dispaired, but that the kynge our soueraigne lorde nowe reignynge, and this realme alway hauynge one prince like unto his highnes, equall to the auncient princis in vertue and courage, it shall be reduced (god so disposynge) unto a publike weale excellynge all other in preeminence of vertue and abundance of thynges necessary. But for as moche as I do wel perceiue that to write of the office or duetie of a soueraigne gouernour or prince, farre excedeth the compasse of my lernyng, holy scripture affirmyng that the hartes of princes be in goddes

Kynge Edgar.

---

[a] The Anglo-Saxon Chronicler, who narrates the deeds of Athelstan and his brother Edmund at the battle of Brunanburh, A.D. 937, says : 'They left behind them the swart raven with horned neb to share the pale-hued carcases ; and the white-tailed eagle with goodly plumage, the greedy war-hawk, and that grey beast the wolf in the weald, the carrion to devour.'—*English Version*, p. 88, note.

[b] 'That Edgar was considered by Anglo-Saxons as the greatest of their kings in power and dominion we find from Elfric, who was nearly his contemporary. He calls Edgar, "of all the kings of the English nation, the most powerful ; and it was the divine will that his enemies, both kings and earls, who came to him desiring peace, should without any battle be subjected to him to do what he willed. Hence he was honoured over a wide extent of land."'—Turner, *Hist. of England*, vol. ii. p. 271. Modern historians have formed on the whole a less favourable opinion of this monarch than the monkish chroniclers whose writings Sir Thomas Elyot must have consulted.

owne handes and disposition,* I wyll therfore kepe my penne within the space that is discribed to me by the thre noble maisters, reason, lernynge, and experience ; and by theyr enseignement or teachyng I wyll ordinately treate of the two partes of a publike weale, wherof the one shall be named Due Administration, the other Necessary Occupation, whiche shall be deuided in to two volumes. In the fyrste shall be comprehended the beste fourme of education or bringing up of noble children from their natiuitie, in suche maner as they may be founde worthy, and also able to be gouernours of a publike weale. The seconde volume, whiche, god grantyng me quietnes and libertie of mynde, I wyll shortly after sende forthe, it shall conteine all the reminant, whiche I can either by lernyng or experience fynde apt to the perfection of a iuste publike weale : in the whiche I shall so endeuour my selfe, that al men, of what astate or condition so euer they be, shall finde therin occasion to be alway vertuously occupied ; and not without pleasure, if they be nat of the scholes of Aristippus or Apicius, of whom the one supposed felicite to be onely in lechery, the other in delicate fedynge and glotony : from whose sharpe talones and cruell tethe, I beseche all gentill reders, to defende these warkes, whiche for theyr commodite is onely compiled.

Due Administration.
Occupation.

CHAPTER III.

That in a publike weale ought to be inferiour gouernours called Magistrates : whiche shall be appoynted or chosen by the soueraigne gouernour.

THERE be bothe reasones and examples, undoutedly infinite, wherby may be proued, that there can be no perfect publike weale without one capital and soueraigne gouernour whiche

---

* Prov. xxi. 1. The king's heart is in the hand of the Lord, as the rivers of water: He turneth it whithersoever He will.

may longe endure or continue. But sens one mortall man can nat haue knowlege of all thynges done in a realme or large dominion, and at one tyme, discusse all controuersies, refourme all transgressions, and exploite ᵃ al consultations, concluded as well for outwarde as inwarde affaires : it is expedient and also nedefull that under the capitall gouernour be sondry meane authorities, as it were aydyng hym in the distribution of iustice in sondry partes of a huge multitude: wherby his labours beinge leuigate and made more tollerable, he shall gouerne with the better aduise, and consequently with a more perfecte gouernance. And, as Jesus Sirach sayth, The multitude of wise men is the welth of the worlde.ᵇ *Sap. vi.* They whiche haue suche authorities to them committed may be called inferiour gouernours, hauynge respecte to theyr office or duetie, wherin is also a representation of gouernance. All be it they be named in latine Magistratus. And herafter I intende to call them Magistratis, lackynge an other more conuenient worde in englisshe ; but that will I do in the seconde

---

ᵃ See the Glossary.

ᵇ 'Jesus the son of Sirach is described in the text of Ecclesiasticus (cap. l.) as the author of that book, which in the LXX and generally, except in the Western Church, is called by his name, the Wisdom of Jesus, the son of Sirach, or simply the Wisdom of Sirach. The same passage speaks of him as a native of Jerusalem, and the internal character of the book confirms its Palestinian origin.'—Smith, *Hist. of the Bible*, sub voc. ' The first distinct quotations occur in Clement of Alexandria, but from the end of the second century the book was much used and cited with respect, and in the same terms as the Canonical Scriptures ; and its authorship was often assigned to Solomon from the similarity which it presented to his writings.'—Ibid. *Ecclesiasticus.* Sir Thomas Elyot is mistaken in referring the quotation to the book of Ecclesiasticus, for the passage occurs in Wisdom, cap. vi. 19, and in a copy of 'The Bokes of Solomon,' in the British Museum, to which the date A.D. 1542 is assigned, the order is as follows : Prouerbia, Ecclesiastes, Sapientia and Ecclesiasticus, *or Jesus the sonne of Syrach* ; but if, as suggested by the writer of the article in Smith's *Dict. of the Bible*, the alternative title of the Wisdom of Sirach is occasionally found, it is not difficult to see how Sir Thomas Elyot may have fallen into an error arising from the application of the same title to two different but not dissimilar works. In ' The Bokes of Salomon ' the verse quoted in the text stands thus : ' But the multitude of the wise is ye welfare of the worlde, and a wyse kynge is the upholdynge of the people.'

parte of this warke, where I purpose to write of theyr sondry offices or effectes of theyr authoritie. But for as moche as in this parte I intende to write of theyr education and vertue in maners, whiche they haue in commune with princes, in as moche as therby they shall, as well by example as by authoritie, ordre well them, whiche by theyr capitall gouernour shall be to theyr rule committed, I may, without anoyance of any man, name them gouernours at this tyme, apropriatynge, to the soueraignes, names of kynges and princes, sens of a longe custome these names in commune fourme of speakyng be in a higher preeminence and estimation than gouernours. That in euery commune weale ought to be a great nombre of suche maner of persons it is partly proued in the chaptre nexte before writen, where I haue spoken of the commodite of ordre. Also reason and commune experience playnly declareth, that, where the dominion is large and populouse, there is hit convenient that a prince haue many inferiour gouernours, whiche be named of

Politic. lib. iii. Aristotel [a] his eien, eares, handes, and legges, whiche, if they be of the beste sorte, (as he further more saythe), it semeth impossible a countrey nat to be well gouerned by good lawes. And excepte excellent vertue and lernynge do inhabile [b] a man of the base astate of the communaltie, to be thought of all men worthy to be so moche auaunced: els suche gouernours wolde be chosen out of that astate of men whiche be called worshipfull, if amonge them may be founden a sufficient nombre, ornate with vertue and wisedome, mete for suche purpose, and that for sondry causes.

Fyrste it is of good congruence that they, whiche be superiour in condition or hauiour, shulde haue also preeminence in

---

[a] See *Pol.* lib. iii. cap. xi. (xvi.): Ἄτοπον δ' ἴσως ἂν εἶναι δόξειεν, εἰ βέλτιον ἴδοι τις δυοῖν ὄμμασι καὶ δυσὶν ἀκοαῖς κρίνων, καὶ πράττων δυσὶ ποσὶ καὶ χερσὶν, ἢ πολλοὶ πολλοῖς· ἐπεὶ καὶ νῦν ὀφθαλμοὺς πολλοὺς οἱ μόναρχοι ποιοῦσιν αὑτῶν καὶ ὦτα καὶ χεῖρας καὶ πόδας· τοὺς γὰρ τῇ ἀρχῇ καὶ αὑτοῖς φίλους ποιοῦνται συνάρχους. μὴ φίλοι μὲν οὖν ὄντες οὐ ποιήσουσι κατὰ τὴν τοῦ μονάρχου προαίρεσιν. εἰ δὲ φίλοι κἀκείνου καὶ τῆς ἀρχῆς· ὅ τε φίλος ἴσος καὶ ὅμιλος. ὥστ', εἰ τούτους οἴεται δεῖν ἄρχειν, τοὺς ἴσους καὶ ὁμοίους ἄρχειν οἴεται δεῖν ὁμοίως.

[b] See the Glossary.

administration, if they be nat inferiour to other in vertue. Also they hauinge of their owne reuenues certeine wherby they haue competent substance to lyue without takyng rewardes: it is lykely that they wyll nat be so desirous of lucre, (wherof may be engendred corruption), as they whiche haue very litle or nothynge so certeyne.

More ouer where vertue is in a gentyll man, it is commenly mixte with more sufferance, more affabilitie, and myldenes, than for the more parte it is in a persone rural, or of a very base linage; and whan it hapneth other wise, it is to be accompted lothesome and monstruous. Furthermore, where the persone is worshypfull, his gouernaunce, though it be sharpe, is to the people more tollerable, and they therwith the lasse grutch, or be dissobedient. Also suche men, hauyng substance in goodes by certeyne and stable possessions, whiche they may aporcionate to their owne liuynge, and bryngynge up of theyr children in lernyng and vertues, may, (if nature repugne nat), cause them to be so instructed and furnisshed towarde the administration of a publike weale, that a poure mannes sonne, onely by his naturall witte, without other adminiculation[a] or aide, neuer or seldome may atteyne to the semblable. Towarde the whiche instruction I haue, with no litle study and labours, prepared this warke,[b] as almighty god be my iuge, without arrogance or any sparke of vayne glorie: but only to declare the feruent zele that I haue to my countrey, and that I desyre only to employ that poure lernyng, that I haue gotten, to the benefite thereof, and to the recreation of all the reders that be of any noble or gentill courage, gyuynge them occasion to eschewe idelnes, beynge occupied in redynge this warke, infarced[c] throughly with suche histories and sentences wherby they shal take, they them selfes confessing, no lytell commodite

---

[a] See the Glossary.
[b] From hence to the end of the chapter is a *hiatus valde deflendus* in all the subsequent editions.
[c] Infarced, *i.e.* 'stuffed full of,' from the Latin *infarcio* or *infercio*; cf. Cic. *Or.* cap. lxix. : 'neque inferciens verba quasi rimas expleat.'

if they will more than ones or twyse rede it. The first reding being to them newe, the seconde delicious, and, euery tyme after, more and more frutefull and excellent profitable.

CHAPTER IV.

The education or fourme of bringing up of the childe of a gentilman, which is to haue authoritie in a publike weale.

FOR as moche as all noble authors do conclude, and also commune experience proueth, that where the gouernours of realmes and cities be founden adourned with vertues, and do employ theyr study and mynde to the publike weale, as well to the augmentation therof as to the establysshynge and longe continuaunce of the same: there a publike weale must nedes be both honorable and welthy. To the entent that I wyll declare howe suche personages may be prepared, I will use the policie of a wyse and counnynge gardener: who purposynge to haue in his gardeine a fyne and preciouse herbe, that shulde be to hym and all other repairynge therto, excellently comodiouse or pleasant, he will first serche throughout his gardeyne where he can finde the most melowe and fertile erth: and therin wil he put the sede of the herbe to growe and be norisshed: and in most diligent wise attende that no weede be suffred to growe or aproche nyghe unto it: and to the entent it may thrive the faster, as soone as the fourme of an herbe ones appereth, he will set a vessell of water by hit, in suche wyse that it may continually distille on the rote swete croppes; and as it spryngeth in stalke, under sette it with some thyng that it breake nat, and alway kepe it cleane from weedes. Semblable ordre will I ensue in the fourmynge the gentill wittes of noble mennes children, who, from the wombes of their mother, shal be made propise or apte to the gouernaunce of a publike weale.

Education of noble wittes.

Fyrste, they, unto whom the bringing up of suche children apperteineth, oughte, againe the time that their mother shall be of them deliuered, to be sure of a nourise whiche shulde be of no seruile condition or vice notable. For, as some aunsient writers do suppose, often times the childe soukethe the vice of his nouryse with the milke of her pappe.[a] And also obserue that she be of mature or ripe age, nat under xx yeres, or aboue xxx, her body also beinge clene from all sikenes or deformite, and hauing her complection most of the right and pure sanguine. For as moche as the milke therof comminge excelleth all other bothe in swetenes and substance.[b] More ouer to the nourise shulde be appointed an other woman of approued vertue, discretion, and grauitie, who shall nat suffre, in the childes presence, to be shewed any acte or tache[c] dishonest, or any wanton or unclene worde to be spoken: and for that cause al men, except physitions only, shulde be excluded and kepte out of the norisery. Perchance some wyll scorne me for that I am so serious, sainge that ther is no suche damage to be fered in an infant, who for tendernes of yeres hath nat the understanding to decerne good from iuell., And yet no man wyll denie, but in that innocency he wyll decerne milke from butter, and breadde from pappe, and er he can speake he wyll with his hande or courttenaunce

Norices, how they oughte to be chosen.

A gouernesse or drye norice.

---

[a] Cicero, *Tusc. Quæst.* iii. cap. 1: ut pæne cum lacte nutricis errorem suxisse videamur.

[b] These delicate questions were by no means confined in the sixteenth century to the ladies and physicians, for Wilson, in his *Arte of Rhetorique*, says: 'Againe the childrens bodies shall be so affected, as the milke is which they receive. Now if the nurse bee of an euill complection, or haue some hid disease, the childe sucking of her breast must needes take parte with her. And if that bee true, whiche the learned doe saie, that the temperature of the minde followes the constitution of the bodie, needes must it bee, that if the nurse be of a naughtie nature, the childe must take thereafter. But if it bee, the nurse bee of a good complexion, of an honest behauiour (whereas contrarywise, Maidens that haue made a scape are commonly called to be nurses), yet can it not be, but that the mother's milke should be much more natural for the childe then the milke of a straunger.'—p. 111.

[c] See the Glossary.

signifie whiche he desireth. And I verily do suppose that in the braynes and hertes of children, whiche be membres spirituall, whiles they be tender, and the litle slippes of reason begynne in them to burgine, ther may happe by iuel custome some pestiferous dewe of vice to perse[a] the sayde membres, and infecte and corrupt the softe and tender buddes, wherby the frute may growe wylde, and some tyme conteine in it feruent and mortal poyson, to the utter destruction of a realme.

And we haue in daily experience that litle infantes assayeth to folowe, nat onely the wordes, but also the faictes and gesture, of them that be prouecte[b] in yeres. For we daylye here, to our great heuines, children swere great othes and speake lasciuious and unclene wordes, by the example of other whom they heare, wherat the leude parentes do reioyce, sone after, or in this worlde, or els where, to theyr great payne and tourment. Contrary wise we beholde some chyldren, knelynge in theyr game before images, and holdyng up theyr lytell whyte handes, do moue theyr praty mouthes, as they were prayeng:[c] other goynge and syngynge as hit were in procession: wherby they do expresse

Infancie.

---

[a] *I.e.* pierce.

[b] *I.e.* advanced, adapted from the Latin proveho. Compare Cicero's use of the word: 'Quamquam eum colere corpi non admodum grandem natu sed tamen jam ætate provectum.'—*De Senect.* 4.

[c] Knight, in his *Life of Colet*, reprints the latter's preface to his Grammar, which concludes with the following sentence: '*And lyfte up your lytell whyte handes for me*, whiche prayethe for you to God; to whom be all honour and imperiall maiesty and glory. Amen.' Knight assigns 1534 as the date of the grammar and Wynkyn de Worde as the printer. It is not a little remarkable that in the two copies in the British Museum the words just quoted are omitted. This fact has apparently escaped the notice of Mr. Seebohm, as although he prints the preface *in extenso* and vouches Knight as his authority he makes no allusion to the omission. The words may have been considered objectionable; they were undoubtedly left out by design, not by accident. Mr. Garnett, of the British Museum, to whose courtesy the editor has been constantly indebted during the preparation of this work for the press, suggests that the discrepancy may be accounted for by the fact that the edition of 1535 (of which copies are in the B. M. library) was printed at Antwerp, possibly under the supervision of Tyndale, and the paragraph in question may have been suppressed as savouring of popery.

theyr disposition to the imitation of those thynges, be they good or iuell, whiche they usually do se or here. Wherfore nat only princis, but also all other children, from their norises pappes, are to be kepte diligently from the herynge or seynge of any vice or euyl tache. And incontinent as sone as they can speake, it behoueth, with most pleasaunt alluryngs, to instill in them swete maners and vertuouse custome. Also to prouide for them suche companions and playfelowes, whiche shal nat do in his presence any reprocheable acte, or speake any uncleane worde or othe, ne to aduaunt[a] hym with flatery, remembrynge his nobilitie, or any other like thyng wherin he mought glory:[b] onlas it be to persuade hym to vertue, or to withdrawe him from vice, in the remembryng to hym the daunger of his iuell example. For noble men more greuously offende by theyr example than by their dede. Yet often remembrance to them of their astate may happen to radycate[c] in theyr hartes intollerable pride, the moost daungerous poyson to noblenes: wherfore there is required to be therein moche cautele[d] and sobrenesse.

CHAPTER V.[e]

The ordre of lernynge that a noble man shulde be trayned in before he come to thaige of seuen yeres.

SOME olde autours holde oppinion that, before the age of seuen yeres, a chylde shulde nat be instructed in letters;[f] but

[a] See the Glossary.
[b] From here to the end of the chapter is *hiatus valde deflendus* in Mr. Eliot's edition.
[c] *I.e.* implant—an adaptation from the Latin. The word *radicor* is only used in an intransitive sense, and by such writers as Pliny and Columella.
[d] The Latin *cautela*, 'caution.'
[e] The whole of this as well as of the following chapter is omitted by Mr. Eliot in his edition of the *Governour*.
[f] Evidently an allusion to the passage in Quintilian, *Instit. Or.* lib. i. cap. i. § 15.:
'Quidam litteris instituendos, qui minores septem annis essent, non putaverunt,

those writers were either grekes or latines, amonge whom all doctrine and sciences were in their maternall tonges; by reason wherof they saued all that longe tyme whiche at this dayes is spente in understandyng perfectly the greke or latyne. Wherfore it requireth nowe a longer tyme to the understandynge of bothe.<u>*</u>] Therfore that infelicitie of our tyme and countray compelleth us to encroche some what upon the yeres of children, and specially of noble men, that they may sooner attayne to wisedome and grauitie than priuate persones, consideryng, as I haue saide, their charge and example, whiche, aboue all thynges, is most to be estemed. Nat withstandyng, I wolde nat haue them inforced by violence to lerne, but accordynge to the counsaile of Quintilian, to be swetely allured therto with praises and suche praty gyftes as children delite in.[b] And their fyrst letters to be paynted or lymned in a pleasaunt maner: where in children of gentyl courage haue moche delectation. And also there is no better allectyue[c] to noble wyttes than to induce them in to a con-

---

quod illa primum ætas et intellectum disciplinarum capere et laborem pati posset. In quâ sententiâ Hesiodum esse plurimi tradunt.' Cf. also Aristotle, *Pol.* lib. vii. cap. xv. (xvii): Ταύτην γὰρ τὴν ἡλικίαν καὶ μέχρι τῶν ἑπτὰ ἐτῶν ἀναγκαῖον οἴκοι τὴν τροφὴν ἔχειν. .... Διελθόντων δὲ τῶν πέντε ἐτῶν, τὰ δύο μέχρι τῶν ἑπτὰ δεῖ θεωροὺς ἤδη γίγνεσθαι τῶν μαθήσεων, ἃς δεήσει μανθάνειν αὐτούς. Δύο δ' εἰσὶν ἡλικίαι, πρὸς ἃς ἀναγκαῖον διῃρῆσθαι τὴν παιδείαν, μετὰ τὴν ἀπὸ τῶν ἑπτὰ μέχρι ἥβης, καὶ πάλιν μετὰ τὴν ἀφ' ἥβης μέχρι τῶν ἑνὸς καὶ εἴκοσιν ἐτῶν.

[a] Hieronymus Wolf, who was rector of a Gymnasium at Augsburg, uses very similar language; he says, in his essay on Education, entitled 'Docendi discendique Ratio,' published about 1576: 'Felices fuisse Latinos qui unam Græcam linguam didicerunt, idque non tam præceptis quàm commercio Græcorum, absque ullâ difficultate: feliciores Græcos, qui suâ linguâ contenti, ac tantum legendi scribendique peritiâ instructi, statim ad artium liberalium et Philosophiæ studium animos adjunxerunt. Nos vero, quibus magna ætatis pars linguis peregrinis discendis elabatur, et tot obices, tot remoræ ante Philosophiæ fores obsistant (sunt enim Latina et Græca lingua non tam ipsa eruditio, quam eruditionis fores aut vestibulum) haud injuria fortunas nostras miserari.'

[b] 'Lusus hic sit: et rogetur, et laudetur, et nunquam non scisse se gaudeat, aliquando ipso nolente doceatur alius, cui invideat; contendat interim, et sæpius vincere se putet; præmiis etiam, quæ capit illa ætas, evocetur.'—Quintilian, *Instit. Orat.* lib. i. cap. i. § 20.

[c] See the Glossary.

tention with their inferiour companions: they somtyme purposely suffring the more noble children to vainquysshe, and, as it were, gyuying to them place and soueraintie, thoughe in dede the inferiour chyldren haue more lernyng.[a] But there can be nothyng more conuenient than by litle and litle to trayne and exercise them in spekyng of latyne: infourmyng them to knowe first the names in latine of all thynges that cometh in syghte, and to name all the partes of theyr bodies: and gyuynge them some what that they couete or desyre, in most gentyl maner to teache them to aske it agayne in latine. And if by this meanes they may be induced to understande and speke latine: it shall afterwarde be lasse grefe to them, in a maner, to lerne any thing, where they understande the langage wherein it is writen. [And, as touchynge grammere, there is at this day better introductions, and more facile, than euer before were made, concernyng as wel greke as latine, if they be wisely chosen.[b]] And hit shal be no reproche to a noble man to instruct his owne children, or at the leest wayes to examine them, by the way of daliaunce or solace, consideryinge that the emperour Octauius Augustus disdayned nat to rede the warkes of Cicero and Virgile to his children and neuewes.[c] And why shulde nat

Instruction in infancie.

---

[a] When it was proposed in 1540 that only the sons of gentlemen should be admitted to the Cathedral School at Canterbury, Cranmer spoke out boldly, and said, 'Poor men's children are many times endued with more singular gifts of nature, which are also the gifts of God, as with eloquence, memory, apt pronunciation, sobriety, and such like; and also commonly more apt to apply their study than is the gentleman's son delicately educated. Wherefore, if the gentleman's son be apt to learning, let him be admitted; if not apt let the poor man's child that is apt enter his room.'—Strype, *Mem. of Cranmer*, vol. i. p. 127.

[b] The words 'if they be wisely chosen' are omitted in all the subsequent editions. Hallam must surely have overlooked this passage, or he would hardly have said 'No Greek grammars or lexicons were yet (*i.e.* down to 1550) printed in England.'—*Lit. of Europe*, vol. i. p. 352, 5th ed.

[c] Suetonius merely says, 'Nepotes et literas, et notare, aliaque rudimenta, per se plerumque docuit.'—*Oct.* 64. But an anecdote narrated by Plutarch to some extent supports the assertion in the text: Πυνθάνομαι δὲ Καίσαρα χρόνοις πολλοῖς ὕστερον εἰσελθεῖν πρὸς ἕνα τῶν θυγατριδῶν· τὸν δὲ βιβλίον ἔχοντα Κικέρωνος ἐν ταῖς χερσὶν ἐκπλαγέντα τῷ ἱματίῳ περικαλύπτειν· ἰδόντα δὲ Καίσαρα λαβεῖν καὶ διελθεῖν

noble men rather so do, than teache their children howe at dyse and cardes, they may counnyngly lese and consume theyr owne treasure and substaunce? Moreouer teachynge repre-

Dionise the tyrant. senteth the auctoritie of a prince: wherfore Dionyse, kynge of Sicile, whan he was for tyranny expelled by his people, he came in to Italy, and there in a commune schole taught grammer,[a] where with, whan he was of his enemies embraided, and called a schole maister, he answered them, that al though Sicilians had exiled hym, yet in despite of them all he reigned,[b] notynge therby the authorite that he had ouer his scholers. Also whan hit was of hym demanded what auailed hym Plato or philosophy, wherin he had ben studious: he aunswered that they caused hym to sustayne aduersitie paciently, and made his exile to be to hym more facile and easy:[c] whiche courage and wysedome consydered of his people, they eftsones restored him unto his realme and astate roiall, where, if he had procured agayne them hostilite or warres, or had returned in to Sicile with any violence, I suppose the people wolde haue alway resysted hym, and haue kepte hym in perpetuall exile: as the romaynes dyd the proude kynge Tarquine, whose sonne rauysshed Lucrece. But to retourne to my purpose, hit shall be expedient that a noble

---

ἰστῶτα μέρος πολὺ τοῦ βιβλίου πάλιν δ' ἀποδιδόντα τῷ μειρακίῳ φάναι· 'Λόγιος ἀνὴρ, ὦ παῖ, λόγιος καὶ φιλόπατρις.'—*Cicero*, 49. Aurelius Victor says: 'Diligebat praeterea Virgilium.'—*Epitome*, cap. i. 17.

[a] Justin says: 'Novissimè ludimagistrum professus, pueros in trivio docebat, ut aut à timentibus semper in publico videretur aut à non timentibus facilius contemneretur.'—Lib. xxi. cap. 5. Compare Valerius Max. lib. vi. cap. ix. ext. 6; Cicero, *Tusc. Quæst.* lib. iii. cap. 12; and Lucian, *Somnium*, cap. xxiii. Ælian describes him as μητραγυρτῶν καὶ κρούων τύμπανα καὶ καταυλούμενος.—*Var. Hist.* lib. ix. § 8.

[b] This incident is not related by Plutarch. Cicero's comment on his occupation as a schoolmaster is, 'usque eo imperio carere non poterat.' It is not improbable that the answer given above is a mere fanciful addition or expansion of this idea.

[c] Τοῦτο δ' ἐν Κορίνθῳ ξένου τινὸς ἀγροικότερον εἰς τὰς μετὰ τῶν φιλοσόφων διατριβὰς, αἷς τυραννῶν ἔχαιρε, χλευάζοντος αὐτὸν καὶ τέλος ἐρωτῶντος, τί δὴ τῆς Πλάτωνος ἀπολαύσειε σοφίας, 'οὐδὲν, ἔφη, σοὶ δοκοῦμεν ὑπὸ Πλάτωνος ὠφελῆσθαι τύχης μεταβολὴν οὕτω φέροντες;'—Plutarch, *Timoleon*, 15.

mannes sonne, in his infancie, haue with hym continually onely suche as may accustome hym by litle and litle to speake pure and elegant latin. Semblably the nourises and other women aboute hym, if it be possible, to do the same : or, at the leste way, that they speke none englisshe but that which is cleane, polite, perfectly and articulately pronounced, omittinge no lettre or sillable, as folisshe women often times do of a wantonnesse, wherby diuers noble men and gentilmennes chyldren, (as I do at this daye knowe), haue attained corrupte and foule pronuntiation.

This industry used in fourminge litel infantes, who shall dought, but that they, (not lackyng naturall witte,) shall be apt to receyue lerninge, whan they come to mo yeres? And in this wise maye they be instructed, without any violence or inforsinge : using the more parte of the time, until they come to the age of vii yeres, in suche disportis, as do appertaine to children, wherin is no resemblance or similitude of vice.

CHAPTER VI.

At what age a tutour shulde be prouided, and what shall appertaine to his office to do.

AFTER that a childe is come to seuen yeres of age, I holde it expedient that he be taken from the company of women : sauynge that he may haue, one yere, or two at the most, an auncient and sad matrone, attendynge on hym in his chambre, whiche shall nat haue any yonge woman in her company : for though there be no perille of offence in that tender and innocent age, yet, in some children, nature is more prone to vice than to vertue, and in the tender wittes be sparkes of voluptuositie : whiche, norished by any occasion or obiecte, encrease often tymes in to so terrible a fire, that therwith all vertue and reason is consumed. Wherfore, to eschewe that daunger, the most sure counsaile is, to withdrawe him from all company of women, and to assigne unto hym a tutor, whiche shulde be an aunciant and worshipfull man, in whom is aproued to be moche gentilnes, mixte with grauitie, and, as nighe as can be, suche one as the childe by imitation folowynge may growe to be excellent. And if he be also lerned, he is the more commendable. Peleus, the father of Achilles, committed the gouernaunce of his sonne to Phenix, which was a straunger borne: who, as well in speakyng elegantly as in doinge valiauntly, was maister to Achilles (as Homere saith [a]) Howe moche profited hit to kynge Philip, father to the great Alexander, that he was deliuered in hostage to the Thebanes? where he was kepte and brought up under the gouernance of Epaminondas,[b] a noble and valiant capitaine: of whom he receiued suche lernynge,

Phenix, Achilles' tutor.

Epaminondas, tutor to kynge Philip.

---

[a] *Il.* ix. 432: foll.

Ὄψε δὲ δὴ μετέειπε γέρων ἱππηλάτα Φοῖνιξ
* * * * * *
πῶς ἂν ἔπειτ' ἀπὸ σεῖο, φίλον τέκος, αὖθι λιποίμην
οἶος; σοὶ δὲ μ' ἔπεμπε γέρων ἱππηλάτα Πηλεὺς
ἤματι τῷ, ὅτε σ' ἐκ Φθίης Ἀγαμέμνονι πέμπε
νήπιον, οὔπω εἰδόθ' ὁμοιίου πολέμοιο,
οὐδ' ἀγορέων, ἵνα τ' ἄνδρες ἀριπρεπέες τελέθουσι.
τοὔνεκά με προέηκε διδασκέμεναι τάδε πάντα,
μύθων τε ῥητῆρ' ἔμεναι, πρηκτῆρά τε ἔργων.

[b] Diodorus Siculus, lib. xvi. cap. 2: Οὗτοι δὲ τῷ Ἐπαμεινώνδου πατρὶ παρέθεντο τὸν νεανίσκον, καὶ προσέταξαν ἅμα τηρεῖν ἐπιμελῶς τὴν παρακαταθήκην καὶ προστατεῖν τῆς ἀγωγῆς καὶ παιδείας. Τοῦ δ' Ἐπαμεινώνδου Πυθαγόρειον ἔχοντος φιλόσοφον ἐπιστάτην, συντρεφόμενος ὁ Φίλιππος μετέσχεν ἐπὶ πλεῖον τῶν Πυθαγορείων λόγων. Ἀμφοτέρων δὲ τῶν μαθητῶν προσενεγκαμένων φύσιν τε καὶ φιλοπονίαν, ὑπῆρξαν ἑκάτεροι διαφέροντες ἀρετῇ. Ὧν Ἐπαμεινώνδας μὲν μεγάλους ἀγῶνας καὶ κινδύνους ὑπομείνας, τῇ πατρίδι παραδόξως τὴν ἡγεμονίαν τῆς Ἑλλάδος περιέθηκεν, ὁ δὲ Φίλιππος, ταῖς αὐταῖς ἀφορμαῖς χρησάμενος, οὐκ ἀπελείφθη τῆς Ἐπαμεινώνδου δόξης—which hardly supports the assertion in the text that Philip was 'brought up *under the governance*' of Epaminondas. The writer of the article on Philip in Smith's *Dict. of Biography* says: 'As for that part of the account of Diodorus which represents Philip as pursuing his studies in company with Epaminondas it is sufficiently refuted by chronology; nor would it seem that his attention at Thebes was directed to speculative philosophy so much as to those more practical points, the knowledge of which he afterwards found so useful for his purposes—military tactics, the language and politics of Greece, and the characters of its people.'

as well in actes martiall as in other liberal sciences, that he excelled all other kynges that were before his tyme in Grece, and finally, as well by wisedome as prowes, subdued all that countray. Semblably he ordayned for his sonne Alexander a noble tutor called Leonidas, unto whom, for his wisedome, humanitie, and lernyng, he committed the rule and preeminence ouer all the maisters and seruantes of Alexander.[a] In whom, nat withstandyng, was suche a familier vice, whiche Alexander apprehending in childhode coulde neuer abandon :[b] some suppose it to be fury and hastines, other superfluous drinking of wyne :[c] whiche of them it were, it is a good warnyng for gentilmen to be the more serious, inserching, nat only for the vertues, but also for

Leonidas, tutor to kynge Alexander.

[a] Πολλοὶ μὲν οὖν περὶ τὴν ἐπιμέλειαν, ὡς εἰκὸς, ἦσαν αὐτοῦ τροφεῖς καὶ παιδαγωγοὶ καὶ διδάσκαλοι λεγόμενοι, πᾶσι δ' ἐφειστήκει Λεωνίδας, ἀνὴρ τό τε ἦθος αὐστηρὸς καὶ συγγενὴς 'Ολυμπιάδος· αὐτὸς μὲν οὐ φεύγων τὸ τῆς παιδαγωγίας ὄνομα καλὸν ἔργον ἐχούσης καὶ λαμπρόν, ὑπὸ δὲ τῶν ἄλλων διὰ τὸ ἀξίωμα καὶ τὴν οἰκειότητα τροφεὺς 'Αλεξάνδρου καὶ καθηγητὴς καλούμενος.—Plut. *Alexander*, 5.

[b] Siquidem Leonides Alexandri pædagogus, ut à Babylonio Diogene traditur, quibusdum eum vitiis imbuit, quæ robustum quoque et jam maximum regem, ab illâ institutione puerili sunt prosecuta.—Quintil. *Instit. Orat.* lib. i. cap. i. § 9. Spalding, in his commentary upon this passage, says that there is no mention, in other writers, of the bad habits which Alexander contracted from his tutor except an allusion to them by a writer of the ninth century, Hincmar Archbishop of Rheims, who says : Et legimus quomodo Alexander in pueritiâ suâ habuit bajulum nomine Leonidem *citatis moribus et incomposito incessu notabilem* quæ puer quasi lac adulterinum ab eo sumpsit.—*Epistolæ*, lib. iii. cap. i. ed. 1602. And in another place he says : Et quia legimus de Alexandro Magno, cujus pædagogus Leonides nomine fuit, *quòd citatos mores et inhonestum incessum habens*, &c.— *Ibid.* lib. ii. cap. 2. Hincmar refers to the passage above quoted from Quintilian, as his authority for the statement ; and Spalding, who has evidently overlooked the passage in Curtius, says : *Citati mores* quid sit ignoro nisi forte sunt mali, famosi. And he repudiates the reading *motibus* for *moribus*, because, he says, Hincmar has used the same expression twice over, but there is very little doubt that Hincmar had in his mind the following passage, although he erroneously refers to Quintilian : Citatiorem gressum Leonidæ vitium fuisse ferunt ; ex ipsius consuetudine id hæsisse Alexandro : quod posteà, cum enixe vellet, corrigere non potuerit.—Q. Curtius, lib. i. cap. 2, § 14.

[c] 'Αλέξανδρον δὲ ἡ θερμότης τοῦ σώματος, ὡς ἔοικε, καὶ ποτικὸν καὶ θυμοειδῆ παρεῖχεν.—Plutarch, *Alexander* 4. 'Ut quidam putant ad vinum iramque pro clivior.'—Q. Curtius, lib. i. cap. 2, § 1 [2].

the vices of them, unto whose tuition and gouernance they will committe their children.

The office of a tutor is firste to knowe the nature of his pupil, that is to say, wherto he is mooste inclined or disposed, and in what thyng he setteth his most delectation or appetite. If he be of nature curtaise, piteouse, and of a free and liberall harte, it is a principall token of grace, (as hit is by all scripture determined.) Than shall a wyse tutor purposely commende those vertues, extolling also his pupill for hauyng of them; and therewith he shall declare them to be of all men mooste fortunate, whiche shall happen to haue suche a maister. And moreouer shall declare to hym what honour, what loue, what commodite shall happen to him by these vertues. And, if any haue ben of disposition contrary, than to expresse the enormities of theyr vice, with as moche detestation as may be. And if any daunger haue therby ensued, misfortune, or punisshement, to agreue[a] it in suche wyse, with so vehement wordes, as the childe may abhorre it, and feare the semblable aduenture.

Office of a tutor.

CHAPTER VII.[b]

In what wise musike may be to a noble man necessarie; and what modestie ought to be therin.

THE discretion of a tutor consisteth in temperance: that is to saye, that he suffre nat the childe to be fatigate with continuall studie or lernyng, wherwith the delicate and tender witte may be dulled or oppressed: but that there may be there with entrelased and mixte some pleasaunt lernynge and exercise, as playenge on instruments of musike, whiche moderately used and without diminution of honour, that is to say, without wanton countenance and dissolute gesture, is nat to be con-

[a] See the Glossary.
[b] The first part of this chapter is entirely omitted in Mr. Eliot's edition.

temned. For the noble kynge and prophete Dauid, kyng of Israell (whom almighty god said that he had chosen as a man accordinge to his harte or desire[a]) duringe his lyfe, delited in musike : and with the swete harmony that he made on his harpe, he constrayned the iuell spirite that vexed kynge Saul to forsake hym, continuynge the tyme that he harped.[b]

The mooste noble and valiant princis of Grece often tymes, to recreate their spirites, and in augmenting their courage, enbraced instrumentes musicall. So dyd the valiaunt Achilles, (as Homere saith), who after the sharpe and vehement contention, betwene him and Agamemnon, for the taking away of his concubine : wherby he, being set in a fury, hadde slayne Agamemnon, emperour of the grekes armye, had nat Pallas, the goddesse, withdrawen his hande;[c] in which rage he, all inflamed, departed with his people to his owne shippes that lay at rode, intendinge to haue retourned in to his countray; but after that he had taken to hym his harpe, (whereon he had lerned to playe of Chiron the Centaure, which also had taught hym feates of armes, with phisicke, and surgery[d]),

Achilles. Homerus, Iliados primo.

Chiron.

[a] Acts xiii. 22 : 'He raised up unto them David to be their king ; to whom also he gave testimony, and said, I have found David the son of Jesse a man after mine own heart which shall fulfil all my will.'

[b] 1 Sam. xvi. 23 : 'And it came to pass when the evil spirit from God was upon Saul that David took an harp and played with his hand : so Saul was refreshed and was well and the evil spirit departed from him.'

[c]
Πηλείωνι δ' ἄχος γένετ'· ἐν δέ οἱ ἦτορ
Στήθεσσιν λασίοισι διάνδιχα μερμήριξεν,
Ἢ ὅγε φάσγανον ὀξὺ ἐρυσσάμενος παρὰ μηροῦ,
Τοὺς μὲν ἀναστήσειεν, ὁ δ' Ἀτρείδην ἐναρίζοι,
Ἦε χόλον παύσειεν, ἐρητύσειέ τε θυμόν.
Ἕως ὁ ταῦθ' ὥρμαινε κατὰ φρένα καὶ κατὰ θυμόν,
Ἕλκετο δ' ἐκ κολεοῖο μέγα ξίφος, ἦλθε δ' Ἀθήνη
Οὐρανόθεν· πρὸ γὰρ ἧκε θεὰ λευκώλενος Ἥρη
Ἄμφω ὁμῶς θυμῷ φιλέουσά τε κηδομένη τε
Στῆ δ' ὄπιθεν, ξανθῆς δὲ κόμης ἕλε Πηλείωνα,
Οἴῳ φαινομένη· τῶν δ' ἄλλων οὔτις ὁρᾶτο.—*Il.* i. 188–198.

[d]
ἐπὶ δ' ἤπια φάρμακα πάσσε
Ἐσθλά, τά σε προτί φασὶν Ἀχιλλῆος δεδιδάχθαι
Ὃν Χείρων ἐδίδαξε, δικαιότατος Κενταύρων.—*Il.* xi. 829.

and, playeng theron, had songen the gestes and actis martial of the aunciente princis of Grece, as Hercules, Perseus, Perithous, Theseus, and his cosin Jason, and of diuers other of semblable value and prowesse, he was there with asswaged of his furie, and reduced in to his firste astate of reason :[a] in suche wyse, that in redoubyng his rage, and that thereby shulde nat remayne to him any note of reproche, he retaynyng his fiers and stourdie countenance, so tempered hym selfe in the entertaynement and answerynge the messagers that came to him from the residue of the Grekes, that they, reputing all that his fiers demeanure to be, (as it were), a diuine maiestie, neuer embrayded hym with any inordinate wrathe or furie.[b] And [c] therfore the great kynge Alexander, whan he had vainquisshed Ilion, where some tyme was set the moste noble citie of Troy, beinge demaunded of one if he wold se the harpe of Paris Alexander, who rauisshed Helene, he therat gentilly smilyng, answered that it was nat the thyng that he moche desired, but that he had rather se the harpe of Achilles, wherto he sange, nat the illecebrous dilectations of Venus, but the valiaunt actes and noble affaires of excellent princis.[d]

Alexander's musyke.

But in this commendation of musike I wold nat be thought to allure noble men to haue so moche delectation therin, that, in playinge and singynge only, they shulde put

[a] Τὸν δ' εὗρον φρένα τερπόμενον φόρμιγγι λιγείῃ,
Καλῇ, δαιδαλέῃ, ἐπὶ δ' ἀργύρεος ζυγὸς ἦεν·
Τὴν ἄρετ' ἐξ ἐνάρων, πτόλιν Ἠετίωνος ὀλέσσας·
Τῇ ὅγε θυμὸν ἔτερπεν, ἄειδε δ' ἄρα κλέα ἀνδρῶν.—*Il.* ix. 186.

[b] Εἰ δέ τοι Ἀτρείδης μὲν ἀπήχθετο κηρόθι μᾶλλον
Αὐτὸς, καὶ τοῦ δῶρα· σὺ δ' ἄλλους περ Παναχαιοὺς
Τειρομένους ἐλέαιρε κατὰ στρατὸν, οἵ σε θεὸν ὣς
Τίσουσ'· ἦ γάρ κέ σφι μάλα μέγα κῦδος ἄροιο.—*Il.* ix. 300.

[c] In Mr. Eliot's edition Chapter VII. begins here.

[d] Ἐν δὲ τῷ περιιέναι καὶ θεᾶσθαι τὰ κατὰ τὴν πόλιν, ἐρομένου τινὸς αὐτὸν εἰ βούλεται τὴν Ἀλεξάνδρου λύραν ἰδεῖν, ἐλάχιστα φροντίζειν ἐκείνης ἔφη, τὴν δ' Ἀχιλλέως ζητεῖν, ᾗ τὰ κλέα καὶ τὰς πράξεις ὑμνεῖ τῶν ἀγαθῶν ἀνδρῶν ἐκεῖνος.—Plutarch, *Alexander*, 15. This reply is also mentioned by Ælian, *Var. Hist.* ix. 30, and Stobæus (*Serm.* vii.).

their holle studie and felicitie: as dyd the emperour Nero, whiche all a longe somers day wolde sit in the Theatre, (an open place where al the people of Rome behelde solemne actis and playes), and, in the presence of all the noble men and senatours, wolde playe on his harpe and synge without cessynge: And if any man hapned, by longe sittynge, to slepe, or, by any other countenance, to shewe him selfe to be weary, he was sodaynly bobbed on the face by the seruantes of Nero, for that purpose attendyng: or if any persone were perceiued to be absent, or were sene to laughe at the folye of the emperour, he was forthe with accused, as it were, of missprision: wherby the emperour founde occasion to committe him to prison or to put hym to tortures.[*] O what misery was it to be subiecte to suche a minstrell, in whose musike was no melodye, but anguisshe and dolour?

Theatre.

Musyke miserable.

It were therfore better that no musike were taughte to a noble man, than, by the exacte knowlege therof, he shuld haue therin inordinate delite, and by that be illected to wantonnesse, abandonyng grauitie, and the necessary cure and office, in the publike weale, to him committed. Kynge

---

[*] 'Mox, flagitante vulgo "ut omnia studia sua publicaret," (hæc enim verba dixere) ingreditur theatrum, cunctis citharæ legibus obtemperans: ne fessus resideret, ne sudorem, nisi ea, quam indutui gerebat veste detergeret: ut nulla oris aut narium excrementa viserentur. Postremo flexus genu, et cœtum illum manu veneratus, sententias judicum opperiebatur ficto pavore. Et plebs quidem urbis, histrionum quoque gestus juvare solita, personabat certis modis plausoque composito. Crederes lætari: ac fortasse lætabantur, per incuriam publici flagitii. Sed qui remotis e municipiis, severamque adhuc et antiqui moris retinentes Italiam, quique per longas provincias, lasciviæ inexperti, officio legationum aut privata utilitate, advenerant, neque aspectum illum tolerare, neque labori inhonesto sufficere; cum manibus nesciis fatiscerent, turbarent gnaros ac sæpe à militibus verberarentur, qui per cuneos stabant, ne quod temporis momentum impari clamore aut silentio segni præteriret. Constitit plerosque Equitum dum per augustias aditus et ingruentem multitudinem enituntur, obtritos, et alios, dum diem noctemque sedilibus continuant, morbo exitiabili correptos: quippe gravior inerat metus, si spectaculo defuissent, multis palam, et pluribus occultis, ut nomina ac vultus, alacritatem, tristitiamque cœuntium scrutarentur. Unde tenuioribus statim irrogata supplicia, adversus illustres dissimulatum ad præsens et mox redditum odium.—Tac. *Ann.* lib. xvi. 4.

Philip, whan he harde that his sonne Alexander dyd singe swetely and properly, he rebuked him gentilly, saynge, But, Alexander, be ye nat ashamed that ye can singe so well and connyngly?[a] whereby he mente that the open profession of that crafte was but of a base estimation. And that it suffised a noble man, hauynge therin knowlege, either to use it secretely, for the refreshynge of his witte, whan he hath tyme of solace: orels, only hearynge the contention of noble musiciens, to gyue iugement in the excellencie of their counnynges. These be the causes where unto hauinge regarde, musike is nat onely tollerable but also commendable. For, as Aristotle saith, Musike in the olde time was nombred amonge sciences, for as moche as nature seketh nat onely howe to be in busines well occupied, but also howe in quietnes to be commendably disposed.[b]

Kynge Philip's wordes to Alexander.

Musike profitable.

And if the childe be of a perfecte inclination and towardnes to vertue, and very aptly disposed to this science, and ripely dothe understande the reason and concordance of tunes, the tutor's office shall be to persuade hym to haue principally in remembrance his astate, whiche maketh hym exempt from the libertie of usinge this science in euery tyme and place: that is to say, that it onely serueth for recreation after tedious or laborious affaires, and to shewe him that a gentilman, plainge or singing in a commune audience, appaireth his estimation: the people forgettinge reuerence, when they beholde him in the similitude of a common seruant or minstrell. Yet, natwithstanding, he shall commende the perfecte understandinge of

[a] Ὁ δὲ Φίλιππος πρὸς τὸν υἱὸν ἐπιτερπῶς ἔν τινι πότῳ ψήλαντα καὶ τεχνικῶς εἶπεν, ʽΟὐκ αἰσχύνῃ καλῶς οὕτω ψάλλων;' Ἀρκεῖ γάρ, ἂν βασιλεὺς ἀκροᾶσθαι ψαλλόντων σχολάζῃ, καὶ πολὺ νέμει ταῖς Μούσαις ἑτέρων ἀγωνιζομένων τὰ τοιαῦτα θεατὴς γιγνόμενος.—Plut. *Pericles*, I. Quintus Curtius also mentions this rebuke, and adds that thenceforth 'velut artem suæ majestati indecoram, negligentius tractare cœpit.'—Lib. i. cap. 3, § 23.

[b] *Pol.* lib. viii. cap. 2: (3) τὴν δὲ μουσικὴν ἤδη διαπορήσειεν ἄν τις· νῦν μὲν γὰρ ὡς ἡδονῆς χάριν οἱ πλεῖστοι μετέχουσιν αὐτῆς· οἱ δ' ἐξ ἀρχῆς ἔταξαν ἐν παιδείᾳ, διὰ τὸ τὴν φύσιν αὐτὴν ζητεῖν, ὅπερ πολλάκις εἴρηται, μὴ μόνον ἀσχολεῖν ὀρθῶς, ἀλλὰ καὶ σχολάζειν δύνασθαι καλῶς.

musike, declaringe howe necessary it is for the better attaynynge the knowlege of a publike weale: whiche, as I before haue saide, is made of an ordre of astates and degrees, and, by reason therof, conteineth in it a perfect harmony: whiche he shall afterwarde more perfectly understande, whan he shall happen to rede the bokes of Plato, and Aristotle, of publike weales: wherin be written diuers examples of musike and geometrye. In this fourme may a wise and circumspecte tutor adapte the pleasant science of musike to a necessary and laudable purpose.

CHAPTER VIII.

That it is commendable in a gentilman to paint and kerue exactly, if nature therto doth induce hym.

IF the childe be of nature inclined, (as many haue ben), to paint with a penne, or to fourme images in stone or tree: he shulde nat be therfrom withdrawen, or nature be rebuked, whiche is to hym beniuolent: but puttyng one to hym, whiche is in that crafte, wherin he deliteth, moste excellent, in vacant tymes from other more serious lernynge, he shulde be, in the moste pure wise, enstructed in painting or keruinge.

⌜And nowe, perchance, some enuious reder wyll hereof apprehende occasion to scorne me, sayenge that I haue well hyed me, to make of a noble man a mason or peynter.⌟ And yet, if either ambition or voluptuouse idelnes wolde haue suffered that reder to haue sene histories, he shuld haue founden excellent princis, as well in payntyng as in keruynge, equall to noble artificers: suche were Claudius,[a] Titus,[b] the

---

[a] 'The undertakings of Claudius were not unworthy of the colossal age of material creations; yet they were not the mere fantastic conceptions of turgid pride and unlimited power.'—Merivale, *Hist. of Rome*, vol. v. p. 504; Suetonius gives a long list of public works executed by direction of Claudius.

[b] 'Besides skill in music and versification, it is specially mentioned that Titus

sonne of Vaspasian, Hadriane,[a] both Antonines,[b] and diuers other emperours and noble princes: whose warkes of longe tyme remayned in Rome and other cities, in suche places where all men mought beholde them: as monuments of their excellent wittes and vertuous occupation in eschewynge of idelnes.

And nat without a necessary cause princis were in their childhode so instructed: for it serued them afterwarde for deuysynge of engynes for the warre: or for making them better that be all redy deuysed. For, as Vitruuius (which writeth of buyldynge to the emperour Augustus) sayth, All turmentes of warre, whiche we cal ordinance, were first inuented by kinges or gouernours of hostes, or if they were deuised by other, they were by them made moche better.[c] Also, by the feate of portraiture or payntyng, a capitaine may discriue the countray of his aduersary, wherby he shall eschue the daungerous passages with his hoste or nauie: also perceyue the

---

was a rapid short-hand writer, and had, moreover, a knack of imitating the writing of others, so that he used to say of himself in jest that he might have made an expert forger.'—Merivale, *Hist. of Rome*, vol. vii. p. 46, note ; Sueton. *Titus*, 3.

[a] 'Hic Græcis literis impensius eruditus à plerisque Græculus appellatus est. Atheniensium studia moresque hausit, potitus non sermone tantum, sed et ceteris disciplinis, canendi, psallendi, medendique scientia, musicus, geometra, pictor, fictorque ex ære vel marmore proximè Polycletos et Euphranoras.'—Victor, *Epitome*, cap. xiv.

[b] Capitolinus says of Antoninus Pius, that he was 'diligens agri cultor.' And of Marcus Aurelius Antoninus 'operam præterea pingendo sub magistro Diogneto dedit. Amavit pugilatum luctamina, et cursum, et aucupatus, et pila lusit adprimè et venatus est.'—Cap. 4.

[c] This proposition is nowhere stated *totidem verbis* by the writer referred to, but it is probable that the passage Sir Thomas Elyot had in his mind is the following: 'Omnis autem est machinatio rerum natura procreata ac præceptrice et magistra mundi versatione instituta. Namque animadvertamus primum et aspiciamus continentem solis, lunæ, quinque etiam stellarum naturam, quæ ni machinata versarentur, non habuissemus interdum lucem nec fructuum maturitates. Cum ergo majores hæc ita esse animadvertissent, è rerum natura sumpserunt exempla et ea imitantes inducti rebus divinis commodas vitæ perfecerunt explicationes itaque comparaverunt, ut essent expeditiora, alia machinis et earum versationibus, nonnulla organis, et ita quæ animadverterunt ad usum utilia esse studiis, artibus institutis, gradatim augenda doctrinis curaverunt.'—Lib. x. cap. 1.

placis of aduauntage, the forme of embataylynge of his
ennemies: the situation of his campe, for his mooste suertie:
the strength or weakenes of the towne or fortresse whiche he
intendeth to assaulte. And that whiche is moost specially to be
considered, in visiting his owne dominions, he shal sette them
out in figure, in suche wise that at his eie shal appere to hym
where he shall employ his study and treasure, as well for the
saulfgarde of his countray, as for the commodite and honour
therof, hauyng at al tymes in his sight the suertie and
feblenes, aduauncement and hyndrance, of the same. And
what pleasure and also utilite is it to a man whiche intendeth
to edifie, hymselfe to expresse the figure of the warke that he
purposeth, accordyng as he hath conceyued it in his owne
fantasie? wherin, by often amendyng and correctyng, he
finally, shall so perfecte the warke unto his purpose, that there
shall neither ensue any repentance, nor in the employment of
his money he shall be by other deceiued. More ouer the
feate of portraiture shall be an allectiue to euery other studie
or exercise. For the witte therto disposed shall alway
couaite congruent mater, wherin it may be occupied. And
whan he happeneth to rede or here any fable or historie,
forthwith he apprehendeth it more desirously, and retaineth
it better, than any other that lacketh the sayd feate: by
reason that he hath founde mater apte to his fantasie. Finally,
euery thinge that portraiture may comprehende will be to him
delectable to rede or here. And where the liuely spirite, and
that whiche is called the grace of the thyng, is perfectly expressed, that thinge more persuadeth and stereth the beholder, and soner istructeth hym, than the declaration in
writynge or speakynge doth the reder or hearer. Experience
we haue therof in lernynge of geometry, astronomie, and cos-
mogrophie, called in englisshe the discription of the worlde.
In which studies I dare affirme a man shal more profite, in
one wike, by figures and chartis, well and perfectly made, than
he shall by the only redyng or heryng the rules of that science
by the space of halfe a yere at the lest; wherfore the late

writers deserue no small commendation whiche added to the autors of those sciences apt and propre figures.

And he that is perfectly instructed in portrayture, and hapneth to rede any noble and excellent historie, wherby his courage is inflamed to the imitation of vertue, he forth with taketh his penne or pensill, and with a graue and substanciall studie, gatherynge to him all the partes of imagination, endeuoureth him selfe to expresse liuely, and (as I mought say) actually, in portrayture, nat only the faict or affaire, but also the sondry affections of euery personage in the historie recited, whiche mought in any wise appiere or be perceiued in their visage, countenance or gesture: with like diligence as Lysippus[a] made in metall kynge Alexander, fightynge and struggling with a terrible lyon of incomparable magnitude and fiersenesse, whom, after longe and difficulte bataile, with wonderfull strength and clene might, at the last he ouerthrewe and vainquisshed;[b] wherin he so expressed the similitude of Alexander and of his lordes standyng about him that they all semed to lyue. Amonge whom the prowes of Alexander appiered, excelling all other: the residue of his lordes after the value and estimation of their courage, euery man set out in suche forwardnes, as they than semed more

Lisippus.

[a] Edicto vetuit, ne quis se præter Apellem
Pingeret, aut alius Lysippo duceret æra
Fortis Alexandri vultum simulantia.—Hor. *Ep.* ii. 1. 239.

[b] This story is related at length by Quintus Curtius: 'Barbaræ opulentiæ in illis locis haud ulla sunt majora indicia, quam magnis nemoribus saltibusque nobilium ferarum greges clausi. Spatiosas ad hoc eligunt sylvas, crebris perennium aquarum fontibus amœnas: muris nemora cinguntur, turresque habent venantium receptacula. Quatuor continuis ætatibus intactum saltum fuisse constabat: quem Alexander cum toto exercitu ingressus "agitari undique feras" jussit. Inter quas cum leo magnitudinis raræ ipsum regem invasurus incurreret; forte Lysimachus, qui postea regnavit, proximus Alexandro, venabulum objicere feræ cœperat. Quo rex repulso et "abire" jusso, adjecit "tam à semet uno quàm à Lysimacho leonem interfici posse." Lysimachus enim quondam cum venaretur in Syria, occiderat eximiæ magnitudinis feram solus: sed lævo humero usque ad ossa laceratus ad ultimum periculi pervenerat. Id ipsum exprobrans ei rex fortius, quam locutus est, fecit: nam feram non excepit modo, sed etiam uno vulnere occidit.'— Lib. viii. cap. 1, § 11–16.

prompt to the helpyng of their maister, that is to say, one lasse a ferde than an other.[a] Phidias the Atheniense, whom all writers do commende, made of yuory the simulachre or image of Jupiter, honoured by the gentiles on the high hille of Olympus: whiche was done so excellently that Pandenus, a counnyng painter, therat admaruailinge, required the craftis man to shewe him where he had the example or paterne of so noble a warke.[b] Than Phidias answered that he had taken it out of thre verses of Homere the poet: the sentence wherof ensueth, as well as my poure witte can expresse it in englisshe:

'Than Jupiter the father of them all
Therto assented with his browes blake,
Shaking his here, and therwith did let fall
A countenance that made al heuen to quake,'[c]

where it is to be noted, that[d] immediately before Thetis the

[a] This appears to be an embellishment by the author, of which we have already seen a somewhat similar instance at p. 34 ante. Plutarch, who evidently refers to the same incident as Curtius, merely says: Τοῦτο τὸ κυνήγιον Κράτερος εἰς Δελφοὺς ἀνέθηκεν εἰκόνας χαλκᾶς ποιησάμενος τοῦ λέοντος καὶ τῶν κυνῶν καὶ τοῦ βασιλέως τῷ λέοντι συνεστῶτος καὶ αὑτοῦ προσβοηθοῦντος, ὧν τὰ μὲν Λύσιππος ἔπλασε, τὰ δὲ Λεωχάρης.—Alexander, 40.

[b] This is narrated by Strabo: ἀπομνημονεύουσι δὲ τοῦ Φειδίου διότι πρὸς τὸν Πάνδεινον εἶπε πυνθανόμενον, πρὸς τί παράδειγμα μέλλοι ποιήσειν τὴν εἰκόνα τοῦ Διός, ὅτι πρὸς τὴν Ὁμήρου, δι' ἐπῶν ἐκτεθεῖσαν τούτων Ἦ καὶ ... Ὄλυμπον, εἰρῆσθαι γὰρ μάλα δοκεῖ καλῶς, ἔκ τε τῶν ἄλλων καὶ τῶν ὀφρύων, ὅτι προκαλεῖται τὴν διάνοιαν ὁ ποιητὴς ἀναζωγραφεῖν μέγαν τινὰ τύπον καὶ μεγάλην δύναμιν ἀξίαν τοῦ Διός, καθάπερ καὶ ἐπὶ τῆς Ἥρας, ἅμα φυλάττων τὸ ἐφ' ἑκατέρῳ πρέπον· ἔφη μὲν γάρ, σείσατο δ' εἰνὶ θρόνῳ, ἐλέλιξε δὲ μακρὸν Ὄλυμπον· τὸ δ' ἐπ' ἐκείνης συμβὰν ὅλῃ κινηθείσῃ, τοῦτ' ἐπὶ τοῦ Διὸς ἀπαντῆσαι ταῖς ὀφρύσι μόνον νεύσαντος, συμπαθούσης δέ τι καὶ τῆς κόμης.—Lib. viii. cap. 3, s. 30.

[c]
Ἦ, καὶ κυανέῃσιν ἐπ' ὀφρύσι νεῦσε Κρονίων
Ἀμβρόσιαι δ' ἄρα χαῖται ἐπερρώσαντο ἄνακτος,
Κρατὸς ἀπ' ἀθανάτοιο· μέγαν δ' ἐλέλιξεν Ὄλυμπον.—Il. i. 528.

[d] In the original the words after 'that' are 'Homere immediatly before had rehersed the consultation had amonge the goddis for the appaising of the two noble princis Achilles and Agamemnon;' but the correction having been made by the author himself and inserted in the errata appended to the original edition, it has been thought advisable, inasmuch as the present edition does not profess to be a fac-simile, to print the passage in accordance with the author's own revision.

mother of Achilles desired Jupiter importunately to inclyne his fauour to the parte of the Troyanes.

Nowe (as I haue before sayde) I intende nat, by these examples, to make of a prince or noble mannes sonne, a commune painter or keruer, whiche shall present him selfe openly stained or embrued with sondry colours, or poudered with the duste of stones that he cutteth, or perfumed with tedious[a] sauours of the metalles by him yoten.[b]

But verily myne intente and meaninge is only, that a noble childe, by his owne naturall disposition, and nat by coertion, may be induced to receiue perfect instruction in these sciences.[c] But all though, for purposis before expressed, they shall be necessary, yet shall they nat be by him exercised, but as a secrete pastime, or recreation of the wittes, late occupied in serious studies, like as dyd the noble princis before named. Al though they, ones beinge attayned, be neuer moche exercised, after that the tyme cometh concerning businesse of greatter importaunce. Ne the lesse the exquisite knowlege and understanding that he hath in those sciences, hath impressed in his eares and eies an exacte and perfecte iugement, as well in desernyng the excellencie of them, whiche either in musike, or in statuary, or paynters crafte, professeth any counnynge, as also adaptinge their saide knowlege to the adminiculation[d] of other serious studies and businesse, as I haue before rehersed : whiche, I doubt nat, shall be well approued by them that either haue redde and understande olde autors, or aduisedly wyll examine my considerations.

The swete[e] writer, Lactantius, saythe in his first

[a] See the Glossary.   [b] See the Glossary.
[c] In the edition of 1546 and all the subsequent editions the remainder of this chapter is omitted. Of all the copies of this work in the British Museum Library there is not one containing the whole of this chapter, which therefore is now, probably for the first time since A.D. 1531, given to the public in an unmutilated shape.
[d] See the Glossary.
[e] 'The style of Lactantius, formed upon the model of the great orator of Rome, has gained for him the appellation of the *Christian Cicero*, and not undeservedly. No reasonable critic indeed would now assert, with Picus of Mirandula, that the

booke[a] to the emperour Constantine agayne the gentiles: 'Of conninge commeth vertue, and of vertue perfect felicite is onely ingendred.'[b] *Lactantius lib. iii.*

And for that cause the gentiles supposed those princis, whiche in vertue and honour surmounted other men, to be goddes. And the Romanes in lyke wise dyd consecrate their emperours,[c] which excelled in vertuous example, in preseruyng or augmentinge the publike weale, and ampliatinge of the empire, calling them *Diui*, whiche worde representeth a signification of diuinitie, they thinkynge that it was excedynge mannes nature to be bothe in fortune and goodnes of suche perfection.

imitator has not only equalled, but even surpassed the beauties of his original. But it is impossible not to be charmed with the purity of diction, the easy grace, the calm dignity, and the sonorous flow of his periods, when compared with the harsh phraseology and barbarous extravagance of his African contemporaries. Some critics absurdly enough, perhaps, have imagined that *Lactantius* is a mere epithet, indicating the milk-like softness and sweetness which characterise the style of this author.'—Smith's *Dict. of Biography*, sub voc.

[a] The reference is erroneous; the passage quoted occurs in the 12th chapter of the third book.

[b] 'Ex scientiâ enim virtus, ex virtute summum bonum nascitur.'

[c] Compare the remarks of Lactantius on this subject: 'Quibus ex rebus, cùm constet illos homines fuisse, non est obscurum, quâ ratione dii cœperint nominari. Si enim nulli reges ante Saturnum vel Uranum fuerunt propter hominum raritatem, qui agrestem vitam sine ullo rectore vivebant: non est dubium quin illis temporibus homines regem ipsum totamque gentem summis laudibus ac novis honoribus jactare cœperint, ut etiam deos appellarent, sive ob miraculum virtutis (hoc verè putabant rudes adhuc et simplices), sive (ut fieri solet) in adulationem præsentis potentiæ, sive ob beneficia quibus erant ad humanitatem compositi. Deinde ipsi reges, cùm cari fuissent iis, quorum vitam composuerant, magnum sui desiderium mortui reliquerunt. Itaque homines eorum simulacra finxerunt, ut haberent aliquod ex imaginum contemplatione solatium; progressique longiùs per amorem meriti, memoriam defunctorum colere cœperunt: ut et gratiam referre bene meritis viderentur, et successores eorum allicerent ad bene imperandi cupiditatem . . . . Hâc scilicet ratione Romani Cæsares suos consecraverunt, et Mauri reges suos. Sic paulatim religiones esse cœperunt, dum illi primi, qui eos noverant, eo ritu suos liberos ac nepotes, deinde omnes posteros imbuerunt. Et hi tamen summi reges ob celebritatem nominis in provinciis omnibus colebantur.'—Lib. i. cap. 15.

E

CHAPTER IX.[a]

What exacte diligence shulde be in chosinge maisters.

AFTER that the childe hathe ben pleasantly trained, and induced to knowe the partes of speche, and can seperate one of them from an other, in his owne langage, it shall than be time that his tutor or gouernour do make diligent serche for suche a maister as is exellently lerned both in greke and latine, and therwithall is of sobre and vertuous disposition, specially chast of liuyng, and of moche affabilite and patience: leste by any uncleane example the tender mynde of the childe may be infected, harde afterwarde to be recouered. For the natures of children be nat so moche or sone aduaunced by thinges well done or spoken, as they be hindred and corrupted by that whiche in actis or wordes is wantonly expressed. Also by a cruell and irous[b] maister the wittes of children be dulled; and that thinge for the whiche children be often tymes beaten is to them euer after fastidious: wherof we nede no better autor for witnes than daily experience.[c] Wherfore the moste necessary thinges to be obserued by a master in his disciples or scholers (as Licon[d] the noble grammarien saide)

---

[a] This and the three next chapters are entirely omitted in Mr. Eliot's edition.

[b] See the Glossary.

[c] Hallam, commenting on this passage, says, 'All testimonies concur to this savage ill-treatment of boys in the schools of this period. The fierceness of the Tudor government, the religious intolerance, the polemical brutality, the rigorous justice, when justice it was of our laws, seem to have engendered a hardness of character, which displayed itself in severity of discipline, when it did not even reach the point of arbitrary or malignant cruelty.' And he gives as the most striking example of this 'severity of discipline' the behaviour of Lady Jane Grey's parents towards one who was 'the slave of their temper in life, the victim of their ambition in death.'—*Literature of Europe*, vol. i. p. 401.

[d] Lycon of Troas, a distinguished Peripatetic philosopher, was the son of Astyanax, and the disciple of Straton, whom he succeeded as the head of the Peripatetic school, B.C. 272; and he held that post for more than forty-four years. He was celebrated for his eloquence and for his skill in educating boys. We are indebted to Diogenes Laertius for what we know of him.

is shamfastnes and praise.[a] By shamfastnes, as it were with a bridell, they rule as well theyr dedes as their appetites. And desire of prayse addeth to a sharpe spurre to their disposition towarde lernyng and vertue. Accordyng there unto Quintilian, instructyng an oratour, desireth suche a childe to be giuen unto hym, whom commendation feruently stereth[b], glorie prouoketh, and beinge vainquisshed wepeth. That childe (saithe he) is to be fedde with ambition, hym a litle chiding sore biteth, in hym no parte of slouthe is to be feared.[c] And if nature disposeth nat the childes witte to receiue lernynge, but rather other wise, it is to be applied with more diligence, and also policie, as chesing some boke, wherof the argument or matter approcheth moste nighe to the childes inclination or fantasie, so that it be nat extremely vicious, and therwith by litle and litle, as it were with a pleasant sauce, prouoke him to haue good appetite to studie. And surely that childe, what so euer he be, is well blessed and fortunate, that findeth a good instructour or maister : whiche was considered by noble kynge Philip, father to the great king Alexander, who immediately after that his sonne was borne wrote a letter to Aristotle, the prince of philosophers, the tenour wherof ensueth.[d]

Aristotle, we grete you well. Lettinge you weete that we haue a sonne borne, for the whiche we gyue due thankes unto god, nat for that he is borne onely, but also for as moche as hit happeneth hym to be borne, you lyuinge. Trusting that it shall happen that he,

The epistel of king Philip to Aristotel.

[a] Ἔφασκε γὰρ δεῖν παραζεῦχθαι τοῖς παισὶ τὴν αἰδῶ καὶ φιλοτιμίαν, ὡς τοῖς ἵπποις μύωπα καὶ χαλινόν.—Diog. Laert. Λύκων.

[b] *I.e.* stirreth.

[c] 'Mihi ille detur puer, quem laus excitet, quem gloria juvet, qui victus fleat. Hic erit alendus ambitu, hunc mordebit objurgatio, hunc honor excitabit, in hoc desidiam nunquam verebor.'—*Instit. Orat.* lib. i. cap. 3, § 7.

[d] 'Philippus Aristoteli salutem dicit. Certiorem te facio, filium mihi genitum esse. Nec perinde Diis gratiam habeo quod omnino natus est, quàm quod te florente nasci illum contigit : à quo educatum institutumque neque nobis indignum spero evasurum, neque successioni tantarum rerum imparem. Satius enim existimo carere liberis, quàm opprobria majorum suorum tollentem in poenam genuisse.'— *Quintus Curtius,* lib. i. cap. 2,

by you taught and instructed, shall be herafter worthye to be named our sonne, and to enioy the honour and substance that we nowe haue prouided. Thus fare ye well.

The same Alexander was wont to say openly, that he ought to gyue as great thankes to Aristotle his mayster as to kynge Philip his father, for of hym he toke the occasion to lyue, of the other he receiued the reason and waye to lyue well.[a] And what maner a prince Alexander was made by the doctrine of Aristotle, hit shall appere in diuers places of this boke: where his example to princes shall be declared. The incomparable benefite of maisters haue ben well remembred of dyuers princes. In so moche as Marcus Antoninus, whiche amonge the emperours was commended for his vertue and sapience, hadde his mayster Proculus (who taught hym grammer[b]) so moche in fauour, that he aduanced hym to be proconsul:[c] whiche was one of the highest dignites amonge the Romanes.

Alexander the emperour caused his maister Julius Fronto to be consul:[d] whiche was the highest office, and in astate nexte the emperour: and also optayned of the senate that the statue or image of Fronto was sette up amonge the noble princes.[e]

[a] 'Ipse quidem prædicavit non minus se debere Aristoteli, quam Philippo: hujus enim munus fuisse, quod viveret; illius, quod honestè viveret.'—*Quintus Curtius*, lib. i. cap. 3, § 10.

[b] 'Usus prætereà grammaticis Græco Alexandro Cotiaensi, Latinis Trosio Apro et Pollione, et Eutychio Proculo Siccensi.'—Capitol. *M. Anton. Phil.* 2.

[c] 'Proculum vero usque ad proconsulatum provexit, oneribus in se receptis.'—*Ibid.*

[d] This is a mistake arising from the author having confounded Julius Frontinus, who is mentioned by Lampridius as instructing Alexander Severus in rhetoric with Cornelius Fronto, who is mentioned by Capitolinus as occupying a similar position as regards oratory towards Marcus Aurelius. Dr. Merivale says, 'Cornelius Fronto, another rhetorician, had attained the consulship as far back as the reign of Hadrian, but declined office in the provinces. He continued in his old age to attend and advise his imperial pupil, who treated him with the highest consideration.'—*Hist. of Rome*, vol. vii. p. 576.

[e] 'Sed multum ex his Frontoni detulit, cui et statuam in senatu petiit.'—Capitol. *M. Anton. Phil.* 2.

THE GOVERNOUR. 53

What caused Traiane to be so good a prince, in so moche that of late dayes whan an emperour receyued his crowne at Rome, the people with a commune crye desired of god that he mought be as good as was Traiane,[a] but that he hapned to haue Plutarche, the noble philosopher, to be his instructour?[b] I agre me that some be good of natural inclination to goodnes: but where good instruction and example is there to added, the naturall goodnes must there with nedes be amended and be more excellent.

CHAPTER X.

What ordre shulde be in lernynge and whiche autours shulde be fyrst redde.

NOWE lette us retourne to the ordre of lernyng apt for a gentyll man. Wherein I am of the opinion of Quintilian[c]

---

[a] 'Hujus tantum memoriæ delatum est, ut usque ad nostram ætatem non aliter in senatu principibus acclametur, nisi "felicior Augusto, melior Trajano."'— *Eutrop.* lib. viii. cap. 5.

[b] 'The statement that Plutarch was the preceptor of Trajan, and that the emperor raised him to the consular rank, rests on the authority of Suidas and a Latin letter addressed to Trajan. But this short notice in Suidas is a worthless authority; and the Latin letter to Trajan, which only exists in the Policraticus of John of Salisbury (lib. v. cap. 1) is a forgery, though John probably did not forge it. John's expression is somewhat singular—"Extat epistola Plutarchi Trajanum instituentis, quæ cujusdam politicæ constitutionis exprimit sensum. Ea dicitur esse hujusmodi;" and then he gives the letter. In the second chapter of this book John says that this Politica Constitutio is a small treatise inscribed "Institutio Trajani," and he gives the substance of part of the work. Plutarch, who dedicated the Ἀποφθέγματα to Trajan, says nothing of the emperor having been his pupil.'— Smith's *Dict. of Biography* : *Plutarch*. Dr. Merivale says, 'The story that he was instructed by Plutarch may be rejected as a fiction founded perhaps on the favour he undoubtedly showed to that philosopher.'—*Hist. of Rome*, vol. vii. p. 213, note.

[c] 'A Græco sermone puerum incipere malo; quia Latinum, qui pluribus in usu est, vel nobis nolentibus perhibet: simul quia disciplinis quoque Græcis prius instituendus est, unde et nostræ fluxerunt. Non tamen hoc adeo superstitiosè velim fieri, ut diu tantum loquatur Græce, aut discat, sicut plerisque moris est; hinc enim accidunt et oris plurima vitia in peregrinum sonum corrupti, et sermonis,

that I wolde haue hym lerne greke and latine autors both at one time: orels to begyn with greke, for as moche as that it is hardest to come by: by reason of the diuersite of tonges, which be fyue in nombre:[a] and all must be knowen, or elles uneth any poet can be well understande. And if a childe do begyn therin at seuen yeres of age, he may continually lerne greke autours thre yeres, and in the meane tyme use the latin tonge as a familiar langage: whiche in a noble mannes sonne may well come to passe, hauynge none other persons to serue him or kepyng hym company, but suche as can speake latine elegantly.[b] And what doubt is there but so may he as sone speake good latin, as he maye do pure frenche, whiche nowe is broughte in to as

The fyrst lerning in chyldehode.

cui quum Græcæ figuræ assidua consuetudine hæserunt, in diversâ quoque loquendi ratione pertinacissimè durant. Non longe itaque Latina subsequi debent, et cito pariter ire: ita fiet ut quum æquali cura linguam utramque tueri cœperimus, neutra alteri officiat.'—*Instit. Orat.* lib. i. cap. 1, § 12.

[a] Quintilian, recording some instances of wonderful memory, says of Crassus, 'quum Asiæ præesset *quinque Græci sermonis differentias* sic tenuit, ut qua quisque apud eum lingua postulasset, eadem jus sibi redditum ferret.'—*Instit. Orat.* lib. xi. cap. 2, § 50. Modern grammarians, however, recognise only four, viz., the Æolic, Doric, Ionic, and Attic, 'because these alone were cultivated and rendered classic by writers.'—*Matthiæ Gr. Gr.* vol. i. p. 4. Professor Müller, indeed, considers the Doric as 'a mere variety of the Æolic,' as the Attic is of the Ionic, and thus reduces the dialects of the Greek language 'into two great classes which are distinguished from each other by characteristic marks.'—*Hist. of Greek Literature*, vol. i. p. 12.

[b] Colet, a contemporary of Sir Thomas Elyot, in the preface to his Latin Grammar, said the best way to learn 'to speak and write clean Latin is busily to learn and read good Latin authors, and note how they wrote and spoke.' The Ciceronianus of Erasmus was written as a protest against the purely classical elegance for which some were at this time contending. 'The primary aim,' says Hallam, 'of these (dialogues) was to ridicule the fastidious purity of that sort of writers who would not use a case or a tense for which they could not find authority in the works of Cicero. A whole winter's night, they thought, was well spent in composing a single sentence; but even then it was to be revised over and over again. Hence they wrote little except elaborated epistles. One of their rules, he tells us, was never to speak Latin if they could help it, which must have seemed extraordinary in an age when it was the common language of scholars from different countries. *It is certain, indeed, that the practice cannot be favourable to very pure Latinity.*'—*Lit. of Europe*, vol. i. p. 324. 4th ed.

many rules and figures, and as longe a grammer as is latine or greke.[a] ⸢I wyll nat contende who, amonge them that do write grammers of greke, (whiche nowe all most be innumerable,) is the beste :[b] but that I referre to the discretion of a wyse mayster.⸥ Alway I wolde aduyse hym nat to detayne the childe to longe in that tedious labours, eyther in the greke or latyne grammer. For a gentyll wytte is there with sone fatigate.

Grammer beinge but an introduction to the understanding of autors, if it be made to longe or exquisite to the lerner, hit in a maner mortifieth his corage: And by that time he cometh to the most swete and pleasant redinge of olde autours, the sparkes of feruent desire of lernynge is extincte with the burdone of grammer, lyke as a lyttel fyre is sone quenched with a great heape of small stickes: so that it can neuer come to the principall logges where it shuld longe bourne in a great pleasaunt fire.

Nowe to folowe my purpose: after a fewe and quicke

---

[a] 'France was not destitute of a few obscure treatises at this time (1520-50), enough to lay the foundations of her critical literature. The complex rules of French metre were to be laid down, and the language was irregular in pronunciation, accent, and orthography. These meaner, but necessary, elements of correctness occupied three or four writers, of whom Goujet has made brief mention; Sylvius or Du Bois, who seems to have been the earliest writer on grammar; Stephen Dolet—better known by his unfortunate fate than by his essay on French punctuation; and though Goujet does not name him, we may add an Englishman, Palsgrave, who published a French Grammar in English as early as 1530.'—*Lit. of Europe*, vol. i. p. 449.

[b] 'The commentaries of Budæus stand not only far above anything else in Greek literature before the middle of the sixteenth century, but are alone in their class. What comes next, but at a vast interval, is the Greek Grammar of Clenardus, printed at Louvain in 1530. It was, however, much beyond Budæus in extent of circulation, and probably for this reason in general utility. This grammar was continually reprinted with successive improvements, and defective as especially in its original state it must have been, was far more perspicuous than that of Gaza, though not perhaps more judicious in principle. It was for a long time commonly used in France; and is, in fact, the principal basis of those lately or still in use among us; such as the Eton Greek Grammar. The proof of this is, that they follow Clenardus in most of his innovations, and too frequently for mere accident in the choice of instances.'—*Lit. of Europe*, vol. i. p. 330.

THE GOVERNOUR.

rules of grammer, immediately, or interlasynge hit therwith, wolde be redde to the childe Esopes [a] fables in greke: in whiche argument children moche do delite.[b] And surely it is a moche pleasant lesson and also profitable, as well for that it is elegant and brefe, (and nat withstanding it hath moche varietie in wordes, and therwith moche helpeth to the understandinge of greke) as also in those fables is included moche morall and politike wisedome. Wherfore, in the teachinge of them, the maister diligently must gader togyther those fables, whiche may be most accommodate to the aduauncement of some vertue, wherto he perceiueth the childe inclined: or to the rebuke of some vice, wherto he findeth his nature disposed. And therin the master ought to exercise his witte, as wel to make the childe plainly to understande the fable, as also declarynge the signification therof compendiously and to the purpose, fore sene alwaye, that, as well this lesson, as all other autours whiche the childe shall lerne, either greke

Esopes fables.

---

[a] Although Mr. Watt, in the *Bibliotheca Britannica*, states, with regard to Æsop, that 'there are, perhaps, few other books of which so many editions were printed prior to 1500,' it appears on perusing his own catalogue that this statement must be taken to apply exclusively to *foreign* editions of the Fables, for the only English edition published prior to the date above mentioned is that of Caxton's Translation, A.D. 1484; it is probable, therefore, that Sir Thomas Elyot's acquaintance with what passed in that age for the fables of Æsop was through the medium of a foreign edition. Modern scholars are of opinion that the fables now extant in prose bearing the name of Æsop are unquestionably spurious. Bentley wrote a dissertation to prove that the present collection is a mere plagiarism from Babrius.

[b] Professor Müller says, 'With regard to the *fable*, it is not improbable that in other countries, particularly in the north of Europe, it may have arisen from a child-like playful view of the character and habits of animals, which frequently suggest a comparison with the nature and incidents of human life. In Greece, however, it originated in an intentional travestie of human affairs. The αἶνος is, as its name denotes, an admonition or rather a reproof, veiled, either from fear of an excess of frankness or from love of fun and jest, beneath the fiction of an occurrence happening among beasts. . . . . It is always some action, some project, and commonly some absurd one, of the Samians, or Delphians, or Athenians, whose nature and consequences Æsop describes in a fable, and thus often exhibits the posture of affairs in a more lucid, just, and striking manner than could have been done by elaborate argument.'—*Hist. of Greek Literature*, vol. i. pp. 191, 192.

or latine, verse or prose, be perfectly had without the boke: wherby he shall nat only attaine plentie of the tonges called Copie, but also encrease and nourisshe remembrance wonderfully.[a]

The nexte lesson wolde be some quicke and mery dialoges, elect out of Luciane, whiche be without ribawdry,[b] or to moche skorning, for either of them is exactly to be eschewed, specially for a noble man, the one anoyeng the soule, the other his estimation concerning his grauitie.[c] The comedies of Aristophanes may be in the place of Luciane, and by reason that they be in metre[d] they be the sooner lerned by harte.[e] I dare make none other comparison betwene them

The ii. lesson to children. Lucian.

Arist.

---

[a] Compare Quintilian's remarks on this subject. 'Nam et omnis disciplina memoria constat, frustraque docemur, si quidquid audimus, præterfluat; et exemplorum, legum, responsorum, dictorum denique factorumque velut quasdam *copias*, quibus abundare, quasque in promptu semper habere debet orator, eadem illa vis repræsentat.'—*Instit. Orat.* lib. xi. cap. 2, § 1.

[b] Müller compares Lucian to Voltaire, but says that the former combined a more sincere, conscientious, and courageous love of the truth for its own sake, and rejects as productions of Lucian the *Philopatris*, the object of which is to cast discredit on Christianity, the *Loves*, the *Images*, and several other pieces which have been attributed to him.

[c] 'Suidas says, with a wonderful vehemence of bigotry, that he was torn to pieces by dogs, because he raved against the truth and blasphemed the name of Christ: "whence," he adds, "he paid an ample penalty in this life, and in the life to come he will inherit eternal fire with Satan." This violence of language and atrocity of statement probably rest on no better foundation than some ecclesiastical tradition, suggested by the belief that Lucian wrote the *Philopatris*, and was a malignant enemy of the faith. But it has long been the opinion of critics that Lucian is not the author of *Philopatris*; and there is no reason to believe that he was more specially opposed to Christianity than he was generally to the forms of oriental superstition, with which he had been led to class the history of our Saviour.'—*Hist. of Gr. Lit.* vol. iii. p. 220.

[d] Müller is of opinion that the great variety of metres employed in comedy were also distinguished by different sorts of gesticulation and delivery, and says: 'Aristophanes had the skill to convey by his rhythms sometimes the tone of romping merriment, at others that of vestal dignity.'—*Hist. of Gr. Lit.* vol. ii. p. 17.

[e] The high estimation in which the works of Aristophanes have been held for educational purposes should rather be attributed to the fact that they were 'based on the whole upon the common conversational language of the Athenians—the Attic dialect as it was current in their colloquial intercourse; comedy expresses

for offendinge the frendes of them both: but thus moche dare I say, that it were better that a childe shuld neuer rede any parte of Luciane than all Luciane.^a

I coulde reherce diuers other poetis whiche for mater and eloquence be very necessary, but I feare me to be to longe from noble Homere: from whom as from a fountaine proceded all eloquence and lernyng.[b] For in his bokes be contained, and moste perfectly expressed, nat only the documentes marciall and discipline of armes, but also incomparable wisedomes, and instructions for politike gouernaunce of people:[c] with the worthy commendation and laude of noble

Homerus.

---

this not only more purely than any other kind of poetry, but even more so than the old Attic prose.'—*Ibid.* p. 18. 'All this abuse and slander, and caricature, and criticism, was conveyed in the most exquisite and polished style: it was recommended by all the refinements of taste and the graces of poetry. It was because of this exquisite elegance and purity, which distinguished the style of the Attic comic writing, as well as its energetic power, that Quintilian recommends an orator to study, as the best model next to Homer, the writings of the old Attic comedy.'—Browne, *Hist. of Classical Literature*, vol. ii. p. 20.

[a] This remark would appear to be applicable *à fortiori* to Aristophanes, but modern scholars deprecate such squeamishness. Thus Dr. Donaldson says, 'So far from charging Aristophanes with immorality, we would repeat in the words which a great and a good man of our own days used when speaking of his antitype Rabelais, that the morality of his works is of the most refined and exalted kind, however little worthy of praise their manners may be; and, on the whole, we would fearlessly recommend any student, who is not so imbued with the lisping and drivelling mawkishness of the present day as to shudder at the ingredients with which the necessities of the time have forced the great comedian to dress up his golden truths, to peruse and re-peruse Aristophanes, if he would know either the full force of the Attic dialect, or the state of men and manners at Athens in the most glorious days of her history.'—*Theatre of the Greeks*, p. 195. 7th ed.

[b] So Quintilian says, 'Igitur, ut Aratus, *ab Jove incipiendum* putat, ita nos rite cœpturi ab *Homero* videmur: hic enim quemadmodum *ex oceano* dicit ipse *amnium vim fontiumque cursus initium capere*, omnibus eloquentiæ partibus exemplum et ortum dedit.'—*Instit. Orat.* lib. x. cap. 1, § 46.

[c] The writer last quoted says of Homer, 'in quo nullius non artis aut præcepta, aut certè non dubia vestigia reperiuntur.'—*Ibid.* lib. xii. cap. 11, § 21. Mr. Gladstone, in considering the political institutions of heroic Greece, embalmed in the poems of Homer, shows that the βουλή or Council, and the ἀγορή or Assembly, 'not only with the king made up the whole machinery both of civil and military administration for that period, but likewise supplied the essential germ, at least, of that form of constitution, on which the best governments of the continent of Europe have, (two

princis: where with the reders shall be so all inflamed, that they most feruently shall desire and coueite, by the imitation of their vertues, to acquire semblable glorie. For the whiche occasion, Aristotel, moost sharpest witted and excellent lerned Philosopher, as sone as he had receiued Alexander from kynge Philip his father, he before any other thynge taught hym the moost noble warkes of Homere: wherin Alexander founde suche swetenes and frute, that euer after he had Homere nat onely with hym in all his iournayes, but also laide hym under his pillowe whan he went to reste:[a] and often tymes wolde purposely wake some houres of the nyght, to take as it were his passe tyme with that mooste noble poete.[b]

For by the redinge of his warke called *Iliados*, where the assembly of the most noble grekes agayne Troy is recited with theyr affaires, he gathered courage and strength agayne his ennemies, wysdome, and eloquence, for consultations, and persuations to his people and army.[c] And by the other warke

of them within the last quarter of a century,) been modelled, with such deviations as experience has recommended, or the change of times has required. I mean the form of government by a threefold legislative body, having for one of its members and for its head, a single person, in whose hands the executive power of the state is lodged. This form has been eminently favoured in Christendom, in Europe, and in England; and it has even survived the passage of the Atlantic, and the transition, in the United States of America, to institutions which are not only republican but highly democratic.'—*Studies on Homer*, vol. iii. p. 94.

[a] Καὶ τὴν μὲν 'Ιλιάδα τῆς πολεμικῆς ἀρετῆς ἐφόδιον καὶ νομίζων καὶ ὀνομάζων ἔλαβε μὲν 'Αριστοτέλους διορθώσαντος, ἣν ἐκ τοῦ νάρθηκος καλοῦσιν, εἶχε δὲ ἀεὶ μετὰ τοῦ ἐγχειριδίου κειμένην ὑπὸ τὸ προσκεφάλαιον, ὡς 'Ονησίκρατος ἱστόρηκε.— Plutarch, *Alex.* 8.

[b] Neither Plutarch nor Quintus Curtius mentions this fact; it would appear, therefore, to be a gratuitous addition of the author, of which a somewhat similar instance was noticed, ante p. 47. Curtius, however, who tells the same story as Plutarch, says, 'Crebra autem lectione totum fere edidicit, ut nemo neque promptius eo familiariùsque uteretur, neque exactiùs de eo judicaret,' lib. i. cap. 4, § 6. Lucian, in the *Dialogues of the Dead*, makes Hannibal say, Καὶ ταῦτα ἔπραξα βάρβαρος ὢν καὶ ἀπαίδευτος παιδείας τῆς 'Ελληνικῆς καὶ οὔτε "Ομηρον ὥσπερ οὗτος ῥαψῳδῶν οὔτε ὑπ' 'Αριστοτέλει τῷ σοφιστῇ παιδευθείς, μόνῃ δὲ τῇ φύσει ἀγαθῇ χρησάμενος. Ταῦτα ἐστιν ἃ ἐγὼ 'Αλεξάνδρου ἀμείνων φημὶ εἶναι.—*Dial. Mort.* xii. 3. (385).

[c] Curtius says, 'Ex omnibus autem ejus carminibus maxime probabat versum

called *Odissea*, whiche recounteth the sondry aduentures of the wise Ulisses, he, by the example of Ulisses, apprehended many noble vertues, and also lerned to eskape the fraude and deceitfull imaginations of sondry and subtile crafty wittes.[a] Also there shall he lerne to ensearche and perceiue the maners and conditions of them that be his familiars, siftinge out (as I mought say) the best from the warst, wherby he may surely committe his affaires, and truste to euery persone after his vertues. Therfore I nowe conclude that there is no lesson for a yonge gentil man to be compared with Homere, if he be playnly and substancially expouned and declared by the mayster.[b]

Nat withstandinge, for as moche as the saide warkes be very longe, and do require therfore a great time to be all lerned

quo boni simul imperatoris, robustique militis laudes Agamemnoni tribuuntur, eumque præcipuum virtutis incitamentum, et veluti morum suorum magistrum habuit.' Lib. i. cap 4, § 7.

[a] Sir Thomas Elyot seems to have formed the same conception of the character of the hero of the *Odyssey* that Horace has summarised in the lines :

Rursus, quid virtus et quid sapientia possit
Utile proposuit nobis exemplar Ulyssen.—*Ep.* I. ii. 18.

Most modern writers have done full justice to the character of Ulysses: thus, while Col. Mure, in the *Language and Literature of Ancient Greece*, has elaborately analysed the original as portrayed by Homer, and shown what a complete metamorphosis it underwent at the hands of the Cyclic poets and Attic dramatists, Mr. Gladstone has pointed out the dual nature ascribed to Ulysses by Homer, and says, 'The depth of emotion in Ulysses is greater than in any other male character of the poems except Achilles ; only it is withdrawn from view because so much under the mastery of his wisdom.'—*Studies on Homer*, vol. iii. p. 599.

[b] A distinguished modern scholar says, 'Homer, if read at our public schools, is, and probably must be, read only, or in the main, for his diction and poetry (as commonly understood) even by the most advanced ; while to those less forward he is little more than a mechanical instrument for acquiring the beginning of real familiarity with the Greek tongue and its inflexions. If, therefore, he is to be read for his theology, history, ethics, politics, for his skill in the higher and more delicate parts of the poetic calling, for his never-ending lessons upon manners, arts, and society ; if we are to study in him the great map of that humanity which he so wonderfully unfolds to our gaze—he must be read at the *universities*, and read with reference to his deeper treasures. He is second to none of the poets of Greece as the poet of boys ; but he is far advanced before them all, even before Æschylus and Aristophanes, as the poet of men.'—Gladstone, *Studies on Homer*, vol. i. p. 19.

and kanned,ᵃ some latine autour wolde be therwith myxte, and specially Virgile; whiche, in his warke called *Eneidos*, is most lyke to Homere, and all moste the same Homere in latine.ᵇ Also, by the ioynynge to gether of those autours, the one shall be the better understande by the other.ᶜ And verily (as I before saide) none one autour serueth to so diuers witts as doth Virgile. For there is nat that affect or desire, wherto any childes fantasie is disposed, but in some of Virgils warkes may be founden matter therto apte and propise.ᵈ

Virgilius.

ᵃ See the Glossary.

ᵇ 'Perhaps Chapman has gone too far when he says, "Virgil hath nothing of his own, but only elocution; his invention, matter and form being all Homer's." Yet no small part of this sweeping proposition can undoubtedly be made good. With an extraordinary amount of admitted imitation and of obvious similarity on the surface, the *Æneid* stands, as to almost every fundamental particular, in the strongest contrast with the *Iliad*. As to metre, figures, names, places, persons, and times, the two works, where they do not actually concur, stand in as near relations one to another, as seems to be attainable without absolute identity of subject; yet it may be doubted whether any two great poems can be named, which are so profoundly discordant upon almost every point that touches their interior spirit; upon everything that relates to the truth of our nature, to the laws of thought and action, and to veracity in the management of the higher subjects, such as history, morality, polity, and religion.'—Gladstone, *Studies on Homer*, vol. iii. p. 502.

ᶜ 'Virgil is at once the copyist of Homer, and for the generality of educated men, his interpreter. In all modern Europe taken together, Virgil has had ten who read him; and ten who remember him, for one that Homer could show. Taking this in conjunction with the great extent of the ground they occupy in common, we may find reason to think that the traditional and public idea of Homer's works, throughout the entire sphere of the Western civilisation, has been formed, to a much greater degree than could at first be supposed, by the Virgilian copies from him.'—*Ibid.* vol. iii. p. 512.

ᵈ 'The variety of incidents,' says Professor Browne, 'the consummate skill in the arrangement of them, the interest which pervades both the plot and the episodes, fully compensate for the want of originality—a defect of which none but learned readers would be aware. What sweeter specimens can be found of tender pathos than the legend of Camilla, and the episode of Nisus and Euryalus? Where is the turbulence of uncurbed passions united with womanly unselfish fondness and queenlike generosity, painted with a more masterly hand than in the character of Dido? Where, even in the *Iliad*, are characters better sustained and more happily contrasted than the weak Latinus, the soldier-like Turnus, the

For what thinge can be more familiar than his bucolikes? [a] nor no warke so nighe approcheth to the commune daliaunce and maners of children, and the praty controuersies of the simple shepeherdes, therin contained, wonderfully reioyceth the childe that hereth hit well declared, as I knowe by myne owne experience. In his Georgikes [b] lorde what pleasaunt varietie

simple-minded Evander, the feminine and retiring Lavinia, the barbarian Mezentius, who to the savageness of a wild beast joined the natural instinct which warmed with the strongest affection for his son?...... In personification nothing is finer than Virgil's portraiture of Fame, except perhaps Spenser's Despair. In description the same genius which shone forth in the *Georgics* embellishes the *Æneid* also; and both the objects and the phenomena of nature are represented in language equally vivid and striking.'—*Hist. of Rom. Class. Lit.* pp. 260, 261.

[a] 'The characters in Virgil's Bucolics are Italians, in all their sentiments and feelings, acting the unreal and assumed part of Sicilian shepherds.....Even the scenery is Sicilian, and does not truthfully describe the tame neighbourhood of Mantua. So long as it is remembered that they are imitations of the Syracusan poet, we miss their nationality, and see at once that they are untruthful and out of keeping; and Virgil suffers in our estimation, because we naturally compare him with the original, whom he professes to imitate, and we cannot but be aware of his inferiority; but if we can once divest ourselves of the idea of the outward form which he has chosen to adopt and forget the personality of the characters, we can feel for the wretched outcast exiled from a happy though humble home, and be touched by the simple narrative of their disappointed loves and child-like woes; can appreciate the delicately veiled compliments paid by the poet to his patron; can enjoy the inventive genius and poetical power which they display; and can be elevated by the exalted sentiments which they sometimes breathe. We feel that it is all an illusion; but we willingly permit ourselves to be transported from the matter of fact realities of a hard and prosaic world.'—*Hist. of Rom. Class. Lit.* p. 244-246.

[b] A modern scholar says, 'The great merit of the Georgics consists in *their varied digressions*, interesting episodes, and sublime bursts of descriptive vigour, which are interspersed throughout the poem. The first book treats of tillage; the second of orchards; the subject of the third, which is *the noblest and most spirited of them, is the care of horses and cattle*; and the fourth, which is the most pleasing and interesting, describes the natural instincts as well as the management of bees...... Dunlop has well observed that Virgil's descriptions are more like landscape-painting than any by his predecessors, whether Greek or Roman; and that it is a remarkable fact that landscape-painting was first introduced in his time. Pliny, in his *Natural History*, informs us that Ludius, who flourished in the lifetime of Augustus, invented the most delightful style of painting, compositions introducing porticoes, gardens, groves, hills, fish-ponds, rivers, and other pleasing objects, enlivened by carriages, animals, and figures. Thus perhaps art inspired poetry.'— Browne, *Hist. of Rom. Class. Lit.* pp. 255, 256, 263.

there is : the diuers graynes, herbes, and flowres that be there described, that, reding therin, hit semeth to a man to be in a delectable gardeine or paradise. What ploughe man knoweth so moche of husbandry as there is expressed? who, delitynge in good horsis, shall nat be therto more enflamed, reding there of the bredyng, chesinge, and kepyng, of them? In the declaration whereof Virgile leaueth farre behynde hym all breders, hakneymen,[a] and skosers.[b]

Is there any astronomer that more exactly setteth out the ordre and course of the celestiall bodies : or that more truely dothe deuine in his pronostications of the tymes of the yere, in their qualities, with the future astate of all thinges prouided by husbandry, than Virgile doth recite in that warke?[c]

If the childe haue a delite in huntyng, what pleasure shall he take of the fable of Aristeus :[d] semblably in the huntynge

[a] See the Glossary.   [b] See the Glossary.

[c] Professor Conington says, ' In the Phænomena and Diosmeia, or Prognostics, of Aratus, we have a specimen of the didactic poetry of the earlier Alexandrian school. Cicero, who translated both works, speaks of him in a well-known passage as a writer who, though ignorant of astronomy, made an excellent poem about the heavenly bodies.......Of the two poems now in question, if they are to be regarded as two, and not as one falling into two parts, Virgil has been but sparingly indebted to the first, the plan of the Georgics not leading him to attempt any description of the stars as they appear in heaven, which is the subject of the Phænomena. But the other work, the Diosmeia, has been laid under heavy contributions to furnish materials for that account of the prognostics of the weather which occupies the latter part of Virgil's first book......The whole of the prognostics, signs of wind, signs of rain, signs of fair weather, signs from sounds by land or by sea, signs from the flight, the motion, or the cry of birds, signs from the actions of beasts, reptiles, and insects, signs from the flames of lamps, and the appearances on water, signs from the sun and moon at their rising and at their setting, are all given nearly as Aratus has given them, though the manner in which they are dealt with is Virgil's own.'—*Introduction to Georgics*, pp. 126, 127.

[d] The story of Aristæus occupies a great portion of the 4th Georgic, v. 317-558. Professor Conington says, ' Whence Virgil derived the story is unknown. Heyne thinks, from the elaboration, that it must have been closely imitated from some Alexandrian writer—possibly from a poem which was extant under the name of Eumelus Βουγονία, as we learn from the *Chronicon* of Eusebius. A brief version of the tale is given by Ovid.'—*Ubi supra.* The different accounts of Aristæus, who once was a mortal and ascended to the dignity of a god through the benefits he had conferred upon mankind, seem to have arisen in different places and independently of

of Dido and Eneas, whiche is discriued moste elegantly in his boke of Eneidos.[a] If he haue pleasure in wrastling, rennyng, or other lyke exercise, where shall he se any more plesant esbatementes,[b] than that whiche was done by Eurealus and other troyans, whiche accompanyed Eneas?[c] If he take solace in hearynge minstrelles, what minstrell may be compared to Jopas, whiche sange before Dido and Eneas?[d] or to blinde Demodocus, that played and sange moste swetely at the dyner, that the kynge Alcinous made to Ulisses:[e] whose dities and melodie excelled as farre the songes of our minstrelles, as Homere and Virgile excelle all other poetes.[f]

---

one another, so that they referred to several distinct beings, who were subsequently identified and united into one. Aristæus is one of the most beneficent divinities in ancient mythology; he was worshipped as the protector of flocks and shepherds, of vine and olive plantations; he taught men to hunt and keep bees, and averted from the fields the burning heat of the sun: he was θεὸς νόμιος, ἀγρεύς, ἀλεξητήρ.

- [a] *Æneid*, iv. 117 foll.   [b] See the Glossary.
- [c] *Æneid*, v. 291 foll.
- [d]
  'Citharâ crinitus Iopas
  Personat auratâ, docuit quem maximus Atlas.
  Hic canit errantem lunam solisque labores;
  Unde hominum genus et pecudes; unde imber et ignes;
  Arcturum pluviasque Hyadas geminosque Triones;
  Quid tantum Oceano properent se tingere soles
  Hiberni, vel quæ tardis mora noctibus obstet;
  Ingeminant plausu Tyrii, Troesque sequuntur.'—*Æn.* i. 740-747.

The name 'Iopas' does not occur anywhere else in Virgil, and Professor Conington suggests that if this is not an error for 'Iarbas,' we must suppose that Virgil here, as elsewhere, has chosen to take a hint from chroniclers, to whom it did not suit him to incur a larger debt. The above passage is referred to by Quintilian lib. i. cap. 10, § 10.

- [e] *Odyssey*, viii. 62, foll.
- [f]
  'Ages elapsed ere Homer's lamp appeared,
  And ages ere the Mantuan swan was heard;
  To carry nature lengths unknown before,
  To give a Milton birth, asked ages more.'—Cowper's *Table Talk*.

These lines are quoted by Mr. Gladstone in the 3rd volume of his *Studies on Homer*, where he enters at great length into the question of the relative position of Homer to some of his successors in epic poetry, in particular Virgil and Tasso. With regard to the former his opinion is thus graphically expressed: 'Homer walks in the open day, Virgil by lamplight. Homer gives us figures that breathe

THE GOVERNOUR. 65

If he be more desirous, (as the most parte of children be,) to here thinges marueilous and exquisite, whiche hath in it a visage of some thinges incredible, wherat shall he more wonder, than whan he shall beholde Eneas folowe Sibille in to helle?[a] What shal he more drede, than the terrible visages of Cerberous,[b] Gorgon,[c] Megera,[d] and other furies and monsters? Howe shall he abhorre tyranny, fraude, and auarice, whan he doth se the paynes of duke Theseus,[e] Prometheus,[f] Sisiphus,[g] and suche other tourmented for their dissolute and vicious lyuyng. Howe glad soone after shall he be, whan he shall beholde, in the pleasant feldes of Elisius,[h] the soules of

---

and move, Virgil usually treats us to waxwork. Homer has the full force and play of the drama. Virgil is essentially operatic. From Virgil back to Homer is a greater distance than from Homer back to life.' With regard to the latter he says, 'There is, it must be confessed, a great and sharp descent from the stature of Homer, as a creative poet, to that of Tasso. Yet he, too, is a classic of Italy, and a classic of the world; and if for a moment we feel it a disparagement to his coun try that she suffers in this one comparison, let her soothe her ruffled recollection by the consciousness that though Tasso has not become a rival to Homer, yet he shares this failure with every epic writer of every land.'—pp. 512, 554.

[a] *Æneid*, vi. 42-55.   [b] *Æn.* vi. 417-423.

[c] 'Gorgones, Harpyiæque et forma tricorporis umbræ.'—*Æn.* vi. 289.

[d] 'Dicuntur geminæ pestes cognomine Diræ
Quas et Tartaream Nox intempesta Megæram
Uno eodemque tulit partu, paribusque revinxit
Serpentum spiris, ventosasque addidit alas.'—*Æn.* xii. 845—848.

[e] 'Sedet æternumque sedebit
Infelix Theseus.'—*Æn.* vi. 617.

Professor Conington says that the ordinary legend of Theseus was that having been fixed in a chair in the shades for his attempt to carry off Persephone, he was released by Heracles, leaving some of his flesh behind him; Virgil, however, has varied the story or followed another.

[f] 'Caucasiasque refert volucres furtumque Promethi.'—*Ecl.* vi. 42.

Hesiod and Æschylus are the authorities for the well known story of Prometheus.

[g] 'Saxum ingens volvunt alii.'—*Æn.* vi. 616.

The traditional punishment of Sisyphus.

[h] 'Devenere locos lætos et amœna vireta
Fortunatorum nemorum sedesque beatas
*   *   *   *   *   *

noble princes and capitaines which, for their vertue, and labours in aduancing the publike weales of their countrayes, do lyue eternally in pleasure inexplicable. And in the laste bokes of Eneidos shall he finde matter to ministre to hym audacite, valiaunt courage, and policie, to take and susteyne noble enterprises, if any shall be nedefull for the assailynge of his enemies.[a]

Finally (as I haue saide) this noble Virgile, like to a good norise, giueth to a childe, if he wyll take it, euery thinge apte for his witte and capacitie: wherfore he is in the ordre of lernyng to be preferred before any other autor latine.[b] I wolde set

> Hic genus antiquum Teucri, pulcherrima proles,
> Magnanimi heroes, nati melioribus annis,
> Ilusque Assaracusque et Troiæ Dardanus auctor.
> * * * * *
> Hic manus ob patriam pugnando vulnera passi,
> Quique sacerdotes casti, dum vita manebat,
> Quique pii vates et Phœbo digna locuti,
> Inventas aut qui vitam excoluere per artes,
> Quique sui memores alios fecere merendo,
> Omnibus his niveâ cinguntur tempora vittâ.'—*Æn.* vi. 638 foll.

According to Professor Conington, Elysium is not a natural place for purgation; it is evidently the everlasting reward of a good life, not a place of temporary sojourn previous to a return to earth. And this view seems to have been anticipated by our author in the text.

[a] Evidently alluding to such passages as that in which Virgil narrates the courageous example exhibited by the heroine Camilla, who undertook to engage the whole Trojan army, and the spirit-stirring speech addressed by her to the commander of the Rutulian troops.—*Æn.* xi. 502 foll.

The 'policie' probably refers to the description of the stratagem devised by Turnus for the purpose of surprising the enemy's forces.—*Æn.* xi. 511 foll.

[b] By Saint Augustine he is called 'Poeta magnus omniumque præclarissimus atque optimus.' But though this tribute is as exaggerated as that paid by Propertius, who considered Virgil superior to Homer, it is not difficult to understand the preference expressed by the author in the text. 'Want of originality,' says Professor Browne 'was not considered a blemish in an age, the taste of which, notwithstanding all its merits, was very artificial; whilst the exquisite polish and elegance which constitute the charm of Latin poetry recommended it both for admiration and imitation. Hence English poets have been deeply indebted to the Romans for their most happy thoughts, and our native literature is largely imbued with a Virgilian and Horatian spirit. The *Georgics* have been frequently taken

nexte unto hym two bokes of Ouid, the one called *Metamorphosios*,[a] whiche is as moche to saye as, chaungynge of men in to other figure or fourme : the other is intitled *De fastis* :[b] where the ceremonies of the gentiles, and specially the Romanes, be expressed : bothe right necessary for the understandynge of other poetes. But by cause there is litell other lernyng in them, concernyng either vertuous maners or policie, I suppose it were better that as fables and ceremonies happen to come in a lesson, it were declared abundantly by the maister than that in the saide two bokes, a longe tyme shulde be spente and almost lost : which mought be better employed on suche autors that do minister both eloquence, ciuile policie, and exhortation to vertue. Wherfore in his place let us bringe in

as a model for imitation, and our descriptive poets have drawn largely from this source.'—*Hist. of Rom. Class. Lit.* p. 256. From the expressions in the text it would rather seem as if the author's grounds for recommending Virgil as a text book were the same as those of his contemporary Sturm, the rector of the college at Strasbourg, who, we are told, 'asserted that the proper end of school education is eloquence, or in modern phrase a masterly command of language ; and, at the same time, assumed that Latin is the language in which eloquence is to be acquired.' One of the most recent, and, at the same time, most severe critics of Virgil, is nevertheless constrained to call the *Æneid* ' perhaps, as a whole, the most majestic poem that the European mind has in any age produced.'—*Studies on Homer*, vol. iii. p. 503.

[a] Professor Browne calls this poem 'Ovid's noblest effort :' and says that in it ' may be traced that study and learning by which the Roman poets made all the treasures of Greek literature their own. In fact, a more extensive knowledge of Greek mythology may be derived from it than from the Greeks themselves, because the books which were the sources of his information are unfortunately no longer extant.'—*Hist. of Rom. Class. Lit.* p. 322.

[b] 'The *Fasti* is an antiquarian poem on the Roman Calendar. It is a beautiful specimen of simple narrative in verse, and displays, more than any of his works, his power of telling a story, without the slightest effort, in poetry as well as prose. As a profound study of Greek mythology and poetry had furnished the materials for his *Metamorphoses* and other poems, so in this he drew principally from the legends which had been preserved by the old poets and annalists of his own country.'—*Ibid.* p. 323. 'With these fair and sounding verses,' says Dr. Merivale, 'the poet satisfied the ecclesiastical spirit of the times, which leant with fond reliance on forms and traditions, and was less a thing to be felt than to be talked about.'—*Hist. of Rome*, vol. iv. p. 605.

Horace, in whom is contayned moche varietie of lernynge and quickenesse of sentence.[a]

This poet may be enterlaced with the lesson of *Odissea* of Homere, wherin is declared the wonderfull prudence and fortitude of Ulisses in his passage from Troy. And if the childe were induced to make versis by the imitation of Virgile and Homere, it shulde ministre to hym moche dilectation and courage to studie:[b] ne the making of versis is nat discom-

---

[a] 'It is in his inimitable Odes that the genius of Horace as a poet is especially displayed. They have never been equalled in beauty of sentiment, gracefulness of language, and melody of versification. *They comprehend every variety of subject suitable to the lyric muse.* They rise without effort to the most elevated topics—the grandest subjects of history, the most gorgeous legends of mythology, the noblest aspirations of patriotism; they descend to the simplest joys and sorrows of every-day life. At one time they burn with indignation, at another they pour forth accents of the tenderest emotions. They present in turn every phase of the author's character; some remind us that he was a philosopher and a satirist; and although many are sensuous and self-indulgent, they are full of gentleness, kindness, and spirituality '—*Hist. of Rom. Class. Lit.* p. 291.

[b] Verse composition formed an important part of the curriculum in Germany as well as in England in the sixteenth century; thus, as Mr. C. S. Parker tells us, Melanchthon, in his report on schools (1528), recommended this exercise as 'a great help to understanding the writings of others, makes the boys rich in words, and gives dexterity in many things;' and while Sturm presided over the school at Strasburg (1538–1583) we find that 'the practice of composition is incessant. Verses are begun in the fifth; the upper forms transpose odes of Horace and Pindar into other metres, and produce poems of their own. . . . Materials as well as models for composition are furnished by constantly reading and learning by heart the best authors, and by systematic excerption of phrases and "flowers."' At Eton, under Udall, in 1560, Latin verses were written on subjects such as might still be set in the lower forms. What a change has come over the spirit of modern schoolmasters and tutors with regard to verse-making as an educational implement we may learn from Mr. Sidgwick's essay on the *Theory of Classical Education*, in which he says, 'Perhaps the most singular assumption is that it is an essential part of the study of Greek and Latin to cultivate the faculty of writing what ought to be poetry in these tongues . . . the imitation that is encouraged at schools in the process of verse-writing is the very worst sort of imitation; it is something which, if it were proposed in respect of any other models than these, we should at once reject as intolerably absurd.' But 'vixere fortes ante Agamemnona,' and as the most recent opponent of the system reminds us, ' Names of the most splendid eminence over a space of two centuries can be quoted in its condemnation; Cowley, Milton, Bacon, Locke, Coleridge, Wordsworth, Macaulay, Thirlwall, Ruskin, Mill—some of our most learned poets, some of our deepest meta-

mended in a noble man : sens the noble Augustus and almost all the olde emperours made bokes in versis.[a]

The two noble poetis Silius,[b] and Lucane,[c] be very expedient to be lerned : for the one setteth out the emulation in qualities and prowesse of two noble and valiant capitaynes, one, enemy to the other, that is to say, Silius writeth of Scipio the Romane, and Haniball duke of

Silius. Lucanus.

physicians, some of our most classical historians, some of our most brilliant scholars —are unanimous in speaking of it with indifference or with contempt.'

[a] 'Poeticam summatim attigit. Unus liber extat, scriptus ab eo hexametris versibus, cujus et argumentum et titulus est "Sicilia." Extat alter æque modicus "Epigrammatum," quæ fere tempore balnei meditabatur.'—Sueton. *Octavius*, 85.

[b] The great work of Silius Italicus, entitled *Punica*, has been described by a modern writer as 'the dullest and most tedious poem in the Latin language.' Professor Browne says, 'the criticism of Pliny the Younger is upon the whole just, "*Scribebat carmina majori curâ quàm ingenio*;" for although it is impossible to read his poem with pleasure as a whole, his versification is harmonious, and will often in point of smoothness bear comparison with that of Virgil.'—*Hist. of Rom. Class. Lit.* p. 464. The *Punica* was first brought to light after the revival of letters by Poggio, the Florentine, who was born in 1381, and died in 1459, having been discovered by him while attending the Council of Constance, 1414-1418 It was, perhaps, owing to its comparatively recent acquisition that Sir Thomas Elyot attached what may appear to modern scholars a somewhat exaggerated importance to this 'ponderous' work. Niebuhr calls him 'the most wretched of all poets,' and says that he 'made only a paraphrase of Livy.'

[c] By modern writers Lucan has been assigned a place at the head of the epic poets who flourished during the silver age. Professor Browne considers the *Pharsalia* (the only one of the poet's works which survives) to be defaced with great faults and blemishes. 'Its arrangement,' he says, 'is that of annals, and therefore it wants the unity of an epic poem ; it has not the connectedness of history, because the poet naturally selected only the most striking and romantic incidents, and yet, notwithstanding these defects in the plan, the historical pictures themselves are beautifully drawn. The characters of Cæsar and Pompey, for example, are masterpieces...... Description forms the principal feature in the poetry of Lucan ; it occupies more than one-half of the *Pharsalia*, so that it might almost as appropriately be termed a descriptive as an epic poem...... Owing to the enthusiasm with which Lucan throws himself into this kind of writing, he abounds in minute detail...... He is not content, as Virgil is, with a sketch— with broad lights and shadows ; he delights in a finished picture ; he possesses the power of placing his subject strongly before the eyes, leaving little or nothing for the imagination to supply...... Virgil sketches, Lucan paints ; the latter describes physically, the former philosophically.'—*Hist. of Rom. Class. Lit.* pp. 455, 459.

Cartaginensis: Lucane declareth a semblable mater, but moche more lamentable: for as moche as the warres were ciuile, and, as it were, in the bowelles of the Romanes, that is to say, under the standerdes of Julius Cesar and Pompei.

Hesiodus, in greke, is more briefe than Virgile, where he writeth of husbandry, and doth nat rise so high in philosophie, but is fuller of fables: and therfore is more illecebrous.[a]

And here I conclude to speke any more of poetis, necessary for the childehode of a gentill man: for as moche as these, I doubt nat, will suffice untill he passe the age of xiii yeres. In which time childhode declineth, and reason waxeth rype, and deprehendeth thinges with a more constant iugement. Here I wolde shulde be remembred, that I require nat that all these warkes shud be throughly radde of a childe in this tyme, whiche were almost impossible. But I only desire that they haue, in euery of the saide bokes, so moche instruction that they may take therby some profite.

[a] A modern writer has used very similar language with regard to Hesiod. 'As the poet's object was not to describe the charms of a country life, but to teach all the means of honest gain which were then open to the Ascræan countryman, he proceeds after having completed the subject of husbandry, to treat with equal detail that of navigation ..... All these precepts relating to the works of industry interrupt somewhat suddenly the succession of economical rules for the management of a family. ..... Mythical narratives, fables, descriptions, and moral apophthegms partly of a proverbial kind, are ingeniously chosen and combined so as to illustrate and enforce the principal idea. .... The opinion that Hesiod received the form of his poetry from Homer cannot well be reconciled with the wide difference which appears in the spirit and character of the two styles of epic poetry...... The Homeric poems among all the forms in which poetry can appear possess in the greatest degree what in modern times is called *objectivity*; that is, a complete abandonment of the mind to the *object*, without any intervening consciousness of the situation or circumstances of the *subject*, or the individual himself. Homer's mind moves in a world of lofty thoughts and energetic actions, far removed from the wants and necessities of the present. There can be no doubt that this is the noblest and most perfect style of composition and the best adapted to epic poetry. *Hesiod, however, never soars to this height.* He prefers to show us his own domestic life, and to make us feel its wants and privations.'—*Hist. of Gr. Lit.* vol. i. pp. 110, 112, 113.

Than the childes courage, inflamed by the frequent redynge of noble poetes, dayly more and more desireth to haue experience in those thinges, that they so vehemently do commende in them, that they write of. *Poetis defended and preysed.*

Leonidas, the noble kynge of Spartanes, beinge ones demaunded, of what estimation in poetry Tirtæus, (as he supposed,) was, it is writen that he answeryng saide, that, for sterynge the myndes of yonge men he was excellent, for as moche as they, being meued with his versis, do renne in to the bataile, regardyng no perile, as men all inflamed in martiall courage.*

And whan a man is comen to mature yeres, and that reason in him is confirmed with serious lernyng and longe experience, than shall he, in redyng tragoedies, execrate and abhorre the intollerable life of tyrantes : and shall contemne the foly and dotage expressed by poetes lasciuious.

Here wyll I leaue to speake of the fyrste parte of a noble mannes studie : and nowe wyll I write of the seconde parte, which is more serious, and containeth in it sondry maners of lernynge.

* Λεωνίδαν μὲν γὰρ τὸν παλαιὸν λέγουσιν ἐπερωτηθέντα, ποῖός τις αὐτῷ φαίνεται ποιητὴς γεγονέναι Τυρταῖος, εἰπεῖν· 'Ἀγαθὸς νέων ψυχὰς κακκανῆν.' Ἐμπιπλάμενοι γὰρ ὑπὸ τῶν ποιημάτων ἐνθουσιασμοῦ παρὰ τὰς μάχας ἠφείδουν ἑαυτῶν.—Plut. *Cleomenes*, 2. Compare Horace in the *Ars Poetica* :

'Tyrtæusque mares animos in Martia bella
Versibus exacuit.'

K. O. Müller says : 'When the Spartans were on a campaign, it was their custom, after the evening meal, when the pæan had been sung in honour of the gods, to recite these elegies. On these occasions the whole mess did not join in the chant, but individuals vied with each other in repeating the verses in a manner worthy of their subject. This kind of recitation was so well adapted to the elegy that it is highly probable that Tyrtæus himself first published his elegies in this manner.'— *Hist. of Gr. Lit.* vol. i. p. 150. It may be observed that the practice of singing patriotic songs has been retained by soldiers down to our own time ; thus the 'Wacht am Rhein' was constantly heard at Prussian bivouacs during the campaign of 1870, whilst the 'Marseillaise' was the favourite song of the French army.

CHAPTER XI.

The moste commodious and necessary studies succedyng ordinatly the lesson of poetes.

AFTER that xiv. yeres be passed of a childes age, his maister if he can, or some other, studiouslye exercised in the arte of an oratour, shall firste rede to hym some what of that parte of logike that is called *Topica*,[a] eyther of Cicero, or els of that noble clerke of Almaine, which late floured, called Agricola:[b] whose warke prepareth inuention, tellynge the places from whens an argument for the profe of any mater may be taken with litle studie: and that lesson, with moche and diligent lernyng, hauyng mixte there with none other exercise, will in the space of halfe a yere be perfectly kanned.

Logike.
Topica.

Immediately after that, the arte of Rhetorike wolde be semblably taught, either in greke, out of Hermo-

Rhetorik.

---

[a] 'C. Trebatius, the celebrated juriconsult, having found himself unable to comprehend the *Topics* of Aristotle, which treat of the invention of arguments, and having failed in procuring any explanation from a celebrated rhetorician whose aid he sought, had frequently applied to Cicero for information and assistance. Cicero's incessant occupations prevented him for a long time from attending to these solicitations; but when he was sailing towards Greece, the summer after Cæsar's death, he was reminded of Trebatius by the sight of Velia, a city with which the lawyer was closely connected, and accordingly, while on board ship, he drew up from recollection the work called *Topica* and dispatched it to his friend from Rhegium, B.C. 44. It is in fact an abstract of the original expressed in plain familiar terms, illustrated by examples derived chiefly from Roman law instead of from Greek philosophy. The editio princeps is believed to have been published at Venice about A.D. 1472.'—Smith's *Dict. of Biography*.

[b] Rodolph Agricola of Groningen was born in 1442. There are but two works of his extant, *De Inventione Dialecticâ*, printed at Louvain, 1516, and an abridgment of ancient history under the title of *Agricolæ Lucubrationes*, published at Cologne in 1539. About 1482 Agricola was invited to the court of the elector-palatine at Heidelberg. He seems not to have been engaged in public instruction, but passed the remainder of his life, unfortunately too short—for he died in 1485—in diffusing and promoting a taste for literature among his contemporaries. 'No German,' says Hallam, 'wrote in so pure a style or possessed so large a portion of classical learning.' Erasmus calls him 'virum divini pectoris, eruditionis reconditæ, stylo minimè vulgari, solidum, nervosum, elaboratum, compositum. In Italiâ summus esse poterat, nisi Germaniam prætulisset.'

gines,[a] or of Quintilian[b] in latine, begynnyng at the thirde boke,[c] and instructyng diligently the childe in that parte of rhethorike, principally, whiche concerneth persuation :[d] for as moche as it is most apte for consultations. There can be no shorter instruction of Rhetorike than the treatise that Tulli wrate unto his sonne, which boke is named the partition of rhetorike.[e] And in good faythe, to speake boldly that I thinke : for him that nedeth nat, or doth nat desire, to be an exquisite oratour, the litle boke made by the famous Erasmus, (whom all gentill wittis are bounden to thanke and

Erasmus.

[a] This celebrated rhetorician flourished in the reign of Marcus Aurelius. His works, five in number, which are still extant, form together a complete system of rhetoric, and were for a long time used in all the rhetorical schools as manuals. It may be mentioned as an interesting fact that the treatise Περὶ τῶν Στάσεων was first printed at Paris the same year in which *The Governour* was published. The work treats of the points and questions which an orator in civil cases has to take into his consideration, and is a useful guide to those who prepare themselves for speaking in the courts of justice. Another treatise, Περὶ Ἰδεῶν, was also printed at Paris in the year 1531, and no doubt Sir Thomas Elyot had access to both these works.

[b] A modern writer considers Quintilian far superior to Cicero as a teacher, although he was inferior to him as an orator, and says, ' He has left, as a monument of his taste and genius, a text-book of the science and art of nations as well as a masterly sketch of the eloquence of antiquity.'—*Hist. of Rom. Class. Lit.* p. 540. His works were discovered by Poggio in the monastery of St. Gall, near Constance, during the sitting of the celebrated council, 1418. Niebuhr considers Quintilian the restorer of a good and pure taste in Roman literature.

[c] ' In the third book, after a short notice of the principal writers on rhetoric, he divides his subjects into five parts, viz. invention, arrangement, style, memory both natural and artificial, and delivery or action. Closely following Aristotle, he then discusses the three kinds of oratory, the demonstrative, deliberative, and judicial.'—*Hist. of Rom. Class. Lit.* p. 537.

[d] ' Affectus ut quae maxime postulat ; nam et concitanda et lenienda frequenter est ira, et ad metum, cupiditatem, odium, conciliationem, impellendi animi ; nonnunquam etiam movenda miseratio, sive ut auxilium obsessis feratur, *suadere* oportebit, sive sociae civitatis eversionem deflebimus . . . quare in suadendo et dissuadendo tria primum spectanda erunt—Quid sit de quo deliberetur ; Qui sint qui deliberent ; Qui sit qui suadeat.'—*Instit. Orat.* lib. iii. cap. 8, §§ 12, 15.

[e] The *De Partitione Oratoriâ* has been correctly described as a catechism of Rhetoric, according to the method of the Middle Academy, by way of question and answer, drawn up by Cicero for the instruction of his son Marcus. The earliest edition of this work in a separate form which bears a date is that by Gabriel Fontana, printed A.D. 1472. Smith's *Dict. of Biography.*

supporte), whiche he calleth *Copiam Verborum et Rerum*,[a] that is to say, plentie of wordes and maters, shall be sufficient.]

Isocrates,[b] concerning the lesson of oratours, is euery where wonderfull profitable, hauynge almost as many wyse sentences as he hath wordes: and with that is so swete[c] and delectable to rede, that, after him, almost all other seme unsauery and

[a] The full title of this work is *De Duplici Copiâ Verborum ac Rerum Commentarii duo.* It was written expressly for Colet's school, as we learn from the preface, which bears the date 1512, though the work itself was probably not published till two years later. The author says: ' Ego sanè non ignarus et quantum Angliæ debeam publicè et quantopere tibi (Colet) privatim sim obnoxius, officii mei sum arbitratus literarium aliquod munusculum in ornamentum scholæ tuæ conferre. Itaque duos novos *De Copiâ* commentarios novæ scholæ nuncupare visum est opus, videlicet cum aptum pueritiæ tum non infrugiferum ni fallor futurum; sed quantum habeat eruditionis, quantumve sit utilitatis allaturus hic labor meus, aliorum esto judicium.' St. Paul's school was founded 1510. In a letter (Epist. lib. x. 18) from Erasmus to Colet, dated Cambridge, Oct. 29, 1513, the former says: ' In absolvendâ *Copiâ* meâ *nunc* sum totus, ut jam ænigmatis instar videri possit me simul et in mediâ *copiâ* et in summâ versari inopiâ. Atque *utinam liceat utramque pariter finire*; nam *Copiæ* brevi finem imponam, si modo Musæ melius fortunarint studia quam hactenus Fortuna rem. Atque id quidem in causâ fuit quo et brevius et indiligentius tuis literis responderim.' Mr. Seebohm (*Oxford Reformers*, p. 216, n.) says the *De Copiâ* was printed May, 1512, but this is evidently a mistake, and he was probably misled by the date at the end of the preface mentioned above. Mr. Seebohm gives, however, a reference to the letter No. 4528, in Mr. Brewer's collection, which should have precluded the possibility of such an error, inasmuch as the date assigned by the latter to Erasmus's letter, corresponds with that given above. The book was several times reprinted.

[b] 'Over and above the great care which he took about the formation of his style, Isocrates had a decided genius for the art of rhetoric; and when we read his periods, we may well believe what he tells us, that the Athenians, alive as they were to beauties of this kind, felt a real enthusiasm for his writings, and friends and enemies vied in imitating their magic elegance. When we read aloud the panegyrical orations of Isocrates, we feel that, although they want the vigour and profundity of Thucydides or Aristotle, there is a power in them which we miss in every former work of rhetoric—a power which works upon the mind as well as upon the ear; we are carried along by a full stream of harmonious diction, which is strikingly different from the rugged sentences of Thucydides and the meagre style of Lysias. The services which Isocrates has performed in this respect reach far beyond the limits of his own school. Without his reconstruction of the style of Attic oratory we could have had no Demosthenes and no Cicero; and through these the school of Isocrates has extended its influence even to the oratory of our own day.'—Müller, *Hist. of Gr. Lit.* vol. ii. p. 153.

[c] Cicero, *De Orat.* iii. 7, attributes 'sweetness' to Isocrates.

THE GOVERNOUR. 75

tedious : and in persuadynge, as well a prince, as a priuate persone, to vertue, in two very litle and compendious warkes, wherof he made the one to kynge Nicocles,[a] the other to his frende Demonicus, wolde be perfectly kanned, and had in continual memorie.

Demosthenes[b] and Tulli,[c] by the consent of all lerned men,

[a] The tract *Nicocles* is an exhortation to the Salaminians to obey their new ruler; and his harangue *To Nicocles* is an exhortation addressed to the young ruler on the duties and virtues of a sovereign. — *Hist. of Gr. Lit.* vol. ii. p. 150, n.

[b] 'The style and characteristics of Demosthenes have furnished the ancient critic Dionysius of Halicarnassus with the materials for a special treatise; and a great modern orator, Lord Brougham, has made this master of ancient eloquence the theme of more than one glowing tribute of praise. As Thucydides was *the* historian and Homer *the* poet of the old grammarians in a special and emphatic sense, so Demosthenes was their orator *par excellence*. Hermogenes places him at the head of all political speakers, and the same was the opinion of Theon. Cicero calls him the prince of orators, and declares that nothing was wanting to his perfection. . . . It appears to us that the main characteristic of the eloquence of Demosthenes—that, in fact, which explains the wonderful effects produced by it on popular assemblies—is this, that he used the common language of his age and country, that he took the greatest pains in choosing and arranging his words, that he aimed at the utmost conciseness, making epithets, even common adjectives, do the work of a whole sentence; and that he was enabled by a perfect delivery and action to give the proper emphasis and the full effect to the terms which he had selected with so much care, so that a sentence composed of ordinary terms sometimes smote with the weight of a sledge-hammer.'—*Hist. of Gr. Lit.* vol. ii. pp. 342, 344. Almost exactly the same thing has been said of an eminent living speaker, Mr. Bright.

[c] Professor Browne says : 'As oratory gave to Latin prose-writing its elegance and dignity, Cicero is not only the representative of the flourishing period of the language, but also the instrumental cause of its arriving at perfection. Circumstances may have been favourable to his influence. The national mind may have been in that stage of progress which only required a master-genius to develop it; but still it was he who gave a fixed character to the language, who showed his countrymen what eloquence especially was in its combination of the precepts of art and the principles of natural beauty; what the vigour of Latin was, and of what elegance and polish it was capable. . . . . . Compared with the dignified energy and majestic vigour of the Athenian orator, the Asiatic exuberance of some of his orations may be fatiguing to the sober and chastened taste of the modern classical scholar; but in order to form a just appreciation, he must transport himself mentally to the excitements of the thronged Forum—to the Senate composed not of aged venerable men, but statesmen and warriors in the prime of life, maddened with the party spirit of revolutionary times—to the presence of the jury of *judices* as numerous as a deliberative assembly, whose office was not merely calmly to

haue preeminence and soueraintie ouer all oratours: the one reignyng in wonderfull eloquence in the publike weale of the Romanes, who had the empire and dominion of all the worlde: the other, of no lasse estimation, in the citie of Athenes, whiche of longe tyme was accounted the mother of Sapience, and the palaice of musis and all liberall sciences. Of whiche two oratours may be attayned, nat onely eloquence, excellent and perfecte, but also preceptes of wisedome, and gentyll maners: with most commodious examples of all noble vertues and pollicie. Wherfore the maister, in redynge them, muste well obserue and expresse the partis and colours of rhetorike in them contayned, accordynge to the preceptes of that arte before lerned.

The utilitie that a noble man shall haue by redyng these oratours, is, that, whan he shall happe to reason in counsaile, or shall speke in a great audience, or to strange ambassadours of great princes, he shall nat be constrayned to speake wordes sodayne and disordred, but shal bestowe them aptly and in their places. Wherfore the moste noble emperour Octauius is highly commended, for that he neuer spake in the Senate, or to the people of Rome, but in an oration prepared and purposely made.*

Octauius.

Also to prepare the childe to understandynge of histories, whiche, beinge replenished with the names of countrayes and townes unknowen to the reder, do make the historie tedious or els the lasse pleasant, so if they be in any wyse knowen, it encreaseth an inexplicable delectation. It shall be therfore, and also for refreshing the witte, a conuenient lesson to beholde the olde tables of

Cosmo-graphie, and the commoditie therof.

---

give their verdict of guilty or not guilty, but who were invested as representatives of the sovereign people with the prerogative of pardoning or condemning. Viewed in this light, his most florid passages will appear free from affectation—the natural flow of a speaker carried away with the torrent of his enthusiasm.'—*Hist. of Rom. Class. Lit.* pp. 328, 342.

* 'Nam deinceps neque in Senatu, neque apud populum, neque apud milites locutus est unquam, nisi meditatâ et compositâ oratione, quamvis non deficeretur ad subita extemporali facultate.'—Sueton. *Octavius*, 84.

Ptholomee,[a] where in all the worlde is paynted, hauynge firste some introduction in to the sphere, wherof nowe of late be made very good treatises, and more playne and easie to lerne than was wonte to be.

All be it there is none so good lernynge as the demonstration of cosmographie by materiall figures and instrumentes, hauynge a good instructour. And surely this lesson is bothe pleasant and necessary. For what pleasure is it, in one houre, to beholde those realmes, cities, sees, ryuers, and mountaynes, that uneth in an olde mannes life can nat be iournaide and pursued:[b] what incredible delite is taken in beholding the diuersities of people, beastis, foules, fisshes, trees, frutes, and herbes: to knowe the sondry maners and conditions of people,

---

[a] 'The system of maps described at the end of Ptolemy's geography exists in some of the manuscripts of the work, in which they are attributed to Agathodæmon of Alexandria, supposed to have lived in the fifth century, and to have derived his materials from the maps drawn up by Ptolemy himself. These maps, which are twenty-seven in number, are elaborately coloured, the sea being green, the mountains red or dark yellow, and the land white.'—*Hist. of Gr. Lit.* vol. iii. p. 269. The climates, parallels, and the hours of the longest day are marked on the east margin of the maps, and the meridians on the north and south. Various errors having in the course of time crept into the copies of the maps, Nicolaus Donis, a Benedictine monk, about A.D. 1470, restored and corrected them, substituting Latin for Greek names. His maps are appended to the Ebnerian MS. of Ptolemy.—Smith's Dict. of Biog. *Agathodæmon.* 'The art of engraving figures on plates of copper was nearly coeval with that of printing, and is due either to Thomas Finiguerra about 1460, or to some German about the same time. It was not a difficult step to apply this invention to the representation of geographical maps; and this we owe to Arnold Buckinck, an associate of the printer Sweynheim. His edition of Ptolemy's geography appeared at Rome in 1478.'—*Lit. of Europe,* vol. i. p. 188. Hallam attributes the increasing attention bestowed upon geographical delineations during the fifteeenth century to two causes, besides the increase of commerce and the gradual accumulation of knowledge: 1st. The translations made early in the century from the cosmography of Ptolemy; 2nd. The discoveries of the Portuguese on the coast of Africa under the patronage of Don Henry, who founded an academy in which nautical charts were first delineated in a manner more useful to sailors by projecting the meridians in parallel right lines instead of curves on the surface of the sphere.—*Ubi supra.*

[b] Hallam says: 'Though these early maps and charts of the fifteenth century are to us but a chaos of error and confusion, it was on them that the patient eye of Columbus had rested through long hours of meditation, while strenuous hope and unsubdued doubt were struggling in his soul.'—*Lit. of Europe,* vol. i. p. 189.

and the varietie of their natures, and that in a warme studie or perler, without perill of the see, or daunger of longe and paynfull iournayes: I can nat tell what more pleasure shulde happen to a gentil witte, than to beholde in his owne house euery thynge that with in all the worlde is contained. The commoditie therof knewe the great kynge Alexander, as some writars do remembre. For he caused the countrayes wherunto he purposed any enterprise, diligently and counningly to be discribed and paynted, that, beholdynge the picture, he mought perceyue whiche places were most daungerous: and where he and his host mought haue most easy and couenable passage.[a]

Semblably dyd the Romanes in the rebellion of France, and the insurrection of theyr confederates, settynge up a table openly, wherin Italy was painted, to the intent that the people lokyng in it, shuld reason and consulte in whiche places hit were best to resiste or inuade their ennemies.[b]

---

[a] Presumably this must be taken to refer to the statement of Strabo, who says, in speaking of the amount of credit to be given to Patrocles: Οὐδὲ τοῦτο δὲ ἀπίθανον τοῦ Πατροκλέους, ὅτι φησὶ τοὺς 'Αλεξάνδρῳ συστρατεύσαντας ἐπιδρομάδην ἱστορῆσαι ἕκαστα, αὐτὸν δὲ 'Αλέξανδρον ἀκριβῶσαι, ἀναγραψάντων τὴν ὅλην χώραν τῶν ἐμπειροτάτων αὐτῷ· τὴν δ' ἀναγραφὴν αὐτῷ δοθῆναί φησιν ὕστερον ὑπὸ Ξενοκλέους τοῦ γαζοφύλακος.—Lib. ii. cap. 1, § 6. Compare Arrian, lib. vi. 24. Pliny mentions 'itinerum mensores' as accompanying the expeditions of Alexander, lib. vi. 21, and vii. 2; and Athenæus cites Bæton, whom he calls 'Αλεξάνδρου βηματιστής and refers to his work, which he styles Σταθμοὶ τῆς 'Αλεξάνδρου πορείας; but none of the above passages can be said to bear out the assertion in the text. Sir Thomas Elyot would seem to have been consulting the *Institutions* of Vegetius *De Re Militari*, which were published not long previously. That author says: 'Primum itineraria omnium regionum, in quibus bellum geritur, plenissimè debet habere perscripta; ita ut locorum intervalla, non solum passuum numero, sed etiam viarum qualitates perdiscat; compendia, diverticula, montes, flumina, ad fidem descripta consideret; usque adeo, ut sollertiores duces itineraria provinciarum, in quibus necessitas gerebatur, non tantum adnotata, *sed etiam picta* habuisse firmentur; ut non solum consilio mentis, verum aspectu oculorum, viam profecturi eligerent.'—Lib. iii. cap. 6.

[b] It is difficult to understand to what this description can apply, unless to the Map of the Empire commenced by Julius Cesar and completed by Agrippa, of whom Pliny tells us 'Agrippam quidem in tanta viri diligentia, præterque in hoc opere cura, orbem cum terrarum orbi spectandum propositurus esset, errasse quis credat, et cum eo Divum Augustum? Is namque complexam eum porticum ex destinatione et commentariis M. Agrippæ à sorore suâ inchoatam peregit.'—*Nat. Hist.*

I omitte, for length of the matter, to write of Cirus,[a] the great kinge of Perse, Crassus[b] the Romane, and dyuers other valiant and experte capitaines: whiche haue lost them selfes and all their army by ignorance of this doctryne.

Wherfore it maye nat be of any wyse man denied, but that Cosmographie is to all noble men, nat only pleasant, but profitable also, and wonderfull necessary.

lib. iii. cap 3. Merivale says: 'Cæsar proposed to execute a complete map of the empire from actual survey. He divided the whole extent of the Roman world into four portions, and appointed men of approved science as commissioners to examine them personally throughout. The work was to be executed in the most minute manner. The Roman land-surveyors had long been familiar with the technical processes by which the inequalities of natural limits are duly measured and registered. Throughout Italy, and in many of the provinces every estate was elaborately marked out on the surface of the soil, and its extent and configuration inscribed on tablets of brass, and preserved with scrupulous care.'—*Hist. of Rome*, vol. ii. p. 422. It is possible that Propertius alludes to this map when he says:

'Cogor et è tabula pictos ediscere mundos
   Qualis et hæc docti sit positura Dei.
Quæ tellus sit lenta gelu quæ putris ab æstu,
   Ventus in Italiam qui bene vela ferat.'—Lib. iv. el. 3. 37.

[a] It was after the death of Cyrus, however, that the ten thousand Greeks encountered the difficulties which form the subject of the Anabasis.

[b] 'Throughout the whole Parthian campaign he (Crassus) exhibited so much imprudence and such a complete neglect of the first principles of military art that premature age may be thought to have impaired his faculties. He was quite uninformed as to the character and resources of the enemy he was going to attack, fancied that he should have an easy conquest over unwarlike people ; that countless treasures lay before him, and that it would be a matter of no difficulty to outstrip the glory of his predecessors, Scipio, Lucullus, and Pompey, and push on his army to Bactria and India. He did not attempt to take advantage of the intestine dissensions in Parthia, did not form any cordial union with the Armenians and other tribes who were hostile to the Parthians, and did not obtain correct information as to the position of the enemy's force and the nature of the country.'— Smith's *Dict. of Biog*. Plutarch says of him : 'Αλλ', ὡς ἔοικε, καὶ τοῖς σπουδάζουσι περὶ αὐτὸν ἐδόκει κατὰ τὸν κωμικὸν ἀνήρ, Ἄριστος εἶναι τἆλλα πλὴν ἐν ἀσπίδι.—*Nic. cum Crass. Comp*. 3. It was at Charrhæ, the Sedan of antiquity, that Crassus met with his death by treachery, and the whole Roman army surrendered ignominiously to the Parthians. It was calculated that 20,000 men perished in this calamitous expedition, and that half that number were made prisoners. 'The names of Charrhæ and Cannæ,' says Merivale, 'were blended together on the bloodiest page of the national annals.'—*Hist. of Rome*, vol. i. p. 532.

In the parte of cosmographie wherwith historie is mingled Strabo[a] reigneth : whiche toke his argument of the diuine poete Homere.[b] Also Strabo hym selfe, (as he saith,) laboured a great part of Africa and Egypte, where undoubtedly be many thinges to be maruailed at.[c] Solinus[d] writeth almost in like forme, and is more brefe, and hath moche more varietie of

[a] Mr. George Long, in his article on Strabo in Smith's *Dict. of Biog.*, says : 'Strabo's work has a particular value to us of the present day, owing to his method of handling the subject ; he has preserved a great number of historical facts, for which we have no other evidence than his work. It forms a striking contrast with the geography of Ptolemæus and the dry list of names, occasionally relieved by something added to them in the geographical portion of the *Natural History* of Plinius. It is in short a book intended for reading, and it may be read ; a kind of historical geography.' Müller says, ' His object was to give an instructive and readable account of the known world, considered from the point of view taken up by a Greek man of letters. Geography is interesting to him from its connexion with history and literature ; places deserve detailed description because they are mentioned in poems, or have been rendered illustrious by the great men, whom they have produced, or the great events of which they have been the scene. To Strabo the world is nothing except as the dwelling-place of the human family.'—*Hist. of Gr. Lit.* vol. iii. p. 135. The first edition of Strabo was by Aldus at Venice, 1516 ; but a Latin translation appeared at Rome, 1469, and was reprinted 1473, more than forty years before the Greek text was published.

[b] Strabo himself says : Καὶ πρῶτον ὅτι ὀρθῶς ὑπειλήφαμεν καὶ ἡμεῖς καὶ οἱ πρὸ ἡμῶν, ὧν ἐστι καὶ Ἵππαρχος, ἀρχηγέτην εἶναι τῆς γεωγραφικῆς ἐμπειρίας Ὅμηρον. Lib. i. cap. 1. § 2.

[c] Τῶν τε Ῥωμαίων καὶ εἰς τὴν εὐδαίμονα Ἀραβίαν ἐμβαλόντων μετὰ στρατιᾶς νεωστί, ἧς ἡγεῖτο ἀνὴρ φίλος ἡμῖν καὶ ἑταῖρος Αἴλιος Γάλλος, καὶ τῶν ἐκ τῆς Ἀλεξανδρείας ἐμπόρων στόλοις ἤδη πλεόντων διὰ τοῦ Νείλου καὶ τοῦ Ἀραβίου κόλπου μέχρι τῆς Ἰνδικῆς, πολὺ μᾶλλον, καὶ ταῦτα ἔγνωσται τοῖς νῦν ἢ τοῖς πρὸ ἡμῶν. Ὅτε γοῦν Γάλλος ἐπῆρχε τῆς Αἰγύπτου, συνόντες αὐτῷ καὶ συναναβάντες μέχρι Συήνης καὶ τῶν Αἰθιοπικῶν ὅρων ἱστοροῦμεν, ὅτι καὶ ἑκατὸν καὶ εἴκοσι νῆες πλέοιεν ἐκ Μυὸς ὅρμου πρὸς τὴν Ἰνδικήν, πρότερον ἐπὶ τῶν Πτολεμαϊκῶν βασιλέων ὀλίγων παντάπασι θαρρούντων πλεῖν καὶ τὸν Ἰνδικὸν ἐμπορεύεσθαι φόρτον.—Lib. ii. cap. 5, § 12.

[d] 'Solinus was the author of a geographical compendium containing a brief sketch of the world as known to the ancients. The arrangement, materials, and frequently the very words are derived almost exclusively from the *Natural History* of Pliny. His work was called *Polyhistor*, and was much studied in the middle ages, and consequently many editions appeared in the infancy of the typographical art. The most notable edition is that of Salmasius, published at Utrecht, 1629, prefixed to his *Plinianæ Exercitationes*, which, according to Hallam, is a mass of learning on the geography and natural history of Pliny in more than 900 pages following the text of the *Polyhistor* of Solinus, who is a mere compiler from Pliny, and contains nothing from any other source.'—*Lit. of Europe*, vol. ii. p. 283.

thinges and maters, and is therfore maruailous delectable: yet Mela is moche shorter, and his stile, (by reason that it is of a more antiquitie,) is also more clene and facile.[a] Wherfore he, or Dionisius,[b] shall be sufficient.

Cosmographie beinge substancially perceiued, it is than tyme to induce a childe to the redinge of histories: but fyrst to set hym in a feruent courage, the mayster in the mooste pleasant and elegant wise expressinge what incomparable delectation, utilitie, and commodite, shal happen to emperours, kinges, princis, and all other gentil men by reding of histories: shewinge to hym that Demetrius Phalareus,[c] a man of excellent wisedome and

Histories and the fourme in redyng of them.

---

[a] Pomponius Mela was the first Roman author who composed a formal treatise upon geography. From internal evidence it is highly probable that he lived in the reign of the Emperor Claudius. Professor Ramsay says: 'As might be expected in a tract which consists chiefly of proper names, the text is often excessively and hopelessly corrupt; *but the style is simple, unaffected, and perspicuous; the Latinity is pure*; all the best authorities accessible at that period, especially Eratosthenes, appear to have been carefully consulted; and although everything is compressed within the narrowest limits, we find the monotony of the catalogue occasionally diversified by animated and pleasing pictures.' The editio princeps of Mela appeared at Milan, 1471, and numerous editions were published before the end of the fifteenth century. Hermolaus Barbarus, a Venetian, who died in 1493, 'boasted that he had corrected more than three hundred passages in the very brief geography of Pomponius Mela.'—*Lit. of Europe*, vol. i. p. 222.

[b] Dionysius of Halicarnassus came to Rome B.C. 29, and remained there for twenty-two years. His work, called *Roman Archæology*, which was published B.C. 7, was intended to take the place of all other works as an introduction to Polybius, and was carried down from the earliest time to B.C. 264, when Polybius really begins. Niebuhr says in his *Lectures*, 'Before Roman history was treated critically Dionysius was neglected, and his work was despised as a tissue of follies.' But from the manner in which he is mentioned in the text it would certainly appear that at any rate Sir Thomas Elyot entertained a proper respect for the great historian.

[c] Demetrius the Phalerian, the disciple of Theophrastus and the friend and fellow-pupil of Menander, had governed Athens as the head of the Macedonian party from B.C. 317 to B.C. 307. When his power was overthrown, he took refuge at the court of Ptolemy Soter, over whom he acquired great influence, insomuch that he engaged the king in the formal patronage of literature, and was even indulged with the favourite occupation of a philosopher, the formation or revision of a code of laws. We are told that he wrote on history and politics, on the poets and on rhetoric, publishing also some of his own speeches; and that

lerninge, and whiche in Athenes had ben longe exercised in the publike weale, exhorted Ptholomee, kyng of Egipt, chiefly aboue all other studyes, to haunte and embrace histories, and suche other bokes, wherin were contayned preceptes made to kynges and princes: sayng that in them he shulde rede those thinges whiche no man durst reporte unto his persone.[a] Also Cicero, father of the latin eloquence,[b] calleth an historie the witnesse of tymes, maistres of life, the lyfe of remembrance, of trouthe the lyght, and messager of antiquite.[c]

Moreouer, the swete Isocrates exhorteth the kynge Nicocles, whom he instructeth, to leaue behynde him statues and images, that shall represent rather the figure and similitude of his mynde, than the features of his body, signifienge therbye the remembraunce of his actes writen in histories.[d]

By semblable aduertisementes shall a noble harte be trayned to delite in histories. And than, accordynge to the counsayle of Quintilian,[e] it is best that he begynne with Titus Liuius, nat onely for his elegancie of writinge, whiche floweth in him like a fountaine of swete

Titus Liuius.

---

besides this he prepared collections of Æsop's *Fables*. He made, therefore, a first beginning of the grammatical and critical literature of his adopted country.—*Hist. of Gr. Lit.* vol. ii. p. 468.

[a] This story is narrated by Plutarch as follows: Δημήτριος ὁ Φαληρεὺς Πτολεμαίῳ τῷ βασιλεῖ παρῄνει τὰ περὶ βασιλείας καὶ ἡγεμονίας βιβλία κτᾶσθαι καὶ ἀναγινώσκειν· ἃ γὰρ οἱ φίλοι τοῖς βασιλεῦσιν οὐ θαρροῦσι παραινεῖν, ταῦτα ἐν τοῖς βιβλίοις γέγραπται.--*Reg. et Imp. Apophtheg.* 189, D. ed. Didot p. 227.

[b] Pliny, eulogising Cicero, says: 'Salve primus omnium parens patriæ appellate, primus in togâ triumphum linguæque lauream merite, et facundiæ Latiarumque literarum parens.'—*Nat. Hist.* lib. vii. cap. 31.

[c] 'Historia vero testis temporum, lux veritatis, vita memoriæ, magistra vitæ, nuntia vetustatis.'—*De Orat.* lib. ii. cap. 9.

[d] Βούλου τὰς εἰκόνας τῆς ἀρετῆς ὑπόμνημα μᾶλλον ἢ τοῦ σώματος καταλιπεῖν. *Ad Nicoclem*, § 36, ed. Didot, 1846.

[e] Ego optimos quidem, et statim, et semper, sed tamen eorum candidissimum quemque, et maxime expositum, velim, ut Livium à pueris magis, quam Sallustium; et hic historiæ major est auctor, ad quem tamen intelligendum jam profectu opus sit.—*Instit. Orat.* lib. ii. cap. 5, § 19. Niebuhr is of the same opinion. 'You cannot study Livy too much,' he says, 'both as scholars and as men who seek and love that which is beautiful.'—*Lectures on Rom. Hist.* xlvii. ed. 1870.

milke :[a] but also for as moche as by redynge that autor he maye knowe howe the mooste noble citie of Rome, of a small and poure begynnynge, by prowes and vertue, litell and litell came to the empire and dominion of all the worlde.[b]

Also in that citye he maye beholde the fourme of a publike weale : whiche, if the insolencie and pryde of Tarquine had nat excluded kynges out of the citie, it had ben the most noble and perfect of all other.[c]

[a] Quintilian's phrase is, 'Livii lactea ubertas.'—*Inst. Orat.* lib. x. cap. 1, § 32.

[b] A modern writer says : 'Rome was now the mistress of the world : her struggles with foreign nations had been rewarded with universal dominion ; so that when the Roman empire was spoken of, no title less comprehensive than "the world" (*orbis*) would satisfy the national vanity. The horrors of civil war had ceased, and were succeeded by an amnesty of its bitter feuds and bloody animosities. Liberty, indeed, had perished, but the people were no longer fit for the enjoyment of it ; and it was exchanged for a mild and paternal rule, under which all the refinements of civilization were encouraged and its subjects could enjoy undisturbed the blessings of peace and security. Rome, therefore, had rest and breathing-time to look back into the past—to trace the successive steps by which that marvellous edifice, the Roman empire, had been constructed. She could do this, too, with perfect self-complacency, for there was no symptom of decay to check her exultation, or to mar the glories which she was contemplating. Livy the good, the affectionate, the romantic, was precisely the popular historian for such times as these.'—Browne, *Hist. of Rom. Class. Lit.* p. 397.

[c] 'Sallust, who in the introduction of his lost history of the period subsequent to the death of Sulla gave, like Thucydides, a brief survey of the moral and political history of his nation, which is preserved in St. Augustin, says that Rome was ruled fairly and justly only so long as there was a fear of Tarquinius ; but that as soon as this fear was removed, the *patres* indulged in every kind of tyranny and arrogance, and kept the *plebes* in servile submission by the severity of the law of debt. In like manner Livy states that the *plebes* who, down to the destruction of of the Tarquins, had been courted with the greatest care, were immediately afterwards oppressed ; that until then the salt which belonged to the *publicum* had been sold at a low price, that tolls had been abolished, and that the king's domain had been distributed among the plebeians ; in short, the φιλάνθρωπα δίκαια of Servius Tullius had been restored .... As long as Tarquinius, who was personally a great man, lived, the patricians hesitated to go to extremes in their innovations, though they insulted the plebeians and deprived them of the *imperia* ; they may even have expelled them from the senate, and they certainly did not fill up with plebeians those places which became vacant by death. But the real oppression did not begin till the fear of an enemy from without was removed.'—Niebuhr, *Lectures on Rom. Hist.* xxvi. ed. 1870.

THE GOVERNOUR.

Xenophon. Xenophon, beynge bothe a philosopher [a] and an excellent capitayne,[b] so inuented and ordred his warke named *Pædia Cyri*, whiche may be interpreted the Childehode or discipline of Cyrus, that he leaueth to the reders therof an incomparable swetenes and example of lyuynge, specially for the conductynge and well ordring of hostes or armyes.[c] And therfore the noble Scipio, who was called Affricanus, as well in peace as in warre was neuer seene without this boke of Xenophon.[d]

With hym maye be ioyned Quintus Curtius,[e] who writeth

[a] Col. Mure says: 'In the allusions to Xenophon's literary character, he is perhaps as frequently honoured with the title of "Philosopher" as with that of "Historian." His pretensions to the former are however feeble, and have been omitted in our catalogue of his sources of celebrity. He is not the author of any properly philosophical work; and the doctrines interspersed in his miscellaneous writings are little remarkable for novelty or depth. His philosophy, if such it can be called, is like his style, simple and familiar; consisting in a pleasing mode of shaping popular views, rather than attempts at original theory.'—*Lang. and Lit. of Greece*, vol. v. p. 260.

[b] The author last quoted says: 'As a soldier he deservedly enjoys a brilliant reputation, in the peculiar kind of warfare in which he is known to have been actively engaged. But it was one affording little opportunity for the highest exercise of strategic talent. His campaigns, however ably conducted, were in so far as known to fame, fought against barbarous enemies. There is no record of his having ever held the responsible command of a large body of regular troops against equally well trained and appointed adversaries.'—*Ibid.* p. 250.

[c] 'The Cyropædia has been commonly assigned by modern critics, to the branch of composition entitled in our own day Historical romance; and this is perhaps as near a definition of its character as our own stock of such technical terms supplies. Of romance, indeed, in the familiar sense, the work contains but little. The main narrative is devoted to affairs of state, civil and military. The illustrative materials, which engross the greater part of the text, consist of disquisitions on the art of war, on political government, and social economy. . . . The main scope of the work is to present the reader with the author's idea of a perfect system of monarchical government. This system he has figured as created or matured by a no less perfect monarch and military commander; with whose life and influence it is so closely identified that as it grew with his youth and manhood, with his death it begins to decay.'—*Ibid.* p. 378.

[d] Sir Thomas Elyot has slightly improved upon Cicero's statement, which is merely 'Itaque semper Africanus Socraticum Xenophontem in manibus habebat.' —*Tusc. Quæst.* lib. ii. cap. 26.

[e] Modern scholars cannot agree as to the time when Quintus Curtius Rufus

the life of kyng Alexander elegantly and swetely. In whom may be founden the figure of an excellent prince, as he that incomparably excelled al other kinges and emperours in wysedome, hardynes, strength, policie, agilite, valiaunt courage, nobilitie, liberalitie and curtaisie: where in he was a spectakle or marke for all princes to loke on.[a] Contrarye wise whan he was ones vainquisshed with voluptie and pride his tiranny and beastly crueltie abhorreth all reders.[b] The comparison of the vertues of these two noble princes, equally described by two excellent writars, well expressed, shall prouoke a gentil courage to contende to folowe their vertues.

Julius Cesar and Salust[c] for their compendious writynge

wrote his work. From the internal evidence Gibbon came to the conclusion that it must have been in the reign of the emperor Gordian. Niebuhr would prefer the reign of Aurelian 'if it were possible that a person could at that time have written such elegant Latin as that of Curtius; but this is impossible.' And he decides eventually on the evidence afforded by the reference to Tyre (lib. iv. 4) in favour of the time of Septimius Severus and Caracalla.—*Lectures on Rom. Hist.* cxl. Professor Browne thinks upon the whole it is most probable that he lived towards the close of the first century.

[a] Arrian has summed up his character as follows: Τό τε σῶμα κάλλιστος καὶ φιλοπονώτατος καὶ ὀξύτατος τὴν γνώμην γενόμενος, καὶ ἀνδρειότατος, καὶ φιλοτιμότατος καὶ φιλοκινδυνότατος καὶ τοῦ θείου ἐπιμελέστατος· ἡδονῶν δὲ τῶν μὲν τοῦ σώματος ἐγκρατέστατος, τῶν δὲ τῆς γνώμης ἐπαίνου μόνου ἀπληστότατος· ξυνιδεῖν δὲ τὸ δέον ἔτι ἐν τῷ ἀφανεῖ ὂν δεινότατος, καὶ ἐκ τῶν φαινομένων τὸ εἰκὸς ξυμβαλεῖν ἐπιτυχέστατος, καὶ τάξαι στρατιὰν καὶ ὁπλίσαι τε καὶ κοσμῆσαι δαημονέστατος· καὶ τὸν θυμὸν τοῖς στρατιώταις ἐπᾶραι καὶ ἐλπίδων ἀγαθῶν ἐμπλῆσαι καὶ τὸ δεῖμα ἐν τοῖς κινδύνοις τῷ ἀδεεῖ τῷ αὑτοῦ ἀφανίσαι, ξύμπαντα ταῦτα γενναιότατος. Καὶ οὖν καὶ ὅσα ἐν τῷ ἀφανεῖ πρᾶξαι, ξὺν μεγίστῳ θάρσει ἔπραξεν· ὅσα τε φθάσας ὑφαρπάσαι τῶν πολεμίων, πρὶν καὶ δεῖσαί τινα αὐτὰ ὡς ἐσόμενα, προλαβεῖν δεινότατος· καὶ τὰ μὲν ξυντεθέντα ἢ ὁμολογηθέντα φυλάξαι βεβαιότατος, πρὸς δὲ τῶν ἐξαπατώντων μὴ ἁλῶναι ἀσφαλέστατος· χρημάτων δὲ ἐς μὲν ἡδονὰς τὰς αὑτοῦ φειδωλότατος, ἐς δέ εὐποιίαν τῶν πέλας ἀφθονώτατος.—Lib. vii. cap. 28.

[b] This is evidently a paraphrase of the passage in Curtius: 'Sed ut primum instantibus curis laxatus est animus, militarium rerum quàm quietis otiique patientior; excepere eum voluptates: et quem arma Persarum non fregerant, vitia vicerunt; intempestiva convivia, et perpotandi pervigilandique insana dulcedo, ludique, et greges pellicum, omnia in externum lapsa sunt morem: quem æmulatus quasi potiorem suo, ita popularium animos oculosque pariter offendit, ut à plerisque amicorum pro hoste haberetur.'—Lib. vi. cap. 2.

[c] One of the most distinguished scholars of the present day says, 'Cæsar's business was the narrative of his campaigns, and he has omitted nearly everything

to the understandynge wherof is required an exact and perfect iugement, and also for the exquisite ordre of bataile and continuinge of the historie without any varietie, wherby the payne of studie shulde be alleuiate, they two wolde be reserued untyll he that shall rede them shall se some experience in semblable matters.* And than shal he finde in them suche pleasure and commodite as therwith a noble and gentyl harte ought to be satisfied. For in them both it shall seme to a man that he is present and hereth the counsayles and exhortations of capitaines, whiche be called *Conciones*,[b]

which did not belong to his purpose.'—Long's *Decline of the Roman Republic*, vol. v. p. 475. Niebuhr says: 'With regard to his (Cæsar's) campaigns in Gaul, I have only to refer you to his own commentaries on the Gallic war, with the supplement of A. Hirtius, a work which every scholar must have read. It is written with such conciseness and brevity that if I attempted to abridge it, as I should be obliged to do if I were to give an account of those campaigns, nothing would be left but a miniature outline. I strongly advise you to read Cæsar's account of his Gallic wars as often as you can, for the oftener you read it the more will you recognise the hand of a great master.'—*Lect. R. H.* cvii. ed. 1870. Professor Browne styles the commentaries 'the materials for history; notes jotted down for future historians.'—*Hist. of Rom. Class. Lit.* p. 379. With regard to Sallust, Niebuhr says, 'The description which Sallust has given of the war (against Jugurtha) is one of the best specimens of ancient literature in either language, and I am almost inclined to prefer it to his Catiline. But both works are peculiar phenomena in Roman literature: they are what we call monographies, which are otherwise unknown among the Romans, except, perhaps, Cælius Antipater's history of the Hannibalian war, of which, however, we know nothing; the memoirs of Fannius were of quite a different nature. The books of Sallust are not written in the form of annals, the character of which he evidently tries to avoid; his intention was to write history in a compact and plastic manner. The works of Sallust are of such a kind that the more we read them the more do we find to admire in them; they are true models of excellent historical composition.' —*Lect. Rom. Hist.* xcii. ed. 1870.

* Mr. Long calls the Commentaries 'a book dull enough to boys, if masters will not sufficiently explain it by making their pupils well acquainted with the geography of the country, and tiresome to all readers who will not take the labour necessary to understand it. Among the great number of illustrious scholars whose names are known, I have found few who have carefully studied the first of Roman writers.' He also says the books on the Civil War 'are not a fit subject for boys to work at.'—*The Decline of the Roman Republic*, vol. v. p. 476, and note. Quintilian's opinion upon this point, in the case of Sallust, has already been quoted ante p. 82, note *.

[b] Rather 'harangues' or 'speeches'; thus Quintilian comparing Thucydides

THE GOVERNOUR. 87

and that he seeth the ordre of hostes whan they be embatayled, the fiers assaultes and encountringes of bothe armies, the furiouse rage of that monstre called warre. And he shall wene that he hereth the terrible dintes of sondry weapons and ordinaunce of bataile, the conducte and policies of wise and expert capitaines, specially in the commentaries of Julius Cesar, whiche he made of his exploiture [a] in Fraunce [b] and Brytayne,[c] and other countraies nowe rekned amonge the prouinces of Germany: [d] whiche boke is studiously to be radde

with Herodotus says, 'Ille concionibus hic sermonibus melior.'—*Instit. Orat.* lib. x. cap. 1, § 73. And the same writer talks of 'concio contra Catilinam.'—*Ibid.* lib. v. cap 11, § 42. There are a few short addresses of Cæsar to his men in the Commentaries.

[a] See the glossary.

[b] 'The old divisions of France before the great revolution of 1789 corresponded in some degree to the divisions of the country in the time of Cæsar, and the names of the people are still retained, with little alteration, in the names of the chief towns or the names of the ante-revolutionary divisions of France. In the country of the Remi, between the Marne and the Aisne, there is the town of Rheims. In the territory of the Suessiones, between the Marne and the Aisne, there is Soissons on the Aisne . . . . The name of the Condrusi is preserved in the country of Condroz or Condrost, in the Pays de Liège, and that of the Pæmani in the Pays de Fammenne, of which country Durburg, Laroche on the Ourthe, and Rochefort on the Homme are the chief towns. These are two signal instances of the permanence of historical evidence.'—Long's *Decline of the Rom. Rep.* vol. iv. p. 46.

[c] Mr. Long's 'conclusion is that the extant authorities to the time of Augustus show that the Greeks and Romans knew very little about Britannia; that Pytheas, if he did navigate the Atlantic, as we can hardly doubt, either did not go so far north as some have supposed, or he was a very careless observer, and reported many things from hearsay; that Cæsar did not know much about Britannia, and has told us even less than he could have done; but that the island had been visited by traders from the French coast, and probably from the Iberian peninsula, for centuries before the Christian era.'—*Ibid.* vol. iv. p. 197.

[d] Pope Pius II., better known as a writer by the name of Æneas Sylvius, in a work published in 1515, contrasts the Germany of his own day with the country of the Germanic tribes known to the Romans in the following manner: 'Comparemus ergo cum veteri novam (Germaniam) et primum de amplitudine dicamus. Danubius ac Rhenus, qui quondam Germaniæ limites clausere, nunc per medios Germanorum dilabuntur agros. Belgica regio, quæ Galliæ prius portio tertia fuit, nunc majori ex parte Germaniæ cessit linguâ et moribus Theutonica. Helvetii quoque, gens anteâ Gallica, in Germanos transivere. Recia tota et ipsum Noricum et quicquid Vindelici nominis inter Alpes Italas ac Danubium fuit, ad Germanos

88   THE GOVERNOUR.

of the princes of this realme of Englande and their counsailors;[a] considering that therof maye be taken necessary instructions concernynge the warres agayne Irisshe men [b] or Scottes,[c] who be of the same rudenes and wilde disposition

deficit. Ita ut etiam Alpes ipsas cœlo vicinas et perpetuâ nive rigentes nomen Germanicum penetrans in Italiâ quoque sedes posuerit, Brixione, Merane, Bubianoque in valle Athesis occupato. Austria quæ apud priscos Pannonici juris fuit, et Norici portio in Germanicum nomen conversa est. Styria quam veteres Valeriam vocavere Theutonicum morem atque imperium subiit. Carni quoque, quos modo Carinthianos Carniolosque nominant, idem fecere ita ut fontes Dravi Savique nominatorum fluminum Theutonici juris existant. Neque Alpes ullæ inter Italiam atque Germaniam sunt, quarum summa cacumina non possideant Theutonici, qui ad Orientem non modo Albim sed Oderam ac Viscellam transmiserunt, et in ipsâ quidem occidentali Sarmaciâ Ulmerigorum et Gepidarum agros invasere: nam et Austria trans Danubium, et Moravia, et quidquid Slessiæ ultra Oderam possident Sarmatici quondam fuit soli. Quin et in Oceano et Baltheo sinû medias insulas sui juris fecere Theutones.'—*Germania*, cap. xxxii. ed. 1515.

[a] 'Cæsar's Commentaries are a manual for a general, the best that was ever written. Many commanders have had their favourite books. Scipio Africanus the Younger was always reading Xenophon. Napoleon, in his captivity at St. Helena, dictated to Marchand his remarks on Cæsar's Commentaries. "The late Marshal Strozzi," says Montaigne, "who took Cæsar for his model, without doubt made the best choice; for, in truth, Cæsar's book ought to be the manual of every general, as it is the true and sovereign example of the military art: and God knows besides with what grace and with what beauty he has set off this rich material, with a manner of expression so pure, so delicate, and so perfect, that to my taste there are no writings in the world which can be compared with his in this respect."'—Long's *Decline of the Roman Republic*, vol. v. p. 473.

[b] Mr. Froude, after describing 'the English pale' at this period, says: 'This narrow strip alone, some fifty miles long and twenty broad, was in any sense English. Beyond the borders the common law of England was of no authority; the king's writ was but a strip of parchment; and the country was parcelled among a multitude of independent chiefs who acknowledged no sovereignty but that of strength, and levied tribute on the inhabitants of the pale as a reward for a nominal protection of their rights, and as a compensation for abstaining from the plunder of their farms. Their swords were their sceptres, their codes of right the Brehon traditions—a convenient system which was called law, but which in practice was a happy contrivance for the composition of felonies.'—*Hist. of Eng.* vol. ii. p. 247.

[c] Mr. Fraser Tytler tells us what the state of Scotland was at the same period. 'James directed his attention to the state of the borders, where the disorders incident to a minority had increased to a degree which threatened the total disruption of these districts. Such excesses were mainly to be attributed to Angus, the late Warden of the Marches, who had secured the friendship of the border chiefs by overlooking their offences, whilst he had bound them to his interests by those

that the Suises[a] and Britons[b] were in the time of Cesar. Semblable utilitie shal be founden in the historie of Titus Liuius, in his thirde Decades, where he writeth of the batayles that the Romanes had with Annibal and the Charthaginensis.[c]

feudal covenants named "bands of manrent," which formed one of the darkest features of the times, compelling the parties to defend each other against the effects of their mutual transgressions. The task, therefore, of introducing order and respect for legal restraints amongst the fierce inhabitants of the marches was one of extreme difficulty. The principal thieves were the border barons themselves, some of whom maintained a feudal state almost royal; whilst their castles, often impregnable from the strength of their natural and artificial defences, defied every attempt to reduce or to storm them.'—*Hist. of Scotland*, vol. iv. p. 205, ed. 1845.

[a] Presumably the Helvetii are thus designated. Merivale, however, says: 'The account which was commonly given of this people and their migration is that they were a pastoral tribe, abounding in wealth, and of a peaceful disposition; it was the example of the Cimbri and Teutones with whom they came in contact that corrupted their natural simplicity, and suggested visions of conquest and rapine. Strabo, vii. 2, following Posidonius. But Cæsar says they were the bravest of the Gauls, from their constant warfare with the Germans on their frontier.'—*Hist. of Rome*, vol. i. p. 279, note.

[b] 'The campaigns of Cæsar in Belgium could not fail to make him acquainted with the existence and character of the inhabitants of the great island which lay within sight of its coasts. It was indeed from their allies on the opposite shore that his enemies had drawn no inconsiderable resources. Questioned as to the relations subsisting between themselves and the natives of Britain, they asserted that many of their own race had emigrated from Gaul during the preceding century, and established themselves beyond the white cliffs just visible in the horizon. They spoke of a population believed by them to be aboriginal upon whom they had intruded themselves, and in whose seats they had gradually fixed their abodes. This primitive people they described as peculiarly rude and barbarous in their social habits. They were almost destitute of clothing, and took a grotesque pleasure in painting or tattooing their bodies with blue woad. They admitted a regulated community of women. They lived almost entirely on milk and flesh; the toil or skill required even for fishing was distasteful to them; and dwelling apart or congregating in a few hovels with a wooden stockade round them, and screened by forests, mountains, or morasses, they possessed nothing which could possess the name of a city.'—*Ibid.* vol. i. pp. 458, 459.

The wretched state of Britain at the time of the Roman invasion is thus commented on by Plutarch. Cæsar is said κακῶσαι τοὺς πολεμίους μᾶλλον ἢ τοὺς ἰδίους ὠφελῆσαι, οὐδὲν γὰρ ὅ τι καὶ λαβεῖν ἦν ἄξιον ἀπ' ἀνθρώπων κακοβίων καὶ πενήτων.—*Cæsar*, 23.

[c] Niebuhr says: 'In the narrative of Livy we can distinguish the different sources from which he derived his information. The account of the first period of the war, and especially the rhetorical description of the siege of Saguntum, are

Also there be dyuers orations, as well in all the bokes of the saide autors as in the historie of Cornelius Tacitus, whiche be very delectable, and for counsayles very expedient to be had in memorie. And in good faythe I haue often thought that the consultations and orations wryten by Tacitus do importe a maiestie with a compendious eloquence therin contained.*

In the lerning of these autors a yonge gentilman shal be taught to note and marke, nat only the ordre and elegancie in declaration of the historie, but also the occasion of the warres, the counsailes and preparations on either part, the estimation

marginal note: Cornelius Tacitus.

---

unquestionably derived from Cælius Antipater; and if his history of the remaining period of the war were not based on better authorities, the whole of his third decade would be worth nothing. But in some parts Livy follows Polybius very carefully; in other parts of this decade, as for instance at the end of a year when he gives a brief summary of the events which occurred during the year, he followed the pontifical annals or some annalist. He evidently wrote this decade with great pleasure, and some portions of it are among the most beautiful things that have ever been written. The points in which he is deficient are a knowledge of facts, experience, an intimate acquaintance with the affairs of real life—he does not step beyond the walls of the school—and a control over his subject. He worked with great ease, and repeated what others had said before him, without toiling and moiling. Wherever he differs from Polybius he deserves no credit at all; and however beautifully his history of the war is written, still it is evident that he could not form a vivid conception of anything. His description of the battle of Cannæ, for instance, is untrue and impossible, whereas that of Polybius is so excellent that it enables the reader to see the locality and to draw a map of it; and the better the locality is known the clearer his description becomes.'—*Lect. on Rom. Hist.* lxxi. ed. 1870. Professor Browne says: 'The third (decade) contains the most beautiful and elaborate passages of the whole work.'—*Hist. of Rom. Class. Lit.* p. 401.

* It may be observed that a modern scholar uses almost precisely similar language. 'It would have been impossible to have satisfied a people whose taste had become more than ever rhetorical, without the introduction of orations. Those of Tacitus are perfect specimens of art; and probably, with the exception of Galgacus, far more true than those of other Roman historians. Still he made use of them, not only to embody traditional acccoụnts of what had really been said on each occasion, but to illustrate his own views of the character of the speaker, and to convey his own political opinions. Full of sagacious observation and descriptive power, Tacitus engages the most serious attention of the reader by the gravity of his condensed and comprehensive style, as he does by the wisdom and dignity of his reflections.'—*Hist. of Rom. Class. Lit.* p. 495.

of the capitaines, the maner and fourme of theyr gouernance, the continuance of the bataile, the fortune and successe of the holle affaires. Semblably out of the warres in other dayly affaires, the astate of the publike weale, if hit be prosperous or in decaye, what is the very occasyon of the one or of the other, the forme and maner of the gouernance therof, the good and euyll qualities of them that be rulers, the commodites and good sequele of vertue, the discommodies and euyll conclusion of vicious licence.

Surely if a noble man do thus seriously and diligently rede histories, I dare affirme there is no studie or science for him of equal commoditie and pleasure, hauynge regarde to euery tyme and age.

By the time that the childe do com to xvii yeres of age, to the intent his courage be bridled with reason, hit were nedefull to rede unto hym some warkes of philoso- *Morall* phie; specially that parte that may enforme him *philoso-* unto vertuous maners, whiche parte of philosophie *phye.* is called morall.* Wherfore there wolde be radde to hym,

---

* This was the course pursued in the Roman system of education. 'At seventeen, or when the fated struggle begins between the moral principles and the instincts of appetite—at the commencement, such as morality and religion have represented it, of the great battle of life between vice and virtue—the youth was transferred to the Academy of the Philosopher to learn the mysteries of the Good, the Fair and the Honourable. While he still continued to exercise himself daily in rhetorical studies and practice, he explored the dark by-ways of morals and metaphysics under accomplished teachers, and traversed the whole circuit of Grecian speculation before he determined in which sect definitively to enrol himself.'—Merivale's *Hist. of Rome*, voL vi. p. 227. Montaigne thought philosophy a fit subject for boys: 'Puisque la philosophie est celle qui nous instruit à vivre, et que l'enfance y a sa leçon comme les aultres aages, pourquoy ne la luy communique lon?

    Udum et molle lutum est; nunc nunc properandus et acri
    Fingendus sine fine rota.

On nous apprend à vivre quand la vie est passee. Cent escholiers ont prins la verole avant que d'estre arrivez à leur leçon d'Aristote De la temperance. Cicero disoit que quand il vivroit la vie de deux hommes, il ne prendroit pas le loisir d'estudier les poëtes lyriques; et ie treuve ces ergotistes plus tristement encores inutiles. Nostre enfant est bien plus pressé; il ne doibt au paidagogisme que les

for an introduction, two the fyrste bokes of the warke of Aristotell, called *Ethicæ*, wherin is contained the definitions and propre significations of euery vertue; and that to be lerned in greke; for the translations that we yet haue be but a rude and grosse shadowe of the eloquence and wisedome of Aristotell. * Forthe with wolde folowe the warke of Cicero, called in Latin *De officiis*, wherunto yet is

Tullie's Offices.

premiers quinze ou seize ans de sa vie; le demourant est deu à l'action. Employons un temps si court aux instructions necessaires. Ce sont abus; ostez toutes subtilitez espineuses de la dialectique dequoy nostre vie ne se peult amender; prenez les simples discours de la philosophie, sçachez les choisir et traicter à point: ils sont plus aysez à concevoir qu'un conte de Boccace; un enfant en est capable au partir de la nourrice, beaucoup mieulx que d'apprendre à lire ou escrire. La philosophie a des discours pour la naissance des hommes comme pour la decrepitude.'—*Essais*, tom. i. p. 225, ed. 1854.

* Nor is this to be wondered at, if we accept M. Bréchillet-Jourdain's account of the method adopted by the translators of Aristotle in the preceding centuries. 'Le chrétien avide de science, se rendait à Tolède, s'attachait à un juif ou à un Sarasin converti, puisait dans sa fréquentation quelque connaisance de la langue maure; quand il voulait traduire un livre, ce maitre le lui expliquait en idiome vulgaire, c'est-à-dire *en espagnol*, et il mettait cette traduction verbale *en latin.*' Speaking of the translations made in the 11th century, M. Jourdain says: 'Les versions portent le caractère d'un âge où la langue latine ne s'écrivait plus avec la même élégance, où le langage d'Aristote était imparfaitement connu. Ce sont de pures versions littérales où le mot latin couvre le mot grec, de même que les pièces dè l'échiquier s'appliquent sur les cases. L'expression originale est rarement rendu par celle qui lui correspond; la contexture de la phrase est grecque beaucoup plus que latine. Enfin, la plupart des termes techniques sont transcrits et non traduits quoiqu'ils eussent pu l'être avec justesse.'—*Recherches sur les traductions d'Aristote*, p. 217, ed. 1843. Ludovicus Vives, tutor to Charles the Fifth, and at one time preceptor to the Princess Mary, daughter of Henry the Eighth, complains bitterly in his treatise, *De Causis corruptarum Artium*, of the impure channels through which the knowledge of Aristotle was filtered into Europe, viz., the commentaries of Averroes. 'Tales sunt illius libri Græci quidem ut ab eo sunt perscripti, nam Latinos ita legimus, ut ænigmata audire te credas, non planum sermonem, atque explicatum, qualem inter se homines consueverunt usurpare. Dicet aliquis grave incommodum, sed ideo tolerabile, quòd adjuvamur bonis interpretibus ac explicatoribus ex Arabiâ usque accitis. Quibus tandem? Versione Arabicâ et commentariis Abenrois. . . . nomen est commentatoris nactus homo, qui, in Aristotele enarrando, nihil minus explicat quàm eum ipsum, quem suscepit declarandum. Itaque videas eum pessimè philosophos omnes antiquos citare, ut qui nullum unquam legerit, ignarus Græcitatis ac Latinitatis; pro polo Ptolemæum ponit, pro Prothagorâ Pythagoram, pro Cratylo Democritum, libros Platonis

THE GOVERNOUR. 93

no propre englisshe worde to be gyuen; but to prouide for it some maner of exposition, it may be sayde in this fourme: 'Of the dueties and maners appertaynynge to men.'[a] But aboue all other, the warkes of Plato wolde be most studiously radde whan the iugement of a man is come to perfection, and by the other studies is instructed in the fourme of speakynge that philosophers used.[b] Lorde god, what incom-

titulis ridiculis inscribit et ita de iis loquitur ut vel cæco perspicuum sit literam eum in illis legisse nullam.'—*Opera*, tom. i. p. 410, ed. 1555. Vives, however, made a strange blunder in assuming that the Arabic copies of Aristotle were derived from Latin originals. 'Aristotelem vero quo modo legit? Non in suâ origine purum et integrum, non in lacunam Latinum derivatum, non enim potuit, linguarum expers, sed *de Latino in Arabicum transvasatum*. In quâ transfusione ex Græcis bonis facta sunt Latina non bona, ut ille dicit, ex Latinis vero malis Arabica pessima.'—*Ubi supra*, p. 411. Ascham, in his *Schoolmaster*, bears testimony to the same effect as the author. 'To speak as I think, I never saw yet any commentary upon Aristotle's Logic, either in Greek or Latin, that ever I liked; because they be rather spent in declaring school-point rules, than in gathering fit examples for use and utterance either by pen or talk.'—*Works*, vol. iii. p. 231, ed. 1864.

[a] The De Officiis has been described by a modern scholar as 'a treatise on moral obligations, viewed nót so much with reference to a metaphysical investigation of the basis on which they rest as to the practical business of the world, and the intercourse of social and political life.'—Smith's *Dict. of Biogr.* sub voc. From the same source we learn that the editio princeps of the De Officiis is one of the oldest specimens of classical typography in existence, having been printed along with the Paradoxa by Fust and Schöffer at Mayence in 1465, and again in 1466. Another edition was published about the latter year at Cologne, by Ulric Zell. Professor Browne says: 'The study of Cicero's philosophical works is invaluable, in order to understand the minds of those who came after him. It must not be forgotten that not only all Roman philosophy after his time, but great part of that of the middle ages, was Greek philosophy filtered through Latin, and mainly founded on that of Cicero.'—*Hist. of Rom. Class. Lit.* p. 357.

[b] Thus Quintilian assigns him the first place amongst the writers whose works he recommends for perusal to a young orator. 'Philosophorum, ex quibus plurimum se traxisse eloquentiæ M. Tullius confitetur, quis dubitet *Platonem* esse præcipuum sive acumine disserendi sive eloquendi facultate divinâ quâdam et Homericâ? Multum enim supra prosam orationem et quam pedestrem Græci vocant, surgit; ut mihi non hominis ingenio sed quodam delphico videatur oraculo instinctus.'—*Instit. Orat.* lib. x. cap. i. § 81. Roger Ascham entertained the same opinion as our author with regard to postponing the time for reading Plato. 'To compare Homer and Plato together, two wonders of nature and art for wit

94 THE GOVERNOUR.

parable swetnesse of wordes and mater shall he finde in the saide warkes of Plato and Cicero ; wherin is ioyned grauitie with dilectation, excellent wysedome with diuine eloquence, absolute vertue with pleasure incredible, and euery place is so infarced [a] with profitable counsaile, ioyned with honestie, that those thre bokes be almoste sufficient to make a perfecte and excellent gouernour. The prouerbes of Salomon with the bokes of Ecclesiastes and Ecclesiasticus be very good lessons. All the historiall partes of the bible be righte necessarye for to be radde of a noble man, after that he is mature in yeres.[b] And the residue (with the newe testament) is to be reuerently touched, as a celestiall iewell or relike, hauynge the chiefe interpretour of those bokes trewe and constant faithe, and dredefully to sette handes theron,[c]

and eloquence, is,' he tells us, 'most pleasant and profitable *for a man of ripe judgment.'—Works*, vol. iii. p. 195, ed. 1864.

[a] See note ante p. 27.

[b] Mr. Seebohm tells us that 'the Scriptures for some generations had been practically ignored at the Universities. . . . A degree in Arts did not, it would seem, entitle the graduate to lecture upon the Bible. . . Before the days of Wiclif the Bible had been free, and Bishop Grosseteste could urge Oxford students to devote their *best morning hours* to Scripture lectures. But an unsuccessful revolution ends in tightening the chains which it ought to have broken. During the fifteenth century the Bible was *not* free. And Scripture lectures, though still retaining a nominal place in the academical course of theological study, were thrown into the background by the much greater relative importance of the lectures on 'the Sentences.'—*The Oxford Reformers*, 2nd edn., pp. 2, 3.

[c] It is impossible in the face of this juxtaposition of Plato and the Scriptures not to see how completely Mr. Seebohm's remarks on this subject are justified. 'It was of necessity,' he says, 'that the sudden reproduction of the Greek philosophy and the works of the older Neo-Platonists in Italy should sooner or later produce a new crisis in religion. A thousand years before, Christianity and Neo-Platonism had been brought into the closest contact. Christianity was then in its youth, comparatively pure, and in the struggle for mastery had easily prevailed. Not that Neo-Platonism was indeed a mere phantom, which vanished and left no trace behind it. By no means. Through the pseudo-Dionysian writings it not only influenced profoundly the theology of mediæval mystics, but also entered largely even into the Scholastic system. It was thus absorbed into Christian theology, though lost as a philosophy. Now, after the lapse of a thousand years, the same battle had to be fought again. But with this terrible difference ; that now Christianity, in the impurest form it had ever assumed—a grotesque perversion of

remembrynge that Oza,[a] for puttyng his hande to the holy shryne that was called *Archa federis*, whan it was broughte by kyng Dauid from the citie of Gaba,[b] though it were waueraynge and in daunger to fall, yet was he stryken of god, and fell deed immediately.[c] It wolde nat be forgoten that the lytell boke of the most excellent doctour Erasmus Roterodamus, (whiche he wrate to Charles, nowe beynge emperour and than prince of Castile[d]) whiche boke is intituled the Institution of a christen prince,[e] wolde be as familyare alwaye with gentilmen, at all tymes, and in euery age, as was Homere with the great king Alexander, or Xenophon with Scipio; for as all men may iuge that haue radde that warke of Erasmus, that there was neuer boke written in latine that, in so lytle a portion, contayned of sentence, eloquence, and vertuous exhortation, a more compendious abundaunce.[f] And here I make an ende

Erasmus of the institution of a christen prynce.

Christianity—had to cope with the purest and noblest of the Greek philosophies. . . . . The leading minds of Italy were once more seeking for a reconciliation between Plato and Christianity in the works of the pseudo-Dionysius, Macrobius, Plotinus, Proclus, and other Neo-Platonists. There was the same anxious endeavour as a thousand years earlier to fuse all philosophies into one. Plato and Aristotle must be reconciled as well as Christianity and Plato. The old world was becoming once more the possession of the new. It was felt to be the recovery of a lost inheritance and everything of antiquity, whether Greek, Roman, Jewish, Persian, or Arabian, was regarded as a treasure.'—*The Oxford Reformers*, pp. 9, 10.

[a] *I.e.* Uzza.

[b] *I.e.* Gibeah. See 2 Sam. vi. 4. Considerable confusion has arisen from the close similarity in the names of the three towns of Benjamin, viz., *Geba*, *Gibeah*, and *Gibeon*, which are all represented in the Septuagint by the same word—Γαβαά.

[c] See 2 Sam. vi. 7.

[d] This was the celebrated Charles the Fifth, grandson of Ferdinand and Isabella, who was born at Ghent, Feb. 24th, 1500. His mother, the infanta Joanna, had married the Archduke Philip, son of the Emperor Maximilian, and sovereign in right of his mother of the Low Countries.

[e] The *Institutio Principis Christiani* was published 1516, and was written 'for the special benefit of Prince Charles, who, then sixteen years old, had succeeded on the death of Ferdinand in the spring of 1516 to the crowns of Castile and Aragon, as well as to the kingdoms of Naples and Sicily, and of the island of Sardinia.'— *The Oxford Reformers*, 2nd ed. p. 368.

[f] 'The position assumed by Erasmus will be best learned by a brief examina-

of the lernynge and studie wherby noble men may attayne to be worthy to haue autorite in a publike weale. Alway I

tion of the "Institutes of a Christian Prince." First, he struck at the root of the notion that a prince having received his kingdom *jure divino* had a right to use it for his own selfish ends. He laid down at starting the proposition that the one thing which "a prince ought to keep in view in the administration of his government is that same thing which a people ought to keep in view in choosing a prince, viz., *the public good*." Christianity in his view was as obligatory on a prince as on a priest or monk. Thus he wrote to Prince Charles—"As often as it comes into your mind that you are a prince, call to mind also that you are a *Christian* prince." . . . . The good of the people was, from the Christian point of view, to override everything else, even royal prerogatives. "If princes were perfect in every virtue, a pure and simple monarchy might be desirable; but as this can hardly ever be in actual practice, as human affairs are now, a *limited monarchy* (monarchia temperata) is preferable—one in which the aristocratic and democratic elements are mixed and united, and so balance one another." And, lest Prince Charles should kick against the pricks and shrink from the abridgment of his autocratic power, Erasmus tells him that "if a prince wish well to the republic, his power will not be restrained but aided by these means." . . . . Proceeding from the general to the particular there is a separate chapter, "De Vectigalibus et Exactionibus," remarkable for the clear expression of the views which More had advanced in his "Utopia," and which the Oxford Reformers held in common, with regard to the unchristian way in which the interests of the poor were too often sacrificed and lost sight of in the levying of taxes. The great aim of a prince, he contended, should be to reduce taxation as much as possible. Rather than increase it, it would be better, he wrote, for a prince to reduce his unnecessary expenditure, to dismiss idle ministers, to avoid wars and foreign enterprises, to restrain the rapacity of ministers, and rather to study the right administration of revenues than their augmentation. If it should be really necessary to exact something from the people, then, he maintained, it is the part of a good prince to choose such ways of doing so as should cause as little inconvenience as possible to those of *slender means*. It may, perhaps, be expedient to call upon the rich to be frugal; but to reduce the *poor* to hunger and crime would be both most inhuman and also hardly *safe*. . . . It requires care also, he continued, lest the inequality of property should be too great; "not that I would wish to take away any property from any one by force, but that means should be taken to prevent the wealth of the multitude from getting into few hands." Erasmus then proceeded to inquire what mode of taxation would prove least burdensome to the people. And the conclusion he came to was that "a good prince will burden with as few taxes as possible such things as are in *common use amongst the lowest classes*, such things as corn, bread, beer, wine, clothes, and other things necessary to life.'. . Erasmus wound up this chapter on taxation by applying the principles of common honesty to the question of *coinage*, in connexion with which many iniquities were perpetrated by princes in the sixteenth century. In the chapter on the "Making and Amending of Laws," Erasmus, in the same way, fixes upon some of the points

shall exhorte tutours and gouernours of noble chyldren, that they suffre them nat to use ingourgitations [a] of meate or drinke, ne to slepe moche, that is to saye, aboue viii houres at the moste. For undoubtedly bothe repletion and superfluous slepe be capitall enemies to studie, as they be semblably to helth of body and soule. Aulus Gellius sayth that children, if they use of meate and slepe ouer moche, *Gell.* lib. iv. be made therwith dull to lerne, and we se that therof slownesse is taken, and the children's personages do waxe uncomely, and lasse growe in stature.[b] Galen wyll nat permitte that pure wyne, without alay of water, shulde in any wyse be gyuen to children, for as moche as it humecteth the body, or

which are so prominently mentioned in the "Utopia." Thus he urges that the greatest attention should be paid, not to the punishment of crimes when committed, but to the prevention of the commission of crimes worthy of punishment. Again there is a paragraph in which it is urged that just as a wise surgeon does not proceed to amputation except as a last resort, so all remedies should be tried before *capital punishment* is resorted to. This was one of the points urged by More. Thus, also, in speaking of the removal of occasions and causes of crime, he urged, just as More had done, that idle people should either be set to work or banished from the realm. The number of priests and monasteries should be kept in moderation. Other idle classes—especially soldiers—should not be allowed. As to the nobility he would not, he said, detract from the honour of their noble birth i their character were noble also. "But if they are such as we see plenty now-a-days—softened by ease, made effeminate by pleasure, unskilled in all good arts, revellers, eager sportsmen, not to say anything worse... why should this race of men be preferred to shoemakers or husbandmen?" In the chapter *De bello suscipiendo* he expressed his well-known hatred of war. It was natural that, holding as he did in common with Colet and More, such strong views against war, he should express them as strongly in this little treatise as he had already done elsewhere... It may be interesting to inquire what remedies or substitutes for war he proposed. He mentioned two. First, the reference of disputes between princes to arbitrators; second, the disposition on the part of princes rather to concede a point in dispute than to insist upon it at far greater cost than the thing is worth.'—*The Oxford Reformers*, p. 371-377. It is somewhat remarkable that Mr. Seebohm takes no notice of the commendation thus bestowed by Sir Thos. Elyot, the contemporary of Erasmus, and one of the best scholars of the day, upon this interesting treatise.

[a] See the Glossary.

[b] Pueros impubes compertum est, si plurimo cibo nimioque somno uterentur, hebetiores fieri, ad veterni usque aut eluci tarditatem; corporaque eorum improcera fieri, minusque adolescere.—*Noct. Attic.* lib. iv. cap. 19.

maketh it moyster and hotter than is conuenient, also it fylleth the heed with fume, in them specially, whiche be lyke as children of hote and moiste temperature. These be well nighe the wordes of the noble Galen.[a]

CHAPTER XII.

Why gentilmen in this present tyme be nat equall in doctryne to the auncient noble men.

NOWE wyll I somwhat declare of the chiefe causes why, in our tyme, noble men be nat as excellent in lernying as they were in olde tyme amonge the Romanes and grekes.[b] Surely, as I haue diligently marked in dayly experience, the principall causes be these. The pride, avarice, and negligence of parentes, and the lacke or fewenesse of suffycient maysters or teachers.[c]

[a] Sane vinum, quàm diutissimè, qui eâ naturâ puer est, ne gustare quidem suaserim. Quippe quod haustum et humectat nimium et calefacit corpus, tum caput halitu replet iis, qui humido calidoque temperamento sunt, quale est ejusmodi puerorum.—*De Sanitate tuendâ*, lib. i. fo. 12, ed. 1538.

[b] 'More's opinion was that in England, in his time, "far more than four parts of the whole (people), divided into ten, could never read English," and probably the education of the other six-tenths was anything but satisfactory.'—*The Oxford Reformers*, p. 353. 'It is stated by a recent historian that as late as the reign of Edward VI. there were peers of Parliament unable to read. Well might Roger Ascham exclaim "The fault is in yourselves, ye noblemen's sons, and therefore ye deserve the greater blame, that commonly the meaner men's children come to be the wisest councillors and greatest doers in the weighty affairs of this realm."'—*Essays on a Liberal Education*, p. 46.

[c] The 'avarice' of parents was without doubt *the cause* of 'the lacke' of masters. Ascham bears witness to the same thing. 'It is pity, that commonly more care is had, yea and that among very wise men, to find out rather a cunning man for their horse, than a cunning man for their children. They say nay in word, but they do so in deed, for to the one they will gladly give a stipend of two hundred crowns by the year, and loth to offer to the other two hundred shillings.'—*Works*, vol. iii. p. 104, ed. 1864. 'When Erasmus broached the subject of an under-master among certain Masters of Arts one said, "Who would be a schoolmaster that could live in any other way?" (Erasmus to Colet.)

As I sayd, pride is the first cause of this inconuenience. For of those persons be some, which, without shame, dare affirme, that to a great gentilman it is a notable reproche to be well lerned [a] and to be called a great clerke: whiche name they accounte to be of so base estymation, that they neuer haue it in their mouthes but whan they speke any thynge in derision, whiche perchaunce they wolde nat do if they had ones layser to rede our owne cronicle of Englande, where they shall fynde that kynge Henry the first, sonne of willyam conquerour, and one of the moste noble [b] princes that euer reigned in this realme, was openly called Henry beau clerke, whiche is in englysshe, fayre clerke, and is yet at this day so named.[c] And wheder that

Henry beau clerk, kynge of Englande.

—*State Papers*, vol. i. no. 4528. Knight, who quotes this letter in his *Life of Colet*, says: 'He had also in a former letter mentioned his fruitless endeavours to serve him in the affair of an usher. And he did, not only in the former of these epistles, but whenever he had an opportunity, encourage men of letters to undertake the laborious care of a grammar school; of which he often speaks in the highest commendation, as what exalts the schoolmaster to the highest dignity; whose business is to season youth in learning and religion, and raise up men for the service of their country. "It may be," says he, "the employment is accounted vile and mean in the opinion of fools, but in itself it is really great and honourable."'—P. 149, ed. 1823.

[a] 'A letter from Pace to Colet about the year 1500, prefixed to the former's *De Fructu*, shows the tone of this class of gentlemen. One is represented as breaking out at table into abuse of letters. "I swear," he says, "rather than my son should be bred a scholar, he should hang. To blow a neat blast on the horn, to understand hunting, to carry a hawk handsomely and train it, that is what becomes the son of a gentleman; but as for book learning, he should leave that to louts."'—*Essays on a Liberal Education*, p. 46.

[b] Suger, the abbé of Saint Denys, who was born in 1081, and was therefore a contemporary, says: Vir prudentissimus Henricus, cujus tam admiranda quàm prædicanda animi et corporis strenuitas et scientia gratam offerrent materiam.'—*Vita Ludovici Grossi*, cap. i. See Migne's *Patrologiæ Cursus*, tom. 186, p. 1258.

[c] Fabyan, who died in 1512, says, that 'for his connyng he was surnamed Bewclerke;' and adds that 'in his youth he plyed him to suche study that he was enstructe in the vii artys lyberallys.'—*Chron.* p. 318, ed. 1559. Matt. Paris calls him 'providus, sed astutus et avarus, patre sic jubente, quia imbellis, officio clericali est addictus, et in eo bene ac expeditenter profecit; et jam legisperitus effectus est;'—*Hist. Angl.* vol. i. p. 31, and adds, 'vir videlicet literis addictus et jam eleganter in grammatica et jure eruditus, mente sagax, corpore decorus, viribus integer.'—*Ubi supra*, p. 163. Ordericus Vitalis calls him *literatus rex*, and the

name be to his honour or to his reproche, let them iuge that do rede and compare his lyfe with his two bretherne, william called Rouse,[a] and Robert le courtoise,[b] they both nat hauyng

English translator of that writer has 'not ventured to put a gloss on the phrase, as there seems to be some doubt respecting Henry's claims to be considered a man of letters in the modern sense of the words, notwithstanding his surname of *Beauclerc*.' 'It is singular,' he adds, 'that neither Henry of Huntingdon nor William of Malmesbury, contemporary writers who have taken extended views of his character, the latter even describing his person, should be altogether silent on the subject of his literary attainments.—Malmesbury, indeed, says incidentally that 'he could not read much aloud, *quamvis ipse nec multum palam legeret*' (lib. v.).—*Bohn's Antiq. Lib.* vol. iii. p. 352. William of Malmesbury, however, gives him credit for more than this, for he says that he was ' Philosophiâ non adeo exiliter informatus. Itaque pueritiam ad spem regni literis muniebat; subinde, patre quoque audiente, jactitare proverbium solitus, " Rex illiteratus asinus coronatus."' And further that ' librorum mella adeo avidis medullis indidit, ut nulli posteà bellorum tumultus, nulli curarum motus eas excutere illustri animo possent.'—*Gesta Reg. Angl.* lib. v. § 390.

[a] By Mat. Paris he is called 'cognomento, capite, et mente, Rufus et vulpinus.'—*Hist. Anglorum*, vol. i. p. 131, Chron. and Mem. Wace calls him 'Willame li Ros' in *Le Roman de Rou*, tom ii. p. 304, ed Pluquet. Robert of Gloucester, 'Wyllam ye rede Kyng,' p. 383, ed. 1724. It is probable that the character of Rufus has received a deeper tinge than it deserved, in consequence of his having incurred the hatred of the clergy, who were also his biographers; thus the French abbot Suger, speaking of his death, says: ' Divinatum est virum divinâ ultione percussum, assumpto veritatis argumento, eo quod pauperum exstiterat intolerabilis oppressor, ecclesiarum crudelis exactor, et si quando episcopi vel prælati decederent, irreverentissimus retentor et dissipator.'—*Vita Ludovici Grossi*, cap. i. See Migne's *Pat. Curs.* tom. clxxxvi. p. 1257.

[b] Fabyan calls him 'Robert the eldest sone of Kynge Wyllyam, the whiche was surnamed Curthose or Shorthose, and Shorte Bote also.'—Cap. ccxxii. p. 245, ed. 1811. And the reason of this nickname being given to him is thus stated by Vitalis: ' Facie obesâ, corpore pingui, brevique staturâ, unde vulgo Gambaron cognominatus est et Brevis-Ocrea.'—Lib. iv. cap. 25. Migne, *Patrol. Curs.* tom. 188. And in another place he says: 'Corpore autem brevis et grossus, ideoque Brevis-Ocrea (Gallicè *Courte-Heuse*) patre est cognominatus.'—Lib. viii. cap. 1. *ubi supra*. Wace gives a somewhat similar explanation of the name:

> Peti fu mult, maiz fu gros,
> Jambes out cortes, gros les os;
> Li Reis por ço le sornomout
> E Corte-Hose l'apelout;
> De cortes hoses ert hosez
> E Corte-Hose ert apelez.
>
> *Le Roman de Rou*, tom. ii. p. 304, ed. Pluquet.

semblable lernyng with the sayd Henry, the one for his dissolute lyuyng and tyranny beynge hated of all his nobles and people, finally was sodaynely slayne by the shotte of an arowe,[a] as he was huntynge in a forest, whiche to make larger and to gyue his deere more lybertie, he dyd cause the houses of lii parisshes to be pulled downe, the people to be expelled, and all beyng desolate to be tourned in to desert, and made onely pasture for beestes sauage;[b] whiche he wolde neuer haue

[a] Sir Thomas Elyot, it will be seen, gives Walter Tyrrel the benefit of the doubt which arose almost immediately, and was subject of grave discussion by subsequent historians. John of Salisbury, who wrote not many years afterwards, says: 'Quis alterutrum miserit telum, adhuc incertum est quidem. Nam Walterus Tyrrellus ille, qui regiæ necis reus à plurimis dictus est, eo quod illi familiaris erat et tunc in indagine ferarum vicinus, et fere singulariter adhærebat, etiam cum ageret in extremis, se à cæde illius immunem esse, invocato in animam suam Dei judicio, protestatus est. Fuerunt plurimi qui ipsum regem jaculum quo interemptum est misisse asserunt et hoc Walterus ille, etsi non crederetur ei, constanter asserebat.'—
—*Vita S. Anselmi*, ed. Migne, p. 1031. The French abbé Suger, who was himself a contemporary of Tyrrell says: 'Imponebatur a quibusdam cuidam nobilissimo viro Galterio Tirello quod eum sagittâ perfoderat. Quem cum nec timeret, nec speraret, jurejurando *sæpius audivimus*, et quasi sacrosanctum asserere quod ea die nec in eam partem silvæ in qua rex venabatur venerit, nec eum in silva omnino viderit.'—*Vita Ludovici Grossi*, cap. i. *ubi supra*. Ordericus Vitalis, who was born in 1075 and died in 1141, and was therefore also a contemporary, attributes the king's death to misadventure. His account is as follows: 'Cumque Rex et Gualterius de Pice cum paucis sodalibus in nemore constituti essent, et armati prædam avidè exspectarent, subito inter eos currente ferâ, rex de statu suo recessit, et Gualterius sagittam emisit. Quæ super dorsum feræ setam radens rapidè volavit, atque regem è regione stantem lethaliter vulneravit.'—Lib. x. cap. 12, ed Migne; and it must be admitted that this account is very rational and bears the marks of truth on the face of it. On the other hand it was only natural, from the hatred with which he was regarded, especially by the clergy, who were also the historians of the event, that his death should be assumed to have been premeditated. Turner says 'It was the misfortune of Rufus that his death benefited so many— Henry, France, and the clergy—that no critical inquiry was made into its cause.' —*Hist. of Eng.* vol. iv. p. 168.

[b] This is exactly the account given by Knyghton, canon of Leicester in the reigns of Edward III., Richard II., and Henry IV., who says: 'Hic Willielmus fecit forestas in multis locis per medium regni et inter Southamtonam et Prioratum de Twynam qui nunc vocatur Crystischyrke prostravit et exterminavit viginti duas ecclesias matrices, cum villis, capellis, et maneriis atque mansionibus, secundum vero quosdam *lii ecclesias parochiales*, et fecit de loco illo Forestam novam quam vocavit

done if he had as moche delyted in good lerning as dyd his brother.

The other brother, Robert le Courtoise, beyng duke of Normandie, and the eldest sonne of wylliam Conquerour, all be it that he was a man of moche prowesse, and right expert in martial affayres, wherfore he was electe before Godfray of Boloigne to haue ben kyng of Hierusalem;[a] yet natwith-

suum novum herbarium et replevit eam cervis, damis, et aliis feris parcens illi per vii annos primos, venatûs gratiâ. Quæ vastaverunt blada et segetes in magnum gravamen compatriotis. Et tantam exercuit per forestas duritiam quod pro damâ hominem suspenderet, pro lepore xxs plecteretur, pro cuniculo xs daret.'—*Decem Scriptores*, fo. 2373, ed. 1652. Ordericus Vitalis makes the number of depopulated parishes still larger : '*plus quam lx parochias* ultro devastavit, ruricolas ad alia loca transmigrare compulit, et silvestres feras pro hominibus, ut voluptatem venandi haberet ibidem constituit.'—Lib. x. cap. 11, ed. Migne. But he attributes the creation of the forest to the first William, whereas Knyghton distinctly states, as we have just seen, that it was made by Rufus ; it is evident, therefore, that Sir Thomas Elyot has adopted his account rather than that of Vitalis. Wilhelmus Gemiticensis, who had been chaplain to the Conqueror, says that Richard, brother to Rufus, had been killed in the lifetime of his father 'in eadem silvâ, dum simili modo venaretur, ictu arboris male evitatæ,' and he adds that it was the common opinion that the sins of the father were visited upon the children, 'quoniam multas villas et ecclesias propter eandem forestam amplificandam in circuitu ipsius destruxerat.'—Lib. vii. cap. 9. Camden's *Anglica Scripta*, ed. 1603. William of Malmesbury mentions the circumstance of Richard's death in the New Forest, which, however, he says 'tabidi aeris nebulâ incurrisse'; and after charging William the Conqueror with the act of devastation, he recounts further proofs of the divine judgment ; 'ibi multa regio generi contigere infortunia, quæ habitatorum præsens audire volentibus suggerit memoria : nam postmodum in eadem silvâ Willelmus filius ejus, et nepos Ricardus, filius Roberti comitis Normanniæ, mortem offenderint : severo Dei judicio ille sagittâ pectus, iste collum trajectus, vel, ut quidam dicunt, arboris ramusculo equo pertranseunte fauces appensus.'— *Gesta Reg. Angl.* lib. iii. § 275, ed. Migne.

[a] This passage seems to furnish additional proof of what was suggested above, that the author had consulted Knyghton's history for the events of this reign, although the story, as reproduced by the learned canon, bears rather a different complexion from that which it originally had. 'In terra sancta,' says Knyghton, 'multa egregia gessit. Ita ubique mirabilis ut nunquam per Christianum aut Paganum de equo dejici potuit. Denique cum in Sabbato Paschali apud *Ierosolymam* inter cæteros astaret Christianos, expectans ignem more solito de supernis in cereum alicujus descendere, cereus ejus divinitùs accensus est, unde et ab omnibus in regem *Ierosolymorum* electus est.'—Twysden, *Decem Scrip.* fo. 2375. Mat. Paris, who narrates the story of the election, embellishes it with the curious addition that on Robert's refusal of the honour, the Crusaders elected Godfrey,

standynge whan he inuaded this realme with sondrie puissaunt armies, also dyuers noble men aydinge hym, yet his noble brother Henry beau clerke, more by wysdome than power, also by lernynge, addyng polycie to vertue and courage, often tymes vaynquisshed hym, and dyd put him to flyght. And after sondry victories finally toke him and kepte hym in prison, hauyng none other meanes to kepe his realme in tranquillitie.[a]

It was for no rebuke, but for an excellent honour, that the emperour Antonine [b] was surnamed philosopher, for by his moste noble example of lyuing, and industrie incomparable,[c]

and conducted him with due solemnity to the Holy Sepulchre, *erubescente duce Roberto.*—*Hist. Anglorum*, vol. i. p. 150.

[a] Vitalis narrates at length the interview at Gisors in Normandy between the Pope Calixtus II. and Henry, when the latter sought to justify the detention of his brother in close custody. He is made to say, 'Frater enim meus incentores totius nequitiæ tuebatur, et illorum concilia, per quos vilis et contemptibilis erat, admodum amplectebatur. Gunherius nimirum de Alneio, et Rogerius de Laceio, Robertus quoque de Belismo, aliique scelesti Normannis dominabantur, et sub imaginatione ducis præsulibus omnique clero cum inermi populo principabantur. Illos siquidem quos ego de transmarinâ regione pro nefariis exturbaveram factionibus, intimos sibi consiliarios, et colonis præsides præfecit innocentibus. Innumeræ cædes et incendia passim agebantur, et dira facinora, quæ inexperti pene incredibilia putant. Fratri meo mandavi sæpius ut meis uteretur consultibus eique totis adminicularer nisibus. Sed ille me contempto meis contra me potitus est insidiatoribus.'—Lib. xii. cap. 12, ed. Migne.

[b] The author has confounded the Emperor Antoninus Pius with his successor Marcus Aurelius Antoninus; it was the latter to whom the epithet of 'the philosopher' was applied. But the mistake is not very surprising, because Victor says of the *former*, 'adeo æqualis, probisque moribus, uti plane docuerit, neque jugi pace, ac longo otio absoluta ingenia corrumpi : eoque demum fortunatas urbes fore, si regna sapientiæ sint.'—*De Cæsaribus*, cap. xv. While on the other hand the biographer of the *latter* says : 'Sententia Platonis semper in ore illius fuit, *Florere civitates, si aut philosophi imperarent, aut imperatores philosopharentur.*'—*Historia Augusta*, tom. i. p. 394, ed. 1671. Eutropius says of Aurelius: 'Philosophiæ deditus Stoicæ, ipse etiam non solum vitæ moribus, sed etiam eruditione Philosophus.'—Lib. viii. cap. 11. And he goes on to tell us: 'Institutus est ad philosophiam per Apollonium Chalcedonium, ad scientiam literarum Græcarum per Sextum Chæronensem, Plutarchi nepotem.'

[c] 'The Stoic philosophy,' says Niebuhr, 'opened to M. Aurelius a completely new world. The letters of Fronto, which are otherwise childish and trifling, throw an interesting light upon young M. Aurelius' state of mind at the

he during all the tyme of his reigne kept the publike weale of the Romanes in suche a perfecte astate, that by his actes he confirmed the sayeng of Plato, That blessed is that publike weale wherin either philosophers do reigne, or els kinges be in philosophie studiouse.[a]

These persones that so moche contemne lernyng, that they wolde that gentilmen's children shulde haue no parte or very litle therof, but rather shulde spende their youth alway (I saye not onely in huntynge and haukyng,[b] whiche moderately

time when he cast rhetoric aside and sought happiness in philosophy; not, indeed, in its dialectic subtleties, but in its fa'th in virtue and eternity. He bore the burdens of his exalted position in the manner in which, according to the precepts of pious men, we ought to take up our cross and bear it patiently. Actuated by this sentiment, M. Aurelius exerted all his powers for the good of the empire, and discharged all his duties, ever active, no less in the military than in the civil administration of the empire. He complains of want of time to occupy himself with intellectual pursuits; but then he consoles himself again with the thought that he is doing his duty and fulfilling his mission.'—*Lectures on Rom. Hist.* cxxxiii. ed. 1870. Another modern historian says: 'The habits of mind which Aurelius had cultivated during the period of his probation were little fitted perhaps to give. him a foresight of the troubles now impending. In presiding on the tribunals, in guiding the deliberations of the senate, in receiving embassies and appointing magistrates, he had shrunk from no fatigue or responsibility; but the distaste he expressed from the first for his political eminence continued, no doubt, to the end: his heart was still with his chosen studies, and with the sophists and rhetoricians who aided him in them. Hadrian, in mere gaiety of heart, turned the prince into an academician, but it was with genuine reluctance and under a strong sense of duty that Aurelius converted the academician into the prince. But the hope that his peculiar training might render him a model to sovereigns—the recollection of the splendid fallacy of Plato, that states would surely flourish were but their philosophers princes or were but their princes philosophers—sustained him in his arduous and unwelcome task, and contributed to his success in it.'—Merivale, *Hist. of Rome*, vol. vii. p. 565.

[a] 'Ἐὰν μή, ἦν δ' ἐγώ, ἢ οἱ φιλόσοφοι βασιλεύσωσιν ἐν ταῖς πόλεσιν ἢ οἱ βασιλῆς τε νῦν λεγόμενοι καὶ δυνάσται φιλοσοφήσωσι γνησίως τε καὶ ἱκανῶς, καὶ τοῦτο εἰς ταὐτὸν ξυμπέσῃ . . . . οὐκ ἔστι κακῶν παῦλα, ὦ φίλε Γλαύκων, ταῖς πόλεσι, δοκῶ δὲ οὐδὲ τῷ ἀνθρωπίνῳ γένει.—*De Rep.* lib. v. cap. 18. It may be here remarked that William of Malmesbury has applied the same sentiment to the reign of Henry the First, whom he evidently regarded as another Antoninus.

[b] 'Hunting and hawking skilfully,' says Strutt, 'were also acquirements that he (*i.e.* an accomplished gentleman) was obliged to possess, and which were usually taught him as soon as he was able to endure the fatigue that they required. Hence it is said of Sir Tristram, a fictitious character held forth as the mirror of

THE GOVERNOUR. 105

used, as solaces ought to be, I intende nat to disprayse) but in those ydle pastymes, whiche, for the vice that is therin, the commaundement of the prince, and the uniuersall consent of the people, expressed in statutes and lawes, do prohibite, I meane, playeng at dyce, and other games named unlefull.*

chivalry in the romance intituled *The Death of Arthur*, that " as he growed in might and strength he laboured ever in hunting and in hawking, so that never gentleman more that ever we heard tell of. And, as the book saith, he began good measures of blowing of beasts of venery and beasts of chase, and all manner of vermains ; and all these terms we have yet of hawking and hunting, and therefore the book of venery of hawking and hunting, is called the book of Sir Tristram."'—Introduction to *Sports and Pastimes*, pp. vii. viii. Strutt also quotes from a document of the time of Henry the Seventh (Harl. MS. 69), the preamble of which states, 'Whereas it ever hath bene of old antiquitie used in this realme of most noble fame, for all lustye gentlemen to passe the delectable season of summer after divers manner and sondry fashions of disports, as in hunting the red and fallowe deer with hounds, greyhounds, and with the bowe : also in hawking with hawks of the tower, and other pastimes of the field.'—*Ibid*. p. xii. Henry the Eighth was exceedingly fond of hunting, hawking, and other field sports. Thus Hall, recording the events of the eighteenth year of his reign, says, 'All this sommer the kyng tooke his pastyme in huntyng.'—*Chron.* fo. cxlix. ed. 1548. Sir Thomas More makes a young gallant say,

'Manhod I am, therefore I me delight
To hunt and hawke, to nourishe up and fede
The grayhounde to the course, the hawke to the flyght,
And to bestryde a good and lusty stede :
These thynges become a very man in dede.'
See Warton's *Hist. of Eng. Poetry*, vol. iii. p. 97.

Hawks were the subject of legislation in the reign of Edw. I.; thus in the Carta de foresta it was enacted that 'every freeman shall have within his own woods ayries of hawks, sparrow-hawks, faulcons, eagles, and herons.' The reader will find more information on this subject in the notes to Chapter XVIII. *infra*.

* The thirty-eighth canon of the Council of Worcester, held in 1240, contains the following prohibition : ' Prohibemus etiam clericis ne intersint ludis inhonestis vel choreis vel ludant ad aleas vel taxillos, nec sustineant ludos fieri de Rege et Regina, nec arietes levari nec palæstras publicas fieri.'—Du Cange, *sub* Ludo. Ordericus Vitalis tells us that in his time even the prelates of the church were in the habit of playing at dice. A still more celebrated writer, John of Salisbury, who lived a little later in the same century, speaks of dice-playing as being then extremely prevalent, and enumerates no less than ten different games, which he names in Latin. See *De nugis Curialium*, lib. i. c. 5. A great deal of curious information on the subject of dice may be found in a treatise called ' Palamedes, sive de tabulâ lusoriâ et aleatoribus,' written by one Daniel Souter in 1622, and

These persones, I say, I wolde shulde remembre, or elles nowe lerne, if they neuer els herde it, that the noble Philip kyng of Macedonia, who subdued al Greece, aboue all the good fortunes that euer he hadde, most reioysed that his sonne Alexander was borne in the tyme that Aristotle the philosopher flourisshed, by whose instruction he mought attaine to most excellent lernynge.[a]

Also the same Alexander often tymes sayd that he was

dedicated to Sir Edward Zouche, who was then Lord Warden of the Cinque Ports and Constable of Dover Castle. By 12 Ric. II. c. 6, servants were prohibited from playing 'at tennis or football, and other games called coits, dice, casting of the stone, kailes, and other such importune games.' And by 11 Hen. VII. c. 2, it was enacted that 'noon apprentice, ne servaunt of husbondry, laborer, ner servaunt artificer pley at the Tables from the xth day of January next commyng, but onely for mete and drinke; ner at the Tenys Closshe, Dise, Cardes, Bowles, nor any other unlawfull game in no wise out of Cristmas, and in Cristmas to pley oonly in the dwelling house of his maister, or where the maister of any the seid servauntes is present.' In the eighteenth year of Henry the Eighth, according to Hall, 'In the moneth of Maie, was a proclamacion made against al unlawfull games accordyng to the statutes made in this behalf, and commissions awarded into every shire for the execution of the same; so that in all places Tables, Dice, Cardes, and Boules wer taken and brent. Wherfore the people murmured against the Cardinall, saying that he grudged at every mannes pleasure savyng his owne; but this Proclamacion small tyme endured, and when young men were forbidden Boules and such other games, some fell to drinkyng, and some to ferettyng of other mennes conies and stealyng of dere in Parkes, and other unthriftiness.'—*Chronicle*, fo. cxlix. ed. 1548; and see further on this subject in the notes to Chapter XX. *infra*.

[a] Aulus Gellius is the authority for this assertion. He says: 'Is Philippus, cum in omni fere tempore negotiis belli victoriisque affectus exercitusque esset, à liberali tamen Musâ et a studiis humanitatis nunquam abfuit; quin lepide comiterque pleraque et faceret et diceret. Feruntur adeo libri Epistolarum ejus munditiæ et venustatis et prudentiæ plenarum: velut sunt illæ literæ, quibus Aristoteli philosopho natum esse sibi Alexandrum nuntiavit. Ea Epistola, quoniam curæ diligentiæque in liberorum disciplinas hortamentum est, exscribenda visa est ad commovendos parentum animos. Exponenda igitur est ad hanc ferme sententiam: "Philippus Aristoteli salutem dicit. Filium mihi genitum scito. Quod equidem Dis habeo gratiam: non proinde quia natus est, quam pro eo quod eum nasci contigit temporibus vitæ tuæ. Spero enim fore, ut eductus eruditusque abs te dignus existat et nobis et rerum istarum susceptione." Ipsius autem Philippi verba hæc sunt: Φίλιππος Ἀριστοτέλει χαίρειν. Ἴσθι μοι γεγονότα υἱόν. πολλὴν οὖν τοῖς θεοῖς χάριν ἔχω, οὐχ οὕτως ἐπὶ τῇ γενέσει τοῦ παιδὸς, ὡς ἐπὶ τῷ κατὰ τὴν σὴν ἡλικίαν αὐτὴν γεγονέναι. ἐλπίζω γὰρ αὐτὸν, ὑπὸ σοῦ τραφέντα καὶ παιδευθέντα, ἄξιον ἔσεσθαι καὶ ἡμῶν καὶ τῆς τῶν πραγμάτων διαδοχῆς.'—*Noct. Att.* lib. ix. cap. 3.

equally as moche bounden to Aristotle as to his father kyng Philip, for of his father he receyued lyfe, but of Aristotle he receyued the waye to lyue nobly.[a]

Who dispraysed Epaminondas, the mooste valiant capitayne of Thebanes, for that he was excellently lerned and a great philosopher?[b] Who euer discommended Julius Cesar for that he was a noble oratour, and, nexte to Tulli, in the eloquence of the latin tonge excelled al other?[c] Who euer

---

[a] This is narrated both by Plutarch and Curtius: the former says: Ἀριστοτέλην δὲ θαυμάζων ἐν ἀρχῇ καὶ ἀγαπῶν οὐχ ἧττον, ὡς αὐτὸς ἔλεγε, τοῦ πατρὸς, ὡς δι' ἐκεῖνον μὲν ζῶν, διὰ τοῦτον δὲ καλῶς ζῶν.—Plutarch, *Alex.* 8. The latter: 'Ipse quidem prædicavit, "non minus se debere Aristoteli quàm Philippo: hujus enim munus fuisse, quod viveret; illius, quod honestè viveret."'—Lib. i. cap. 3. Bishop Thirlwall says: 'When we consider the shortness of the time, and the early age to which this part of Alexander's education was limited, we might be inclined to think that Aristotle's influence over his mind and character can scarcely have been very considerable. Nevertheless, it is at least certain that their connection lasted long enough to impress the scholar with a high degree of attachment and reverence for the master—of whom he used to say that he loved him no less than his father; for to the one he owed life, to the other *the art of living*—and even with some interest in his philosophical pursuits.'—*Hist. of Greece*, vol. vi. p. 132, where it is to be noticed that the modern historian has omitted to translate the word which Sir Thomas Elyot perceived to be the most expressive in the Greek as well as in the Latin.

[b] Eruditus autem sic, ut nemo Thebanus magis. Nam et citharizare, et cantare ad chordarum sonum doctus est à Dionysio: qui non minore fuit in musicis gloria, quam Damon, aut Lamprus; quorum pervulgata sunt nomina: carmina cantare tibiis ab Olympiodoro, saltare a Calliphrone. At philosophiæ præceptorem habuit Lysim Tarentinum, Pythagoreum: cui quidem sic fuit deditus, ut adolescens tristem et severum senem omnibus æqualibus suis in familiaritate anteposuerit: neque prius eum à se dimiserit, quam in doctrinis tanto antecesserit condiscipulos, ut facile intelligi posset, pari modo superaturum omnes in ceteris artibus. . . . Itaque cum in circulum venisset, in quo aut de republicâ disputaretur, aut de philosophiâ sermo haberetur, nunquam inde prius discessit, quam ad finem sermo esset adductus. . . . Fuit etiam disertus, ut nemo Thebanus ei par esset eloquentiâ: neque minus concinnus in brevitate respondendi, quàm in perpetuâ oratione ornatus.—Cornel. Nepos. *Epaminondas*, 2, 5.

[c] 'C. vero Cæsar si foro tantum vacasset, non alius ex nostris contra Ciceronem nominaretur; tanta in eo vis est, id acumen, ea concitatio, ut illum eodem animo dixisse, quo bellavit, appareat; exornat tamen hæc omnia mira sermonis, cujus proprie studiosus fuit, elegantiâ.'—Quintilian, *Instit. Orat.* lib. x. cap. i. § 114. Mr. Long says: 'The two roads to distinction at Rome were oratory and military ability; and Cæsar was both a soldier and an orator. . . . His first

reproued the emperour Hadriane for that he was so exquisitely lerned, nat onely in greke and latine,[a] but also in all sciences liberall, that openly at Athenes, in the uniuersall assembly of the greatteste clerkes of the worlde, he by a longe tyme disputed with philosophers and Rhetoriciens, whiche were estemed mooste excellent, and by the iugement of them that were present had the palme or rewarde of victorie?[b] And yet, by the gouernance of that noble emperour,

oration, which was against Cn. Dolabella, who was charged with the offence of Repetundæ in Macedonia, was spoken when Cæsar was still a very young man. Dolabella was acquitted; but Cæsar's prosecution was the foundation of his reputation as an orator. Cæsar's orations were not collected by himself; and though they were extant, or some of them at least, long after his death, we have only a few fragments. The speech which Sallustius attributes to Cæsar, when he spoke of the punishment of the conspirators in B.C. 63, is generally supposed to be the historian's own composition.'—*Decline of the Roman Republic*, vol. v. p. 477. Cicero says that Cæsar spoke Latin perhaps best of all the Roman orators. His words are these: 'De Cæsare et ipse ita judico, et de hoc hujus generis acerrimo æstimatore sæpissime audio, illum omnium ferè oratorum Latinè loqui elegantissimè; nec id solum domesticâ consuetudine, ut dudum de Læliorum et Muciorum familiis audiebamus, sed quamquam id quoque credo fuisse, tamen ut esset perfecta illa benè loquendi laus, multis literis, et iis quidem reconditis et exquisitis, summoque studio et diligentiâ est consequutus.'—*Brutus*, cap. 72. And in another place he says: 'Cæsar autem rationem adhibens, consuetudinem vitiosam et corruptam, purâ et incorruptâ consuetudine emendat. Itaque quum ad hanc elegantiam verborum Latinorum (quæ, etiamsi orator non sis, et sis ingenuus civis Romanus, tamen necessaria est) adjungit illa oratoria ornamenta dicendi, tum videtur tamquam tabulas bene pictas collocare in bono lumine: hanc quum habeat præcipuam laudem in communibus, non video cui debeat cedere: splendidam quamdam, minimeque veteratoriam rationem dicendi tenet, voce, motu, formâ etiam magnificâ et generosâ quodammodo.'—*Ibid.* cap. 75.

[a] 'Facundissimus Latino sermone, Græco eruditissimus fuit.'—*Eutropius*, lib. viii. cap. 7. Merivale says: 'For five years he was placed under the fashionable teachers of letters and philosophy in Greece, and the success which attended him in these and other kindred studies, the boast of the city of Minerva, gained him the familiar nickname of Græculus. *He became imbued,* we are assured, *with the true spirit of the Athenians, and not only acquired their language, but rivalled them in all their special accomplishments—in singing, in playing, in medicine, in mathematics, in painting, and in sculpture, in which he nearly equalled a Polycletus and a Euphranor*' (Victor, *Epit.* 28).—*Hist. of Rome*, vol. vii. p. 405.

[b] This appears to go rather beyond the statements of Victor and Spartianus,

THE GOVERNOUR. 109

nat only the publik weale florisshed but also diuers rebellions were suppressed, and the maiesty of the empire hugely increased.[a] Was it any reproche to the noble Germanicus [b] (who by the assignement of Augustus [c] shulde haue succeded

i.e. if it refers to the passage of the former quoted in the last note, it is a very liberal interpretation of the phrase 'potitus non sermone tantum sed et ceteris disciplinis,' &c. And if Sir Thomas Elyot is referring to the life of Hadrian by Spartianus in the Augustan history, the only passage which could afford any justification for so strong an assertion would seem to be the following : ' Et quamvis esset oratione et versu promptissimus, et in omnibus artibus peritissimus, tamen professores omnium artium semper ut doctior risit, contempsit, obtrivit. Cum his ipsis professoribus et philosophis, libris vel carminibus invicem editis, sæpe certavit. Et Favorinus quidem, cum verbum ejus quoddam ab Hadriano reprehensum esset, atque ille cessisset, arguentibus amicis quod male cederet Hadriano, de verbo quod idonei auctores usurpassent, risum jucundissimum movit. Ait enim, "Non recte suadetis, familiares, qui non patimini me illum doctiorem omnibus credere qui habet triginta legiones."'—*Hist. Aug.* tom. i. p. 148, ed. 1671. The author last quoted says indeed 'apud *Alexandriam* in Museo multas quæstiones professoribus proposuit et propositas ipse dissolvit.' —*Ibid.* p. 182.

[a] Niebuhr says : 'No Roman emperor before him had looked upon himself as the real master of the world, but merely as the sovereign of Rome, or, at most, of Italy. His reign passed almost without any wars ; and if we except the insurrection of the Jews, we hear only of trifling military operations, that, for example, against the revolted Mauretanians, whom he reduced very speedily. . . . This war (with the Jews) was the only shock which the Roman Empire experienced in the reign of Hadrian, but it was, after all, of no great importance. His reign, which lasted nearly twenty-two years, was thus free from any remarkable calamity ; and, as it passed away in almost uninterrupted peace, it may be regarded as one of the happiest periods of the empire.'—*Lect. Rom. Hist.* cxxxii. ed. 1870.

[b] Merivale says : 'The large training of the highest Roman education had fitted him, amidst these public avocations, to take a graceful interest in literature. His compositions in Greek and Latin verse were varied, and perhaps more than respectable for school exercises, with which only they should be compared.' And adds in a note, ' The Greek comedy of Germanicus (Sueton. *Calig.* 3) was probably a mere scholastic imitation, such as was generally the character of the Greek verses of the young Roman nobles. His translation of Aratus (which I believe to be genuine) may have served to relieve the dulness of the study of astronomy without the aid of telescopes or the Principia. But Ovid solicits his patronage for the most learned of his own works, at a time when such applications were not merely compliments.'—*Hist. of Rome*, vol. v. p. 24.

[c] 'At hercule Germanicum, Druso ortum, octo apud Rhenum legionibus imposuit, ascirique per adoptionem a Tiberio jussit ; quanquam esset in domo Tiberii filius juvenis ; sed quo pluribus munimentis insisteret.'—Tacitus, *Annales*, lib. i. cap. 3.

Tiberius in the empire, if traitorous enuy had nat in his flourysshynge youth bireft hym his lyfe)[a] that he was equall to the moost noble poetes of his time, and, to the increase of his honour and moost worthy commendation, his image was set up at Rome, in the habite that poetes at those dayes used?[b] Fynally howe moche excellent lernynge commendeth, and nat dispraiseth, nobilitie, it shal playnly appere unto them that do rede the lyfes of Alexander called Seuerus,[c] Tacitus,[d] Probus

[a] Whether he died by a natural death or by poison is a question upon which the ancients themselves are not agreed. Niebuhr is 'inclined to believe that his death was a natural one; for the statements brought forward against Piso refer to sorcery rather than to poison: of the former there seem to have been proofs, and superstition was then very prevalent, and a person who could resort to sorcery would not be likely to attempt poison.'—*Lectures on Rom. Hist.* cxxiv. While Merivale says: 'It results clearly, from the acknowledgments of the narrator, whose hostility to the third Cæsar is strongly marked, that the evidence advanced to prove the murder of Germanicus was completely nugatory. Still less does there appear any reasonable ground to implicate Tiberius himself in participation in the schemes of Piso, even supposing the guilt of the latter in this respect to be still matter of question.'—*Hist. of Rome*, vol. v. p. 108.

[b] There is no allusion to this in Tacitus, who enumerates the various honours which were decreed. 'Honores, ut quis amore in Germanicum aut ingenio validus, reperti decretique: ut nomen ejus Saliari carmine caneretur; sedes curules Sacerdotum Augustalium locis, superque eas querceæ coronæ statueientur; ludos Circenses eburna effigies præiret; neve quis Flamen aut Augur in locum Germanici, nisi gentis Juliæ, crearetur. . . . . . Statuarum locorumve, in quis colerentur, haud facile quis numerum inierit. Cum censeretur clypeus auro et magnitudine insignis, inter auctores eloquentiæ, asseveravit Tiberius, solitum paremque ceteris dicaturum; neque enim eloquentiam fortuna discerni: et satis illustre, si veteres inter scriptores haberetur.'—*Annal.* lib. ii. cap. 83.

[c] 'The dryness of business was relieved by the charms of literature; and a portion of time was always set apart for his favourite studies of poetry, history, and philosophy. The works of Virgil and Horace, the Republics of Plato and Cicero, formed his taste, enlarged his understanding, and gave him the noblest ideas of man and government.'—*Decline and Fall of Rom. Empire*, vol. i. p. 287. According to Lampridius, 'Ne unum quidem diem sponte sua transire passus est, quo se non et ad litteras et ad militiam exerceret' (cap. 3); and he gives a long list of the young prince's instructors, but, curiously enough, he goes on to say, 'Sed in Latinis non multum profecit, ut ex ejusdem orationibus apparet quas in senatu habuit, vel in contionibus quas apud milites vel apud populum; nec valde amavit Latinam facundiam, sed amavit litteratos homines vehementer,' for which he gives a very sufficient reason—'*eos etiam reformidans ne quid de se asperum scriberent.*'

[d] The greatest of modern historians says: 'If we can prefer personal merit to

Aurelius,[a] Constantine,[b] Theodosius,[c] and Charles the gret, surnamed Charlemaine,[d] all being emperours, and do compare

accidental greatness, we shall esteem the birth of Tacitus more truly noble than that of kings. He claimed his descent from the philosophic historian whose writings will instruct the last generations of mankind. From the assiduous study of his immortal ancestor he derived the knowledge of the Roman constitution and of human nature.'—*Decline and Fall of Rom. Empire*, vol. ii. pp. 35, 36. Vopiscus records an interesting fact. 'Cornelium Tacitum scriptorem historiæ Augustæ, quod parentem suum eundem diceret, in omnibus bibliothecis conlocari jussit : et ne lectorum incuria deperiret librum per annos singulos decies scribi publicitus in evicosarchis jussit et in bibliothecis poni.'—*Hist. Aug.* tom. ii. p. 612.

[a] M. Aurelius Probus was emperor from A.D. 276-282. Professor Ramsay says : 'History has unhesitatingly pronounced that the character of Probus stands without a rival in the annals of imperial Rome, combining all the best features of the best princes who adorned the purple ; exhibiting at once the daring valour and martial skill of Aurelian, the activity and vast conceptions of Hadrian, the justice, moderation, simple habits, amiable disposition, and cultivated intellect of Trajan, the Antonines, and Alexander. We find no trace upon record of any counterbalancing vices or defects.'—Smith's *Dict. of Biogr. sub voc.*

[b] Eutropius gives the following character to Constantine : 'Vir primo imperii tempore optimis principibus, ultimo mediis comparandus. Innumeræ in eo animi corporisque virtutes claruerunt ; militaris gloriæ appetentissimus, fortuna in bellis prospera fuit : verum ita, ut non superaret industriam. Nam etiam Gothos, post civile bellum, varie profligavit, pace ad postremum datâ ; ingentemque apud barbaras gentes memoriæ gratiam collocavit. Civilibus artibus et studiis liberalibus deditus : affectator justi amoris, quem omni sibi et liberalitate et docilitate quæsivit ; sicut in nonnullos amicos dubius, ita in reliquos egregius : nihil occasionum prætermittens quo opulentiores eos clarioresque præstaret. Multas leges rogavit, quasdam ex bono et equo, plerasque superfluas, nonnullas severas ; primusque urbem nominis sui ad tantum fastigium evehere molitus est ut Romæ æmulam faceret.'—*Hist. Rom.* lib. x. cap. 7.

[c] Gibbon says : 'Posterity will confess that the character of Theodosius might furnish the subject of a sincere and ample panegyric. Every art, every talent of an useful or even of an innocent nature was rewarded by his judicious liberality ; and except the heretics, whom he persecuted with implacable hatred, the diffusive circle of his benevolence was circumscribed only by the limits of the human race. The government of a mighty empire may assuredly suffice to occupy the time and the abilities of a mortal ; yet the diligent prince, without aspiring to the unsuitable reputation of profound learning, always reserved some moments of his leisure for the instructive amusement of reading. History, which enlarged his experience, was his favourite study.'—*Decline and Fall of Rom. Empire*, vol. iii. pp. 386-7.

[d] 'The literary merits of Charlemagne are attested by the formation of schools, the introduction of arts, the works which were published in his name, and his

them with other, whiche lacked or had nat so moche of doctrine. Verily they be ferre from good raison, in myne opinion, whiche couaite to haue their children goodly in stature, stronge, deliuer,[a] well synging, wherin trees, beastes, fysshes, and byrdes, be nat only with them equall, but also ferre do excede them. And connynge, wherby onely man excelleth all other creatures in erthe, they reiecte, and accounte unworthy to be in their children. What unkinde appetite were it to desyre to be father rather of a pece of flesshe, that can onely meue and feele, than of a childe that shulde have the perfecte fourme of a man? What so perfectly expresseth a man as doctrine? Diogines the philosopher seing one without lernynge syt on a stone, sayde to them that were with him, beholde where one stone sytteth on an other;[b] whiche wordes, well considered and tried, shall appere to contayne in it wonderfull matter for the approbation of doctrine, wherof a

---

familiar connection with the subjects and strangers whom he invited to his court to educate both the prince and people. His own studies were tardy, laborious, and imperfect; if he spoke Latin and understood Greek, he derived the rudiments of knowledge from conversation, rather than from books; and in his mature age the emperor strove to acquire the practice of writing, which every peasant now learns in his infancy. The grammar and logic, the music and astronomy, of the times were only cultivated as the handmaids of superstition; but the curiosity of the human mind must ultimately tend to its improvement, and the encouragement of learning reflects the purest and most pleasing lustre on the character of Charlemagne.'—*Decline and Fall of Rom. Empire*, vol. vi. p. 172.

[a] See the Glossary.

[b] Sir Thomas Elyot appears to be quoting from memory, and has altogether missed the point of the story which is told, not of the cynic, but of Aristippus, and will be found in the life of that philosopher by Diogenes Laertius; it is as follows: ἐρωτηθεὶς ὑπό τινος τί αὐτοῦ ὁ υἱὸς ἀμείνων ἔσται παιδευθείς, 'καὶ εἰ μηδὲν ἄλλο, εἶπεν, ἐν γοῦν τῷ θεάτρῳ οὐ καθεδεῖται λίθος ἐπὶ λίθῳ.'—Diog. Laert. *Aristippus*, cap. 4, p. 50, ed. Didot, 1850. There is a kind of pun, too, implied in the word λίθος which is incapable of translation into English. Compare Plato, Hippias Major 292 D.:—αὐτὸ γὰρ ἔγωγε, ὦ ἄνθρωπε, κάλλος ἐρωτῶ, ὅ τι ἐστί, καὶ οὐδέν σοι μᾶλλον γεγωνεῖν δύναμαι ἢ εἴ μοι παρεκάθησο λίθος, καὶ οὗτος μυλίας, μήτε ὦτα μήτ' ἐγκέφαλον ἔχων. The word πέτρος is used in a somewhat similar way in a fragment of Sotion, νῷ πέτρος ὁ τῆσδε πιὼν where πέτρος is said to mean ἀναίσθητος τῇ ψυχῇ.—See Westermann, Παραδοξογράφοι, p. 187, ed. 1839.

wyse man maye accumulate ineuitable argumentes, whiche I of necessite, to auoide tediousnes, must nedes passe ouer at this tyme.

CHAPTER XIII.

The seconde and thirde decay of lernyng amonge gentilmen.

THE seconde occasion wherfore gentylmens children seldome haue sufficient lernynge is auarice. For where theyr parentes wyll nat aduenture to sende them farre out of theyr propre countrayes, partly for feare of dethe, whiche perchance dare nat approche them at home with theyr father; partly for expence of money, whiche they suppose wolde be lesse in theyr owne houses or in a village, with some of theyr tenantes or frendes; hauyng seldome any regarde to the teacher, whether he be well lerned or ignorant. For if they hiare a schole maister to teche in theyr houses, they chiefely enquire with howe small a salary he will be contented, and neuer do inserche howe moche good lernynge he hath, and howe amonge well lerned men he is therin estemed, usinge therin lasse diligence than in takynge seruantes, whose seruice is of moche lasse importance, and to a good schole maister is nat in profite to be compared.[a] A gentil man, er he take a cooke in to

---

[a] This is corroborated by Peacham, who, writing some years later, says, 'Such is the most base and ridiculous parsimony of many of our gentlemen (if I may so terme them) that if they can procure some poore Batcheler of Art from the Uniuersitie to teach their children say grace and serue the Cure of an Impropriation, who, wanting meanes and friends, will be content upon the promise of ten pounds a yeare at his first comming, to be pleased with fiue; the rest to be set off in hope of the next aduouson (which perhaps was sold before the young man was born), or if it chance to fall in his time, his Ladie or Master tels him, "Indeed, Sir, wee are beholden unto you for your paines, such a liuing is lately fallen, but I had before made a promise of it to my Butler or Bailiffe for his true and extraordinarie seruice;" when the truth is he hath bestowed it upon himselfe for fourscore or an hundred peeces, which indeede his man two daies before had fast hold of, but could not keepe. It is not commonly seene that the most gentlemen will give

I

his seruice, he wyll firste diligently examine hym, howe many sortes of meates, potages, and sauces, he can perfectly make, and howe well he can season them, that they may be bothe pleasant and nourishynge; yea and if it be but a fauconer, he wyll scrupulously enquire what skyll he hath in feedyng, called diete, and kepyng of his hauke from all sickenes, also how he can reclaime her and prepare her to flyght. And to suche a cooke or fauconer, whom he findeth expert, he spareth nat to gyue moche wages with other bounteous rewardes.* But of a schole maister, to whom he will committe his childe, to be fedde with lernynge and instructed in vertue, whose lyfe shall be the principall monument of his name and honour, he neuer maketh further enquirie but where he may haue a schole maister; and with howe litel charge; and if one be perchance founden, well lerned, but he will nat take paynes to teache without he may haue a great

---

better wages and deale more bountifully with a fellow who can but teach a dogge or reclaime an hawke then upon an honest learned and well qualified man to bring up their children. It may be hence it is that dogges are able to make syllogismes in the fields, when their young masters can conclude nothing at home, if occasion of argument or discourse be offered at the table.'—*The Compleat Gentleman*, p. 31.

* We learn from the Household book of the Earl of Northumberland that at the beginning of the sixteenth century the wages paid quarterly to a clerk of the kitchen were 5 marks, and of a falconer, 'if he be yoman,' 40 shillings, 'and if he be grome,' 20 shillings (see p. 48). In the same establishment the quarterly stipend of a chaplain 'graduate' was only 5 marks, and of one 'not graduate,' 40 shillings; but while these 'clerics' were remunerated at the same rate as the cooks and falconers, it is interesting to find that the services of a schoolmaster *teaching grammar* were estimated to be worth 100 shillings. It would seem, indeed, that the clerical income had remained stationary, while that of other occupations had increased, for Bishop Fleetwood states in the *Chronicon Preciosum* that 'in the council held at Oxford, 1222, it was decreed that where the churches had no greater revenues than 5 marks per ann., they should be conferred on none, but such as should constantly reside in person, on the place,' and he adds 'a single priest might therefore subsist on 5 marks, but he could not afford to keep a curate.'—Chap. v. p. 107. Besides their regular wages, the cooks in the royal and other large households came in for handsome presents. Thus we find in the Privy Purse Expenses of the Princess Mary this entry :—" Item geuen to the cooks to their *withe* at Easter, xxs.," the word in italics signifying an accustomed *fee*, according to Sir Frederick Madden.—p. 275.

salary, he than speketh nothing more, or els saith, What shall so moche wages be gyuen to a schole maister whiche wolde kepe me two seruantes?* to whom maye be saide these wordes, that by his sonne being wel lerned he shall receiue more commoditie and also worship than by the seruice of a hundred cokes and fauconers.

The thirde cause of this hyndrance is negligence of parentes, whiche I do specially note in this poynt; there haue bene diuers, as well gentill men as of the nobilitie, that deliting to haue their sonnes excellent in lernynge haue prouided for them connynge maysters, who substancially haue taught them gramer, and very wel instructed them to speake latine elegantly, wherof the parentes haue taken moche delectation; but whan they haue had of grammer sufficient and be comen to the age of xiiii yeres, and do approche or drawe towarde the astate of man, whiche age is called mature or ripe, (wherin nat onely the saide lernyng continued by moche experience shal be perfectly digested, and confirmed in perpetuall remembrance, but also more seriouse lernyng contayned in other lyberall sciences, and also philosophy, wolde than be lerned) the parentes, that thinge nothinge regarding, but being suffised that their children can onely speke latine proprely, or make verses with out mater or sentence, they from thens forth do suffre them to liue in idelnes, or els, putting them to seruice, do, as it were, banisshe them from all vertuous study or exercise of that whiche they before lerned; so that we may beholde diuers yonge gentill men, who in their infancie and childehode were wondred at for their aptness to lerning and prompt speakinge of elegant latine, whiche nowe, beinge men, nat onely haue forgotten their congruite, (as is the commune

---

* At a time when the Lord Chancellor of England received as his salary 100 marks, with a similar sum for the commons of himself and his clerk, making in all 133*l.* per annum, Colet offered to the high-master of his school 35*l.* per annum, and a house to live in besides. This was practical proof that Colet meant to secure the services of more than a mere common grammarian.'—*The Oxford Reformers*, p. 219, 2nd edn.

worde), and unneth can speake one hole sentence in true latine, but, that wars is, hath all lernynge in derision, and in skorne therof wyll, of wantonnesse, speake the moste barberously that they can imagine.[a]

Nowe some man will require me to shewe myne opinion if it be necessary that gentilmen shulde after the age of xiiii yeres continue in studie. And to be playne and trewe therein, I dare affirme that, if the elegant speking of latin be nat added to other doctrine, litle frute may come of the tonge; sens latine is but a naturall speche, and the frute of speche is wyse sentence, whiche is gathered and made of sondry lernynges.

And who that hath nothinge but langage only may be no more praised than a popiniay, a pye, or a stare, whan they speke featly. There be many nowe a dayes in famouse scholes and uniuersities whiche be so moche gyuen to the studie of tonges onely, that, whan they write epistles, they seme to the reder that, like to a trumpet, they make a soune without any purpose, where unto men do herken more for the noyse than for any delectation that therby is meued. Wherefore they be moche abused that suppose eloquence to be only in wordes or coulours of Rhetorike, for, as Tulli saith, what is so furiouse or mad a thinge as a vaine soune of wordes of the best sort and most ornate, contayning neither connynge *What elo-* nor sentence?[b] Undoubtedly very eloquence is in *quence is.* euery tonge where any mater or acte done or to be done is expressed in wordes clene, propise, ornate, and

---

[a] Ascham makes the same complaint. 'From seven to seventeen,' he says, 'young gentlemen commonly be carefully enough brought up, but from seventeen to seven and twenty (the most dangerous time of all in a man's life, and most slippery to stay well in), they have commonly the rein of all license in their own hand, and especially such as do live in the court. And that which is most to be marvelled at, commonly the wisest and also best men, be found the fondest fathers in this behalf.'—*Works*, vol. iii. p. 123, ed. 1864.

[b] 'Quid est enim tam furiosum, quàm verborum, vel optimorum atque ornatissimorum, sonitus inanis, nullâ subjectâ sententiâ, nec scientiâ?'—Cic. *de Oratore*, lib. i. cap. 12.

comely : whereof sentences be so aptly compact that they by
a vertue inexplicable do drawe unto them the mindes and
consent of the herers, they beinge therwith either perswaded,
meued, or to delectation induced. Also euery man is nat an
oratour that can write an epistle or a flatering oration in latin :
where of the laste, (as god helpe me,) is to moche used. For
a right oratour may nat be without a moche better furniture.
Tulli saienge that to him belongeth the explicating or un-
foldinge of sentence, with a great estimation in gyuing counsaile concerninge maters of great importaunce, also to him
appertaineth the steringe and quickning of people languisshe-
inge or dispeiringe, and to moderate them that be rasshe and
unbridled.[a] Wherfore noble autours do affirme that, in the
firste infancie of the worlde, men wandring like beastes in
woddes and on mountaines, regardinge neither the religion due
unto god, nor the office pertaining unto man, ordred all thing
by bodily strength : untill Mercurius (as Plato supposeth)
or some other man holpen by sapience and eloquence, by
some apt or propre oration, assembled them to geder and
perswaded to them what commodite was in mutual conuersation and honest maners.[b] But yet Cornelius Tacitus *Corn. Ta.*
describeth an oratour to be of more excellent qualities, *de Orat.*

[a] 'Hujus est in dando consilio de maximis rebus cum dignitate explicata
sententia : ejusdem et languentis populi incitatio, et effrænati moderatio.'—Cic. *de
Oratore*, lib. ii. cap. 9.

[b] Ἐπειδὴ δὲ ὁ ἄνθρωπος θείας μετέσχε μοίρας, πρῶτον μὲν διὰ τὴν τοῦ θεοῦ συγγέν-
ειαν ζῴων μόνον θεοὺς ἐνόμισε, καὶ ἐπεχείρει βωμούς τε ἱδρύεσθαι καὶ ἀγάλματα θεῶν·
ἔπειτα φωνὴν καὶ ὀνόματα ταχὺ διηρθρώσατο τῇ τέχνῃ, καὶ οἰκήσεις καὶ ἐσθῆτας καὶ
ὑποδέσεις καὶ στρωμνὰς καὶ τὰς ἐκ γῆς τροφὰς εὕρετο. οὕτω δὴ παρεσκευασμένοι κατ'
ἀρχὰς ἄνθρωποι ᾤκουν σποράδην, πόλεις δὲ οὐκ ἦσαν. ἀπώλλυντο οὖν ὑπὸ τῶν θηρίων
διὰ τὸ πανταχῇ αὐτῶν ἀσθενέστεροι εἶναι, καὶ ἡ δημιουργικὴ τέχνη αὐτοῖς πρὸς μὲν
τροφὴν ἱκανὴ βοηθὸς ἦν, πρὸς δὲ τὸν τῶν θηρίων πόλεμον ἐνδεής· πολιτικὴν γὰρ
τέχνην οὔπω εἶχον, ἧς μέρος πολεμική. ἐζήτουν δὴ ἀθροίζεσθαι καὶ σώζεσθαι κτίζοντες
πόλεις. ὅτ' οὖν ἀθροισθεῖεν, ἠδίκουν ἀλλήλους ἅτε οὐκ ἔχοντες τὴν πολιτικὴν τέχνην,
ὥστε πάλιν σκεδαννύμενοι διεφθείροντο. Ζεὺς οὖν δείσας περὶ τῷ γένει ἡμῶν, μὴ ἀπόλοιτο
πᾶν, Ἑρμῆν πέμπει ἄγοντα εἰς ἀνθρώπους αἰδῶ τε καὶ δίκην, ἵν' εἶεν πόλεων κόσμοι τε
καὶ δεσμοὶ φιλίας συναγωγοί.—Plato, *Protagoras*, cap. xii. Compare with this account of the origin of society the idea of the gradual development of communities
at the beginning of the 3rd book of 'the Laws.'

saynge that, an oratour is he that can or may speke or raison in euery question sufficiently elegantly: and to persuade proprely, accordyng to the dignitie of the thyng that is spoken of, the oportunitie of time, and pleasure of them that be herers.[a] Tulli, before him, affirmed that, a man may nat be an oratour heaped with praise, but if he haue gotten the knowlege of all thynges and artes of greattest importaunce.[b] And howe shall an oratour speake of that thynge that he hath nat lerned? And bicause there may be nothynge but it may happen to come in praise or dispraise, in consultation or iugement, in accusation or defence: therfore an oratour, by others instruction perfectly furnisshed, may, in euery mater and lernynge, commende or dispraise, exhorte or dissuade, accuse or defende eloquently, as occasion hapneth.[c] Wherfore in as moche as in an oratour is required to be a heape of all maner of lernyng: whiche of some is called the worlde of science, of other the circle of doctrine, whiche is in one worde of greke *Encyclopedia*:[d]

[a] 'Sed is est orator, qui de omni quæstione pulchrè et ornatè et ad persuadendum aptè dicere, pro dignitate rerum, ad utilitatem temporum, cum voluptate audientium possit.'—Tac. *de Oratoribus*, cap. 30.

[b] 'Ac meâ quidem sententiâ nemo poterit esse omni laude cumulatus orator, nisi erit omnium rerum magnarum atque artium scientiam consecutus.'—Cic. *de Oratore*, lib. i. cap. 6.

[c] Wilson, following the order of Quintilian, says there are five things to be considered in an oratour—Invention of Matter, Disposition of the same, Elocution, Memory, and Utterance; and concludes his dissertation on this subject as follows: 'Thus we see that euery one of these must goe together, to make a perfite oratour, and that the lack of one is a hinderance of the whole, and that as well all maie be wantyng as one, if wee looke to haue an absolute oratour.'—*Arte of Rhetorique*, p. 7.

[d] This expression is used by Quintilian, who says, 'Orbis ille doctrinæ, quam Græci ἐγκύκλιον παιδείαν vocant.'—*Instit. Orat.* lib. i. cap. 10, § 1. Gentilis deprecates the acquirement of such 'a heap of all manner of learning' by an ambassador. 'Nec oportere Nicephoro auscultari censeo, qui n legato rerum omnium, omniumque linguarum cognitionem, et quidem excellentem requirit. Quæ igitur illarum disciplinarum (ostende, qui adseris de cœlestibus, Plato) in legatione utilitas? Sed (ut diximus) nec possibilis est comparatio: egregiè enim et verè illic Cicero: "Quibus in rebus summa ingenia philosophorum plurimo cum labore consumpta ntelligimus, eas sicut aliquas parvas res oratori attribuere magna amentia est."

therfore at this day may be founden but a very few oratours. For they that come in message from princes be, for honour, named nowe oratours, if they be in any degre of worshyp: [a] onely poore men hauyng equall or more of lernyng beyng called messagers. Also they whiche do onely teache rhetorike, whiche is the science wherby is taught an artifyciall fourme of spekyng,[b] wherin is the power to persuade, moue,

Sed et mediocriter doctos magnos in republicâ, multosque viros commemorant, et nos scimus fuisse tales, qualis numquam ullus hujusmodi *enciclopædicus* extitit. Verùm et alibi disputatum à nobis est plenius adversus istos, qui *orbem* ubique crepant *scientiarum*, contra quos mirum quàm multus sæpeque est Xenophon, et in hoc maximè nostro Politices argumento.'—*De Legationibus*, lib. iii. cap. 1.

[a] Albericus Gentilis, in his treatise, *De Legationibus*, published in 1585, gives a reason why noblemen should be employed in embassies. 'Virum ignobilem posse nobilis, adeoque principis personam præstare, vix est verisimile. Nobilitas enim ipsa est ille stimulus, quo ad res præclaras urgemur; et plebeium genus, quin abjectè se et humiliter non gerat, rarum est.' lib. iii. cap. 4. And as a principal qualification he says: 'Oratoriis excultum virtutibus legatum desideramus, et nomen ipsum oratoris commune desiderat.' Latin was naturally the language of diplomacy in the sixteenth century, and therefore Gentilis says: 'Et nunc quidem si legatus linguam Latinam teneret benè prospectum ei opinor, quoniam longè hæc est hodie in universâ Europâ notior quam fuerit Græca.' A knowledge of modern languages was, however, desirable. 'Si tamen et eas cognosceret, *quæ nunc virunt*, ubi futurus legatus est, magis atque magis probarem, nam, ut alia omittam, afficere quemadmodum volet poterit legatus regem sanè certius, si hujus ipsum patrio sermone alloquitur.'—*Ubi supra*, cap. 7. Abraham de Wicquefort, whose elaborate treatise on the functions of ambassadors was translated into English by Mr. Digby at the beginning of the eighteenth century, tells us that the quality of an orator was considered so indispensable for the purposes of diplomacy, that when ambassadors of noble birth were found to be deficient in that respect they had an *orator* allowed them, who made a speech for them and pronounced it in their presence. He says, 'I cannot tell whether the men of letters are fitter for embassy than tradesmen, but I shall not scruple to say that an Embassador is not better formed in the college than in the shop. When I say men of letters I would be understood to mean them who have contracted too great a familiarity with books, who are too much wedded to the prejudicate opinions of the Doctors, and have more reading than good sense: in fine, to say all in one word, who are either pedants by profession or have pedantick sentiments.'—*The Embassador*, p. 50, ed. 1716.

[b] The earliest treatise on Rhetoric in the English language is *The Arte or Crafte of Rhethoryke*, by Leonard Cox, who dedicated it 'to the lorde Hughe Faryngton, Abbot of Redynge.' It was published, according to Hallam, about 1524, and it appears from the preface that the author was a tutor or master in the grammar school of Reading. This was followed by a larger work by Thomas

and delyte,ᵃ or by that science onely do speke or write, without any adminiculation of other sciences, ought to be named rhetoriciens,ᵇ declamatours, artificiall spekers, (named in Greeke *Logodedali*ᶜ), or any other name than oratours. Semblably they that make verses, expressynge therby none other lernynge but the craft of versifyeng, be nat of auncient writers named poetes, but onely called versifyers.ᵈ For the name of a poete, wherat nowe, (specially in this realme,) men haue suche indignation, that they use onely poetes and poetry in the contempte of eloquence,ᵉ was in auncient tyme in hygh

Wilson, in 1553. The latter gives the following definition of his subject: 'Rhetorique is an Arte to set forthe by utteraunce of wordes, matter at large, or (as Cicero doth saie) it is learned, or rather an artificiall declaration of the mynde, in the handelyng of any cause, called in contention, that maie through reason largely be discussed.'—P. 1.

ᵃ 'Three thynges are required of an orator: to teache, to delight, and to persuade.'—*Arte of Rhetorique*, p. 2.

ᵇ Wilson was keenly alive to the pedantic character of the scholarship of his day. 'I knowe,' he says in his quaint way, 'them that thinke *Rhetorique* to stande wholie upon darke woordes, and he that can catche an ynke horne terme by the taile, him thei coumpt to bee a fine Englisheman and a good *Rhetorician*.'—*Arte of Rhetorique*, p. 165, ed. 1584.

ᶜ This phrase is used by Plato in the Phædrus, cap. li.: καὶ πίστωσιν οἶμαι καὶ ἐπιπίστωσιν λέγειν τόν γε βέλτιστον λογοδαίδαλον B.ζάντιον ἄνδρα. ΦΑΙ. τὸν χρησ ὃν λέγεις Θεόδωρον; a passage which is referred to by Cicero in his *Orator*, cap. 12, as follows: 'Hæc tractasse Thrasymachum Chalcedonium primum et Leontinum ferunt Gorgiam; Theodorum inde Byzantium, multosque alius, quos λογοδαιδάλους appellat in Phædro Socrates.' And also by Quintilian, who says, 'Et Theodorus Byzantius, ex iis et ipse, quos Plato appellat λογοδαιδάλους.'—*Instit. Orat.* lib. iii. cap. i. § 11.

ᵈ So Æneas Sylvius, in his *Tractatus de Liberorum Educatione*, after mentioning Virgil, Ovid, Lucan, and Statius, says: 'Cæteri qui carmine scribunt heroico, remotissimi ab his sunt, *versificatorumque magis quàm poetarum* nomine sunt appellandi.'—*Opera*, p. 984, ed. 1551. Puttenham, however, applies the term to 'translators,' as distinguished from poets. 'Euen so the uery Poet makes and contriues out of his owne braine both the verse and matter of his poeme, and not by any foreine copie or example, as doth the translator; who, therefore, may well be sayd a *versifer*, but not a poet.'—*The Arte of English Poesie*, lib. i. chap. i. Quintilian, who calls Cornelius Severus 'versificator quàm poeta melior,' may perhaps be the ancient writer referred to by the author.

ᵉ Even fifty years after 'the Governour' was published, Sir Philip Sidney, in his *Apologie for Poetrie*, laments that he is obliged 'to make a pittiful defence of

estimation; in so moche that all wysdome was supposed to be therein included, and poetry was the first philosophy that euer was knowen :* wherby men from their childhode were

poore Poetry, which from almost the highest estimation of learning is fallen to be the laughing stocke of children.' He is driven to inquire 'why England (the Mother of excellent mindes) should bee growne so hard a step-mother to Poets, who certainly in wit ought to passe all other ;' and complains 'that Poesie thus embraced in all other places should onely finde in our time a hard welcome in England. I thinke the very earth lamenteth it, and therfore decketh our soyle with fewer laurels than it was accustomed.' Puttenham, writing about the same time, says: 'But in these dayes (although some learned Princes may take delight in them) yet uniuersally it is not so. For as well Poets as Poesie are despised, and the name become of honorable infamous, subiect to scorne and derision, and rather a reproch than a prayse to any that useth it; for commonly who so is studious in th' Arte or shewes him selfe excellent in it, they call him in disdayne a *phantasticall*: and a light headed or phantasticall man (by conversion) they call a Poet. And this proceedes through the barbarous ignoraunce of the time and pride of many gentlemen and others, whose grosse heads not being brought up or acquainted with any excellent Arte, nor able to contriue or in manner conceiue any matter of subtiltie in any businesse or science they doe deride and scorne it in all others as superfluous knowledges and vayne sciences, and whatsoeuer deuise be of rare inuention they terme it *phantasticall*, construing it to the worst side : and among men such as be modest and graue, and of little conuersation, nor delighted in the busie life and vayne ridiculous actions of the popular, they call him in scorne a *Philosopher* or *Poet*, as much to say as a phantasticall man very iniuriously (God wot) and to the manifestation of their own ignoraunce, not making difference betwixt termes.'—*Arte of Eng. Poesie*, lib. i. chap. viii., and, strangely enough, he seems to consider that poets were in higher estimation at the beginning of the century, for he mentions Sternhold and 'one Gray' as enjoying especial favour under Henry the Eighth.

* Puttenham uses very similar language. He says : 'So as the Poets were also from the beginning the best perswaders, and their eloquence the first Rethoricke of the world. Then, forasmuch as they were the first obseruers of all naturall causes and effects in the things generable and corruptible, and from thence mounted up to search after the celestiall courses and influences, and yet penetrated further to know the diuine essences and substances separate, as is sayd before, they were the first Astronomers and Philosophists and Metaphisicks. Finally, because they did altogether endeuor them selues to reduce the life of man to a certaine method of good maners, and made the first differences betweene vertue and vice, and then tempered all these knowledges and skilles with the exercise of a delectable musicke by melodious instruments, which withall serued them to delight their hearers and to call the people together by admiration to a plausible and vertuous conversation, *therefore were they the first Philosophers Ethick*, and the first artificial musicians of the world. Such was Linus, Orpheus, Amphion, and Museus, the

brought to the raison howe to lyue well, lernynge therby nat onely maners and naturall affections, but also the wonderfull werkes of nature, mixting serious mater with thynges that were pleasaunt: as it shall be manifest to them that shall be so fortunate to rede the noble warkes of Plato and Aristotle, wherin he shall fynde the autoritie of poetes frequently alleged: ye and that more is, in poetes was supposed to be science misticall and inspired, and therfore in latine they were called *Vates*, which worde signifyeth as moche as prophetes.[a] And therfore Tulli in his Tusculane questyons supposeth that a poete can nat abundantly express verses sufficient and complete, or that his eloquence may flowe without labour wordes wel sounyng and plentuouse, without celestiall instinction,[b] whiche is also by Plato ratified.[c]

Ci. Tusc.
Quest. i.

most ancient Poets and Philosophers of whom there is left any memorie by the prophane writers.'—*Arte of English Poesie*, lib. i. chap. iv.

[a] Sir Philip Sidney says: 'Among the Romans a Poet was called *Vates*, which is as much as a Diuiner, Fore-seer, or Prophet, as by his conioyned wordes *Vaticinium* and *Vaticinari* is manifest: so heauenly a title did that excellent people bestow upon this hart-rauishing knowledge... For that same exquisite obseruing of number and measure in words, and that high-flying liberty of conceit proper to the poet, did seeme to haue some dyuine force in it.'—*Apologie for Poetrie*, p. 23.

[b] 'Ut ego aut poetam grave plenumque carmen sine cœlesti aliquo mentis instinctu putem fundere, aut eloquentiam sine quâdam vi majore fluere, abundantem sonantibus verbis, uberibusque sententiis.'—Cic. *Tusc. Quæst.* lib. i. cap. 26. Compare with the above passage *De Oratore*, lib. ii. cap. 46: 'Sæpe enim audivi poetam bonum neminem (id quod a Democrito et Platone in scriptis relictum esse dicunt) sine inflammatione animorum existere posse, et sine quodam afflatu quasi furoris.'

[c] Πάντες γὰρ οἵ τε τῶν ἐπῶν ποιηταὶ οἱ ἀγαθοὶ οὐκ ἐκ τέχνης, ἀλλ' ἔνθεοι ὄντες καὶ κατεχόμενοι, πάντα ταῦτα τὰ καλὰ λέγουσι ποιήματα, καὶ οἱ μελοποιοὶ οἱ ἀγαθοὶ ὡσαύτως, ὥσπερ οἱ κορυβαντιῶντες οὐκ ἔμφρονες ὄντες ὀρχοῦνται, οὕτω καὶ οἱ μελοποιοὶ οὐκ ἔμφρονες ὄντες τὰ καλὰ μέλη ταῦτα ποιοῦσιν, ἀλλ' ἐπειδὰν ἐμβῶσιν εἰς τὴν ἁρμονίαν καὶ εἰς τὸν ῥυθμόν, καὶ βακχεύουσι καὶ κατεχόμενοι, ὥσπερ αἱ βάκχαι ἀρύτονται ἐκ τῶν ποταμῶν μέλι καὶ γάλα κατεχόμεναι, ἔμφρονες δὲ οὖσαι οὔ, καὶ τῶν μελοποιῶν ἡ ψυχὴ τοῦτο ἐργάζεται, ὅπερ αὐτοὶ λέγουσι..... κοῦφον γὰρ χρῆμα ποιητής ἐστι καὶ πτηνὸν καὶ ἱερόν, καὶ οὐ πρότερον οἷός τε ποιεῖν, πρὶν ἂν ἔνθεός τε γένηται καὶ ἔκφρων καὶ ὁ νοῦς μηκέτι ἐν αὐτῷ ἐνῇ· ἕως δ' ἂν τουτὶ ἔχῃ τὸ κτῆμα, ἀδύνατος πᾶς ποιεῖν ἐστιν ἄνθρωπος καὶ χρησμῳδεῖν.—Plato, *Ion*, cap. v.

But sens we be nowe occupied in the defence of Poetes, it shall nat be incongruent to our mater to shewe what profite may be taken by the diligent reding of aunciant poetes, contrary to the false opinion, that nowe rayneth, of them that suppose that in the warkes of poetes is contayned nothynge but baudry, (suche is their foule worde of reproche,) and unprofitable leasinges.*

But first I wyll interprete some verses of Horace, wherin he expresseth the office of poetes, and after wyll I resorte to a more playne demonstration of some wisdomes and counsayles contayned in some verses of poetes. Horace, in his seconde booke of epistles, sayth in this wyse or moche lyke:

> The poete facyoneth by some pleasant mene *Horat.*
> The speche of children tendre and unsure : *ep. lib.*
> Pullyng their eares from wordes unclene, *ii. ep'la.*
> Gyuing to them preceptes that are pure : *ad Augustum.*
> Rebukying enuy and wrathe if it dure :
> Thinges wel done he can by example commende :
> The nedy and sicke he dothe also his cure
> To recomfort, if aught he can amende.*

But they whiche be ignoraunt in poetes wyll perchaunce obiecte, as is their maner, agayne these verses, sayeng that in Therence and other that were writers of comedies, also Ouide, Catullus, Martialis, and all that route of lasciuious poetes that wrate epistles and ditties of loue, some called in latine *Elegiæ*

---

* So half a century later, Sir Philip Sidney tells us, the critics said, 'How much it (poetry) abuseth men's wit, trayning it to wanton sinfulnes and lustfull loue: the Comedies rather teach than reprehend amorous conceits; the Lirick is larded with passionate sonnets. The Elegiack weepes the want of his mistresse, and euen to the Heroical *Cupid* hath ambitiously climed.'—*Apologie for Poetrie,* p. 53.

ᵇ 'Os tenerum pueri balbumque poeta figurat;
    Torquet ab obscænis jam nunc sermonibus aurem;
    Mox etiam pectus præceptis format amicis,
    Asperitatis et invidiæ corrector et iræ;
    Rectè facta refert; orientia tempora notis
    Instruit exemplis; inopem solatur et ægrum.'
                            Hor. *Epist.* lib. ii. i. 126-131.

and some *Epigrammata*, is nothyng contayned but incitation to lechery.[a]

First, comedies, whiche they suppose to be a doctrinall of rybaudrie,[b] they be undoutedly a picture or as it were a mirrour of man's life,[c] wherin iuell is nat taught but discouered ;

[a] Thus it is related of Ignatius Loyola, by his biographer, that 'in scholis Terentium explicari, (ni perpurgatus esset,) quamquam optimum Latinitatis auctorem et Romanæ Comœdiæ principem, vetuit nominatim, quod eum videlicet parum verecundum ac parum pudicum arbitraretur. Noluit igitur eâ lectione puerorum animos imbui ne plus moribus noceret quàm prodesset ingeniis.'— Maffei *in Vitâ Ignatii*, lib. iii. cap. 8, p. 432, ed. 1590. And Æneas Sylvius, in an essay entitled *De Liberorum Educatione*, which he wrote A.D. 1450, and dedicated to Ladislaus, King of Hungary and Bohemia, says of Ovid, 'Ubique tristis, ubique dulcis est, in plerisque tamen locis nimium lascivus.' He recommends Horace, but adds 'sunt tamen in eo quædam quæ tibi nec legere voluerim, nec interprætari ;' and in marking out a course of study for boys he says, 'Martialis perniciosus quamvis floridus et ornatus, ita tamen spinis densus est ut legi rosas absque punctione non sinat. *Elegiam qui scribunt omnes puero negari debent, nimium enim sunt molles.* Tibullus, Propertius, Catullus, et quæ translata est apud nos Sapho, raro namque non amatoria scribunt, desertosque conqueruntur amores. Amoveantur igitur, aut ad firmius ætatis robur reserventur.' It is curious to observe the consideration, which induces him to except Juvenal from this category : 'Juvenalis alto ratis ingenio pleraque nimis licenter locutus est in aliquibus autem satyris, *tam religiosum se præbuit ut nostræ fidei doctoribus in nullo cedere judicatur.*'—*Opera*, p. 984, ed. 1551. Ludovicus Vives would find consolation even in the loss of some of the elegiac poets. 'Imo vero amissa sunt tot philosophorum et sacrorum autorum monimenta, et grave erit ac non ferendum facinus, si Tibullus pereat aut Ars Amandi Nasonis ?'—*De Tradendis Disciplinis*, p. 474, ed. 1555.

[b] John Heywood, who was beloved and rewarded by Henry the Eighth for his buffooneries, has been styled the first writer of English comedies ; but Warton points out that this distinction can only be conferred upon him by those who 'confound comedies with moralities and interludes.' His comedies, most of which appeared before 1534, are 'destitute of plot, humour, or character, and give us no very high opinion of the festivity of this agreeable companion. They consist of low incident and the language of ribaldry.'—*Hist. of Engl. Poetry*, vol. iii. p. 86. To Udall, the head-master of Eton, must be attributed the production of the first real comedy in the English language, which was certainly in existence, as Mr. Collier points out, in 1551, if not earlier. (*Hist. of Dram. Poetry*, vol. ii. p. 445.) For though Wood in his 'Athenæ Oxon.' mentions a comedy called 'Piscator, or the Fisher Caught,' written by one John Hoker about 1540, Warton suspects this to have been written in Latin. (*Hist. of Engl. Poetry*, vol. iii. p. 83.)

[c] Ludovicus Vives gives a sketch of the rise and development of comedy, which, as coming from the pen of a contemporary, is worth quoting : 'Venit in

THE GOVERNOUR. 125

to the intent that men beholdynge the promptnes of youth unto vice, the snares of harlotts and baudes laide for yonge myndes, the disceipte of seruantes, the chaunces of fortune contrary to mennes expectation, they beinge therof warned may prepare them selfe to resist or preuente occasion. Semblably remembring the wisedomes, aduertisements, counsailes, dissuasion from vice, and other profitable sentences, most eloquently and familiarely shewed in those comedies, undoubtedly there shall be no litle frute out of them gathered.*

scenam poesis populo ad spectandum congregato, et ibi sicut pictor tabulam proponit multitudini spectandam, ita poeta *imaginem quandam vitæ*, ut merito Plutarchus de his dixerit, poema esse picturam loquentem, et picturam poema tacens, ita magister est populi, et pictor, et poeta. Corrupta est hæc ars quòd ab insectatione flagitiorum et scelerum transiit ad obsequium pravæ affectionis, ut quemcunque odisset poeta, in eum linguæ ac styli intemperantiâ abuteretur. Cui injuriæ atque insolentiæ itum est obviam, primum à divitibus potentia sua et opibus : hinc legibus, quibus cavebatur, ne quis in alium noxium carmen pangeret. Tum involucris cœpit tegi fabula : paulatim res tota ad ludicra, et in vulgum plausibilia est traducta ad amores, ad fraudes meretricum, ad perjuria lenonis, ad militis ferociam, et glorias : quæ quum dicerentur cuneis refertis puerorum, puellarum, mulierum, turba opificum hominum et rudium, mirum quàm vitiabantur mores civitatis admonitione illâ et quasi incitatione ad flagitia : præsertim quum comici semper catastrophem lætam adderent amoribus et impudicitiæ. *Nam si quando addidissent tristes exitus deterruissent ab iis actibus spectatores, quibus eventus esset paratus acerbissimus.* In quo sapientior fuit qui nostrâ linguâ scripsit *Celestinam* tragi-comœdiam. Nam progressui amorum et illis gaudiis voluptatis exitum annexuit amarissimum, nempe amatorum, lenæ, lenonum, casus et neces violentas. Neque vero ignorarunt olim fabularum scriptores turpia esse quæ scriberent et moribus juventutis damnosa. .... Recentiores in linguis vernaculis multo, meâ quidem sententiâ, excellunt veteres in argumento deligendo. *Nullæ ferè exhibentur nunc publicæ fabulæ quæ non delectationem utilitate conjungant.'—De Causis Corrupt. Artium*, p. 367, ed. 1555. The play referred to by Vives is evidently the same as that mentioned in the following passage, which occurs in a treatise called 'A Second and Third Blast of Retrait from Plaies and Theaters,' published in 1580 : 'The nature of these comedies are for the most part after one manner of nature, like the *Tragical Comedie* of Calistus, where the bawdresse *Scelestina* inflamed the maiden Melibeia with her sorceries.'—*English Drama and Stage*, by W. C. Hazlitt, p. 143, ed. 1869.

* Sir P. Sidney says : 'Comedy is an imitation of the common errors of our life, which he representeth in the most ridiculous and scornefull sort that may be. So as it is impossible that any beholder can be content to be such a one. Now, as in Geometry, the oblique must bee knowne as wel as the right, and in Arith-

And if the vices in them expressed shulde be cause that myndes of the reders shulde be corrupted: than by the same argumente nat onely entreludes in englisshe, but also sermones, wherin some vice is declared, shulde be to the beholders and herers like occasion to encreace sinners.*

metick the odde as well as the euen, so in the actions of our life who seeth not the filthiness of euil wanteth a great foile to perceiue the beauty of vertue. This doth the Comedy handle so in our priuate and domestical matters as with hearing it we get as it were an experience what is to be looked for of a nigardly *Demea*: of a crafty *Davus*: of a flattering *Gnato*: of a vaine glorious *Thraso*: and not onely to know what effects are to be expected, but to know who be such by the signifying badge giuen them by the comedian. And little reason hath any man to say that men learne euill by seeing it so set out: sith as I sayd before, there is no man liuing but by the force trueth hath in nature, no sooner seeth these men play their parts but wisheth them in *Pistrinum*: although perchance the sack of his owne faults lye so behinde hys back that he seeth not himselfe daunce the same measure, wherto yet nothing can more open his eyes then to finde his own actions contemptibly set forth.'—*Apologie for Poetrie*.

* That sermons of the period were often of a questionable character appears pretty plain from Burnet's account of Bonner's 'Injunctions,' which were published in 1542. 'These Injunctions,' he says, 'especially when they are considered at their full length, will give great light into the temper of men at that time, and particularly inform us of the design and method in preaching as it was then set forward; concerning which the reader will not be ill-pleased to receive some information. In the time of popery there had been few sermons but in Lent, for their discourses on the holydays were rather panegyrics on the saint, or the vain magnifying of some of their relics which were laid up in such or such places. In Lent there was a more solemn and serious way of preaching; and the friers, who chiefly maintained their credit by their performances at that time, used all the force of their skill and industry to raise the people into heats by passionate and affecting discourses. And the design of their sermons was rather to raise a present heat, which they knew afterwards how to manage, than to work a real reformation on their hearers.'—*Hist. of the Reformation*, vol. i. p. 500, ed. 1865. One of the Injunctions above referred to expressly forbade the acting of plays or interludes 'in the churches.' Another directed 'That there should be no sermons preached that had been *made within these two hundred or three hundred years*. But when they preached they should explain the whole Gospel and Epistle for the day, according to the mind of some good doctor allowed by the Church of England. And chiefly to insist on those places that might stir up the people to good works and to prayer, and to explain the use of the ceremonies of the Church. That there should be no railing in sermons; but the preacher should calmly and discreetly set forth the excellencies of virtue and the vileness of sin, and should also explain the prayers for that day, that so the people might pray with one heart. And should teach them the use of the sacra-

And that by comedies good counsaile is ministred: it appiereth by the sentence of Parmeno, in the seconde comedie of Therence

> In this thinge I triumphe in myne owne conceipte, *Therent.*
> That I have founden for all yonge men the way *in Eunu.*
> Howe they of harlottes shall knowe the deceipte,
> Their wittes, their maners, that therby they may
> Them perpetually hate; for so moche as they
> Out of theyr owne houses be fresshe and delicate,
> Fedynge curiousely; at home all the daye
> Lyuinge beggarly in moste wretched astate.*

There be many mo words spoken whiche I purposely omitte to translate, nat withstandynge the substance of the hole sentence is herin comprised. But nowe to come to other poetes, what may be better saide than is written by Plautus in his firste comedie?

> Verily Vertue dothe all thinges excelle. *Plautus in*
> For if libertie, helthe, lyvyng and substance, *Amphit.*
> Our countray, our parentes and children do well *Alc.*
> It hapneth by vertue; she doth all aduance. *loq'tur.*
> Vertue hath all thinge under gouernaunce,

---

ments, particularly of the mass, but should avoid *the reciting of fables or stories for which no good writer could be vouched.*'— *Ibid.* Wilson, in his *Arte of Rhethoryke*, throws some light on this subject. He says: 'Euen these auncient Preacher must now and then plaie the fooles in the pulpit to serue the tickle eares of their fleting audience, or els they are like sometymes to preache to the bare walles,' p. 3. ed. 1584.

* 'Id vero est, quod ego mihi puto palmarium,
Me reperisse, quo modo adolescentulus
Meretricum ingenia et mores posset noscere;
Mature ut cum cognorit, perpetuo oderit.
Quæ dum foris sunt, nihil videtur mundius;
Nec magis compositum quicquam, nec magis elegans:
Quæ, cum amatore suo cum cœnant, liguriunt.
Harum videre ingluviem, sordes, inopiam;
Quàm inhonestæ solæ sint domi, atque avidæ cibi;
Quo pacto ex jure hesterno panem atrum vorent;
Nosse omnia hæc, salus est adolescentulis.'
Ter. *Eunuch.* act v. sc. iv. l. 8-18.

> And in whom of vertue is founden great plentie,
> Any thinge that is good may neuer be deintie.[a]

Also Ouidius, that semeth to be moste of all poetes lasciuious, in his mooste wanton bokes hath righte commendable and noble sentences; as for proufe therof I will recite some that I haue taken at aduenture.

Ouidius de reme. amoris.
> Time is in medicine if it shall profite;
> Wyne gyuen out of tyme may be anoyaunce.
> A man shall irritate vice if he prohibite
> Whan tyme is nat mete unto his utterance.
> Therfore, if thou yet by counsaile arte recuperable,
> Flee thou from idlenesse and alway be stable.[b]

Martialis, whiche, for his dissolute wrytynge, is mooste seldome radde of men of moche grauitie, hath nat withstandynge many commendable sentences and right wise counsailes, as amonge diuers I will reherce one whiche is first come to my remembrance.

Martialis li. xii. ad Julium.
> If thou wylte eshewe bytter aduenture,
> And auoide the gnawynge of a pensifull harte,
> Sette in no one persone all holy thy pleasure,
> The lasse ioy shalte thou haue but the lasse shalt thou smarte.[c]

---

[a]
> 'Virtus præmium est optimum:
> Virtus omnibus rebus anteit profecto.
> Libertas, salus, vita, res, parentes,
> Patria et prognati tutantur, servantur:
> Virtus omnia in se habet: omnia assunt bona, quem penes est virtus.'—Plaut. *Amphitruo*, act ii. sc. ii. l. 17-21.

[b]
> 'Temporis ars medicina fere est: data tempore prosunt,
> Et data non apto tempore vina nocent.
> Quin etiam accendas vitia, irritesque vetando;
> Temporibus si non aggrediare suis.
> Ergo, ubi visus eris nostræ medicabilis arti,
> Fac monitis fugias otia prima meis.'—Ovid. *Rem. Amor.* 131-136.

[c]
> 'Si vitare velis acerba quædam,
> Et tristes animi cavere morsus,
> Nulli te facias nimis sodalem.
> Gaudebis minus, et minus dolebis.'
> Martial. *Epigram*, lib. xii. 34.

I coulde recite a great nombre of semblable good sentences out of these and other wanton poets, who in the latine do expresse them incomparably with more grace and delectation to the reder than our englisshe tonge may yet comprehende.*

Wherfore sens good and wise mater may be picked out of these poetes, it were no reason, for some lite mater that is in their verses, to abandone therefore al their warkes, no more than it were to forbeare or prohibit a man to come into a faire gardein, leste the redolent sauours of swete herbes and floures shall meue him to wanton courage, or leste in gadringe good and holsome herbes he may happen to be stunge with a nettile. No wyse man entreth in to a gardein but he sone espiethe good herbes from nettiles, and treadeth the nettiles under his feete whiles he gadreth good herbes. Wherby he taketh no damage, or if he be stungen he maketh lite of it and shortly forgetteth it. Semblablye if he do rede wanton mater mixte with wisedome, he putteth the warst under foote and sorteth out the beste, or, if his courage be stered or prouoked, he remembreth the litel pleasure and gret detriment that shulde ensue of it, and

---

* Puttenham has a higher appreciation of his own language. 'If th' art of Poesie,' he says, 'be but a skill appertaining to utterance, why may not the same be with us as wel as with them, our language being no lesse copious, pithie, and significatiue than theirs, our conceipts the same, and our wits no lesse apt to deuise and imitate than theirs were? If, againe, Art be but a certaine order of rules prescribed by reason and gathered by experience, why should not Poesie be a vulgar Art with us as well as with the Greeks and Latines, our language admitting no fewer rules and nice diuersities than theirs? But, peradventure, moe by a peculiar, which our speech hath in many things differing from theirs: and yet in the generall points of that Art allowed to go in common with them: so as if one point perchance which is their feete whereupon their measures stand, and, in deede, is all the beautie of their Poesie, and which feete we haue not, nor as yet neuer went about to frame, (the nature of our language and wordes not permitting it,) we haue in stead thereof twentie other curious points in that skill more than they euer had, by reason of our rime and tunable concords or symphonie, which they neuer obserued. Poesie, therefore, may be an Art in our vulgar, and that verie methodicall and commendable.'—*The Arte of English Poesie*, lib. i. chap. ii.

withdrawynge his minde to some other studie or exercise shortly forgetteth it.

And therfore amonge the iewes, though it were prohibited to children untill they came to rype yeres to reade the bokes of Genesis, of the iuges, *Cantica Canticorum*, and some parte of the boke of Ezechiel the prophete, for that in them was contayned some matter whiche moughte happen to incense the yonge mynde. Wherin were sparkes of carnall concupiscence, yet after certayne yeres of mennes ages it was lefull for euery man to rede and diligently studie those warkes.*

* Jerome, in the preface to his commentaries upon Ezekiel, says: 'Aggrediar Ezechielem prophetam cujus *difficultatem* Hebræorum probat traditio. Nam nisi quis apud eos ætatem sacerdotalis ministerii, id est, tricesimum annum impleverit, nec principia *Geneseos* nec *Canticum Canticorum*, nec *hujus voluminis exordium et finem* legere permittitur : ut ad perfectam scientiam et mysticos intellectus plenum humanæ naturæ tempus accedat.'—*Opera*, tom. iv, p. 434. Ed. 1571. Romæ. It will be seen from this that the author has interpolated the book of Judges amongst the prohibited writings, Jerome making no mention of it, and that he has assigned a totally different reason for such prohibition to that given by the father. Mr. Horne says: 'Ezekiel is more vehement than Jeremiah in reproving the sins of his fellow-countrymen, and abounds more in visions, which render some passages of his book exceedingly difficult to be understood.'—*Introd. to Old Test.* p. 829. 'It is remarkable,' says Professor Bush, 'that Daniel is excluded from the number of prophets, and that his writings, with the rest of the Hagiographa, were not publicly read in the Synagogues, as the Law and the Prophets were. This is ascribed to the singular minuteness with which he foretold the coming of the Messiah before the destruction of the city, and the apprehension of the Jews lest the public reading of his predictions should lead any to embrace the doctrines of Christianity.'—*Notes on Genesis*, Introduction, p. 8. It is not unlikely that some such 'apprehension' may have had as much to do with the prohibition mentioned by Jerome in the case of Ezekiel, as the intrinsic difficulty of the interpretation, inasmuch as a portion of his book is filled with denunciations against the Jewish people; and he foretold the destruction of Jerusalem and its inhabitants. With regard to Canticles, Origen says: 'Aiunt enim observari etiam apud Hebræos quod nisi quis ad ætatem perfectam maturamque pervenerit *libellum hunc* ne quidem in manibus tenere permittatur. Sed et illud ab eis accepimus custodiri, quandoquidem moris est apud eos omnes scripturas à doctoribus et a sapientibus tradi pueris simul et eas quas δευτερώσεις appellant, ad ultimum quatuor ista reservari, id est Principium Genesis, in quo mundi creatura describitur, et Ezechielis Prophetæ principia, in quibus de Cherubim refertur, et finem in quo templi ædificatio continetur, et hunc Cantici Canticorum librum.'—*Prologus in Cantica Canticorum*. It is not a little remarkable that neither this passage from Origen nor the one quoted above from Jerome is referred to by Whiston,

So all thoughe I do nat approue the lesson of wanton poetes to be taughte unto all children, yet thynke I conuenient and necessary that, whan the mynde is become constante and courage is asswaged, or that children of their naturall disposition be shamfaste and continent, none aunciente poete wolde be excluded from the leesson of suche one as desireth to come to the perfection of wysedome.

But in defendynge of oratours and poetes I had all moste forgoten where I was. Verily there may no man be an excellent poet nor oratour unlasse he haue parte of all other doctrine, specially of noble philosophie. And to say the trouth, no man can apprehende the very delectation that is in the leesson of noble poetes unlasse he have radde very moche and in diuers autours of diuers lernynges. Wherfore, as I late said, to the augmentation of understandyng, called in latine *Intellectus et mens*, is required to be moche redyng and vigilaunt studie in euery science, specially of that parte of philosophie named morall, whiche instructeth men in vertue and politike gouernaunce. Also no noble autour, specially of them that wrate in greke or latine before xii. C. yeres passed, is nat for any cause to be omitted. For therin I am of Quintilianes opinion, that there is fewe or none aunciente warke that yeldethe nat some frute or commoditie to the diligent reders.[a] And it is a very grosse or obstinate witte that by readyng moche is nat some what amended.

Concernynge the election of other autours to be radde I haue (as I truste) declared sufficiently my conceipt and opinion in the x and xi chapiters of this litle treatise.[b]

---

who wrote an essay expressly to prove that 'this book was written by Solomon in the loose and wicked part of his life,' and that consequently it ought to be excluded from the canon. See *A Supplement to an Essay towards Restoring the True Text of the Old Testament*, 1723.

[a] 'Paucos et vix ullum ex his, qui vetustatem pertulerunt, existimo posse reperiri, quin judicium adhibentibus allaturus sit utilitatis aliquid.'—*Instit. Orat.* ib. x. cap. 1, § 40.

[b] In the original, as printed, this paragraph ended as follows: 'in the firste

Finally, like as a delicate tree that cometh of a kernell, whiche as sone as it burgeneth out leues, if it be plucked uppe or it be sufficiently rooted, and layde in a corner, it becometh drye or rotten and no frute cometh of it, if it be remoued and sette in an other ayre or erthe, which is of contrary qualities where it was before, it either semblably diethe or beareth no frute, or els the frute that cometh of it leseth his verdure and taste, and finally his estimation. So the pure and excellent lerning wherof I haue spoken, thoughe it be sowen in a childe neuer so tymely, and springeth and burgeneth neuer so pleasauntly, if, byfore it take a depe rote in the mynde of the childe, it be layde a syde, either by to moche solace or continuall attendaunce in seruice, or els is translated to an other studie whiche is of a more grose or unpleasaunt qualitie before it be confirmed or stablisshed by often reding or diligent exercise, in conclusion it vanissheth and cometh to no thing.

Wherfore lete men replie as they list, but, in myne opinion, men be wonderfully disceyued nowe a dayes, (I dare nat saye with the persuasion of auarice,) that do put their children at the age of xiiii or xv yeres to the studie of the lawes of the realme of Englande.* I will shewe to them reasonable causes

boke of this little treatise,' but the correction appears among the errata of the first edition, and for the reason given in note⁴, p. 47 *ante*, has been inserted in its proper place in accordance with the author's directions.

* Was this, as Blackstone would seem to suggest, out of deference to the example of ancient Rome, where, as Cicero informs us (*De Legg.* lib. ii. cap. 23), the very boys were obliged to learn the twelve tables by heart as a *carmen necessarium* or indispensable lesson, to imprint on their tender minds an early knowledge of the laws and constitution of their country? Fortescue, who was Lord Chief Justice and afterwards Lord Chancellor, shows us that at any rate in his time (*i.e.* in the reign of Henry VI.) the Inns of Court were more like Universities than they have ever been since, and that only the sons of rich men could afford such an expensive education. He says: 'Sunt namque in eo decem Hospitia minora, et quandoque vero plura, quæ nominantur Hospitia Cancellariæ. Ad quorum quodlibet pertinent centum studentes ad minus, et ad aliqua eorum major in multo numerus, licet non omnes semper in eis simul conveniant. Studentes etenim isti, pro eorum parte majori, juvenes sunt. Originalia et quasi Legis Elementa addiscentes, qui in illis proficientes, ut ipsi maturescunt, ad majora

why, if they wyll paciently here me, infourmed partely by myne owne experience.

CHAPTER XIV.

Howe the studentes in the lawes of this realme maye take excellent commoditie by the lessons of sondrie doctrines.

IT may nat be denyed but that al lawes be founded on the depest parte of raison,[*] and, as I suppose, no one lawe so

Hospitia studii illius, quæ *Hospitia Curiæ* appellantur, assumuntur. Quorum majorum quatuor sunt in numero et ad minimum eorum pertinent in formâ prænotatâ ducenti studentes aut prope. In his enim majoribus Hospitiis, nequaquam potest studens aliquis sustentari minoribus expensis in anno quam octoginta scutorum (= 20 marks), et si servientem sibi ipse ibidem habuerit ut eorum habet pluralitas, tanto tunc majores ipse sustinebit expensas. *Occasione vero sumptuum hujusmodi ipsi nobilium filii tantùm in Hospitiis illis Leges addiscunt. Cum pauperes et vulgares pro filiorum suorum exhibitione tantos sumptus nequeant sufferre.* Et mercatores raro cupiant tantis oneribus annulis attenuare Mercandisas suas. *Quo fit ut vix doctus in Legibus illis reperiatur in regno, qui non sit nobilis et de nobilium genere egressus.* Unde magis aliis consimilis status hominibus ipsi nobilitatem curant et conservationem honoris et famæ suæ. In his revera Hospitiis majoribus etiam et minoribus, ultra studium Legum, est quasi Gymnasium omnium morum qui nobiles decent. Ibi cantare ipsi addiscunt similiter, et se exercent in omni genere Harmoniæ. Ibi etiam tripudiare ac jocos singulos nobilibus convenientes, qualiter in Domo Regiâ exercere solent, enutriti. In ferialibus diebus, eorum pars major legalis disciplinæ studio, et in Festivalibus Sacræ Scripturæ et Cronicorum lectioni post divina obsequia se confert. Ibi quippe disciplina virtutum est, et vitiorum omnium exilium. Ita ut propter virtutis acquisitionem, vitii etiam fugam, Milites, Barones alii quoque Magnates, et nobiles regni, in Hospitiis illis ponunt filios suos, quamvis non gliscunt eos Legum imbui disciplinâ, nec ejus exercitio vivere, sed solum ex patrociniis suis.'—*De Laud. Leg. Angl.* cap. 49.

[*] Cicero's definition of the law of nature is as follows: 'Lex est *ratio* summa insita in naturâ, quæ jubet ea quæ facienda sunt prohibetque contraria. Eadem *ratio* quum est in hominis mente confirmata et confecta Lex est.'—*De Legg.* lib. i. cap. 6. Blackstone says: 'This law of nature, being coeval with mankind and dictated by God himself, is, of course, superior in obligation to any other. It is binding over all the globe, in all countries, and at all times: no human laws are of any validity if contrary to this, and such of them as are valid derive all their force and all their authority mediately or immediately from this original. But in order to apply this to the particular exigencies of each individual, it is still neces-

moche as our owne;[a] and the deper men do inuestigate raison the more difficile or harde muste nedes be the studie. Also that reuerende studie is inuolued in so barbarouse a langage, that it is nat onely voyde of all eloquence,[b] but also beynge

[a] sary to have recourse to *reason* ; whose office it is to discover, as was before observed, what the law of nature directs in every circumstance of life, by considering what method will tend the most effectually to our own substantial happiness. And if our reason were always, as in our first ancestor before his transgression, clear and perfect, unruffled by passions, unclouded by prejudice, unimpaired by disease or intemperance, the task would be pleasant and easy—we should need no other guide but this. But every man now finds the contrary in his own experience ; that his reason is corrupt and his understanding full of ignorance and error. This has given manifold occasion for the benign interposition of divine providence, which, in compassion to the frailty, the imperfection, and the blindness of human reason, hath been pleased at sundry times and in divers manners to discover and enforce its laws by an immediate and direct revelation. The doctrines thus delivered we call the revealed or divine law, and they are to be found only in the Holy Scriptures. .... Upon these two foundations, the law of nature and the law of revelation, depend all human laws : that is to say, no human laws should be suffered to contradict these.'—*Commentaries*, p. 40, 15th ed.

[a] 'The first ground of the law of England is the law of *reason*..... It is not used among them that be learned in the laws of England to reason what thing is commanded or prohibited by the law of *nature*, and what not, but all the reasoning in that behalf is under this manner. As when anything is grounded upon the law of nature they say that *reason* will that such a thing be done ; and if it be prohibited by the law of nature they say it is against *reason*, or that *reason* will not suffer that to be done.'—*Doctor and Student*, chap. v. By Coke the common law of England is called 'the absolute perfection of reason;' (*Second Instit*. cap. xii.) and in another place the same learned judge says, 'This is another strong argument in law, *nihil quod est contra rationem est licitum* ; for reason is the life of the law, nay, the common law itselfe is nothing else but reason ; which is to be understood of an artificiall perfection of reason, gotten by long study, observation, and experience, and not of every man's naturall reason.'—*Co. Litt.* 97 b. Plowden asserts that the common law 'is no other than pure and tried reason.'—*The Case of Mines*, Rep. p. 316.

[b] Fulbecke, who wrote in 1599 the earliest treatise in English on the study of the law, says : 'Cicero, when he treateth of matters of law, speaketh like a lawyer, and a lawyer must speak as the law doth speak ; therefore Baro saith well the writers of the law would not have left to posterity so many law books if they had affected a choice phrase of speech. And surely if when the Latin tongue did most flourish the Cæsars and Cicero himself did not use any gorgeous and filed kind of speech in matters of law, shall we desire it of Bartolus, Bracton, Britton, and Glanvill, when eloquence was in the eclipse or wane, and exceedingly decayed ? Varro saith that by the diverse mixtures of people and

seperate from the exercise of our lawe onely, it serueth to no commoditie or necessary purpose, no man understandyng it but they whiche haue studyed the lawes.*

nations old words grow out of use and are changed, and new do take place: how can it then be but that the common law should have harsh, obscure, difficult, and strange terms by the commixtion of the several languages of the Saxons, Danes, and Normans, the authors of the same?'—*Preparative to the Study of the Law*, p. 54, ed. 1829. Sir John Doderidge, a sixteenth century lawyer, defending the use of Law Latin, says: 'Secondly may be objected that since the time that the Latine tongue was vulgarly used among the Romans and other the nations that they subdued to that empire (for they much endeavoured the propagation of their language), sundry new things have beene invented, whereof those ancient people had either no intelligence or no use; and, therefore, where such things doe occurre there doe want words proper and peculier in the Latine tongue to denote the same, and men must of necessity bee enforced either to use barbarous words, farre from the purity of the Latine speech, or to invent new to express their meaning. . . . . . Lastly, there remaineth this scruple: where it hath been affirmed that there is much respect had of the true propriety of Latine words, it seemeth nothing lesse, for those formes are conceived in a base stile, farre removed from purity of speech; so that the professors of law within this land can challenge no great commendation in this kinde. To this is answered that the Lawes of this Land neither doe nor desire to affect Eloquence in the Latine tongue, for wee have no use of the speech thereof in our arguments, for as much as the statute made 36 E. III. cap. 15, hath ordained that all pleadings and all arguments and disputations of Law should thenceforth be performed in the English tongue; whereas formerly, as it seemeth, it was put in ure in the French, remaining untill that time as a badge of the Norman captivity, whereof there is now no use but in the arraigning of an Assize and an Appeale, and such French arguments as are used for exercise in the Houses and Societies of Court and Chancery.'—*The English Lawyer*, p. 49, edn. 1631.

* 'From the conquest till the latter half of the fourteenth century the pleadings in courts of justice were in Norman French; but in the 36 Ed. III. it was ordained by the king "that all plees which be to be pleded in any of his courts, before any of his justices, or in his other places, or before any of his other ministers, or in the courts and places of any other lords within the realm, shall be pleded, shewed, and defended, answered, debated, and judged in the English tongue, and that they be entred and enrolled in Latine." Long before this wise measure of reform was obtained by the urgent wishes of the nation, the French of the law courts had become so corrupt and unlike the language of the invaders, that it was scarcely more intelligible to educated natives of France than to most Englishmen of the highest rank. A jargon, compounded of French and Latin, *none save professional lawyers could translate it with readiness or accuracy*. And, whilst it unquestionably kept suitors in ignorance of their own affairs, there is reason to believe that it often perplexed the most skilful of those official interpreters who were never weary of extolling its lucidity and precision.'--

Than children at xiiii or xv yeres olde, in whiche tyme springeth courage, set all in pleasure, and pleasure is in nothyng that is nat facile or elegaunt, beyng brought to the moste difficulte and graue lernyng whiche hath no thynge illecebrouse or delicate to tickyll their tender wyttes and alure them to studie, (onles it be lucre, whiche a gentyll witte lytle estemeth,) the more parte, vainquisshed with tediousenesse, either do abandone the lawes and unwares to their frendes do gyue them to gamyng and other (as I mought saye) idle busynesse nowe called pastymes;[a] or els if they be in any wyse therto constrayned, they apprehendyng a piece therof, as if they beyng longe in a derke dungeon onely dyd se by the light of a candell,[b] than if after xx or xxx yeres studie they

Jeaffreson's *Book about Lawyers*, vol. ii. p. 98. Fabyan says that in 38 Ed. III. an ordinance was made that serjeants and 'prentyses of the lawe' should plead their pleas *in their mother tongue*, but adds that 'this stood but a short while.'—*Chron.* p. 247, ed. 1559.

[a] What the pastimes were to which the students of the author's day were addicted we learn from Dugdale, who, speaking of the Inner Temple, says: 'In 13 Hen. VIII. it was ordered that none of the society should, within this House, exercise the play of *Shoffe-grote* or *Slyp-grote* upon pain of 6s. 8d.'—*Origines*, p. 149. The following passage in the *Archæologia*, under date 1763, may perhaps be considered to support the strictures of the author unless we refer the 'pastime,' of which such conclusive proof is given, to the latter half of the succeeding century, when the ruling passion was probably still stronger : 'In new paving the hall of the Middle Temple in London, *about forty years ago*, was taken up a silver gilt enamelled box containing near one hundred pair of small ivory dice, scarce more than two-thirds of the modern size.'—Vol. viii. p. 427. Dugdale, speaking of Lincoln's Inn, says : 'Touching their sports and corporal exercises, it was ordered in 32 Eliz. that not only all the sportings, late watchings, and exercises before that time yearly used on the *Hunting Night*, but also their repair usually at a certain day yearly to Kentish Town, and the Dining, with sports and assemblies, before that time used, should be taken away and no more exercised.'—*Origines*, p. 245, ed. 1680. From the same source we learn that the members of the Middle Temple were 'wont to be entertained with *Post Revels*, performed by the better sort of the young gentlemen of the Society, with galliards, corrantoes, and other dances, or else with stage playes.'—*Ibid.* p. 205.

[b] Sir William Blackstone, in his inaugural lecture 'On the Study of the Law,' delivered at Oxford, 25 Oct., 1758, uses very similar language with regard to the preparation for the profession in his own time. '.We may appeal,' he says, 'to the experience of every sensible lawyer whether anything can be more hazardous or discouraging than the usual entrance on the study of the law. A raw and un-

happen to come amonge wyse men, hering maters commened of concerning a publike weale or outwarde affaires betwene princes, they no lasse be astonied than of commyng out of a darke house at noone dayes they were sodaynly striken in the eyen with a bright sonne beame.[a] But I speke nat this in reproche of lawyers, for I knowe dyuers of them whiche in consultation wyll make a right vehement raison, and so do some other whiche hath neither lawe nor other lernyng, yet the one and the other, if they were fournisshed with excellent doctrine, their raison shulde be the more substanciall and certayne.[b]

experienced youth, in the most dangerous season of life, is transplanted on a sudden into the midst of allurements to pleasure, without any restraint or check but what his own prudence can suggest; with no public direction in what course to pursue his inquiries; no private assistance to remove the distresses and difficulties which will always embarrass a beginner. In this situation he is expected to sequester himself from the world, and, by a tedious, lonely process, to extract the theory of law from a mass of undigested learning; or else, by an assiduous attendance on the courts, to pick up theory and practice together sufficient to qualify him for the ordinary run of business. How little, therefore, is it to be wondered at that we hear of so frequent miscarriages: *that so many gentlemen of bright imaginations grow weary of so unpromising a search, and addict themselves wholly to amusements or other less innocent pursuits; and that so many persons of moderate capacity confuse themselves at first setting out, and continue ever dark and puzzled during the remainder of their lives.*'—*Commentaries*, vol. i. p. 31, 15th edition.

[a] Speaking of the custom that prevailed more than two hundred years later, Blackstone says : 'If practice be the whole he is taught, practice must also be the whole he will ever know; if he be uninstructed in the elements and first principles upon which the rule of practice is founded, the least variation from established precedents will totally distract and bewilder him : *ita lex scripta est* is the utmost his knowledge will arrive at; he must never aspire to form, and seldom expect to comprehend, any arguments drawn *à priori* from the spirit of the laws and the natural foundations of justice.'—*Commentaries*, vol. i. p. 32, 15th edn. The reproach of the sixteenth century has, it is to be feared, not been entirely removed in the nineteenth. Witness the evidence given before the Royal Commission appointed (1854) to inquire into the arrangements of the Inns of Court. 'One of the gentlemen who was thought worthy of passing by the Council had never heard of the Spanish Armada; another, who had never heard of Lord Clarendon, was selected some time ago for an honourable notice. The gentleman who had never heard of the Spanish Armada was allowed to hold rank in a profession supposed to consist of educated men.'—*Rep.* p. 122.

[b] The most distinguished lawyer of this time was, undoubtedly, Sir Thomas

There be some also whiche by their frendes be coarted [a] to aplye the studie of the lawe onely, and for lacke of plentuouse exhibition be let of their lybertie, wherfore they can nat resorte unto passetyme; these of all other be moste caste awaye, for nature repugnyng, they unneth taste any thing that may be profytable, and also their courage is so mortifyed (whiche yet by solace perchaunce mought be made quicke or apte to some other studie or laudable exercise) that they lyue euer after out of all estimation.[b]

Wherfore Tulli sayeth we shulde so indeuour our selfes that we striue nat with the uniuersall nature of man, but that beynge conserued, lette us folowe our owne propre natures, that thoughe there be studies more graue and of more importaunce, yet ought we to regarde the studies wherto we be by our owne nature inclined.[c] And that this sentence is

More, who was appointed Lord Chancellor three years previous to the publication of *The Governour*. Amongst other celebrated contemporaries were Shelley, Brooke, Cholmley, Fitz-Herbert (the author of various legal works), Chiistopher Hales, who was Attorney-General, and afterwards Master of the Rolls, 1536, and Fitz-James, Chief Justice of the King's Bench, whose character Mr. Foss shows to have been unjustly depreciated by Lord Campbell. It is possible that the insinuation in the text, of lack of learning, coupled with vehemence, may be intended to apply to such men as Lord Rich, of whom Mr. Foss says: 'As his name is not to be discovered in the Year-Books or in any other reports, it is difficult otherwise to attribute his advancement to the bench of that society (the Middle Temple), than to the influence of opulent friends and *a mixture of that subtleness and insolence in his bearing* which he exhibited in after life.'—*Judges of England*, vol. v. p. 318.

[a] See the Glossary.

[b] Dugdale, in describing how at this time (*i.e.* temp. Hen. VIII.) the practice of the law was commenced too early, quotes a passage from a MS. in the Cotton Library curiously resembling that in the text: 'First, there is no land nor revenues belonging to the House whereby any learner or student mought be holpen and encouraged to study, by means of some yearly stipend or salary; which is the occasion that many a good witt, *for lack of exhibition*, is compelled to give over and forsake study before he have any perfyt knowledge in the law, and to fall to practi-ing, and become a Typler in the Law.'—*Origines*, p. 193, ed. 1680.

[c] 'Sic enim est faciendum, ut, contra universam naturam nihil contendamus; eâ tamen conservatâ, propriam naturam sequamur; ut, etiam si sint alia graviora atque meliora, tamen nos studia nostra nostræ naturæ regulâ metiamur.'—Cic. *De Officiis*, lib. i. cap. 31. It must never be forgotten that unless Gibbon had

THE GOVERNOUR. 139

true we haue dayly experience in this realme specially. For how many men be there that hauyng their sonnes in childhode aptly disposed by nature to paynte, to kerue, or graue, to embrawder, or do other lyke thynges, wherin is any arte commendable concernynge inuention, but that, as sone as they espie it, they be therwith displeased, and forthwith byndeth them apprentises[a] to taylours, to wayuers,[b] to towkers,[c] and somtyme to coblers,[d] whiche haue ben the inestimable losse of

acted on the principle mentioned in the above passage, literature would have been bereft of one of her most brilliant ornaments. The historian himself tells us, 'Mrs. Gibbon, with seeming wisdom, exhorted me to take chambers in the Temple, and devote my leisure to the study of the law. I cannot repent of having neglected her advice. Few men, without the spur of necessity, have resolution to force their way through the thorns and thickets of that gloomy labyrinth. Nature had not endowed me with the bold and ready eloquence which makes itself heard amidst the tumult of the bar. And I should probably have been diverted from the labours of literature without acquiring the fame or fortune of a successful pleader.'—*Memoirs*, p. 59.

[a] It is clear, however, that this was not in former times considered derogatory, for in the *Liber Albus*, which was compiled in 1419, we read: 'Antiquitùs nullus factus fuit apprenticius, nec saltem admissus fuit in libertatem dictæ civitatis, nisi cognitus fuerat esse *liberæ conditionis*; sive, si postquam liberatus fuerat, innotesceret quod erat servilis conditionis, *eo ipso* civitatis perdidit libertatem.'—*Chron. and Mem.* p. 33. And Stow, in his *Survey*, which was written in 1598, says: 'But because the apprentices of London were often children of gentlemen and persons of good quality, they did affect to go in costly apparel, and wear weapons, and frequent schools of dancing, fencing, and music; therefore, by an Act of Common Council in May, anno 1582, these things were thought fit to be forbidden.'—Vol. ii. p. 329.

[b] See note p. 7 *ante*.
[c] See the Glossary.
[d] Mr. Froude would apparently consider this as an additional proof of the national hatred of the 'abominable sin of idleness;' but it hardly supports to the full extent his view that it was 'the State, which promising for itself that all able-bodied men should be found in work, *and not allowing any man to work at a business for which he was unfit*, insisted as its natural right that children should not be allowed to grow up in idleness, to be returned at mature age upon its hands. Every child, so far as possible, was to be trained up in some business or calling, idleness 'being the mother of all sin,' and the essential duty of every man being to provide honestly for himself and his family. The educative theory, for such it was, was simple but effective: it was based on the single principle that, next to the knowledge of a man's duty to God, and as a means towards doing that duty, the first essential of a worthy life was the ability to maintain it in independence. Varieties

many good wittes, and haue caused that in the said artes englisshmen ·be inferiors to all other people, and be constrayned, if we wyll haue any thinge well paynted, kerued, or embrawdred, to abandone our owne countraymen and resorte unto straungers,* but more of this shall I speke in the nexte volume.

of inapplicable knowledge might be good, but they were not essential. Such knowledge might be left to the leisure of after years, or it might be dispensed with without vital injury. Ability to labour could not be dispensed with, and this, therefore, the state felt it to be its own duty to see provided.'—*Hist. of Eng.* vol. i. p. 43. It is abundantly clear from the evidence not only of Sir Thos. Elyot, but of other 16th century writers, that it was not *the State* acting upon the general principle that idleness is abominable and sinful, but the parents themselves, acting from merely selfish motives, who apprenticed their children to trades. It must be remembered that in pre-Reformation times the Universities offered few inducements to any but members of the monastic orders. The Inns of Court, as Fortescue tells us, were expensive, and frequented exclusively by the rich and noble. One result of the Reformation was to divert the stream which had hitherto flowed through the Inns of Court into another channel flowing through the Universities to the secure haven of clerical preferment bestowed by lay patronage. The Universities now held out inducements to the scions of noble houses; *per contra* the middle classes were attracted to the Inns of Court. Ferne, writing at the end of the 16th century, complains that 'A worthy maintenaunce of the yonger brethren of Gentle and Noble houses (*especiallye since the desolucion that was iustly layd upon Collegiat Churches and Chapters*) is mightely diminished. For by that free accesse, now permitted to yeomanrye and Merchauntes, to set their broode to the studye of common lawes, that faculty is so pestered, yea many worthy offices, and places of high regarde in that vocation (in olde time left to the support of gentle linage) are now preoccupated and usurped by ungentle and base stocke.'—*The Blazon of Gentrie*, p. 93, ed. 1586.

* Another cause has, however, been assigned for this lack of native talent, and perhaps a more probable one. 'When we look into the history of the great schools of Italy, and consider how much they are indebted for their rise and prosperity to the influence of the Roman Church, it may account in some degree for the stagnation of the Arts in England, that this source of encouragement was cut off when it might have been an important aid to the favourable circumstances in which they were at length placed by the patronage of the sovereign, and the more general desire to cultivate them for their own sake, which would necessarily follow the spread of literature and refinement. . . . In the gradual development of the arts of painting and sculpture England had taken no share; and as regards the former especially, our history presents a total blank during the whole period of its advancement in Italy. When, therefore, an epoch at length arrived favourable to the appreciation of the art, it presented itself for the first time in a perfect form to

But to resorte unto lawyars. I thinke verily if children were broughte uppe as I haue written, and continually were retayned in the right studie of very philosophy untyll* they passed the age of xxi yeres, and than set to the lawes of this realme *

the few in whom superior education and wealth united the will with the means of encouraging it. In the eyes of this class, who may rather be said to have purchased than patronised it, art assumed the character of a foreign luxury, and they were at first too impatient, and soon learned to be too fastidious, to attend to the tedious process of cultivating what they could readily import. Thus was established, and thus has been perpetuated, the predilection for foreign art and foreign artists, which so long pressed like an incubus upon native talent, and condemned it to move in the humble track of imitation. Walpole designates the state of native art in the sixteenth century as genius struggling with barbarism. He should have said genius struggling with prejudice, the influence of which he might have extended down to his own time.'—*Pict. Hist. of Engl.* vol. ii. p. 851. The king was himself a munificent patron of the arts; his connexion with Holbein is well known, and he likewise employed Raphaell, Pietro Torregiano, a Florentine sculptor of very superior talent; Benedetto Rovezzano, who was selected to design a magnificent royal tomb, which was never completed; Jerome de Trevisi, Luca Penni, and other artists of less note.

* Blackstone, addressing the University of Oxford, says: 'The inconveniences here pointed out (*i.e.* of justice being administered by illiterate persons) can never be effectually prevented but by making academical education a previous step to the profession of the common law, and at the same time making the rudiments of the law a part of academical education. For sciences are of a sociable disposition, and flourish best in the neighbourhood of each other; nor is there any branch of learning but may be helped and improved by assistances drawn from other arts. If, therefore, the student in our laws hath formed both his sentiments and style by perusal and imitation of the purest classical writers, among whom the historians and orators will best deserve his regard; if he can reason with precision, and separate argument from fallacy, by the clear, simple rules of pure unsophisticated logic; if he can fix his attention and steadily pursue truth through any the most intricate deduction by the use of mathematical demonstrations; *if he has enlarged his conceptions of nature and art by a view of the several branches of genuine experimental philosophy*; if he has impressed on his mind the sound maxims of the law of nature, the best and most authentic foundation of human laws; if, lastly, he has contemplated those maxims reduced to a practical system in the laws of Imperial Rome; if he has done this or any part of it (though *all* may be easily done under as able instructors as ever graced any seats of learning), a student thus qualified may enter upon the study of the law with incredible advantage and reputation. And if at the conclusion or during the acquisition of these accomplishments he will afford himself here a year or two's farther leisure, to lay the foundation of his future labours in a solid, scientifical method, without thirsting too early to attend that practice which it was impossible he should rightly comprehend, he will after-

(being ones brought to a more certayne and compendiouse studie, and either in englisshe, latine, or good french, written in a more clene and elegant stile *) undoughtedly they shuld

> wards proceed with the greatest ease, and will unfold the most intricate points with an intuitive rapidity and clearness.'—*Commentaries*, vol. i. p. 33, 15th edn. Lord Bolingbroke enunciates the same sentiments in his *Letters on the Study and Use of History;* he says, 'A lawyer now is nothing more, I speak of ninety-nine in a hundred at least, to use some of Tully's words, '*nisi leguleius quidam cautus, et acutus præco actionum, cantor formularum, auceps syllabarum.*' But there have been lawyers that were orators, philosophers, historians; there have been Bacons and Clarendons, my Lord. There will be none such any more, till, in some better age, true ambition or the love of fame *prevails over avarice*: and till men find leisure and encouragement to prepare themselves for the exercise of this profession, by climbing up to the vantage ground, so my Lord Bacon calls it, of science, instead of grovelling all their lives below, in a mean, but gainful application to all the little arts of chicane. Till this happen, the profession of the law will scarce deserve to be ranked among the learned professions: and whenever it happens, one of the vantage grounds to which men must climb is metaphysical, and the other historical, knowledge. They must pry into the secret recesses of the human heart, and become well acquainted with the whole moral world, that they may discover the abstract reason of all laws; and they must trace the laws of particular states, especially of their own, from the first rough sketches to the more perfect draughts, from the first causes or occasions that produced them, through all the effects, good and bad, that they produced.'—P. 132, ed. 1777.
>
> * The lawyers generally, however, were quite contented with their barbarous jargon. Fulbecke, writing quite at the end of the century, says in his *Direction or Preparative to the Study of the Law*, 'If the received words of the Law should be altered it may well be presumed that many ancient books of the Civil law, and the old year books, would in short time be hardly understood. And I am surely persuaded that if the ancient terms of the law should be changed for more polite and familiar novelties, the new terms would be nothing so emphatical and significant as the old. .... The fine Rhetorician will say *Absurda consuetudo disrumpenda est ;* the Lawyer, he will say *Usus contra rationem annullandus est ;* he will say that it is not Roman Latin; it is most true, therefore, will he conclude it is not well spoken nor congrue. The argument halteth. The Muscovite will speak of a thing after one sort; the Fleming after another sort will utter the same thing: neither of them speak in Latin, but in their own language. Do they not, therefore, speak right? Yes, they speak right and congrue in their own language, and so do the lawyers in their own dialect and language proper to their art. Doth any man think that these words, *Bellum, Exul, Sylva, Proscriptio, manus injectio*, were unknown to the ancient writers of the law? Yet sometime they do not use these, but instead of them they say *Guerra, Bannitus, Boscus, Attinctura, Arrestum*. But it is convenient that they should use these latter words, being proper to their art or science. Neither is it meet that they should change them for the words of

become men of so excellent wisedome that throughout all the worlde shulde be founden in no commune weale more noble counsaylours,* our lawes nat onely comprehendyng most ex-

a strange language. . ¯ . . And the common law being derived from the Normans and other nations, doth conveniently retain the words of the first inventors. And because amongst lawyers Latin words be used many times in another sense than they are vulgarly and commonly taken, it is not good to have the interpretation of such words from any other than the lawyers themselves. . . I do not think any exquisite skill of the Latin tongue to be necessary in a lawyer; but hold it sufficient if he know so much thereof, and in such manner, as the common sort of men which are conversant in the reading of Latin books. . . The ancient reporters and handlers of the Law, whilst they wrote of Fines, Vouchers, Remitters, Restitution, Releases, and such intricate matters, had no leisure to note the properties and rules of the Latin tongue in Cicero, Pliny, Plautus, and Varro; they inquired not what was good Latin, but what was good law.'—*Preparative to the Study of the Law*, pp. 56, 57. Roger North, the younger brother of the Lord Keeper Guildford, at a still later period preferred the old style, for in his *Discourse on the Study of the Laws*, he insists upon the necessity of a student's early application to learn the old law French. 'Some may think that because the law French is no better than the old Norman corrupted, and now a deformed hotchpotch of the English and Latin mixed together, it is not fit for a polite spark to foul himself with; but this nicety is so desperate a mistake that lawyer and law French are coincident—one will not stand without the other. All the ancient books that are necessary to be read and understood are in that dialect; and the law itself is not in its native dress, nor is, in truth, the same thing in English. During the English times as they are called, when the Rump abolished Latin and French, divers books were translated, as the great work of Coke's Reports, &c.; but upon the revival of the law, those all died, and are now but waste paper. Even the modern Reports mostly are in French, and, as I said, all the ancient as well as divers authentic tracts, as Fitz-Herbert's *Natura Brevium*, Staunford's *Pleas of the Crown*, Crompton's *Jurisdiction of Courts*, &c., are only to be had in French, and will any man pretend to be a lawyer without it, when that language should be as familiar to him as his mother-tongue? Now it is not the least use of these initiatory books that they are to be read in French, for thereby a student with his slow steps gains ground in the language as well as in the law; and by that time as he shall be capable to understand other books, he will be capable to read them, therefore I should absolutely interdict reading Littleton, &c., in any other than French; and, however it is translated and the English con-columned with it, it should be used only as subsidiary, to give light to the French where it is obscure, and not as a text. For really the Law is scarce expressible properly in English, and when it is done it must be *Françoise* or very uncouth.'—P. 11, ed. 1824.

* Sir Edward Coke says there are two things to be avoided by the student 'as enemies to learning—*præpostera lectio* and *præpropera praxis.*'—*Co. Litt.* 70 b,

cellent raisons, but also beyng gadred and compacte (as I mought saye) of the pure mele or floure syfted out of the best lawes of all other countrayes, as somwhat I do intende to proue euidently in the nexte volume,* wherin I wyll rendre myne offyce or duetie to that honorable studie wherby

which he also assigns in another place (*Pref. to Ninth Reports*) as 'two causes of the uncertainty of the law.' That by the former phrase he means to imply a desultory mode of reading appears pretty plain from his use of a similar expression in the *Institutes*, part ii. cap. 46, where, in his note on the Statute of Westm. 1st, he says, 'The mischief before this statute was in respect of preposterous *or disorderly* hearing of causes.' With regard to the latter phrase, *præpropera praxis*, it may be observed that Sir Edward Coke's own career affords the best commentary to his text, for we are told that after being six years a student, 'in consideration of his great proficiency in the law, he was permitted to be called to the bar, though the usual period of probation was then eight years. The flattering compliment thus paid by the heads of his profession to his learning and talents was, of itself, a sufficient recommendation to ensure him early opportunities for bringing himself further into notice. Accordingly, we find him engaged as counsel in a case of some importance so early as 1578, that is, in the twenty-eighth year of his age. He was also appointed reader or lecturer at Lyon's Inn, an office which he held during three years; and his readings (which were not given as it is usual to give them at present, merely for the sake of observing an antiquated form) were so assiduously attended and so generally admired that he rapidly attained a degree of repute much greater than that of any other barrister of the same age and standing at the bar.'—*Library of Useful Knowledge*. Blackstone says, with reference to the study of the Law in his own time, 'The evident want of some assistance in the rudiments of legal knowledge has given birth to a practice which, if ever it had grown to be general, must have proved of extremely pernicious consequence. I mean the custom by some so very warmly recommended, of dropping all liberal education, as of no use to students in the law: and placing them in its stead at the desk of some skilful attorney, *in order to initiate them early in all the depths of practice*, and render them more dexterous in the mechanical part of business. A few instances of particular persons (men of excellent learning and unblemished integrity) who, in spite of this method of education, have shone in the foremost ranks of the bar, have afforded some kind of sanction to this illiberal path to the profession, and biassed many parents of short-sighted judgment in its favour; not considering that there are some geniuses formed to overcome all disadvantages, and that from such particular instances no general rules can be formed; nor observing that those very persons have frequently recommended, by the most forcible of all examples, the disposal of their own offspring, a very different foundation of legal studies—a regular academical education.'—*Commentaries*, vol. i. p. 31, 15th edn.

* This intention, however, as the reader will presently see, was not carried out by the author.

my father was aduaunced to a iuge, and also I my selfe haue attayned no lytle commoditie.[a]

I suppose dyuers men ther be that will say, that the swetnesse that is contayned in eloquence and the multitude of doctrines, shulde utterly withdrawe the myndes of yonge men from the more necessary studie of the lawes of this realme. To them wyll I make a briefe answere, but true it shalbe, and I trust sufficient to wise men. In the gret multitude of yonge men, whiche alway will repayre, and the lawe beinge ones brought in to a more certayne and perfect langage, will also increase in the reuerent studie of the lawe, undoughtedly there shall neuer lacke but some by nature inclyned, dyuers by desyre of sondrie doctrines, many for hope of lucre or some other aduancement,[b] will effectuelly studie the lawes, ne will be therfrom withdrawen by any other lesson whiche is more eloquent. Example we haue at this present tyme of diuers excellent lerned men, bothe in the lawes ciuile as also in phisike, whiche being exactly studyed in all partes of eloquence, bothe in the Greeke tonge and latine,[c] haue nat wit-

[a] See the Life of the Author, prefixed to the present edition.

[b] Wilson says: 'After we haue perswaded our freend that the lawe is honest, drawyng our argumentes from the heape of vertues, wee must goe further with hym, and bryng hym in good beleeue that it is very gainfull. For many one seeke not the knowledge of learning for the goodnesse sake, but rather take paines for the gaine which thei see doeth arise by it. Take awaie the hope of lucre, and you shall see fewe take any paines; no, not in the Vineyarde of the Lorde. For although none should followe any trade of life for the gaine sake, but euen as he seeth it is most necessarie for the aduauncement of God's glorie, and not passe in what estimation thynges are had in this worlde, yet because we are all so weake of witte in our tender yeres, that wee cannot weigh with our selues what is best, and our bodie so neshe, that it looketh euer to be cherished, we take that whiche is moste gainefull for us, and forsake that altogether whiche wee ought moste to followe. So that for lacke of honest meanes, and for want of good order, the best waie is not used, neither is God's honour in our first yeares remembred. I had rather (saied one) make my childe a Cobler, then a Preacher, a Tankerd bearer, then a Scholer. For what shall my sonne seeke for learning when he shall neuer gett thereby any liuyng? Sett my sonne to that whereby he maie get some what. The law, therfore, not onely bringeth much gaine with it, but also aduanceth men both to worship, renowne, and honour.'—*Arte of Rhet.* p. 36.

[c] The honour of restoring Greek learning in England must be divided between

standing radde and perused the great fardelles and trusses of the most barbarouse autours, stuffed with innumerable gloses,[a]

Linacre, Grocyn, and William Lilye. 'Their claims,' says the biographer of the first-named, 'are nicely balanced. In the year 1518 letters patent were granted to John Chamber, Thomas Linacre, and Fernandus de Victoria, the acknowledged physicians to the king, together with Nicholas Halsewell, John Francis, Robert Yaxley, and all men of the same faculty in London, to be incorporated as one body and perpetual community or college.'—Johnson's *Life of Linacre*, pp. 150, 279, ed. 1835. This was the foundation of the College of Physicians, of which Linacre was the original president. 'His primary object,' says Hallam, 'was to secure a learned profession, to rescue the art of healing from mischievous ignorance, and to guide the industrious student in the path of real knowledge, which at that time lay far more through the regions of ancient learning than at present. It was important, not for the mere dignity of the profession, but for its proper ends, to encourage the cultivation of the Greek langage, or to supply its want by accurate versions of the chief medical writers.'—*Lit. of Europe*, vol. i. p. 459, 4th ed. Even at this early stage of medical science there were some ladies who made it their study; thus we are told that in the household of Sir Thomas More, 'Margaret Gige, though not one of his naturall children, yet brought up with his other children even from her youth, was furnished with the knowledge of both the Greek and Latin tongues, and had good skill in phisicke, as by this you may see. It happened that Sir Thomas, some yeares before his death, had an ague, and had passed two or three fitts. After, he had a fitt out of course, so strange and merveilous, that a man would thinke it impossible; for he felt himself at one time bothe hote and cold, throughoute all his bodie, and not in one part hote, and in another colde, for that is not strange; but he felt sensiblie and painfullie, at one time in one place, both contrarie qualities. He asked the physitians how it might be possible. They answered it could not be. Then this little maide (for then shee was verie younge, yet had read Galen) told Sir Thomas, that there was such a kind of fever; and forthwith she shewed a book of Galen, *De Differentiis Febrium*, where he avoucheth as much. This gentlewoman after married Doctor John Clement, famous for his singular skill in Greek, and in phisicke.'—Wordsworth's *Eccles. Biog.* vol. ii. p. 122, 4th. ed.

[a] Sir John Doderidge, speaking of the commentators, says: 'What horrid and incompt words hath Logicke and Philosophy endured, introduced by their Dunces devices, as *Ens, entitas, quidditas, causalitas*, with a multitude of others impertinent to be remembered? With what improper tearmes and barbarous speeches have the schoolmen daubed Divinity? What hath beene in this kinde brought in upon the pure and cleare fountaines of the Digests of the Civill Lawes? which being compiled out of sundry most excellent sentences, drawne out of the workes and passages of the ancient Romane lawyers, *doe retaine the same purity and conformity of a cleane and neat stile, as though all had beene penned by one man*; and yet are in a manner defiled by the Feudary Tenurist writers of the middle age in their *Glosses* and commentaries, as those learned Lawyers of this latter age, Alciatus, Budæus, Cujacius, and the rest have undergone an Herculean

wherby the moste necessary doctrines of lawe and phisike be mynced in to fragmentes, and in all wise mens opinions, do perceyue no lasse in the said lernynges than they whiche neuer knewe eloquence, or neuer tasted other but the fecis or dragges of the sayd noble doctrines. And as for the multitude of sciences can nat indamage any student,[a] but if he be

labour to clense the same.'—*The English Lawyer*, p. 52, ed. 1631. The idea contained in the sentence marked by italics in this passage had been already anticipated by Laurentius Valla, who says: 'Cui (*i.e.* the general conformity of the Roman law writers) simile quiddam (ut de ultimâ tantum parte quæ ad nos pertinet dicam), in epistolis Ciceronis admirari solebam, quæ quum a pluribus scribantur, omnes tamen ab uno eodemque audacius dixerim, si personas sustuleris, ab uno Cicerone scriptæ judicentur, ita verba ac sententiæ characterque ipse dicendi ubique sui est similis. Quod eo magis Jurisconsultis est admirandum ; quòd illi eâdem ætate cuncti extiterunt, in eodem quasi ludo ac scholâ instituti, hi vero inter se etiam seculis distant, licet omnes post Ciceronem, ideoque quibusdam in verbis ab eo differentes, quales omnes a Virgilio usque ad Livium fuerunt.'—*Elegantiarum*, lib. iii. *in procemio*, ed. 1562. Selden in his Preface to the *Titles of Honour* criticises the labours of the commentators upon the Civil Law in the following terms : 'In things of this nature, to be extracted out of story and philology, they cease to be Doctors, nay, are scarce *Alphabetarians*, even the whole rank of them, until you come to the most learned Budè, Alciat, Hotomon, Cujas, Wesenbeck, Brisson, the Gentiles, and some few more of this age, before whom the body of that profession was not amiss compared to a fair robe of cloth of gold, or of richest stuff and fashion, *qui fust* (saving all mannerly respect to you, reader) *brodée de merde*. The reason of the similitude is known to any who sees such impudent barbarism in the glosses on so neat a text, which from Justinian (he died 565) until Lothar II. (he was emperor 1125) lay hidden and out of use in the Western Empire, nor did any there all that time profess or read it.'—*Opera*, tom. iii. pars. 1, p. 95, ed. 1726. Hallam says that 'the labours of the older jurists in accumulating glosses or short marginal interpretations were more calculated to multiply than to disentangle the intricacies of the Pandects.'—*Lit. of Europe*, vol. i. p. 409, 4th ed.

[a] Sir John Doderidge was equally in favour of a liberal education for a lawyer. 'It may well bee affirmed that the knowledge of the Law is truly stiled *Rerum divinarum humanarumque scientia*, and worthily imputed to be the Science of Sciences; and that therein lies hid the knowledge almost of every other learned science. But yet I pray consider, that those forraine knowledges are not inherent or inbred in the Lawes, but rather as a borrowed light, not found there, but brought thither, and learned elsewhere by them that have adorned and polished the studies of the Lawes. For since the materiall subject of the Law is so ample (as indeed it is), containing all things that may be controverted, the study of the Lawes, then, must of necessity stretch out her hand and crave to be holpen and assisted almost of all other sciences. Therefore this objection may well bee in-

meued to studie the lawe by any of the sayd motions by me before touched, he shal rather increase therin than be hyndred, and that shall apere manifestly to theym that either will gyue credence to my reporte, or els will rede the warkes that I wyll alledge; whiche if they understande nat, to desyre some lerned man by interpretinge to cause them perceyue it. And first I wil begyn at oratours, who beare the principall tytle of eloquence.

The Arte of Retorycke in mooitng. It is to be remembred that in the lernyng of the lawes of this realme, there is at this daye an exercise, wherin is a maner, a shadowe, or figure of the auncient rhetorike. I meane the pleadynge used in courte and Chauncery called motes;[a] where fyrst a case is appoynted verted against them that doe urge the same, and proveth rather that the Professor of the Lawes should be furnished with the knowledge of all good literature of most of the Sciences liberall; for if a man may observe the use of those sciences to lie hidden in the Law, who then may better use them or observe them, then he which is already furnished with them. And if the knowledge of the Law doe receive ornament by those eruditions (as I think no man can denie), it shall be very expedient and well befitting the student of the Lawes to have first familiarity and acquaintance with them, and to bee instructed in the same.'—*Engl. Lawyer*, p. 34. Coke was quite of the same opinion:—' Now what arts and sciences are necessary for the knowledge and understanding of these laws? I say that, seeing these laws do limit, bound and determine all other human laws, arts and sciences, I cannot exclude the knowledge of any of them from the professors of these laws; the knowledge of any of them is necessary and profitable.'—*Pref. to Reports*, Part III.

[a] From Chamberlayne's *Present State of England* we learn that ' Utter Barristers are such as from their learning and standing are called by the Benchers to plead and argue in the society *doubtful cases and questions* which are called *Moots* (from *meeting*, the old Saxon word for the French *assemble*, or else from the French *mot*, a word). And whilst they argue the said cases they sit *uttermost* on the forms or benches which they call the Bar. Out of these Mootmen are chosen Readers for the Inns of Chancery belonging to the Inns of Court, whereof they are Members, where in Term time and grand Vacations they argue cases in the presence of attorneys and clerks. All the rest are accounted Inner Barristers, who for want of learning or time are not to argue in these Moots. And yet in a Moot before the Benchers two of these Inner Barristers, sitting on the same form with the Utter Barristers, do for their exercises *recite by heart* the pleading of the same Moot case in Law French, which Pleading is the Declaration at large of the said Moot case, the one taking the part of the Plaintiff and the other of the Defendant,' Part II. p. 225, ed. 1679.

THE GOVERNOUR. 149

to be moted by certayne yonge men, contaynyng some doubtefull controuersie, which is in stede of the heed of a declamation called *thema*. The case beinge knowen, they whiche be appoynted to mote, do examine the case, and inuestigate what they therin can espie, whiche may make a contention, wherof may ryse a question to be argued,[a] and that of Tulli is called *constitutio*,[b] and of Quintilian *status causæ*.[c]

Also they consider what plees on euery parte ought to be made, and howe the case maye be reasoned, whiche is the fyrste parte of Rhetorike, named *Inuention*; than appoynte they howe many plees maye be made for euery parte, and in what formalitie they shulde be sette, whiche is the seconde parte of Rhetorike, called *disposition*, wherin they do moche approche unto Rhetorike: than gather they all in to perfecte remembrance, in suche ordre as it ought to be pleaded, whiche is the parte of Rhetorike named *memorie*. But for as moche as the tonge wherin it is spoken, is barberouse, and the sterynge of affections of the mynde in this realme was neuer used,[d] ther-

---

[a] Fulbecke, writing in 1599, recommends this practice as a preparation for the profession. He says: 'Gentlemen students of the Law ought by domesticall Moots to exercise and conforme themselves to greater and waighter attempts, for it is a point of warlike policie, as appeareth by *Vegetius*, to traine younge souldiours by sleight and small skirmishes for more valorous and haughty proceedings, for such a shadowed kind of contention doth open the way and giue courage unto them to argue matters in publicke place and Courts of Recorde.'— *Preparative to the Study of the Law*, p. 41, ed. 1620. In practice, indeed, it was found, at a time when books were scarce and beyond the reach of many, the readiest way to acquire a sound knowledge of law. Thus Wilson says: 'I haue knowne diuers, that by familiar talking and *moutyng* together, haue come to right good learnyng, without any greate booke skill, or muche beatyng of their braine by any close studie or secrete musing in their Chambers.'—*Arte of Rhet.* p. 39.

[b] 'Omnis res quæ habet in se positam in dictione aut disceptatione aliquam controversiam, aut facti, aut nominis, aut generis, aut actionis continet quæstionem. Eam igitur quæstionem, ex quâ causa nascitur, Constitutionem appellamus.'—*De Inventione*, lib. i. cap. 8.

[c] 'Quod nos *statum*, id quidam *constitutionem* vocant, alii *quæstionem*, alii *quod ex quæstione appareat*.'—*Instit. Orat.* lib. iii. cap. 6, § 2.

[d] Wilson, in his *Arte of Rhetorique*, says: 'There are three maner of stiles or inditynges. The great or mightie kinde, when we use greate wordes or vehement figures. The small kinde, when wee moderate our heate by meaner

fore there lacketh *Eloquution* and *Pronunciation*, two the principall partes of rhetorike.ᵃ Nat withstanding some lawyars, if they be well retayned, wyll in a meane cause pronounce right vehemently.ᵇ Moreouer there semeth to be in the sayd

_{wordes, and use not the moste stirryng sentences. The *lawe kinde*, when we use no *Metaphores* nor translated wordes, nor yet use any amplifications, but goe plainly to worke, and speake altogether in common wordes.'—P. 172. But he was quite aware of the advantage of appealing to the passions, for he says elsewhere, 'Now in mouyng pitie, and stirryng men to mercie, the wrong done must first bee plainly tolde ; or if the Judges haue sustained the like extremitie, the best were to wil them to remember their owne state, how they haue beene abused in like maner, what wronges they haue suffered by wicked doers, that by hearyng their owne, they maie the better hearken to others.'—*Ubi supra*, p. 135.}

ᵃ The above passage is quoted by Mr. Forsyth (*Hortensius*, p. 314) in confirmation of his statement that forensic eloquence was at a very low ebb in England at this period ; but, curiously enough, he misquotes it, and substitutes ' nature ' for ' realme,' thereby weakening the force of what he intended for (as it is in fact) an apt illustration of his position. Mr. Forsyth says in another place : ' It must indeed be admitted that eloquence has always been rare amongst the advocates of England, and it may be interesting to consider whether there have been causes to account for this. Perhaps one reason is the excessive degree of technicality which formerly pervaded every part and parcel of the English law. Of all the systems that ever were invented to cramp and confine the intellect, that of special pleading seems to have been the most admirably adapted to attain that end. We need not deny that its principles were based in rigid logic, but the development of those principles produced such a luxuriant crop of artificial and wiredrawn distinctions, that the most subtle intellect found it difficult to understand them. It was a miserable exercise of perverted ingenuity to make plain statements unintelligible by involved verbiage, and while affecting to exclude all ambiguity of expression, to ransack the English language for expletives and synonyms, the result of which was a mass of obscure phraseology such as even a tutored intellect could hardly comprehend.'—*Ubi supra*, p. 341.

ᵇ Under the head of 'Ambiguities,' Wilson gives us a picture of the way in which cases were got up in his day. ' The Lawiers lacke no cases to fill this parte ful of examples. For rather then faile, they will make doubtes oftentymes, where no doubt should be at all. "Is his Lease long enough ?" (quoth one). "Yea, sir, it is very long," saied a poore Housbandman. "Then (quoth he) let me alone with it ; I will finde a hole in it I warrant thee."' He is careful to add, however, ' In all this talke I excepte alwaies the good Lawiers, and I maie wel spare them, for they are but a fewe.'—*Arte of Rhet.* p. 98. Some idea of the fees paid to counsel may be culled from the 'Household and Privy Purse Expenses of the Le Stranges of Hunstanton,' published in the *Archæologia*. Amongst other items is a fee of 6s. 8d. paid to Mr. Serjeant Spelman (afterwards one of the Judges of the King's Bench), 'for his counsell in putting in of the

pledinges certayne partes of an oration, that is to say for *Narrations, Partitions, Confirmations* and *Confutations*, named of some *Reprehensions*,[a] they haue *Declarations, Barres, Replications* and *Reioyndres*,[b] onely they lacke pleasaunt

---

answer.' Similar fees of 3*s*. 4*d*. are afterwards given to Mr. Knightley and Mr. Whyte for 'counsell,' but in 1534 Mr. Yelverton had 20*s*. 'for his counsell.' Sir Thomas More was made under sheriff of London at the age of twenty-eight, and we are told that 'by this office and learned counsaile, (for there was not any matter of weight or importance in any of the prince's courts that he was not retained for counsaile on the one partie or the other) without grudge of conscience, or injurie to anie man, he gained above four hundred pounds yearlie.'—*Wordsworth Eccles. Biog.* vol. ii. p. 57, 4th ed.

[a] According to Quintilian's definition, 'Nunc de judiciali genere . . . . cujus partes, ut plurimis auctoribus placuit, quinque sunt, *proœmium, narratio, probatio, refutatio, peroratio*. His adjecerunt quidam *partitionem, propositionem, excessum*, quarum priores duæ probationi succedunt.'—*Instit. Orat.* lib. iii. cap. 9. § 1. Cicero says: 'Reprehensio est, per quam argumentando adversariorum confirmatio diluitur, aut infirmatur aut allevatur.'—*De Invent.* lib. i. cap. 42. Wilson divides an oration into seven parts as follows, viz. '1. The Enterance or beginnyng. 2. The Narration. 3. The Proposition. 4. The Deuision or seuerall partyng of thinges. 5. The Confirmation. 6. The Confutation. 7. The Conclusion.' And he explains each part *seriatim* thus: 1 'is the former parte of the Oration, whereby the will of the standers by, or of the Judge, is sought for and required to heare the matter.' 2 is 'a plaine and manifest pointyng of the matter, and an euident settyng forth of all thynges that belong unto the same, with a breefe rehersall grounded upon some reason.' 3 is 'a pithie sentence comprehended in a smal roome, the somme of the whole matter.' 4 is 'an openyng of thynges, wherein wee agree and rest upon, and wherein wee sticke and stande in trauers, shewyng what we haue to saie in our owne behalfe.' 5 is 'a declaration of our owne reasons, with assured and constant proofes.' 6 is 'a dissoluyng or wyping awaie of all suche reasons as make against us.' 7 is 'a clarkly gatheryng of the matter spoken before and a lappyng up of it altogether.'—*The Arte of Rhetorique*, p. 7. One of the earliest books on pleading is called *Novæ Narrationes*, or 'the newe tales,' evidently deriving its title from the Latin name of the plaintiff's formal allegation, *narratio*, which was called *counte* or *conte* in French. We see from the text that the rules of oratory laid down by Cicero and Quintilian must have exercised considerable influence upon the forms and terminology of the early English pleaders.

[b] Rastell, in 1564, published his 'Colleccion of entrees, of declaracions, barres, replicacions, reioinders, issues, verdits, iudgementes, executions, proces, contynuances, essoynes, and diuers other matters.' The modern editor of the year books confirms Mr. Stephens's view that the reign of Edward I. marks the period at which pleading was 'first methodically formed and cultivated as a science.' Mr. Horwood thinks that the writings of Duns Scotus (who lectured at

fourme of begynnyng, called in latine *Exordium*,* nor it maketh therof no great mater; they that haue studied rhe-

Oxford) and of Alexander de Hales, to say nothing of Thomas Aquinas and other foreign schoolmen, must have been a good preparation for the subtleties of pleading. Sir Matthew Hale says that 'tho' pleadings in the time of Hen. VI., Edw. IV., and Hen. VII. were far shorter than afterwards, *especially after Henry VIII.*, yet they were much longer than in the time of King Edw. III., and the Pleaders, yea, and the Judges too, became somewhat too curious therein, so that art or dexterity of pleading, which in its use, nature, and design was only to render the fact plain and intelligible, and to bring the matter to judgment with a convenient certainty, began to degenerate from its primitive simplicity and the true use and end thereof, and to become a piece of nicety and curiosity.'—*Hist. of the Common Law*, p. 173.

* The pleadings down to the time of Edward III. were *vivâ voce*, and those who pleaded orally would no doubt pursue the method first recommended by Quintilian in his Institutes, and afterwards adopted by later Rhetoricians. Thus Wilson says, 'An enteraunce (i.e. *exordium*) is two waies deuided. The first is called a plaine beginning, when the hearer is made apt to giue good eare out of hande, to that whiche shall followe. The seconde is a priuie twining, or close creeping in, to win fauour with muche circumstaunce, called insinuation. For in all matters that men take in hande, this consideration ought first to be had, that we first diligently expend the cause, before we go through with it, that we maie be assured whether it be lawfull or otherwise. And not onely this, but also wee must aduisedly marke the men before whom wee speake, the men against whom we speake, and al the circumstaunces which belong unto the matter. If the matter be honest, godly, and such as of right ought to be wel liked, we maie use an open beginning, and wil the hearers to reioyce, and so go through with our parte. If the cause be lothsome, or suche as will not be well borne with all, but needeth much helpe and fauour of the hearers, it shal be the speaker's part priuely to get fauour, and by humble talk to win their good willes. First requiryng them to giue hym the hearyng, and next not streightly to giue iudgement, but with mercie to mitigate all rigour of the Lawe. . . . . Notwithstandyng I thinke it not amisse often to rehearse this one point, that euermore *the beginnyng* be not ouermuche laboured, nor curiously made, but rather apt to the purpose, seeming upon present occasion, euermore to take place, and so to bee deuised, as though wee speake altogether, without any greate studie, framing rather our tale to good reason than our tongue to vaine painting of the matter. In all which discourse I haue framed all the lessons and euery enterance properly *to serue for pleading at the barre.*'—*Arte of Rhetorique*, pp. 101, 107. When written pleadings were introduced there was no longer any necessity for a 'pleasant form of beginning,' because the count or declaration then became, as Sir E. Coke tells us, 'an exposition of the writ, and addeth time, place, and other necessary circumstances, that the same may be triable. The count must be agreeable and conforme to the writ, the barre to the count, &c., and the judgement to the count, for none of them must be narrower or broader than the other.'—*Co. Litt.* 303 a, b.

torike shal perceyue what I meane. Also in arguynge their cases, in myn opinion, they very litle do lacke of the hole arte; for therin they do diligently obserue the rules of Confirmation and Confutation, wherin resteth proufe and disproufe,[a] hauyng almoste all the places wherof they shall fetche their raisons, called of Oratours *loci communes*,[b] which I omitte to name, fearinge to be to longe in this mater. And verily I suppose, if there mought ones happen some man, hauying an excellent wytte, to be brought up in suche fourme as I haue hytherto written, and maye also be exactly or depely

[a] Wilson defines Confirmation thus: 'When we haue declared the cheef pointes whereunto we purpose to referre all our reasons, wee must heape matter, and finde out argumentes to confirme the same to the uttermoste of our power, making first the strongest reasons that wee can, and next after, gathering all the probable causes together, that being in one heape, they maie seeme strong and of great waight. And whatsoeuer the aduersarie hath said against us, to answere thereunto as tyme and place maie best serue. That if his reasons bee light, and more good maie be done in confuting his, than in confirming our owne, it were best of all to set upon him, and put awaie by arte all that he hath fondly saied without wit. Now in trying the troth, by reasons gathered of the matter, we must first mark what was done at that time by the suspected person; when suche and suche offences were committed; yea, what he did before this act was done. Againe the tyme must be marked, the place, the maner of doyng, and what harte he bare him. As the oportunitie of doyng, and the power he had to doe this deede. The which, all set together, shall either acquit him, or finde him giltie. These arguments serue to confirme a matter in iudgement for any hainous offence. In *confuting* of causes, the like maie bee had as we used to proue, if we take the contrary of the same. For as thinges are alledged, so they may be wrested, and as houses are builded, so they be ouerthrown. What though many coniectures bee gathered, and diuers matters framed to ouerthrowe the defendant, yet wit maie finde out bywaies to escape, and suche shiftes maie be made, either in auoiding the daunger by plaine deniall, or els by obiections, and rebounding againe of reasons made, that small harme shall turne to the accused person, though the presumptions of his offence bee greate, and bee thought by good reason to be faultie.'—*Arte of Rhetorique*, pp. 114, 115.

[b] 'Hæc ergo argumenta, quæ transferri in multas causas possunt, *locos communes* nominamus: nam locus communis aut certæ rei quandam continet amplificationem, ut si quis hoc velit ostendere, eum, qui parentem necarit, maximo supplicio esse dignum: quo loco, nisi perorata et probata causa, non est utendum: aut dubiæ, quæ ex contrario quoque habeat probabiles rationes argumentandi; ut suspicionibus credi oportere, et contra, suspicionibus credi non oportere.'—*Cic. de Invent.* lib. ii. cap. 15.

lerned in the arte of an Oratour, and also in the lawes of this realme, the prince so willyng and therto assistinge, undoughtedly it shulde nat be impossible for hym to bring the pleadyng and reasonyng of the lawe, to the auncient fourme of noble oratours;[a] and the lawes and exercise therof beyng in pure latine or doulce frenche, fewe men in consultations shulde (in myne opinion) compare with our lawyars, by this meanes beinge brought to be perfect orators, as in whome shulde

[a] Sir Henry Maine says: 'It is not because our own jurisprudence and that of Rome were *once* alike that they ought to be studied together—it is because they *will be* alike. It is because all laws, however dissimilar in their infancy, tend to resemble each other in their maturity; and because we in England are slowly, and perhaps unconsciously or unwillingly, but still steadily and certainly accustoming ourselves to the same modes of legal thought, and to the same conceptions of legal principle, to which the Roman jurisconsults had attained after centuries of accumulated experience and unwearied cultivation.'— *Cambridge Essays*, 1856, p. 2. Mr. Stephen has pointed out that the oratorical analysis of Quintilian exhibits exactly the principle of the English pleading, 'and when,' he says, 'it is considered that the logic and rhetoric of antiquity were the favourite studies of the age in which that science was principally cultivated, and that the Judges and pleaders were doubtless men of general learning according to the fashion of their times, it is perhaps not improbable that the method of developing the point in controversy was improved from these ancient sources.'— *Principles of Pleading*, Appendix, note 23, ed. 1843. This position is further confirmed if we refer to the earliest English writers on Rhetoric. Thus Wilson says: ' In matters criminall, where iudgement is required, there are two persones at the least, whiche muste through contrarietie stande and reste uppon some *issue*. As for example, a seruyng man is apprehended by a Lawier for Felonie, uppon suspition. The Lawier saieth to the seruing manne, thou hast dooen this roberie. Naye (saieth he), I haue not doen it. Upon this conflicte and matching together ariseth this State, whether this seruing man hath doon this robberie or no. Upon whiche pointe the Lawier must stand and seeke to proue it to the uttermoste of his power. A State therfor, in matters of Judgement, is that thyng whiche doeth arise upon the first demaunde, and deniall made betwixt men, whereof the one part is the accuser, and the other part the persone or persones accused. It is called a State, because we doe stande and rest upon some one poincte, the which must wholie and onely be proued of the one side, and denied of the other. I can not better terme it in Englishe then by the name of an *Issue*, the whiche not onely ariseth upon much debatyng, and long trauers used, whereupon al matters are saied *to come to an issue*, but also els where an issue is saied to be then and so often as bothe partes stande upon one pointe, the whiche dooeth as well happen at the first beginnyng, before any probations are used, as it dooeth at the latter endyng, after the matter hath at large been discussed.'—*Arte of Rhetorique*, p 90.

than be founden the sharpe wittes of logitians, the graue sentences of philosophers, the elegancie of poetes, the memorie of ciuilians, the voice and gesture of them that can pronounce commedies, which is all that Tulli, in the person of the most eloquent man Marcus Antonius, coulde require to be in an oratour.[a] *Ci. de oratore,* li. i.

But nowe to conclude myne assertion, what let was eloquence to the studie of the lawe in Quintus Sceuola, whiche being an excellent autour in the lawes ciuile, was called of al lawiars moste eloquent?[b] Or howe moche was eloquence minisshed by knowlege of the lawes in Crassus, whiche was called of all eloquent men the beste lawiar?[c]

Also Seruus Sulpitius, in his tyme one of the moste noble oratours next unto Tulli, was nat so let by eloquence but that on the ciuile lawes he made notable commentes, and many noble warkes by all lawyars approued.[d] Who redeth the text

[a] 'In oratore autem acumen dialecticorum, sententiæ philosophorum, verba prope poetarum, memoria jurisconsultorum, vox tragædorum, gestus pæne summorum actorum est requirendus.'—*De Oratore,* lib. i. cap. 28.

[b] Cicero says of him: 'Q. Scævola, æqualis et collega meus, homo omnium et disciplinâ juris civilis eruditissimus, et ingenio prudentiâque acutissimus, et oratione maxime limatus atque subtilis, atque, ut ego soleo dicere, juris peritorum eloquentissimus, eloquentium juris peritissimus.'—*De Oratore,* lib. i cap. 39.

[c] Lucius Licinius Crassus was born B.C. 150. Cicero institutes the following comparison between him and Scævola: 'Hic ego, Noli, inquam, Brute, existimare his duobus quicquam fuisse in nostrâ civitate præstantius: nam, ut paulo ante dixi, consultorum alterum disertissimum, disertorum alterum consultissimum fuisse; sic in reliquis rebus ita dissimiles erant inter sese, statuere ut tamen non posses, utrius te malles similiorem. Crassus erat elegantium parcissimus, Scævola parcorum elegantissimus. Crassus in summâ comitate habebat etiam severitatis satis, Scævolæ multâ in severitate non deerat tamen comitas.'—*De claris Orator.,* cap. 40.

[d] Servius Sulpicius Rufus was consul B.C. 51. Cicero says: 'Fuit enim Sulpicius vel maxime omnium, quos quidem ego audiverim, grandis et, ut ita dicam, tragicus orator: vox cum magna, tum suavis, et splendida: gestus et motus corporis ita venustus, ut tamen ad forum, non ad scenam institutus videretur; incitata et volubilis, nec ea redundans tamen nec circumfluens, oratio' (*De claris Orator.* cap. 55), and asserts that he had often heard Sulpicius declare that he was not accustomed and was unable to write. Pomponius, however, tells quite a different tale. 'Servius, cum in causis orandis primum locum *aut pro certo post Marcum Tullium* obtineret, traditur ad consulendum Quintum Mucium de re amici sui pervenisse; cumque eum sibi respondisse de jure Servius parum intel-

of Ciuile, called the *Pandectes* or *Digestes*,[a] and hath any commendable iugement in the latine tonge, but he wyll affirme that Ulpianus, Sceuola, Claudius, and all the other there named, of whose sayenges all the saide textis be assembled, were nat only studious of eloquence, but also wonderfull exercised: for as moche as theyr stile dothe approche nerer to the antique and pure eloquence, than any other kinde of writars that wrate aboute that tyme?[b]

lexisset, iterum Quintum interrogasse, et à Quinto Mucio responsum esse, nec tamen percepisse, et ita objurgatum esse a Quinto Mucio; namque eum dixisse, turpe esse patricio et nobili, et causas oranti, jus in quo versaretur ignorare. Eâ velut contumeliâ Servius jactatus operam dedit juri civili, et plurimum eos, de quibus locuti sumus, audiit: institutus à Balbo Lucilio, instructus autem maximè a Gallo Aquilio, qui fuit Cercinæ; itaque libri complures ejus exstant Cercinæ confecti. Hic cum in legatione perisset, statuam ei populus Romanus pro rostris posuit et hodieque exstat pro rostris Augusti. *Hujus volumina complura exstant; reliquit autem prope centum et octoginta libros.'—De Orig. Juris.*, § 43, ed. 1848.

[a] Hallam says: 'The general voice of Europe has always named Andrew Alciati of Milan as the restorer of the Roman law. He taught from the year 1518 to his death in 1550, in the Universities of Avignon, Milan, Bourges, Paris, and Bologna. Literature became with him the handmaid of law; the historians of Rome, her antiquaries, her orators and poets, were called upon to elucidate the obsolete words and obscure allusions of the Pandects; to which, the earlier as well as the more valuable and extensive portion of the civil law, this method of classical interpretation is chiefly applicable. Alciati was the first who taught the lawyers to write with purity and elegance. Erasmus has applied to him the eulogy of Cicero on Scævola, that he was the most jurisprudent of orators and the most eloquent of lawyers.'—*Lit. of Europe*, vol. i. p. 411, 4th ed.

[b] Sir Henry Maine says: 'Those who have penetrated deepest into the spirit of the Ulpians, Papinians and Pauluses are ready to assert that in the productions of the Roman lawyers they discover all the grand qualities which we identify with one or another in the list of distinguished Englishmen. They see the same force and elegance of expression, the same rectitude of moral view, the same immunity from prejudice, the same sound and masculine sense, the same sensibility to analogies, the same keen observation, the same nice analysis of generals, the same vast sweep of comprehension over particulars. Unless we are prepared to believe that for five or six centuries the world's collective intellect was smitten with a paralysis which never visited it before or since, we are driven to admit that the Roman jurisprudence may be all which its least cautious encomiasts have ventured to pronounce it, and that the language of conventional panegyric may even fall short of the unvarnished truth.'—*Cam. Essays*, 1856, p. 29. Gibbon passes almost the same judgment as our author. 'Perhaps if the pre-

Semblably Tulli, in whom it semeth that Eloquence hath sette her glorious Throne, most richely and preciousely adourned for all men to wonder at, but no man to approche it, was nat let from beinge an incomparable oratour, ne was nat by the exacte knowlege of other sciences withdrawen from pleadyng infinite causes before the Senate and iuges, and they beinge of moste waightye importance.* In so moche as Cornelius Tacitus, an excellent oratour, historien, and lawiar, saithe, Surely in the bokes of Tulli, men may deprehende, that in hym lacked nat the knowlege of geometrye, ne musike, ne grammer, finally of no maner of art that was honest: he of logike perceiued the subtiltie, of that

Corn. Ta. de Orator.

ceptors and friends of Cicero were still alive, our candour would acknowledge that, except in purity of language, their intrinsic merit was excelled by the school of Papinian and Ulpian.'—*Decline and Fall of the Roman Empire*, vol. v. p. 284. Laurentius Valla held the same opinion: 'Nam Servii Sulpicii atque Mutii Scævolæ nihil extat, sed alterius Mutii recentioris. Et prisci illi quidem Jurisconsulti quales quantique in eloquendo fuerint, judicare non possumus, quippe quorum nihil legimus. His autem, qui inter manus versantur, nihil est, meâ sententiâ, quod addi adimive posse videatur, non tam eloquentiæ (quam quidem materia illa non magnopere patitur) quàm Latinitatis atque elegantiæ, sine quâ cæca omnis doctrina est, et illiberalis, præsertim in jure civili.'—*Elegant.*, lib. iii. p. 200, ed. 1562.

* 'He had learnt the rudiments of Grammar and languages from the ablest teachers, gone through the studies of humanity and the politer letters with the poet Archias, been instructed in Philosophy by the principal Professors of each sect, Phædrus the Epicurean, Philo the Academic, Diodotus the Stoic, acquired a perfect knowledge of the law from the greatest lawyers as well as the greatest statesmen of Rome, the two Scævolas, all which accomplishments were but ministerial and subservient to that on which his hopes and ambition were singly placed —the reputation of an Orator. Thus adorned and accomplished he offered himself to the Bar about the age of twenty-six, not as others generally did, raw and ignorant of their business, and wanting to be formed to it by use and experience, but finished and qualified at once to sustain any cause which should be committed to him... After he had given a specimen of himself to the City in this (cause of P. Quinctius) and several other private causes, he undertook the celebrated defence of S. Roscius of Ameria in his twenty-seventh year... Roscius was acquitted to the great honour of Cicero, whose courage and address in defending him was applauded by the whole city, so that from this moment he was looked upon as an Advocate of the first class, and equal to the greatest causes.'—Middleton's *Life of Cicero*, vol. i. p. 36-39, ed. 1755.

parte that was morall all the commoditie, and of all thinges the chiefe motions and causis.[a]

And yet for all this abundance, and as it were a garnerde heaped with all maner sciences, there failed nat in him substanciall lernying in the lawes Ciuile,[b] as it may appiere as wel in the bokes, whiche he him selfe made of lawes,[c] as also and most specially, in many of his most eloquent orations; whiche if one well lerned in the lawes of this realme dyd rede and wel understande, he shulde finde, specially in his orations called *Actiones* agayne Verres,[d] many places where he shulde espie, by likelihode, the fountaynes, from whense proceded diuers groundes of our commune lawes.[e] But I wyll nowe leue to speake any more therof at this tyme.

[a] 'Itaque Hercule in libris Ciceronis deprehendere licet, non geometriæ, non musicæ, non grammaticæ, non denique ullius ingenuæ artis scientiam ei defuisse. Ille dialecticæ subtilitatem, ille moralis partis utilitatem, ille rerum motus causasque cognovit.'—*De Oratoribus*, cap. 30.

[b] 'He studied civil law under the able guidance of Q. Mucius Scævola, whose house was thronged by clients who resorted to the great jurist for advice in legal difficulties.'—*Hortensius*, p. 146, 2nd ed.

[c] 'These laws are generally taken from the old constitution or custom of Rome, with some little variation and temperament contrived to obviate the disorders to which that Republic was liable, and to give it a stronger turn towards the Aristocratical side; in the other books which are lost, he had treated, as he tells us, of the particular rights and privileges of the Roman people.'—Middleton's *Life of Cicero*, vol. ii. p. 162, edn. 1755.

[d] Mr. Forsyth considers that 'the great case against Verres, of all the trials of antiquity, bears the nearest resemblance to the impeachment of Warren Hastings.' —*Hortensius*, p. 139, 2nd ed.

[e] 'The historical connexion between the Roman jurisprudence and our own, appears to be now looked upon as furnishing one very strong reason for increased attention to the civil law of Rome. The fact, of course, is not now to be questioned. The vulgar belief that the English Common Law was indigenous in all its parts was always so easily refuted by the most superficial comparison of the text of Bracton and Fleta with the *Corpus Juris*, that the honesty of the historians who countenanced it can only be defended by alleging the violence of their prejudices; and now that the great accumulation of fragments of ante-Justinianean compendia, and the discovery of the MSS. of Gaius, have increased our acquaintance with the Roman law in the only form in which it can have penetrated into Britain, the suspicion of an earlier filiation amounts almost to a certainty.'— *Camb. Essays*, 1856, p. 1. Mr. Finlason has written an elaborate essay on this

THE GOVERNOUR. 159

All[a] that I haue writen well considered, it shall seme to wise men, that neither eloquence, nor knowlege of sondry doctrines, shall utterly withdrawe all men from studie of the lawes. But all though many were allected unto those doctrines by naturall disposition, yet the same nature, whiche wyll nat (as I mought saye) be circumscribed within the boundes of a certayne of studies, may as well dispose some man, as well to desire the knowlege of the lawes of this realme, as she dyd incline the Romanes, excellently lerned in all sciences, to apprehende the lawes ciuile ; [b] sens the lawes

subject. He says : 'It is the opinion of those whose researches into our early history give their opinions highest authority, that after the decline of the Roman Empire, and the withdrawal of the Roman legionaries, the Romanised Britons (the two races having been so long together that they must to a great extent have become blended) retained, as might be expected, the Roman ideas of government, and the Roman laws and institutions, and that these were likewise in a similar way transmitted to subsequent races of barbarian invaders, who, before their conquests were complete, became blended with the Romanised inhabitants of the island. Nothing is more remarkable in the history of this country than the gradual blending of the successive races and their laws and institutions, and one of the most remarkable, though perhaps least recognised illustrations of this is afforded by the manner in which the Roman occupation paved the way for the Saxon invasion, and, on the other hand, prepared the way for the adoption by the Saxons of the Roman institutions. There would therefore, it is manifest, be every reasonable probability that the Roman laws and institutions would be adopted in this country, and would continue to exist here even after the Roman rule was at an end. Nor is it left to probability ; it is converted to the positive certainty of historic truth by the actual existence of the laws of the Romanised Britons, compiled at a period posterior to the termination of the Roman rule in the island, and anterior to the later Saxon laws.'—*Reeves' Hist. of Engl. Law,* Introduc. p. xxxvi. ed. 1869. Mr. Stephen has pointed out (what M. Houard had previously noticed) the resemblance between the forms of the *precepts* given by Marculfus in the 7th century and the forms of the writs of our own courts, and he justly thinks that the pedigrees of our forms may be traced up to the old Roman formulæ. See *Year Books* 32-33 Ed. I., *Preface,* p. xi. Sir John Doderidge, at the end of the sixteenth century, had already remarked 'the great conformity' between the Roman law and our own, but he seems to have thought that this was merely a coincidence arising from the fact that the 'laws of the Empire' and the 'Law of this Land' agreed 'in the principles of nature and reason.'— *The English Lawyer,* p. 158.

[a] The following passage, down to the words 'heedes of the lawes,' is omitted in all the subsequent editions.

[b] Blackstone, in recommending a more general study of the law, says in his

of this realme, beinge well gathered and brought in good latine,* shal be worthy to haue like praise as Tulli gaue to the lawes comprehended in the xii tables, from whens all ciuile lawe flowed, whiche praise was in this wise. Al

inaugural address as Vinerian Professor, 'The Roman Pandects will furnish us with a piece of history not unapplicable to our present purpose. Servius Sulpicius, a gentleman of the patrician order, and a celebrated orator, had occasion to take the opinion of Quintus Mutius Scævola, the then oracle of the Roman law, but for want of some knowledge in that science, could not so much as understand even the technical terms which his friend was obliged to make use of. Upon which Mutius Scævola could not forbear to upbraid him with this memorable reproof: "That it was a shame for a patrician, a nobleman, and an orator of causes to be ignorant of that law in which he was so peculiarly concerned." This reproach made so deep an impression on Sulpicius that he immediately applied himself to the study of the law, wherein he arrived to that proficiency that he left behind him about an hundred and fourscore volumes of his own compiling upon the subject, and became, in the opinion of Cicero, a much more complete lawyer than even Mutius Scævola himself. I would not be thought to recommend to our English nobility and gentry to become as great lawyers as Sulpicius, though he together with this character sustained likewise that of an excellent orator, a firm patriot, and a wise indefatigable senator; but the inference which arises from the story is this, that ignorance of the laws of the land hath ever been esteemed dishonourable in those who are entrusted by their country to maintain, to administer, and to amend them.'—*Comment.* vol. i. p. 11, 15th ed.

* Before the end of the century, however, the lawyers defended the barbarisms which passed current in the profession for Latin words. Thus Sir John Doderidge says: 'The entries and enrollments of our Writs, Pleas, and all other our Law proceedings are neither base, abject, or horrid, as hath beene imported, for our Originall Writs of set forme are from ancient memory, have ever beene preserved in the booke called the Register, from the which our Clerkes may not swerve, to avoyd the infinite variety of formes which might otherwise ensue, and were first conceived and devised in as proper Latine, as the times wherein they were first invented, and the matter it selfe was able to beare. And as touching the other mentioned proceedings entered in the Latine tongue, although not eloquent, yet *satis laudato forensi stilo* as in any other kingdome perspicuous and significant.' —*The Engl. Lawyer*, p. 52. Fulbecke did 'not thinke any exquisite skill of the Latine tongue to bee necessary in a Lawyer;' and Selden, whose own Latin was remarkably uncouth, excuses the usage of such peculiar forms as '*implacitare, alodium, forisfacta* et ejusmodi forsan paucula alia quæ fastidientis forsan stomachi grammaticis, qui ad nascentis Cæsariani imperii ævum ita omnia ridiculè exigunt, ut res ipsas imprimis utiles, libentius ignorari velint quàm delicatulis auribus per vocabula Cicerone, Salustio, Tacito, Livio, aut aliis scriptoribus qui tunc floruere classicis, minimè reperta immitti.'—*Opera*, tom. ii. pars. 2, col. 1594, ed. 1726.

though men will abraide at it, I wyll say as I thinke, the one litle boke of the xii tables semeth to me to surmounte the libraries of all the philosophers in waighty auto- ritie, and abundance of profite, beholde who so wyll the fountaines and heedes of the lawes.[a] *Ci. de oratore, li. i.*

More ouer, whan yonge men haue radde lawes, expouned in the orations of Tulli, and also in histories of the begynnynge of lawes, and in the warkes of Plato, Xenophon, and Aristotell, of the diuersities of lawes and publike weales, if nature (as I late saide) wyll dispose them to that maner studie, they shall be therto the more incensed, and come unto it the better prepared and furnisshed. And they whom nature therto nothinge meueth, haue nat only saued all that time, which many now a dayes do consume in idlenesse,[b] but also haue wonne suche a treasure, wherby they shall alway be able to serue honourably theyr prince, and the publike weale of theyr countray, principally if they conferre al their

---

[a] 'Fremant omnes licet: dicam quod sentio: bibliothecas, mehercule, omnium philosophorum unus mihi videtur xii tabularum libellus, si quis legum fontes et capita viderit, et auctoritatis pondere, et utilitatis ubertate superare.'—*De Oratore*, lib. i. cap. 44. The laws of the Twelve Tables 'were compiled by the Decemvirs at the beginning of the fourth century of Rome, and consisted of a revision of the then existing laws, and some new ones which, according to a very questionable tradition, had been imported from Greece by three Commissioners, who had been sent there for the purpose of collecting notices of such laws and customs as might be useful to the Romans. In the adaptation of these they are said to have been assisted by an Ionian Greek, named Hermodorus of Ephesus. The new code, when completed, was engraved on twelve tablets of ivory or brass, and set up publicly in front of the Rostra in the Comitium, that the enactments might be seen and read by all the citizens. These were in the strictest and most technical sense *leges*, and may be considered as the early statute law of Rome.'—*Hortensius*, p. 56, 2nd ed.

[b] 'Idleness,' according to Mr. Froude, was the crying evil of that age. Wilson, writing in 1553, says, 'Mary, unto them that had rather slepe all daie then wake one hour, chosing for any labour slothful idlenesse, thinkyng this life to be none other but a continuall restyng place, unto such pardie it shall seeme painefull to abide any labour. To learne *Logique*, to learne the lawe, to some it semeth so harde that nothyng can enter into their heddes, and the reason is that thei want a will and an earnest minde to doe their endeuour.'—*Arte of Rhetorique*, p. 31.

doctrines to the moste noble studie of morall philosophie, whiche teacheth both vertues, maners, and ciuile policie:[a] wherby at the laste we shulde haue in this realme sufficiencie of worshypfull lawyars, and also a publike weale equiualent to the grekes or Romanes.[b]

[a] 'And as the study and practice of Morall Philosophy (as Art doth witnesse) it not fittest for men over yong, so likewise the study of the Law, *which hath his foundation in Morall Philosophy (both having one end generall, namely the rectifying of our manners)* doth require some maturity of yeeres, and not to bee set upon by infants in yeeres, judgment, and carriage.'—*English Lawyer*, p. 38, ed. 1631.

[b] Sir John Doderidge, writing at the end of the century, says: 'In our owne times in scorne some have called the crew of unlearned Lawyers, *doctum quoddam genus indoctorum hominum*. But to returne that reproach from whence it sprang, to the honour of the study of our Lawes be it spoken, that the Profession of our Lawes hath *now*, and formerly hath had, great numbers of students that have had as long and as ample institution in those sciences, called liberall, as any of them. And if I might remember old Originalls, from the time of the Norman Conquest untill the latter dayes of King Henry the third, as well the Judges itinerate through the counties, as those that were sedentarie in the King's High Courts of Justice, (which then for the most part followed his person,) were men excellently skilled in all generall good learning, as doe witnesse the works of that worthy Judge Henry de Bracton, and John Britton, sometimes a learned Bishop of Hereford, skilfull in the Lawes of this Realme, who writ a treatise by commandement, and writ of King Edward the first, as an Institution to the study of the Lawes of this Realme, serving that time. So also was Martyn de Patchull, sometimes Deane of Paul's in London, of whom the said Bracton maketh honourable mention, together with divers other noted men of rare learning, not only in the Lawes of this Realme, but in all forraine knowledge fit for their places. And these men exercised Judiciall functions in the Temporall Courts of this Realme, whereof our records, being *et vetustatis et veritatis vestigia*, the lively representations of time and truth, and reputed the Treasures of the Kingdome, doe yeeld plentifull testimony. What should I further commemorate the names and revive the memories of our worthy ancestors, Herle, Bereford, Thorpe, Finden, Belknap, flourishing in the victorious times of King Edward the Third? whose deepe, short, subtile, pithie and learned Law-Arguments argue moreover thus much, that they were sufficiently furnished in that schoole learning which in those times was in most esteeme. Let me not here forget or passe over in silence those excellent Judges in the raigne of King Henry the sixt, Newton, Prisott, Fortescue, which man last named was first Chauncellor to the Prince, and after Chiefe Justice of the King's Bench, and was excellently learned in Divinity, Philosophy, Law both Ecclesiasticall and the Lawes of this Realme, as the little Treatise written by him in the praise of our Lawes in the Latine tongue, and some other Manuscripts I have seene of his worke of a higher subject doe, evidently declare.'—*English Lawyer*, p. 33.

CHAPTER XV.

For what cause at this day there be in this realme fewe perfecte schole maisters.

LORDE god, howe many good and clene wittes of children be nowe a dayes perisshed by ignorant schole maisters.[a] Howe litle substancial doctrine is apprehended by the fewenesse of good gramariens? Not withstanding I knowe that there be some well lerned, whiche haue taught, and also do teache, but god knoweth a fewe, and they with small effecte, hauing therto no comforte, theyr aptist and moste propre scholers, after they be well instructed in speakyng latine, and understanding some poetes, being taken from theyr schole by their parentes,[b] and either be brought to the courte, and made lakayes or pages, or els are bounden prentises;[c] wherby the worshyp that the

---

[a] This is confirmed by Ascham, who says: 'There is no one thing that hath more either dulled the wits, or taken away the will of children from learning, than the care they have to satisfy their masters in the making of Latins. For the scholar is commonly beat for the making, when the master were more worthy to be beat for the mending, or rather marring of the same, the master many times being as ignorant as the child what to say properly and fitly to the matter.'—*Works*, vol. iii. pp. 88, 89, ed. 1864. Erasmus complains of the brutality and ignorance of schoolmasters of the period in language almost identical with that in the text. 'Jam hinc mihi conjecta, vir egregie, *quam multa felicissima ingenia perdant isti carnifices indocti*; sed doctrinæ persuasione tumidi, morosi, vinolenti, truces, et vel animi gratiâ cædentes, nimirum ingenio tam truculento, ut ex alieno cruciatu capiant voluptatem. Hoc genus homines lanios aut carnifices esse decuit, non pueritiæ formatores. Nec ulli crudelius excarnificant pueros, quàm qui nihil habent quod illos doceant. Hi quid agant in scholis nisi ut plagis et jurgiis diem extrahant?'—*De Pueris Instit.* Opera, tom. i. p. 435, ed. 1540. While Peacham says 'For one discreete and able Teacher, you shall finde twenty ignorant and carelesse, who (among so many fertile and delicate wits as England affoordeth) whereas they make one Scholler, they marre Ten.'—*The Compleat Gentleman*, p. 22, ed. 1622.

[b] From Erasmus we learn that the masters were frequently changed. 'Nihil inutilius quàm frequenter mutare præceptorem. Ad eum enim modum Penelopes tela texitur ac retexitur. At ego novi pueros, qui ante annum duodecimum, plusquam quatuordecim præceptoribus usi sunt, idque parentum incogitantiâ.'—*Opera*, tom. i. p. 429.

[c] Ascham also refers to this custom of the times. 'And when this sad-natured and

maister, aboue any reward, couaiteth to haue by the praise of his scholer, is utterly drowned; wherof I haue herde schole maisters, very well lerned, of good righte complayne. But yet (as I sayd) the fewenesse of good gramariens is a great impediment of doctrine.[a] (And here I wolde the reders shulde marke that I note to be fewe good gramariens, and not none.) I call nat them gramariens, whiche onely can teache or make rules, wherby a childe shall onely lerne to speake congrue latine,[b] or to make sixe versis standyng in one fote, wherin perchance shal be neither sentence nor eloquence.[c] But I

hard-witted child is bet from his book, and becometh after either student of the common law, or page in the court, or serving man, or bound prentice to a merchant or to some handicraft, he proveth in the end wiser, happier, and many times honester too, than many of those quick wits do by their learning.'—*Schoolmaster*, p. 102, ed. 1864.

[a] 'The last act of Erasmus's kindness to the dean's (Colet) school was to find out at Cambridge (where he then was) an usher, or second master, according to the founder's desire, to be under Mr. William Lilye. He inquired among the masters of arts there; but could meet with none, it seems, that cared for, or were fit for that place, who would engage in it. They did not affect so laborious an employment, however honourable the terms might be. One of the seniors said in a flouting way, "*Who would lead such a slavish life among boys in a school if he can have any other way of living ?*"—Knight's *Life of Colet*, pp. 147, 148.

[b] Erasmus gives the following picture of these grammarians. 'Nunc quibus ambagibus ac difficultatibus excruciantur pueri, dum ediscunt literarum nomina priusquàm agnoscant figuras, dum in nominum ac verborum inflexionibus coguntur ediscere quot casibus modis ac temporibus eadem vox respondeat, veluti Musæ, genitivo et dativo singulari, nominativo et vocativo plurali. Legeris à legor, à legerim, et à legero. Quæ carnificina tum perstrepit in ludo quum hæc à pueris exiguntur.'—*Opera*, tom. i. p. 441. And Pace takes evident pleasure in ridiculing the labours of these precisians. 'Ad ultimum de Grammaticis (adeo in omnibus et verbis et dictionibus dissident) piget loqui. Nam aliqui admittunt verba neutralia, aliqui excludunt. Aliqui diphthongos in scribendo apponunt, aliqui detrahunt. Aliqui in scribendis dictionibus duplicibus utuntur literis, aliqui simplicibus; adeò ut in ipsâ quoque literâ scribendâ dissensio sit inter eos qualis est inter omnes, et Aldum solum in scribendâ causâ, nam is solus alteram addit S.'—*De Fructu*, p. 53.

[c] Erasmus seems to allude to this practice: 'L. Arbitror tibi frequenter ex majoribus auditum, fuisse tempus quo pueri multis annis discruciabantur modis significandi, et quæstiunculis ex quâ vi, et aliis indoctissimis næniis, magnâque ambitione dictabatur, ediscebatur, exponebatur Ebrardus et Florista, *quod supererat temporis ridiculis versiculis transigebatur.*'—*Dial. de Pronuntiatione*, Opera, tom.

name hym a gramarien, by the autoritie of Quintilian, that speakyng latine elegantly, can expounde good au- tours, expressynge the inuention and disposition of the mater, their stile or fourme of eloquence, explicating the figures as well of sentences as wordes, leuyng nothyng, persone, or place, named by the autour, undeclared or hidde from his scholers.[a] Wherfore Quintilian saith, it is nat inough for hym to haue rad poetes, but all kyndes of wrytyng must also be sought for; nat for the histories only, but also for the propretie of wordes, whiche communely do receiue theyr autoritie of noble autours. More ouer without musike gramer may nat be perfecte; for as moche as therin muste be spoken of metres and harmonies, called *rythmi* in greke. Neither if he haue nat the knowlege of sterres, he may understande poetes, whiche in description of times (I omitte other things) they traicte of the risinge and goinge downe of planettes. Also he may nat be ignorant in philosophie, for many places that be almooste in euerye poete fetched out of the most subtile parte of naturall questions. These be well nighe the wordes of Quintilian.[b]

Fab. Quintilian, li. i.

Than beholde howe fewe gramariens after this description be in this realme.

Undoubtedly ther be in this realme many well lerned,

---

i. p. 773. And in another place he exclaims. 'Deum immortalem! quale seculum erat hoc, quum magno apparatu disticha Joannis Garlandini adolescentibus, operosis ac prolixis commentariis, enarrabantur. Quum ineptis versiculis dictandis, repetendis, et exigendis magna pars temporis absumebatur.'—*De Pueris Instit.*, Opera, tom. i. p. 444, ed. 1540. We learn from Harrison that in his day (*i.e.* about 1577), 'the rules of versifieng' formed part of the curriculum at the public schools.—*Descript. of Eng.* p. 151.

[a] See *Quintil. Instit. Orat.* lib. i.

[b] 'Nec poetas legisse satis est: executiendum omne scriptorum genus, non propter historias modo, sed verba, quæ frequenter jus ab auctoribus sumunt. Tum nec citra musicen grammatice potest esse perfecta, quum ei de metris rhythmisque dicendum sit: nec si rationem siderum ignoret, poetas intelligat; qui ut alia mittam, toties ortu occasuque signorum in declarandis temporibus utuntur: nec ignara philosophiæ, cum propter plurimos in omnibus ferè carminibus locos, ex intimâ quæstionum naturalium subtilitate repetitos.'—*Instit. Orat.* lib. i. cap. 4, § 4.

whiche if the name of a schole maister were nat so moche had in contempte,[a] and also if theyr labours with abundant salaries mought be requited,[b] were righte sufficient and able to induce their herers to excellent lernynge, so they be nat plucked away grene, and er they be in doctrine sufficiently rooted. But nowe a dayes, if to a bachelar or maister of arte studie of philosophie waxeth tediouse, if he haue a spone full of latine, he wyll shewe forth a hoggesheed without any lernyng, and offre

[a] Erasmus, in his Dialogue *De Pronuntiatione*, says: 'L. Plerique turpe putant quenquam semper in grammatices professione manere. U. Quinam id turpius quàm pictorem nihil aliud profiteri quàm pictorem? Quanquam fieri non potest ut grammaticus nihil sit quàm grammaticus, etiamsi in cæteris disciplinis non perinde excellat.... Et pulchrum est probri causâ dicere grammatico nihil aliud es quàm grammaticus? Est aliquid et ventre contemptius, per quod ejiciuntur crassiora corporis excrementa. Contemnat hoc qui volet, et videat quàm floreant cætera membra.'—*Opera*, tom. i. p. 771, ed. 1540.

[b] Ascham says that grooms were better paid than schoolmasters. 'It is pity that commonly more care is had, yea and that among very wise men, to find out rather a cunning man for their horse than a cunning man for their children. They say nay in word, but they do so in deed, for to the one they will gladly give a stipend of two hundred crowns by the year, and loth to offer to the other two hundred shillings. God that sitteth in heaven laugheth their choice to scorn, and rewardeth their liberality as it should, for he suffereth them to have tame and well-ordered horses, but wild and unfortunate children, and therefore in the end they find more pleasure in their horse than comfort in their children.'—*Schoolmaster*, p. 104, ed. 1864. Erasmus makes the same comparison as Ascham: 'Sunt quos animus sordidus deterret à conducendo præceptore idoneo, *et pluris educitur equiso quàm filii formator.*'—*De Pueris Instit.*, Opera, tom. i. p. 428. And in another place he says, 'Ad hujus aut illius commendationem quemvis ludo præficimus, ferè indoctum, interdum et moribus improbis, non huc spectantes, ut rei charissimæ civium liberis omnibus consulamus, sed ut unius famelici ventriculo prospiciamus. *Accuratiùs circumspicientes cui committamus unum equum, aut canem venatorem, quàm cui credamus totius civitatis pignora.*'—Opera, tom. i. p. 766. Mulcaster, the head master of St. Laurence Pountney School, pleading fifty years afterwards the cause of his profession, says: 'For whom in consideration of sufficient abilitie and faithfull trauell I must still pray for good entertainement, which will alway procure most able persons. For it is a great daunting to the best able man, and a great cutting off of his diligent paynes, when he shall finde his whole dayes trauell not able to furnish him of necessarie prouision, to do good with the best, and to gaine with the basest, nay, much lesse than the lowest, who may entend to shift, when he must entend his charge; and enrich himselfe, nay, hardly feede himselfe, with a pure and poore conscience.'—*Positions*, p. 237, ed. 1581.

to teache grammer and expoune noble writers, and to be in the roome of a maister: he wyll, for a small salarie, sette a false colour of lernyng on propre wittes, whiche wyll be wasshed away with one shoure of raine.[a] For if the children be absent from schole by the space of one moneth, the best lerned of them will uneth tell wheder *Fato*, wherby Eneas was brought in to Itali, were other a man, a horse, a shyppe, or a wylde goose.[b] Al thoughe their maister wyll perchance auaunte hym selfe to be a good philosopher. *Vergilius Aeneid versu secundo.*

Some men perauenture do thinke that, at the begynning

---

[a] Erasmus draws a still more painful picture of the schoolmasters of the period: 'Quàm igitur belle prospicitur his pueris, qui vix dum quadrimi mittuntur in ludum literarium, ubi præsidet præceptor ignotus, agrestis, ac moribus parum sobriis, interdum ne cerebri quidem sani, frequenter lunaticus, aut morbo comitiali obnoxius, aut lepræ, quam nunc vulgus scabiem gallicam appellat. Neminem enim hodie tam abjectum, tam inutilem, tam nullius rei videmus, quem vulgus non existimet idoneum moderando ludo literario.'—*De Pueris Instit.*, Opera, tom. i. p. 434. Mulcaster advocated the foundation of a college for training masters : ' Why should not teachers be well prouided for, to continue their whole life in the schoole, as Diuines, Lawyers, Physicians do in their seuerall professions? Thereby iudgement, cunning, and discretion will grow in them: and maisters would proue olde men, and such as Xenophon setteth ouer children in the schooling of Cyrus. Wheras now, the schoole being used but for a shift, afterward to passe thence to the other professions, though it send out very sufficient men to them, itselfe remaineth too too naked, considering the necessitie of the thing. I conclude, therfore, that this trade requireth a particular college.'— *Positions*, p. 251. In another place Erasmus says: 'Jam illud in pædagogiis pene solenne est, ut aut tenues, quibus non est unde vivant, aut puerum aliquem nudiustertius magistelli nomine donatum, pueris grammaticen docendis præficiant, tantum in hoc ut vivat.'—*Dial. de Pronuntiatione*, Opera, tom. i. p. 771.

[b] Erasmus says : ' Pueros nostros ultra pubertatem domi detinemus, ac otio, luxu, deliciisque corruptos, vix tandem in scholam publicam mittimus. Illic ut res bene cedat, degustant aliquid grammatices, mox simul atque norunt inflectere voces, et suppositum apposito recte jungere, perdidicere grammaticam, et ad perturbatam dialecticen admoventur, ubi si quid etiam recte loqui didicerunt, dediscant oportet. Sed infelicior erat ætas, quæ me puero modis significandi et questiunculis ex quâ vi, pueros excarnificabat nec aliud interim docens quàm perperam loqui. Nimirum præceptores illi ne puerilia docere viderentur, grammaticen, dialectices ac metaphysices difficultatibus obscurabant, nimirum ut præposterè jam provectiores post majores disciplinas grammaticen discerent. Quod nunc videmus aliquod Theologis evenire cordatioribus, ut post tot laureas, post omnes titulos, ut jam illis liberum non sit quicquam nescire, ad eos libros redire cogantur, qui pueris solent prælegi.'—*De Pueris Instit.* Opera, tom. i. p. 443.

of lernynge, it forceth nat, all thoughe the maisters haue nat so exacte doctrine as I haue reherced; but let them take good hede what Quintilian saith, that it is so moche the better to be instructed by them that are beste lerned, for as moche as it is difficultie to put out of the mynde that whiche is ones settilled, the double bourden beinge painfull to the maisters that shal succede, and verily moche more to unteache than to teache. Wherfore it is writen that Timothe, the noble musitian, demaunded alway a gretter rewarde of them whom other had taught, than of them that neuer any thinge lerned. These be the wordes of Quintilian or like.[a]

Fab. Quint. lib. i.

Also commune experience teacheth that no man will put his sonne to a botcher to lerne, or he bynde hym prentise to a taylour: or if he wyll haue hym a connyng goldsmith, wyll bynde hym firste prentise to a tynkar: in these thynges poure men be circumspect, and the nobles and gentilmen, who wolde haue their sonnes by excellent lerning come unto honour, for sparynge of coste, or for lacke of diligent serche for a good schole maister, wilfully distroy their children, causinge them to be taught that lerninge, whiche wolde require sixe or seuen yeres to be forgoten[b]: by whiche tyme the more parte of

---

[a] 'Quanto sit melius optimis imbui, quantaque in eluendis, quæ semel insederint, vitiis, difficultas consequatur; quum geminatum onus succedentes premat, et quidem dedocendi gravius ac prius, quàm docendi. Propter quod Timotheum clarum in arte tibiarum, ferunt duplices ab iis, quos alius instituisset, solitum exigere mercedes, quàm si rudes traderentur.'—*Instit. Orat.* lib. ii. cap. 3, § 2.

[b] Some parents, indeed, considered that learning was altogether an unfit occupation for a *gentleman*. Pace, in his letter to Colet, in which he dedicates to the latter his book *De Fructu*, published at Basle in 1517, tells a story characteristic of some of the foxhunting squires of that day. 'Quum duobus annis plus minus jam præteritis, ex Romanâ urbe in patriam rediissem, interfui cuidam convivio multis incognitus. Ubi quum satis fuisset potatum, unus, nescio quis, ex convivis, non imprudens, ut ex verbis vultuque conjicere licuit, cœpit mentionem facere de liberis suis bene instituendis. Et primum omnium bonum præceptorem illis sibi quærendum, et scholam omnino frequentandam censuit. Aderat forte unus ex his, quos nos *generosos* vocamus, et qui semper cornu aliquod a tergo pendens gestant, acsi etiam inter prandendum venarentur. Is, auditâ literarum laude, percitus repentinâ irâ furibundus prorupit in hæc verba. "Quid nugaris," inquit, "Amice? Abeant in malam rem istæ stultæ literæ; omnes docti sunt mendici; etiam Erasmus ille doc-

that age is spente, wherin is the chiefe sharpnesse of witte called in latine *acumen*, and also than approcheth the stubborne age, where the childe broughte up in pleasure disdayneth correction.

Nowe haue I all declared (as I do suppose) the chiefe impechementes of excellent lernynge: of the reformation I nede nat to speake, sens it is apparant, that by the contraries, men pursuinge it ernestly with discrete iugement and liberalitie, it wolde sone be amended.

CHAPTER XVI.
Of sondry fourmes of exercise necessary for euery gentilman.

ALL thoughe I haue hitherto aduaunced the commendation of lernyng, specially in gentil men, yet it is to be considered that continuall studie without some maner of exercise, shortly exhausteth the spirites vitall,[*] and hyndereth naturall decoction and digestion, wherby mannes body is the soner corrupted and brought in to diuers sickenessis, and finallye the life is therby made shorter: where contrayrye wise by exercise, whiche is a vehement motion (as Galene prince of phisitions defineth) the helthe of man is preserued, and his strength increased: for as moche the membres by meuyng and mutuall touching, do waxe more harde, and naturall heate in all the body is therby augmented. More ouer it maketh the spirites of a man more stronge and valiant, so that, by the hardnesse of the membres,

tissimus (ut audio) pauper est, et in quâdam suâ epistolâ vocat τὴν κατάρατον πενίαν uxorem suam, id est, execrandam paupertatem, et vehementer conqueritur se non posse illam humeris suis usque in βαθυκήτεα πόντον, id est, profundum mare, excutere. (Corpus Dei juro) volo filius meus pendeat potius quàm literis studeat. Decet enim generosorum filios apte inflare cornu, perite venari, accipitrem pulchre gestare et educare. *Studia vero literarum rusticorum filiis sunt relinquenda.*"¹ P. 15.

[*] This was also the opinion of Montaigne, who says: 'Nostre leçon, se passant comme par rencontre, sans obligation de temps et de lieu, et se meslant à toutes nos actions, se coulera sans se faire sentir : les jeux mesmes et les exercices seront une bonne partie de l'estude ; la course, la luicte, la musique, la danse, la chasse, le maniement des chevaulx et des armes.'—*Essais*, tom. i. p. 229, ed. 1854.

all labours be more tollerable; by naturall hete the appetite is the more quicke; the chaunge of the substance receiued is the more redy; the nourisshinge of all partes of the body is the more sufficient and sure. By valiaunt motion of the spirites all thinges superfluous be expelled, and the condutis of the body densed.[a] Wherfore this parte of phisike is nat to be contemned or neglected in the education of children, and specially from the age of xiiii yeres upwarde, in whiche tyme strength with courage increaseth.[b] More ouer there be diuers maners of exercises; wherof some onely prepareth and helpeth digestion; some augmenteth also strength and hardnesse of body; other serueth for agilitie and nymblenesse; some for celeritie or spedinesse.[c] There be also whiche ought to be used for necessitie

[a] 'Nam quoniam vehementior motus exerçitatio est, necesse quidem est tria hæc ab eâ perfici in corpore exercitando, membrorum duritiem ex mutuo ipsorum attritu, genuini caloris augmentum, et spiritus citatiorem motum. Sequi vero hæc reliqua omnia privatim commoda quæ corpus exercitiis accepta refert: utique ex membrorum duritiâ, tum ut minus ex labore afficiantur, tum ad labores robur. Ex calore, tum deducendorum in corpus validum attractum, tum immutationem magis expeditam, tum nutritionem magis fælicem, tum ut singulæ corporis partes sint (ut ita dicam) perfusæ. Cujus affectus beneficio et solida mollescere, et humida tenuari et exiguos coporeæ molis meatus laxiores fieri accidit. At ex spiritus valentiore impetu et purgari hos omnes meatus necesse est, et excrementa expelli.'—*De Sanitate tuendâ*, lib. ii. fo. 19, ed. 1538.

[b] 'Cui vero optimi status corpus contigit, is ad quartumdecimum usque annum, jam traditam victus rationem observet, illo tamen in exercitatione servato modo, ut neque immodicè se neque violenter exerçitet, ne corporis id incremento sit in morâ. Hoc ætatis animum quoque finxisse aptissimum est, idque potissimum probis consuetudinibus, et gravibus disciplinis, quæ animo modestiam pariant. Quippe ad ea quæ sequente ætate circa corpus ejus moliri oportebit, maximo compendio sit animi modestia, et ad parendum facilitas. *A secundo vero septennio usque ad expletum tertium*, si quidem ad robustissimum corporis habitum provehere hominem cupis, aut militem eum strenuum, aut luctatorem, aut alias viribus insignem destinans, utique de iis animi dotibus quæ ad scientiam sapientiamque pertinent minus laborabis. Quæ enim ad mores spectant: hâc maxime ætate perfici absolvique convenit.'—*De San. tuend.* lib. i. fo. 13 a.

[c] 'Jam singulas exercitationum seorsum persequi tempestivum videtur: illo præsertim prius significato quòd in his quoque complures differentiæ inveniantur. Quippe interim aliam partem aliud alio magis exercitium fatigat. Et quædam lente motis fiunt, quædam ocyssime agitatis, et quædam robore ac nixu adhibitis, quædam sine his. Ad hæc, quædam cum robore pariter et celeritate, quædam languidè. Ac quod violenter quidem sine velocitate exercetur, εὔτονον, id est valens,

only. All these ought he that is a tutor to a noble man to haue in remembrance, and, as opportunitie serueth, to put them in experience. And specially them whiche with helth do ioyne commoditie (and as I moughte say) necessitie: consideryng that be he neuer so noble or valiant, some tyme he is subiecte to perile, or (to speake it more pleasauntly) seruant to fortune. Touching suche exercises, as many be used within the house, or in the shadowe, (as is the olde maner of speking.[a]), as deambulations, laborynge with poyses made of leadde or other metall, called in latine *Alteres*,[b] liftynge and throwyng the heuy stone or barre, playing at tenyse, and diuers semblable exercises, I will for this tyme passe ouer; exhortyng them which do understande latine, and do desire to knowe the commodities of sondrye exercises, to resorte to the boke of Galene, of the gouernance of helth, called in latine *De Sanitate tuendâ*, where they shal be in that mater abundantly satisfied, and finde in the readynge moche delectation; whiche boke is translated in to latine, wonderfull eloquently by doctor Linacre, late mooste worthy phisition to our mooste noble soueraigne lorde kynge Henry the VIII.[c]

voco; quod violenter et cum celeritate σφόδρον, id est, vehemens. Violenter autem robustève dicere, nihil referat. Fŏdere ergo, valens robustaque exercitatio est. Simili modo et si quis quatuor simul equos habenis coerceat, impensè robusta exercitatio est, non tamen celeris. . . . . . Superest ut de iis dicamus quæ celeritate peraguntur citraque robur et violentiam. Id genus sunt cursus, et umbratilis armorum meditatio, et cum duo summis manibus concertant, ἀκροχειρισμους Græci vocant, tum quæ per corycum et pilam exercitatio fit, utique cum à distantibus et currentibus administratur.'—*De San. tuend*. lib. ii. fo. 30, 31.

[a] 'Quæ vero ab iis quæ extrinsecus sunt posita, ducuntur, ejusmodi sunt, quod aut sub dio exercitatio fit, aut sub tecto, aut in mistâ umbrâ quam ὑποσυμμιγῆ Græci vocant.'—*De San. tuend*. lib. ii. fo. 29 b.

[b]   'Quid pereunt stulto fortes altere lacerti?
      Exercet melius vinea fossa viros.'—*Martial*, lib. xiv. 49.
      'Gravesque draucis
      Alteras facili rotat lacerto.'—*Ibid*. lib. vii. 67.
' Idque multo certe magis fiet, seorsum si quis summis manibus, utraque apprehenso pondere (cujusmodi sunt qui in palæstrâ *Alteres* dicuntur), porrectis his aut in sublimè erectis, eodem habitu persistat.'—Galen, *De San. tuen*. lib. ii. fo. 30 b.

[c] Thomas Linacre was born in 1460, and died in 1524. Paulus Jovius, a con-

THE GOVERNOUR.

And I wyll nowe only speake of those exercises, apt to the furniture of a gentilmannes personage, adapting his body to hardnesse, strength, and agilitie, and to helpe therwith hym selfe in perile, whiche may happen in warres or other necessitie.

temporary, pays him the following compliment: 'Inter alia vero præclara ejus ingenii monumenta vel illud Galeni *De Sanitate tuendâ*, opus è Græco summâ Latini sermonis elegantiâ felicissimè traductum, immortalem sibi apud posteros laudem comparavit.'—*Descript. Brit.* p. 49. And Pace, the friend of Colet, also shows in what high estimation the learned Doctor was held. 'Est enim is summus medicus, et par orator, ut tum experientiâ tum libris felicissimè editis, manifestum fecit omnibus, et te non nisi aliud agens, et ἐν παρέργῳ, id est horis supervacaneis, aggressus est, ac quidam ex amantissimis ejus persæpe sunt mirati, quod quum natus sit ad altissima quæque, non recusaverit ad ista infima descendere, ut contenderet cum Tryphone, vel nescio quo alio grammatico, de quibusdam minutiis casus vocativi. Contendit tum ille feliciter, quia vicit. Sed mallem victoriam fuisse illustriorem et similem illi quem Patavii olim reportavit. Nam quum in gymnasio Patavino professionis artis medicæ ei (ut nunc moris est) darentur insignia, publice non sine summâ laude disputavit, et seniorum medicorum adversaria argumenta acutissimè refellit.'—*De Fructu*, p. 76. It is stated by Johnson, Linacre's biographer, that the first edition of the translation referred to in the text was printed at Paris by Guillaume Rubé, in 1517, and that presentation copies of the same edition were sent to Wolsey, and Fox, Bishop of Winchester, of which one is still preserved in the British Museum, and the other in the College (of Physicians?) Library. The author of the *Repertorium Bibliographicum* has fallen into an error (which has been perpetuated by M. Brunet in his valuable *Manuel du Libraire*), in saying that there are two presentation copies on vellum of Linacre's translation of the *Methodus Medendi* in the Brit. Mus., one dedicated to Henry VIII. and the other to Wolsey. The fact is only one of the volumes referred to is a copy of this work, the other being a translation of the *De Sanitate tuendâ*, but both are dedicated to the king, although it appears from the prefatory epistle inscribed in each copy that *both* were *presented* to the Cardinal. Johnson's description of the latter volume as 'a magnificent specimen of the art of embellishment in the 16th century' is far more applicable to the copy of the *Methodus Medendi*. It is rather surprising to find that Hallam, who refers to Johnson's *Life of Linacre* on more than one occasion, says in view of the above facts, 'Though a first edition of his translation of Galen has been supposed to have been printed at Venice in 1498, *it seems to be ascertained that none preceded that of Cambridge in* 1521;' *Lit. of Eur.* vol. i. p. 321, for, as we have seen, Linacre's translation of the *De Sanitate tuendâ* was printed in 1517 at Paris, and this was quickly followed by a translation of the *Methodus Medendi*, published at Paris in 1519: a translation of the *De Temperamentis*, published as early as 1498, is ascribed to Linacre by Hoffmann (see *Bibliographisches Lexicon*, Part. ii. p. 134), who, however, makes no mention of the famous Cambridge edition of 1521. And it was probably this omission on the part of Hoffmann which caused Hallam to make the remark above quoted.

CHAPTER XVII.

Exercises wherby shulde growe both recreation and profite.

WRASTLYNGE is a very good exercise in the begynnynge of youthe, so that it be with one that is equall in strengthe, or some what under, and that the place be softe, that in fallinge theyr bodies be nat brused.[a]

There be diuers maners of wrastlinges, but the beste, as well for helthe of body as for exercise of strengthe, is whan layeng mutually their handes one ouer a nothers necke, with the other hande they holde faste eche other by the arme, and claspyng theyr legges to gether, they inforce them selfes with strengthe and agilitie to throwe downe eche other, whiche is also praysed by Galene.[b] And undoubtedly it shall be founde profitable in warres, in case that a capitayne shall be constrayned to cope with his aduersary hande to hande, hauyng his weapon broken or loste. Also it hath ben sene that the waiker persone, by the sleight of

Wrastlynge. Galenus.

---

[a] Strutt says, 'The citizens of London in times past are said to have been expert in the art of wrestling, and annually upon St. James's day they were accustomed to make a public trial of their skill.' *Sports and Pastimes*, p. 63, ed. 1801. The amusement seems to have been carried on to such an extent as to become a public nuisance, for in the twelfth year of Henry IV., A.D. 1411, proclamation was made on the Friday next before the feast of St. Bartholomew (the 24th August) in the following form: 'That no manere man ne child, of what estate or condicioun that he be, be so hardy to wrestell, or make ony wrastlyng, within the Seintuary ne the boundes of Poules, ne in non other open place within the Citee of Londone, up peyne of emprisonement of fourty dayes, and makyng fyn unto the Chaumbre, after the discrecioun of the Mair and Aldermen.'—Riley's *Memorials of London*, p. 580, ed. 1868.

[b] 'Quæ vero luctantes inter se moliuntur cum robori augendo student, hæc aut pulverem altum, aut palestram desiderant. Ea sunt ejusmodi: cum uterque luctantium ambobus cruribus alterum alterius crus complectitur, deinde manibus inter se collatis, altera cervici violenter incumbat, utique quæ e regione impediti cruris est, altero brachio. Licebit et circa summum caput manibus injectis violenter retrorsum se agat ac revellat. Ejusmodi lucta utriusque luctatoris robur exercet: quemadmodum et ea quæ altero alterum cruribus cingente, vel ambo per ambo mittente, fiunt. Nam hæc quoque utrumque ad robur præparant. Infinitæ aliæ ejusmodi robustæ exercitationes in palestrâ sunt.'—*De San. tuend.* lib. ii. fo. 31 a.

wrastlyng, hath ouerthrowen the strenger, almost or he coulde fasten on the other any violent stroke.

Rennynge. Also rennyng is bothe a good exercise and a laudable solace.[a] It is written of Epaminondas the valiant capitayne of Thebanes, who as well in vertue and prowesse as in lerninge surmounted all noble men of his tyme, that daily he exercised him selfe in the mornyng with rennyng and leaping, in the euening in wrastling, to the intent that likewise in armure he mought the more strongly, embracinge his aduersary, put hym in daunger. And also that in the chase, rennyng and leaping, he mought either ouertake his enemye, or beyng pursued, if extreme nede required, escape him.[b] Semblably be-

[a] Galen explains the foot-races in vogue in his own day. 'Est autem ἐκπλεθρίειν cum in plethro, id est in sextâ parte stadii, quis prorsum retrorsumque vicissim, idque sæpe, in utramque partem sine flexu cursitans, unoquoque cursu breve quiddam de spatio demit, quoad denique in unico gressu constiterit.'—*De San. tuend.* lib. ii. fo. 31. Strutt quotes from an ancient MS. entitled *Of Knyghthode and Batayle*, supposed to have been written early in the 15th century, and now in the Cottonian Library, Titus, A. xxiii. pt. i. p. 6, the following verses in praise of this exercise:

'In rennynge the exercise is good also,
To smyte first in fight, and also whenne
To take a place our foemen will forrenne,
And take it erst; also to serche or sture,
Lightly to come and go, rennynge is sure.
Rennyng is also right good at the chace;
And for to lepe a dike is also good:
For mightily what man may renne and lepe,
May well devict, and safe his party kepe.'

A comparison with the following passage of Vegetius would seem to show that the writer of the MS. borrowed largely from this source: 'Sed ad cursum præcipue assuefaciendi sunt juniores, ut majore impetu in hostes procurrant, ut loca opportuna celeriter, quum usus venerit, occupent : vel adversariis idem facere volentibus præoccupent : ut ad explorandum alacriter pergant, alacrius redeant : ut fugientium terga facilius comprehendant. Ad saltum etiam quo vel fossæ transiliuntur, vel impediens aliqua altitudo superatur, exercendus est miles.'—*De Re Militari*, lib. i. cap. 9.

[b] 'Postquam ephebus factus est, et palæstræ dare operam cæpit: non tam magnitudini virium servivit, quàm velocitati. Illam enim ad athletarum usum; hanc ad belli existimabat utilitatem pertinere. Itaque exercebatur plurimum currendo et luctando, ad eum finem, quoad stans complecti posset, atque contendere. In armis plurimum studii consumebat.'—Corn. Nepos, *Epaminon.* cap. 2. It will be seen from the account given in the text that the Author's translation

fore him dyd the worthy Achilles, for whiles his shippes laye at rode, he suffred nat his people to slomber in ydlenesse, but daily exercised them and himselfe in rennyng, wherin he was most excellent and passed all other, and therfore Homere, throughout all his warke, cálleth hym swifte foote Achilles.[a]

The great Alexander beyng a childe, excelled all his companions in rennyng; wherfore on a tyme one demaunded of hym if he wolde renne at the great game of Olympus, wherto, out of all partes of Grece, came the moste actife and valiant persons to assay maistries; wherunto Alexander answered in this fourme, I wold very gladly renne ther, if I were sure to renne with kinges, for if I shulde contende with a priuate person, hauing respect to our bothe astates, our victories shulde nat be equall.[b] Nedes muste rennynge be taken for a laudable exercise, sens one of the mooste noble capitaynes of all the

of the above passage is enriched with some details which were apparently unknown to Nepos. It is not a little remarkable that Plutarch has given us a description the very reverse of this; for in comparing the great Theban captain with Pelopidas, he says, Ἦσαν δὲ καὶ πρὸς πᾶσαν ἀρετὴν πεφυκότες ὁμοίως, πλὴν ὅτι τῷ γυμνάζεσθαι μᾶλλον ἔχαιρε Πελοπίδας, τῷ δὲ μανθάνειν Ἐπαμεινώνδας, καὶ τὰς διατριβὰς ἐν τῷ σχολάζειν ὁ μὲν περὶ παλαίστρας καὶ κυνηγέσια, ὁ δὲ ἀκούων τι καὶ φιλοσοφῶν ἐποιεῖτο.—*Pelopidas*, cap. 4.

[a] It was not, however, for the purpose of keeping his men in good training, but to do honour to the dead Patroclus, that Achilles instituted the races described in the twenty-third book of the Iliad, in which moreover it is expressly mentioned that he did *not* himself take part. Mr. Gladstone says, 'We may observe how closely it belonged to the character of the greatest heroes to excel in every feat of gymnastic strength as well as in the exercises of actual warfare. The kings and leading chiefs all act in the Games, with the qualified exception of Agamemnon, whose dignity could not allow him to be actually judged by his inferiors, but yet who appears as a nominal candidate, and receives the compliment of a prize, though spared the contest for it; and with the exception also of Achilles, who could not contend for his own prizes.'—*Studies on Homer*, vol. i. p. 324.

[b] Ποδωκέστατος γὰρ τῶν ἐφ᾽ ἡλικίας γενόμενος νέων, καὶ τῶν ἑταίρων αὐτὸν ἐπ᾽ Ὀλύμπια παρορμώντων, ἠρώτησεν, εἰ βασιλεῖς ἀγωνίζονται· τῶν δὲ οὐ φαμένων, ἄδικον εἶπεν εἶναι τὴν ἅμιλλαν, ἐν ᾗ νικήσει μὲν ἰδιώτας, νικηθήσεται δὲ βασιλεύς.—Plutarch, *De Alex. Virt.* 9. Curtius tells the story rather differently. 'Ergo dicentibus, "quoniam cursu plurimum valeret, debere profiteri nomen suum inter eos, qui Olympicis ludis certaturi essent, cognominis sibi regis exemplo; magnam eâ re per Græciam sibi famam comparaturum." "Facerem," inquit, "si reges haberem adversarios."'—Lib. i. cap. 2, § 17.

Romanes toke his name of rennyng, and was called *Papirius Cursor*, which is in englisshe, Papirius the Renner.[a] And also the valiant Marius the Romane, whan he had bene seuen tymes Consul, and was of the age of foure score yeres, exercised him selfe dayly amonge the yonge men of Rome, in suche wyse that there resorted people out of ferre partes to beholde the strength and agilitie of that olde Consul, wherin he compared with the yonge and lusty soudiours.[b]

There is an exercise whiche is right profitable in exstreme daunger of warres, but by cause there semeth to be some perile in the lernynge therof, and also it hath nat bene of longe tyme moche used, specially amonge noble men, perchance some reders wyll litle esteme it, I meane swymmynge.[c] But nat withstandyng, if they reuolue the imbecilitie

Swymmynge.

---

[a] The author had apparently read the following passage in Livy: 'Inde ad triumphum decessisse Romam Papirium Cursorem scribunt, qui eo duce Luceriam receptam Samnitesque sub jugum missos auctores sunt. Et fuit vir haud dubie dignus omni bellicâ laude, non animi solum vigore, sed etiam corporis viribus excellens. Præcipua pedum pernicitas inerat, quæ cognomen etiam dedit : victoremque cursu omnium ætatis suæ fuisse ferunt.'—Lib. ix. cap. 16.

[b] Οὐ μὴν ἀλλὰ Μάριος φιλοτίμως πάνυ καὶ μειρακιωδῶς ἀποτριβόμενος τὸ γῆρας καὶ τὴν ἀσθένειαν, ὁσημέραι κατέβαινεν εἰς τὸ πεδίον καὶ μετὰ τῶν νεανίσκων γυμναζόμενος ἐπεδείκνυε τὸ σῶμα κοῦφον μὲν ὅπλοις, ἔποχον δὲ ταῖς ἱππασίαις, καίπερ οὐκ εὐσταλὴς γεγονὼς ἐν γήρᾳ τὸν ὄγκον, ἀλλ' εἰς σάρκα περιπληθῆ καὶ βαρεῖαν ἐνδεδωκώς. Ἐνίοις μὲν οὖν ἤρεσκε ταῦτα πράττων, καὶ κατιόντες ἐθεῶντο τὴν φιλοτιμίαν αὐτοῦ καὶ τὰς ἁμίλλας.'—Plutarch, *Marius*, 34.

[c] Probably the earliest treatise devoted specially to this subject is one called *De Arte Natandi*, by Everard Digby, which was published in 1587. The author, a Cambridge Master of Arts, apologises in his preface for writing a book on the subject, which he asserts is 'nuper enata facultas aut saltem calamo nostro ab infimis umbris revocata (cum sit jocus recens prorsus ac juvenilis),' but explains that the number of deaths amongst the undergraduates by drowning in the Cam warrants him in recommending the scientific teaching of swimming. 'Evidentius hujus veritatis ususque simul natandi præ ceteris insignis, clarum nobis et apertum exhibent testimonium, *tot quotannis aquis Cantabrigiensibus clari generis absorpti iuvenes et pereuntes funditùs*. Qui arte isthâc orbati prorsus ac destituti, horæ momento, vitalia simul lumina, et triste nobis et eorum desiderium reliquerunt. Horum necem immaturam interitumque violentum (humanum cum sit humanis casibus ingemiscere) misericordiâ multoties prosecutus, dolebam equidem, et vehementer angebar artem natandi tam diu tot tantorumque magno cum dispendio delituisse orbam, parvam, ignotam. Hinc primum traduxit originem pia isthæc

of our nature, the hasardes and daungers of batayle, with the examples which shall herafter be showed, they wyll (I doubt nat) thinke it as necessary to a capitayne or man of armes, as any that I haue yet rehersed. The Romanes, who aboue all thinges had moste in estimation martiall prowesse, they had a large and spaciouse felde without the citie of Rome, whiche was called Marces felde, in latine *Campus Martius*, wherin the youth of the citie was exercised. This felde *Campus* adioyned to the ryuer of Tyber, to the intent that *Martius*. as well men as children shulde wasshe and refresshe them in the water after their labours, as also lerne to swymme.* And nat men and children only, but also the horses, that by suche usaige they shulde more aptely and boldly passe ouer great riuers, and be more able to resist or cutte the

erga patriam industria nostra, et brevis tractatûs hujus regulas paucas, veras, salu tares, demonstrationemque lucidam ac apertam continentis calamus noster primum initium derivavit.' In the MS. before alluded to, entitled *The Book of Knyghthode and Batayle*, there are some verses in praise of swimming, evidently a mere metrical translation of a passage of Vegetius, which, for the purpose of comparison, is printed below. The editor is not aware that this fact has been remarked by any previous writer.

> 'To swymme is eek to lerne in sommer seson,
> Men fynde not a brugge as ofte as flood ;
> Swymming to voyde and chace an oste wil eson ;
> Eke after reyn the Ryvers gothe wood (*i.e.* rage).
> That every man in th'ost con swymme is good,
> Knyght, squyer, footman, cook and cosynere,
> And grome and page for swymmyng is to lere.'

'Natandi usum æstivis mensibus omnis æqualiter debet tiro condiscere. Non enim semper flumina pontibus transeuntur : sed et cedens et insequens natare cogitur frequenter exercitus: sæpe repentinis imbribus vel niveis solent exundare torrentes.' —*De Re Militari*, lib. i. cap. 10. And again 'Seu mare seu fluvius vicinus est sedibus, æstivo tempore, ad natandum cogendi sunt omnes.'—*Ibid.* lib. iii. cap. 4.

* 'Ideoque Romani veteres, quos tot bella et continuata pericula ad omnem rei militaris erudierant artem, campum Martium vicinum Tiberi delegerant, in quo juventus post exercitium armorum, sudorem pulveremque delueret, ac lassitudinem cursûs natandi labore deponeret. Non solùm autem pedites, sed et equites ipsosque equos vel lixas, quos galearios vocant, ad natandum exercere percommodum est, ne quid imperitis, quum necessitas imminebit, eveniat.'—Vegetius, *De Re Militari*, lib. i. cap. 10.

waues, and nat be aferde of pirries* or great stormes. For it hath ben often tymes sene that, by the good swimminge of horses, many men haue ben saued, and contrary wise, by a timorouse royle* where the water hath uneth come to his bely, his legges hath foltred, wherby many a good and propre man hath perisshed. What benefite receiued the hole citie of Rome by the swymmynge of Oratius Cocles, whiche is a noble historie and worthy to be remembred. After the Romanes had expelled Tarquine their kynge, as I haue before remembred, he desired ayde of Porsena, kynge of Thuscanes, a noble and valiant prince, to recouer eftsones his realme and dignitie; who with a great and puissant hoste besieged the citie of Rome, and so sodaynely and sharpely assaulted it, that it lacked but litle that he ne had entred into the citie with his host ouer the bridge called *Sublicius*; where encountred with hym this Oratius with a fewe Romanes. And whiles this noble capitayne, beinge alone, with an incredible strengthe resisted all the hoste of Porcena that were on the bridge, he commaunded the bridge to be broken behynde hym, where with all the Thuscanes theron standyng fell in to the great riuer of Tiber, but Oratius all armed lepte in to the water and swamme to his company, al be it that he was striken with many arowes and dartes, and also greuouslye wounded.[b] Nat withstandynge by his noble courage and feate of swymmyng he saued the citie of Rome from perpetuall seruitude, whiche was likely to haue ensued by the returne of the proude Tarquine.

Oratius Cocles.

* See the Glossary.

[b] The author has followed the account given by Plutarch: ''Ωθουμένων δὲ τῶν πολεμίων διὰ τῆς ξυλίνης γεφύρας ἐκινδύνευσεν ἡ Ῥώμη κατὰ κράτος ἁλῶναι. Πρῶτος δὲ Κόκλιος Ὁράτιος καὶ σὺν αὐτῷ δύο τῶν ἐπιφανεστάτων ἀνδρῶν, Ἑρμήνιος καὶ Λάρτιος, ἀντέστησαν περὶ τὴν ξυλίνην γέφυραν. Οὗτος ἑστὼς πρὸ τῆς γεφύρας ἡμύνετο τοὺς πολεμίους, ἄχρις οὗ διέκοψαν οἱ σὺν αὐτῷ κατόπιν τὴν γέφυραν. Οὕτω δὲ μετὰ τῶν ὅπλων ἀφεὶς ἑαυτὸν εἰς τὸν ποταμὸν ἀπενήξατο καὶ προσέμιξε τῇ πέραν ὄχθῃ δόρατι Τυῤῥηνικῷ βεβλημένος τὸν γλουτόν.—*Poplicola*, 16. Livy, on the contrary, says: 'Multisque superincidentibus telis *incolumis* ad suos tranavit, rem ausus plus famæ habituram ad posteros, quàm fidei,' lib. ii. cap. 10, and he is supported by Valerius Maximus, lib. iii. cap. 2, § 1.

Howe moche profited the feate in swymmynge to the valiant Julius Cesar, who at the bataile of Alexandri, on a bridge beinge abandoned of his people for the multitude of his enemyes, whiche oppressed them, whan he moughte no lenger sustaine the shotte of dartes and arowes, he boldly lepte in to the see, and, diuynge under the water, escaped the shotte and swamme the space of CC pasis to one of his shyppes, drawynge his cote armure with his teethe after hym, that his enemies shulde nat attayne it. And also that it moughte some what defende hym from theyr arowes. And that more maruaile was, holdynge in his hande aboue the water certayne lettres, whiche a litle before he had receyued from the Senate.[a]

Julius Cesar swymmyng.

Before hym Sertorius, who of the spanyardes was named the second Anniball for his prowesse, in the bataile that Scipio faughte agayne the Cimbres, whiche inuaded Fraunce. Sertorius, when, by negligence of his people, his enemyes preuailed and put his hoste to the warse, he beinge sore wounded, and his horse beinge lost, armed as he was in a gesseron, holdyng in his handes a tergate, and his sworde, he lepte in to the ryuer of Rone, whiche is wonderfull swyfte, and, swymmyng agayne the streme, came to his company, nat without greatte wondryng of all his enemies, whiche stode and behelde hym.[b]

Sertorius.

---

[a] 'Alexandriæ, circa oppugnationem pontis, eruptione hostium subitâ compulsus in scapham, pluribus eodem præcipitantibus, cum desiluisset in mare, nando per ducentos passus evasit ad proximam navem, elatâ lævâ, ne libelli quos tenebat madefierent; paludamentum mordicus trahens, ne spolio potiretur hostis.'—Sueton. *Julius*, 64. Plutarch has rather a different version of the same feat, as follows. Περὶ τῇ Φάρῳ μάχης συνεστώσης, κατεπήδησε μὲν ἀπὸ τοῦ χώματος εἰς ἀκάτιον καὶ παρεβοήθει τοῖς ἀγωνιζομένοις, ἐπιπλεόντων δὲ πολλαχόθεν αὐτῷ τῶν Αἰγυπτίων ῥίψας ἑαυτὸν εἰς τὴν θάλασσαν ἀπενήξατο μόλις καὶ χαλεπῶς. Ὅτε καὶ λέγεται βιβλίδια κρατῶν πολλὰ μὴ προέσθαι βαλλόμενος καὶ βαπτιζόμενος, ἀλλ' ἀνέχων ὑπὲρ τῆς θαλάσσης τὰ βιβλίδια τῇ ἑτέρᾳ χειρὶ νήχεσθαι· τὸ δὲ ἀκάτιον εὐθὺς ἐβυθίσθη.—Plut. *Julius Cæsar*, 49.

[b] Πρῶτον μὲν οὖν, Κίμβρων καὶ Τευτόνων ἐμβεβληκότων εἰς Γαλατίαν, στρατευόμενος ὑπὸ Καιπίωνι, κακῶς ἀγωνισαμένων τῶν Ῥωμαίων καὶ τροπῆς γενομένης,

The great kynge Alexander lamented that he had nat lerned to swimme. For in Inde whan he wente agayne the puissaunt kynge Porus, he was constrayned, in folowynge his entreprise, to conuay his hoste ouer a ryuer of wonderfull greatnesse; than caused he his horse men to gage the water, whereby he firste perceiued that it came to the brestis of the horsis, and, in the myddle of the streme, the horsis wente in water to the necke, wherwith the fotemen beinge aferde, none of them durst auenture to passe ouer the ryuer. That perceiuynge Alexander with a dolorouse maner in this wyse lamented. O howe moste unhappy am I of all other that haue nat or this tyme lerned to swymme? And therwith he pulled a tergate from one of his souldiours, and castynge it in to the water, standynge on it, with his spere conuaied hym selfe with the streme, and gouernyng the tergate wysely, broughte hym selfe unto the other side of the water;* wherof his people beinge abasshed, some assayed to swymme, holdyng faste by the horses, other by speares and other lyke weapons, many upon fardels and trusses, gate ouer the ryuer; in so moche as nothinge was perisshed sauue a litle bagage, and of that no great quantitie lost.

What utilitie was shewed to be in swymmynge at the firste warres whiche the Romanes had agayne the Carthaginensis? It happened a bataile to be on the see betwene them, where they of Carthage beinge vainquisshed, wolde haue sette up their sailes to haue fledde, but that perceiuynge diuers yonge Romanes, they threwe them selfes in to the see, and swymmynge unto the shippes, they enforced theyr ennemies to stryke on lande, and there assaulted them so asprely, that

ἀποβεβληκὼς τὸν ἵππον καὶ κατατετρωμένος τὸ σῶμα, τὸν Ῥοδανὸν διεπέρασεν αὐτῷ τε τῷ θώρακι καὶ θυρεῷ πρὸς ἐναντίον ῥεῦμα πολὺ νηχόμενος· οὕτω τὸ σῶμα ῥωμαλέον ἦν αὐτῷ καὶ διάπονον τῇ ἀσκήσει.—Plut. *Sertorius*, 3.

* This is another and still more remarkable instance of the way in which the author has improved (?) upon history. The allusion is evidently to the following passage in Plutarch. Τῇ δὲ καλουμένῃ Νύσῃ τῶν Μακεδόνων ὀκνούντων προσάγειν (καὶ γὰρ ποταμὸς ἦν πρὸς αὐτῇ βαθύς) ἐπιστὰς, 'Τί γάρ, εἶπεν, ὁ κάκιστος ἐγὼ νεῖν οὐκ ἔμαθον;' Καὶ ἤδη τὴν ἀσπίδα ἔχων περᾶν ἠθέλησεν.—*Alexander*, 58.

the capitaine of the Romanes, called Luctatius, mought easily take them.[a]

Nowe beholde what excellent commoditie is in the feate of swymmyng; sens no kyng, be he neuer so puissaunt or perfecte in the experience of warres, may assure hym selfe from the necessities whiche fortune sowethe amonge men that be mortall. And sens on the helth and saulfe garde of a noble capitayne, often tymes dependeth the weale of a realme, nothing shulde be kepte from his knowlege, wherby his persone may be in euery ieoperdie preserued.

Amonge these exercises it shall be conuenient to lerne to handle sondrye waipons,[b] specially the sworde and the batayle axe, whiche be for a noble man moste conuenient. But the most honorable exercise, in myne opinion, and that besemeth the astate of euery noble persone, is to ryde suerly and clene on a great horse and a roughe,[c] whiche undoubtedly nat onely importeth a maiestie and drede to inferiour *Defence with waipons.* *Rydynge and vauntynge of horsis.*

---

[a] 'Qualis deinde roboris illi milites, qui vehementi ictu remorum concitatam fugæ Punicam classem, nantes lubrico pelagi, quasi camporum firmitate, pedites in littus retraxerunt?'—Val. Max. lib. iii. cap. 2, § 10. It will be seen that the name of the Roman general has been supplied by the author, with other details according to his fancy. It is curious to observe how subsequent writers have appropriated the result of Sir Thomas Elyot's labours without acknowledging their obligation; thus this passage, along with some other portions of *The Governour*, has been transferred bodily by Peacham to the pages of his 'Compleat Gentleman,' published in 1622.

[b] Fencing must have formed a necessary part of a young nobleman's education in the author's time. In a letter to Secretary Cromwell from his son's tutor, we read: 'The order of his studie, as the houres lymyted for the Frenche tongue, writinge, *plaienge att weapons*, castinge of accomptes, pastimes of instruments, and suche others, hath bene devised and directed by the prudent wisdome of Mr. Southwell. . . . Mr. Cheney and Mr. Charles in lyke wise endevoireth and emploieth themselves, accompanienge Mr. Gregory in lerninge, amonge whome ther is a perpetuall contention, strife, and conflicte, and in maner of an honest envie who shall do beste, not oonlie in the ffrenche tongue, but also in writynge, *playenge at weapons*, and all other theire exercises.'—Ellis's *Orig. Letters*, 3rd Series, vol. i. p. 342.

[c] We learn from Wilson that the sons of noblemen were skilful riders at a very

persones, beholding him aboue the common course of other men, dauntyng a fierce and cruell beaste, but also is no litle socour, as well in pursuete of enemies and confoundyng them, as in escapyng imminent daunger, whan wisdome therto exhorteth. Also a stronge and hardy horse dothe some tyme more domage under his maister than he with al his waipon: and also settethe forwarde the stroke, and causethe it to lighte with more violence.

Bucephal, the horse of great kynge Alexander, who suffred none on his backe saulfe onely his maister, at the bataile of Thebes beinge sore wounded, wolde nat suffre the kinge to departe from hym to another horse, but persistyng in

Bucephal.

---

early age. Speaking of the young Duke of Suffolk, nephew of Henry the Eighth, he says: 'In this tyme (besides his other giftes of the mynde whiche passed all other and were almoste incredible) folowyng his father's nature, he was so delited with ridyng and runnyng in armour upon horsebacke, and was so comely for that facte, and could do so well in chargyng his staffe, beyng but xiv yeres of age, that menne of warre, even at this houre, mone muche the want of suche a worthie gentleman. Yea, the Frenche men that first wondered at his learnyng, when he was there among them, and made a notable oracion in Latine, were much more astonied when thei saw his comely ridyng, and litle thought to finde these twoo ornamentes ioyned bothe in one, his yeres especially beyng so tender and his practise of so small tyme.'—*Arte of Rhetorique*, p. 16. King James I. recommends this form of exercise to his son, 'for it becommeth a Prince best of any man to be a faire and good horse-man. Use, therefore, to ride and danton great and couragious horses, that I may say of you as Phillip saide of Great Alexander, his sonne, Μακεδονία οὐ σὲ χωρεῖ. And specially use such games on horse-backe as may teach you to handle your armes thereon, such as the tilt, the ring, and lowe-ryding for handling of your sworde.'—Βασίλικον Δῶρον, lib. iii. p. 121. The reader will probably be of opinion that 'The Governour' must have been carefully studied by the Royal author. Ascham, a few years later, said: 'Fond schoolmasters neither can understand, nor will follow this good counsel of Socrates, but wise riders in their office can and will do both; which is the only cause that commonly the young gentlemen of England go so unwillingly to school, and run so fast to the stable. For in very deed, fond schoolmasters, by fear, do beat into them the hatred of learning, and wise riders, by gentle allurements, do breed up in them the love of riding. They find fear and bondage in schools, they feel liberty and freedom in stables; which causeth them utterly to abhor the one, and most gladly to haunt the other. And I do not write this, that in exhorting to the one, I would dissuade young gentlemen from the other; yea, I am sorry with all my heart that they be given no more to riding than they be. For of all outward qualities, to ride fair is most comely for

his furiouse courage, wonderfully continued out the bataile, with his fete and tethe betyng downe and destroyenge many enemies.[a] And many semblable maruailes of his strength he shewed. Wherfore Alexander, after the horse was slayne, made in remembrance of hym a citie in the countray of India and called it Bucephal, in perpetual memorie of so worthy a horse, whiche in his lyfe had so well serued hym.[b]

What wonderfull enterprises dyd Julius Cesar achieue by the helpe of his horse? Whiche nat onely dyd excell all other horsis in fiercenesse and swyfte rennynge, but also was in some parte discrepant in figure from other horsis, hauing his fore hoeues like to the feete of a man. And in that figure Plinius writeth that he sawe hym kerued before the temple of Venus.[c]

Other remembrance there is of diuers horsis by whose monstruous power men dyd exploite incredible affaires: but

---

himself, most necessary for his country; and the greater he is in blood, the greater is his praise, the more he doth exceed all other therein. It was one of the three excellent praises amongst the noble gentlemen of the old Persians, 'Always to say truth, to ride fair, and shoot well,' and so it was engraven upon Darius's tomb, as Strabo beareth witness,

'Darius the king lieth buried here,
Who in riding and shooting had never peer.'

—*Schoolmaster*, p. 113, ed. 1864.

[a] Pliny, whom Sir Thomas Elyot had evidently read, does not relate this last circumstance. He merely says: 'Neminem hic alium, quàm Alexandrum, regio instratus ornatu, recepit in sedem, alios passim recipiens. Idem in prœliis memoratæ cujusdam perhibetur operæ, Thebarum oppugnatione vulneratus in alium transire Alexandrum non passus.'—*Nat. Hist.* lib. viii. cap. 64. But Plutarch describes the peculiar devotion of the horse rather differently, and Sir Thomas Elyot has apparently confused the two accounts. Ὁ δὲ Βουκεφάλας γυμνὸς μὲν ἂν παρεῖχεν ἀναβῆναι τῷ ἱπποκόμῳ, κοσμηθεὶς δὲ τοῖς βασιλικοῖς προκοσμίοις καὶ περιδεραίοις οὐδένα προσίετο, πλὴν αὐτὸν Ἀλέξανδρον· τοῖς δ' ἄλλοις, εἰ πειρώμενοι προσίοιεν, ἐναντίος ἐπιτρέχων ἐχρεμέτιζε μέγα καὶ συνήλλετο, καὶ κατεπάτει τοὺς μὴ πρόσω ἴεσθαι μηδ' ἀποφεύγειν φθάσαντας.—*De Solert. Animal.* cap. 14.

[b] Multa præterea ejusdem modi, propter quæ rex defuncto ei duxit exequias: urbemque tumulo circumdedit nomine ejus.—*Ubi supra*. Καὶ πόλιν οἰκίσας ἐπ' αὐτῷ παρὰ τὸν Ὑδάσπην Βουκεφαλίαν προσηγόρευσε.—Plutarch. *Alex.* 61.

[c] 'Nec Cæsaris dictatoris quenquam alium recepisse dorso equus traditur: idemque humanis similes pedes priores habuisse, hâc effigie locatus ante Veneris genetricis ædem.'—*Ubi supra*.

by cause the reporte of them contayneth thinges impossible, and is nat writen by any approued autour: I will nat in this place reherce them: sauyng that it is yet supposed that the castell of Arundell in Sussex was made by one Beauuize, erle of South hamton, for a monument of his horse called Arundell,* whiche in ferre countrayes had saued his maister from many periles. Nowe considerynge the utilitie in rydynge greatte horses, hit shall be necessary (as I haue sayd),

Arundell.

* The Romance of Bevis, or, as he is more commonly styled, Sir Bevis of Southampton, was one of the most popular and best known legends in the middle ages. There is good ground, however, for supposing that Sir Thomas Elyot was the first *writer* of any note who connected Bevis with the Castle through the medium of his horse. It is a curious fact that the editor has been unable to find among the numerous writers who have treated either of the legend of Sir Bevis or of the topography of Arundel, a single instance in which the authority of Sir Thomas Elyot in reference to the above statement is quoted, though, as will be seen presently, one writer, who was himself a cotemporary of the author, has appropriated his language wholesale without acknowledgment, and has apparently down to the present time escaped detection. In order that the reader may form his own opinion of the extent of this plagiarism, and as the work in which it occurs is not generally accessible, it has been deemed expedient to print the passage *in extenso*. It occurs in Legh's *Accidens of Armory*, which was published in 1562, only thirty years after the first appearance of 'The Governour.' In describing a coat of armes which bears 'a horse argent upon a field gules,' Legh says: '*Bucephalus, the horse of the great kyng Alexaunder, in battale, wolde suffer no man to come on his backe, but onely the kynge. And beyng sore wounded wolde not suffer hym to departe from him and take an other horse, but wonderfully continued out the battayle; with his feete beating downe and his teathe biting he destroied many enemies. Wherefore Alexaunder, after the horse was slayne, made in the remembraunce of him a citie in the countrey of India, and called it Bucephala. What wonderfull enterprises did Julius Cesar acheve by the helpe of his horse, the which had his fore feete like the feete of a man, as Plinie writeth.* The horse Arundel, of no littell fame in Britaine lande, amongst these is worthy to be remembered, for whose good seruice the olde renowmed Beauice of South hampton buylded the castell of Arundel in Southsex. O most worthy to be put in Fame's Boke, that wolde not forgett the seruice of a beast, where nowe in this tyme they be that do forgett the seruice of men. Yea, some there be, that make no remembraunce of their owne fathers, who tenderly fostered them not with forgettfulnes unto there dying day,' p. 94. On comparing the words in italics in the above passage with those of the text the reader will not fail to see that Legh's final apostrophe ought to have recoiled with increased force upon his own head. Camden, in his 'Britannia,' the first edition of which was published in 1586, repudiates the etymology which found favour with Elyot, but makes no allusion to the latter. He says: 'Causa nominis nec ab Arundelio Beuesii fabulosi equo, nec ex *Charudo* Cimbricæ Chersonensi promontario, quod

that a gentilman do lerne to ride a great and fierce horse whiles he is tender and the brawnes and sinewes of his thighes

Goropius per quietem vidit, sed ex valle in quâ sedit ad Arun flumen,' &c., p. 157. In 1722, a new edition of the 'Britannia' came out under the auspices of Gibson, who, without mentioning any names, says : ' However *there are those* who, on one hand, contend for the story of Bevis's horse, and on the other hand will by no means admit this derivation from Arun, and they offer their reasons for both. That Bevis was founder of the Castle (*they say*) *is a current opinion handed down by tradition*, and there is a tower in it still known by the name of Bevis's Tower, which they tell you was his own apartment. Besides, they think it natural enough to imagine, that the name of a horse might be Arundel, from his swiftness, since that word in French signifies a swallow, and the present arms of the town (which is corporate by prescription) are a swallow. Now why (*say they*) *might not Bevis's Arundel as well have the honour of naming a town wherein his master had a particular interest as Alexander's Bucephalus had of a city?*'—*Ibid.* vol. i. p. 244. The anonymous author of 'Magna Britannia,' a work published in 1730, mentions what he calls 'the current opinion concerning the foundation of the Castle,' but he contents himself with following Gibson's exposition of it, and cites no authorities for the story. In 1789 Mr. Gough revised and continued the work which Gibson had initiated, and for the latter's note upon the etymology substituted the following statement : ' In favour of the derivation of its name from Bevis's horse Arundel *it is urged* that there is still a tower in the castle called after Bevis's name, and *said to be built by him*, and his horse might have his name from his swiftness, answering to the French *hirondelle* (a swallow), which is the arms of the town, but this is a mere rebus. *Alexander's horse gave his name to a city in India.*'—Vol. i. p. 196. It is certainly a remarkable circumstance that from Camden downwards not one of these antiquarians should have referred to Sir Thomas Elyot as the original writer, who it is evident, from the numerous editions of *The Governour,' must have done more than anyone else to give currency to the legend. It is still more surprising that not one of the modern writers, Dallaway, Tierney, Lower, &c., who have made the antiquities of Arundel their special study, has condescended to refer to this passage in the text, though it would have been interesting, if for no other reason, as showing that, in the opinion of a man of such extensive learning as Sir Thomas Elyot, the tradition, commonly received in his day, was entitled to a higher degree of respect than should be accorded to stories, which were not vouched (to use his own words) ' by any approved author.' It may be mentioned as a curious coincidence that while the armorial bearings of the town of Arundel display, as has been already stated, a swallow, one of the heraldic supporters of the Dukes of Norfolk is 'the white horse of Arundel.' In Dallaway's *History of Sussex* this coat of arms is depicted, but unaccompanied by any reference to the legend. His Grace the Duke of Norfolk, to whom the editor applied for information on the subject, states in a letter dated the 19th January, 1876, that ' the sword said to have belonged to Bevis is now hanging in the gallery here. It is nearly eight feet long, it is two-edged, and intended to be used with both hands. The tradition is that when Bevis was dying he threw his sword from the battlements of the tower, saying that he wished to be buried where it fell. A large grave-shaped mound in

nat fully consolidate.[a] There is also a ryght good exercise which is also expedient to lerne, whiche is named the vauntynge of a horse: that is to lepe on him at euery side without stiroppe or other helpe, specially whiles the horse is goynge. And beinge therin experte, than armed at all poyntes to assay the same; the commoditie wherof is so manifest that I nede no further to declare it.[b]

CHAPTER XVIII.

The auncient huntyng of Greekes and Romanes.

BUT nowe wyll I procede to write of exercises whiche be nat utterly reproued of noble auctours, if they be used with oportunite and in measure, I meane huntyng, hauking, and daunsyng. In huntynge may be an imitacion of batayle, if it be suche as was used amonge them of Persia, wherof Xenophon, the noble and moste eloquent philosopher, maketh a dilectable mention in his booke called the doctrine of Cirus: and also maketh another speciall boke, contayning the hole discipline of the auncient huntynge of the Grekes: and in that fourme beyng used, it is a laudable exercise, of the whiche I wyll nowe somwhat write.

a valley in the downs now enclosed in the park is said to be his grave on the spot where the sword fell.' Thus, however little credit we may feel disposed to attach to the *story*, there remains an indisputable witness of *fact*. For the gigantic sword still preserved in the castle must at some period or other have belonged to a real man capable of wielding it.

[a] Galen says children should be taught to ride at seven years old. 'Septennes vero etiam valentiora exercitia tolerant, ita ut equitare jam assuescant.'—*De San. tuend*. lib. i. fo. 9.

[b] Xenophon recommends this practice in his treatise called *Hipparchicus*. Τῶν γε μὴν ἵππων ὑπαρχόντων οἵων δεῖ τοὺς ἱππέας αὖ ἀσκητέον, πρῶτον μὲν ὅπως ἐπὶ τοὺς ἵππους ἀναπηδᾶν δύνωνται· πολλοῖς γὰρ ἤδη ἡ σωτηρία παρὰ τοῦτο ἐγένετο.—Cap. i. § 5. Sir Thomas Wilson, in speaking of the education of a nobleman, says: 'Againe I maie commende hym for plaiyng at weapons, for runnyng uppon a great horse, for chargyng his staffe at the Tilt, for *vawting*, for playing upon instrumentes, yea, and for paintyng, or drawyng of a Plat, as in olde tyme noble Princes muche delited therein.'—*Arte of Rhetorique*, p. 13.

Cirus and other auncient kynges of Persia (as Xenophon writeth)* used this maner in all their huntyng. First, where as it semeth, there was in the realme of Persia but one citie, whiche as I suppose, was called Persepolis, there were the children of the Persians, from their infancie unto the age of seuentene yeres, brought up in the lernyng of iustice and temperance, and also to obserue continence in meate and drinke: in so moche that, whyder so euer they went, they toke with them for their sustenaunce but onely breed and herbes, called Kersis, in latine *Nasturtium*, and for their drinke, a disshe to take water out of the ryuers as they passed. Also they lerned to shote and to caste the darte or iauelyn. Whan they came to the age of xvii yeres, they were lodged in the palaises that were there ordayned for the kynge and his nobles, whiche was as well for the sauegarde of the citie, as for the example of temperance that they dayly had at their eyes gyuen to them by the nobles, whiche also mought be called Peeres, by the signification of the greeke worde, wherin they were called, *Omotimi*. More ouer they were accustomed to ryse alway in the first spring of the day, and paciently to sustayne alwaye bothe colde and heate. And the kyng dyd se them exercised in goynge and also in rennyng. And whan he

The huntynge of Persians. Xenophon pædia Cyri li. i.

---

* Διδάσκουσι δὲ τοὺς παῖδας καὶ σωφροσύνην· μέγα δὲ συμβάλλεται εἰς τὸ μανθάνειν σωφρονεῖν αὐτοὺς ὅτι καὶ τοὺς πρεσβυτέρους ὁρῶσιν ἀνὰ πᾶσαν ἡμέραν σωφρόνως διάγοντας. Διδάσκουσι δὲ αὐτοὺς καὶ πείθεσθαι τοῖς ἄρχουσι· μέγα δὲ καὶ εἰς τοῦτο συμβάλλεται ὅτι ὁρῶσι τοὺς πρεσβυτέρους πειθομένους τοῖς ἄρχουσιν ἰσχυρῶς. Διδάσκουσι δὲ καὶ ἐγκρατεῖς εἶναι γαστρὸς καὶ ποτοῦ· μέγα δὲ καὶ εἰς τοῦτο συμβάλλεται ὅτι ὁρῶσι τοὺς πρεσβυτέρους οὐ πρόσθεν ἀπιόντας γαστρὸς ἕνεκα πρὶν ἂν ἀφῶσιν οἱ ἄρχοντες, καὶ ὅτι οὐ παρὰ μητρὶ σιτοῦνται οἱ παῖδες, ἀλλὰ παρὰ τῷ διδασκάλῳ, ὅταν οἱ ἄρχοντες σημήνωσι. Φέρονται δὲ οἴκοθεν σῖτον μὲν ἄρτον, ὄψον δὲ κάρδαμον, πιεῖν δὲ, ἤν τις διψῇ, κώθωνα, ὡς ἀπὸ τοῦ ποταμοῦ ἀρύσασθαι. Πρὸς δὲ τούτοις μανθάνουσι καὶ τοξεύειν καὶ ἀκοντίζειν. Μέχρι μὲν δὴ ἓξ ἢ ἑπτακαίδεκα ἐτῶν ἀπὸ γενεᾶς οἱ παῖδες ταῦτα πράττουσιν, ἐκ τούτου δὲ εἰς τοὺς ἐφήβους ἐξέρχονται. Οὗτοι δ' αὖ οἱ ἔφηβοι διάγουσιν ὧδε. Δέκα ἔτη ἀφ' οὗ ἂν ἐκ παίδων ἐξέλθωσι κοιμῶνται μὲν περὶ τὰ ἀρχεῖα, ὥσπερ προείρηται, καὶ φυλακῆς ἕνεκα τῆς πόλεως καὶ σωφροσύνης· δοκεῖ γὰρ αὕτη ἡ ἡλικία μάλιστα ἐπὶ μελείας δεῖσθαι· παρέχουσι δὲ καὶ τὴν ἡμέραν ἑαυτοὺς τοῖς ἄρχουσι χρῆσθαι, ἤν τι δέωνται ὑπὲρ τοῦ κοινοῦ. Καὶ ὅταν μὲν δέῃ, πάντες μένουσι περὶ

intended in his owne persone to hunte, whiche he dyd comenly euery monethe, he toke with him the one halfe of the company of yonge men, that were in the palaises. Than toke euery man with him his bowe and quiuer with arowes, his sworde or hache of steele, a lytell tergate, and two dartes. The bowe and arowes serued to pursue beestes that were swyfte, and the dartes to assayle them and all other beestes. And whan their courage was chaufed, or that by fiersenesse of the beest they were in daunger, than force constrayned them to stryke with the sworde, or hache, and to haue good eye at the violent assaulte of the beest, and to defende them if nede were with their tergates, wherin they accounted to be the truest and moste certayne meditation of warres. And to this huntyng the kyng dyd conducte them, and he him selfe first hunted suche beestes as he hapned to encounter. And whan he had taken his pleasure, he than with moste diligence dyd sette other forwarde, beholdynge who hunted valiauntly, and refourmynge them whom he sawe negligent or slouthfull. But er they went forthe to this huntyng, they dyned competently, and duryng their huntyng they dyned no more : for if, for any occasion, their huntyng continued aboue one daye, they toke the sayd dyner for their souper, and the next daye, if they kylled no game, they hunted untyll souper tyme, accountyng

τὰ ἀρχεῖα· ὅταν δὲ ἐξίῃ βασιλεὺς ἐπὶ θήραν, τὰς ἡμισείας φυλὰς καταλείπει· ποιεῖ δὲ τοῦτο πολλάκις τοῦ μηνός. Ἔχειν δὲ δεῖ τοὺς ἐξιόντας τόξα καὶ παρὰ τὴν φαρέτραν ἐν κολεῷ κοπίδα ἢ σάγαριν, ἔτι δὲ γέρρον καὶ παλτὰ δύο, ὥστε τὸ μὲν ἀφεῖναι, τῷ δ' ἂν δέῃ, ἐκ χειρὸς χρῆσθαι. Διὰ τοῦτο δὲ δημοσίᾳ τοῦ θηρᾶν ἐπιμέλονται καὶ βασιλεὺς ὥσπερ καὶ ἐν πολέμῳ ἡγεμὼν αὐτοῖς ἐστι καὶ αὐτός τε θηρᾷ καὶ τῶν ἄλλων ἐπιμελεῖται ὅπως ἂν θηρῶσιν, ὅτι ἀληθεστάτη αὐτοῖς δοκεῖ αὕτη ἡ μελέτη τῶν πρὸς τὸν πόλεμον εἶναι. Καὶ γὰρ πρωὶ ἀνίστασθαι ἐθίζει καὶ ψύχη καὶ θάλπη ἀνέχεσθαι, γυμνάζει δὲ καὶ ὁδοιπορίαις καὶ δρόμοις, ἀνάγκη δὲ καὶ τοξεῦσαι θηρίον καὶ ἀκοντίσαι ὅπου ἂν παραπίπτῃ· Καὶ τὴν ψυχὴν δὲ πολλάκις ἀνάγκη θήγεσθαι, ὅταν τι τῶν ἀλκίμων θηρίων ἀνθιστῆται· παίειν μὲν γὰρ δήπου δεῖ τὸ ὁμόσε γιγνόμενον, φυλάξασθα δὲ τὸ ἐπιφερόμενον· ὥστε οὐ ῥᾴδιον εὑρεῖν ἐν τῇ θήρᾳ τί ἄπεστι τῶν ἐν πολέμῳ παρόντων. Ἐξέρχονται δὲ ἐπὶ τὴν θήραν ἄριστον ἔχοντες πλεῖον μὲν, ὡς τὸ εἰκὸς, τῶν παίδων τἄλλα δὲ ὅμοιον. Καὶ θηρῶντες μὲν οὐκ ἂν ἀριστήσαιεν, ἢν δέ τι δεήσῃ ἢ θηρίου ἕνεκα ἐπικαταμεῖναι ἢ ἄλλως βουληθῶσι διατρίψαι περὶ τὴν θήραν, τὸ ἄριστον τοῦτο δειπνήσαντες τὴν ὑστεραίαν αὖ θηρῶσι μέχρι δείπνου, καὶ μίαν ἄμφω τούτω τὼ ἡμέρα λογίζονται, ὅτι μιᾶς ἡμέρας σῖτον δαπανῶσι. Τοῦτο δὲ ποιοῦσι τοῦ ἐθίζεσθαι ἕνεκα, ἵνα ἐάν τι καὶ ἐν πολέμῳ δεήσῃ

those two dayes but for one. And if they toke any thyng, they ete it at their souper with ioye and pleasure. If nothynge were killed, they ete onely breed and Kersis, as I byfore rehersed, and dranke therto water. And if any man wil disprayse this diete, lette him thinke what pleasure there is in breed, to him that is hungry, and what dilectation is in drinkynge water, to him that is thursty. Surely this maner of huntyng maye be called a necessary solace and pastyme, for therin is the very imitation of batayle, for nat onely it dothe shewe the courage and strength as well of the horse as of him that rydeth, trauersynge ouer mountaynes and valeys, encountringe and ouerthrowyng great and mighty beestes, but also it increaseth in them bothe agilitie and quicknesse, also sleight and policie to fynde suche passages and straytes, where they may preuent or intrappe their enemies. Also by continuance therin they shall easily sustayne trauaile in warres, hunger and thurst, cold and heate. Hytherto be the wordes of Xenophon, althoughe I haue nat set them in lyke order as he wrate them.

The chiefe hunting of the valiaunt Grekes was at the lyon, the lybarde,[a] the tigre, the wilde swyne, and the beare, and somtyme the wolfe and the harte. Theseus, whiche was companyon to Hercules, attayned the greatest parte of his renome for fightynge with the great bore, whiche the Grekes called *Phera*, that wasted and consumed the feldes of a great countray.[b]

The huntynge of the Grekes.

δύνωνται τοῦτο ποιεῖν. Καὶ ὄψον δὲ τοῦτο ἔχουσιν οἱ τηλικοῦτοι ὅ τι ἂν θηράσωσιν, εἰ δὲ μὴ, τὸ κάρδαμον. Εἰ δέ τις αὐτοὺς οἴεται ἢ ἐσθίειν ἀηδῶς, ὅταν κάρδαμον μόνον ἔχωσιν ἐπὶ τῷ σίτῳ, ἢ πίνειν ἀηδῶς, ὅταν ὕδωρ πίνωσιν, ἀναμνησθήτω πῶς ἡδὺ μὲν μᾶζα καὶ ἄρτος πεινῶντι φαγεῖν, πῶς δὲ ἡδὺ ὕδωρ διψῶντι πιεῖν.—Xen. *Cyr.* lib. i. cap. 2.

[a] See the Glossary.

[b] Ἡ δὲ Κρομμυωνία σῦς, ἣν Φαιὰν προσωνόμαζον, οὐ φαῦλον ἦν θηρίον, ἀλλὰ μάχιμον καὶ χαλεπὸν κρατηθῆναι. Ταύτην, ὁδοῦ πάρεργον, ὡς μὴ δοκοίη πάντα πρὸς ἀνάγκην ποιεῖν, ὑποστὰς ἀνεῖλε· καὶ ἅμα, τῶν μὲν ἀνθρώπων τοῖς πονηροῖς ἀμυνόμενον οἰόμενος δεῖν τὸν ἀγαθὸν προσφέρεσθαι, τῶν δὲ θηρίων καὶ προεπιχειροῦντα τοῖς γενναίοις μάχεσθαι καὶ διακινδυνεύειν.—Plut. *Theseus*, 9. Crommyón was on the border dividing Corinth from Megara.

Meleager likewise for sleyng of the great bore in Calidonia, whiche in greatnesse and fiercenesse exceded all other bores, and had slayne many noble and valiaunt persones.[a]

The great Alexander, in tymes vacaunt from bataile, delyted in that maner huntinge. On a tyme he faughte alone with a lyon wonderfull greatte and fierce, beinge present amonge other straungers, the ambassadour of Lacedemonia, and, after longe trauaile, with incredible might he ouerthrewe the lyon, and slewe him; wherat the said ambassadour wondring meruaylously sayde to the kinge, I wolde to god (noble prince) ye shulde fight with a lyon for some great empire.[b] By whiche wordes it semed that he nothing approued the valiauntnesse of a prince by fighting with a wylde beest, wherin moche more was aduentured than mought be by the victorie goten.

Al be it Pompei,[c] Sertorius,[d] and diuers other noble

[a]
Ἡ δὲ χολωσαμένη, δῖον γένος ἰοχέαιρα,
Ὦρσεν ἐπὶ χλούνην σῦν ἄγριον, ἀργιόδοντα,
Ὃς κακὰ πόλλ' ἔρδεσκεν, ἔθων Οἰνῆος ἀλωήν·
Πολλὰ δ' ὅγε προθέλυμνα χαμαὶ βάλε δένδρεα μακρά
Αὐτῇσιν ῥίζῃσι, καὶ αὐτοῖς ἄνθεσι μήλων.
Τὸν δ' υἱὸς Οἰνῆος ἀπέκτεινεν Μελέαγρος,
Πολλέων ἐκ πολίων θηρήτορας ἄνδρας ἀγείρας,
Καὶ κύνας· οὐ μὲν γάρ κε δάμη παύροισι βροτοῖσιν·
Τόσσος ἔην, πολλοὺς δὲ πυρῆς ἐπέβησ' ἀλεγεινῆς.
Homer, *Iliad*, ix. 534-542.

According to Strabo, the dam of this boar was the sow slain by Theseus. Ἡ δὲ Κρομμυών ἐστι κώμη τῆς Κορινθίας, πρότερον δὲ τῆς Μεγαρίδος, ἐν ᾗ μυθεύουσι τὰ περὶ τὴν Κρομμυωνίαν ὗν, ἣν μητέρα τοῦ Καλυδωνίου κάπρου φασί, καὶ τῶν Θησέως ἄθλων ἕνα τοῦτον παραδιδόασι τὴν τῆς ὑὸς ταύτης ἐξαίρεσιν.—Lib. viii. cap. 6, § 22.

[b] Ἐπέτεινεν οὖν ἔτι μᾶλλον αὐτὸς ἑαυτὸν ἐν ταῖς στρατείαις καὶ ταῖς κυνηγεσίαις κακοπαθῶν καὶ παραβαλλόμενος, ὥστε καὶ Λάκωνα πρεσβευτὴν παραγενόμενον αὐτῷ λέοντα καταβάλλοντι μέγαν εἰπεῖν· Καλῶς γε, Ἀλέξανδρε, πρὸς τὸν λέοντα ἠγώνισαι περὶ τᾶς βασιλείας.—Plut. *Alexander*, 40.

[c] Χρώμενος δὲ τῇ τύχῃ καὶ τῇ ῥώμῃ τοῦ στρατεύματος εἰς τὴν Νομαδικὴν ἐνέβαλε· καὶ πολλῶν ὁδὸν ἡμερῶν ἐλάσας καὶ πάντων κατακρατήσας οἷς ἐνέτυχε, καὶ τὸ πρὸς Ῥωμαίους δέος ἤδη τῶν βαρβάρων ἐξερρηνκὸς αὖθις ἰσχυρὸν καὶ φοβερὸν ἐγκαταστήσας, οὐδὲ τὰ θηρία δεῖν ἔφη τὰ τὴν Λιβύην κατοικοῦντα τῆς τῶν Ῥωμαίων ἄπειρα ῥώμης καὶ τόλμης ἀπολιπεῖν. Ὅθεν ἐν θήραις λεόντων καὶ ἐλεφάντων ἡμέρας διέτριψεν οὐ πολλάς.—Plut. *Pompeius*, 12.

[d] Πλάνοις δὲ χρώμενος ἀεὶ καὶ κυνηγεσίοις, ὁπότε σχολάζοι, πάσης διεκδύσεως

Romanes, whan they were in Numidia, Libia, and suche other countrayes, which nowe be called Barbary[a] and *The huntynge of the Romanes.* Morisco,[b] in the vacation season from warres, they hunted lions, liberdes, and suche other bestis, fierce and sauage,[c]

φεύγοντι καὶ διώκοντι κυκλώσεως ἀβάτων τε καὶ βασίμων τόπων ἐμπειρίαν προσειλήφει.—Plut. *Sertorius*, 13.

[a] Puttenham, writing in 1589, says: 'That part of Affricke hath *but of late* receiued the name of Barbarie, and some others rather thinke that of this word Barbarous, that countrey came to be called Barbaria, *and but few yeres in that respect agone*. Others, among whom is Ihan Leon, a Moore of Granada, will seeme to derive Barbaria from this word Bar, twise iterated, thus Barbar, as much to say as flye, flye, which chaunced in a persecution of the Arabians by some seditious Mahometanes, in the time of their Pontif, Habdul Mumi, when they were had in the chase and driuen out of Arabia westward into the countreys of Mauritania, and during the pursuite cried one upon another flye away, flye away, or passe, passe, by which occasion they say, when the Arabians which were had in chase came to stay and settle themselves in that part of Affrica, they called it Barbar, as much to say the region of their flight or pursuite.'—*Arte of English Poesie*, lib. iii. cap. 22. The beginning of the 16th century saw the rise of a horde of pirates, who from their lawless inroads became formidable to Europe, and gave to the history of Barbary an interest unknown to earlier times. The famous Barbarossa was at this time Viceroy of Algiers, and his fleets scoured the Mediterranean, and struck terror into all the maritime nations of Europe. In 1541 Charles the Fifth led an expedition in person against Algiers, and landed 20,000 infantry and 6,000 cavalry, but the result was most disastrous; for a violent storm arising, the greater part of the fleet was wrecked, no less than 86 ships and 15 galleys being lost in less than half an hour, and scarcely one-third of the troops who had landed were brought off again. Several Englishmen took part as volunteers in this expedition, amongst others Sir Henry Knevet, the English Ambassador to the Court of Spain, Sir Thomas Chaloner, Messrs. Knolles, Isham, &c. The wonderful escape of Sir T. Chaloner from drowning, by holding on to a cable with his teeth, is recorded by Hackluyt, vol. ii. p. 99. A very graphic account of the sufferings endured by Charles and his army, written shortly after by one of the survivors, Nicolas Durand de Villegagnon, was translated into English in 1542, and may be read in the *Harleian Miscellany*, vol. iv. p. 532.

[b] *I.e.* Morocco—the ancient Mauritania Tingitana. The two kingdoms of Morocco and Fez, which now form one empire, are situated on the north-western coast of Barbary. Morisco was the name applied in the 16th and 17th centuries to the Moors, who were settled in Spain previous to 1492. Thus it is said by an old writer, 'the main body of the inhabitants of the kingdoms of Granada, Murcia, and Valencia were Moriscoes.'—*Mahometism Explained*, vol. ii. p. 276, ed. 1725.

[c] These have never been entirely extirpated, and in 1792 the English Consul at Tripoli, Mr. Tully, reported as follows, 'A part of the great western road

to thentent therby to exercise them selfes and their souldiours. But all myghty god be thanked, in this realme be no suche cruel bestis to be pursued.* Not withstandyng in the

from Tunis to Tripoli cannot be passed without great danger, on account of wild beasts, which not unfrequently attack passengers in spite of the precautions taken to prevent their approach.'—*Narrative of Ten Years' Residence in Tripoli*, p. 288, ed. 1816. Murray's Handbook for Algeria, published 1874, in describing Bordj Bouira, a small village 126 kilomètres from Algiers, describes it as being 'one of the few districts in the province of Algiers where lions are still to be found, and at times they do considerable damage. While the writer is penning these lines on the spot, a report is brought in that last night fourteen sheep were killed in one enclosure by a lion close to the village. A cub was shot a few days previously, and the mother wounded shortly afterwards.'—P. 122.

* Harrison, however, says : 'Lions we haue had verie manie in the north parts of Scotland, and those with maines of no lesse force than they of Mauritania were sometimes reported to be, but how and when they were destroied as yet I do not read ;' but the lack of indigenous beasts seems at any rate to have been supplied by importation from abroad, for the same writer tells us that King Henry I., 'disdaining (as he termed them) to follow or pursue cowards, cherished of set purpose sundrie kinds of wild beasts, as bears, libards, ounces, lions, at Woodstocke and one or two other places in England, which he walled about with hard stone, an. 1120, and where he would often fight with some one of them hand to hand, when they did turne againe and make anie raise upon him ; but cheeflie he loued to hunt the lion and the bore, which are both verie dangerous exercises, especiallie that with the lion, except some policie be found wherwith to trouble his eie sight in anie manner of wise.'—*Descript. of Eng.* pp. 225, 226. Camden mentions bears and wild boars as having been found in Wales, and many places still retain the name of *Pennarth*, or the bear's head. 'It does not appear,' says Mr. Pennant, 'how long they continued in that principality ; but there is proof of their infesting Scotland so late as the year 1057, when a Gordon, in reward for his valour in killing a fierce bear, was directed by the king to carry three *bears' heads* on his banner.'—*British Zoology*, vol. i. p. 65, ed. 1776. With regard to wolves, the author last cited says : 'We find that some centuries after the reign of King Edgar these animals were again increased to such a degree, as to become the object of royal attention. Accordingly Edward I. issued out his mandate to Peter Corbet to superintend and assist in the destruction of them in the several counties of Gloucester, Worcester, Hereford, Salop, and Stafford.'—*Ubi supra*, p. 63. A charter of liberties of John, as Earl of Morton, to the county of Devonshire, the original of which was formerly in the possession of the Dean and Chapter of Exeter, but had been removed therefrom by the late Bishop and was restored to its proper custody only in the present year (1876), in consequence, curiously enough, of inquiries with regard to it made by the editor for the purpose of this work, confirms the right 'quod capiant Capreolum, Vulpem, Cattum, *Lupum*, Leporem, Lutram, ubicunque illa invenerint extra regardum forestæ meæ,' from which it may fairly

huntyng of redde dere and falowe, mought be a great parte of semblable exercise used by noble men,[a] specially in forestis[b] which be spaciouse, if they wold use but a fewe nombre

[a] be inferred that these animals were not then extirpated even in that southern county. The existence of this interesting document was unknown to the learned Deputy Keeper of the Public Records, Sir T. Duffus Hardy. By the kindness of the Ven. Archdeacon of Barnstaple, the editor has been favoured with a sight of a photograph of the original charter, which appears to be in good preservation. We read too that as late as temp. 11 Henry VI., 'Sir Robert Plumpton, Knight, was seised of one bovate of land in Mansfield Woodhouse, in the county of Nottingham, called Wolf-hunt-land, held by the service of winding a horn, and chasing (driving) or frightening the wolves in the forest of Sherwood.'—Blount's *Tenures of Land*, p. 213, ed. 1874.

[a] Deer were at this time so numerous in England as to be most destructive. Thus Harrison says: 'Although that of themselves they are not offensiue at all, yet their great numbers are thought to be verie preiudiciall, and therfore justlie reproued of many. Of these also the stag is accounted for the most noble game, the fallow deere is the next, then the roe, whereof we haue indifferent store.' He also tells us that 'King Henry the fifth, in his beginning, thought it a meere scofferie to pursue anie fallow deere with hounds or greihounds, but supposed himselfe alwaies to haue done a sufficient act when he had tired them by his owne trauell on foot, and so killed them with his hands in the upshot of that exercise and end of his recreation... And yet I denie not, but rather grant willinglie that the hunting of the red deere is a right princelie pastime.'—*Ubi supra*, p. 226. Henry the Eighth was extremely fond of hunting. Thus Sir Philip Draycott, in a letter to the Earl of Shrewsbury, says: 'To acerten yow of the Kyng's progres after your departyng. The first was to Otlond (Oatlands), and ther in the meds under Cherssey (Chertsey) was kyllyng of staggys, holdyn in for the purpos, on after an oder, all the after non, so yt theye were warnyd by the trumpetts, and knoen theyreby yff theye dyd entter any dere of prys. And they was not only cowrssyd with sum grewnds, but also with horsmen with darts and sperys, and many so sleyne ; the most pryncele sport yt hath ben sene : and many dyd escap over the Temys, and to the forrest after theye passyd there.'—*Lodge's Illustrations*, vol. i. p. 6. Hall, narrating the events of the year 1522, when Charles V. visited England, says : 'On Monday thei dyned in Southwarke with the Duke of Suffolke, and hunted there in the Parke, and roade to the Manor of Richemond to their lodgyng, and the next day to Hampton Court, where they had great cheere, and from thence on thursday to Wyndsore, where he hunted Fryday. On Fryday they departed out of Wyndsore, and by easy iorneys came to Wynchester the xxii day of June, and in the way thether the Emperor hunted the Hart.'—*Chronicle*, p. 641, ed. 1809. Again in the 18th year of his reign the same writer tells us, 'All this sommer the kyng tooke his pastyme in huntyng,' *i.e.*, no doubt, stag-hunting.

[b] The king's passion for his favourite sport led to the creation of the 'Honor of Hampton Court,' which was the last instance of the creation of a Royal Forest

of houndes, onely to harborowe*, or rouse, the game, and by their yorning ᵇ to gyue knowlege whiche way it fleeth; the remenant of the disporte to be in pursuyng with iauelyns and other waipons, in maner of warre. And to them whiche, in this hunting, do shewe moste prowesse and actyuytie, a garlande or some other lyke token to be gyuen, in signe of victorie, and with a ioyfull maner to be broughte in the presence of him that is chiefe in the company; there to receiue condigne prayse for their good endeuour. I dispraise nat the huntynge of the foxe with rennynge houndes, but it is nat to be compared to the other hunting in commoditie of exercise. Therfore it wolde be used in the deepe wynter, whan the other game is unseasonable.ᶜ

in England. The preamble of the statute creating it, 31 Hen. VIII. cap 5, declares that 'His Grace ensuynge the avanncement and amplificacion of his reasonable and princelie commodities to be nye unto his saide Mannor, heretofore of late hath assigned and lymitted a certen territory or grounde for a chace thereof to be made, for norisshinge, generacion, and feeding of beasts of venery and of fowles of warren.' In the same reign it was made a felony, and therefore punishable with death, to 'take, kill or slee any Deere within anny parke or closed ground used for Deere,' if the poacher had 'his face hid or coverid with hoode or visar, or with his face paintid, or himself otherwise disguysid.'—32 Hen. VIII. cap. 11. Harrison says: 'Certes it should seeme, that forrests and franke chases haue alwaies beene had, and religiouslie preserued in this iland for the solace of the prince and recreation of his nobilitie. Howbeit I read not that euer they were inclosed more than at this present, or otherwise fensed than by usuall notes of limitation, whereby their bounds were remembred from time to time, for the better preseruation of such venerie and vert of all sorts as were nourished in the same.'— *Description of England*, p. 206, ed. 1587.

* See the Glossary.
ᵇ See the Glossary.
ᶜ Fox-hunting was formerly not in such repute as hare-hunting. Thus the *Book of St. Albans*, which, according to Strutt, contains the first treatise upon the subject of hunting that ever appeared from the press, 'has minute instructions with regard to stag and hare-hunting, but none whatever as to the fox. It mentions, however, that 'the season of the fox is from the Natiuitie till the Annunciation of our Lady.' Harrison says, 'Of foxes we have some, but no great store,' and apparently it was not usual at this time for fox-hunters to be mounted. In a book called the *Countrie Farm*, printed in 1600, we are told that 'the killing of foxes and brockes bring neither pleasure nor profite to the hunters, taking profite in this place for meate and nourishment, for the fox his flesh (and much less the brocks) is

Huntyng of the hare with grehoundes is a righte good solace for men that be studiouse, or them to whom nature hath nat gyuen personage or courage apte for the warres.[a] And also for gentilwomen, whiche fere neither sonne nor wynde for appairing their beautie. And perauenture they shall be there at lasse idell, than they shulde be at home in their chambres.[b]

nothing pleasant to eate, in as much as it hath an unsauorie, strong, and wilde kinde of taste;' and the author proceeds to show how 'some subtile foxe hunters take the foxe without any helpe of dogs.' Turberville, however, writing in 1575, says: 'The hunting of the Foxe is pleasant, for he maketh an excellent crye, because his sent is verie hote, and he neuer fleeth farre before the houndes, but holdeth the strongest couerts, and fleeth from the fielde as a beast which trusteth not in his legges nor yet in his strength.'—*The Booke of Hunting*, p. 188.

[a] The author last quoted gives the following reasons for preferring coursing to all other kinds of hunting: 'I might well mainteine that of all chases, the hare maketh greatest pastime and pleasure, and sheweth most cunning in hunting, and is meetest for gentlemen of all other huntings, for that they may find them at all times, and hunt them at most seasons of the yeare, and that with small charges. And againe bicause their pastime shall be alwayes in sight, whereby they may iudge the goodnesse of their houndes without great paines or trauell. Also it is great pleasure to beholde the subtiltie of the little poore beaste, and what shift she can make for hir selfe.'—*The Booke of Hunting*, p. 162, ed. 1575.

[b] Harrison speaks rather contemptuously of hare and stag hunting, 'all which,' he says, ' (notwithstanding our custom,) are pastimes more meet for ladies and gentlewomen to exercise (whatsoeuer Franciscus Patritius saith to the contrarie in his institution of a prince) than for men of courage to follow, whose hunting should practise their armes in tasting of their manhood, and dealing with such beasts as eftsoones will turne againe and offer them the hardest, rather than their horsses feet which manie times may carrie them with dishonour from the field.'—P. 226. Queen Elizabeth, it is well known, set an example to the ladies of her day. Thus Mr. Rowland Whyte, writing on Sept. 1, 1600, says: 'The Court is now given to hunting and sports. Upon Thursday her Majesty dines and hunts at Hanworth Parke; upon Tuesday she dines at Mr. Drake's, and this day she huntes in the new lodge in the forest.' Under date Sept. 12 he writes: 'Her Majesty is very well and excellently disposed to hunting, for every second day she is on horseback, and continues the sport long: it is thought she will remayne in Oatlands till fowle weather drives her away.'—Nichols' *Progresses of Q. Eliz.* vol. iii. p. 513. And in the account of Her Majesty's Progress in 1591, we are told that 'Hir Grace rode to Cowdrey to dinner, and aboute sixe of the clocke in the evening, from a turret sawe sixteen buckes (all having fayre lawe) pulled downe with greyhoundes, in a laund.' —*Ubi supra*, p. 91. Leland tells us that on the 27th July, 1503, the Queen of Scotland arrived at Alnwick, and 'two mylle from the sayd place the said Erle (of

Kylling of dere with bowes or grehundes serueth well for the potte, (as is the commune saynge,) and therfore it muste of necessitie be some tyme used.[a] But it contayneth therin no commendable solace or exercise, in comparison to the other fourme of hunting, if it be diligently perceiued.[b]

As for haukyng, I can finde no notable remembrance that it was used of auncient tyme amonge noble princes.[c] I call

Northumberland) cam and mett hyr, well accompayned, and brought hyr thorough hys Park, wher she kylde a Buk with her bow.'—*Collectanea*, vol. iv. p. 278.

[a] 'Though hunting had ceased to be a necessary means of procuring food, it was a very convenient resource, on which the wholesomeness and comfort, as wel as the luxury of the table depended. Before the natural pastures were improved, and new kinds of fodder for cattle discovered, it was impossible to maintain the summer stock during the cold season. Hence a portion of it was regularly slaughtered and salted for winter provisions. We may suppose, that when no alternative was offered but these salted meats, even the leanest venison was devoured with relish.'—*Hist. of the Middle Ages*, vol. iii. p. 312, 12th ed. James I. called it 'a theivish forme of hunting to shoote with gunnes and bowes.'—*Basilikon Doron*.

[b] This species of sport was therefore adapted for ladies. When Queen Elizabeth was at Cowdray in Sussex, in 1591, we are told: 'At 8 of the clock in the morning her Highness took horse with all her traine, and rode into the parke, where was a delicate bowre prepared, under the which were her Highness's musicians placed, and a crossbowe by a nymph with a sweet song delivered to her hands, to shoote at the deere (about some thirtie in number) put into a paddock, of which number she killed three or four, and the Countess of Kildare one.'—Nichols' *Progresses*, vol. iii. p. 91. So Surflet says: 'The hunting of fower-footed beasts, as the stag; the wild bore, the roebucke, and the hare is performed principally with dogs, horses, and strength of bodie, sometimes with ropes and nets, and sometimes with toiles; but these two sorts of taking of beasts are more fit for holidaie men, milke sops, and cowards then for men of valour, which delight more in the taking of such beasts in respect of the exercise of their bodie and pleasure, then for the filling of the bellie.'—*The Countrie Farme*, p. 837, ed. 1600.

[c] Warton says, 'Hawking is often mentioned in the capitularies of the eighth and ninth centuries. The *grand fauconnier* of France was an officer of great eminence. His salary was four thousand florins; he was attended by a retinue of fifty gentlemen and fifty assistant falconers, and allowed to keep three hundred hawks. He licensed every vender of falcons in France, and received a tribute for every bird that was sold in that kingdom, even within the verge of the court. The king of France never rode out on any occasion without this officer.'—*Hist. of English Poetry*, vol. ii. p. 406, note. 'In Doomsday Book, a *hawk's airy* is returned among the most valuable articles of property, which proves the high estimation these birds were held in at the commencement of the Norman government; and

auncient tyme before a thousande yeres passed, sens whiche tyme vertue and noblenesse hath rather decayed than increased. Nor I coulde neuer knowe who founde firste that disporte.[a]

Plinius makethe mention, in his viii boke of the historie of nature,[b] that in the partes of grece, called Thracia, men and

probably some establishment like that above mentioned was made for the royal falconer in England.'—Strutt's *Sports and Pastimes*, p. 22.

[a] It is interesting to observe that Sir Thomas Elyot's opinion, that this sport was a modern institution, is quite confirmed, after the lapse of three-centuries, by the careful researches of the most learned of modern historians. 'The favourite diversions of the middle ages, in the intervals of war, were those of hunting and hawking. The former must in all countries be a source of pleasure; but it seems to have been enjoyed in moderation by the Greeks and the Romans. With the northern invaders, however, it was rather a predominant appetite than an amusement; it was their pride and their ornament, the theme of their songs, the object of their laws, and the business of their lives. Falconry, *unknown as a diversion to the ancients*, became from the fourth century an equally delightful occupation. From the Salic and other barbarous codes of the fifth century to the close of the period under our review, every age would furnish testimony to the ruling passion for these two species of chase, or, as they were sometimes called, the mysteries of woods and rivers. A knight seldom stirred from his house without a falcon on his wrist, or a greyhound that followed him. Thus are Harold and his attendants represented in the famous tapestry of Bayeux. And in the monuments of those who died anywhere but on the field of battle it is usual to find the greyhound lying at their feet or the bird upon their wrists. Nor are the tombs of ladies without their falcon; for this diversion, being of less danger and fatigue than the chase, was shared by the delicate sex.'—*Hist. of the Middle Ages*, vol. iii. p. 310, 12th. ed. Laurentius Valla was of the same opinion as the author. In his dialogue with Antonius Raudensis occurs the following passage: 'R. Nola est sonalium accipitrum. L. Si nola nomen vetus est, non potest esse id, quod accipitres nunc ferunt, cum veteres ne venaticas quidem aves mansuefecissent, et ad prædam instituissent, ut nos facimus, nedum tintinnabulis ornarent.'—*Opera*, p. 433, ed. 1543. Peacham says, 'Hawking was a sport utterly unknowne to the ancients, as Blondinus and P. Jovius, in the second booke of his Historie, where he entreateth of the Muscouitish affaires, witnesseth, but was inuented and first practised by Fredericke Barbarossa, when he besieged Rome; yet it appeareth by Firmicus that it was knowne twelve hundred yeares since, where he speaketh of falconers and teachers of other birds; and, indeed, beyond him I thinke it can no where be found that Falconrie was knowne.'—*Compleat Gentleman*, p. 183, ed. 1622.

[b] The passage referred to occurs not in the eighth but in the tenth book of Pliny's *Natural History*. 'In Thraciæ parte super Amphipolim, homines atque accipitres societate quâdam aucupantur. Hi ex sylvis et arundinetis excitant aves:

haukes, as it were by a confederacie, toke byrdes to gether in this wyse. The men sprange the birdes out of the busshes, and the haukes, sorynge ouer them, bete them downe, so that the men mought easily take them. And than dyd the men departe equally the praye with the faukons, whiche beinge well serued, eftsones, and of a custome, repayred to suche places, where, beinge a lofte, they perceued men to that purpose assembled. By which rehersall of Plinius we may coniecte, that from Thracia came this disporte of hauking.* And I

---

illi supervolantes deprimunt. Rursus captas aucupes dividunt cum iis. Traditum est missas in sublime sibi excipere eos, et, cum tempus sit capturæ, clangore ac volatûs genere invitare ad occasionem.'—*Nat. Hist.* lib. x. cap. 10. It may be observed that Pliny himself seems to have copied Aristotle, who says: Ἐν δὲ Θρᾴκῃ τῇ καλουμένῃ ποτὲ Κεδρειπόλει ἐν τῷ ἕλει θηρεύουσιν οἱ ἄνθρωποι τὰ ὀρνίθια κοινῇ μετὰ τῶν ἱεράκων· οἱ μὲν γὰρ ἔχοντες ξύλα σοβοῦσι τόν κάλαμον καὶ τὴν ὕλην, ἵνα πέτωνται τὰ ὀρνίθια, οἱ δ᾽ ἱέρακες ἄνωθεν ὑπερφαινόμενοι καταδιώκουσιν· ταῦτα δὲ φοβούμενα κάτω πέταται πάλιν πρὸς τὴν γῆν· οἱ δ᾽ ἄνθρωποι τύπτοντες τοῖς ξύλοις λαμβάνουσι, καὶ τῆς θήρας μεταδιδόασιν αὐτοῖς· ῥίπτουσι γὰρ τῶν ὀρνίθων, οἱ δ᾽ ὑπολαμβάνουσιν.—*De Animal. Hist.* lib. ix. cap. 36. Ælian, who, as Professor Beckmann says, 'seldom relates anything without some alteration or addition,' also gives an account of this method of fowling, but says nets were used as well. Ἀκούω δὲ ὅτι ἐν τῇ Θρᾴκῃ καὶ ἀνθρώποις εἰσὶ σύνθηροι ἐν ταῖς ἑλείοις ἄγραις· καὶ ὁ τρόπος. Οἱ μὲν ἄνθρωποι τὰ δίκτυα ἁπλώσαντες ἡσυχάζουσιν, οἱ δὲ ἱέρακες ὑπερπετόμενοι καὶ φοβοῦσι τοὺς ὄρνις καὶ συνωθοῦσιν εἰς τὰς τῶν δικτύων περιβολάς. Τῶν οὖν ᾑρημένων οἱ Θρᾷκες μέρος ἀποκρίνουσι καὶ ἐκείνοις, καὶ ἔχουσιν αὐτοὺς πιστούς· μὴ δράσαντες δὲ τοῦτο ἑαυτοὺς τῶν συμμάχων ἐστέρησαν.—*De Nat. Animal.* lib. ii. cap. 42.

* Ælian, however, on the authority of Ctesias, says that hares and foxes were hunted in India by means of falcons. Τοὺς λαγὼς καὶ τὰς ἀλώπεκας θηρῶσιν οἱ Ἰνδοὶ τὸν τρόπον τοῦτον. Κυνῶν εἰς τὴν ἄγραν οὐ δέονται, ἀλλὰ νεοττοὺς συλλαβόντες ἀετῶν καὶ κοράκων καὶ ἰκτίνων προσέτι, τρέφουσι, καὶ ἐκπαιδεύουσι τὴν θήραν. Καὶ ἔστι τὸ μάθημα· πρᾴῳ λαγῷ καὶ ἀλώπεκι τιθασῷ κρέας προσαρτῶσι, καὶ μεθιᾶσι θεῖν, καὶ τοὺς ὄρνιθας αὐτοῖς κατὰ πόδας ἐπιπέμψαντες, τὸ κρέας ἀφελέσθαι συγχωροῦσιν· Οἱ δὲ ἀνὰ κράτος διώκουσι, καὶ ἑλόντες ἢ τὸν ἢ τήν, ἔχουσιν ὑπὲρ τοῦ καταλαβεῖν ἆθλον τὸ κρέας καὶ τοῦτο μὲν αὐτοῖς δέλεαρ ἐστι καὶ μάλα ἐφολκόν. Οὐκοῦν ὅταν ἀκριβώσωσι τὴν σοφίαν τὴν θηρατικήν, ἐπὶ τοὺς ὀρείους λαγὼς μεθιᾶσιν αὐτοὺς καὶ ἐπὶ τὰς ἀλώπεκας τὰς ἀγρίας. Οἱ δὲ ἐλπίδι τοῦ δείπνου τοῦ συνήθους, ὅταν τι τούτων φανῇ, μεταθέουσι καὶ αἱροῦσιν ὤκιστα, καὶ τοῖς δεσπόταις ἀποφέρουσιν, ὡς λέγει Κτησίας. Καὶ ὅτι ὑπὲρ τοῦ τέως προσηρτημένου κρέως αὐτοῖς τὰ σπλάγχνα τῶν ᾑρημένων τὸ δεῖπνόν ἐστιν, ἐκεῖθεν καὶ τοῦτο ἴσμεν.—*De Nat. Animal.* lib. iv. cap. 26. 'It seems, therefore, that the Greeks received from India and Thrace the first information respecting the method of fowling with birds of prey; but it does not appear

doubt nat but many other, as wel as I, haue sene a semblable experience of wilde hobies,[a] whiche, in some countrayes that be champaine, wyll sore and lie a lofte, houeringe ouer larkes and quailes, and kepe them downe on the grounde, whiles they whiche awayte on the praye do take them. But in what wise, or where so euer, the beginninge of hauking was, suerly it is a right delectable solace,[b] thoughe therof com-

that this practice was introduced among them at a very early period. In Italy, however, it must have been very common, for Martial and Apuleius speak of it as a thing everywhere known. The former calls a hawk a fowler's servant, and the latter makes use of a kind of pun on the word *accipiter*, which signified also a species of fish. It cannot, indeed, be said that this art was ever forgotten, but, like other inventions, though at first much admired, it was afterwards neglected, so that it remained a long time without improvement. It is, however, certain that it was at length brought to the utmost degree of perfection. It is mentioned in the Roman laws, and in writers of the fourth and fifth centuries.'—Beckmann's *History of Inventions*, vol. i. p. 201, ed. 1846.

[a] 'The hobbie is the least of all haukes, in respect of bodie, except the merlin, and is likewise for the lure and not for the fist, being of the number of those that sore aloft, as the faulcon, the lanier, and the sacre. This birde is sufficiently knowne euerie where, for there is not any countrie where the hobbies do not follow the hunters, inasmuch as it is the proper worke of the hobbie to make her praie of the little birdes as they flie, as by name, the larke; this is his speciall propertie, that hauing founde the hunters in the fielde, going to hunt the hare or the partridge, he keepeth them companie, still flying ouer their heades, hoping to meete with some one little birde or other which the dogs shall put up; but for the most part these little birds doe rather choose to become a praie unto the dogges, or else to find out some meanes to saue themselues amongst the horses, or to be taken aliue, then to commit themselues to the mercie of the hobbie, their mortall aduersarie. But, howsoeuer, the hobbie will not followe the hunters longer than a certaine time, as though he had his houres limited him: for leauing them he goeth to looke out the place of his rest amongst the woodes of high timber trees, where they keepe and pearch ordinarilie. He hath a blewe beake, yellow legs and feete, the feathers under his eies verie blacke, the top of his head betwixt blacke and a darke yellow, two white spots aboue his necke, but underneath his throat and on either side of his temples russet ones, his wings very blew, his backe, traine, and wings blacke on the upper side, his traine very much consisting of variable colours underneath by reason of red spots traced ouerthwart amongst the blacke. If you see him flying in the aire he may be perceiued to be somewhat red under his traine and betwixt his legs. The hobbie is so quicke and swift, as that he dare aduenture upon the rauen, and giue him many a drie bob in the aire.'—*The Countrie Farme*, p. 876, ed. 1600.

[b] The English translator of a French treatise, written in 1582, says: 'This skill

meth nat so moche utilitie, (concerning exercise,) as there dothe of huntinge.* But I wolde our faukons mought be satisfied with the diuision of their pray, as the faukons of Thracia were; that they neded nat to deuour and consume the hennes of this realme in suche nombre, that unneth it be shortly considred, and that faukons be brought to a more homely diete, it is right likely that, within a shorte space of yeres, our familiar pultrie shall be as scarce [b], as be nowe partriche and fesaunt.[c] I speake nat this in dispraise of the faukons,

is now a daies so highly honored, as that the great nobles of the worlde will that it should be consecrated wholie to themselues, as reseruing it for a pastime onely beseeming them ; and in this our countrie of France it is had in such price, as that the gentleman which is ignorant in this skill, and that other of hunting, is lightly prized, as though he lackt the two things which of all other (chiualrie and martiall skill excepted) are the most rare and excellent.'—*Maison Rustique*, p. 870.

* It was probably because this sport did not entail any violent exercise that ladies frequently took part in it. Thus Paulus Jovius describing the manners and customs of the English, says, 'Adservare et ardeas mos est, quibuscum hierofalcones volatu et unguibus contendant, et in stagnis passim atque fluviolis magnus anatum pictarum numerus reperitur, quæ inde adnatantium canum assultu latratuque exturbatæ, opimam jucundamque prædam falconibus præbent, neque ulla est in his exercitationibus plenior voluptas, nisi fœminæ laboris et prædæ comites accesserint.'—*Descript. Britann.* p. 16, ed. 1548.

[b] Harrison mentions the ravages committed by numerous birds of prey, which must have been more dreaded by farmers' wives than foxes are now. 'Of other rauenous birds we haue also verie great plentie, as the bustard, the kite, the ringtaile, dunkite, and such as often annoie our countrie dames by spoiling of their young breeds of chickens, duckes, and goslings, whereunto our verie rauens and crowes haue learned also the waie ; and so much are our rauens giuen to this kind of spoile that some idle and curious heads of set purpose haue manned, reclaimed, and used them in steed of hawkes, when other could not be had.'—*Description of England*, p. 227. We learn from the Northumberland Household Book, that at this period the price of chickens was 'one obol apiece,' and of good hens 'twopence apiece.'

[c] The writer above quoted declares 'that there is no nation under the sunne which hath alreadie in the time of the yere more plentie of wild foule than we, for so manie kinds as our Iland doth bring forth, and much more would haue, if those of the higher soile might be spared but one yeare or two from the greedie engins of couetous foulers, which set onlie for the pot and purse,' and he enumerates a great many, among which he specifies 'the woodcocke, partrich, and feasant ; ' and then he concludes, ' but as these serue not at all seasons, so in their seuerall turnes there is no plentie of them wanting, whereby the tables of the nobilitie and gentrie should seeme at anie time furnisht.'—*Ubi supra*, p. 222. The English translator of *La Maison*

but of them whiche kepeth them like coknayes.[a] The meane gentilmen and honest housholders, whiche care for the gentill entertainement of their frendes, do finde in their disshe that I saye trouthe, and noble men shall right shortly espie it, whan they come sodainly to their frendes house, unpuruaied for lacke of longe warning.[b]

Rustique, which was written by M. Liebault, in 1582, says: 'It is a point of great curiositie to keepe feasants, which Columella calleth hens of Numidia, but he that can do it, hath both pleasure and profit. Men of old time were woont to fat their fesant cocks and hens for feastiuall daies, or bankets and feastes onely, and not for broode, and gaue unto them the first day honied water and strong wine, to cause them to forget their naturall place; after that, of the flowre of barlie, tempered with water, of ground beanes, and of cleane harley, of whole millet, of turnip seede, and linseed boiled and dried, mixt with the flowre of barlie; and for to heate and clense their stomackes they gaue them mustard seed for fiue daies, and so fatted them up in their coupes for threescore daies. This is the thing that diuers cookes of Paris, with certaine other rich vittailers, do know very well to do; and they must (as saith Columella) giue them their meate to eate to the end they may be fat when they are used in bankets, for but few of these wilde fesant hens do giue themselues to lay, and bear the yoke of seruitude both togither.'—Pp. 112, 113. This allusion to the skill of the Parisians in preparing pheasants for the table will perhaps explain the following item in the *Privy Purse Expenses of Henry VIII.*, under date 22 Dec., 1532, 'Paid to the frenche Preste, the fesaunt breder, for to bye him a gowne and other necesarys . . . xls.' In this and other similar books of the period there are many entries of payments to persons who brought presents of pheasants and partridges to the royal larder; but we may believe our author, when he says they were a rarity at ordinary tables, for, as a celebrated ornithologist says, 'Phasiani itaque cùm quia rari sunt, tum quia sapore jucundissimi, ditissimorum mensis duntaxat nati videntur, fuerunt enim semper in supremo honoris culmine habiti.' At an earlier period these birds would appear to have been much more scarce, for Mr. Thorold Rogers, who has carefully investigated the domestic economy of the fourteenth century, says, 'I have never found any entry of the sale or purchase of hares or pheasants;' but, he adds, 'I do not doubt that they existed, as they are mentioned in chronicles and recited in deeds, but they never form part of the accounts which have come before me.'—*Agriculture and Prices*, vol. i. p. 33, ed. 1866. He says, however, that at the same period 'Partridges were plentiful enough, and were, it appears, generally captured by hawks, and occasionally in nets.'—*Ibid.* p. 65. The English probably learned in their French campaigns to appreciate these delicacies, for, according to Willoughby, 'Galli certè perdicum carnes tanti faciunt, ut si hæ defuerint, instructissimas etiam mensas et lautissimos conviviorum apparatus nihili ducant.'—*Ornithologia*, p. 120, ed. 1676.

[a] See the Glossary.

[b] All the old writers bear witness to the profuse hospitality of the time; thus

But nowe to retourne to my purpose: undoubtedly haukyng, measurably used, and for a passetyme, gyueth to a man good appetite to his souper. And at the leest waye withdraweth hym from other daliance, or disportis dishonest, and to body and soule perchance pernicious.[a]

Nowe I purpose to declare somthyng concerning daunsing,[b] wherin is merite of prayse and dispraise, as I shall expresse it in suche forme, as I trust the reder shal finde therin a rare and singuler pleasure, with also good lerning in thinges nat yet communely knowen in our vulgare.[c] Which if it be radde of

---

Harrison, who was evidently a *bon vivant*, complacently protests, 'We are not so miserable in England (a thing onelie granted unto us by the especiall grace of God and libertie of our Princes), as to dine or sup with a quarter of a hen, or to make so great a repast with a cocks combe, as they do in some other countries, but if occasion serue, the whole carcasses of manie capons, hens, pigeons, and such like do oft go to wracke, beside beefe, mutton, veale, and lambe; all whiche at euerie feast are taken for necessarie dishes amongest the communaltie of England.'—*Description of England*, p. 223.

[a] Peacham in the same way strongly recommends hunting for the same reason; 'for there is no one exercise,' he says, 'that enableth the body more for the warre than hunting, by teaching you to endure heate, cold, hunger, thirst, to rise early, watch late, lie and fare hardly.'—*The Compleat Gentleman*, p. 182. But this exercise was not considered necessary for any but noblemen and rich men, for Surflet says, 'there is no neede that a good housholder should trouble his braine with much hunting.'—*The Countrie Farme*, p. 3. James I. recommended hawking as a pastime for his son, in the cautious tone adopted by Sir T. Elyot: 'As for hawkinge, I condemn it not; but I must praise it more sparingly, because it neither resembleth the warres so neere as hunting doeth, in making a man hardie and skilfully ridden in all grounds, and is more uncertain and subject to mischances; and, which is worst of all, is there through an extreme stirrer up of the passions.'—*Basilikon Doron*, lib. iii. p. 122.

[b] Ascham, in his *Schoolmaster*, recommends the same course of exercises as Elyot. He says: 'Therefore, to ride comely, to run fair at the tilt or ring, to play at all weapons, to shoot fair in bow or surely in gun, to vault lustily, to run, to leap, to wrestle, to swim, to dance comely, to sing and play on instruments cunningly, to hawk, to hunt, to play at tennis, and all pastimes generally which be joined with labour (used in open place and on the daylight), containing either some fit exercise for war or some pleasant pastime for peace, be not only comely and decent but also very necessary for a courtly gentleman to use.'—Vol. iii. p. 139, ed. 1864.

[c] As might be expected, the art of dancing as an accomplishment was imported from France, for, as Mr. Wright says, 'We know little of the Anglo-Saxon mode

hym that hath good opportunitie and quiete silence, I doubt nat, but he shall take therby suche commoditie, as he loked nat to haue founden in that exercise, whiche of the more parte of sadde men is so litle estimed.

CHAPTER XIX.

That all daunsinge is nat to be reproued.

I AM nat of that opinion that all daunsinge generallye is repugnant unto vertue: al though some persones excellently lerned, specially diuines,* so do affirme it, whiche alwaye haue

---

of dancing, but to judge by the words used to express this amusement, *hoppan* (to hop), *saltian* and *stellan* (to leap), and *tumbian* (to tumble), it must have been accompanied with violent movements.' However, very soon after the Norman invasion, 'the girls and women seem to have been passionately fond of the dance, which was their common amusement at all public festivals.'—*Domestic Manners in England during the Middle Ages*, pp. 35, 111. Under these circumstances it is not surprising to find that the earliest printed treatise on the art is a translation from the French, entitled, 'The maner of dauncynge of base daunces after the use of fraunce and other places, translated out of frenche in englysshe by Robert Coplande, 1521.' Dibdin calls this 'without doubt a very curious as well as uncommon volume,' a remark justified by the fact that no copy of this work is to be found in the British Museum. No English writer had attempted to treat the subject *ab ovo* until Sir Thomas Elyot devoted to it this and the six following chapters of *The Governour*; while the learned treatise of Meursius, *De Saltationibus Veterum*, was not published till 1618, and is only a detailed list of the dances known to the ancients, not entering at all into the history or ethics of the art. The most important of the early works on this subject is the *Orchesographie* of Thoinot Arbeau, or rather of one Jean Tabourot, who wrote under the former *nom de plume*. This book, which is now very rare, was published in 1589. In more recent times M. Burette, in his 'Mémoires pour servir à l'histoire de la danse des anciens,' printed in the 1st vol. of the *Académie des Inscriptions*, 1719, and M. de Cahusac, in *La Danse Ancienne et Moderne*, 1754, have treated the subject fully, in a critical and philosophical spirit.

* Whether Sir Thomas Elyot had any particular preachers in his mind it is of course impossible to say, but Prynne, in his *Histriomastix*, pp. 226, 227, gives a long list of writers and preachers who denounced the passion for dancing. This list includes such names as Erasmus, Ludovicus Vives, Rodolphus Gualterus, and Calvin, besides a host of less note. It is most probable, indeed, that the righteous horror

in theyr mouthes (whan they come in to the pulpet) the sayeng of the noble doctor saincte Augustine, That better it were to delue or to go to ploughe on the sonday than to daunse:[a] which moughte be spoken of that kynde of daunsinge whiche was used in the tyme of saincte Augustine,[b] whan euery thing

with which some of the clergy regarded dancing was due to the influence of Geneva; for, as Fuller tells us, dancing was held as 'a grievous crime in that church, and condemned by their last form of discipline.'—*Church Hist.* vol. v. p. 112, ed. 1845. And it is curious to note how the Puritan doctrines, which were destined to prevail during a considerable part of the next century, were already giving indications of their gathering strength. But even the church itself was not averse from indulging in the popular pastime, for Alexander Barclay tells us that—

'The prestis and clerkes to daunce haue no shame;
The frere or monke in his frocke and cowle
Must daunce in his dortor (*i.e.* dormitory), lepynge to play the fole.'
Ship of Fools, vol. i. p. 294, ed. 1874.

[a] 'Melius est enim arare quàm saltare.'—*In Psalmum* xci., *Op.* tom. viii. p. 212, ed. 1531. 'Melius enim utique totâ die foderent, quàm totâ die saltarent.'—*In Psal.* xxxii., *ibid.* p. 44. Migne's ed. tom. iv. coll. 281, 1172.

[b] All the fathers of the church condemned dancing. Thus St. Ambrose says: 'Debet igitur bene consciæ mentis esse lætitia, non inconditis comessationibus, non nuptialibus excitata symphoniis; ibi enim intuta verecundia, illecebra suspecta est, ubi comes deliciarum est extrema saltatio. Ab hâc virgines Dei procul esse desidero. Nemo enim, ut dixit quidam sæcularium'doctor, saltat sobrius nisi insanit. Quod si juxta sapientiam sæcularem, saltationis aut temulentia auctor est aut amentia, quid divinarum scripturarum cautum putamus exemplis, cum Joannes prænuntius Christi, saltatricis optione jugulatus, exemplo sit plus nocuisse saltationis illecebram quàm sacrilegi furoris amentiam?'—*De Virginibus*, lib. iii. cap. 5. Chrysostom says: "Ἔνθα γὰρ ὄρχησις ἐκεῖ διάβολος· οὐδὲ γὰρ εἰς τοῦτο ἔδωκεν ἡμῖν πόδας ὁ Θεός, ἀλλ' ἵνα εὔτακτο βαδίζωμεν· οὐχ ἵνα ἀσχημονῶμεν, οὐχ ἵνα κατὰ τὰς καμήλους πηδῶμεν (καὶ γὰρ καὶ ἐκεῖναι ἀηδεῖς ὀρχούμεναι, μήτιγε δὴ γυναῖκες), ἀλλ' ἵνα σὺν ἀγγέλοις χορεύωμεν. Εἰ γὰρ τὸ σῶμα αἰσχρὸν τοιαῦτα ἀσχημονοῦν, πολλῷ μᾶλλον ἡ ψυχή. Τοιαῦτα ὀρχοῦνται οἱ δαίμονες· τοιαῦτα ἐπιτωθάζουσιν οἱ τῶν δαιμόνων διάκονοι.— *In Matt. Homil.* xlviii. Migne's ed. tom. vii. And Augustine says: 'Melius feminæ eorum die sabbati lanam facerent, quàm toto die in mæniianis suis impudice saltarent.' —*Sermo* ix. cap. 3. Migne's ed. tom. v. col. 77. And again, 'Isti enim infelices et miseri homines, qui balationes et saltationes ante ipsas basilicas sanctorum exercere nec metuunt nec erubescunt, etsi christiani ad ecclesiam venerint, pagani de ecclesiâ revertuntur, quia ista consuetudo balandi de paganorum observatione remansit.'— *Sermo de Tempore*, 215 (Migne's ed. tom. v. Appendix, *Sermo* cclxv.) It may be observed that from this verb, *balare* or *ballare* (= *saltare*), is derived our substantive Ball, through the French *le bal*. The Greek βαλλίζειν was used in a kindred sense, which Suicer explains thus: 'βαλλίζειν proprie est jacere vel jactare. Hinc

with the empire of Rome declined from their perfection, and the olde maner of daunsinge was forgoten, and none remayned but that whiche was lasciuiouse,* and corrupted the myndes

βαλλίζειν χεῖρας et βάλλειν χεῖρας manus jactare, quod saltantes faciunt. Manus enim jactare, saltare est. Ovidius: "Et faciles jactant ad sua verba manus." '— *Thesaurus Ecclesiasticus,* sub voc. The 53rd canon of the Council of Laodicea decrees, "Ὅτι οὐ δεῖ Χριστιανοὺς εἰς γάμους ἀπερχομένους βαλλίζειν ἢ ὀρχεῖσθαι, ἀλλὰ σεμνῶς δειπνεῖν ἢ ἀριστᾶν, ὡς πρέπει Χριστιανοῖς.—Bingham's *Antiq. of Christian Ch.* vol. vi. p. 448, note, ed. 1855. And in the royal edict confirming the Third Council of Toledo we read, 'Quod ballimathiæ et turpia cantica prohibenda sunt à sanctorum solenniis.'—Crabbe, *Concilia,* tom. ii. p. 172, ed. 1551, where ballimathiæ = saltationes.

* Juvenal and Martial describe the character of the dancing which was in vogue in their day.

> 'Forsitan expectes, ut Gaditana canoro
> Incipiat prurire choro, plausuque probatæ
> Ad terram tremulo descendant clune puellæ,
> Irritamentum Veneris languentis, et acres
> Divitis urticæ.'—*Sat.* xi. 162.

> 'Nec de Gadibus improbis puellæ
> Vibrabunt sine fine prurientes
> Lascivos docili tremore lumbos.'—Martial, *Epig.* lib. v. 78.

What it became afterwards we learn from later writers. Thus Arnobius, who wrote at the close of the third century, says: 'Idcirco animas misit, ut res sancti atque augustissimi nominis symphoniacas agerent et fistulatorias hic artes, ut inflandis bucculas distenderent tibiis, cantionibus ut præirent obscœnis, numerosos iterarent scabillorum concrepationibus sonores, quibus animarum alia lasciviens multitudo incompositos corporum dissolveretur in motus, saltitaret et cantaret, orbes saltatorios verteret, et ad ultimum clunibus et coxendicibus sublevatis lumborum crispitudine fluctuaret?'—*Adv. Gentes,* lib. ii. § 42, Migne's ed. col. 881. The same writer gives us a picture of the stage dancing which found favour in his day. 'Sedent augures interpretes divinæ mentis et voluntatis, necnon et castæ virgines, perpetui nutrices et conservatrices ignis, sedet cunctus populus et senatus. Consulatibus functi patres Diis proximi, atque augustissimi reges, et quod nefarium esset auditu, gentis illa genitrix Martiæ regnatoris et populi procreatrix amans saltatur Venus, et per affectus omnes meretriciæ vilitatis impudicâ exprimitur imitatione, bacchari. Saltatur et Magna sacris compta cum infulis Mater, et contra decus ætatis illa Pessinuntia Dindymene in bubulci unius amplexu flagitiosâ fingitur appetitione gestire.'—*Ubi supra,* lib. iv. § 35, Migne's ed. We may compare with this the remarks of Saint Augustin, who says: 'Quid sunt ad hoc malum Mercurii furta, Veneris lascivia, stupra ac turpitudines cæterorum, quæ proferremus de libris, nisi quotidie cantarentur et saltarentur in theatris?'—*De Civit. Dei,* lib. vii. cap. 26, Migne's ed. tom. vii. col. 216. And Jerome says: 'Quomodo in theatralibus scenis unus atque idem histrio, nunc Her-

of them that daunsed, and prouoked sinne, as semblably some do at this day.* Also at that tyme Idolatry was nat clerely

culem robustus ostendit, nunc mollis in Venerem frangitur, nunc tremulus in Cybelem.'—*Epist.* xliii. *Ad Marcellam*, Migne's ed. tom. i. § 193. Another writer, we are told by Gibbon, 'complains with decent indignation that the streets of Rome were filled with crowds of females, who might have given children to the state, but whose only occupation was to curl and dress their hair, and "jactari volubilibus gyris, dum exprimunt innumera simulacra, quæ finxere fabulæ theatrales."'—*Decline and Fall of Rom. Empire*, vol. iv. p. 87, note.

* Amongst other contemporary writers, Ludovicus Vives, complaining of this amusement, says: 'What good dothe all that daunsynge of yonge women, holden upon men's armes that they may hop the hygher? What meaneth that shakynge unto mydnyght, and neuer wery, whiche if they were desyred to go but to the nexte churche, they were nat able, except they were caryed on horse backe or in a charette? Who wolde nat thinke them out of their wyttes? I remember that I harde upon a tyme saye, that there were certeyne men brought out of a farre countrey into our partes of the worlde, whiche whan they sawe women daunce, they rounne away wonderly afrayde, cryeng out that they thought the women were taken with an unked kynd of fransy. And to say good sothe, who wolde not reken women frantycke whan they daunce, if he had neuer sene women daunce before? And it is a worlde to se, how demurely and sadly some syt beholdyng them that daunce, and with what gesture, pase, and mouynge of the body, and with what sobre fotynge som of them daunce.'—*Instruction of a Christian Woman*, p. 47, ed. 1541. Erasmus also, in his *De Contemptu Mundi*, says: 'Postea ubi eos epularum satietas cepit, ad choreas surgitur. Cujus animus sic compositus, sic firmus, sic marmoreus, quem lascivi illi motus, agitataque in numerum brachia, citharæ cantus, voces puellares, non corrumpant, non labefactent, non emolliant? Adde quod ea sæpe carmina sunt quibus incendi jam frigidus ævo Laomedontiadis et Nestoris hernia possent. At ubi choraules (citharâ ex more tactâ) quiescendi signum dedit, rusticus habeberis, ni eam cujus lævam complexus saltasti, disuaviatus fueris. Cæteri lusus his impudentiores, atque ad meram lasciviam excogitati, à me non dicentur, utinam ab illis non agerentur.'—Cap. vii. Sebastian Brant devotes a special place to dancers in his *Ship of Fools*. Henry Cornelius Agrippa, styled by Hallam a 'meteor of philosophy,' devotes a chapter of his *De Vanitate Scientiarum* to this subject. He says: 'Itaque saltationem necesse est omnium vitiorum esse postremum, neque enim facile dictu quæ mala hic visus hauriunt et auditus quæ pariant colloquia et tactus. Saltatur inconditis gestibus, et monstroso pedum strepitu, ad molles pulsationes, ad lascivas cantilenas, ad obscœna carmina, contrectantur matronæ et puellæ impudicis manibus, et basiis, meretriciisque complexibus, et quæ abscondit natura, velavit modestia, ipsâ lasciviâ tunc sæpe nudantur, ludi tegmine obducitur scelus. Exercitium profecto non à cælis exortum, sed à malis dæmonibus excogitatum in injuriam Divinitatis.'—Cap. xviii. ed. 1531. This list of witnesses to the character of the dancing which prevailed in the 16th century may be fitly closed with the evidence of one whose sympathies would naturally be enlisted on

extincte, but diuers fragmentes therof remained in euery region.ᵃ And perchance solempne daunsis, whiche were celebrate unto the paynyms false goddes, were yet continued;ᵇ for as moche as the pure religion of Christe was nat in all places consolidate,ᶜ and the pastors and curates dyd wynke at suche

the side of youth and gaiety, and whose evidence is therefore doubly valuable—the poet Petrarch. He says: 'Veneris præludium illud quidem; sono stupidas ac misellas circumducere, atque urgere, et stringere, ac specie urbanitatis atterere, liberæ ibi manus, liberi oculi, liberæ volant voces, pedum strepitus, et multorum cantus dissoni et tubarum clangor, concursatio, et pulvis et quæ sæpe ludis additur, hostis pudicitiæ et amica scelerum, nox ipsa. Hæc sunt quæ timorem ac pudorem pellunt, hi sunt libidinum stimuli, hæc laxamenta licentiæ. Et hæc est, ni me falli facilem putes, illa delectatio, quam simpliciter et velut innocuè, chorearum appellatione profitemini et, ludi tegmine, crimen obnubitis. Tolle radicitus hanc speciem ingeniosam, atque improbam: tolle libidinem, sustuleris et choream.'—*De remed. utriusque fortunæ*, lib. i. dial. 24.

ᵃ Theodosius died A.D. 395, St. Augustin not till A.D. 430; and, according to Gibbon, 'so rapid, yet so gentle, was the fall of Paganism, that only twenty-eight years after the death of Theodosius the faint and minute vestiges were no longer visible to the eye of the legislator.'—*Decline and Fall of Rom. Empire*, vol. iii. p. 426. But Dean Milman has pointed out that Paganism maintained its ground for a considerable time in the rural districts, and that in the middle of the fifth century Maximus, Bishop of Turin, wrote against the heathen deities, as if their worship was still in full vigour in the neighbourhood of his city.'—*Ubi supra*, p. 422, note. 'The Pagans traced the calamities of the empire to the prevalence of Christianity, and to confute this accusation against Christianity was the design of Augustine's twenty two books, *De Civitate Dei*, addressed to Marcellus.'—Mosheim's *Eccles. Hist.* vol. i. p. 413, note, ed. 1845.

ᵇ 'After the conversion of the Imperial city, the Christians still continued, in the month of February, the annual celebration of the Lupercalia; to which they ascribed a secret and mysterious influence on the genial powers of the animal and vegetable world. The bishops of Rome were solicitous to abolish a profane custom so repugnant to the spirit of Christianity, but their zeal was not supported by the authority of the civil magistrate; the inveterate abuse subsisted *till the end of the fifth century*, and Pope Gelasius, who purified the capital from the last stain of idolatry, appeased by a formal apology the murmurs of the senate and people.' —*Decline and Fall of Rom. Empire*, vol. iv. p. 282.

ᶜ Amongst other instances of the vitality of Pagan ceremonies, M. Beugnot mentions the fact that the worship of Bacchus continued throughout the sixth century, but had assumed at this late epoch the character of mere rustic revelry and sport. 'Les fêtes de Bacchus continuèrent pendant toute la durée de ce siècle à être célébrées dans la Gaule; mais il faut reconnaître que le caractère religieux de ces fêtes avait presque totalement disparu; elles n'existaient plus que comme

recreations, fearyng that if they shulde hastily haue remeued it, and induced sodaynely the seueritie of goddis lawes, they shulde stere the people therby to a generall sedition; to the imminent daunger and subuertion of Christis hole religion, late sowen amonge them, and nat yet sufficiently rooted.[a] But the wyse and discrete doctor saincte Augustine, usinge the arte of an oratour, wherin he was right excellent, omitting all rigorous menace or terrour, dissuaded them by the moste easiste way from that maner ceremony belonging to idolatrie; preferring before it bodily occupation; therby aggrauatyng the offence to god that was in that ceremonie, sens occupation, which is necessary for mannes sustinance, and in due tymes vertuous, is nat withstanding prohibited to be used on the sondayes.[b] And yet in these wordes of this noble doctor is nat so generall dispraise to all daunsinge as some men do

une occasion fournie aux paysans de déployer, à l'époque des vendanges, leur goût pour une joie licencieuse et grossière.'—*Destruction du Paganisme*, tom. ii. p. 324.

[a] This view is quite confirmed by modern writers. M. Beugnot, for example, says: 'Quand le christianisme devint la religion dominante, ses docteurs comprirent qu'ils allaient être forcés de céder également sur la forme extérieure du culte, et qu'ils ne seraient pas assez forts pour contraindre cette multitude de païens qui embrassaient le christianisme avec une sorte d'enthousiasme irréfléchi et peu durable, à oublier un système d'actes, de cérémonies, et de fêtes, dont l'empire sur leurs idées et leurs mœurs était immense.'—*Ubi supra*, tom. ii. p. 261. The list of festivals for the whole Christian Church was swelled by the consecration of the day of *the purification of the Holy Virgin Mary*, that the people might not miss their *Lupercalia*, which they were accustomed to celebrate in the month of February, and by the day of *our Saviour's conception*, 'the *birthday of St. John*, and some others.—Mosheim, *Eccles. Hist.* vol. ii. p. 49, ed. 1845. And Schlegel points out that the Romans had been accustomed about this time (the 24th of June), to keep the feast of Vesta with kindling a new fire, amid *dances* and other sports.—*Ubi supra*, note 9. According to Gibbon, 'the most respectable bishops had persuaded themselves that the ignorant rustics would more cheerfully renounce the superstitions of Paganism, if they found some resemblance, some compensation, in the bosom of Christianity.'—*Decline and Fall of Rom. Empire*, vol. iii. p. 433.

[b] 'Observemus ergo diem dominicam, fratres, et sanctificemus illam, sicut antiquis præceptum est de sabbato, dicente Legislatore, *A vespere usque ad vesperam celebrabitis sabbata :vestra*. Videamus ne otium nostrum vanum sit, sed à vesperâ diei sabbati usque ad vesperam diei dominici, sequestrati à rurali opere et ab omni negotio, soli divino cultui vacemus.'—*Serm. de Tempore*, 251. Migne's ed. tom. v. Appendix, *Sermo* cclxxx.

suppose. And that for two causis. Firste in his comparison he preferreth nat before daunsing or ioyneth therto any viciouse exercise, but annecteth it with tillynge and diggynge of the erthe, whiche be labours incident to mannes lyuynge, and in them is contained nothynge that is vicious. Wherfore the preeminence therof aboue daunsing qualifieng the offence, they beinge done out of due tyme, that is to say, in an holy day, concludeth nat daunsinge to be at all tymes and in euery maner unlaufull or vicious, considerynge that in certayne casis of exstreme necessitie menne mought bothe ploughe and delue without doinge to god any offence.[a] Also it shall seme to them that seriousely do examine the said wordes that therin saincte Augustine doth nat prohibite daunsinge so generally as it is taken, but onely suche daunsis whiche (as I late saide) were superstitious and contained in them a spice of idolatrie,[b] or els dyd with unclene motions or countinances irritate the myndes of the dauncers to venereall lustes, wherby fornication and auoutrie were daily increased.[c] Also in those daunces were enterlased dities of

[a] The Code of Justinian, although prohibiting business in the city, permitted agricultural operations to be carried on in the country, if necessary, on the Lord's day. 'Omnes judices, urbanæque plebes, et cunctarum artium officia venerabili die solis quiescant. Ruri tamen positi agrorum culturæ libere licenterque inserviant: quoniam frequenter evenit, ut non aptius alio die frumenta sulcis, aut vineæ scrobibus mandentur: ne occasione momenti pereat commoditas cœlesti provisione concessa.'—L. 3, tit. 12, *de Feriis*, leg. 3.

[b] Thus Augustine mentions the dancing at the tomb of St. Cyprian, the first African bishop who obtained the crown of martyrdom, which was evidently of this nature. 'Istum tam sanctum locum, ubi jacet tam sancti Martyris corpus, sicut meminerunt multi qui habent ætatem, locum, inquam, tam sanctum invaserat pestilentia et petulantia saltatorum. Per totam noctem cantabantur hic nefaria, et cantantibus saltabatur. Quando voluit Dominus per sanctum fratrem nostrum episcopum vestrum, ex quo hic cæperunt sanctæ vigiliæ celebrari, illa pestis aliquantulum reluctata, postea cessit diligentiæ, erubuit sapientiæ.'—*Sermo* cccxi. Migne's ed. tom. v. col. 1415.

[c] Cyril of Alexandria, speaking of the dancing of his day, says: 'Πορνικὸν δὲ τὸ ἐπιτήδευμα, καὶ βδελυρίας ἀπόδειξις τῆς ἐσχάτης. Ὅπου γὰρ ὁ τῶν ποδῶν κτύπος εὐρύθμοις ᾄσμασι συνηχεῖ, ἐκεῖ που πάντως καὶ αὐτὸς ὁ διὰ χειρῶν ἀνακτυπεῖ κρότος, και πᾶν εἶδος αἰσχρῶν ἐπιτηδευμάτων, καὶ πρόκλησις τοῖς

wanton loue ᵃ or ribaudry, with frequent remembrance of the moste vile idolis Venus and Bacchus, as it were that the daunce were to their honour and memorie, whiche most of all abhorred from Christes religion, sauerynge the auncient errour or paganysme.ᵇ I wolde to god those names were nat at this

δρῶσιν εἰς ἀκαθαρσίαν.'—*In Isaiam*, lib. i. orat. 3, Migne's ed. tom. iii. § 69. And Salvian of Marseilles, speaking of the stage in the fifth century, says : 'Talia enim sunt quæ illic fiunt, ut ea non solum dicere, sed etiam recordari aliquis sine pollutione non possit. Quæ quidem omnia tam flagitiosa sunt, ut etiam explicare ea quispiam atque eloqui, salvo pudore, non valeat. Quis enim integro verecundiæ statu dicere queat, illas rerum turpium imitationes, illas vocum ac verborum obscænitatis, illas motuum turpitudines, illas gestuum fœditates? Itaque in illis imaginibus fornicationum omnis omnino plebs animo fornicatur. Et qui forte ad spectaculum puri venerant, de theatro adulteri revertuntur.'—*De Gubernatione Dei*, lib. vi. Migne's ed. § 117. Gibbon tells us that at this time 'the vast and magnificent theatres of Rome were filled by three thousand female dancers.'

ᵃ Quintilian, describing the manners and morals of his age, says: 'Omne convivium obscœnis canticis strepit.'—*Instit. Orat.* lib. i. cap. 2, § 8. Compare Horace :

'Ludisque, et bibis impudens,
Et cantu tremulo pota Cupidinem
Lentum sollicitas.'—*Carm.* lib. iv. 13.

And Juvenal:

'Nota Bonæ secreta Deæ, cum tibia lumbos
Incitat, et cornu pariter vinoque feruntur,
Attonitæ, crinemque rotant, ululantque Priapi
Mænades.'—*Sat.* vi. 314-317.

Also Persius :

'Hic neque more probo videas neque voce serenâ
Ingentes trepidare Titos, cum carmina lumbum
Intrant, et tremulo scalpuntur ubi intima versu.'—*Sat.* i. 20.

Theodosius endeavoured to purify the Roman entertainments by getting rid of the professional singers : 'Prohibueritque lege ministeria lasciva psaltriasque commessationibus adhiberi.'—Victor, *Epit.*, cap. xlviii. § 10.

ᵇ These names were therefore most repugnant to the fathers of the Church. Tertullian says : 'Theatrum proprie sacrarium Veneris est. Hoc denique modo id genus operis in sæculo evasit. Nam sæpe censores renascentia cum maxime theatra destruebant, moribus consulentes, quorum scilicet periculum ingens de lasciviâ providebant, ut jam hinc ethnicis in testimonium cedat sententia ipsorum nobiscum faciens, et nobis in exaggerationem disciplinæ etiam humanæ prærogativa. Itaque Pompeius Magnus solo theatro suo minor, cum illam arcem omnium turpitudinem extruxisset, veritus quandoque memoriæ suæ censoriam animadversionem, Veneris ædem superposuit, et ad dedicationem edicto populum

day used in balades[a] and ditties in the courtes of princes and noble men, where many good wittes be corrupted with semblable fantasies, whiche in better wise employed mought haue bene more necessarye to the publike weale and their princes honour.[b] But nowe wyll I leue this seriouse mater to diuines

vocans, non theatrum, sed Veneris templum nuncupavit. Cui subjecimus, inquit, gradus spectaculorum, ita damnatum et damnandum opus templi titulo prætexit, et disciplinam superstitione delusit. Sed Veneri et Libero convenit. Duo ista dæmonia conspirata et conjurata inter se sunt, ebrietatis et libidinis. Itaque theatrum Veneris, Liberi quoque domus est. Nam et alios ludos scenicos Liberalia proprie vocabant, præterquam Libero devotos, quod sunt Dionysia penes Græcos, etiam à Libero institutos. Et est plane in artibus quoque scenicis Liberi et Veneris patrocinium. Quæ privata et propria sunt scenæ de gestu et flexu corporis mollitiæ Veneris et Liberi immolant : illi per sexum, illi per luxum, dissolutis quæ vero voce, et modis, et organis, et lyris transiguntur. Appollines, et Musas, et Minervas, et Mercurios mancipes habent.'—*De Spectaculis*, cap. 10.

[a] Gascoigne, in his *Notes of Instruction concerning the making of Verse or Rhyme in English*, which was published in 1575, says this 'propre name was (I thinke) deriued of this worde in Italian *Ballare*, whiche signifieth to daunce. And indeede those kinds of rimes serue beste for daunces or light matters.'—p. 10.

[b] Puttenham tells us that 'the Lord Nicholas Vaux, a noble gentleman and much delighted in vulgar making, and a man otherwise of no great learning, but hauing herein a maruelous facillitie, made a dittie representing the battayle and assault of Cupide excellently well.'—*Arte of English Poesie*, lib. iii. p. 200. From the same source we learn that in this reign there 'sprong up a new company of courtly makers, of whom Sir Thomas Wyat th' elder and Henry Earle of Surrey were the two chieftaines, who hauing trauailed into Italie, and there tasted the swete and stately measures and stile of the Italian poesie, as nouices newly crept out of the schooles of Dante, Arioste, and Petrarch, they greatly pollished our rude and homely maner of vulgar Poesie, from that it had been before, and for that cause may iustly be sayd the first reformers of our English meeter and stile.' —*Ubi supra*, lib. i. chap. 31. Warton remarks that 'So many of the nobility, and principal persons about the court, writing sonnets in the Italian style, is a circumstance which must have greatly contributed to circulate this mode of composition, and to encourage the study of the Italian poets,' and adds to the list of courtiers already mentioned the name of Edmund Lord Sheffield, created a baron by King Edward the Sixth, and said by Bale to have written sonnets in the Italian manner.—*Hist. of Engl. Poetry*, vol. iii. p. 63, ed. 1840. The author's strictures in the text may possibly refer to the unfortunate Earl of Surrey, though he was not beheaded till 1547, and at the time of the publication of *The Governour* must have been at the zenith of his fame; but the example set by this distinguished man of fashion was doubtless followed at a great distance by a whole host of courtiers of lesser note, to whom Sir Thomas Elyot's remarks would more appropriately apply.

to persuade or dissuade herein accordinge to their offices.[a] And sens in myn opinion saint Augustine that blessed clerke reproueth nat so generally all daunsinge, but that I may laufully reherce some kynde therof whiche may be necessary and also commendable, takyng it for an exercise,[b] I shall nowe procede to speake of the firste begynnynge therof, and in howe great estimation it was had in diuers regions.

[a] In the latter half of the 16th century dancing was severely animadverted upon by the clergy, perhaps the best known work being that of John Northbrooke, a preacher at Bristol, who in 1578 published *A treatise wherein Dicing, Dauncing, Vaine Playes or Enterluds, with other idle pastimes, &c., commonly used on the Sabbath Day, are reproved by the Authoritie of the Word of God and Auncient Writers*. This was quickly followed by the *Schoole of Abuse*, first published in 1579, by Stephen Gosson, Rector of Great Wigborough, in Essex. The sermons of the period were also directed against dancing as an accompaniment of wakes and May games. In France the Protestant clergy inveighed strongly against the practice, and the subject is elaborately handled in a work entitled *Traité des Danses auquel est amplement resolue la question à sauoir s'il est permis aux Chrestiens de danser*, published in 1580. There is a very curious chapter on this head in the English translation of Perrin's *History of the Waldenses*, but modern investigations, particularly those of Mr. Bradshaw, the University librarian, at Cambridge, have gone far to depreciate this history as a work of authority, and the articles of Discipline especially (in which the chapter against dancing appears), are said to be much garbled by Perrin.

[b] The old French writer, Thoinot Arbeau, makes the following remarks upon the practice of this art : ' La dance ou saltation est un art plaisant et proffitable, qui rend et conserue la santé, convenable aux ieusnes, aggreable aux vieux, et bien seant a tous, pourueu qu'on en use modestement, en temps et lieu, sans affectation vicieuse ; je dis en temps et lieu, parce qu'elle apporteroit mespris a celluy qui, comme un pillier de salle, y seroit trop assidu.'—*Orchesographie*, p. 5, ed. 1588. Galen notices the advantages of dancing as an exercise: 'Veluti statim saltantium prævegeti motus, in quibus nimirum quàm maximè saliunt, ac celerrimè circumacti vertuntur, et genu prius posito mox emicant, et crura tum attrahunt, tum maximè divaricant, et summatim in quibus ocyssimè moventur, gracile, musculosum, durum, compactum, prætereà vegetum, corpus reddunt.'—*De San. tuend.* lib. ii. fo. 33, b.

CHAPTER XX.

Of the firste begynnyng of daunsing and the olde estimation therof.

THERE be sondry opinions of the originall begynnyng of daunsing.[a] The poetes do faine that whan Saturne, whiche deuoured diuers his children, and semblably wolde haue done with Jupiter, Rhea the mother of Jupiter deuised that *Curetes*,[b] (whiche were men of armes in that countray) shuld daunse in armour,[c] plainge with their swordes and sheldes, in suche fourme as by that newe and pleasant deuise they shulde assuage the melancoly of Saturne, and in the meane tyme Jupiter was conuaied in to *Phrigia*, where Saturne also pursuyng hym, Rhea semblably taught the people there called *Coribantes*,[d] to daunse in a nother fourme, wherwith Saturne was eftsones demulced and

Curetes.

Chori- bantes.

---

[a] Lucian for example says : Καὶ πρῶτόν γε ἐκεῖνο πάνυ ἠγνοηκέναι μοι δοκεῖς, ὡς οὐ νεώτερον τὸ τῆς ὀρχήσεως ἐπιτήδευμα τοῦτό ἐστιν οὐδὲ χθὲς καὶ πρῴην ἀρξάμενον, οἷον κατὰ τοὺς προπάτορας ἡμῶν ἢ τοὺς ἐκείνων, ἀλλ' οἵ γε τἀληθέστατα ὀρχήσεως περὶ γενεαλογοῦντες ἅμα τῇ πρώτῃ γενέσει τῶν ὅλων φαῖεν ἄν σοι καὶ ὄρχησιν ἀναφῦναι τῷ ἀρχαίῳ ἐκείνῳ Ἔρωτι συναναφανεῖσαν· ἡ γοῦν χορεία τῶν ἀστέρων καὶ ἡ πρὸς τοὺς ἀπλανεῖς τῶν πλανήτων συμπλοκὴ καὶ εὔρυθμος αὐτῶν κοινωνία καὶ εὔτακτος ἁρμονία τῆς πρωτογόνου ὀρχήσεως δείγματά ἐστι. Κατ' ὀλίγον δὲ αὐξανομένη καὶ τῆς πρὸς τὸ βέλτιον ἀεὶ προσθήκης τυγχάνουσα, νῦν ἔοικεν ἐς τὸ ἀκρότατον ἀποτετελέσθαι καὶ γεγενῆσθαι ποικίλον τι καὶ παναρμόνιον καὶ πολύμουσον ἀγαθόν.—*De Saltatione*, § 7.

[b] Τούτους δ' ὠνόμαζον Κουρῆτας, νέους τινὰς ἐνόπλιον κίνησιν μετ' ὀρχήσεως ἀποδιδόντας, προστησάμενοι μῦθον τὸν περὶ τῆς τοῦ Διὸς γενέσεως, ἐν ᾧ τὸν μὲν Κρόνον εἰσάγουσιν εἰθισμένον καταπίνειν τὰ τέκνα ἀπὸ τῆς γενέσεως εὐθύς, τὴν δὲ Ῥέαν πειρωμένην ἐπικρύπτεσθαι τὰς ὠδῖνας καὶ τὸ γεννηθὲν βρέφος ἐκποδὼν ποιεῖν καὶ περισώζειν εἰς δύναμιν, πρὸς δὲ τοῦτο συνεργοὺς λαβεῖν τοὺς Κουρῆτας, οἳ μετὰ τυμπάνων καὶ τοιούτων ἄλλων ψόφων καὶ ἐνοπλίου χορείας καὶ θορύβου περιέποντες τὴν θεὸν ἐκπλήξειν ἔμελλον τὸν Κρόνον καὶ λήσειν ὑποσπάσαντες αὐτοῦ τὸν παῖδα.—*Strabo*, lib. x. cap. 3, § 11.

[c] Ἐνόπλιος δὲ αὐτῶν ἡ ὄρχησις ἦν, τὰ ξίφη μεταξὺ κροτούντων πρὸς τὰς ἀσπίδας καὶ πηδώντων ἔνθεόν τι καὶ πολεμικόν.—Lucian, *De Saltat.* § 8.

[d] Πιθανὸν δέ φησιν ὁ Σκήψιος, Κουρῆτας μὲν καὶ Κορύβαντας εἶναι τοὺς αὐτούς, οἳ περὶ τὰς τῆς μητρὸς τῶν θεῶν ἁγιστείας πρὸς ἐνόπλιον ὄρχησιν ᾔθεοι καὶ κόροι τυγχάνουσι παρειλημμένοι. Καὶ Κορύβαντας δὲ ἀπὸ τοῦ κορύπτοντας βαίνειν ὀρχηστικῶς, οὓς καὶ βητάρμονας λέγει ὁ ποιητής· δεῦτ' ἄγε Φαιήκων βητάρμονες, ὅσσοι ἄριστοι. τῶν δὲ Κορυβάντων ὀρχηστικῶν καὶ ἐνθουσιαστικῶν ὄντων, καὶ τοὺς μανικῶς κινουμένους

appaysed, whiche fable hath a resemblaunce to the historie of the bible in the first boke of kyngs, where it is remembred that Saule (whom god chase from a keper of asses to be kynge of iewes, who in stature excelled and was aboue all other men by the heed), declining from the lawes and preceptes of god, was possessed of an iuell spirite whiche often tymes turmented and vexed him, and other remedie founde he none but that Dauid, whiche after hym was kynge, beinge at that tyme a propre childe and playinge swetelye on a harpe, with his pleasant and perfect harmonie reduced his minde in to his pristinate estate, and durynge the tyme that he played the spirite cessed to vexe him, which I suppose hapned nat only of the efficacie of musike (all be it therin is moche power, as well in repressing as exciting naturall affectes [a]), but also of the vertue ingenerate in the childe Dauid that played, whom

κορυβαντιᾷν φαμεν.—*Strabo*, lib. x. cap. 3, § 21. Euripides makes mention of both in the *Bacchæ*.

 ᾿Ω θαλάμευμα Κουρή-
 των, ζάθεοί τε Κρῆτες
 Διογενέτορες ἔναυλοι,
 ἔνθα τρικόρυθες ἄντροις
 βυρσότονον κύκλωμα τόδε
 μοι Κορύβαντες εὗρον,
 ἀνὰ δὲ βάκχια συντόνῳ
 κέρασαν ἡδυβόᾳ Φρυγίων
 αὐλῶν πνεύματι, ματρός τε 'Ρέας
 εἰς χέρα θῆκαν, κτύπον εὐάσμασι Βακχᾶν.—v. 120-129.

Lucian says: Πρῶτον δέ φασι 'Ρέαν ἡσθεῖσαν τῇ τέχνῃ ἐν Φρυγίᾳ μὲν τοὺς Κορύβαντας, ἐν Κρήτῃ δὲ τοὺς Κουρῆτας ὀρχεῖσθαι κελεῦσαι, καὶ οὐ τὰ μέτρια ὤνατο τῆς τέχνης αὐτῶν, οἵ γε περιορχούμενοι διεσώσαντο αὐτῇ τὸν Δια, ὥστε καὶ σῶστρα εἰκότως ἂν ὁ Ζεὺς ὀφείλειν ὁμολογοίη αὐτοῖς ἐκφυγὼν διὰ τὴν ἐκείνων ὄρχησιν τοὺς πατρῴους ὀδόντας.—*De Saltatione*, § 8.

[a] Music seems to have been somewhat neglected a few years later, for Ascham says in his *Toxophilus*, 'Of them that come daily to the University where one hath learned to sing six hath not.' And Puttenham complains in his *Arte of Poesie* 'that it is hard to find in these dayes of noblemen or gentlemen any excellent musitian.'—P. 16. Yet, according to Peacham, Henry the Eighth 'could not only sing his part sure, but of himself composed a service of four, five, and six parts, as Erasmus in a certain epistle testifieth of his own knowledge.'—*Compleat Gentleman*, p. 99, ed. 1622.

god also had predestinate to be a great kyng, and a great prophete. And for the soueraigne gyftes of grace and of nature, that he was endowed with, All mightye god sayde of him that he had founde a man after his harte and pleasure. But nowe to retourne to speake of daunsinge.

Some interpretours of poets do imagine that Proteus, who is supposed to haue turned him selfe in to sondry figures, as some tyme to shewe him selfe like a serpent, some tyme like a lyon, other whiles like water, a nother time like the flame of fire, signifieth to be none other, but a deliuer and crafty daunser, which in his daunse coulde imagine the inflexions of the serpente, the softe and delectable flowynge of the water, the swiftnes and mounting of the fire, the fierce rage of the lyon, the violence and furie of the libarde ;[a] which exposition is nat to be dispraised, sens it discordeth nat from reason. But one opinion there is whiche I wyll reherce, more for the mery fantasie that therin is contained, than for any faithe or credite that is to be giuen therto.[b]

Proteus.

---

[a] Δοκεῖ γάρ μοι ὁ παλαιὸς μῦθος καὶ Πρωτέα τὸν Αἰγύπτιον οὐκ ἄλλο τι ἢ ὀρχηστήν τινα γενέσθαι λέγειν, μιμητικὸν ἄθρωπον καὶ πρὸς πάντα σχηματίζεσθαι καὶ μεταβάλλεσθαι δυνάμενον, ὡς καὶ ὕδατος ὑγρότητα μιμεῖσθαι καὶ πυρὸς ὀξύτητα ἐν τῇ τῆς κινήσεως σφοδρότητι, καὶ λέοντος ἀγριότητα καὶ παρδάλεως θυμὸν καὶ δένδρου δόνημα, καὶ ὅλως ὅτι καὶ θελήσειεν.—Lucian, *de Saltatione*, § 19. Scaliger says that the dance called μορφασμὸς was so styled, 'cum plurimis subinde figuris Protei mutationes referebat.'—*Poetices*, lib. i. cap. 18, ed. 1607.

[b] The story which follows is evidently a translation of the passage in Ælian given in the next note. But, it may be asked, how came the name of Hiero to be introduced in connexion with it? Ælian merely says Τρύζος τις τύραννος. The Editor has endeavoured to find some explanation of a mistake, which it will be seen has been perpetuated through successive centuries, and suggests the following as the most probable. Scheffer in a note on this passage in the edition of 1685, says : 'Quis hic fuerit non invenio, dubitoque an bene scriptum sit hoc nomen,' but in another note he unconsciously supplies a link in the chain of circumstantial evidence by which alone we can decide the reason for the introduction of the name of Hiero. As a commentary upon the words καὶ ἀλλήλοις ἔνευον, κ.τ.λ., Scheffer gives a reference to the epistle of Saint Jerome, *de Vitando Suspecto Contubernio* (*Epistola*, cxvii. tom. i. § 787, Migne's edition), in which occurs a somewhat similar expression. 'Loquetur nutibus, et quidquid metuit dicere, significabit affectibus.' Now is it not possible that the discovery of this parallel passage in S. Jerome may have been made by some much earlier commentator, who would write

Hiero the kynge of Sicile.

Ouer Syracusis (a great and auncient citie in Sicile) there raigned a cruel tirant called Hiero,* whiche by horrible tyrannies and oppressions brought him selfe in to the indignation and hatered of all his people, whiche he

in the margin of his MS. the word Hieron as an abbreviation for Hieronymus, with the appropriate reference? Subsequent transcribers may then have omitted the reference and taken Hieron for a gloss, and so the word Hieron or Hiero might eventually have been regarded as the name of the tyrant of whom the story is told. The Editor ventures to suggest another but less probable reason why Sir Thomas Elyot should adopt the name of Hiero. In the edition of Ælian, printed at Venice in 1550, and therefore possibly in some of the earlier editions, after the words 'Æliani de variâ historiâ,' the title-page has 'adjuncta est et Ode Pindari quæ inscribitur in Hieronem Celete.' Thus the name Hiero may have been unconsciously associated in the mind of the author (especially if writing from memory, without the book before him) with the story given by Ælian. It is curious, however, to observe how subsequent writers have fallen into the same trap. Thus Menestrier, in his work entitled *Des Ballets anciens et modernes*, published in 1682, says at p. 41: ' *Quelques uns ont crû* que Hieron, un des tyrans de Syracuse, donna occasion à ces dances figurées,' and then he gives in a few words the same story as that referred to by Sir Thomas Elyot. But M. Bonnet, who copied largely from Menestrier, has fallen into a still more ludicrous error. At p. 28 of his *Histoire générale de la Danse*, published in 1724, he says, '*Eunapius Historien a crû, aussi bien que quelques autres*, que Hieron, Roi de Syracuse et de Sicile, dans la lxxv. Olympiade, donna occasion aux danses figurées,' &c. Now the way in which Bonnet fell into such a grievous mistake was evidently this. Menestrier, in a paragraph preceding the reference to Hiero, had said, 'Ainsi si Eunapius a dit agréablement que l'âme dansoit dans les yeux, parce qu'il est peu de passions qui ne s'expriment par leurs mouvemens et qui ne deviennent sensibles,' &c., and gave a marginal reference to Eunapius. (The original passage τῶν ὀφθαλμῶν ἑρμηνευόντων χορεύουσαν ἔνδον τὴν ψυχὴν περὶ τὰ δόγματα, will be found in the life of Chrysanthius by Eunapius, p. 502, ed. Boissonade, 1849). Bonnet apparently thought the marginal reference was the authority for the story about Hiero, and did not give himself the trouble to verify it, but simply copied and distorted Menestrier with certain additions (*e.g.* the Olympiad given above), which are only the 'merry fantasies' of his own imagination. It is not improbable that Menestrier had read the story originally in *The Governour*, an hypothesis to some extent favoured by his expression '*quelques uns* ont crû.'

* Ὅτι Τρύζος τις τύραννος, βουλόμενος ἐξελεῖν τὰς συνωμοσίας καὶ τὰς κατ' αὐτοῦ ἐπιβουλὰς, ἔταξε τοῖς ἐπιχωρίοις, μηδένα μηδενὶ διαλέγεσθαι μήτε κοινῇ μήτε ἰδίᾳ. Καὶ ἦν τὸ πρᾶγμα ἀμήχανον καὶ χαλεπόν. Ἐσοφίσαντο οὖν τὸ τοῦ τυράννου πρόσταγμα, καὶ ἀλλήλοις ἔνευον, καὶ ἐχειρονόμουν πρὸς ἀλλήλους, καὶ ἐνεώρων δριμύ, καὶ αὖ πάλιν γαληναῖον καὶ φαιδρόν· καὶ ἐπὶ τοῖς σκυθρωποῖς καὶ ἀνηκέστοις ἕκαστος αὐτῶν συνωφρυωμένος ἦν δῆλος, τὸ τῆς ψυχῆς πάθος ἐκ τοῦ προσώπου τῷ πλησίον διαδεικνύς. Ἐλύπει τὸν τύραννον καὶ ταῦτα, καὶ ἐπίστευε τέξεσθαί τι αὐτῷ πάντως

perceiuing, lest by mutuall communication they shulde conspire agayne hym any rebellion, he prohibited all men under terrible menacis, that no man or woman shulde speke unto a nother, but in stede of wordes, they shulde use in their necessarye affaires, countenances, tokens, and mouinges with their feete, handes, and eien, whiche for necessite firste used, at the laste grewe to a perfecte and delectable daunsinge. And Hiero, nat withstanding his folisshe curiositie, at the laste was slayne of his people moste miserably. But all though this historie were true, yet was nat daunsing at this time first begon, for Orpheus and Museus, the most aunciente of poetes,[a] and also Homere,[b] whiche were longe afore Hiero, do make mention of daunsinge. And in Delus, whiche was the moste aunciente temple of Apollo, no solemnitie was done without daunsinge.[c]

κακὸν καὶ τὴν σιωπὴν διὰ τὸ τῶν σχημάτων ποικίλον. Ἀλλ' οὖν ἐκεῖνος καὶ τοῦτο κατέπαυσε. Τῶν τις οὖν ἀχθομένων τῇ ἀμηχανίᾳ καὶ δυσφορούντων καὶ τὴν μοναρχίαν καταλῦσαι διψώντων ἀφίκετο εἰς τὴν ἀγοράν, εἶτα ἔκλαε στὰς πολλοῖς ἅμα καὶ θαλεροῖς τοῖς δακρύοις. Περιέστησαν οὖν αὐτὸν καὶ περιῆλθον τὸ πλῆθος, καὶ ὀδυρμῷ κἀκεῖνοι συνείχοντο. Ἥκεν ἀγγελία παρὰ τὸν τύραννον, ὡς οὐδεὶς αὐτῶν χρῆται νεύματι οὐκέτι, δάκρυα δὲ αὐτοῖς ἐπιχωριάζει. Ὁ δὲ ἐπειγόμενος καὶ τοῦτο παῦσαι, μὴ μόνον τῆς γλώττης καταγινώσκων δουλείαν, μηδὲ μόνον τῶν νευμάτων, ἀλλ' ἤδη καὶ τοῖς ὀφθαλμοῖς τὴν ἐκ φύσεως ἀποκλείων ἐλευθερίαν, ᾗ ποδῶν εἶχεν, ἀφίκετο σὺν τοῖς δορυφόροις, ἵνα ἀναστείλῃ τὰ δάκρυα. Οἱ δὲ οὐκ ἔφθασαν ἰδόντες αὐτόν, καὶ τὰ ὅπλα τῶν δορυφόρων ἁρπάσαντες τὸν τύραννον ἀπέκτειναν.—Ælian, *Var. Hist.* lib. xiv. cap. 22.

[a] Ἐῶ λέγειν ὅτι τελετὴν οὐδὲ μίαν ἀρχαίαν ἔστιν εὑρεῖν ἄνευ ὀρχήσεως, Ὀρφέως δηλαδὴ καὶ Μουσαίου, τῶν τότε ἀρίστων ὀρχηστῶν, καταστησαμένων αὐτάς, ὥς τι κάλλιστον καὶ τοῦτο νομοθετησάντων σὺν ῥυθμῷ καὶ ὀρχήσει μυεῖσθαι.—Lucian, *de Saltatione*, § 15.

[b] Lucian, alluding to *Iliad* xiii. 637, says: Ὁ μὲν γὰρ Ὅμηρος τὰ ἥδιστα καὶ κάλλιστα καταλέγων, ὕπνον καὶ φιλότητα καὶ μολπὴν καὶ ὄρχησιν, ταύτην μόνην ἀμύμονα ὠνόμασε, προσμαρτυρήσας νὴ Δία καὶ τὸ ἡδὺ τῇ μολπῇ, ἅπερ ἀμφότερα τῇ ὀρχηστικῇ πρόσεστι, καὶ ᾠδὴ γλυκερὰ καὶ ὀρχηθμὸς ἀμύμων, ὃν σὺ νῦν μωμᾶσθαι ἐπινοεῖς.—*De Salt.* § 23. Athenæus says: Οἱ Φαίακες δὲ παρ' Ὁμήρῳ καὶ ἄνευ σφαίρας ὠρχοῦντο, καὶ ὀρχοῦνταί που ἀνὰ μέρος πυκνῶς· τοῦτο γάρ ἐστι τό, Τάρφε ἀμειβόμενοι. Lib. i. cap. 27

[c] Ἐν Δήλῳ δέ γε οὐδὲ αἱ θυσίαι ἄνευ ὀρχήσεως, ἀλλὰ σὺν ταύτῃ καὶ μετὰ μουσικῆς ἐγίγνοντο.—Lucian, *de Saltat.* § 16. Athenæus says: Οὕτως δ' ἦν ἔνδοξον καὶ σοφὸν ἡ ὄρχησις, ὥς τε Πίνδαρος τὸν Ἀπόλλω ὀρχηστὴν καλεῖ·

Ὀρχηστά, ἀγλαΐας ἀνάσσων,
εὐρυφάρετρ' Ἄπολλον.—Lib. i. cap. 40.

Also in Inde, where the people honoureth the sonne, they assemble to gether, and whan the sonne first appereth, ioyned all in a daunse they salute him, supposinge that for as moche as he moueth without sensible noyse, it pleseth him best to be like wise saluted, that is to say with a pleasant motion and silence.[a] The interpretours of Plato[b] do thinke that the wonderfull and incomprehensible ordre of the celestial bodies, I meane sterres and planettes, and their motions harmonicall, gaue to them that intentifly, and by the deepe serche of raison beholde their coursis, in the sondrye diuersities of nombre and tyme, a fourme of imitation of a semblable motion, whiche they called daunsinge or saltation; wherfore the more nere they approched to that temperance and subtile modulation of the saide superiour bodies, the more perfecte and commendable is their daunsinge, whiche is moste like to the trouthe of any opinion that I have hitherto founden.[c]

[a] Καὶ τί σοι τοὺς Ἕλληνας λέγω, ὅπου καὶ Ἰνδοὶ ἐπειδὰν ἕωθεν ἀναστάντες προσεύχωνται τὸν Ἥλιον, οὐχ ὥσπερ ἡμεῖς τὴν χεῖρα κύσαντες ἡγούμεθα ἐντελῆ ἡμῶν εἶναι τὴν εὐχήν, ἀλλ' ἐκεῖνοι πρὸς τὴν ἀνατολὴν στάντες ὀρχήσει τὸν Ἥλιον ἀσπάζονται σχηματίζοντες ἑαυτοὺς σιωπῇ καὶ μιμούμενοι τὴν χορείαν τοῦ θεοῦ· καὶ τοῦτό ἐστιν Ἰνδῶν καὶ εὐχὴ καὶ χοροὶ καὶ θυσία. Διὸ καὶ τούτοις ἱλεοῦνται τὸν θεὸν δὶς καὶ ἀρχομένης καὶ δυομένης τῆς ἡμέρας.—Lucian, de Saltat. § 17.

[b] Perhaps the following passage may have given countenance to this idea: ἐξῆν δὲ ἀνθρώπῳ γε ἐπὶ τὰ καλλίω καὶ βελτίω καὶ φίλα τιθεμένῳ λαμβάνειν, ὡς διὰ τοῦτο αὐτὸ ἔμφρον δεῖ νομίζειν, τὸ κατὰ ταὐτὰ καὶ ὡσαύτως καὶ διὰ ταὐτὰ πρᾶττον ἀεί, τοῦτο δ' εἶναι τὴν τῶν ἄστρων φύσιν, ἰδεῖν μὲν καλλίστην, πορείαν δὲ καὶ χορείαν πάντων χορῶν καλλίστην καὶ μεγαλοπρεπεστάτην χορεύοντα πᾶσι τοῖς ζῶσι τὸ δέον ἀποτελεῖν.—Epinomis, cap. vi. 982 E. Cf. Timæus, 40 C.

[c] Ἡ γοῦν χορεία τῶν ἀστέρων καὶ ἡ πρὸς τοὺς ἀπλανεῖς τῶν πλανήτων συμπλοκὴ καὶ εὐρυθμος αὐτῶν κοινωνία καὶ εὔτακτος ἁρμονία τῆς πρωτογόνου ὀρχήσεως δείγματά ἐστι. Κατ' ὀλίγον δὲ αὐξανομένη καὶ τῆς πρὸς τὸ βέλτιον ἀεὶ προσθήκης τυγχάνουσα νῦν ἔοικεν ἐς τὸ ἀκρότατον ἀποτετελέσθαι καὶ γεγενῆσθαι ποικίλον τι καὶ παναρμόνιον καὶ πολύμουσον ἀγαθόν.—Lucian, de Saltat. § 7. M. Burette, however, thinks there is no need to resort to these fanciful analogies, and that the origin of dancing is to be found in the natural and invincible tendency of man to movement and imitation. The first dances were probably nothing more than mere gestures—the outward expression of mental excitement. 'Mais on ne tarda guéres à assujettir ces mouvements aux loix d'une mesure, et d'une cadence réglée, qui a sa source dans la Nature, c'est-à-dire, dans une certaine disposition machinale de nos organes, d'où dépend cette inclination à répéter avec quelque sorte d'égalité, les

Other fables there be whiche I omitte for this present time. And nowe I will expresse in what estimation daunsing was had in the auncient time. And also sondry fourmes of daunsinge, nat all, but suche as had in them a semblance of vertue or kunnyng.

Whan the arke of god (wherin was put the tables of the commaundementes, the yerde wherwith Moisis deuided *Archa* the redde see, and dyd the miracles in the presence of *federis.* Pharao, kynge of Egypte, also a parte of manna, wherwith the children of Israel were fedde fourtie yeres in deserte), was recouered of the Philisties, and broughte unto the citie of Gaba,[a] the holy kynge Dauid, wearing on him a *Kynge Dauid* linen surplesse, daunsed before the saide arke, folowing *daunsing* him a great nombre of instrumentes of musike. *openly.* Wherat his wife Micol, the daughter of kyng Saule, disdained and scorned him, wherwith (as holy scripture saith[b]) all mighty god was moche displeased. And Dauid, not cessinge, daunsed[c] ioyousely through the citie, in that maner

---

· mêmes sons et les mêmes gestes, comme on peut l'observer dans les enfans, et dans les animaux mêmes. On marqua d'abord cette cadence ou par le son de la voix ou par la percussion de quelque corps, et c'est une espéce de cadence qui n'est pas ignorée encore aujourd'hui des peuples les plus barbares.'—Académie des Inscript. *Mem- de Lit.* tom. i. p. 131. A.D. 1719. This view of the origin of dancing has been also adopted by M. Blasis. See *The Art of Dancing,* translated by R. Barton, p. 6, ed. 1830. It ought to be observed, however, that this theory had been anticipated ages before by Plato, who says in the *Laws*: φησὶ δὲ τὸ νέον ἅπαν ὡς ἔπος εἰπεῖν τοῖς τε σώμασι καὶ ταῖς φωναῖς ἡσυχίαν ἄγειν οὐ δύνασθαι, κινεῖσθαι δὲ ἀεὶ ζητεῖν καὶ φθέγγεσθαι, τὰ μὲν ἁλλόμενα καὶ σκιρτῶντα, οἷον ὀρχούμενα μεθ' ἡδονῆς καὶ προσπαίζοντα, τὰ δὲ φθεγγόμενα πάσας φωνάς. Τὰ μὲν οὖν ἄλλα ζῷα οὐκ ἔχειν αἴσθησιν τῶν ἐν ταῖς κινήσεσι τάξεων οὐδὲ ἀταξιῶν, οἷς δὴ ῥυθμὸς ὄνομα καὶ ἁρμονία· ἡμῖν δὲ οὓς εἴπομεν τοὺς θεοὺς συγχορευτὰς δεδόσθαι, τούτους εἶναι καὶ τοὺς δεδωκότας τὴν ἔνρυθμόν τε καὶ ἐναρμόνιον αἴσθησιν μεθ' ἡδονῆς, ᾗ δὴ κινεῖν τε ἡμᾶς καὶ χορηγεῖν ἡμῶν τούτους, ᾠδαῖς τε καὶ ὀρχήσεσιν ἀλλήλοις ξυνείροντας, χοροὺς τε ὠνομακέναι τὸ παρὰ τῆς χαρᾶς ἔμφυτον ὄνομα.— Lib. ii. 653 E.

[a] See ante p. 95, note b.

[b] 'Therefore Michal, the daughter of Saul, had no child unto the day of her death.'—2 *Sam.* vi. 23.

[c] The Fathers of the Church excepted this from their usual animadversions on the amusement. Thus S. Ambrose says: 'Sed etiam et corporis saltatio in honorem Dei laudabilis habetur.'—*In Psalm cxviii. ad v.* 54, Migne's ed. tom.

honouringe that solemne feaste, whiche amonge the iewes was one af the chiefe and principall, wherwith god was more pleased than with all the other obseruances that than were done unto hym at that tyme.

I wyll nat trouble the reders with the innumerable ceremonies of the gentiles, whiche were comprehended in daun-

ii. § 1052. 'Cantavit David et ante arcam Domini non pro lasciviâ, sed pro religione saltavit. Ergo non histrionicis motibus sinuati corporis saltus, sed impigra mentis, et religiosa corporis agilitas designatur.'—*In Luc.* lib. vi. ad v. 32, Migne *ubi supra*, § 1385. And in another place, 'Sed hæc quæ corporeo aspectu fiunt turpia, sacrosanctæ religionis contemplatione reverenda sunt.'— *Epistol.* lviii. tom. iii. § 1014. And again, ' Hæc gloriosa sapientis saltatio quam saltavit David.'—*Ibid.* S. Gregory Nazianzen, addressing Julian the Apostate, says : Εἰ καὶ ὀρχήσασθαι δεῖ σὲ, ὡς πανηγυριστὴν καὶ φιλέορτον, ὀρχῆσαι μὲν, ἀλλὰ μὴ τὴν Ἡρωδιάδος ὄρχησιν τῆς ἀσχήμονος, ἧς ἔργον Βαπτιστοῦ θάνατος· ἀλλὰ τὴν Δαυὶδ ἐπὶ τῇ καταπαύσει τῆς κιβωτοῦ, ἣν ἡγοῦμαι τῆς εὐκινήτου καὶ πολυστρόφου κατὰ Θεὸν πορείας εἶναι μυστήριον.—*Oratio,* v. cap. 35, Migne ed. tom. i. col. 709. Some, like S. Cyprian, refuted those who would draw from this example a precedent in favour of the dancing in vogue in his day. 'Quod David in conspectu Dei choros egit nihil adjuvat in theatro sedentes Christianos fideles : nulla enim obscœnis motibus membra distorquens desaltavit Græcæ libidinis fabulam. Nabulæ, cynaræ, tibiæ, tympana, citharæ, Domino servierunt, non idolis.'—*De Spectaculis,* cap. 3, Migne's ed. col. 782. The Calvinists in the 16th century adopted a similar line of argument. Listen to one of them : 'Or maintenant faisons comparaison de ces danses là à celles d'auiourd'huy, pour voir si elles se rapportent. Celles là donc pour toutes fins auoyent une affection vehemente de donner louange à Dieu, auec tous tesmoignages de liesse saincte, et celles cy ne tendent ailleurs, qu'à prendre et donner du plaisir. C'estoyent là mouuements de personnes touchees et esmues d'une douce iouissance des benefices de Dieu : et ce sont ici danses apres des banquets, de personnes le plus souuent plaines de vin et de viandes, ou de cœurs vains et follastres, ou faisans l'amour. Là les sons estoyent suiets sacrez, cantiques et actions de graces, pour conduire les pas à ce qu'il n'y eust rien de profane : ici les chansons les plus folles et les plus ordes et vilaines sont les mieux receuës : afin que tout d'un bransle les cœurs et les corps ne s'esmeuuent qu'à follastreries et vanitez. Là les hommes n'estoyent point auec les femmes, il n'y auoit point d'embrassemens, de baisers, de deuis, icy tous y sont pesle-mesle ensemble, auec toute priuauté, licence et abandon. Bref, les effects de celles-là ne pouuoyent estre que saincts et bons, les causes et circonstances y estans toutes sainctes, et n'y auoit apparence d'incònuenient ; mais ici les causes et les façons estans telles que nous auons dites, ne peuuent produire que tous pernicieux effects. Voila la difference comme du iour à la nuict.'—Lambert Daneau. *Traité des Danses*, p. 82, ed. 1580. A learned German, John Ernest Muller, published in 1687 a dissertation, 'de Davide ante arcam federis saltante,' which will be found in the 32nd vol. of the great work of Ugolinus.

singes, sens they ought to be noumbred amonge superstitions.[a] But I wyll declare howe wise men and valiant capitaines imbraced daunsinge for a soueraigne and profitable exercise.

Licurgus, that gaue first lawes to the Lacedemones (a people in Grece), ordayned that the children there shulde be taught as diligently to daunse in armure, as to fight. And that in time of warres, they shulde meue them in bataile againe their enemies in fourme and maner of daunsinge.[b]

Semblably the olde inhabitantes of Ethiopia, at the ioyninge of their batailes, and whan the trumpettes and other instrumentes soune, they daunse; and in stede of a quiuer, they haue their dartes set about their heddes, like to rayes or bemes of the sonne, wherwith they beleue that they put their ene-

[a] The Rev. J. B. Deane, in his observations on Dracontia and the Druidical remains at Carnac in Brittany, mentions the existence of a very curious custom still observed at Erdeven. 'At an annual festival held on the day of the Carnival, the villagers unite in a general *dance*, which by its figure *describes accurately the Ophite hierogram of the Circle and Serpent*. The dancers commence in a circle, and, having performed a few revolutions, wheel off to the right and left in the same manner as their temple recedes from Kerlescant. They call this dance *par excellence* "Le Bal." Now this word may mean nothing more than the common French word "bal"—a public dancing. But it is *possible* that it may be *the original sacred dance of Baal*, from whom it may take its name, which, in process of time, and through change of religions and manners, became used more generally to signify *a Ball*, in the present acceptation of the word. *Dancing* was one of the most ordinary and most important of the idolatrous rites in all heathen religions; and the *circular dance* was preferred to all others. A tradition of this circular dancing peeps through the fables which we before noticed as common respecting the Druidical temples in England, namely, that the stones were human beings petrified in the midst of a *dance*. Now all the temples to which such superstitions are attached are *circular*. May not then the *circular dance*, similar to that practised at Erdeven, have been the ordinary accompaniment of an Ophite festival?'—*Archæologia*, vol. xxv. p. 217.

[b] Λακεδαιμόνιοι μὲν ἄριστοι Ἑλλήνων εἶναι δοκοῦντες παρὰ Πολυδεύκους καὶ Κάστορος καρυατίζειν μαθόντες—ὀρχήσεως δὲ καὶ τοῦτο εἶδος ἐν Καρύαις τῆς Λακωνικῆς διδασκόμενον—ἅπαντα μετὰ Μουσῶν ποιοῦσιν ἄχρι τοῦ πολεμεῖν πρὸς αὐλὸν καὶ ῥυθμὸν καὶ εὔτακτον ἔμβασιν τοῦ ποδός· καὶ τὸ πρῶτον σύνθημα Λακεδαιμονίοις πρὸς τὴν μάχην ὁ αὐλὸς ἐνδίδωσι. Τοιγαροῦν καὶ ἐκράτουν ἁπάντων μουσικῇ αὑτοῖς καὶ εὐρυθμίας ἡγουμένης. Ἴδοις δ' ἂν νῦν ἔτι καὶ τοὺς ἐφήβους αὑτῶν οὐ μεῖον ὀρχεῖσθαι ἢ ὁπλομαχεῖν μανθάνοντας.—Lucian, *de Saltat*. § 10.

mies in feare.[a] Also it was nat lefull for any of them to cast any darte at his enemie but daunsing. And nat only this rude people estemed so moche daunsing, but also the moste noble of the grekes, whiche for their excellencie in prowesse and wisedome were called halfe goddes. As Achilles, and his sonne Pirrhus,[b] and diuers other. Wherfore Homere, amonge the highe benefites that god gyueth to man, he reciteth daunsinge. For he saithe in the firste boke of Iliados :[c]

> 'God graunteth to some man prowesse martiall,
> To a nother daunsinge, with songe armonicall.'

Suppose ye that the Romanes, whiche in grauitie of maners passed the Grekes, had nat great pleasure in daunsinge?[d] Did nat Romulus,[e] the firste kinge of Romanes, and builder of the citie of Rome, ordaine certaine prestes and ministers to the god Mars (whome he aduaunted to be his

---

[a] Αἰθίοπες δέ γε καὶ πολεμοῦντες σὺν ὀρχήσει αὐτὸ δρῶσι, καὶ οὐκ ἂν ἀφείη τὸ βέλος Αἰθίοψ ἀνὴρ ἀφελὼν τῆς κεφαλῆς—ταύτῃ γὰρ ἀντὶ φαρέτρας χρῶνται περιδέοντες αὐτῇ ἀκτινηδὸν τὰ βέλη— εἰ μὴ πρότερον ὀρχήσαιτο καὶ τῷ σχήματι ἀπειλήσειε καὶ προεκφοβήσειε τῇ ὀρχήσει τὸν πολέμιον.—Lucian, de Saltat. § 18.

[b] Πολλοὺς δὲ καὶ ἄλλους τῶν ἡρώων εἰπεῖν ἔχων τοῖς αὐτοῖς ἐγγεγυμνασμένους καὶ τέχνην τὸ πρᾶγμα πεποιημένους ἱκανὸν ἡγοῦμαι τὸν Νεοπτόλεμον, 'Αχιλλέως μὲν παῖδα ὄντα, πάνυ δὲ διαπρέψαντα ἐν τῇ ὀρχηστικῇ καὶ εἶδος τὸ κάλλιστον αὐτῇ προστεθεικότα, Πυρρίχιον ἀπ' αὐτοῦ κεκλημένον.—Ibid. § 9.

[c] The reference is erroneous; the verses quoted are evidently a translation of the following:

Ἄλλῳ μὲν γὰρ ἔδωκε θεὸς πολεμήϊα ἔργα·
Ἄλλῳ δ' ὀρχηστύν, ἑτέρῳ κίθαριν καὶ ἀοιδήν.—Il. xiii. 730.

[d] 'Caton, le plus sevère des Romains, à l'age de plus de soixante ans, crut devoir se faire recorder ses danses, afin de paroître moins gauche dans un Bal de Rome.' —Cahusac, La Danse, Ancienne et Moderne, tom. i. p. 74.

[e] It was not Romulus, but Numa, who instituted the Salii. Σάλιοι δὲ ἐκλήθησαν, οὐχ, ὡς ἔνιοι μυθολογοῦσι, Σαμόθρᾳκος ἀνδρὸς ἢ Μαντινέως, ὄνομα Σαλίου, πρώτου τὴν ἐνόπλιον ἐκδιδάξαντος ὄρχησιν, ἀλλὰ μᾶλλον ἀπὸ τῆς ὀρχήσεως αὐτῆς ἁλτικῆς οὔσης, ἣν ὑπορχοῦνται διαπορευόμενοι τὴν πόλιν, ὅταν τὰς ἱερὰς πέλτας ἀναλάβωσιν ἐν τῷ Μαρτίῳ μηνί, φοινικοῦς μὲν ἐνδεδυμένοι χιτωνίσκους, μίτραις δὲ χαλκαῖς ὑπεζωσμένοι πλατείαις καὶ κράνη χαλκᾶ φοροῦντες, ἐγχειριδίοις δὲ μικροῖς τὰ ὅπλα κρούοντες.—Plut. Numa, 13.

father [a])? Which prests, for as moche as certaine times they daunsed [b] about the citie with tergates, that they imagined to falle from heuen, were called in latine *Salii*, which in to englisshe may be translated daunsers, who continued so longe time in reuerence amonge the Romanes, that unto the tyme that they were christned, the noble men and princes children there, usinge moche diligence and sute, couayted to be of the college of the saide daunsers.[c]

More ouer the emperours that were moste noble,[d] delited

[a]   —'placet Ilia Marti ;
Teqne parit, gemino juncte Quirine Remo.
Ille suos semper Venerem Martemque parentes
Dixit : et emeruit vocis habere fidem.'—Ov. *Fasti*, lib. iv. 55.

Livy's account is more cautious. 'Vi compressa Vestalis, quum geminum partum edidisset, seu ita rata, seu quia deus auctor culpæ honestior erat, Martem incertæ stirpis patrem nuncupat.'—Lib. i. cap. 4. And Justin is as doubtful as Livy. 'Igitur clausa in luco Marti sacro, duos pueros, incertum stupro, an ex Marte conceptos, enixa est.'—Lib. xliii. cap. 2.

[b] It was Ovid who first gave the derivation of the name from their occupation.

'Jam dederat Saliis (à saltu nomina ducunt)
Armaque, et ad certos verba canenda modos.'
Fasti, lib. iii. 387.

'Salios item duodecim Marti Gradivo legit, tunicæque pictæ insigne dedit, et super tunicam æneum pectori tegumen, cælestiaque arma, quæ ancilia appellantur, ferre, ac per Urbem ire canentes carmina cum tripudiis solennique saltatu jussit.'—Liv. lib. i. cap. 20.

[c] Neither Plutarch, Dionysius, nor Livy go quite so far as to assert this, but no doubt it is not an unreasonable inference from the statements of these writers. Dionysius of Halicarnassus, for instance, speaks of them as Οὓς αὐτὸς ὁ Νόμας ἀπέδειξεν ἐκ τῶν πατρικίων δώδεκα τοὺς εὐπρεπεστάτους ἐπιλεξάμενος νέους.—Lib. cap. 70. And again he says : Χρῆν δὲ τούτους ἐλευθέρους τε εἶναι καὶ αὐθιγενεῖς καὶ ἀμφιθαλεῖς.—Lib. ii. cap. 71. Lucan calls them 'lecta juventus Patricia.'—*Pharsalia*, lib. ix. 478. Lucian also mentions their noble birth, but says nothing about the competition to be elected into the college. Ἐπὶ τούτοις δίκαιον μηδὲ τῆς Ῥωμαίων ὀρχήσεως ἀμνημονεῖν, ἣν οἱ εὐγενέστατοι αὐτῶν τῷ πολεμικωτάτῳ τῶν θεῶν Ἄρει οἱ Σάλιοι καλούμενοι—ἱερωσύνης δὲ τοῦτο ὄνομα—ὀρχοῦνται σεμνοτάτην τε ἅμα καὶ ἱερωτάτην.—*De Saltatione*, § 20.

[d] Lucian says that this art made special progress in the reign of Augustus. Ἡ νῦν ὄρχησις καθεστῶσα, οὐ πάλαι ἀρξαμένη ἐς τοσοῦτον κάλλος ἐπιδιδόναι, ἀλλὰ κατὰ τὸν Σεβαστὸν μάλιστα.—*De Saltatione*, § 34. Yet it was Augustus who sternly prohibited 'the practice in which knights and even senators had sometimes indulged, of

in daunsyng, perceyuing therin to be a perfecte measure, whiche maye be called modulation, wherin some daunsers of olde tyme so wonderfully excelled, that they wolde plainly expresse in daunsynge, without any wordes* or dittie, histories, with the hole circumstaunce of affaires in them contayned, wherof I shall reherce two maruailouse experiences. At Rome, in the tyme of Nero, there was a philosopher called Demetrius, whiche was of that secte, that for as moche as they abandoned all shamfastnes in their wordes and actes, they were called *Cinici*, in englisshe doggishe. This Demetrius, often reprouing daunsing, wolde saye that there was nothing therin of any importaunce, and that it was none other but a counterfayting with the feete and handes of the armonie that

---

showing their skill in dancing and acting upon the public stage.'—Merivale, *Hist. of Rome*, vol. iv. p. 47. Tiberius expelled the players from the city; and though Caligula, 'the first of the Roman emperors, did not forbear from singing and dancing in public,' his character hardly entitles him to the epithet in the text. Domitian revived the laws of his predecessors against the singers and dancers of the theatres, and we are told that he even went so far as to expel a senator of quæstorian rank from that illustrious assembly, 'quòd gesticulandi saltandique studio teneretur.'—Suet. *Domit.* 8.

* M. Baron, who has investigated this subject in his *Lettres sur la Danse*, says: 'J'aurai occasion de vous parler quelque jour des efforts inutiles que nous avons faits pour noter la danse comme on note la musique. Les anciens, plus heureux, étaient parvenus à noter et le geste, et l'espèce de danse appelée *Saltation*, celle qui consistait à représenter la démarche, les attitudes, en un mot tous les mouvemens dont on accompagne les discours. Cet art de la saltation, qui est perdu, et dont on ne peut plus parler que par conjecture, fut porté à un si haut degré, qu'on crut pouvoir se passer entièrement des paroles, et jouer toutes sortes de pièces de théâtre *sans ouvrir la bouche*. Diverses circonstances contribuèrent à la création de ce nouveau genre d'imitation, que l'on appela *pantomime*. Un nommé Livius Andronicus, Grec de naissance, comme presque tous les acteurs de Rome, bon poète d'ailleurs, excellent tragédien, ayant perdu la voix par accident, prétendit exprimer par ses gestes les idées qu'il animait auparavant de sa diction. L'essai plut au peuple, il fut perfectionné, et la mort d'Ésope et de Roscius, les Garrick et les Lekain du siècle d'Auguste, ayant laissé dans la déclamation théâtrale un vide qui ne put jamais être comblé, Pilade de Cilicie et Bathylle d'Alexandrie, deux hommes non moins extraordinaires, attirèrent toute l'attention sur la pantomime, et les auteurs tragiques et comiques devinrent en Italie ce qu'ils y sont encore aujourd'hui, depuis que la musique a fait oublier tout le reste.'—P. 127, ed. 1824.

was shewed before in the rebecke,[a] shalme,[b] or other instrument, and that the motiones were but vaine and seperate from all understanding, and of no purpose or efficacie. Wherof herynge a famouse daunser, and one, as it semed, that was nat without good lernyng, and had in remembraunce many histories, he came to Demetrius and saide unto him, Sire, I

[a] The rebec, Italian *ribeca*, was a species of violin with three strings. The old French form of the word was rebèbe, rubèbe, or rebelle, and Larousse traces the derivation to the word rabâb, which is applied by the Arabians to an instrument of similar shape. Chaucer probably intended to designate this when he wrote, 'and pleyen songes on a smal rubible.'—*Miller's Tale*, Works, vol. ii. p. 103, ed. 1866. Warton, in his note on this line, *Hist. of Eng. Poetry*, vol. ii. p. 194, ed. 1840, calls it 'a species of guitar,' but refers to a poem never printed, called '*Reason and Sensuallite*, compylled by Ihon Lydgate,' in which mention is made of

'Lutys, ribibis (ribibles), and geternes,
More for estatys than tavernes.'

Thomas Langley, whose translation of Polydore Vergil's *De Inventoribus* was first published in 1546, says: 'Thucydides writeth that the Lacedemonians used first in war Shalmes, Clarions, and Rebeckes.'—Lib. i. cap, 12. The word occurs in Drayton's *Eclogues*—'He turned his rebec to a mournful note.' Milton, too, in his *L'Allegro*, has—

'When the merry bells ring round,
And the jocund rebecks sound
To many a youth and many a maid
Dancing in the chequer'd shade.'

M. Georges Kastner, in *Les Danses des Morts*, has an elaborate dissertation upon this instrument. He says: 'Il est certain qu'on faisait principalement usage de la rubèbe (rebec), pour faire danser. Il parait avoir plus particulièrement joué son rôle dans les fêtes bourgeoises, populaires, et champêtres, et dans les mains des ménétriers de second ordre, au service du premier venu. Tous les instruments à archet, à deux et à trois cordes, ont été dans ce cas; en France, en Angleterre, en Allemagne, en Russie, en Italie, en Espagne, et jusque chez les Orientaux, ils ont toujours défrayé les concerts du peuple. . . Peu à peu le nom de *rebec* fut généralement appliqué à toute vielle ou viole propre à faire danser.'—P. 249-251, ed. 1852. The word is at least as old as the 10th century, for Du Cange cites from a MS. of that date the following lines:

'Quidam *rebecam* arcuabant,
Muliebrem vocem confingentes.'

[b] In Richardson's *Dict.* (*sub voc.* Rebec) this word is erroneously printed *shaline*. It is derived from the French chalemelle, chalemel, or chalumeau, the Latin *calamus*. In fact, Gower, in his *Confessio Amantis*, which was written quite at the end of the 14th century, actually uses the French form *shalmele*; but then we know from Puttenham that it was Gower's habit 'not to sticke to put in a

humbly desire you refuse nat to do me that honestie with your presence, in beholding me daunce, whiche ye shall se me do without soune of any instrument. And than if it shall seme to you worthy dispraise, utterly banisshe and confounde my science. Wherunto Demetrius graunted.[a] The yonge man

---

plaine French word for an English.' See *Arte of Eng. Poesie*, p. 67. He combines it with another French word, the cornmuse, and so does Chaucer:

> 'That maden lowde menstralcies,
> In cornmuse and *shalymes*,
> And many other maner pipe.'
> *The House of Fame*, b. iii. Works, vol. v. p. 246, ed. 1866.

Langley, in his translation of Polydore Vergil, says: 'Some refer the originall of the Harp and Pipe to Apollo, for his image in Delos (as they say) hath in the right hand a bow and in the left hand the goddesses of favour. Whereof one hath a harp, another a shalm, the third a pipe. Shalms were at the beginning made of cranes' legs, and after of great reeds. Dardanus Trezenius used first to play and sing with them.'—Lib. i. cap. 12. Guillaume de Marhault, a minstrel of the 14th century, gives a very long list of the musical instruments used in his day in his poem entitled *Le Temps Pastour*, amongst which he mentions together, 'cornemuses et chalemelles.' Other passages from romances and poems of the 12th, 13th, 14th, and 15th centuries, in which the same word occurs variously spelt, are quoted by M. Kastner, who says: 'Ces instruments, appelés aujourd'hui flûtes, flageolets, chalumeaux, hautbois, cornemuses, musettes, étaient désignés au moyen âge par un assez grand nombre de termes, qu'on transportait souvent de l'un à l'autre, ou qu'on employait d'une manière collective. Tels sont les suivants tirés des écrivains de la basse latinité, *fistula, pipa, calamus, calamellus, calamella, cieramela, cabreta, musa*, &c.; et ceux-ci particuliers aux vieux poëtes français, *fistule, frestel* ou *frestiau, pipe, pipeau, calamel, chalemelle*, ou *chalemie, muse*, &c. La plupart de ces dénominations s'appliquaient à de simples tubes semblables aux sifflets et aux chalumeaux des campagnards.'—*Ubi suprà*, p. 194. In England the word was more usually spelt *shawme*. In Mr. Wright's *Domestic Manners in England during the Middle Ages*, a drawing is given of an angel playing on the shalm from the Royal MS. 14 E. iii. Possibly there is some connexion between this word and the Hebrew word *Schalischim*. Ugolinus says, '*Schalischim* aliud est musicum instrumentum quod Septuaginta reddunt *cymbala*, S. Hieronymus sistra. Semel tantum occurrit in Sacrâ Scripturâ (1 *Sam*. xviii. 6, where the A. V. has merely *instruments of music*). Fœminæ venientibus Sauli et Davidi occurrerunt cum tympanis et *schalischim*.'—*Thes. Ant. Sac.* tom. xxxii. p. 796.

[a] Ὁ δὴ καὶ Δημήτριον τὸν Κυνικὸν παθεῖν λέγουσιν· ἐπεὶ γὰρ καὶ αὐτὸς ὁμοιά σοι κατηγόρει τῆς ὀρχηστικῆς, λέγων τοῦ αὐλοῦ καὶ τῶν συρίγγων καὶ τῶν κτύπων πάρεργον, τι τὸν ὀρχηστὴν εἶναι, μηδὲν αὐτὸν πρὸς τὸ δρᾶμα συντελοῦντα, κινούμενον δὲ ἄλογον ἄλλως κίνησιν καὶ μάταιον, οὐδενὸς αὐτῇ νοῦ προσόντος, τῶν δ' ἀνθρώπων τοῖς περὶ τὸ πρᾶγμα γοητευομένων, ἐσθῆτι Σηρικῇ καὶ προσωπείῳ εὐπρεπεῖ, αὐλῷ τε καὶ

daunsed the aduoutry of Mars and Venus, and therin expressed howe Vulcane, husbonde of Venus, therof beyng aduertised by the sonne, layde snares for his wife and Mars; also howe they were wounden and tyed in Vulcanes nette; more ouer howe all the goddes came to the spectacle; finally howe Venus, all ashamed and blusshing, ferefully desired her louer Mars to delyuer her from that perill, and the residue contayned in the fable; whiche he dyd with so subtile and crafty gesture, with such perspicuitie and declaration of euery acte in the mater (whiche of all thing is moste difficile) with suche a grace and beautie, also with a witte so wonderfull and pleasaunt, that Demetrius, as it semed, therat reioysing and deliting, cried with a loude voice, O man, I do nat only se, but also here, what thou doest, and it semeth also to me that with thy handes thou spekest. Whiche sayinge was confirmed by all them that were at that tyme present.

The same yonge man songe and daunsed on a time before the emperour Nero,[a] whan there was also present a straunge

τερετίσμασι καὶ τῇ τῶν ὀδόντων εὐφωνίᾳ, οἷς κοσμεῖσθαι μηδὲν ὂν τὸ τοῦ ὀρχηστοῦ πρᾶγμα· ὁ τότε κατὰ τὸν Νέρωνα εὐδοκιμῶν ὀρχηστὴς οὐκ ἀσύνετος, ὥς φασιν, ἀλλ' εἰ καί τις ἄλλος ἔν τε ἱστορίας μνήμῃ καὶ κινήσεως κάλλει διενεγκὼν ἐδεήθη τοῦ Δημητρίου εὐγνωμονεστάτην, οἶμαι, τὴν δέησιν, ἰδεῖν ὀρχούμενον, ἔπειτα κατηγορεῖν αὐτοῦ, καὶ ὑπέσχετό γε ἄνευ αὐλοῦ καὶ ᾀσμάτων ἐπιδείξασθαι αὐτῷ· καὶ οὕτως ἐποίησεν· ἡσυχίαν γὰρ τοῖς τε κτυποῦσι καὶ τοῖς αὐλοῦσι καὶ αὐτῷ παραγγείλας τῷ χορῷ αὐτὸς ἐφ' ἑαυτοῦ ὠρχήσατο τὴν 'Αφροδίτης καὶ Ἄρεως μοιχείαν, Ἥλιον μηνύοντα καὶ Ἥφαιστον ἐπιβουλεύοντα καὶ τοῖς δεσμοῖς ἀμφοτέρους, τήν τε 'Αφροδίτην καὶ τὸν Ἄρη, σαγηνεύοντα καὶ τοὺς ἐφεστῶτας θεοὺς ἕκαστον αὐτῶν, καὶ αἰδουμένην μὲν τὴν 'Αφροδίτην, ὑποδεδοικότα δὲ καὶ ἱκετεύοντα τὸν Ἄρη καὶ ὅσα τῇ ἱστορίᾳ ταύτῃ πρόσεστιν, ὥστε τὸν Δημήτριον ὑπερησθέντα τοῖς γιγνομένοις τοῦτον ἔπαινον ἀποδοῦναι τὸν μέγιστον τῷ ὀρχηστῇ· ἀνέκραγε γὰρ καὶ μεγάλῃ τῇ φωνῇ ἀνεφθέγξατο, Ἀκούω, ἄνθρωπε, ἃ ποιεῖς, οὐχ ὁρῶ μόνον, ἀλλά μοι δοκεῖς ταῖς χερσὶν αὐταῖς λαλεῖν.—Lucian, de Saltatione, § 63.

[a] Ἐπεὶ δὲ κατὰ τὸν Νέρωνά ἐσμεν τῷ λόγῳ, βούλομαι καὶ βαρβάρου ἀνδρὸς τὸ ἐπὶ τοῦ αὐτοῦ ὀρχηστοῦ γενόμενον εἰπεῖν, ὅπερ μέγιστος ἔπαινος ὀρχηστικῆς γένοιτ' ἄν· τῶν γὰρ ἐκ τοῦ Πόντου βαρβάρων βασιλικός τις ἄνθρωπος κατά τι χρέος ἥκων ὡς τὸν Νέρωνα ἐθεᾶτο μετὰ τῶν ἄλλων τὸν ὀρχηστὴν ἐκεῖνον οὕτω σαφῶς ὀρχούμενον, ὡς καίτοι μὴ ἐπακούων τὰ τῶν ᾀδομένων—ἡμιέλλην γάρ τις ὢν ἐτύγχανε—συνεῖναι ἁπάντων· Καὶ δὴ ἀπιὼν ἤδη ἐς τὴν οἰκείαν, τοῦ Νέρωνος δεξιουμένου καὶ ὅ τι βούλοιτο αἰτεῖν κελεύοντος καὶ δώσειν ὑπισχνουμένου, Τὸν ὀρχηστήν, ἔφη, δοὺς τὰ μέγιστα εὐφρανεῖς. Τοῦ δὲ Νέρωνος ἐρομένου, Τί ἄν σοι χρήσιμος γένοιτο ἐκεῖ; Προσοίκους, ἔφη, βαρβάρους

kynge, whiche understode none other langage but of his owne countray; yet nat withstanding the man daunsed so aptely and playnely, as his custome was, that the straunge kynge, all thoughe he perceiued nat what he said, yet he understode euery dele of the mater. And whan he had taken his leue of the emperour to departe, the emperour offered to gyue to hym any thynge that he thoughte mought be to his commoditie. Ye may (sayd the kynge) bounteousely rewarde me, if ye lende me the yonge man that daunsed before your maiestie. Nero wondring and requiring of him why he so importunately desired the daunser, or what commodite the daunser mought be unto him, Sir, said the king, I haue diuers confins and neighbours that be of sondry languages and maners, wherfore I haue often tymes nede of many interpretours. Wherfore if I had this man with me, and shulde haue anything to do with my neighbours, he wolde so with his facion and gesture expresse euery thinge to me, and teche them to do the same, that from hensforth I shulde nat haue nede of any interpretour. Also the auncient philosophers commended daunsing; in so moche as Socrates, the wysest of all the grekes in his time, and from whom all the sectes of philosophers, as from a fountaine, were deriuied, was nat ashamed to account daunsinge amonge the seriouse disciplines, for the commendable beautie, for the apte and proportionate meuinge, and for the craftie disposition and facionyng of the body.[a] It is to be considered that in the saide auncient tyme there were diuers maners of daunsing,[b] whiche varied in the names, lyke wyse as they dyd

ἔχω, οὐχ ὁμογλώττους, καὶ ἑρμηνέων οὐ ῥᾴδιον εὐπορεῖν πρὸς αὐτούς· ἢν οὖν τινος δέωμαι, διανεύων οὗτος ἕκαστά μοι ἑρμηνεύσει. Τοσοῦτον ἄρα καθίκετο αὐτοῦ ἡ μίμησις τῆς ὀρχήσεως, ἐπίσημός τε καὶ σαφὴς φανεῖσα.—Lucian, de Saltatione, § 64.

[a] Ὁ Σωκράτης δὲ σοφώτατος ἀνὴρ οὐ μόνον ἐπῄνει τὴν ὀρχηστικὴν, ἀλλὰ καὶ ἐκμαθεῖν αὐτὴν ἠξίου μέγιστον ἀπονέμων εὐρυθμίᾳ καὶ εὐμουσίᾳ καὶ κινήσει ἐμμελεῖ καὶ εὐσχημοσύνῃ τοῦ κινουμένου, καὶ οὐκ ᾐδεῖτο γέρων ἀνὴρ ἐν τῶν σπουδαιοτάτων μαθημάτων καὶ τοῦτο ἡγούμενος εἶναι.—Lucian, de Saltatione, § 25.

[b] Meursius, in his treatise entitled *Orchestra sive de Saltationibus Veterum*, published A.D. 1618, and which is printed in the 8th volume of the *Thesaurus Græcarum Antiquitatum* of Gronovius, has collected with infinite pains 189 different

in tunes of the instrument, as semblably we haue at this daye.ᵃ But those names, some were generall, some were speciall;ᵇ the generall names were gyuen of the uniuersall fourme of daunsinge, wherby was represented the qualities or conditions of sondry astates; as the maiestie of princes was shewed in that daunse whiche was named *Eumelia*,ᶜ and belonged to tragedies; dissolute motions and wanton countenaunces in that whiche was called *Cordax*,ᵈ and pertained to

names of dances known to the Greeks. But Meursius had been anticipated by many writers of antiquity, even before Lucian, whose writings have not come down to us. Οὐ γάρ με λέληθεν ὅτι πολλοὶ πρὸ ἡμῶν περὶ ὀρχήσεως συγγεγραφότες τὴν πλείστην διατριβὴν τῆς γραφῆς ἐποιήσαντο πάντα τῆς ὀρχήσεως τὰ εἴδη ἐπεξιόντες καὶ ὀνόματα αὐτῶν καταλέγοντες καὶ οἷα ἑκάστη καὶ ὑφ' ὅτου εὑρέθη, πολυμαθείας ταύτην ἐπίδειξιν ἡγούμενοι παρέξειν.—Lucian, *de Saltat.* § 33. Athenæus and Julius Pollux have preserved for us the names of several kinds of dances, but they have not thrown much additional light upon the subject. The elder Scaliger also devoted a chapter (the 18th) of his first book of *Poetics* to the enumeration of the various kinds of ancient dances; and, according to M. Burette, he specifies some which have escaped the attention even of Meursius, and it is consequently to be regretted that he has not left us a more complete treatise upon the subject.

ᵃ 'Il y en avoit qui régloient leur Cadence et leur Mesure, tantôt sùr celle du Chant, tantôt sur celle de quelque instrument de musique, tel que la flûte ou la lyre, quelquefois sur le Chant soûtenu de la Symphonie. Il y en avoit d'autres qui n'étoient accompagnées ni du Chant, ni des Instruments. Les unes étoient graves, sérieuses, et modestes, les autres gayes, folâtres, et deshonnêtes.'—Acad. des Inscriptions, *Mém. de Lit.* tom. i. p. 152, Hague, ed. 1719. Speaking of the dances in vogue in the 16th century, Arbeau says: 'Il y auoit deux sortes de basses dances, les unes communes et regulières, les aultres irregulières. Les regulières estoient appropriées aux chansons regulières et les irregulières aux chansons irregulières.'—*Orchesographie*, fo. 24 b.

ᵇ M. Burette divides the ancient Greek dances into four principal classes, 'selon qu'elles étoient destinées: 1, aux Cérémonies de la Réligion; 2, aux Exercices de la Guerre; 3, aux Spectacles du Théâtre; 4, aux Nôces, aux Festins, et à semblables réjouissances.'—*Mém. de Lit.*, *ubi supra*, p. 153.

ᶜ Δοκεῖς δέ μοι, ὅταν κωμῳδίαν καὶ τραγῳδίαν ἐπαινῇς, ἐπιλελῆσθαι ὅτι καὶ ἐν ἑκατέρᾳ ἐκείνων ὀρχήσεώς ἐστιν ἴδιόν τι εἶδός ἐστιν, οἷον τραγικῇ μὲν ἡ ἐμμέλεια, κωμῳδικῇ δὲ ὁ κόρδαξ, ἐνίοτε δὲ καὶ τρίτης σικινίδος προσλαμβανομένης.—Lucian, *de Saltat.* § 26.

ᵈ Athenæus thus distinguishes these dances: Ὁ μὲν κόρδαξ παρ' Ἕλλησι φορτικὸς, ἡ δ' ἐμμέλεια σπουδαία.—Lib. xiv. cap. 30. And Demosthenes evidently considered the Cordax indecent, for he says, Εἰ δέ τις σώφρων ἢ δίκαιος ἄλλως, τὴν καθ' ἡμέραν ἀκρασίαν τοῦ βίου καὶ μέθην καὶ κορδακισμοὺς οὐ δυνάμενος φέρειν, παρεῶσθαι καὶ ἐν οὐδενὶ εἶναι μέρει τὸν τοιοῦτον.—*Olynth.* ii. § 18.

comedies, wherin men of base hauiour only daunsed. Also the fourme of bataile and fightyng in armure was expressed in those daunsis [a] which were called *Enopliæ*. Also there was a kynde of daunsinge called *Hormus*,[b] of all the other moste lyke to that whiche is at this time used; wherin daunsed yonge men and maidens, the man expressinge in his motion and countenance fortitude and magnanimitie apt for the warres, the maiden moderation and shamefastnes, which represented a pleasant connexion of fortitude and temperance. In stede of these we haue nowe base daunsis, bargenettes, pauions, turgions, and roundes.[c] And as for the speciall names, they

---

[a] These were also called Pyrrhic dances. Ἡ δὲ ἐνόπλιος ὄρχησις στρατιωτική, καὶ ἡ πυρρίχη δηλοῖ καὶ ὁ Πύρριχος, ὅν φασιν εὑρετὴν εἶναι τῆς τοιαύτης ἀσκήσεως τῶν νέων καὶ τὰ στρατιωτικά.—Strabo, lib. x. cap. 3, § 8. Compare Plato's description of this dance: Τὴν πολεμικὴν δὴ τούτων, ἄλλην οὖσαν τῆς εἰρηνικῆς, πυρρίχην ἂν τις ὀρθῶς προσαγορεύοι, τάς τε εὐλαβείας πασῶν πληγῶν καὶ βολῶν ἐκνεύσεσι καὶ ὑπείξει πάσῃ καὶ ἐκπηδήσεσιν ἐν ὕψει καὶ ξὺν ταπεινώσει μιμουμένην καὶ τὰς ταύταις ἐναντίας τὰς ἐπὶ τὰ δραστικὰ φερομένας αὖ σχήματα ἔν τε ταῖς τῶν τόξων βολαῖς καὶ ἀκοντίων καὶ πασῶν πληγῶν μιμήματα ἐπιχειρούσας μιμεῖσθαι.—*Leges*, lib. vii. cap. 18, 815 A. It was also styled the Cretan dance. 'Saltationem armatam Curetes docuere, Pyrrhichen Pyrrhus, utramque in Creta.'—Pliny, lib. vii. cap. 57.

[b] Ὁ δὲ ὅρμος ὄρχησίς ἐστι κοινὴ ἐφήβων τε καὶ παρθένων, παρ᾽ ἕνα χορευόντων καὶ ὡς ἀληθῶς ὁρμῷ ἐοικότων· καὶ ἡγεῖται μὲν ὁ ἔφηβος τὰ νεανικὰ ὀρχούμενος καὶ ὅσοις ὕστερον ἐν πολέμῳ χρήσεται, ἡ παρθένος δὲ ἕπεται κοσμίως τὸ θῆλυ χορεύειν διδάσκουσα, ὡς εἶναι τὸν ὅρμον ἐκ σωφροσύνης καὶ ἀνδρείας πλεκόμενον.—Lucian, *de Saltatione*, § 12.

[c] The old French writer, Thoinot Arbeau, already quoted, says: 'Quant aux dances anciennes, je n'en scaurois que dire, car l'injure du temps, ou la paresse des hommes, ou la difficulté de les descripre, a esté cause de nous en oster la cognoissance, et aussi vous n'en debuez auoir soucy, parce que tel les façons de dancer sont hors de practique, voires nous auons veu du temps de noz pères, aultres dances que celles de présent lesquelles en sont de mesmes, tant sont les hommes amateurs de nouueaultez; il est vray que nous pouuons comparer *l'emmelie* a noz pauanes et basse dances; *le cordax* aux gaillardes, tordions, voltes, corantes, gauottes, bransles de champaigne et de bourgoigne, bransles gayz et bransles couppez. *Le Siccinnis* aux bransles doubles et bransles simples. *La pirrichie* à la dance que nous appellons bouffons ou matachins.'—*Orchesographie*, fo. 5. Puttenham speaks of 'the ordinary Musickes amorous, such as might be song with voice or to the Lute, Citheron, or Harpe, or daunced by measures, as the Italian Pauan and galliard are at these daies in Princes' Courts and other places of honourable or ciuill assembly.'—*Arte of English Poesie*, lib. i. cap. 23, p. 37, ed. 1811.

were taken as they be nowe,[a] either of the names of the firste inuentors, or of the measure and nombre that they do containe, or of the firste wordes of the dittie, whiche the songe comprehendeth wherof the daunse was made.[b] In euery of the said daunsis, there was a concinnitie of meuing the foote and body, expressing some pleasaunt or profitable affectes or motions of the mynde.[c]

Here a man may beholde what artifice and crafte there was in thauncient tyme in daunsinge, whiche at this day no man can imagine or coniecte.[d] But if men wolde nowe applie the

---

[a] The Pavane derived its name from the fact that the dancers formed a circle like the tail of a peacock; 'les danseurs font la roue l'un devant l'autre comme les Paons, font avec leurs queues, d'où lui est venu le nom.'—M. Compan. *Dict. de Danse*, ed. 1787. The Courante or Corranto was so called 'à cause des allées et des venues dont elle est remplie, plus qu'aucune autre.'—*Ibid.* On the other hand, 'La gaillarde,' says Thoinot Arbeau, 'est appellée ainsi parce qu'il fault estre gaillard et dispos pour la dancer,' fo. 39 b. From the same authority we learn that 'Le branle morgué appellé le branle des Lauandieres se danse par mesure binaire, et est ainsi appellé parce que les danceurs y font du bruit auec le tappement de leurs mains, lequel represente celuy que font les batoirs de celles qui lauent les buées sur la riuiere de Seyne à Paris.'—*Orchesographie*, fo. 83. What the dance was which the author calls *bargenette* it is impossible to discover; by *turgion* no doubt the French *tordion* is intended, which according to Arbeau 'n'est aultre chose qu'une gaillarde par terre.'—*Ubi supra*, fo. 28 b.

[b] Thus Athenæus says with regard to the dance called Sicinnis: Καλεῖται δ' ἡ μὲν Σατυρικὴ ὄρχησις, ὥς φησιν Ἀριστοκλῆς ἐν ὀγδόῳ τῶν περὶ Χορῶν σίκιννις καὶ οἱ Σάτυροι, σικιννισταί. Τινὲς δέ φασι Σίκιννόν τινα βάρβαρον εὑρετὴν αὐτῆς γενέσθαι, ἄλλοι δὲ Κρῆτα λέγουσι τὸ γένος εἶναι Σίκιννον. Ὀρχησταὶ δ' οἱ Κρῆτες, ὥς φησιν Ἀριστόξενος. Σκάμων δ' ἐν πρώτῳ περὶ Εὑρημάτων, σίκιννιν αὐτὴν εἰρῆσθαι ἀπὸ τοῦ σείεσθαι.—Lib. xiv. cap. 28.

[c] Aristotle considered dancing a purely imitative art, for he says: Αὐτῷ δὲ τῷ ῥυθμῷ μιμοῦνται χωρὶς ἁρμονίας οἱ τῶν ὀρχηστῶν· καὶ γὰρ οὗτοι διὰ τῶν σχηματιζομένων ῥυθμῶν μιμοῦνται καὶ ἤθη καὶ πάθη καὶ πράξεις.—*Poetica*, cap. I, § 6. Plutarch draws a comparison between dancing and poetry, and says that as poets make use of figures and metaphors to express ideas, Οὕτως ἐν ὀρχήσει, τὸ μὲν σχῆμα μιμητικόν ἐστι μορφῆς καὶ ἰδέας, καὶ πάλιν ἡ φορὰ πάθους τινὸς ἐμφαντικὸν, ἢ πράξεως, ἢ δυνάμεως· ταῖς δὲ δείξεσι κυρίως αὐτὰ δηλοῦσι τὰ πράγματα, τὴν γῆν, τὸν οὐρανὸν, αὐτοὺς τοὺς πλησίον.—*Quæst. Conviv.* lib. ix. 15, § 6.

[d] 'Il résulte de tout cela, que la Danse, selon Platon, Aristote, et même Plutarque, n'étoit qu'une veritable Imitation, accomplie par les seuls mouvemens du corps, et que les danseurs ne s'y proposoient pour but princ}pal, que de représenter les Actions et les Passions humaines, soit en les imitant, par des marches et par des

firste parte of their youthe, that is to say from seuen yeres to twentie, effectuelly in the sciences liberall, and knowlege of histories, they shulde reuiue the aunceint fourme as well of daunsing,* as of other exercises, wherof they mought take nat only pleasure, but also profite and commoditie.

figures, soit en les indiquant par des Signes, le tout, en s'assujettissant à une Cadence reglée. Les Grecs avoient tellement perfectionné leur Danse, par raport à cette imitation des Passions, que les sculteurs les plus habiles (à ce que nous aprend Athénée), ne croyoient pas perdre leur tems en allant étudier, et même dessiner les différentes atitudes que prenoient les danseurs dans les Spectacles publics, et ils tâchoient ensuite d'exprimer vivement ces atitudes dans leurs figures, qui doivent sans doute à ce secours, emprunté de la Danse, leurs plus grandes beautez.'—Acad. des Inscr., *Mém. de Lit.* tom. i. p. 148. A modern master of the art denies the superiority of the ancient mode of dancing, and says that 'the Italians were the first to subject the arms, legs, and body to certain rules; which regulation took place in the sixteenth century. Before that time they danced, in my opinion, much in the same manner as the Greeks and Romans had done before them, which was by giving high leaps, making extravagant contortions, uncouth and indelicate motions, and resting in the most unbecoming attitudes. A commonplace practice was the only instruction such dancers received. The greater or less pleasure they enjoyed in their performance occasioned them more or less to excel. Dancing (as an art) was then only in its infancy.—M. Blasis, *The Art of Dancing*, p. 11, ed. 1830.

* The licentiousness which characterised the stage dances in the latter days of the Roman Empire doubtless threw discredit, especially in the eyes of the Christian converts, upon all forms of dancing. During many centuries the art seems to have languished, in company with the sister arts of Music, Poetry, and Painting, and it was not till the end of the fifteenth century that it reappeared in the graceful form which has rendered it popular with the most highly civilised nations of the world. Modern dancers should know to whom they are indebted for the revival of this favourite pastime. 'Le nom de Berganzo Botra brille à la tête des annales de la danse moderne. Une fête qu'il donna dans la ville de Tortone en 1489, à Galéas, duc de Milan, et Isabelle d'Arragon, son épouse, fut la véritable origine des carrousels et des ballets.'—M. Baron, *Lettres sur la Danse*, p. 137. From Italy the art quickly passed to France, where an unforeseen circumstance enabled it to occupy a still more prominent place as a national amusement. The unfortunate death of Henry II. in 1559, the result of an accident at a tournament, led to the abandonment of the chivalrous exercise. From that time, according to M. de Cahusac, 'les Bals, les Mascarades, et sur tout les Ballets qui n'entraînoient après eux aucun danger, et que la Reine Catherine de Médicis avoit connus à Florence, furent pendant plus de cinquante ans, la ressource de la galanterie, et de la magnificence Françoise.'—*La Danse Ancienne et Moderne*, tom. ii. p. 126, ed. 1754.

CHAPTER XXI.

Wherfore in the good ordre of daunsinge a man and a woman daunseth to gether.

IT is diligently to be noted that the associatinge of man and woman in daunsing, they bothe obseruinge one nombre and tyme in their meuynges, was nat begonne without a speciall consideration, as well for the necessarye coniunction of those two persones, as for the intimation of sondry vertues, whiche be by them represented.[a] And for as moche as by the association of a man and a woman in daunsinge may be signified matrimonie,[b] I coulde in declarynge the dignitie and com-

---

[a] The ideas here expressed are evidently borrowed from Plato's proposition in the *Laws*, to place music and dancing under the supervision of a select committee, whose duty it would be to pay especial regard to the different qualities of the two sexes. Ἔστι δὲ ἀμφοτέροις μὲν ἀμφότερα ἀνάγκη κατεχόμενα ἀποδιδόναι, τὰ δὲ τῶν θηλειῶν αὐτῷ τῷ τῆς φύσεως ἑκατέρου διαφέροντι τούτῳ δεῖ καὶ διασαφεῖν. τὸ δὴ μεγαλοπρεπὲς οὖν καὶ τὸ πρὸς τὴν ἀνδρείαν ῥέπον ἀρρενωπὸν φατέον εἶναι, τὸ δὲ πρὸς τὸ κόσμιον καὶ σῶφρον μᾶλλον ἀποκλῖνον θηλυγενέστερον ὡς ὂν παραδοτέον ἔν τε τῷ νόμῳ καὶ λόγῳ.—Lib. vii. cap. 10. 802 E. It remained for a Frenchman, celebrated *par excellence* for his skill and proficiency in that accomplishment which has been described by another of his countrymen as 'un art charmant, un art tout français,' to assign a reason, far from *spirituel*, for the associating of man and woman in dancing. According to this authority, 'Les danses sont practiquées pour congnoistre si les amoureux sont sains et dispos de leurs membres, à la fin desquelles il leur est permis de baiser leurs maistresses, affin que respectiuement ilz puissent sentir et odorer l'un l'aultre, silz ont l'alaine souefue, et silz sentent une senteur mal odorant, que l'on nomme l'espaule de mouton, de façon que de cêt endroict, oultre plusieurs commoditez qui reussissent de la dance, elle se treuve necessaire pour bien ordonner une societé.'—*Orchesographie*, fo. 2 b.

[b] The old French writer last quoted has some very practical ideas upon this point. He says quaintly enough, 'Naturellement le masle et la femelle se recherchent, et n'y a chose qui plus incite l'homme à estre courtois, honneste, et faire acte genereux que l'amour, et si voulez vous marier, vous debuez croire qu'une maistresse se gaigne par la disposition et grace qui se voit en une dance, car quant à l'escrime et au ieu de paulme, les dames n'y veuillent assister de craincte d'une espée rompue, ou d'un coup d'estoeuf, qui les pourroit endommager.'—*Orchesographie*, fo. 2 b. The Reformers, however, retorted that the practice of dancing involved something less innocent than is here implied. 'Deinde aiunt matrimonia nonnunquam hâc occasione honesta conciliari. Non pia hæc est atque honesta matrimonia

moditie of that sacrament make intiere volumes, if it were
nat so communely knowen to all men, that almoste euery
frere lymitour carieth it writen in his bosome.* Wherfore,

ineundi ratio : quin contrà ipsa experientia docet ὡς ἐπὶ τὸ πλεῖστον (id quod in
omnibus rebus potissimum est considerandum), hujusmodi saltationibus et multa
temeraria atque illegitima matrimonia contrahi, et justè contracta fœdari, et stupra
atque adulteria ex iis promanare.'—Stuckius, *Antiq. Conviv.* lib. iii. cap. 21,
p. 615, ed. 1695. And Lambert Daneau, writing in 1580, says : 'Mais entre
tous les proufits et commoditez de la danse, il n'y en a point qu'ils magnifient da-
uantage que ceste cy, asçauoir, que c'est l'acheminement et preparatif à beaucoup
de mariages, pour ce que les ieunes gens et autres se voyent là de pres, et s'amou-
rachent tant que lon vient à en parler, que les bons baladins maintesfois y ont esté
desirez, et par là sont paruenus à de grands partis, les filles semblablement. Voila
les belles utilitez que les meres principalement nous chantent tous les iours,
pour auoir licence d'apprendre a leurs filles à bien danser et les produire là
comme sur un theatre. Or ils ne nous sçauroyent mieux dire, et en plus clair
langage, qu'il n'y a rien plus propre à remuer les cœurs et affections des personnes,
et enflammer les conuoitises que les danses.'—*Traité des Danses*, p. 76, ed. 1580.

* Chaucer gives us a striking picture of these friars.

    'I speak of many hundred years ago,
    For now can no man see non elves mo.
    For now the great charity and prayers
    Of *lymytours* and other holy freres,
    That serchen every land and every stream,
    As thick as motis in the sunne-beam,
    Blessing halls, chambers, kitchens, and bowers,
    Cities and burghs, castles high and towers,
    Thorps and barns, shippons and dairies,
    This maketh that there been no fairies.
    For there as wont to walken was an elf,
    There walketh now the *lymytour* himself,
    In undermeles and in mornwenings,
    And sayeth his matins and his holy things
    As he goeth in his *lymytacion*.'—*Wife of Bath's Tale.*

And Spenser says :

    'I mean me to disguise,
    In some strange habit after uncouth wize,
    Or like a pilgrim or a *lymytour*.'—*Hubb. Tale.*

Mr. Cutts, in his sketch of the religious orders, says : 'The constitutions required
that no one should be licensed as a general preacher until he had studied theology
for three years ; then a provincial or general chapter examined into his character
and learning, and, if these were satisfactory, gave him his commission, either
limiting his ministry to a certain district (whence he was called in English a *limi-*

lest in repetyng a thinge so frequent and commune my boke shulde be as fastidious or fulsome to the reders as suche marchaunt preachours[a] be nowe to their custumers, I wyll reuerently take my leue of diuines. And for my parte I wyll endeuour my selfe to assemble, out of the bokes of auncient poets and philosophers, mater as well apte to my purpose as also newe or at the lest waies infrequent, or seldome herde of them that haue nat radde very many autours in greke and latine.

But nowe to my purpose. In euery daunse, of a moste auncient custome, there daunseth to gether a man and a woman, holding eche other by the hande [b] or the arme, whiche

tour, like Chaucer's Friar Hubert), or allowing him to exercise it where he listed (when he was called a *lister*).'—*Scenes and Characters of Mid.Ages*, p. 38, ed. 1872. In a sermon preached before Edward VI. at Greenwich, 1552, Bernard Gilpin, the Rector of Houghton, in Durham, said: 'A thousand pulpits in England are covered with dust; some have not had foure sermons these fifteene or sixteene yeares since Friers left their *limitations*, and few of these were worthy the name of sermons.'

[a] So called because, as belonging to the mendicant orders, they begged alms and thus made *merchandise* of their preaching.

'I found ther the fryers, all the four orders,
Preached to the people for profite of themselves.'—*Piers Plowman*.

The Dominicans were specially distinguished by the title of 'Friars Preachers.' 'The authority to preach,' says Mr. Cutts, 'and exercise other spiritual functions necessarily brought the friars into collision with the parochial clergy; and, while a learned and good friar would do much good in parishes which were cursed with an ignorant, or slothful, or wicked pastor, on the other hand, the inferior class of friars are accused of abusing their position by setting the people against their pastors, whose pulpits they usurped, and interfering injuriously with the discipline of the parishes into which they intruded.'—*Scenes, &c., of the Middle Ages*, p. 38. Matthew Paris, who, as a Benedictine of the great Monastery of St. Albans, delights in denouncing the faults of the new orders, tells us that the mendicants, within a quarter of a century of their first settlement in England, had degenerated more than any of the older monastic orders in three or four centuries; and a letter written in the name of the secular clergy to Henry III. contrasts their profession with their practice by saying that 'although having nothing they possess all things, and although without riches they grow richer than all the rich.'—Robertson's *Hist. of the Church*, vol. iii. p. 593, ed. 1866.

[b] It may well be doubted, however, if the custom of men and women dancing *together* is as ancient as the author supposes. The Puritan writers, at any rate,

betokeneth concorde. Nowe it behouethe the daunsers and also the beholders of them to knowe all qualities incident to a man, and also all qualities to a woman lyke wyse appertaynynge.

A man in his naturall perfection is fiers, hardy, stronge in opinion, couaitous of glorie, desirous of knowlege, appetiting by generation to brynge forthe his semblable. The good nature of a woman is to be milde, timerouse, tractable, benigne, of sure remembrance, and shamfast. Diuers other qualities of eche of them mought be founde out, but these be moste apparaunt, and for this time sufficient.

Wherfore, whan we beholde a man and a woman daun-

---

were at great pains to disprove this assertion. Thus Northbrooke says: 'Also here is to be noted in these examples, that you alledge for Dauncing, that Miriam and the other women, and Jephtah his daughter, the women that daunced in meeting Saul, and Judeth that daunced with the other women of Israel for ioye of their delivery, &c., daunced not with yong men, but apart by themselues, among women and maydens (which celebrated their victories), but seuerally by them selues among men.'—*Treatise against Dauncing*, p. 117. Another writer says: 'Præstereà pleræque Christianorum saltationes mixtim fiunt confuso sexu, quales pleræque veterum non erant (seorsim enim viri, seorsim mulieres saltabant), ac proinde multo majora sunt lasciviæ, Veneris, atque libidinum irritamenta quàm illæ veterum fuerint.'—Stuckius, *Antiq. Conviv.* lib. iii. p. 613, ed. 1695. Prynne, who investigated the subject most carefully from the Puritan point of view, says: 'These dances which we read of in Scripture were all single, consisting altogether of men, or of women only (which kind of single measures were anciently in use among the Persians and Grecians, and are yet retained among the Brasilians and others); whereas our moderne dances are for the most part mixt, both men and women dancing promiscuously together by selected couples.'—*Histriomastix*, p. 252, ed. 1633. It is probable that the age of chivalry, which did so much to render the position of women more tolerable, encouraged them to employ this new means of asserting their superiority in a pastime common to both sexes. Arbeau recognises the advantage of dancing as an exercise for women in the following quaint manner: 'Elle sert grandement à la santé, mesmement des ieusnes filles, lesquélles estans ordinairement sedentaires, et ententiues à leur lanifice, broderies, et ouurages desguille, font amas de plusieurs mauluaises humeurs, et ont besoing de les faire exhaler par quelque exercice temperé. La dance leur est un exercice propre, car elles n'ont pas liberté de se promener, et aller çà et la dehors et dedans les villes, ainsi que nous pouuons faire sans reprehension, tellement que n'en auons besoing comme elles.'—*Orchesographie*, fo. 6 b.

singe to gether, let us suppose there to be a concorde of all the saide qualities,ᵃ beinge ioyned to gether, as I haue set them in ordre. And the meuing of the man wolde be more vehement, of the woman more delicate, and with lasse aduauncing of the body,ᵇ signifienge the courage and strenthe that oughte to be in a man, and the pleasant sobrenesse that

<blockquote>
'The richest Jewell in all the heau'nly Treasure,
That euer yet unto the Earth was showne,
Is perfect Concord, th' onely perfect pleasure
That wretched Earth-borne men haue euer knowne,
For many harts it doth compound in one,
That what so one doth will, or speake, or doe,
With one consent they all agree thereto.

Concord's true Picture shineth in this Art,
Where diuers men and women ranked be,
And euery one doth daunce a seuerall part,
Yet all as one in measure doe agree,
Obseruing perfect uniformitie :
All turne together, all together trace,
And all together honor and embrace.'

Sir John Davies, *Orchestra*, ed. 1622.
</blockquote>

ᵇ This was quite in accordance with the strict rules of the art, as laid down by its professors. '*Capriol:* Vous me venez de proposer six manieres de contenances et mouuements, lesquelles treuuez vous les plus decentes? *Arbeau:* L'une de celles qui ont le pied oblique me semble plus belle, car nous voyons és medalles et statues antiques, que les Monopodes sont treuuez plus artistes et plus aggreables. Et quand aux pieds ioincts ou aux pieds eslargis directement, ils sentent leur contenance fœminine. Et tout ainsi qu'il est mal-sceant à une Damoiselle d'auoir une contenance hommace, aussi doibt l'homme euiter les gestes muliebres. Ce que vous pouuez aperceuoir aux reuerences, car à les faire, les hommes portent brusquement le pied croisé en derrier, et les Damoiselles plient les deux genoulx doulcement et se releuuent de mesme.'—*Orchesog.* fo. 42 b. M. Burette has expressed very nearly the same idea in enumerating the advantages of dancing. 'La Danse, de même que la Poësie, la Musique, la Peinture, et la Sculpture n'étant qu'une véritable imitation, et ne se proposant pour but principal, que de représenter au naturel les diverses actions des Hommes, et de peindre par des gestes mesurez les différentes Passions qui les agitent : qui ne voit, qu'en tournant cette imitation du côté des actions vertueuses, et n'exposant aux yeux, dans cette Peinture mobile et animée, que des Tableaux de Passions utiles à la Société, on n'en puisse faire un usage merveilleux, pour réveiller, dans les cœurs, des sentimens de Piété, de Compassion, de Courage, de Générosité et d'autres vertus semblables.'—Acad. des Inscript. *Mém. de Lit.* tom. i. p. 129, Hague, ed. 1719.

shulde be in a woman. And in this wise *fiersenesse* ioyned with *mildenesse* maketh *Seueritie;* *Audacitie* with *timerositie* maketh *Magnanimitie;* wilfull opinion and *Tractabilitie* (which is to be shortly persuaded and meued) makethe *Constance* a vertue; *Couaitise of Glorie,* adourned with *benignitie* causeth honour; *desire of knowlege* with *sure remembrance* procureth *Sapience; Shamfastnes* ioyned to *Appetite of generation* maketh *Continence,* whiche is a meane betwene *Chastitie* and *inordinate luste.* These qualities, in this wise beinge knitte to gether, and signified in the personages of man and woman daunsinge, do expresse or sette out the figure of very nobilitie; whiche in the higher astate it is contained, the more excellent is the vertue in estimation.

CHAPTER XXII.

Howe daunsing may be an introduction unto the firste morall vertue, called prudence.

As I haue all redye affirmed, the principall cause of this my litle enterprise is to declare an induction or meane, howe children of gentill nature or disposition may be trayned in to the way of vertue with a pleasant facilitie. And for as moche as it is very expedient that there be mixte with studie some honest and moderate disporte, or at the lest way recreation, to recomforte and quicken the vitall spirites,[b] leste they longe

[a] 'Lo this is Dauncing's *true nobilitie,*
Dauncing, the child of Musicke and of Loue,
Dauncing it selfe both loue and harmony,
Where all agree, and all in order moue;
Dauncing the Art that all Arts doe approue,
The faire caracter of the World's consent,
The Heau'n's true figure, and th' Earth's ornament.'
    Sir John Davies, *Orchestra.*

[b] Ascham lays great stress upon this in his *Schoolmaster.* 'Some men will say that children, of nature, love pastime and mislike learning; because, in their kind, the one is easy and pleasant, the other hard and wearisome. Which is an

trauailyng, or beinge moche occupied in contemplation or remembrance of thinges graue and seriouse, moughte happen to be fatigate, or perchance oppressed. And therfore Tulli, who uneth founde euer any tyme vacaunt from studie, permitteth in his firste boke of offices that men maye use play and disporte, yet nat withstandinge in suche wyse as they do use slepe and other maner of quiete, whan they haue sufficiently disposed ernest maters and of waighty importaunce.[a] *Off. i.*

Nowe by cause there is no passe tyme to be compared to that, wherin may be founden both recreation and meditation of vertue, I haue amonge all honest passe times, wherin is exercise of the body, noted daunsinge[b] to be of an excellent utilitie, comprehendinge in it wonderfull figures, or, as the grekes do calle them, *Ideae*, of vertues and noble qualities, and specially of the commodiouse vertue called prudence, whom Tulli defineth to be the knowlege of thinges whiche oughte to be desired and folowed, and also of them whiche ought to be fledde from or exchewed.[c] And *Ci. Off. i.*

opinion not so true as some men ween. For the matter lieth not so much in the disposition of them that be young, as in the order and manner of bringing up by them that be old; nor yet in the difference of learning and pastime. For, beat a child if he dance not well, and cherish him though he learn not well, you shall have him unwilling to go to dance and glad to go to his book; knock him always when he draweth his shaft ill, and favour him again though he fault at his book, you shall have him very loth to be in the field, and very willing to go to school.'— P. 115, ed. 1864. So Montaigne says, 'Les ieux mesmes et les exercices seront une bonne partie de l'estude; la course, la luicte, la musique, *la danse*, la chasse, le maniement des chevaulx et des armes.'—*Essais*, tom. i. p. 229, ed. 1854.

[a] 'Ludo autem et joco uti illo quidem licet; sed (sicut somno, et quietibus ceteris) tum, cum gravibus seriisque rebus satisfecerimus.'—*De Officiis*, lib. i. cap. 29.

[b] A modern writer has expressed precisely the same opinion: 'Outre que la danse donne au corps les dispositions les plus convenables, pour mieux réussir à presque tous les exercises utiles dans la Paix et dans la Guerre, elle a encore cet avantage, qu'en offrant aux Hommes *un honnête amusement*, elle peut aider à leur inspirer les passions les plus louables, et par là contribuer en quelque façon au règlement des Mœurs.'—Burette, Acad. des Inscript. *Mém. de Lit.* p. 128.

[c] 'Princepsque omnium virtutum est illa sapientia, quam σοφίαν Græci vocant:

it is named of Aristotel the mother of vertues;[a] of other philosophers it is called the capitayne or maistres of vertues; of some the house wyfe, for as moche as by her diligence she doth inuestigate and prepare places apt and conuenient, where other vertues shall execute their powers or offices.[b]

Prouerb xxvii. Wherfore, as Salomon saithe, like as in water be shewed the visages of them that beholde it,[c] so unto men that be prudent the secretes of mennes hartes be openly discouered. This vertue beinge so commodiouse to man, and, as it were, the porche of the noble palaice of mannes reason, wherby all other vertues shall entre, it semeth to me right expedient, that as sone as oportunitie may be founden, a childe or yonge man be therto induced. And by cause that the studie of vertue is tediouse for the more parte to them that do florisshe in yonge yeres, I haue deuised howe in the fourme of daunsinge, nowe late used in this realme amonge gentilmen,[d] the hole description of this vertue prudence may

---

prudentiam enim, quam Græci φρόνησιν dicunt, aliam quandam intelligimus; quæ est rerum expetendarum fugiendarumque scientia.'—*De Off.* lib. i. cap. 43.

[a] Apparently this refers to the following passage: 'Ἀλλά, φησίν, αὕτη ἐπιμελεῖται πάντων, καὶ κυρία ἐστὶ προστάττουσα. Ἀλλ' ἴσως ἔχει ὥσπερ ἐν οἰκίᾳ ὁ ἐπίτροπος. Οὗτος γὰρ πάντων κύριος καὶ πάντα διοικεῖ· ἀλλ' οὔπω οὗτος ἄρχει πάντων, ἀλλὰ παρασκευάζει τῷ δεσπότῃ σχολήν, ὅπως ἂν ἐκεῖνος μὴ κωλυόμενος ὑπὸ τῶν ἀναγκαίων ἐκκλείηται τοῦ τῶν καλῶν τι καὶ προσηκόντων πράττειν. Οὕτω καὶ ὁμοίως τούτῳ ἡ φρόνησις ὥσπερ ἐπίτροπος τίς ἐστι τῆς σοφίας, καὶ παρασκευάζει ταύτῃ σχολὴν καὶ τὸ ποιεῖν τὸ αὑτῆς ἔργον, κατέχουσα τὰ πάθη καὶ ταῦτα σωφρονίζουσα.—*Magna Moral.* lib. i. cap. 35. In another place Aristotle says: Οὔτε γὰρ ἄνευ τῆς φρονήσεως αἱ ἄλλαι ἀρεταὶ γίνονται, οὔθ' ἡ φρόνησις τελεία ἄνευ τῶν ἄλλων ἀρετῶν, ἀλλὰ συνεργοῦσί πως μετ' ἀλλήλων ἐπακολουθοῦσαι τῇ φρονήσει.—*Ibid.* lib. ii. cap. 3.

[b] We may compare with the above the following modern definition: 'Prudence is a Virtue, not of the Speculative Reason, which contemplates Conceptions, but of the Practical Reason, which guides our Actions.'—Whewell, *Elements of Morality*, p. 88, 4th ed.

[c] 'As in water face answereth to face, so the heart of man to man.'—*Prvv.* xxviii. 19.

[d] As before stated, there are hardly any works extant in English on dancing of an earlier date than *The Governour*; and it is therefore exceedingly difficult to collect information on the subject. It is probable, however, that the dances in vogue in France were adopted generally in this country, and we must therefore refer to the authority so often quoted, the *Orchesographie* of Arbeau, to learn not

be founden out and well perceyued, as well by the daunsers as by them whiche standinge by, wyll be diligent beholders and markers, hauyng first myne instruction suerly grauen in the table of their remembrance. Wherfore all they that haue their courage stered towarde very honour or perfecte nobilitie, let them approche to this passe tyme, and either them selfes prepare them to daunse, or els at the leste way beholde with watching eien other that can daunse truely, kepynge iuste measure and tyme.[a] But to the understanding of this instruction, they must marke well the sondry motions and measures, which in true fourme of daunsing is to be specially obserued.

The first meuyng in euery daunse is called honour,[b] whiche is a reuerent inclination or curtaisie, with a longe deliberation or pause, and is but one motion, compre- *honour in daunsing.*

only the names but the style of the various dances of the period in question. Arbeau, on being asked to describe the dances of his youth, replies : 'On dançoit pauanes, basse-dances, branles, et courantes ; les basse-dances sont hors d'usage depuis quarante ou cinquante ans. Mais ie preuoy que les matrones sages et modestes les remettront en usage, comme estant une sorte de dance pleine d'honneur et modestie. *C.* Ie treuue ces pauanes et basse-dances belles et graues, et bien seantes aux personnes honorables, principalement aux dames et damoiselles. *A.* Le Gentilhomme la peult dancer ayant la cappe et léspee. Et vous aultres vestuz de voz longues robes, marchants honnestement auec une grauité posee. Et les damoiselles auec une contenance humble, les yeulx baissez, regardans quelques fois les assistans auec une pudeur virginale. Et quant à la pauane, elle sert aux Roys, Princes et Seigneurs graues, pour se monstrer en quelque iour de festin solemnel, auec leurs grands manteaux et robes de parade. Et lors les Roynes, Princesses et Dames les accompaignent, les grands queues de leurs robes abaissees et traisnans, quelques fois portees par damoiselles. Et sont les dites pauanes iouees par haulbois et saquebouttes, qui l'appellent le grand bal, et la font durer iusques à ce que ceux qui dancent ayent circuit deux ou trois tours la salle ; si mieulx ils n'ayment la dancer par marches et desmarches. On se sert aussi desdictes pauanes quant on veult faire entrer en une mascarade chariotz triumphantz de dieux et deesses, Empereurs ou Roys, plains de maiesté.'—*Orchesographie,* ff. 24 b, 29.

[a] 'Il fault que les gestes des membres accompaignent les cadances des instruments musicaulx, et ne fault pas que le pied parle d'un, et l'instrument daultre.'— *Orchesographie,* fo. 5.

[b] Elaborate directions for the proper execution of this step are given by Thoinot Arbeau as follows : 'Le premier mouuement est la reuerence. Au commence-

R

hendinge the tyme of thre other motions,[a] or settyng forth of the foote. By that may be signified that at the begynning of all our actes, we shulde do due honour to god, whiche is the roote of prudence; whiche honour is compacte of these thre thinges, feare, loue, and reuerence.[b] And that in the begynnynge of all thinges we shulde aduisedly, with some tracte of tyme, beholde and for se the successe of our entreprise.

By the seconde motion, whiche is two in nombre, may be signified celeritie and slownesse, whiche two, all be it they seme to discorde in their effectes and naturall propreties,[c] and therfore they may be well resembled to the braule [d] in daunsinge (for in our englisshe tonge we say men do braule, whan betwene them is altercation in wordes), yet of them two springeth an excellent

Celeritie and slownes.

A braule.

ment d'une gaillarde, il fault presupposer, que le danceur tenant la Damoiselle par la main, faict la reuerence lorsque les ioueurs d'instrumens commencent à sonner, laquelle, reuerence faicte, se renge en une contenance belle et decente. Pour faire la reuerence, vous tiendrez le pied gaulche ferme à terre, et pliant le iarret de la iambe droicte, porterez la pointe de l'arreil de la semelle droicte derrier ledict pied gaulche, ostant vostre bonnet ou chappeau, et saluant vostre Damoiselle et la compagnie. Aprez que la reuerence est ainsi faicte, redresserez le corps, et recouurant vostre teste, retirerez vostre dict pied droict, et vous mettrez et poserez les deulx pieds ioincts, que nous entendons estre contenance decente, quand les deulx pieds sont tellement disposez, quilz sont l'un au droict de l'aultre, comme vous voyez en la figure cy dessoubz, les arreils desquels sont dirigez en ligne droicte et soubstiennent egallement le corps du danceur.'—*Orchesographie*, ff. 25 b, 40.

[a] 'Il vous fault auparauant sçauoir que les chansons des basse dances sont iouees par mesure *ternaire*, et à chacune mesure le tabourin pour s'accorder auec la flutte, faict la mesure *ternaire* aussi.'—*Ibid.* fo. 24 b.

[b] 'When the moral attributes of God are more s adily apprehended, Fear receives a mixture of Love, and becomes Revere .e; and in proportion as the Goodness of God becomes more and more fixed in man's belief, Love predominates over Fear in the feelings which they have respecting him.'—*Elements of Morality*, p. 292, 4th ed.

[c] 'Per quod monebat, ut ad rem agendam simul adhiberetur et industriæ celeritas et diligentiæ tarditas, ex quibus duobus contrariis fit *maturitas*.'—A. Gell. *Noct. Att.* lib. x. cap. 11.

[d] In Cotgrave's *Dict.* the word *bransle* is translated 'a brawle or daunce wherein many (men and women), holding by the hands, sometimes in a ring and otherwhiles at length, move all together.' But properly speaking it was, as explained in the text, the second movement in the basse dance. It is thus explained by

vertue where unto we lacke a name in englisshe. Wherfore I am constrained to usurpe a latine worde, callyng it *Maturitie*: whiche worde, though it be strange and darke, yet by declaring the vertue in a fewe mo wordes, the name ones brought in custome, shall be as facile to understande as other wordes late commen out of Italy and Fraunce, and made denizins amonge us.[a]

Arbeau : 'Le branle est appellé par Arena *congedium*, et croy qu'il le nomme ainsi, pource qu'à veoir le geste du danceur, il sembleroit qu'il voulust finir et prendre *congé*, et neantmoins apres le branle, il continue ses marches et mouuements comme ils sont escrits ésdits memoires. Le dit branle se faict en quatre battements de tabourin, qui accompaignent quatre mesures de la chanson iouee par la flutte, en tenant les pieds ioincts, remuant le corps doucement du cousté gauche pour la premiere mesure, puis du cousté droit, en regardant les assistans modestement pour la deuxieme mesure, puis encor du cousté gauche pour la troisieme mesure. Et pour la quatrieme mesure du cousté droit, en regardant la Damoiselle d'une œillade desrobee doulcement et discretement.'—*Orchesographie*, fo. 27. Sir John Davies, whose philosophical poems are praised by Hallam for their perspicuity, was the author of an ode already quoted, entitled *Orchestra*, the subject of which is the antiquity and excellence of dancing. From the dedication it would seem to have been first composed in the reign of Edward VI., and republished in that of Elizabeth. In it occurs the following stanza, descriptive of the dance in question

'Then first of all he (*Love*) doth demonstrate plaine
The motions seauen that are in nature found—
Upward and *downward*, *forth*, and *backe againe*,
To this side and *to that*, and *turning round*,
Whereof a thousand *brawles* he doth compound,
Which he doth teach unto the multitude,
And euer with a turne they must conclude.'

[a] 'Puttenham, in his *Arte of English Poesie*, lib. iii. cap. 4, gives many instances of foreign words, or words derived from the Latin, which were gradually becoming acclimatised in this country. The following are a few examples : *Major-domo*, 'borrowed of the Spaniard and Italian, and therefore new and not usuall, but to them that are acquainted with the affaires of Court.' *Politien*, 'receiued from the Frenchmen, but at this day usuall in Court and with all good Secretaries.' *Conduict*, 'a French word, but well allowed of us, and long since usuall.' *Idiome*, 'taken from the Greekes, yet seruing aptly.' *Significatiue*, 'borrowed of the Latine and French, but to us brought in first by some Nobleman's Secretarie as I thinke, yet doth so well serue the turne as it could not now be spared.' *Penetrate, indignitie, sauage, obscure*, &c., &c. Wilson, however, finds fault with the habit affected by some *dilettanti* of introducing foreign words at random. 'Some farre iournied ientlemen,' he says, 'at their returne home, like as

Maturitie is a meane betwene two extremities, wherin nothing lacketh or excedeth, and is in suche astate that it may neither encrease nor minisshe without losinge the denomination of Maturitie. The grekes in a prouerbe do expresse it proprely in two wordes, whiche I can none other wyse interprete in englisshe, but speede the slowly.[a]

Also of this worde Maturitie, sprange a noble and preciouse sentence, recited by Salust in the bataile againe Cataline, whiche is in this maner or like, Consulte before thou enterprise any thing, and after thou hast taken counsaile, it is expedient to do it maturely. *Maturum* in latine maye be enterpreted ripe or redy, as frute whan it is ripe, it is at the very poynte to be gathered and eaten, and euery other thinge, whan it is redy, it is at the instante after to be occupied.[c] Therfore that worde maturitie is translated to the actis of man, that whan they be done with suche moderation, that nothing in the doinge may be

marginal: Priusquam incipias consulto. Maturum.

---

thei loue to go in forrein apparell, so thei wil pouder their talke with ouersea language. He that cometh lately out of Fraunce will talke French-Englishe, and neuer blushe at the matter. Another choppes in with Angleso-Italiano; and applieth the Italian phrase to our English speaking, the which is, as if an Oratour, that professeth to utter his mind in plaine Latine, would needes speake Poetrie, and farre fetched colours of straunge antiquitie. The Lawyer wil store his stomack with the pratyng of pedlers. The Auditour, in makyng his accompt and rekenyng, cometh in with *sise sould* and *cater denere* for vi*s*. iv*d*. The unlearned or foolishe phantasticall, that smelles but of learnyng (suche felowes as haue seen learned men in their daies), will so Latine their tongues that the simple cannot but wonder at their talke, and thynke surely thei speake by some Reuelacion.'—*Arte of Rhet.* p. 164, ed. 1584. Montaigne makes the same complaint with regard to his own countrymen: 'Il ne s'y veoid qu'une miserable affectation d'estrangeté, des desguisements froids et absurdes, qui, au lieu d'eslever, abbattent la matiere : pourveu qu'ils se gorgiasent en la nouvelleté, il ne leur chault de l'efficace ; pour saisir un nouveau mot, ils quittent l'ordinaire, souvent plus fort et plus nerveux.'— *Essais*, tom. iii. p. 444, ed. 1854.

[a] Σπεῦδε βραδέως.

[b] 'Nam et prius quam incipias, consulto, et ubi consulueris, mature facto opus est.'—*Catilina*, cap. i.

[c] 'Nam et in frugibus et in pomis "matura" dicuntur quæ neque cruda et immitia sunt, neque caduca et decocta, sed tempore suo adulta maturaque.'—Aulus Gellius, *Noct. Att.* lib. x. cap. 11.

sene superfluous or indigent, we may saye, that they be maturely done :[a] reseruyng the wordes ripe and redy to frute and other thinges seperate from affaires, as we haue nowe in usage. And this do I nowe remembre for the necessary augmentation of our langage.[b]

In the excellent and most noble emperour Octauius Augustus, in whom reigned all nobilitie, nothinge is more commended than that he had frequently in his mouthe this worde *Matura*, do maturely.[c] As he shulde haue saide, do neither to moche ne to litle, to soone ne to late, to swiftly nor slowely, but in due tyme and measure.

Nowe I trust I haue sufficiently expounde the vertue called Maturitie, whiche is the meane or mediocritie betwene slouthe and celeritie, communely called spedinesse; and so haue I declared what utilitie may be taken of a braule in daunsinge.

[a] 'Quoniam autem id, quod non segniter fiebat, "mature" fieri dicebatur, progressa plurimum verbi significatio est ; et non jam quod non segnius, sed quod festinantius fit, id fieri "mature" dicitur.'—Aulus Gellius, *ubi supra*.

[b] Wilson, though averse to the employment of what he calls 'inkhorn terms,' admits that the poverty of the language is an excuse for the process of engrafting foreign words upon the parent stock. ' Now whereas wordes be receiued as well Greke as Latine to set furthe our meanyng in thenglisshe tongue, either for lacke of store or els because we would enriche the language, it is well doen to use them, and no man therin can be charged for any affectacion, when all other are agreed to folowe the same waie. There is no man agreued when he heareth (Letters Patents), and yet *Patentes* is Latine, and signifieth open to all men. The Communion is a fellowship or a commyng together, rather Latine than Englishe ; the Kynges Prerogatiue declareth his power royall aboue all other, and yet I knowe no man greued for these terms beeyng used in their place, nor yet any one suspected for affectacion when suche generall wordes are spoken. The folie is espied when either we will use suche wordes as fewe men doo use, or use them out of place when another might serue muche better.'—*Arte of Rhetorique*, p. 167, ed. 1584.

[c] ' Nihil autem minus in perfecto duce, quàm festinationem temeritatemque convenire arbitrabatur. Crebro itaque illa jactabat : Σπεῦδε βραδέως, et 'Ασφαλὴς γὰρ ἐστ' ἀμείνων, ἢ θρασὺς στρατηλάτης, et 'Sat celeriter fieri, quicquid fiat satis bene.'—Sueton. *Oct.* 25. Aulus Gellius says, ' Illud vero Nigidianum rei atque verbi temperamentum Divus Augustus duobus Græcis verbis elegantissimè exprimebat : nam et dicere in sermonibus et scribere in epistolis solitum esse aiunt, σπεῦδε βραδέως.'— *Noct. Att.* lib. x. cap. 11.

CHAPTER XXIII.

The thirde and fourth braunches of prudence.

THE thirde motion, called singles,[a] is of two unities seperate in pasinge forwarde; by whom may be signified prouidence and industrie; whiche, after euerye thinge maturely achieued, as is before writen, maketh the firste pase forwarde in daunsinge. But it shall be expedient to expounde what is the thing called Prouidence, for as moche as it is nat knowen to euery man.

Sengles in daunsing.

Prouidence is wherby a man nat only foreseeth commoditie and incommoditie, prosperitie and aduersitie, but also consulteth, and therewith endeuoureth as well to repelle anoyaunce, as to attaine and gette profite and aduauntage. And the difference betwene it and consideration is that consideration only consisteth in pondering and examining thinges conceiued in the mynde,[b] Prouidence in helpinge them with counsaile

Prouidence, what it is.

Consideration, what it is.

---

[a] A translation of the French *simples*, which was the third movement in the basse dance. 'La troisieme sorte de mouuement sont deux simples. *Capriol.* Deux simples suyuent le branle, comment fault-il les faire? *Arbeau.* Vous marcherez en auant du pied gauche pour la premiere mesure. Puis mettrez le pied droit ioinct auec ledict gauche pour la deuxieme mesure. Puis auancerez le pied droit pour la troisieme mesure : et à la quatrieme mesure et battement ioindrez le pied gauche auec le dict pied droit, et ainsi sera parfaict le mouuement des deux simples. Et se fault donner garde de faire les auonces des pieds si grandes qu'il semble qu'on veuille mesurer la longueur de la salle, ioinct que la Damoiselle ne pourroit honnestement faire de si grandes passees comme vous feriez. Arena et aultres de sa sequelle font le simple d'un mesme pied, marquant pour la premiere mesure du pied gauche a cousté du droit, puis aduanceant le dit gauche. Et aultant du pied droit. Mais il me souuient que mon maistre de Poictiers impreuuoit ceste mode, disant qu'il estoit plus décent de finir les deux simples par les pieds ioincts, que par l'aduance de l'un des pieds.'—*Orchesographie*, ff. 26, 27.

[b] The following is a modern definition of this faculty : 'That man has some power over his own thoughts is evident. He can retain an object of thought in his mind, contemplate it in various aspects and bearings, scrutinize it, deliberate upon it. This is Inquiry and *Consideration*, and by this proceeding he can often discover means to an end, and consequences of an act, which escape his notice in

and acte. Wherfore to consideration pertaineth excogitation and aduisement, to prouidence prouision and execution. For like as the good husbande, whan he hath sowen his grounde, settethe up cloughtes [a] or thredes, whiche some call shailes,[b] some blenchars,[c] or other like showes, to feare away birdes,

a more rapid and slight mode of regarding the subject.'—Whewell, *Elements of Morality*, p. 136, 4th ed.

[a] This word is more often spelt *clout*, and, according to Richardson, is derived from *cleofian* = findere, and means anything cloven or torn into small pieces. In Johnson's *Dict.*, the first meaning assigned to this word is 'a cloth for any mean use,' and the following illustration from Spenser's *Fairy Queen* is given :

'His garment, nought but many ragged *clouts*,
With thorns together pinn'd and patched was.'

In Cotgrave's *Dict.* the word *Espouentail* is translated 'a man of clouts to feare birds with.' Is it not possible that there is some connection with the French word *clouet*, a little nail or tin-tack, as pieces of tin or nails are often seen strung on threads at the present day for the very purpose described in the text? It is remarkable that though Somner in his *Dict. Sax.-Lat.-Angl.*, and Skinner in his *Etymologicon Linguæ Anglicanæ* both derive *Clout* from the A. S. *Clut* = Pittacium, Sutura, the latter says, 'Clouted shoon, *i.e.* vir rusticus à Fr. G. *clouet*, clavulus seu parvus clavus diminutivo τοῦ *clou*, clavus, et inde *clouette*, q. d. qui calceos parvis clavis confixos habet,' a derivation which seems to some extent to justify the present suggestion.

[b] In Sherwood's *Eng.-Fren. Dict.*, ed. 1650, the equivalent given for the word 'shales' is *cossats* or *finfreluches*, meaning husks or shells of beans, &c. In Johnson's Dict. 'shale' is said to be a corruption for *shell*, but this seems to have been doubted by Grose. It is worthy of note that the spelling in the text is *shail*, not *shale*, and it would seem therefore to be connected with the French écaille, which is in German *schale*. Now écaille or escaille = *haillon*; and Cotgrave translates the latter 'a clowt, a tatter, a rag,' which is precisely the meaning attached to the word 'shaile' by Sir Thos. Elyot.

[c] It is worthy of note that one of the meanings in Johnson's Dict. assigned to the word 'clout' is 'the mark of *white* cloth at which archers shot' (Fr. *clouette*), and an illustration is given from Shakespeare's *Hen. IV.*, 'he would have clapt in the *clout* at twelve score.' Mr. Todd, in his edition of Johnson's *Dict.*, derives *blenchars* from the verb *to blench*, and explains it as 'that which may frighten or cause to start,' and cites the passage in the text and one other from Beaumont and Fletcher's *Love's Pilgrimage*. Is not blenchar, however, merely the French *blancheur, blanchet?* Cotgrave translates the latter 'a *white* woollen cloth,' but Du Cange gives also as a meaning of *Blanchet*, '*blanc, but auquel on vise en tirant*,' tom. vii. p. 64, and, in the Glossary, under *blanchetus*, quotes the following passage from a writer of the 15th century: 'Le suppliant joua et

whiche he foreseeth redy to deuoure and hurte his corne. Also perceiuinge the improfitable weedes apperynge, whiche wyll anoye his corne or herbes, forthewith he wedeth them clene out of his grounde, and wyll nat suffre them to growe or encrease. Semblably it is the parte of a wyse man to forsee and prouide, that either in suche thinges as he hath acquired by his studie or diligence, or in suche affaires as he hath in hande, he be nat indomaged or empeched by his aduersaries.

In lyke maner a gouernour of a publike weale ought to prouide as well by menaces, as by sharpe and terrible punisshementes, that persones iuell and improfitable do nat corrupte and deuoure his good subiectes.* Finally there is in prouidence suche an admiration and maiestie, that nat

---

tira d'un arc ... par deux ou trois cops ouprès du *Blanchet*, qui estoit opposé esdites butes, ainsi qu'il est accoustumé. Ubi *album* seu scopus est vulgo *Blanc*.' It would seem from the context that blenchars might be interpreted as 'rags of *white* cloth' used as 'scarecrows,' and if this suggestion be adopted, then it would hardly be going too far to assume that *clouts*, *shailes*, and *blenchars* are all of them adaptations from the French, which at this period was, as has been already noticed, a very common practice with English writers. In Cowel's Law Dict. '*Blench*' is said to be 'a kind of tenure of land, as to hold land in *blench* is by payment of a sugar-loaf, a bever-hat, a couple of capons, and such like, if it be demanded in the name of *blench*, *i.e.* nomine *albæ firmæ*.' The *blenchar* may, therefore, have been the name jocularly applied to the man of clouts, crowned with an old bever hat, by whom the land was defended against the birds. It seems, however, on the whcle, clear that the notion of a *white* colour is implied, as being most effective for the purpose described. Cotgrave says that *Blanchards* were 'an ordre of Friers who go ordinarily in *white* sheets, and wear neither hats nor shoes.' Now a scarecrow consisting of a white sheet stretched on a pole might easily be imagined to bear a fanciful resemblance to a member of this order, and as friars were constantly a subject of derision, it is possible the word so used ook its origin from this fact. It must be confessed, however, that both derivations seem rather far fetched.

* 'He who has authority ought to issue commands, not only kind, but also prudent and wise. He has faculties by which he is enabled to judge of such characters in Rules of Action, and he is bound to employ these faculties as well as his Affections in the performance of his Duty. Thus there are Duties which belong to these faculties. We may term them generally Duties of the Intellectual Faculties, but we may conveniently distinguish among them the *Duty of Prudence* and the *Duty of Wisdom*.'—Whewell's *Elements of Morality*, p. 135.

onely it is attributed to kinges and rulers, but also to god, creatour of the worlde.[a]

Industrie hath nat ben so longe tyme used in the englisshe tonge as Prouidence; wherfore it is the more straunge, and requireth the more plaine exposition.[b] It is a *Industrie.* qualitie procedyng of witte and experience, by the whiche a man perceyueth quickly, inuenteth fresshly, and counsayleth spedily. Wherfore they that be called Industrious, do moste craftily and depely understande in all affaires what is expedient, and by what meanes and wayes they maye sonest exploite them.[c] And those thinges in whome other men trauayle, a person industrious lightly and with facilitie spedeth, and fyndeth newe wayes and meanes to bring to effecte that he desireth.

[a] 'We must conceive ourselves and the world to be under the government of God. God must be the Governor, as he is the Creator, of the world; for as the Creator, he formed and placed in it those springs of Progress by which its course is carried on and regulated. We cannot help believing that, like all other parts of the Creation, the course of the world of human doing and suffering, must have a Purpose, and this Purpose must be in harmony with the Moral Government of God. The course of this world, we cannot but believe, is directed by God's Providence.'—*Elements of Morality,* pp. 256, 257, 4th ed.

[b] It is a curious coincidence that this word appears conspicuously in the Statutes of the Realm of this very year (1532), with the modern meaning of occupation or handicraft, a meaning which does not appear to have been previously implied in such records. Thus the preamble of the 24 Hen. VIII. cap. 4, after noticing the fact of the increasing importation of linen cloth, runs as follows: 'By reason wherof not only the said straunge Countres where the seid Lynnen Clothe is made, by the policie and *industrie* of makyng and ventyng therof are greately enriched, and a marvelous greate nombre of theyr peple, men, women and children, sett on work and occupacion and kepte from idelnes, but also contrarie wise the inhabitauntez and subjectes of this Realme, for lake of like policie and *industrie* aboute the inventing, practisyng, and puttyng in exercise like occupacion, beyng compelled to bye all or the moost parte of the said Lynnen Clothe, &c.' But, in 26 Hen. VIII. cap. 19, the preamble recites that the King's most loving subjects 'consyderyng the great *industrye,* labor, peyne and travayle, with the excessive and inestimable charges whiche his Highness hath bene att,' &c.; have granted to the King's Highness one whole 15th and 10th. Where the word is used in its ordinary sense, it, however, does not appear often in the Statute Book during this reign.

[c] It will be noticed that the author employs this word in a sense quite different to that which we are accustomed to ascribe to it. It is not so much the exercise

250   THE GOVERNOUR.

Alcibiades. Amonge diuers other remembred in histories, such one amonge the grekes was Alcibiades, who being in childehode moste amiable[a] of all other, and of moste subtile witte, was instructed by Socrates.[b] The saide Alcibiades, by the sharpnesse of his witte, the doctrine of Socrates, and by his owne experience in sondrie affaires in the commune weale of the Athenienses, became so industrious, that were it good or iuell that he enterprised, no thinge almoste eskaped[c] that he acheued nat, were the thing neuer so difficile (or as who saythe) impenitrable, and that many sondrie thinges, as well for his countray, as also agayne it, after that he, for his inordinate pride and lechery, was out of Athenes exiled.[d]

of volition as an intellectual faculty. It is an efficient rather than an instrumental cause. So used it answers as nearly as possible to what would now be called 'cleverness,' a word unknown in the author's day. In Elyot's own Dictionary the meaning assigned to *industria* is 'a vertue comprehendynge bothe study and diligence,' and *industrius* is translated, 'He that is wytty and actyue.'

[a] 'Affabilis, blandus, temporibus callidissimè inserviens.'—Corn. Nep. *Alcibiades*, 1.

[b] Ὑπ' εὐφυίας ἐγνώρισε Σωκράτη καὶ προσήκατο διασχὼν τοὺς πλουσίους καὶ ἐνδόξους ἐραστάς. Ταχὺ δὲ ποιησάμενος συνήθη καὶ λόγων ἀκούσας οὐχ ἡδονὴν ἄνανδρον ἐραστοῦ θηρεύοντος οὐδὲ φιλημάτων καὶ ψαύσεως προσαιτοῦντος, ἀλλ' ἐλέγχοντος τὸ σαθρὸν τῆς ψυχῆς αὐτοῦ καὶ πιεζοῦντος τὸν κενὸν καὶ ἀνόητον τῦφον.—Plut. *Alcibiad.* 4.

[c] Sir Thomas Elyot has apparently followed the account given of Alcibiades by Corn. Nepos. 'Constat enim inter omnes, qui de eo memoriæ prodiderunt, nihil eo fuisse excellentius, vel in vitiis, vel in virtutibus . . . . . Nihil enim eum non efficere posse ducebant. Ex quo fiebat, ut omnia minus prospere gesta ejus culpæ tribuerent, cum eum aut negligenter aut malitiosè fecisse loquerentur.'—*Alcibiades*, 1, 7. Thirlwall says he possessed 'a mind of singular versatility, a spirit which, like that of the people itself, shrank from no enterprise and bent before no obstacle.'—*Hist. of Greece*, vol. iii. p. 311, ed. 1846. Grote compares him to Themistocles and styles him 'essentially a man of action.'

[d] It is interesting to compare his picture, as drawn by a great modern historian: 'There are few characters in Grecian history who present so little to esteem, whether we look at him as a public or as a private man. His ends are those of exorbitant ambition and vanity: his means rapacious as well as reckless, from his first dealing with Sparta and the Spartan envoys down to the end of his career. The manœuvres whereby his political enemies first procured his exile were indeed base and guilty in a high degree. But we must recollect that if his enemies were

Amonge the romanes, Caius Julius Cesar, whiche first toke upon him the perpetuall rule and gouernaunce of the empire, is a noble example of industrie, for in his incomparable warres and busynesse incredible (if the autoritie and faithe of the writers were nat of longe tyme approued) he dyd nat onely excogitate moste excellent policies and deuises to vainquisshe or subdue his enemies, but also prosecuted them with suche celeritie and effecte, that diuers and many tymes he was in the campe of his enemies, or at the gates of their townes or fortresses, whan they supposed that he and his hoste had ben two dayes iournay from thens,*

Julius Cesar.

more numerous and violent than those of any other politician in Athens, the generating seed was sown by his own overweening insolence, and contempt of restraints, legal as well as social.'—Grote's *Hist. of Greece*, vol. vi. pp. 22, 23.

* This was especially the case during his seventh campaign. Mr. George Long, reviewing the events of the year B.C. 52, says: 'It was the coldest time of the year, and the Cevennes were covered with snow to the depth of six feet, but by hard work the soldiers cut a road through the snow and reached the country of the Arverni. . . . . . The Arverni were surprised at the appearance of Cæsar's troops, for they thought that the Cevennes were a sufficient protection, and the mountains had never been crossed at this season of the year even by single travellers. Cæsar taking advantage of this alarm ordered his cavalry to spread themselves over the country and to strike terror into the people. . . . .' Cæsar again crossed the mountains at this inclement season, probably by the same road, and travelling at a great rate he reached Vienna (Vienne) on the East side of the Rhone, to which place he had sent forward many days before the cavalry which he had recently raised. Continuing his journey day and night northwards through the country of the Ædui he reached the Lingones, where two of the legions were wintering. By these rapid movements he anticipated any hostile designs that the Ædui might form against him, and sending his orders to the other legions he got them all together at Agendicum (Sens) before the Arverni could be informed of his arrival in these parts.'—*Decline of Roman Republic*, vol. iv. p. 291. And a little later in the same campaign, Merivale tells us that 'Cæsar rushed to the defence of the Boii, although the season of the year and the scarcity of provisions presented serious obstacles to the movements of an army. His first object was to march upon Genabum, the possession of which place would intercept the communication of the northern and southern states of the confederacy. With his usual celerity he advanced to the walls before the defenders were apprised of his movements. The meditated assault was only postponed for the moment by the late hour of his arrival. But the Gauls within, astounded at the unexpected apparition of their restless enemy, were preparing to evacuate the town by the bridge which crosses the Loire.'—*Hist. of Rome*, vol. ii. p. 11, ed. 1850.

leauing to them no tyme or layser to consulte or prepare agayne him sufficient resistence. And ouer that, this qualitie industrie so reigned in him, that he him selfe wolde ministre to his secretaries at one tyme and instante, the contentes of thre sondrie epistles or lettres.[a] Also it is a thing wonderfull to remembre that he, beynge a prince of the moste auncient and noble house of the romanes, and from the tyme that he came to mans astate, almoste contynuelly in warres,[b] also of glorie insatiable, of courage inuincible, coulde in affaires of suche importaunce and difficultie, or (whiche is moche more to be meruayled at nowe) wolde so exactly write the historie of his owne actes and iestes, that for the natiue and inimitable eloquence in expressing the counsailes, deuises, conuentions, progressions, enterprises, exploitures, fourmes, and

---

[a] Pliny and Plutarch do not quite agree in their description of this wonderful effort of memory, and Sir Thomas Elyot has adopted neither version. The former says: 'Epistolas vero tantarum rerum *quaternas* pariter librariis dictare: aut, si nihil aliud ageret, septenas.'—*Nat. Hist.* lib. vii. cap. 25. Plutarch says: 'Ἐν ἐκείνῃ δὲ τῇ στρατείᾳ προσεξήσκησεν ἱππαζόμενος τὰς ἐπιστολὰς ὑπαγορεύειν καὶ δυσὶν ὁμοῦ γράφουσιν ἐξαρκεῖν, ὡς δὲ Ὄππιός φησι, καὶ πλείοσι.—*Cæsar*, 17. The same feat has been accomplished in modern times by an eminent English statesman. We are told in the *Greville Memoirs* that 'Canning's industry was such that he never left a moment unemployed; and such was the clearness of his head that he could address himself almost at the same time to several different subjects with perfect precision, and without the least embarrassment. He wrote very fast, but not fast enough for his mind, composing much quicker than he could commit his ideas to paper. He could not bear to dictate, because nobody could write fast enough for him; but on one occasion when he had the gout in his hand and could not write, he stood by the fire and dictated at the same time a despatch on Greek affairs to George Bentinck and one on South American politics to Howard de Walden, each writing as fast as he could, while he turned from one to the other without hesitation or embarrassment.'—Vol. i. p. 106, 1st ed.

[b] Mr. George Long says: 'His literary occupations were continued during his campaigns, and employed his leisure hours. He was the most diligent of men, always busy with something. . . . He must have had plenty to do in looking after his commissariat, raising money and troops among his Gallic allies, forming his plans, and corresponding with his friends in Rome; but he found leisure to write also the history of his campaigns, to which he gave the modest title of Commentarii.'—*Decl. of Rom. Rep.*, vol. v. pp. 472, 473.

facions of imbatailynge, he semeth to put all other writers of like mater to silence.*

Here is the perfecte paterne of Industrie, whiche I trust shal suffice to make the propre signification therof to be understande of the reders. And consequently to incende them to approche to the true practising therof.

So is the sengles declared in these two qualities, Prouidence and Industrie; which, seriousely noted and often remembred of the daunsers and beholders, shall acquire to them no litle frute and commoditie, if there be in their myndes any good and laudable mater for vertue to warke in.

CHAPTER XXIV.

Of the fifthe braunche, called circumspection, shewed in reprinse.

COMUNELY nexte after sengles in daunsing is a reprinse, whiche is one mouing only, puttynge backe the ryght fote to his felowe. And that may be well called circumspection, whiche signifieth as moche as beholdynge *Reprinse in daunsinge.*

---

* Montaigne was of the same opinion. 'On récite de plusieurs chefs de guerre, qu'ils ont eu certains livres en particuliere recommendation, comme le grand Alexandre, Homere; Scipion Africain, Xenophon; Marcus Brutus, Polybius; Charles cinquieme, Philippe de Comines; et dict on, de ce temps, que Machiavel est encores allieurs en credit. Mais le feu mareschal Strozzi, qui avoit prins Cæsar pour sa part, avoit sans doubte bien mieulx choisi; car à la verité, ce deburoit estre le breviaire de tout homme de guerre, comme estant le vray et souverain patron de l'art militaire : et Dieu sçait encores de quelle grace et de quelle beauté il a fardé cette riche matiere, d'une façon de dire si pure, si delicate, et si parfaicte, qu'à mon goust il n'y a aulcuns escripts au monde qui puissent estre comparables aux siens en cette partie.'—*Essais*, tom. iii. p. 212, ed. 1854. Cicero himself paid a high compliment to Cæsar's ability as a writer when he said, 'Sanos quidem homines à scribendo deterruit. Nihil enim est in historiâ purâ et illustri brevitate dulcius.'— *De Claris Orat.* cap. 75.

b In Cotgrave's *Dictionary* one of the meanings assigned to this word is 'a turn in the daunsing of a measure.' Neither Johnson nor Richardson, however, though referring constantly to *The Governour* for illustrations, notice this use of the word

on euery parte, what is well and sufficient, what lackethe, howe and from whens it may be prouided. Also what hath caused profite or damage in the tyme passed, what is the astate of the tyme present, what aduauntage or perile maye succede or is imminent. And by cause in it is contained a deliberation, in hauing regarde to that that foloweth, and is also of affinitie with prouidence and industrie, I make hym in the fourme of a retrete.[a]

In this motion a man may, as it were on a mountaine or place of espial,[b] beholde on euery syde farre of, measuring and estemyng euery thing, and eyther pursue it, if it be commendable, or abandone it or escheue it, if it be noyfull. This qualite (lyke as prouidence and industrie be) is a braunche of Prudence, whiche some calle the princesse of vertues;[c] and it is nat onely expedient, but also nedefull to euery astate and degree of men, that do contynue in the lyfe called actife.

In the Iliados of Homere, the noble duke Nestor, a man
Nestor. of maruaylous eloquence and longe experience, as

Reprise, and it is probable, therefore, that both these authorities considered that it had never become naturalised in the English language. It is equally ignored by Furetière, Larousse, and even Littré, and it is only in the work of Thoinot Arbeau that we find an interpretation parallel to that in the text. The writer last mentioned says in his *Orchesographie*: 'Le mouuement appellé *reprise*, precede ordinairement le branle, et quelquefois le double, et tient quatre mesures du tabourin aussi bien comme les aultres mouuements, lequel vous ferez en remuant un peu les genoux, ou les pieds, ou les arroils seullement, comme si les pieds vous fremioient. Sçauoir sur la premiere mesure les arroils du pied droit, puis encor les dits arroils du pied droit sur la second mesure, puis les arroils du pied gauche sur la troisieme mesure, et les arroils du dit pied droit sur la quatrieme mesure. Et en ces quatre mouuements demeure accomplie *la reprise*, et le danceur prest à faire le branle ou les aultres mouuements qui suyuent.'—Fo. 28.

[a] This word seems to be merely a translation of, or at any rate a synonym for, reprinse.

[b] This word is sometimes used *pro personâ*; thus Holinshed in his 'History of Henry the Seventh' says: 'The king then aduertised not onelie by his *espials* upon their returne, but also from other his trustie freends, determined with all speed to haue the fraud published.'—*Chron.* vol. iii. p. 777.

[c] Justice is called by Cicero 'Hæc enim una virtus omnium est domina et regina virtutum.'—*De Off.* lib. iii. cap. 6.

he that lyued thre mennes lyues,[a] as he there auaunteth in the counsayle that he gaue to Agamemnon, to reconcile to him Achilles, the moste stronge of all the grekes, he persuadyd Agamemnon specially to be circumspect; declaringe howe that the priuate contention betwene them shulde replenisshe the hooste of the grekes with moche dolour,[b] wherat kynge Priamus and his children shulde laughe, and the resydue of the Troyanes in their myndes shulde reioyce and take courage.[c]

Amonge the Romanes Quintus Fabius for this qualitie is soueraignely extolled amonge historiens; and for that cause he is often tymes called of them *Fabius cunctator*,[d] that is to saye the tariar or delayer, for in the warres

Fabius.

[a] Τῷ δ' ἤδη δύο μὲν γενεαὶ μερόπων ἀνθρώπων
  'Εφθίαθ', οἵ οἱ πρόσθεν ἅμα τράφεν ἠδ' ἐγένοντο
  'Εν Πύλῳ ἠγαθέῃ, μετὰ δὲ τριτάτοισιν ἄνασσεν.—*Il.* i. 250-253.

And in the *Odyssey* we are told

  Τρὶς γὰρ δή μιν φασὶν ἀνάξασθαι γένε' ἀνδρῶν.—Lib. iii. 245.

Mr. Gladstone arrives at the conclusion that by γενεή a term of about thirty years is implied, and says that 'Homer has been careful to mark, by an appropriate change of expressions, the difference between Nestor's age in the two poems respectively. In the *Iliad* he is exercising the kingly office *among* the third generation since his birth. In the *Odyssey* he is said to have exhausted the three terms.'—*Studies on Homer*, vol. iii. p. 450.

[b] Πολλῶν δ' ἀγρομένων, τῷ πείσεαι, ὅς κεν ἀρίστην
  Βουλὴν βουλεύσῃ· μάλα δὲ χρεὼ πάντας 'Αχαιοὺς
  'Εσθλῆς καὶ πυκινῆς, ὅτι δήιοι ἐγγύθι νηῶν
  Καίουσιν πυρὰ πολλά· τίς ἂν τάδε γηθήσειε;
  Νὺξ δ' ἥδ' ἠὲ διαρραίσει στρατὸν, ἠὲ σαώσει.—*Il.* ix. 74-78.

[c] These words are an addition of the author by way of antithesis, a practice to which, as we have seen, he was much addicted.

[d] 'Ut Fabius inter plures imperatorias virtutes *Cunctator* est appellatus.'— Quintil. *Instit. Orat.* lib. viii. cap. 2, § 11, Cicero says: 'Hic et bella gerebat, ut adolescens, quum plane grandis esset; et Hannibalem juveniliter exsultantem patientiâ suâ molliebat; de quo præclare familiaris noster Ennius:

  'Unus, qui nobis cunctando restituit rem.
  Non ponebat enim rumores ante salutem.
  Ergo postque, magisque viri nunc gloria claret.'

  De Senect. cap. 4.

bytwene the romanes and Anniball, he knowynge all costes [a] of the countray, continuelly kept him and his hoste on mountaynes and high places, within a small distaunce of Hanniballes armie ; so that neither he wolde abandon his enemies nor yet ioyne with them batayle. By whiche wonderfull policie he caused Anniball so to trauayle, that some tyme for lacke of vitayle and for werynesse, great multitudes of his hoste perisshed. Also he oftentymes awayted them in daungerous places, unredy, and than he skirmisshed with them, as longe as he was sure to haue of them aduauntage ; and after he repayred to the hyghe places adioyning, usyng his accustomed maner to beholde the passage of Anniball.[b] And by this meanes this moste circumspecte capitaine Fabius wonderfully infeblyd the powar of the said Anniball : whiche is no lasse estemed in praise, than the subduing of Cartage by the valiaunt Scipio.[c] For if Fabius had nat so fatigate Anniball and his hoste, he had shortly subuerted the cite of Rome, and than coulde nat Scipio haue ben able to attayne that entreprise.

What more clere mirrour or spectacle can we desire of circumspection,[d] than kyng Henry the seuenth, of most noble memorie, father unto our mooste dradde soueraigne lorde, whose worthy renome, like the sonne

Kynge Henry the vii.

---

[a] *I.e.* coasts.

[b] Αὐτὸς δὲ πάσας θέμενος ἐν αὑτῷ τὰς τῆς νίκης ἐλπίδας, ὡς καὶ τοῦ θεοῦ τὰς εὐπραξίας δι' ἀρετῆς καὶ φρονήσεως παραδιδόντος, τρέπεται πρὸς Ἀννίβαν, οὐχ ὡς διαμαχούμενος, ἀλλὰ χρόνῳ τὴν ἀκμὴν αὐτοῦ καὶ χρήμασι τὴν ἀπορίαν καὶ πολυανθρωπίᾳ τὴν ὀλιγότητα τρίβειν καὶ ὑπαναλίσκειν βεβουλευμένος. Ὅθεν ἀεὶ μετέωρος ἀπὸ τῆς ἵππου τῶν πολεμίων ἐν τόποις ὀρεινοῖς στρατοπεδεύων ἐπηωρεῖτο, καθημένου μὲν ἡσυχάζων, κινουμένου δὲ κατὰ τῶν ἄκρων κύκλῳ περιιὼν καὶ περιφαινόμενος ἐκ διαστήματος ὅσον ἀκοντὶ μὴ βιασθῆναι μάχεσθαι καὶ φόβον ὡς μαχησόμενος τοῖς πολεμίοις ἀπὸ τῆς μελλήσεως αὐτῆς παρέχειν.—Plut. *Fabius,* 5.

[c] The writer of the article on Fabius in Smith's *Dict. of Biog.* says : 'Marcellus and Scipio restored the republic to its military eminence, whereas Fabius made it capable of restoration.' It must be remembered, however, that Fabius was at a later period vehemently opposed to the intention of Scipio, of carrying the war into Africa, which resulted in the destruction of Carthage.

[d] It is not a little curious that Lord Bacon distinctly denies him the possession of this quality, and says that he was, 'in his nature and constitution of mind, not very apprehensive or forecasting of future events afar off, but an entertainer of fortune

in the middes of his sphere, shyneth and euer shall shyne in mennes remembrance? What incomparable circumspection was in hym alway founden, that nat withstandynge his longe absence out of this realme,[a] the disturbance of the same by sondrye seditions amonge the nobilitie,[b] Ciuile warres and batayles, wherin infinite people were slayne, besyde skirmisshis and slaughters in the priuate contentions and factions

by the day.'—*Works*, vol. iii. p. 110, ed. 1825. Holinshed, however, says 'that in great perils, doubtfull affaires, and matters of importance' he was 'supernaturall, and in maner diuine, for he ordered all his doings aduisedlie, and with great deliberation.'—Vol. iii. p. 797. A modern historian, writing under no apprehension of incurring the royal displeasure, is necessarily more chary of his compliments. Dr. Lingard considers that the credit which Henry the Seventh obtained with contemporary writers for political wisdom, or as our author calls it, 'circumspection,' arose from nothing higher than the naturally crafty bent of 'a mind dark and mistrustful, tenacious of its own secrets, and adroit in divining the secrets of others.' And then he quotes, in support of this contention, a passage from Sir Thomas More (see Holinshed's *Chron.* vol. iii. p. 734), which, however, has no reference to Henry VII. at all, but to Richard III. The fact that Sir Thomas More's history was written in the reign of the son of the king whose character Dr. Lingard supposes to be thus painted, would almost of itself preclude such a supposition, but a careful perusal of the whole passage with the context, shows conclusively that the 'covert demeanour' was not intended to apply to Henry. Hall, Grafton, and Stow, as well as Holinshed, print the passage verbatim; but the former omits the significant words 'in late days.' And while Hall, in the next paragraph, adheres to the original style, viz., 'the noble prince kynge Henrye the VII.,' Grafton, writing in the lifetime of the grand-daughter, styles him 'the late noble prince of famous memorie.' Thus the weight of evidence, as well as probability, is against such an inference as is drawn by Dr. Lingard. It is singular, however, that another distinguished writer, Mr. Sharon Turner, has adopted precisely the same view. See his *Hist. of Engl.* vol. vii. p. 60.

[a] We learn from Stow that Henry, then Earl of Richmond, and his uncle, the Earl of Pembroke, fled into Brittany in the month of September, 1471, and that he sailed in the Kalends of August, 1485, 'from Harefleete (*i.e. Harfleur*), with so prosperous a winde that the seuenth day after he arriued in Wales in the euening, at a port called Milforde Hauen, and incontinent tooke land and came to a place called Dale.'—*Annales*, pp. 425, 469, ed. 1615. According to this computation he was absent from England just fourteen years. Commines says: 'Ce comte (*i.e.* Henry VII.) avoit esté *quinze ans ou environ*, prisonnier en Bretagne, du duc François dernier mort, esquelles mains il vint par tempeste de mer, cuidant fuir en France, et le comte de Pennebroc, son oncle, avec luy.'—*Mémoires*, liv. v. chap. 18.

[b] Notably the insurrection of Lord Lovell and the partisans of the pretended Earl of Warwick, and of Perkin Warbeck.

S

of diuers gentilmen, the lawes layde in water (as is the prouerbe),[a] affection and auarice subduinge iustice and equitie;[b] yet by his moste excellent witte, he in fewe yeres, nat onely broughte this realme in good ordre and under due obedience, reuiued the lawes, auaunced Justice,[c] refurnisshed his dominions, and repayred his manours;[d] but also with suche circumspection traited with other princes and realmes, of

[a] Plato has ἐν ὕδατι γράφειν in the *Phædrus*, cap. lxi, p. 276 c., but this is hardly an equivalent expression to that in the text, the meaning intended to be conveyed being better represented by the phrase of Lucretius, 'Religio *pedibus subjecta* vicissim obteritur,' or by Livy's 'Qui omnia jura populi obtrisset,' and Cicero's 'Leges ac jura labefactat.' The editor is not aware of any phrase, either in Greek or Latin, which would be accurately translated as above; and though Stephens quotes a line, "Ὅρκον δ' ἐγὼ γυναικὸς εἰς ὕδωρ (οἶνον) γράφω (cf. *Athen*. lib. x. p. 441), which he says = 'nihili facere,' it is obvious that this does not represent the full force of the English phrase.

[b] Bacon, accounting for the defection, and consequent impeachment and execution, of Sir William Stanley, says that Henry, out of gratitude for his services at the battle of Bosworth, had given him 'great gifts, made him his counsellor and chamberlain, and, somewhat contrary to his nature, had winked at the great spoils of Bosworth-field, which came almost wholly to this man's hands, to his infinite enriching. Yet, nevertheless, blown up with the conceit of his merit, he did not think he had received good measure from the king, at least not pressing down and running over, as he expected. And his ambition was so exorbitant and unbounded, as he became suitor to the king for the Earldom of Chester: which ever being a kind of appanage to the principality of Wales, and using to go to the king's son, his suit did not only end in a denial but in a distaste: the king perceiving thereby, that his desires were intemperate, and his cogitations vast and irregular, and that his former benefits were but cheap, and lightly regarded by him.'—*Works*, vol. iii. p. 299, ed. 1825.

[c] This is confirmed by the testimony of a still more eminent lawyer than the author, Lord Chancellor Bacon, who observes 'Certainly his times, for good commonwealth's laws, did excel. So as he may justly be celebrated for the best lawgiver to this nation, after King Edward the First; for his laws, whoso marks them well, are deep and not vulgar; not made upon the spur of a particular occasion for the present, but out of providence of the future, to make the estate of his people still more and more happy, after the manner of the legislators in ancient and heroical times.'—*Ubi supra*, p. 233.

[d] Bacon says: 'As to his expending of treasure, he never spared charge which his affairs required, and in his buildings was magnificent; but his rewards were very limited, so that his liberality was rather upon his own state and memory than upon the deserts of others.'—*Ubi supra*, p. 409.

leages, of aliaunce,[a] and amities, that during the more parte of his reigne, he was litle or nothyng inquieted with outwarde hostilitie or martiall businesse.[b] And yet all other princes either feared hym or had hym in a fatherly reuerence. Whiche praise, with the honour thereunto due, as inheritaunce discendeth by righte unto his most noble sonne, our moste dere soueraigne

---

[a] A modern historian, reviewing this reign, says: 'Henry made an alliance with Ferdinand and Isabella, against France. He made also alliances with the duke of Milan, the king of Naples, the bishop of Liege, the archduke Philip, (whom his father Maximilian had set over the Low Countries), and the duke of Saxony, the governor of Friesland. He concluded a perpetual peace with the king of Denmark, and with Portugal, and treaties of commerce with the republic of Florence, and with the Low Countries. He also negotiated with the city of Riga, concerning some of its ships, which English cruisers had taken. He was empowered to assist Ladislaus, king of Hungary, with money, against the Turks. The pacification with Scotland ended, after much negotiation, in a marriage between its sovereign, James IV., and Margaret, the eldest daughter of Henry—an important union, as it occasioned the house of Stewart to succeed to the English crown. The marriage of Catherine, the princess of Spain, with Arthur, was also accomplished.'—Turner's *Hist. of Eng.* vol. vii. p. 87.

[b] Stow says: 'Notwithstanding many and great occasions of trouble and war, he kept his Realme in right good order, for the which he was greatly reuerenced of forraine princes.'—*Annales*, p. 471, ed. 1615. And Bacon assigns as a reason for this his skill in diplomacy: 'As for little envies, or emulations upon foreign princes, which are frequent with many kings, he had never any' but went substantially to his own business. Certain it is that though his reputation was great at home, yet it was greater abroad. For foreigners that could not see the passages of affairs, but made their judgments upon the issues of them, noted that he was ever in strife, and ever aloft. It grew also from the airs which the princes and states abroad received from their ambassadors and agents here; which were attending the court in great number; whom he did not only content with courtesy, reward, and privateness, but, upon such conferences as passed with them, put them in admiration, to find his universal insight into the affairs of the world: which though he did suck chiefly from themselves, yet that which he had gathered from them all seemed admirable to every one. So that they did write ever to their superiors in high terms concerning his wisdom and art of rule; nay, when they were returned, they did commonly maintain intelligence with him. Such a dexterity he had to impropriate to himself all foreign instruments.'—*Works*, vol. iii. p. 411. Mr. Brewer, however, contrasting the position of England under Henry VII. with what it afterwards became under his son, contends that 'during his reign England rose to no higher estimate on the continent than a third or fourth-rate power.'—*Preface to Letter and Papers of the Reign of Henry VIII.* p. xxi.

lorde that nowe presently raigneth.[a] For, as Tulli saithe, the best inheritance that the fathers leue to their children, excellynge all other patrimonie, is the glorie or praise of vertue and noble actis.[b] And of suche faire inheritance his highnesse may compare with any prince that euer raigned :[c] whiche he

[a] Lord Bacon, in his fragment of the reign of Henry VIII., says : 'He was inheritor of his father's reputation, which was great throughout the world.'—*Works*, vol. iii. p. 419. A modern writer, eminently qualified, by his examination of those sources of information which were unknown to previous historians, to express an authoritative opinion, has said that 'if Henry VIII. had died previous to the first agitation of the divorce, his loss would have been deplored as one of the heaviest misfortunes which had ever befallen the country ; and he would have left a name which would have taken its place in history by the side of that of the Black Prince or of the conqueror of Agincourt.'—Froude, *Hist. of Eng.* vol. i. p. 157, ed. 1856. Another equally competent authority says: 'He was the most popular, the most wealthy, the most envied of monarchs.'—Brewer, vol. ii. pt. i. p. cxcviii.

[b] 'Optima autem hæreditas à patribus traditur liberis, omnique patrimonio præstantior, gloria virtutis, rerumque gestarum.'—*De Off.* lib. i. cap. 33.

[c] Such, too, was the opinion of Fulwell, who, writing in 1575, nearly thirty years after Henry's death, says : ' Among the most fortunate kynges and princes that ever raigned, let the fortunes of King Henry the Eyght have a speciall place ; whose happie successe in his affaires was comparable unto the events of the mightie conqueror, Kyng Phillip's sonne of Macedon. There were in his tyme raigning more puissant princes together then ever were lyving in any age before ; and yet, amongst them all, not one of them equall to the Kyng of Englande in prowess. . . . . A man he was in all gifts of nature, of fortune, and of grace, peerles ; and, to conclude, a man above all prayses.' This language of panegyric is, of course, open to the observation that it was employed in the lifetime of a sovereign who was the daughter of the man so eulogised, but we may well agree with the writer when he goes on to say, ' Suche a kyng did God set to raigne over England, whereof this realme may well vaunt above other nations, whose worthines is more treated of by forreign wryters than by any of our owne countrey men : which may justly redownd to the reproche of all our English poets and historiographers.'—*Harleian Miscellany*, vol. ix. p. 342, ed. 1812. This last assertion indeed is fully borne out by the documents recently published under the direction of the Master of the Rolls. From this source we learn the unbiassed opinion of the Papal Nuncio, Francesco Chieregato, who in a letter to the Marchioness of Mantua, dated 10 July, 1517, styles Henry 'this most invincible king, whose acquirements and qualities are so many and excellent that I consider him to excel all who ever wore a crown ; and blessed and happy may this country (England) call itself in having as its lord so worthy and eminent a sovereign, whose sway is more bland and gentle than the greatest liberty under any other.'—*Venetian State Papers*, vol. ii. p. 400. Even Cardinal Pole, Henry's bitterest detractor and most uncompro-

dayly augmenteth, adding therto other sondry vertues, whiche I forbeare nowe to reherce, to the intent I wyll exclude all suspition of flaterye, sens I myselfe in this warke do speciallye reproue it. But that whiche is presently knowen, and is in experience, nedeth no monument. And unto so excellent a prince there shall nat lacke here after condigne writers to registre his actes, with mooste eloquent stile in perpetuell remembrance.[a]

mising opponent, is himself compelled to make the following admission in the *Apology*, which he dedicated to the Emperor Charles V.: 'Ego mentior si olim talem (*sc.* indolem) fuisse dicam ex quâ præclara omnia sperari possent. Fuit enim aliquando prorsus regia. Summum in eo pietatis studium apparebat et religionis cultus, magnus amor justitiæ, non abhorrens tamen natura, ut tum quidem videbatur, à clementiâ, tantum liberalitatis specimen, ut non solum, ubi opus esset, libenter daret sed multos ultro ad virtutem præmiis invitaret, et virtute præditos muneribus honestaret ; neque in hoc discrimen poneret, suus ne, id est ex regno, an externus esset, sed in quibuscumque virtutem elucere videret, dignam præmio judicabat, et præmiis afficiebat. Ex quo effectum est, ut etiam exteri multi ad eum confluerent, qui literis, qui aliis artibus præstantes erant, tanquam ad virtutis æstimatorem optimum et præmiatorem liberalissimum. Ob quas causas non tam nostris, quàm multis exteris nationibus, cœpit esse ut celebris, ita maxime carus, ejusque nomen illustrari.'—*Epistol. Reg. Poli*, pars i. p. 86, ed. 1744, Brixiæ.

[a] Mr. Turner says : 'When we reflect on the copious amplifications of abuse with which the memory of Henry has been as pertinaciously as indiscriminately assailed, the common candour of that impartial feeling, and that moral justice, which every one who exists in society is bound by mutual interest, as well as by higher principles, to exercise towards others, leads us at the outset of his history to ask, what was the general estimation of him by his associates and contemporaries who knew him well, and who judged of him without vindictive resentments. They had the best means of perceiving the truth, and are the safest guides to us in discriminating it from the clouds and falsehoods with which hostility, too violent to be honest, has deformed and concealed it.'—*Hist. of Engl.* vol. ix. p. 28. To the labours of Mr. Brewer and Mr. Froude the present generation is indebted for that clear and impartial insight into the character of this king, which, by the unaccountable neglect of previous historians to consult the abundant materials, unassorted it is true, but well worthy to be explored, and only needing patient investigation, in our national archives, had been rendered well nigh impossible. Mr. Froude, in his concluding summary, says : 'The history of the reign of Henry VIII. is a palimpsest in which the original writing can still be read ; and I have endeavoured only to reinstate the judgment upon his motives and his actions— which was entertained by all moderate Englishmen in his own and the succeeding generation—which was displaced only by the calumnies of Catholic or antinomian fanatics when the true records were out of sight ; and when in the establishment of

CHAPTER XXV.

Of the sixte, seuenth, and eighte braunches of prudence.

A DOUBLE in daunsinge is compacte of the nombre of thre,[a] wherby may be noted these thre braunches of prudence; election, experience, and modestie. By them the saide vertue of prudence is made complete, and is in her perfection. Election is of an excellent powar and autoritie,[b] and hath suche a maiestie, that she will nat be approched unto of euery man. For some there be to whom she denieth her presence, as children, naturall fooles,[c] men beinge frantike, or subdued with

a new order of things, the hesitating movements, the inconsistencies and difficulties inevitable in a period of transition could no longer be understood without an effort.'—*Hist. of England,* vol. iv. p. 531, ed. 1858.

[a] This, however, is not quite in accordance with the rules laid down by Arbeau. 'Le double se faict en *quatre* mesures et battements du tabourin. Sur la premiere mesure fault auancer le pied gauche. Sur la seconde mesure, il fault aduancer le pied droit. Sur la troisiesme mesure, il fault encor auancer le pied gauche ; et sur la quatrieme mesure, il fault ioindre le droit auéc ledit gauche. Et ainsi en 4 mesures sera complet le double.'—*Orchesographie,* fo. 27. b.

[b] The Latin word *electio* is very rarely used by classical writers, although the verb from which it is derived is constantly to be met with. It is most commonly to be met with in the writings of the Fathers, who, like the Calvinists at a later period, attached a special doctrinal meaning to it. Richardson gives several illustrations of the use of this word by early English writers—Chaucer, Gower, Lord Berners, and others. It occurs several times in the English translation of the Bible.

[c] 'Lord Coke has enumerated four different classes of persons who are deemed in law to be *non compotes mentis*. The first is an idiot, or fool natural; the second is he who was of good and sound memory, and by the visitation of God has lost it ; the third is a lunatic, *lunaticus qui gaudet lucidis intervallis*, and sometimes is of a good and sound memory, and sometimes *non compos mentis* ; and the fourth is *non compos mentis* by his own act, as a drunkard. In regard to drunkenness, the writers upon natural and public law adopt it, as a general principle, that contracts made by persons in liquor, even though their drunkenness be voluntary, are utterly void ; because they are incapable of any deliberate consent, in like manner as persons who are insane, or *non compotes mentis*. Cases of an analogous nature may easily be put, where the party is subjected to undue influence, although in other respects of competent understanding. As where he does an act, or makes a contract, when he is under duress, or the influence of extreme terror, or of threats, or of apprehensions short of duress. For, in cases of this

affects, also they that be sublectes to flaterers and proude men. In these persones reason lacketh libertie, whiche shuld prepare their entrie unto election. This Election, whiche is a parte, and as it were a membre, of prudence,^a is best described by Oportunitie,^b whiche is the principall parte of counsaile, and is compacte of these thinges folowynge. *Election. Oportunitie.*

The importaunce of the thinge consulted. The facultie and power of hym that consulteth. The tyme whan. The fourme howe. The substance wherwith to do it. The dispositions and usages of the countrayes. For whom and agayne whom it oughte to be done. All these thinges prepensed and gathered to gether seriousely, and, after a due examination, euery of them iustely pondred in the balance of reason, immediately cometh the autoritie of Election, who taketh on her to appoynt what is to be effectuelly folowed or pursued, reiectynge the residue.^c

---

sort, he has no free will, but stands *in vinculis*. On this account courts of equity watch with extreme jealousy all contracts made by a party while under imprisonment; and if there is the slightest ground to suspect oppression or imposition in such cases, they will set the contracts aside. Circumstances, also, of extreme necessity and distress of the party, although not accompanied by any direct restraint or duress, may, in like manner, so entirely overcome his free agency as to justify the court in setting aside a contract made by him, on account of some oppression, or fraudulent advantage, or imposition, attendant upon it.—Story's *Equity Jurisprudence*, vol. i. sec. 230-239, 10th edn.

^a 'Prudentia (cernitur) in *delectu* bonorum et malorum.'—Cic. *de Fin.* lib. v. cap. 23.

^b This definition, it will be seen, is much more comprehensive than that of the ancient philosophers. Cicero, for example, says: 'Locum autem actionis, opportunitatem temporis esse dicunt. Tempus autem actionis opportunum Græce εὐκαιρία, Latinè appellatur "occasio."'—*De Off.* lib. i. cap. 40.

^c 'Election,' in a legal and technical sense, 'is the obligation imposed upon a party to choose between two inconsistent or alternative rights or claims, in cases where there is clear intention of the person, from whom he derives one, that he should not enjoy both. Every case of election, therefore, presupposes a plurality of gifts or rights, with an intention, express or implied, of the party, who has a right to control one or both, that one should be a substitute for the other. The party, who is to take, has a choice; but he cannot have the benefits of both. Before any presumption of an election can arise, it is necessary to show that the party acting or acquiescing was cognisant of his rights. When this is ascertained

And than ought experience to be at hande, to whom is committed the actual execution.[a] For without her Election is frustrate, and all inuention of man is but a fantasie. And therfore who aduisedly beholdeth the astate of mannes life, shall well perceiue that all that euer was spoken or writen, was to be by experience executed: and to that intent was speche specially gyuen to man, wherin he is moste discrepant from brute beastis, in declaring what is good, what viciouse, what is profitable, what improfitable,[b] by them whiche by clerenesse of witte do excelle in knowlege, to these that be of a more inferior capacitie.[c] And what utilitie

Expe-rience.

affirmatively, it may be further necessary to consider, whether the party intended an election; whether the party was competent to make an election; for a *feme covert*, an infant, or a lunatic, will not be bound by an election. Questions have also arisen in Courts of Equity, as to the time when, and the circumstances under which, an election may be required to be made. The general rule is, that the party is not bound to make any election until all the circumstances are known, and the state, and condition, and value of the funds are clearly ascertained; for until, so known and ascertained, it is impossible for the party to make a discriminating and deliberate choice, such as ought to bind him to reason and justice.'—Story's *Equity Jurisprudence*, vol. ii. chap. 30, secs. 1075, 1097, 1098, 10th edn.

[a] ' Per varios usus artem *experientia* fecit
Exemplo monstrante viam.'—Manilius, *Astron.* lib. i. 61.

And Columella has a very similar expression:

' Hæc ne ruricolæ paterentur monstra, salutis
Ipsa novas artes varia *experientia* rerum
Et labor ostendit miseris, ususque magister
Tradidit agricolis.'—Lib. x. 337.

[b] Puttenham, in his *Arte of Poesie*, says: ' Utterance also and language is giuen by nature to man for perswasion of others, and aide of them selues, I meane the first abilitie to speake. For speech it selfe is artificiall and made by man, and the more pleasing it is, the more it preuaileth to such purpose as it is intended for.' —Lib. i. chap. iv. p. 5, ed. 1811.

[c] A distinguished modern writer has drawn attention to the immense importance of speech in the earliest ages, and the degree in which the faculty was cultivated by the specimens exhibited in the poems of Homer. ' The trait,' says Mr. Gladstone, ' which is truly most worthy of note in the polities of Homeric Greece, is also that which is so peculiar to them; namely, the substantive weight and influence which belonged to speech as an instrument of government; and of this power by much the most remarkable development is in its less confined and more popular application to the Assembly. This power of speech was essentially

shulde be acquired by suche declaration, if it shulde nât be experienced with diligence ?

The philosopher Socrates had nat bene named of Appollo the wyseste man of all Gracia,[a] if he had nat daylye practised the vertues, whiche he in his lessons commended. Julius Cæsar, the firste emperour, all thoughe there were in hym moche hydde lernynge ; in so moche as he firste founde the ordre of our kalandre, with the Cikle and bisexte, called the lepe yere ;[b] yet is he nat so moche honoured for his lernynge as he is for his diligence, wherwith he exploited or brought to conclusion those counsailes, whiche as well by his excellent lerning and wisedome, as by the aduise of other experte counsailours were before traited, and (as I mought saye) ventilate.[c]

Socrates.

Julius Cæsar.

a power to be exercised over numbers, and with the safeguards of publicity, by man among his fellow men. It was also essentially an instrument addressing itself to reason and free will, and acknowledging their authority. No government which sought its power in force, as opposed to reason, has at any time used this form of deception. The world has seen absolutism deck itself with the titles and mere forms of freedom, or seek shelter under its naked abstractions ; but from the exercise of free speech as an instrument of state, it has always shrunk with an instinctive horror.' The speeches in Homer, says the same writer, 'contain specimens of transcendant eloquence which have never been surpassed, they evince the most comprehensive knowledge, and the most varied and elastic use, of all the resources of the art.'—*Studies on Homer*, vol. iii. pp. 102, 107, ed. 1858.

[a] Τῆς γὰρ ἐμῆς, εἰ δή τίς ἐστι σοφία καὶ οἵα, μάρτυρα ὑμῖν παρέξομαι τὸν θεὸν τὸν ἐν Δελφοῖς. Χαιρεφῶντα γὰρ ἴστε που. Οὗτος ἐμός θ' ἑταῖρος ἦν ἐκ νέου, καὶ ὑμῶν τῷ πλήθει ἑταῖρός τε καὶ ξυνέφυγε τὴν φυγὴν ταύτην καὶ μεθ' ὑμῶν κατῆλθε. Καὶ ἴστε δὴ, οἷος ἦν Χαιρεφῶν, ὡς σφοδρὸς ἐφ' ὅ τι ὁρμήσειε. Καὶ δή ποτε καὶ εἰς Δελφοὺς ἐλθὼν ἐτόλμησε τοῦτο μαντεύσασθαι καὶ—ὅπερ λέγω, μὴ θορυβεῖτε, ὦ ἄνδρες—ἤρετο γὰρ δὴ, εἴ τις ἐμοῦ εἴη σοφώτερος. ἀνεῖλεν οὖν ἡ Πυθία μηδένα σοφώτερον εἶναι.—Plato, *Apolog.* cap. 5.

[b] Ἡ δὲ τοῦ ἡμερολογίου διάθεσις καὶ διόρθωσις τῆς περὶ τὸν χρόνον ἀνωμαλίας φιλοσοφηθεῖσα χαριέντως ὑπ' αὐτοῦ καὶ τέλος λαβοῦσα γλαφυρωτάτην παρέσχε χρείαν.—Plut. *Cæsar*, 59.

[c] Cicero calls Cæsar 'Hoc *τέρας* horribili vigilantiâ, celeritate, diligentiâ.'— *Epist. ad Att.* lib. viii. 9. 'While other illustrious men,' says Merivale, 'have been reputed great for their excellence in some one department of human genius, it was declared by the concurrent voice of antiquity that Cæsar was excellent in all. He had genius, understanding, memory, taste, reflection, industry, and exactness.'—*Hist. of Rome*, vol. ii. p. 494, ed. 1850.

Who wyll nat repute it a thinge vayne and scornefull, and more lyke to a may game,[a] than a mater seriouse or commendable, to beholde a personage, whiche in speche or writyng expresseth nothing but vertuous maners, sage and discrete counsailes, and holy aduertisementes, to be resolued in to all vices, folowyng in his actis no thinge that he hym selfe in his wordes approuethe and teacheth to other?[b]

Who shall any thynge esteme their wysedome, whiche with great studies finde out remedies and prouisions necessary for thinges disordred or abused; and where they themselfes may execute it, they leue it untouched; wherby their deuises, with the soune that pronounced them, be vanisshed and come to nothing? Semblably it is to be thought in all other doctrine. Wherfore, as it semed, it was nat without consideration affirmed by Tulli, that the knowlege and con-

---

[a] Polydore Vergil (*De Rerum Inventoribus*, lib. v. cap. 2) derives these dances or games from the Roman Floralia, and says that 'at the Kalends of May the youth, as well men as women, are wont to go a Maying in the fields, bring home boughs and flowers to garnish their houses and gates, and in some places the churches.' Stubbs in his *Anatomie of Abuses*, describes the ceremonies which accompanied the bringing home of the Maypole, and says: 'This stinking idoll thus being reared up, with handkerchiefes and flagges streaming on the top, they strawe the ground round about, bind green boughes about it, set up summer halls, bowers, and arbours hard by it. And then fal they to banquet and feast, to leape and daunce about it, as the heathen people did at the dedication of their idolles, whereof this is a perfect patterne, or rather the thinge it selfe. I haue heard it crediblie reported (and that *vivâ voce*) by men of great grauity, credite, and reputation, that of fourtie, threescore, or a hundred maides going to the wood ouernight, there haue scarcely the third part of them returned home againe undefiled.'—P. 109, ed. 1595. Northbrooke mentions other reasons for discouraging this once popular pastime. 'What adoe make our yong men at the time of May?' he says, 'Do they not use night watchings to rob and steale yong trees out of other men's grounds, and bring them home into their parish with minstrels playing before? And when they haue set it up they will decke it with floures and garlandes, and daunce rounde (men and women togither, most unseemely and intollerable, as I have proued before) about the tree, like unto the children of Israell that daunced about the golden calfe that they had set up.'—*A Treatise against Dauncing*, p. 140.

[b] This reads like a paraphrase of the well-known line,

'Video meliora proboque,
Deteriora sequor.'

templation of Natures operations were lame and in a maner imperfecte, if there followed none actuall experience.[a] Of this shall be more spoken in the later ende of this warke.

Here with wolde be conioyned, or rather mixte with it, the vertue called Modestie, whiche by Tulli is defined to be the knowlege of oportunitie of thinges to be done *Off. i.* or spoken, in appoyntyng and settyng them in tyme or place to them conuenient and propre.[b] Wherfore it semeth to be moche like to that whiche men communely call discretion. Al be it *discretio* in latine signifieth Separation,[c] wherin it is more like to Election; but as it is communely used, it is nat only like to Modestie, but it is the selfe Modestie.[d] For he that forbereth to speake, all though he can do it bothe wisely and eloquently, by cause neither in the time nor in the *Discretion.* herers he findethe oportunitie, so that no frute may succede of his speche, he therfore is vulgarely called a discrete persone. Semblably they name him discrete, that punissheth an offendour lasse than his merites do require, hauyng regarde to the waikenes of his persone, or to the aptnesse of his

[a] 'Etenim cognitio contemplatioque naturæ manca quodam modo atque inchoata sit, si nulla actio rerum consequatur.'—*De Off.* lib. i. cap. 43.

[b] 'Itaque, ut eandem nos modestiam appellemus, sic definitur à Stoicis, ut modestia sit scientia earum rerum, quæ agentur aut dicentur, loco suo collocandarum.'—*De Off.* lib. i. cap. 40.

[c] Thus Lactantius, speaking of the separation of the soul from the body, says: 'Cum vis aliqua utrumque discreverit, quæ *discretio* mors vocatur.'—Lib. vii. cap. 12. Cicero places the adverbs discretè and electè in juxtaposition in the *De Inventione*, and contrasts them with their opposites, confusè and permixtè. Thus he says: 'In præsentia tantummodo numeros, et modos, et partes argumentandi confuse et permixte dispersimus: post discrete et electe in genus quodque causæ, quid cuique conveniat, ex hâc copiâ digeremus.'—Lib. i. cap. 30. The word *discretio*, however, is not used by any classical writer. The German philologist Nolten, in his *Lexicon Latinæ Linguæ Antibarbarum*, says: '*Discretio* non nisi sequioris ætatis scriptores v. g. Augustinum, Prudentium, et Avienum pro auctoribus agnoscat.'—Tom. i. col. 509, ed. 1780.

[d] Nolten defines this word as follows: 'Discretus pro *modesto*, seu *eo qui rerum momenta observat; qui cuncta prudenter discernit; seu qui est ἐπιεικὴς; qui ἐπιείκειαν exercet; qui de suo jure remittit*, barbare; quemadmodum etiam hâc notione *discrete et discretio*, item *indiscretus* pro *impudente*, et *indiscrete* pro *impudenter*, et *indiscretio* pro *rusticitate* et *malitiâ* eodem passu ambulant.'—*Ubi supra.*

amendement. So do they in the vertue called Liberalitie, where in gyuynge, is had consideration as well of the condition and necessite of the persone that receiuethe, as of the benefite that comethe of the gyfte receyued. In euery of these thinges and their semblable is Modestie; whiche worde nat beinge knowen in the englisshe tonge, ne of al them which under stode latin, except they had radde good autours, they improprely named this vertue discretion. And nowe some men do as moche abuse the worde modestie, as the other dyd discretion. For if a man haue a sadde countenance at al times, and yet not beinge meued with wrathe, but pacient, and of moche gentilnesse, they whiche wold be sene to be lerned, wil say that the man is of a great modestie; where they shulde rather saye that he were of a great mansuetude;[a] whiche terme, beinge semblably before this time unknowen in our tonge, may be by the sufferaunce of wise men nowe receiued by custome, wherby the terme shall be made familiare. That lyke as the Romanes translated the wisedome of Grecia in to their citie,[b]

Modestie abused.

---

[a] The word *mansuetudo* is frequently used by Cicero, and generally in connexion with clementia or misericordia. Tacitus uses it in opposition to *comitas*; thus he says: 'Tanta illi comitas in socios, mansuetudo in hostes.'—*Annales*, lib. ii. cap. 72. And Sallust says: 'Eâ mansuetudine atque misericordiâ Senatum Populumque Romanum semper fuisse, ut nemo unquam ab eo frustra auxilium petiverit.'— *Catilina*, cap. 34. Quintilian considers mansuetum the equivalent of the Greek τὸ ἥμερον, and connects it with 'fas, justum, pium, æquum.'—*Instit. Orat.* lib. iii. cap. 8, § 26. Chaucer uses the word in *The Persones Tale*: 'Remedye agayns ire, is a vertue that men clepe *mansuetude*, that is deboneirté.'—*Poetical Works*, vol. iii. p. 321, ed. 1866. And also the adjective *mansuete* in *Troylus and Cryseyde*, lib. v. stanza 28.

'She seyde ek she was fayn with hym to mete,
And stood forth muwet, mylde, and *mansuete*.'—*Ibid.* vol. v. p. 9.

[b] 'Et nova fictaque nuper habebunt verba fidem, si
Græco fonte cadant, parcè detorta.'—Hor. *Ars Poet.* 52.

Quintilian says: 'Multa ex Græco formata nova ac plurima à Sergio Flavio, quorum dura quædam admodum videntur, ut *ens* et *essentia*: quæ cur tantopere aspernemur, nihil video, nisi quod iniqui judices adversus nos sumus, ideoque paupertate sermonis laboramus.'—*Instit. Orat.* lib. viii. cap. 3, § 33. Such words

we may, if we liste, bringe the lernynges and wisedomes of them both in to this realme of Englande, by the translation of their warkes; sens lyke entreprise hath ben taken by frenche men, Italions, and Germanes, to our no litle reproche for our negligence and slouth.

And thus I conclude the last parte of daunsinge, whiche diligently beholden shall appiere to be as well a necessary studie as a noble and vertuouse pastyme, used and continued in suche forme as I hiderto haue declared.[a]

CHAPTER XXVI.

Of other exercises, whiche if they be moderately used, be to euery astate of man expedient.

I HAUE showed howe huntynge and daunsing may be in the nombre of commendable exercises, and passe tymes, nat repugnant to vertue. And undoubted it were moche better to be occupied in honest recreation than to do nothynge.[b] For it

---

as bibliotheca, rhetor, ephippium, exantlare, triclinium, were adopted by the Romans from the Greeks.

[a] Ascham says in his *Schoolmaster*: 'The Muses, besides learning, were also ladies of dancing, mirth, and minstrelsy.' And he mentions amongst other accomplishments, 'very necessary for a courtly gentleman,' the being able 'to dance comely, to sing, and play on instruments cunningly.'—*Works*, vol. iii. p. 139, ed. 1864. Locke, writing a century and a half after Sir Thomas Elyot, says: 'Since nothing appears to me to give children so much becoming confidence and behaviour, and so to raise them to the conversation of those above their age, as *dancing*, I think they should be taught to dance as soon as they are capable of learning it. For though this consist only in outward gracefulness of motion, yet, I know not how, it gives children manly thoughts and carriage more than any thing.' —*Thoughts on Education*, p. 67, ed. 1693. The skill displayed by the English in this accomplishment seems to have produced an impression upon foreigners for Hentzner, a German, who travelled in England, in 1598, recording his impressions says, 'In saltationibus et arte Musicâ excellunt.'—*Itinerarium*, p. 165, ed. 1617.

[b] Cicero expresses a similar idea: 'Mihi enim, qui nihil agit, esse omnino non videtur.'—*De Nat. Deor.* lib. ii. cap. 16.

is saide of a noble autour, In doinge nothinge men lerne to do iuel;[a] and Ouidius the poete saith

Ouid de remedio amoris.   If thou flee idleness Cupide hath no myghte; His bowe lyeth broken, his fire hath no lyghte.'[b]

Idlenesse. It is nat onely called idlenes, wherin the body or minde cesseth from labour, but specially idlenes is an omission of al honest exercise.[c] The other [d] may be better called a vacacion from seriouse businesse, whiche was some tyme embraced of wise men and vertuous.

[a] 'Nam illud verum est M. Catonis oraculum, Nihil agendo homines male agere discunt.'—Columella, *de Re Rusticâ*, lib. xi. cap. 1.

[b] 'Otia si tollas, periere Cupidinis arcus, Contemptæque jacent, et sine luce, faces.'
Rem. Amor. 139.

[c] From the following passage in Northbrooke's *Treatise against Idlenesse* the reader will see how much the Puritan divine was indebted to Sir Thomas Elyot: 'Idlenesse is a wicked will giuen to rest, and slothfulnesse, from all right necessarie, godly, and profitable works. *Also ydlenesse is not onely of the body or mynde to cease from labour, but especially an omission or letting passe negligentlye all honest exercises*;' for no day ought to be passed ouer without some good profitable exercises to the prayse of God's glorious name, to our brethrens profite, and to our selues commoditie and learning.'—P. 50. In this very year (1530-1) an Act (22 Hen. VIII. cap. 12) was passed for the punishment of beggars and vagabonds, the preamble of which ran as follows: 'Where in all places throughe out this realme of Englande vacabundes and beggers have of longe tyme increased, and dayly do increase, in great and excessyve nombres by the occasyon of ydlenes, *mother and rote of all vyces*, whereby hathe insurged and spronge, and dayly insurgeth and spryngeth contynuall theftes, murders, and other haynous offences and great enormytes, to the high displeasure of God, the inquyetacion and damage of the Kyngs people, and to the marvaylous disturbance of the Comon Weale of this realme.'

[d] *I.e.* recreation. The word in its original sense, as used by Latin writers, signified a recovery from sickness; thus Pliny says: 'Ab ægritudine recreationi efficax in cibo.'—*Nat. Hist.* lib. xxii. cap. 49. But by the end of the 15th century the modern signification had become well established. Chaucer, Gower, &c., employ the word in its present sense. The following passage in Locke's *Thoughts on Education* seems so nearly identical with that in the text that it may fitly be presented here for comparison: 'Recreation is not being idle (as every one may observe), but easing the wearied part by change of business.'—P. 245, ed. 1693.

THE GOVERNOUR. 271

It is writen to the praise of Xerxes [a] kynge of Persia, that in tyme vacaunt from the affaires of his realme, he with his owne handes hadde planted innumerable trees, whiche longe or he died brought fourth abundance of frute; and for the craftie and dilectable ordre in the settyng of them, it was to al men beholdyng the princes industrie, exceding maruailous.[b]

Kynge Xerxes.

But who abhorreth nat the historie of Serdanapalus, kynge of the same realme?[c] whiche hauynge in detestation all princely affaires, and leuynge all company of men, enclosed hym selfe in chambers with a great multitude of concubynes. And for that he wolde seme to be some time occupied, or els that wanton pleasures and quietnesse became to hym tediouse, he was founde by one of his lordes

Serdanapalus.

[a] This is a mistake of the author; the story is told not of Xerxes, but of Cyrus. Northbrooke has copied this passage word for word in his *Treatise against Idlenesse*, p. 49.

[b] Οὗτος τοίνυν ὁ Κῦρος λέγεται Λυσάνδρῳ, ὅτε ἦλθεν ἄγων αὐτῷ τὰ παρὰ τῶν συμμάχων δῶρα, ἄλλα τε φιλοφρονεῖσθαι, ὡς αὐτὸς ἔφη ὁ Λύσανδρος ξένῳ ποτέ τινι ἐν Μεγάροις διηγούμενος, καὶ τὸν ἐν Σάρδεσι παράδεισον ἐπιδεικνύναι αὐτὸν ἔφη. Ἐπεὶ δὲ ἐθαύμαζεν αὐτὸν ὁ Λύσανδρος ὡς καλὰ μὲν τὰ δένδρα εἴη, δι' ἴσου δὲ τὰ πεφυτευμένα ὀρθοὶ δὲ οἱ στίχοι τῶν δένδρων, εὐγώνια δὲ πάντα καλῶς εἴη, ὀσμαὶ δὲ πολλαὶ καὶ ἡδεῖαι συμπαρομαρτοῖεν αὐτοῖς περιπατοῦσι, καὶ ταῦτα θαυμάζων εἴπεν, Ἀλλ' ἐγώ τοι, ὦ Κῦρε, πάντα μὲν ταῦτα θαυμάζω ἐπὶ τῷ κάλλει, πολὺ δὲ μᾶλλον ἄγαμαι τοῦ καταμετρήσαντός σοι καὶ διατάξαντος ἕκαστα τούτων. Ἀκούσαντα δὲ ταῦτα τὸν Κῦρον ἡσθῆναί τε καὶ εἰπεῖν, Ταῦτα τοίνυν, ὦ Λύσανδρε, ἐγὼ πάντα καὶ διεμέτρησα καὶ διέταξα, ἔστι δ' αὐτῶν, φάναι, ἃ καὶ ἐφύτευσα αὐτός.—Xen. *Œconom.* cap. iv. § 20.

[c] The author has, it will be seen, slightly altered the story as it is narrated by Justin. 'Postremus apud eos regnavit Sardanapalus, vir muliere corruptior. Ad hunc videndum (quod nemini ante eum permissum fuerat) præfectus ipsius, Medis præpositus, nomine Arbaces, cum admitti magnâ ambitione ægre obtinuisset, invenit eum inter scortorum greges purpuram colo nentem, et muliebri habitu cum mollitiâ corporis et oculorum lasciviâ omnes fœminas anteiret, pensa inter virgines partientem. Quibus visis, indignatus tali fœminæ tantum virorum subjectum, tractantique lanam, ferrum et arma portantes parere; progressus ad socios, quid viderit, refert: negat "se ei parere posse, qui se fœminam malit esse, quàm virum." Fit igitur conjuratio: bellum Sardanapalo infertur. Quo ille audito, non ut vir regnum defensurus, sed, ut metu mortis mulieres solent, primo latebras circumspicit: mox deinde cum paucis et incompositis in bellum proreditur. Victus, in regiam se recipit, ubi exstructâ incensâque pyrâ, *et se et divitias suas in incendium mittit; hoc solo imitatus virum.*'—Lib. i. cap. 3.

in a womans atyre, spinnyng in a distafe amonge persones defamed; whiche knowen abrode, was to the people so odiouse, that finally by them he was burned, with all the place wherto he fledde for his refuge. And I suppose there is nat a more playne figure of idlenesse than playinge at dise.[*] For besides that, that therin is no maner of exercise of the body or mynde, they whiche do playe therat must seme to haue

Playing at dise.

[*] This passage is appropriated *verbatim* by Northbrooke at p. 88 of his *Treatise against Dice-playing*, published in 1578, without any acknowledgment. And we shall have occasion to notice other instances in which he has reproduced not only our author's ideas, but the very language in which they are clothed. Dice-playing appears to have been so prevalent, and to have been considered so injurious to the State, that it was made the subject of legislation at a very early period of our Constitution. The first statute directed against this popular amusement is the 12th Ric. II. cap. 6, which enacts that 'Servants and labourers shall leave all playing at this, and other such importune games.' The 17th Ed. IV. cap. 3, includes this amongst other 'unlawful games which are daily used in divers parts of this land, as well by persons of good reputation as of small having, to their own impoverishment and such evil-disposed persons by their ungracious procurement and encouraging do bring others to such games till they be utterly undone and impoverished of their goods, to the pernicious example of divers of the King's liege people if such unprofitable games should be suffered long to continue; because that by the means thereof divers and many murders, robberies, and other heinous felonies be oftentimes committed and done in divers parts of this realm, to the great inquieting and trouble of many good and well-disposed persons, and the importune loss of their goods; which players in their said offences be daily supported and favoured by the governors and occupiers of divers houses, tenements, gardens, and other places where they use and occupy their said ungracious and incommendable games.' In 1535 an Act (27 Hen. VIII. cap. 25) was passed which, among other things, enacted 'that no personne nor personnes, at any tyme after the feaste of Seint John Baptiste nexte commyng, shall use, kepe, and mayntene any open playeng house, or place for commen bowling, *dysyng*, carding, closhe, tenys, or other unlawfull games, taking money for the same, or other gayne, in any place of this realme, upon payne to forfaite fyve markes for every moneth that any such unlawfull houses or games shall so be openly kepte, used, and mayntened in any place within this realme.' A later statute (33 Hen. VIII. cap. 9) prohibited *artificers and servants* from playing at dice 'out of Christmas,' under a penalty of 20s. for every such offence, but at the same time enabled 'every master' to license his servants to play at dice with their master, 'or with any other gentleman repayringe to their saide maister, openly in his house or in his presence, accordinge to his discrecion.' And noblemen and others, having lands, &c., in their own or their wives' right, to the yearly value of 100l., could license their families and households to play at dice within the precincts of their 'houses, gardens, or orchards.'

no portion of witte or kunnyng, if they will be called faire plaiars, or in some company auoide the stabbe of a dagger, if they be taken with any crafty conueiaunce. And by cause alwaye wisedome is therin suspected, there is seldome any playinge at dise, but therat is vehement chidyng and braulyng, horrible othes, cruell, and some tyme mortall, menacis.[a] I omitte strokes, whiche nowe and than do happen often tymes betwene bretherne and most dere frendes, if fortune brynge alwaye to one man iuell chaunces, whiche maketh the playe of the other suspected. O why shulde that be called a playe, whiche is compacte of malice and robry?[b] Undoubtedly they that write of the firste inuentions of thinges, haue good cause to suppose Lucifer, prince of deuilles, to be the first inuentour of

[a] 'Suche folowe this game, stryuynge nyght and day,
Tournynge the dyse somtyme by polecy
Them falsly settynge, assaynge if they may
Some vyle auauntage for to obtayne therby.
But than, if they nat set them craftely,
Anone begynneth brawlynge and debate,
Blasfemynge, and othes, the pot about the pate.'
Ship of Fools, vol. ii. p. 71, ed. 1874.

Another writer of the 16th century says: 'If there bee any cogging panion, or shifting mate, that by sleight and paltry goeth about to help the chaunce, or strike the dyce, (as many foysting coseners and deceiptfull packers in playing both can do and use to do), such an one is accoumpted for a lewd felowe and a cogging verlet, and being once knowne or taken with the maner, hee is worthilie expelled and abandoned of all men, out of all honest companies. These cogging trickes and subtile shiftes in playe, whosoeuer useth, is euer the causer of much brabbling, wrangling, skoulding, and fighting.'—Daneau's *Treatise touching Dyceplay*, ch. vi. Whetstone, speaking of the same period (1586), says: 'But this I am assured, and many a gentleman's undoyng witnesseth as muche, that these expert shifters, by false dice, slipperie castynge, or some other nice sleight, althoughe all the daye they dallye with younge nouices as a catte doeth with a mouse, yet before bedde tyme they wyll make their purses as emptie of money as the catte the mouse's headde of braynes.' - *Mirror for Magistrates*, p. 26. The term 'cogging' was used to denote the method of cheating at dice by fastening them in a box as they were dropped *in*, thus enabling them to drop *out* with the required face upwards.

[b] The author seems to have had Justinian's words in his mind: 'Quis enim ludos appellet eos ex quibus crimina oriuntur?'—*Præfationes, Digest*. *I*. § 9. It may be observed that Northbrooke has copied almost *verbatim* the passage in the text at p. 88 of his *Treatise against Diceplay*.

dise playinge, and helle the place where it was founden,[a] although some do write that it was first inuented by Attalus.[b]

[a] Plato ascribes the invention to an Egyptian deity, whom he calls Theuth. "Ἥκουσα τοίνυν περὶ Ναύκρατιν τῆς Αἰγύπτου γενέσθαι τῶν ἐκεῖ παλαιῶν τινα θεῶν, οὗ καὶ τὸ ὄρνεον τὸ ἱερόν, ὃ δὴ καλοῦσιν Ἶβιν· αὐτῷ δὲ ὄνομα τῷ δαίμονι εἶναι Θεῦθ. Τοῦτον δὲ πρῶτον ἀριθμόν τε καὶ λογισμὸν εὑρεῖν καὶ γεωμετρίαν καὶ ἀστρονομίαν, ἔτι δὲ πεττείας τε καὶ κυβείας.—*Phædrus*, cap. 59. Herodotus gives some colour to the assertion in the text, for he describes King Rhampsinitus as passing the time in Hades in this amusement. Μετὰ δὲ ταῦτα ἔλεγον τοῦτον τὸν βασιλέα ζωὸν καταβῆναι κάτω ἐς τὸν οἱ Ἕλληνες ᾅδην νομίζουσι εἶναι, κἀκεῖθι συγκυβεύειν τῇ Δήμητρι, καὶ τὰ μὲν νικᾶν αὐτήν, τὰ δὲ ἑσσοῦσθαι ὑπ' αὐτῆς.—Lib. ii. cap. 122. In the treatise *de Aleatoribus*, which by some has been attributed to S. Cyprian, the writer says: 'Aleæ tabulam dico, ubi diabolus præsto est. Cum enim quidam studio litterarum bene eruditus, multum meditando hoc malum et tam perniciosum studium adinvenit, instinctu solius Zabuli, qui eum artibus suis repleverat; hanc ergo autem ostendit, quam et colendam sculpturis cum suâ imagine fabricavit.'— Migne, *Patrol. Cursus*, tom. iv. col. 831, 832. The learned German, Cornelius Agrippa, before quoted in a chapter upon dice-play, says: 'Hæc ars mendaciorum, perjuriorum, furtorum, litium, injuriarum, homicidiorumque mater est, vere malorum dæmonum inventum.'—*De Vanitate Scientiarum*, cap. 14, ed. 1531. The casuistical writers of the 15th and 16th centuries condemned it as a diabolical invention. Thus Angelus de Clavasio, one of the most famous, who died 1495, says: 'Est et tertius ludus qui est diabolicus, quòd operatione diabolicâ est inventus ad inducendos homines ad peccatum. Et iste est in triplici differentiâ. Primus consistit in ludibriis, quod ludibria sunt rerum inhonestarum demonstrationes. Secundus ludus est ludus aleæ, et sub isto comprehenditur omnis ludus qui innititur solum fortunæ, ut ludus chartarum, taxillorum, et hujusmodi. Tertius ludus est mixtus, quòd partim innititur fortunæ et partim industriæ, ut ludus tabularum cum taxillis.'—*Summa Angelica*, tit. Ludus, § 3, ed. 1513. In *The Ship of Fools* a *terrestrial* fury, more wicked than the infernal trio, is represented as being responsible for the mischief.

'Sayth poetis that in hell ar Furyes thre,
The folys to punysshe that ar sende to the same,
For theyr nat lyuynge here in equyte,
It nedyth nat them here to count by name.
The fourth Fury is encresyd by this game,
Which (than the other) is more furious and bad,
For here in erth it makyth folys mad.'—Vol. ii. p. 70, ed. 1874.

The author of *The Gaming Table* tells us that gambling-houses first received the name of *Enfers* in France, in the reign of Louis XV., and were soon after designated by the name of 'Hells' in England. They were previously known as 'Ordinary-Tables.'

[b] The author had evidently studied the works of the learned monk John of Salisbury, who wrote in the 12th century and who is responsible for the fol-

For what better allectiue coulde Lucifer deuise to allure or bringe men pleasauntly in to damnable seruitude, than to purpose to them in fourme of a playe, his principall tresory; wherin the more parte of synne is contained, and all goodnesse and vertue confounded?

The firste occasion to playe is tediousnes of vertuous occupation.[a] Immediately succedeth couaiting of an other mans goodes, whiche they calle playinge; therto is annected auarice and straite kepynge, whiche they call wynnyng; sone after cometh sweryng in rentyng the membres of god,[b] whiche they name noblenesse, (for they wyll say he that sweareth depe, sweareth like a lorde); than folowethe furye or rage, whiche they

---

lowing statement: 'Attalus Asiaticus, si gentilium historiis creditur, hanc ludendi lasciviam dicitur invenisse, ab exercitio numerorum paululum deflexa materia.'— *Polycraticus*, lib. i. cap. 5. Northbrooke has copied, *verbatim*, this passage in his *Treatise against Dice Play*. See pp. 87, 88, 89.

[a] Nicolas de Lyra, a celebrated Franciscan of the 14th century, in a work called *Præceptorium*, which was, however, not printed till 1505, alleges nine specific reasons for prohibiting dice-play amongst Christians: '1. Est desiderium lucrandi, ecce cupiditas, quæ est radix omnium malorum. 2. Est voluntas spoliandi proximum, ecce rapina. 3. Est usura maxima, quæ attendit non solum in anno vel in mense, sed in eodem die. 4. Est multiplicia mendacia et verba vana et ociosa, quæ in talibus ludis frequenter contingunt. 5. Est execrabilis juratio et blasphemia, quæ in talibus ludis frequenter in Deum et in sanctos refunditur, ecce heresis. 6. Est corruptio multiplex proximorum, qui ad ludum de malâ consuetudine conveniunt et respiciunt. 7. Est scandalum bonorum, quod ex prædictis conditionibus nephandis incurritur. 8. Est contemptus prohibitionis sanctæ matris ecclesiæ, nam glosa dicit quod hujusmodi ludi sunt prohibiti non tantum dissuasi. 9. Est amissio temporis et omnium actuum bonorum, quod in illo tempore quis facere potuisset.'—*Septimum Præcept.* Northbrooke has translated this passage of the *Præceptorium* at p. 101 of his *Treatise*.

[b]
    'But in the mean season, if that any discorde
    Amonge them fall, the woundes of God ar sworne,
    His armys, herte and bonys, almost at euery worde
    Thus is our Sauyour amonge these caytyfs torne,
    And wordes of malyce, myschefe, and great scorne
    They throwe to God, renounsynge oft his name,
    Whan that mysfortune doth bacwarde gyde theyr game.'
                      Ship of Fools, vol. ii. p. 72.

More than a century after the publication of *The Governour*, the game seems to have retained the same accompanyment. 'Blaspheming, drunkenness, and swearing are here so familiar that civility is, by the rule of contrarieties, accounted

calle courage;[a] amonge them cometh inordinate watche,[b] whiche they name paynfulnesse; he bringethe in glotonie, and that is good fellowshippe; and after cometh slepe superfluous, called amonge them naturall reste; and he some tyme bringeth in lechery, whiche is nowe named daliance.[c] The name of this Tresorie is verily idlenesse, the dore wherof is lefte wyde open to dise plaiers; but if they happe to bringe in their company, lerninge, vertuouse busines, liberalitie, pacience, charitie, temperance, good diete, or shamefastnes, they muste leue them without the gates. For Euill custome, which is the porter, will nat suffre them to entre.

Alas what pitie is it that any christen man shulde by wanton company be trayned,[d] I will no more saye in to this Treasorie, but in to this lothesome dungeon where he

[a] vice. I do not mean swearing, when there is occasion to attest a truth, but upon no occasion, as "God damn me, how dost? What a clock is it, by God?" &c.'—*The Nicker Nicked*, printed in 1669; see *Harl. Miscell.* vol. ii. p. 109.

[a] Northbrooke says: 'It is a world to see and to behold the wicked people, how they wrest and turne the names of good things unto the names of vices. If a man can dice-play and daunce hee is named a proper and a fyne nimble man; if he wil loyter and liue idlely upon other men's labours, and sit al day and night at cards and dice, he is named a good companion and a shopfellow; if he can sweare and stare they say he hath good courage.'—*Treatise against Dicing*, Introduction, p. 2.

[b]   'Exces of watchynge doth players great damage,
    And in that space oft Venus doth them blynde,
    Makynge them hoore longe or they come to age.
       *   *   *   *   *
    Watchynge without season tyll theyr wyt be past,
    Ye two nyghtes or thre, as folys voyde of grace,
    No thyrst nor hunger can moue them from that place.'
                                    Ship of Fools, vol. ii. p. 71.

[c] In the original there is a side note here, followed a few lines lower by two other side notes, but as they are merely an exact repetition of the first three side notes of Chap. xxiii. it is manifest that they have simply been misplaced by an error in printing; and it has therefore not been thought worth while to reproduce them n this edition.

[d] Johannes Gallensis, otherwise Gualensis or Wallensis (see Oudin. *De Script. Eccles.* tom. iii. col. 494), but who is styled by Dupin *John of Galles* of the order of Minor Friars (see *Eccles. Writers*, vol. ii. p. 437, ed. 1724), a writer of the 13th century, complains in his *Communiloquium* or *Summa Collationum* of the bad

shal lye fetored in giues of ignorance, and bounden with the stronge chayne of obstinacie, harde to be losed but by grace?

The[a] most noble emperour Octauius Augustus, who hath amonge writers in diuers of his actes an honorable remembraunce, only for playing at dise[b] and that but seldome, sustaineth note of reproche.

The lacedemones sent an ambassade to the citie of Corinthe,[c] to haue with them aliaunce; but whan the am-

example set by the *magnates moderni*, and says: 'Et non solum nobiles intendentes talibus sibi nocent, sed etiam multis aliis, quibus dant audaciam et exemplum talibus vacandi, et etiam liberos suos et heredes exemplo suo ad talia provocant.'— Pars i. distinc. 10, cap. 7, ed. 1489. Cornelius Agrippa, in his treatise *De Vanitate Scientiarum*, which was published in the same year as *The Governour*, says: '*Hodie* regum et nobilium hic exercitatissimus ludus est.'—Cap. xiv.

[a] Northbrook has copied this passage almost word for word at p. 99 of his *Treatise against Diceplay*.

[b] 'Aleæ rumorem nullo modo expavit, lusitque simpliciter et palam oblectamenti causâ, etiam senex, ac, præterquam Decembri mense, aliis quoque festis profestisque diebus.'—Sueton. *Octav.* 71.

[c] The only authority for this story appears to be John of Salisbury, already referred to, who relates it as follows: 'Chilon Lacedæmonius jungendæ societatis causâ missus Corinthum, duces et seniores populi ludentes invenit in aleâ. Infecto itaque negotio reversus est, dicens se nolle 'gloriam Spartanorum, quorum virtus constructo Byzantio clarescebat, hâc maculare infamiâ, ut dicerentur cum aleatoribus contraxisse societatem.'—*Polycraticus*, lib. i. cap. 5. Chaucer expanded John's account in a metrical version in *The Pardoneres Tale*:—

> 'Stilbon, that was i-holde a wis embasitour,
> Was sent unto Corinthe with gret honour
> Fro Lacidome, to make hir alliaunce;
> And whan he cam, him happede *par chaunce*,
> That alle the grettest that were of that lond
> Playing atte hasard he hem fond.
> For whiche, as soone as it mighte be,
> He stal him hoom ayein to his contré,
> And saide ther, " I nyl nought lese my name,
> I nyl not take on me so gret diffame,
> Yow for to allie unto noon hasardoures.
> Sendeth othere wiser embasitoures,
> For by my trouthe, me were lever dye,
> Than I yow scholde to hasardours allye.

bassadours founde the princes and counsailours playeng at dyse, they departed without exploytinge their message, sayeng that they wolde nat maculate the honour of their people with suche a reproche, to be sayde that they had made aliaunce with disars.

Also to Demetrius the kynge of Parthians sent golden dise in the rebuke of his litenesse.[a]

Euerythihg is to be estemed after his value. But who hering a man, whom he knoweth nat, to be called a disar, anone supposeth him nat to be of light credence,[b] dissolute,

---

> For ye, that ben so glorious in honoures,
> Schal not allie yow with hasardoures,
> As by my wil, ne as by my treté."
> This wise philosophre thus sayd he.'
>
> *Poetical Works*, vol. iii. p. 94, ed. 1866.

It is curious to observe the change which the original Greek name has undergone in the hands of the English poet. In a *Treatise touching Dyceplay*, written by a Frenchman, Lambert Daneau, and translated by Thomas Newton, which was published in 1586, Chilo is further metamorphosed into *Gobilo* (see chap. vii.), a mistake apparently copied from the *De Vanitate Scientiarum* of H. Cornelius Agrippa.

[a] ' Tunc quoque uxori et liberis donatus, in Hyrcaniam, pœnalem sibi civitatem, remittitur, talisque aureis ad exprobrationem puerilis levitatis donatur.'—*Justin.* lib. xxxviii. cap. 9. Our author, however, has evidently derived this story from the same source as the last, viz. the *Polycraticus* of John of Salisbury, where the two narratives follow each other in the precise order adopted in the text. This will at once appear on comparing John's version, which is as follows : ' Regi quoque Demetrio in opprobrium puerilis levitatis, tali aurei à rege Parthorum dati sunt.'— Lib. i. cap. 5. It is very remarkable that Chaucer had, in the *Pardoneres Tale*, observed the same sequence :

> ' Loke eek that to the king Demetrius
> The king of Parthes, as the book saith us,
> Sent him a paire dees of gold in scorn,
> For he had used hasard there to-forn ;
> For which he hield his gloir and his renoun
> At no valieu or reputacioun.'—*Ubi supra*, vol. iii. p. 95.

[b] Northbrooke quotes this passage *in extenso* at pp. 90, 101 of his *Treatise*, but, contrary to his usual practice, with an acknowledgment of the author. Stubbs also refers to it at p. 132 of his *Anatomie of Abuses*.

vayne, and remisse?[a] Who almoste trusteth his brother, whom he knoweth a dise player?[b] Ye among themselfes they laugh, whan they perceyue or here any doctrine or vertuouse worde procede from any of their companyons, thynking that it becommeth nat his persone, moche more whan he dothe any thing with deuotion or wisedome.[c] Howe many gentilmen, howe many marchauntes, haue in this damnable passe tyme consumed their substaunce,[d] as well by their owne labours, as

[a] Publius Syrus had said long before, 'Aleator quanto in arte est melior tanto est nequior.' An opinion erroneously attributed to Seneca by John of Galles in the work before mentioned.

[b] Alexander of Hales tells us the same thing, and that gamblers were not content until they had literally *denuded* those with whom they played of everything. 'Vult enim aleator spoliare proximum suum, immo et amicum, et magistrum vel dominum suum, rêbus suis, scilicet auro, argento, tunicâ immo, et si potest camisiâ et bracis, quod non faceret aliquis de latronibus qui spoliant peregrinos in nemoribus.'—*Destructorium Vitiorum*, pars iv. cap. 23, ed. 1496. Mr. Wright, in his *Domestic Manners*, has a woodcut which represents this process very literally. 'One, who is evidently the more aged of the two players, is already perfectly naked, whilst the other is reduced to his shirt.'—*Ubi supra*, p. 216. Vives quotes the gambler's proverb, 'Ibi quærendam esse togam, ubi amiseris.'—*Opera*, tom. i. p. 48, ed. 1555.

[c] Northbrooke bears testimony to the same thing : ' If a gentleman haue in him any humble behauiour, then the Roysters cal such a one by the name of a Loute, a Clinchpoup, or one that knoweth no fashions : if a man talke godly and wisely, the worldlings deride it, and say the yong Fox preacheth, beware your geese, and of a yong saint groweth an old deuil ; if a man will not dice and play, then he is a nigard and a miser, and no good fellow.'—*Treatise against Diceplay*, Introd.

[d]
'There is almoste no maner of degre,
Man, childe, woman, pore man, or estate,
Olde or yonge, that of this game ar fre,
Nor yet the clargy, both pore preste and prelate,
They use the same almoste after one rate,
Whan by great los they brought ar in a rage,
Right fewe haue reason theyr madnes to asswage.'
Ship of Fools, vol. ii. p. 72.

Mr. Wright says : 'The pernicious rage for gambling had been extending itself ever since the beginning of the 15th century.'—*Dom. Man. in Eng.* p. 483. The king himself was addicted to the game, for a writer in the succeeding century declared, 'You may read in our histories how Sir Miles Partridge played at dice, with King Henry the Eighth, for Jesus Bells so called, which were the greatest in

by their parentes,[a] with great studie and painfull trauaille in a longe tyme acquired, and fynisshed their lyfes in dette and penurie? Howe many goodly and bolde yemen hath it brought unto thefte, wherby they haue preuented the course of nature, and dyed by the ordre of lawes miserably?[b] These be the frutes

England, and hung in a tower of St. Paul's Church, and won them; whereby he brought them to ring in his pocket; but the ropes afterwards catched about his neck, for in Edward the Sixth's days he was hanged for some criminal offences.'— *Harl. Miscel.* vol. ii. p. 110.

[a] Whetstone, writing at the end of the 16th century, complains bitterly of the allurements held out to the young students of the Inns of Court by the proximity of the gambling houses. 'By reason of Dicyng houses and other allectiues to unthriftinesse, the good father which is at charge to make his sonne a Lawier to do his country seruice, throughe the loosenesse of the sonne, many times spendeth his money to the undooyng of his posterytie.' And he asserts that 'These wicked houses first nusleth our young gentlemen in pride, and acquainteth them with sundrie shifting companions, whereof one sort couseneth him at dice and cardes, an other sort consume him with lecherie, an other sort by brocadge bringeth him in debt and out of credit, then awayteth couetousnesse and usurie to sease upon his liuing, and the unciuill Sergeant upon his libertie. To ruine is thus brought the gentleman, a great estate and strength of this Realme, principally by the frequenting of dicing houses.'—*Mirror for Magistrates*, ff. 25 b., 31. And Daneau, writing about the same time, says: 'We haue heard of some, read of others, yea and knowen not a few, that by this wicked game haue played away their Lordshippes, Dukedomes, Seigniories, mannors, houses, and landes, ouer and besides their horses, apparell, gold, siluer, jewelles, houshold stuffe, and all that they had beside or could borrowe. Yea we reade of some that haue set their own bodies at the stake, and throwen for the propertie of their owne selues at a cast at Dyce in steede of money when they haue lacked it, and loosing the chaunce, and thereby themselues, haue afterwarde lead the remaunder of their daies, as slaues, in miserable seruitude at the discretion of the winners.'—*A Treatise touching Dyce-play*, cap. ix. ed. 1586.

[b] 'And to be playne, great inconuenyences
Procedyth to many by this unlawfull game,
And by the same oft youth doth sue offences
To his destruccion and all his frendes shame.
For whan all theyr good is wastyd by the same
Often some by foly fallyth to be a thefe,
And so ende in shame sorowe and myschefe.'
Ship of Fools, vol. ii. p. 73.

and reuenues of that diuilysshe marchandise, besyde the fynall rewarde, whiche is more terrible; the reporte wherof I leaue to diuines, suche as fere nat to showe their lerninges,[a] or fille nat their mouthes so full with swete meates, or benefices, that their tonges be nat let to speake trouth;[b] for that is their duetie and office, excepte I with many other be moche disceyued.

[a] Such as Latimer, who Strype tells us, 'being a bold man, would speak his mind with great freedom. His practice was, in his sermons at Court, to declaim against the vices there. And against the vices of the common people, when he happened to preach before them in London and elsewhere. And against the vices of the ecclesiastics, when he came up before them.'—*Eccles. Mem.* vol. i. pt. i. p. 261. It was Latimer who, being at Cambridge at Christmas, 1527, preached his famous 'card-sermons,' making use of the game which was especially in vogue at that season to point his moral, but it does not appear that he expressed any disapprobation of this form of amusement. In opposition to Latimer, the prior of the Black Friars, one Buckenham, 'thinking,' as Foxe says, 'to make a great hand against Master Latimer, brought out his Christmas *dice*, casting there to his audience, *cinque* and *quatre*; meaning by the *cinque* five places in the New Testament, and the four doctors by the *quatre*; by which his *cinque quatre* he would prove that it was not expedient the Scripture to be in English, lest the ignorant and vulgar sort, through the occasion thereof, might haply be brought in danger to leave their vocation, or else to run into some inconvenience.'—*Acts and Monuments*, vol. vii. p. 449, ed. 1847. The reader will find a more modern parallel to this in Mr. Chatto's book, at p. 321, ed. 1848.

[b] That there were many of the clergy to whom this insinuation was applicable appears certain. Strype says: 'The great neglect of their parishes added also to their disrepute. For they made them only serve as means to accumulate wealth to themselves, without any conscience to discharge their duties there. For they for the most part followed divers trades and occupations secular, some were surveyors of lands, some receivers, some stewards, some clerks of the kitchen, many gardeners, and orchard makers. And commonly this was the trade; the better the benefice, and the cure the more, the seldomer was the Parson or Vicar resident at home. If they wanted now and then sermons to be preached in their churches, they got friars to do it for them.'—*Eccles. Mem.* vol. i. pt. i. p. 607. While the latter, to gain the favour of their audience, too often 'suppressed the truth, taught fables and falsehoods, and to extort money preached the matters contrary to the true faith.'—Fosbroke's *Brit. Monachism*, p. 170, ed. 1843. Half a century later, indeed, we find the clergy, such men as Northbrooke, Stockwood, Spark, Rainolds, Gosson, &c., preaching against card-playing and stage-playing indiscriminately.

Playing at cardes[a] and tables[b] is some what more

[a] Mr. Barrington cannot have been acquainted with this passage, or he would hardly have said that 'during the reigns of Henry VIII. and Edward VI. this amusement (card-playing) seems not to have been very common in England.' —*Archæologia*, vol. viii. p. 141. And Mr. Chatto, although dissenting from this view, appears equally to have overlooked such an excellent opportunity for supporting his assumption that 'card-playing was common in England, both in the cottage and the palace,' at this period. These omissions furnish a convincing proof of the neglect with which this work has been treated by writers professing to give an insight into the life and manners of the time in which the author lived. Ludovicus Vives gives us a graphic picture of a game as played at this time, and from him we learn that the cards used were either of French or Spanish make. 'Chartæ enim Hispanæ, quemadmodum et Gallicæ, in quatuor sunt genera seu familias divisæ. Hispanæ habent aureos nummos, carchesia, baculos, enses; Gallicæ corda, rhombulos, trifolia, vomerculos, seu palas, seu spicula. Est in quâque familiâ rex, regina, eques, monas, dyas, trias, quaternio, pentas, senio, heptas, ogdoas, enneas. Gallicæ habent etiam decades; et Hispanis aurei et carchesia potiora sunt pauciora, contrà enses et baculi ; Gallis autem plura sunt semper meliora.'—*Opera*, tom. i. p. 48, ed. 1555. Northbrooke says : 'The Kings and Coate cardes that we use nowe, were in olde time the images of idols and false gods, which since they that woulde seeme Christians haue chaunged into Charlemaine, Launcelot, Hector, and such like names, bicause they would not seeme to imitate their idolatrie therein.'—P. 111. The King himself was passionately fond of cards, and 'to show the extent to which that passion was carried, it is sufficient to state that the whole amount paid for his losses at cards, dice, tennis and other games, together with those lost in wagers, amounted in three years to 3,243*l*. 5*s*. 10*d*.' —*Privy Purse Expenses of Henry VIII.* Introd. p. xxiii.

[b] A game called tabula or tabulæ was known to the ancients. Thus Juvenal says :
'Neque enim loculis comitantibus itur
Ad casum tabulæ, positâ sed luditur arcâ.'—*Sat.* i. 89, 90.
One of Martial's epigrams is devoted to *Tabula lusoria*, which is thus described :
'Hic mihi bis seno numeratur tessera puncto :
Calculus hic gemino discolor hoste perit.'—*Epig.* lib. xiv. 17.
Seneca mentions a game by this name. 'Ludebat latrunculis, quum centurio, agmen periturorum trahens, illum quoque excitari jubet. Vocatus numeravit calculos, et sodali suo; "Vide," inquit, "ne post mortem meam mentiaris te vicisse." Tum annuens centurioni, "Testis," inquit, "eris, uno me antecedere." Lusisse tu Canum illâ tabulâ putas? Illusit.'—*De Tranquill. Animi*, cap. 14. Isidore, who lived early in the 7th century after Christ, says : 'Tabula luditur pyrgo, calculis, tesserisque' and 'Tabulam ternis descriptam dicunt lineis.'— *Etymologiarum*, lib. xviii. cap. 60, 64. By Justinian's law, the penalty for playing at tables is changed from deprivation to a triennial suspension into a monastery for the performance of repentance. Some, perhaps, will wonder at the severity

tollerable, only for as moche as therin wytte is more used, and lasse truste is in fortune,* all be hit therin is neither laudable study nor exercise. But yet men delitinge in vertue mought with cardes and tables deuyse games, where in moughte

of these laws in prohibiting the exercise of the tables under such a penalty, but their wonder will cease when they are told that it was equally prohibited to the laity under pain of excommunication. For the Council of Eliberis (about A.D. 305) orders 'that a Christian playing at dice or tables shall not be admitted to the holy communion, but after a year's penance and abstinence, and his total amendment.'—Bingham's *Antiq. of Christian Church*, vol. ii. p. 205. At first the game appears to have been played with only one board, but at a later period with two. 'It was probably this construction which caused the name to be used in the plural; and as the Anglo-Saxons always used the name in the singular, as is the case also with John of Salisbury in the 12th century, whilst the plural is always used by the writers of a later date, we seem justified in concluding that the board used by the Anglo-Saxons and Anglo-Normans consisted of one table, and that this was afterwards superseded by the double board.'—*Domestic Manners in England*, p. 218, ed. 1862. Mr. Wright adds: 'It is hardly necessary to point out that the mediæval game of tables was identical with our modern backgammon, or rather, we should perhaps say, that the game of backgammon as now played is one of the games played on the tables.' In the *Privy Purse Expenses of Henry VIII*. we find an entry on one occasion of the sum of 4*l*. 13*s*. 4*d*. 'delivered to the King's grace to playe at tabulls with maister Weston,' and another entry of the same sum for the King to play with Robert Seymore, at Dover.

* This is quite in accordance with the view of the casuists. Thus John Baptista Trovamala in *Summa Rosella*, printed about 1483, says, 'Tres sunt species ludi. Nam quidam est consistens in ingenio, ut ludus scachorum; quidam est consistens in fortunâ, ut ludus azarri; quidam est mixtus, participans de utroque, ut ludus tabularum cum taxillis.'—*Sub voc.* Ludus, § 1. It was doubted at one time by casuists whether games of skill were lawful or not, and whether the winner at such games was bound (as in games of chance) to make restitution, but in the *Summa Rosella*, we find the first point resolved in the affirmative and the second in the negative. 'Concessus videtur omnis ludus qui fit gratiâ virtutis experiendæ. Et dicunt quidam quòd in hoc casu, id quod vincitur non subjacet restitutioni, cùm non submittunt se homines fortunæ, immo bonum exinde provenit cum exerceant se ingenio.'—*Sub voc.* Ludus, § 11. Northbrooke says: 'Playing at Tables is farre more tollerable (although in all respectes not allowable) than dyce and cardes are, for that it leaneth partlye to chaunce, and partly to industrie of the mynde. For although they cast indeed by chaunce, yet the castes are gouerned by industrie and witte. In that respecte Plato affirmed that the life of manne is lyke unto the playe at Tables. For euen as (sayeth he) in Table playe, so also in the lyfe of man, if anye thinge go not verye well, the same must bee by arte corrected and amended, as when a caste is euill it is holpen agayne by the wysedome and cunning of the player.'—P. 111.

be moche solace, and also study commodiouse; as deuising a bataile, or contention betwene vertue and vice, or other like pleasaunt and honest inuention.[a]

The chesse, of all games wherin is no bodily exercise, is mooste to be commended; for therin is right subtile engine, wherby the wytte is made more sharpe and remembrance quickened.[b] And it is the more commendable and also commodiouse if the players haue radde the moralization of the

---

[a] Ludovicus Vives recommends cards as combining amusement and instruction for boys. 'Permittendus interdum quoque lusus foliorum longiusculus, qui ingenium, et judicium, et memoriam exerceat, quemadmodum etiam latrunculorum et acierum.'—*Opera*, tom. i. p. 472, ed. 1555. And Peacham declares that he had seen French cards, the four suits of which represented the four quarters of the globe, the court cards being portraits of the sovereigns, &c., in appropriate costume, 'which ingenious deuice,' he says, 'cannot be but a great furtherance to a young capacitie,' and adds with less show of reason, 'and some comfort to the infortunate gamester when what he hath lost in money he shall have dealt him in land or wit.'—*The Compleat Gentleman*, p. 65. Lambert Daneau tells us that in his day the 'coatcards' were called by the name of Charlemagne, Lancelot, &c.

[b] Burton, in the *Anatomy of Melancholy*, says: 'Chesse play is a good exercise of the minde for some kinde of men, and fit for such melancholy, as Rhasis holds, as are idle, and haue extravagant impertinent thoughts or are troubled with cares, nothing better to distracte their mind and alter their meditations; invented (some say) by the generall of an army in a famine, to keepe his souldiers from mutiny. But if it proceed from ouermuch study, in such a case it may doe more harme then good; it is a game too troublesome for some men's braines, too full of anxiety, all out as bad as study, and besides it is a testy cholericke game, and very offensiue to him that looseth the Mate.'—P. 230, ed. 1624. The Rhasis here mentioned is doubtless the Arabian writer referred to by Dr. Hyde, who, in his elaborate work on the origin and etymology of the game of chess, quotes two books, one entitled *Apologeticus pro ludentibus al Shatrangj*, and the other, *De Arte Nerdiludii*, the author of each being a certain 'Al Râzi, qui vulgo Rasis dictus.'—*Historia Shahiludii*, pp. 182, 275, ed. 1694. James I. was apparently much of the same opinion as Burton, for in his instructions to his son he says: 'As for the chesse, I thinke it ouer fonde, because it is ouer wise and philosophicke a follie. For where all such light plaies are ordained to free men's heads for a time from the fashious thoughts on their affaires, it by the contrarie filleth and troubleth men's heads with as many fashious toyes of the playe, as before it was filled with thoughts on his affaires.'—Βασιλικὸν Δῶρον, p. 125, ed. 1603. Montaigne too seems not to have properly appreciated the noble game, for he styles it 'ce niais et puerile jeu,' and 'cet amusement ridicule.'—*Essais*, liv. i. chap. 50.

chesse, and whan they playe do thinke upon hit; whiche bokes be in englisshe.* But they be very scarse, by cause fewe men do seeke in plaies for vertue or wisedome.

* The book here referred to is of course Caxton's *Game of the Chesse*, printed in 1475, and famous from being formerly supposed to be the first specimen of English typography. It was a translation from a French work entitled 'Les moralitez du livre du jeu des echecs traduit du Latin en François, par F. Jehan *de* Vignay, hospitalier de l'ordre du Haut pas.' Warton calls the French writer John *du* Vignay, and describes him rather oddly as 'a monk hospitaler of Saint James du Haut-page;'—(*Hist. Eng. Poet.* vol. ii. p. 260), but Echard informs us that it was the order 'S. Jacobi de Altopassu Parisiis, quorum Ecclesia etiamnum extat illo eodem nomine vocata,' and he gives amongst other works of this writer a MS. with the above title, to which he adds this note: 'Quam versionem Johanni duci Normanniæ, Philippi VI. Valesii dicti regis Galliæ filio nuncupavit.'—*Script. Ord. Prædic.* tom. i. p. 742. And it was, no doubt, another copy of this MS. which is referred to by M. de Vulson, who says: 'J'ay vû un vieux manuscrit dans la bibliothèque de M. du Chesne, qui traite de la moralité de l'échiquier, et du jeu des échecs, composé par un Religieux nommé Frère Jean de Vignay, hospitalier de l'ordre du Haut-pas, dédié à tres-noble et tres-excellent Prince Jean de France, Duc de Normandie, fils aîné du Roy Philippe. Il compare l'echiquier à un Royaume, et les echecs au Roy, à la Reine, aux nobles Chevaliers, aux Conseillers, et au menu peuple, et discourt avec beaucoup de moralité, comme il est nécessaire que tous ces ordres se comportent, pour rendre un Regne parfait, et un Royaume paisible et fleurissant.'—*La Science Héroïque*, p. 159, ed. 1669. Warton is wrong in saying that this French work was written 'about the year 1360,' for Philip of Valois died in 1350. M. l'Abbé Lebeuf says that John was living in 1330, and as Philip came to the throne in 1328 this is probably about the time at which it was written. It is curious that Dibdin has made the confusion still worse by saying 'Warton (*Hist. Eng. Poet.* vol. ii. p. 313, note u, ed. 1843) assigns to a copy of his translation the date 1382.'—*Typ. Ant.* edit. Ames, vol. i. p. 32. But what Warton was referring to was not *Le Jeu des Echecs*, but a translation by Vignay of the *Legenda Aurea* of Jacques de Voragine. Warton's date, however, of this translation is equally wrong, and the correct one is no doubt that given by Echard, viz., 1348. It is remarkable also that M. l'Abbé Lebeuf, who speaks of this as well as of his translation of the *Speculum Ecclesiæ* (Acad. Roy. des Ins. *Hist. et Mém.* tom. xvii. pp. 742, 743), makes no allusion to the *Jeu des Echecs*, which from one point of view at least is the most interesting of all. Jean de Vignay was apparently unknown to MM. Richard et Giraud, who do not mention him, although they give an account of his order and say, 'Il y a une paroisse à Paris, qui en a retenue le nom.'—*Bibl. Sacrée*, tom. xiv. p. 34, ed. 1824. It is to be observed that Caxton, in his preface to the second edition of *The Game of Chess*, speaks of 'an excellent doctour of dyuynyte in the royame of fraunce, of the ordre of thospytal of Saynt Johns of Jherusalem,' as having 'made a book of the chesse moralysed.' This is manifestly a misdescription, but the error may perhaps be

CHAPTER XXVII.

That shotyng in a longe bowe is principall of all other exercises.

TULLI saithe in his firste boke of Officis, we be nat to that intent brought uppe by Nature, that we shuld seme to be

explained by the fact that the order of St. Jacques du Haut-pas was one of the military orders. Dibdin says : 'The earliest *French* impression of de Vignay's book which I have discovered is the one printed by Michel le Noir at Paris in 1505.'—*Ubi supra*, p. 35 note. If this were so it would seem that Caxton must have translated from a MS. copy, and he goes on to say 'After all it does not seem improbable that Caxton's edition of 1474 was *the first book ever printed* on the subject of chess.' Another work in French on the same subject was written by Jean Ferron ; and Prosper Marchand says, 'C'est sur l'une de ces Traductions Françoises qu'a été faite l'Angloise, comme il paroit par le titre,' but he adds 'il seroit bien difficile de dire sur laquelle des deux.'—*Dict. Hist.* art. *Cessoles.* p. 181 note. Dibdin says : 'Most probably de Vignay's book was the immediate original of Caxton's,' whilst a still later authority says, 'On comparing the English and the two French versions, it is evident that Caxton must have been well accquainted with both. His prologue addressed to the Duke of Clarence contains, *nominibus mutatis*, the whole of Jean de Vignay's dedication to Prince John of France ; while chapters i. and iii. are taken entirely from the translation of Jean Faron. The remainder of the book is from the version of Jehan de Vignay, with one or two special insertions, evidently from the pen of Caxton himself.'—Blade's *Life of Caxton*, vol. ii. p. 10, ed. 1863. Dr. Hyde, in his *Hist. Shahiludii*, gives as the date of Caxton's book 'circa annum 1480,' but Mr. Blades, with far better materials for forming an opinion, has arrived at a different conclusion and assigns it to 1475. It may be observed that *The Game of Chess* is only a translation of a translation. For both the French writers above-mentioned had merely copied and translated a work written in Latin by Jacobus de Cessolis, who lived at the end of the 13th or beginning of the 14th century, the title of which was 'De moribus hominum et de officiis nobilium super ludo scacchorum.' Warton says 'Jacobus de Casulis or of Casali in *Italy*, a French Dominican friar, about the year 1290 wrote a Latin treatise on Chess' (*Hist. E. P.* vol. ii. p. 260), but this description is erroneous, for the name was derived from the birthplace of the writer, Cessoles, a village in the Diocese of Laon, in the district of the Province of Picardy, bordering upon Champagne (Prosper Marchand *ubi supra*). Hyde says that the work was written 'ante annum 1200,' but Echard fixes the date 'sub finem sæculi xiii vel initia sequentis,' and the birthplace, on the authority of a notice by Pignon, who was not only a native of the same place, but a member of the same order, having been lecturer of the College of Dominicans at Rheims before 1403. Marchand mentions a folio edition of de Cessolis, which was apparently unknown to Echard and other bibliographers, and he observes that this was not the most ancient work on the subject, as was believed

made to playe and disporte, but rather to grauitie, and studies

by the Duke of Brunswick (who himself wrote a book on chess in 1617), 'car sans parler de Phasis, mort vers l'an 1000 (this is no doubt a misprint for Rhasis mentioned above) dès l'an 1198 le Pape Innocent III. avoit déjà tiré de ce jeu des Leçons de Morale ainsi que Cessoles.'—*Ubi supra*, p. 181 note. Elsewhere he tells us that these Moral Lessons are preserved in the form of Latin MSS. in the libraries of S. John's Coll., Oxford, and S. Benet (?) at Cambridge, and he also says that Ludovicus Jacob, in his *Bibliotheca Pontificia*, ed. 1643, at p. 119, Oldoinus, in his *Athenæum Romanum*, 1676, at p. 463, and G. J. Eggs, in his *Pontificium Doctum*, 1718, at p. 425, 'sont les ceuls qui fassent mention de cet ouvrage.' —Dict. Hist. *sub voc.* Murner, tom. ii. p. 98 note. Mr. Twiss says that these MSS. agree with one in the Brit. Mus. (Bibl. Reg. 12 E. xxi. P. 210), which 'appears to have been written about the year 1400,' and 'as it is the earliest MS. on the subject extant,' he inserts a translation. The Editor, however, believes he is in a position to show that this 'moralisation,' which has always hitherto been attributed to Innocent III., was not in reality the work of that Pontiff. Dr. Hyde says: 'Moralizatio Scaccarii quæ *nimis temere* Innocentio III. tribuitur, proculdubio scripta est ab aliquo ejusdem nominis Monacho Anglo, uti constat tam ex aliis quam ex vocibus *check* et *mayte*, &c., quæ Angliam, non vero Italiam redolent.'—P. 179. And he says that the Moralization is printed by Dr. Prideaux at the end of his Logic. This last appears to be a scarce work, and there is no copy of it in the B. M. Library, but by the courtesy of Mr. H. O. Coxe of the Bodleian Library the Editor has had an opportunity of seeing the passage referred to by Hyde, which is at p. 375 of Dr. Prideaux's *Hypomnemata, Logica, Rhetorica*, &c. Mr. Coxe, in answer to the Editor's inquiries on the subject, says, 'There is no date to the work, but as it was printed by Lichfield it was probably between 1645-55.' Hyde's own book was printed in 1694. Dr. Prideaux says: 'Ob argumenti similitudinem visum est subjicere Innocentii III. de Scaccario Moralitates ex MSo. publicæ Bibliothecæ Oxoniensis, nunquam (quod sciam) antehac excusas,' and then he gives *in extenso*, 'Moralitas de Scaccario secundum Dominum Innocentium Tertium.' Twiss gives at pp. 4-7 of vol. ii. of his work on chess a translation of the Brit. Mus. MS. above mentioned, and the Editor finds, on comparing this translation with the Oxford copy, that there are several points of difference. The Editor, however, on examining the work called *Communiloquium* of Johannes Gallensis before mentioned (pars i. distinctio 10, cap. 7) has discovered what he believes to be the original of the Morality attributed to Innocent. It is almost exactly like the MS. in the Brit. Mus., and differs but little from the Oxford. The whole passage occurs again in the *Destructorium* of Alexander of Hales, who quotes it as the composition of a writer whom he calls indifferently Ruallensis and Vuallerensis (pars iv. cap. 23, fo. 124). Now this is especially interesting, for John of Galles has hitherto been assumed to have lived 'about 1260,' but Alexander *died* in 1245, therefore Johannes Gallensis must certainly have written the above work anterior to this latter date. Innocent III. died in 1216, and the Moralization was no doubt written between 1216 and 1245; and as we know that John passed a considerable

of more estimation.[a] Wherfore it is writen of Alexander, emperour of Rome, for his grauitie called *Seuerus*,[b] that in his chyldehode, and before he was taught the letters of greke or latine, he neuer exercised any other play or game, but only one, where in was a similitude of iustice, and therfore it was called in latine *Ad Judices*, whiche is in englisshe to the iuges.[c] But the forme therof is nat expressed by the sayde autor,[d]

portion of his life abroad, it is not unlikely that it should have been ascribed to the Pope, who was himself the author of numerous works. Anyhow, the author of the *Destructorium* unhesitatingly ascribes the authorship of it to 'Vuallerensis,' and on comparing the passage in the former with that in the *Communiloquium*, no one can doubt that 'Vuallerensis,' 'Ruallensis' and 'Gallensis' are the same person. Moreover Oudin writes the same name indifferently Gualensis and Wallensis. It is not a little curious that on looking at the MS. in the B. M. the Editor found that it was bound up with another work of Johannes Gallensis, the *Tractatus de Virtutibus*. This, of course, may be merely accidental. But it will be a satisfaction to the Editor if his researches are the means of showing, after the lapse of nearly two centuries, that the learned Dr. Hyde was right in suspecting the Pope's Morality to have been written by an Englishman, though not of the same name as the Pontiff.

[a] 'Neque enim ita generati à naturâ sumus, ut ad ludum et jocum facti esse videamur, sed ad severitatem potius, et ad quædam studia graviora atque majora.' Cic. *de Off.* lib. i. cap 29.

[b] This is a mistake of the author; the story is told by Ælius Spartianus of Septimius Severus, not Alexander Severus.

[c] 'In primâ pueritiâ priusquam Latinis Græcisque literis imbueretur, quibus eruditissimus fuit, nullum alium inter pueros ludum nisi ad judices exercuit, quum ipse prælatis fascibus ac securibus, ordine puerorum circumstante, sederet ac judicaret.'—*Hist. Aug.* tom. i. p. 589, ed. 1671.

[d] Although we do not know the precise nature of this game, yet from other sources we learn that it was the habit of children, then as now, to mimic the actions of their elders. Thus Trebellius Pollio uses the expression 'Pueri fingunt per ludibria potestates.' See *Hist. August.* tom. ii. p. 194, ed. 1671. And Suetonius tells us that Nero ordered his stepson Rufius Crispinus to be drowned, 'impuberem adhuc, quia ferebatur ducatus et imperia ludere.'—*Nero*, 35. Again, Plutarch in his life of Cato gives us a picture of the precocity of the children of those days. Πάλιν δὲ συγγενοῦς τινος ἐν γενεθλίοις καλέσαντος ἐπὶ δεῖπνον ἄλλους τε παῖδας καὶ τοὺς περὶ Κάτωνα, σχολὴν ἄγοντες ἔν τινι μέρει τῆς οἰκίας ἔπαιζον αὐτοὶ καθ' ἑαυτοὺς ἀναμεμιγμένοι νεώτεροι καὶ πρεσβύτεροι, τὸ δὲ παιζόμενον ἦν δίκαι καὶ κατηγορίαι καὶ ἀγωγαὶ τῶν ἁλισκομένων.—*Cato Minor*, 2. This would seem to have resembled the 'playing at judges' alluded to in the text. Seneca enumerates various childish games. 'Non ideo quidquam inter illos puerosque interesse quis dixerit, quod illis talorum nucumque et æris minuti avaritia est, his auri

nor none other that I haue yet radde; wherfore I wyll repaire againe to the residue of honest exercise.

And for as moche as Galene, in his seconde boke of the preseruation of helth, declareth to be in them these qualities or diuersities, that is to say, that some be done with extendinge of myght, and as hit were violently, and that is called valiaunt exercise; some with swyfte or hasty motion, other with strength and celerite, and that maye be called vehement.[a] The particular kyndes of euery of them he describethe, whiche were to longe here to be rehersed.

But in as moche as he also saithe, that he that is of good astate in his body, ought to knowe the power and effecte of euery exercise, but he nedethe nat to practise any other but that whiche is moderate and meane betwene euery extremite;[b] I wil now brefely declare in what exercise nowe in custome amonge us, maye be mooste founde of that mediocritie, and maye be augmented or mynysshed at the pleasure of hym

---

argentique et urbium; quod illi inter ipsos magistratus gerunt, et prætextam fascesque ac tribunal imitantur, hi eadem in campo, foroque, et in curiâ serio ludunt; illi in litoribus arenæ congestu simulacra domuum excitant, hi ut magnum aliquid agentes, in lapidibus ac parietibus, et tectis moliendis occupati, ad tutelam corporum inventa in periculum verterunt?'—*De Constantia Sapientis*, cap. 12. And Chrysostom alludes to the ever favourite pastime of 'playing at soldiers' in his *Homilies on the Corinthians*. Οὐχ ὁρᾶτε τοὺς παῖδας, ὅταν παίζοντες τάξιν ποιῶσι, καὶ στρατιώτας, καὶ προηγῶται αὐτῶν, κήρυκες καὶ ῥαβδοῦχοι, καὶ μέσος ὁ παῖς ἐν χώρᾳ ἄρχοντος βαδίζῃ, ὡς παιδικὰ τὰ γινόμενα; —*In Epist. I. ad Cor. Hom. i.* (Migne ed. tom. x. p. 16.)

[a] 'Jam singulas exercitationum seorsum persequi tempestivum videtur: illo præsertim prius significato, quòd in his quoque complures differentiæ inveniantur. Quippe interim aliam partem aliud alio magis exercitium fatigat. Et quædam lentè motis fiunt, quædam ocyssimè agitatis, et quædam robore ac nixu adhibitis, quædam sine his. Ad hæc quædam cum robore pariter et celeritate, quædam languidè. Ac quod violenter quidem sine velocitate exercetur, εὔτονον, id est *valens* voco; quod violenter et cum celeritate, σφοδρόν, id est *vehemens.*'—*De Sanit. tuend.* lib. ii. fo. 30, ed. 1538.

[b] 'Ergo gymnastes propositi nobis adulescentis utique qui optimum corporis statum est sortitus, omnium quidem exercitationum vires pernovit, deligit vero ex omni genere quod moderatum, mediumque inter utrumque excessum est.'—*Ubi supra*, fo. 33, l. 71.

that dothe exercise, without therby appairinge any part of dilectation or commodite therof.

And in myn oppinion none may be compared with shootinge in the longe bowe, and that for sondry utilities that come therof, wherin it incomparably excelleth all other exercise.* For in drawyng of a bowe, easie

The commendation of shoting.

---

* Ascham in his *Toxophilus*, which was not written till several years after the publication of *The Governour*, takes credit to himself for being the first who had composed a treatise on the subject of archery. He says, complacently enough, 'I am (I suppose) the first which hath said anything in this matter.'—*Toxophilus*, p. 5, ed. 1864. But it is not unreasonable to suppose that Sir Thomas Elyot's commendation of the exercise, and the large space he devoted to it in his popular work, inspired Ascham with a desire to employ his own pen in furtherance of the same object, viz., the rescue of archery from the decay which was then imminent. This is, indeed, placed almost beyond doubt by the fact that he records a conversation on the subject with the author of *The Governour*. 'As I was once in company with Sir Thomas Elyot, knight (which surely for his learning in all kind of knowledge, brought much worship to all the nobility of England), I was so bold to ask him, if he at any time had marked any thing as concerning the bringing in of shooting into England. He answered me gently again, he had a work in hand, which he nameth *De rebus memorabilibus Angliæ*, which I trust we shall see in print shortly, and for the accomplishment of that book, he had read and perused over many old monuments of England, and in seeking for that purpose he marked this of shooting in an exceeding old chronicle, the which had no name, that what time as the Saxons came first into this realm, in King Vortiger's days, when they had been here a while, and at last began to fall out with the Britons, they troubled and subdued the Britons with nothing so much as with their bow and shafts, which weapon being strange and not seen here before, was wonderful terrible unto them: and this beginning I can think very well to be true.'—*Toxophilus*, p. 77. Upon this passage Mr. Roberts remarks in his *English Bowman*, 'In support of what Sir Thomas Elyot notices, we may refer to an authority (probably the very authority alluded to by him), which is Henry of Huntingdon, who informs us that in the twenty-second year of the reign of Kenrick and Ceaulin (Saxon monarchs) a great battle was fought between the Saxons and English, in which the English disposed their *archers* (*viris sagittariis*) and light armed troops after the manner of the Romans; this battle happened about the year 560.'—P. 10, ed. 1801. Mr. Roberts, however, must surely be mistaken in thinking that Henry of Huntingdon was the authority alluded to by Sir Thos. Elyot, for in the first place it is to be observed that the latter says it was 'in King Vortiger's days.' Now Vortigern was killed A.D. 455, whereas the battle mentioned by Henry of Huntingdon was not fought till A.D. 552, and in the second place, the chronicle, according to Elyot, said it was the *Saxons* who subdued the Britons with their bow and shafts, and gave as a reason that it was 'a new and strange weapon;'

and congruent to his strength, he that shoteth dothe moderately exercise his armes, and the ouer parte of his body; and if his bowe be bygger, he must adde to more strength; wherin is no lasse valiaunt exercise than in any other wherof Galene writeth.

In shootynge at buttes, or brode arowe markes, is a mediocritie of exercise of the lower partes of the body and legges, by goinge a litle distaunce a mesurable pase.

At rouers or prickes,* it is at his pleasure that shoteth,

but Henry says that it was the *Britons* who employed archers against the Saxons. Independently of these contradictions, however, it is hardly likely that Sir Thos. Elyot would speak of Henry of Huntingdon's work, which was well known to, and much read by historians of the 16th century, although it was not *printed* till 1596, as 'an exceeding old chronicle which had no name.' But this description exactly applies to a translation of Higden's *Polychronicon*, the Latin text of which, according to Dr. Babington, was never printed till it formed a part of the series of publications now being brought out under the direction of the Master of the Rolls, except certain portions which were printed by Gale in 1691, and which, therefore, were of course unknown in that form to Sir T. Elyot. Now in the 16th century the author of *Polychronicon* was 'unknown.' Dr. Babington says: 'We may mention the names of Wycliffe, Purvey, and Thorpe among the Lollards; also of John Capgrave, Richard of Cirencester, and Thomas of Elmham, among the chroniclers; all of whom wrote before Caxton's edition appeared in 1482. None of these authors, however, so far as I know, mention Higden by name.'—Introduction, p. xliv. In Trevisa's translation 'the name of Higden is not so much as mentioned in the MS. at all.'—*Ubi supra*, p. lvi. This MS., which is now printed by Dr. Babington for the first time, is preserved in the library of St. John's College, Cambridge; and the present Editor thinks it not unlikely that this may be the 'exceeding old chronicle' referred to by Sir Thos. Elyot, who, as the reader will see on referring to the life prefixed to the present work, must have had ample opportunity for ransacking the Cambridge libraries. Now there is a passage in Trevisa's translation (vol. v. p. 263 *Chron. and Mem.* ed.) which, although really bearing quite a different interpretation, from the difficulty of reading it in the MS. may have appeared to Sir T. Elyot to refer to weapons of war. Moreover, at p. 273 of the same vol. it is said: 'Hengistus usede a newe manere of tresoun,' and these passages occur before the narration of the death of Vortigern. For these reasons it seems probable that the chronicle referred to was *not* that of Henry of Huntingdon, but a translation of *Polychronicon* in MS.

* Carew, in his *Survey of Cornwall*, says: 'To give you some taste of the Cornishmen's former sufficiency that way, for long shooting, their shaft was a cloth yard, their pricks twenty-four score; for strength they would pierce any ordinary armour: and one Master Robert Arundell (whom I well knew) could shoot twelve

howe faste or softly he listeth to go. And yet is the praise of the shooter neither more ne lasse, for as farre or nighe the marke is his arowe, whan he goethe softly, as whan he runneth.

Tenese, seldome used, and for a little space, is a good exercise for yonge men, but it is more violent than shoting, by reason that two men do play. Wherfore neither of them is at his owne libertie to measure the exercise.* For if the one

score with his right hand, with his left, and from behind his head. Lastly, for near and well-aimed shooting, buts made them perfect in the one, and roving in the other, for pricks, *the first corrupter of archery, through too much preciseness*, were then scarcely known, and little practised.'—P. 194, ed. 1811. Gervase Markham, who wrote in the reign of Elizabeth, says: 'The markes to shoote at are three—Butts, Pricks, or Roauers. The Butte is a leuell marke, and therefore would haue a strong arrowe with a very broad feather; the Pricke is a mark of compasse, yet certaine in the distance, therefore would have nimble, strong arrowes with a middle feather, all of one weight and flying; and the Roauer is a marke incertaine, sometimes long, sometimes short, and therefore must haue arrowes lighter or heauier, according to the distance of place.'—*Country Contentments*, p. 108, ed. 1615. And Ascham says: 'Methinks that the customable shooting at home, specially at butts and pricks, make nothing at all for strong shooting, which doth most good in war.'—*Toxophilus*, p. 82, ed. 1864. Drayton, describing Robin Hood and his band, says:

> 'Of archery they had the very perfect craft,
> With Broad-arrow, or But, or Prick, or Rouing shaft,
> At Markes full fortie score, they used to Prick and Roue,
> Yet higher then the breast, for Compasse neuer stroue.'
> *Polyolbion*, Song xxvi. p. 122, ed. 1622.

The prick or *preke* (Saxon) was the mark in the centre of the target, and prickshafts are arrows considerably lighter than those used in other kinds of shooting. By Statute 33 Henry VIII. cap. 9 it was enacted, 'that noe man under thage of xxiv yeres shall shoote at any standinge pricke except it be at a Rover, whereat he shall chaunge at every shoote his marke, uppon payne for everye shoote doinge the contrarie fower pence; and that noe person above the saide age of xxiv yeres shall shoote at any marke of a leaven (xi) score yardes or under, with anye prick shafte or fleight, under the peyne to forfeyt for everie shoote six shillings and eight pence.' Sir John Maundevile, who wrote in the fourteenth century, in his description of Tartary, says: 'Men of that contree ben alle gode Archeres, and schooten righte welle, bothe men and women, als wel on Hors bak, *prykynge*, as on Fote, rennynge.'—*Voiage and Travaile*, p. 301, ed. 1727.

* This seems always to have been a fashionable game. Henry VIII. was very fond of this, as he was of all manly sports. Sebastian Giustinian, in his report of

stryke the balle harde, the other that intendeth to receyue
him, is than constrained to use semblable violence, if he wyll

England to the Venetian Senate, speaking of the king, who was then twenty-nine
years old (A.D. 1519), says, after describing his passion for field sports : 'He was
also fond of tennis, at which game it was the prettiest thing in the world to see him
play ; his fair skin glowing through a shirt of the finest texture.'—*Cal. of Stat.
Papers (Venetian)*, vol. ii. p. 559. In the *Privy Purse Expenses* there are numerous items of sums lost by the king at this game. And Hall tells us that in the
second year of his reign he 'was moche entysed to playe at tennes and at dice,
which appetite certayn craftie persones about hym perceyuynge, brought in Frenchmen and Lombardes, to make wagers with hym, and so he lost moch money ; but
when he perceyued their crafte, he exchuyd their compaignie, and let them go.'
However, twelve years later, the same chronicler records the fact that 'the kyng
and the Emperor played at tennice, at the Bayne, against the princes of Orenge and
the Marques of Brandenborow, and on the Princes syde *stopped* the Erle of Deuonshyre, and the lorde Edmond on the other syde, and they departed euen handes
on bothe sydes after eleven games fully played.'—*Chronicle*, vol. ii. fo. 98 b. ed.
1548. The Emperor above-mentioned was Chas. V., for whom the king had rebuilt his 'newe palace of Brydewell,' of which 'the Bayne' formed a part. When
Whitehall become a royal residence, the king, according to Stow, built 'divers
fair Tennis-courts, Bowling-allies, and a cock-pit out of certain old tenements.'—
Survey of London, lib. vi. p. 6, ed. 1720. But the royal example notwithstanding, we
find tennis enumerated amongst the 'unlawful games' which were prohibited by
statute in 1541. The reason of this severity was doubtless the excessive gambling
which the game encouraged, and which is so strongly reprobated by Puritan
writers at the end of the century. Northbrooke, however, whilst inveighing
against cards, dice, &c., classes tennis with chess amongst 'honest and lawful
games,' so that they be played 'at conuenient times and that moderately without
any excesse.'—*Treatise against Diceplay*, p. 98. Peacham, describing the amusements of the French, says : 'Their exercises are for the most part Tennise play,
Pallemaile, shooting in the Crossebow or Peece, and Dancing.'—*Compleat Gentleman*, p. 204. The *jeu de paume*, however, which answered to our Fives, was
more popular in France than tennis. James the First, amongst the exercises
which he would have his son 'to use, although but moderately, not making a craft
of them,' recommends 'playing at the caitche or tennise.'—Βασιλικὸν Δῶρον, lib.
iii. p. 121, ed. 1603. Daneau, the French writer previously quoted, whose
treatise was translated by Thomas Newton in 1586, after laying it down that
money won at play could not be recovered at law, makes an exception in favour
of money won at 'the Tenise play, (which hath found so much fauour to be specially priuiledged in some cities and places, by the priuate lawes of their countrey)
that if a man do winne thereat some little portion or smal pittaunce of money
(as namely a groate, or sixe pence, or thereaboutes), he may iudicially demaund
and recouer the same. Which Play seemeth hereupon to haue found this speciall
fauour, for that there is in it (as Galene affirmeth) an excellent good and wholesome

retourne the balle from whens it came to him. If it trille fast on the grounde, and he entendeth to stoppe, or if it rebounde a great distaunce from hym, and he wolde eftesones retourne it, he can nat than kepe any measure in swiftnesse of mocion.

Some men wolde say, that in mediocritie, whiche I haue so

exercise of the bodie, and no lesse industrie of the mynde.'—*Treatise touching Dyceplay*. As showing how popular the game once was in this country, the reader will be surprised to find an allusion to it in a most unlikely quarter, viz. the dry and somewhat pedantic work of Nathaniel Bacon, intitled *An Historical and Political Discourse of the Laws and Government of England*, where, speaking of the changes introduced by the Danes into the Saxon commonwealth, he says : 'And as at Tennis, the Dane and Bishop "served" each other with the fond countryman, that whether Lord Dane or Lord Bishop was the greater burthen is hard to be determined.'—P. 69, ed. 1760. Ludovicus Vives gives the following description of the game as played in Spain in the 16th century : 'Cabanillius. "Hàc inde ad sphæristerium Barzii, seu mavis Masconorum." Borgia. "In Galliâ habetisne ad hunc modum ludos in publico?" Scintilla. "De aliis Galliæ urbibus non possem tibi respondere; Lutetiæ scio nullum esse, sed in privato multa, velut in suburbiis Divi Jacobi, D. Marcelli, D. Germani." Cab. "Et in ipsâ civitate famosissimum, quod vocant Bracchæ." Bor. "Luditur eâdem illic ratione, quâ hìc?" S. "Eâdem prorsum, nisi quòd magister ludi præbet illic calceos et pileos lusorios." B. "Cujusmodi sunt?" S. "Calcei sunt coactilitii." B. "Non essent hìc utiles." C. "Videlicet in viâ lapidosâ, in Franciâ vero et Belgicâ luditur super pavimentum lateribus constratum, planum, et æquabile." S. "Pilei sunt æstate leviores, in hyeme autem crassi, profundi, cum offendice sub mento, ne in agitatione vel elabantur ex capite, vel decidant in oculos." B. "Offendimento hìc non utimur, nisi quum est ventus vehementior, sed quales habent pilas?" S. "Nullos ferè folles ut hìc ; sed sphærulas minores vestratibus, et multo duriores, ex corio albo ; tomentum est, non ut in vestris, lanugo è pannis tonsa, sed pili ferè canini, eamque ob causam raro luditur palmâ." B. "Quomodo ergo percutiunt pilam? pugno ut folles?" S. "Ne sic quidem sed reticulo." B. "Confecto ex filo?" S. "Ex fidibus crassiusculis, quales ferè sunt sextæ in testudine, habent funem tensum et reliqua ut hìc in ludis domesticis. Sub funem misisse globum, vicium est seu peccatum. Signa sunt bina, seu mavis metas. Numeri quaterni, quindecim, triginta, quadraginta quinque, seu antegressio, æqualitas numerorum ; victoria quæ est duplex, ut cum dicitur vicimus signum, et vicimus ludum. Pila autem vel ex volatu remittitur, vel ex primo resultu, ex secundo enim ictus est invalidus, et ibi fit signum, ubi pila est percussa."'—*Opera*, tom. i. p. 51, ed. 1555. It is somewhat singular that Strutt makes no allusion to this chapter of *The Governour*, and indeed, like many other modern writers, he seems to have overlooked this most interesting picture of 16th century life and manners.

moche praised in shootynge, why shulde nat boulynge, claisshe, pynnes, and koytyng be as moche commended?[a] Verily as for two the laste, be to be utterly abiected of al noble men, in like wise foote balle,[b] wherin is nothinge but beastly furie

[a] The origin of the word 'claisshe' or 'closh' is lost in obscurity. Strutt says it was exceedingly like the game called kayles, which seems to have resembled that now known as 'nine pins,' and which is probably referred to by Sir Thomas Elyot under the designation of 'pynnes.' For 'bowlinge, Coytinge, Cloyshe and Cayles' are mentioned together as 'unlawfull games' in 33 Hen. VIII. cap. 9. In another section of the same statute this word is spelt 'clashe.' In 1389 an Act was passed (12 Ric. II. cap. 6) forbidding 'les jeues as pelotes si bien a meyn come a pice, et les autres jeues appellez coytes, dyces, gettre de pere, keyles et autres tielx jeues importunes,' which in the English translations of the statutes appears as 'all playing at Tennis or Football and other games called Coits, Dice, Casting of the Stone, Kailes, and other such importune games.' This prohibition was re-enacted by 2 Henry IV. cap. 4, but in 17 Edw. IV. cap. 3, Closh and Kailes are described as being 'new imagined games.' In Cotgrave's Dict. the French word Quille is translated 'a keyle, a big peg, a pin of wood used at ninepins or keyles,' which sufficiently indicates the origin of the term.

[b] James I., whilst commending some athletic exercises to the notice of his son as suitable for a young Prince, says, 'But from this count I debarre all rough and violent exercise, as the foot ball, meeter for laming than making able the users thereof.'—Βασιλικὸν Δῶρον, lib. iii. p. 120, ed. 1603. It is curious that Strutt, who quotes this passage twice, viz. at pp. xv. and 80, prints 'court' for 'count,' which seems a very unnecessary correction; as the game, quite apart from the King's discouragement of it, is unlikely to have been patronised by courtiers. The King, however, had manifestly read, marked, and inwardly digested *The Governour* before sitting down to transcribe these precepts for the benefit of his son. Carew, whose *Survey of Cornwall* was first published in 1602, gives an elaborate description of 'Hurling,' which appears to have resembled the game of Football, as played at Rugby in the nineteenth century, and he calls it 'A play, verily, both rude and rough, and yet such as is not destitute of policies, in some sort resembling the feats of war; for you shall have companies laid out before, on the one side, to encounter them that come with the ball, and of the other party to succour them, in manner of a foreward . . . . . The ball in this play may be compared to an infernal spirit, for whosoever catcheth it, fareth straightways like a madman, struggling and fighting with those that go about to hold him; and no sooner is the ball gone from him, but he resigneth this fury to the next receiver, and himself becometh peaceable as before. I cannot well resolve, whether I should more commend this game for the manhood and exercise, or condemn it for the boisterousness and harms which it begetteth; for as on the one side it makes their bodies strong, hard, and nimble, and puts a courage into their hearts to meet an enemy in the face, so on the other part it is accompanied with many dangers, some of which do ever fall to the players share: for proof whereof, when the Hurling is ended, you shall see them retiring

and exstreme violence; wherof procedeth hurte, and consequently rancour and malice do remaine with them that be wounded; wherfore it is to be put in perpetuall silence.[a]

In classhe is emploied to litle strength;[b] in boulyng often times to moche;[c] wherby the sinewes be to moche strayned, and the vaines to moche chafed. Wherof often tymes is sene to ensue ache, or the decreas of strength or agilitie in the armes: where, in shotyng, if the shooter use the strength of

home as from a pitched battle, with bloody pates, bones broken, and out of joint, and such bruises as serve to shorten their days; yet all is good play, and never attorney nor coroner troubled for the matter.'—Pp. 197, 198.

[a] In Scotland it was thought necessary to suppress football and golf, in order to promote the practice of archery. The Parliament of James II., in 1458, 'decreed and ordained that the displays of weapons be held by the lords and barons, spiritual and temporal, four times in the year, and that the foot ball and golf be utterly cried down, and not to be used.'—Pinkerton's *Hist. of Scot.*, vol. i. p. 426, ed. 1797. M. Misson, who travelled in England in the 17th century, and afterwards published the result of his observations, says: 'En hyver le *Foot-ball* est un exercise utile et charmant. C'est un balon de cuir, gros comme la tête, et rempli de vent; cela se balotte avec le pied dans les rues par celui qui le peut attraper; il n'y a point d'autre science.'—*Mémoires et Observations faites par un Voyageur*, p. 255, ed. 1698.

[b] Strutt says that this game was 'played with pins, which were thrown at with a bowl instead of a truncheon, and probably differed only in name from the nine-pins of the present time.'—*Sports and Pastimes*, p. 202, ed. 1801.

[c] Markham says: 'There is another recreation, which howsoeuer unlawfull in the abuse thereof, yet exercised with moderation is euen of Physicions themselues helde exceeding wholsome, and hath beene prescribed for a recreation to great Persons, and that is bowling; in which a man shall finde great art in choosing out his ground, and preuenting the winding, hanging, and many turning aduantages of the same, whether it bee in open wilde places or in close allies; and in this sport the chusing of the bowle is the greatest cunning; your flat bowles being the best for allies, your round byazed bowles for open grounds of aduantage, and your round bowles like a ball for green swarthes that are plaine and leuell.'—*Country Contentments*, lib. i. p. 108, ed. 1615. The game, however, seems to have been attended with certain disadvantages when played in town, for Gosson says, 'Common Bowling Allyes are priuy Mothes that eate uppe the credite of many ydle Citizens, whose gaynes at home are not able to weighe downe theyr losses abroad, whose shoppes are so farre from maintaining their play, that their wiues and children cry out for bread and go to bed supperlesse ofte in the yeere.' —*Schoole of Abuse*, p. 45. And Whetstone speaks of 'these shames of good citizens' who 'trade but to a dycing house, or at the furthest trauail to a bowling alley.' —*Mirrour for Magistrates*, p. 29, ed. 1584.

his bowe within his owne tiller,[a] he shal neuer be therwith grieued or made more feble.

Also in shootyng is a double utilitie, wherin it excelleth all other exercises and games incomparably.[b] The one is that it is, and alway hath ben, the moste excellent artillerie for warres,[c] wherby this realme of Englande hath bene

[a] Barwick, 'un vieux mousquetaire' of the sixteenth century, who advocated the use of firearms in opposition to Sir John Smythe, says : ' But as touching the certaintie of shooting at markes or enemies, let it be with Harquebuze or musket, considered but with the archer himselfe : whether a Cros-bowe or a Long-bowe *in a Tyller* shoot more certainely, either at marke or pricke, than dooth the Long-bowe that from the hand of the bowman is deliuered ; and then I thinke it will be allowed, that when the Harquebuze or musket do take the leuel from the button of his sight unto the pin in the fore ende of his peece, that he may shoote with more and surer leuell then can either loose Long-bowe, *Tiller-bowe*, or Cros-bowe, and specially the musket, who hath his rest to stay his peece upon right steadfastly.'— *Discourse concerning Weapons of Fire*, p. 11. In an account of a procession Sept. 17, 1583, we are told that there were forty pages, 'every one bearing a *tiller-bow* or cross-bow, and broad arrows in their hands.'—Roberts, *English Bowman*, p. 261, ed. 1801.

[b] The King himself was a first-rate shot, a fact which is corroborated by several independent witnesses. Paulus Jovius the Italian says : 'Nemo ipso Rege Britannicum ingentem arcum contentius flexit, nemo certiùs atque validiùs sagittavit.'—*Descript. Brit.* fo. 18 b. And John Taylor, clerk of the Parliament, tells us in his Diary which he kept whilst he was with the English army in France, in 1513, that three ambassadors came to the king, 'who was practising archery in a garden with the archers of his guard. He cleft the mark in the middle, and surpassed them all, as he surpasses them in stature and personal graces.'—Brewer's *Lett. and Pa.* vol. i. p. 623. These archers were part of the king's bodyguard, every gentleman 'spere' being obliged to furnish 'two good archers, well horsed and harnessed,' and these archers were only to be appointed after personal presentation to His Majesty. See Grose's *Mil. Antiq.* vol. i. p. 110, note, ed. 1812.

[c] Ascham, in the *Toxophilus*, says : 'Artillery, now-a-days, is taken for two things, guns and bows.'—P. 55, ed. 1864. In the old ballad of *Robin Hood and the Curtall Fryer* it is said—

'Then some would leape, and some would runne,
And some would use *artillery* ;
"Which of you can a good bow draw,
A good archer for to be ? " '—Ritson's *Collect.* vol. ii. p. 62, ed. 1832.

The word was, of course, introduced from France. So far as the editor has been able to ascertain, the first occasion on which it is used in the Statutes of the Realm is in the title of the Act 33 Hen. VIII. cap. 9, which was passed in 1541. The origin of the Artillery Company shows that the word was at first applied to

nat only best defended from outwarde hostilitie, but also in other regions a fewe englisshe archers haue ben seene to preuayle agayne people innumerable,* also wonne

manual weapons, for Stow informs us that 'King Hen. VIII., anno regni 29, granted by patent to Sir Christopher Morris, Maister of his Ordinance, Anthony Knevyt and Peter Mewtas, Gentlemen of his Privy Chamber (who were overseers of the Fraternity or Guild of St. George), that they should be overseers of the science of artillery, *that is* for long bows, cross bows, and hand guns.'—Stow's *Survey of London*, lib. i. p. 250. M. Daniel traces the origin of the word to the Latin *ars, artis,* 'parce qu'il y avoit beaucoup d'artifice dans ces machines,' and he quotes from a document which he calls a 'statute' of Edward II. King of England, but which in the margin is styled *De Officio Senescalli Aquitaniæ*, the following application of the term : 'Item ordinatum est, quòd sit unus *artillator*, qui faciat ballistas, carellos, arcos, sagittas, lanceas, spiculas, et alia arma necessaria pro garnisionibus castrorum.' And he calls attention to the fact that in France the title of Grand Master or Master of Artillery was in use long before the invention of fire-arms.'—*Hist. de la Milice Françoise*, tom. i. p. 143, ed. 1724.

* Sir John Smythe, a veteran of the 16th century and an enthusiastic admirer of the long bow, gives in his *Discourses upon Weapons*, published in 1590, several instances of this, beginning with the battle of Crecy, where the French 'were six at the least, for euerie one of the English;' Poitiers, where the English army numbered only 8,000, 'of the which there were 6,000 Archers and 2,000 armed men,' whilst the French army consisted of 'aboue threescore thousand horsemen and footmen, of the which there were aboue 10,000 men at armes, and of horsemen of all sorts aboue 30,000.' 'The famous victorie and battaile of Agincourt also, of later years fought by King Henry the fift against the whole power of France, doth euidentlie shewe the most excellent effectes and execution of Archers, where with the grace of God and incredible volees of arrowes, the French king's army was ouerthrown, which consisted of aboue 40,000 horsemen and footmen, of the which there were 10,000 men at armes, all knightes, esquiers, and gentlemen ; whereas King Henrie's army did consist but of 10,000 Archers, 1,500 Launces, and 2,000 footmen of other weapons.' To descend to skirmishes, this writer tells us that 'in King Henrie the Sixts time, John Lord of Bellay, being accompanied with 200 Launces at the least, and taking his way to a towne called Mans, met by chaunce with an English Captaine, called Berry, that had to the number of fourscore Archers, who, perceiuing the French men, presentlie reduced his men into a "hearse," turning their backes to a hedge, because the Launces might not charge them in back, but onlie in frunt, and so giuing their volees of arrowes at the French Launces charging, did so wound and kill their horses, that they ouerthrewe them, and slewe and tooke diuers of them prisoners.' On another occasion, 'Sixe score (French) launces charged sixteene or twentie English archers, when the volees of arrowes of those fewe Archers wrought such notable effect against the French horsmen that they brake and ouerthrew them, in such sort that there were diuers of the French slaine and taken prisoners.'—P. 31-34.

inpreignable cities and stronge holdes, and kepte them in the myddes of the strength of their enemies. This is the feate, wherby englisshe men haue ben most dradde and had in estimation with outwarde princes, as well enemies as alies.[a] And the commoditie therof hath bene approued as

[a] Philip de Comines, in the preceding century, speaking of archers, said : 'Mon advis est que la souveraine chose du monde pour les batailles, sont les Archiers: mais qu'ils soient à milliers (car en petit nombre ne valent rien), et que ce soient gens mal montez, à ce qu'ils n'ayent point de regret à perdre leurs chevaux, ou du tout n'en ayent point : et valent mieux pour un jour en cet office ceux qui jamais ne veirent rien, que les bien exercitez. Et aussi telle opinion tiennent les Anglois, *qui sont la fleur des Archiers du monde.*'—*Mémoires,* tom. i. p. 22, ed. 1706. Barbaro, the Venetian ambassador at the Court of Henry VIII., in his report to the Senate on the English army, wrote that 'The infantry is formed of taller men (than the light cavalry), and divided into four sorts. The first is of archers, who abound in England, and are very excellent both by nature and from practice, so that the archers alone have often been seen to rout armies of 30,000 men.'—*Cal. St. Pap. (Venetian),* vol. v. p. 350. In 1507 the Spanish ambassador in England wrote to Ferdinand that 'the manner of fighting as practised by the English is very peculiar, and very well calculated for a war in Africa. They use bows and arrows with wonderfull dexterity. It is believed in England that the English bowmen could, in a few years, conquer the whole of Africa.'—*Cal. St. Pa. (Spanish),* vol. i. p. 438. It is curious, however, to read King Ferdinand's opinion a few years afterwards, viz., in 1513, that 'English soldiers are strong and courageous, but for a long time past they have not been accustomed to warlike operations. If English archers were intermixed with German pikemen, they would certainly render good service; but it is not probable that English archers alone could resist German troops in a pitched battle.'—*Ubi supra,* vol. ii. p. 94. The French historian, Gabriel Daniel, in his description of the battle of Agincourt, calls the English archers 'milice redoubtable, et qui n'avoit point d'égale en son espéce dans les autres nations,' and says that they received the charge of the French cavalry 'avec une grêle effroyable de fléches.' He also mentions that 'Ces Archers étoient armez à la légere, et marchoient lestement.'—*Histoire de France,* tom. iii. pp. 873, 874, ed. 1720. The Italian, Paulus Jovius, in his *Description of Britain,* written in 1548, says : 'Hâc unâ ratione Joannes Galliæ Rex, apud Pictavos ingenti prælio victus captusque est, et Philippus ad Sammorabrinam acceptâ magnâ clade profligatus, apparuitque eâ in pugnâ sagittarios Ligures, qui scorpionibus arcuferreis uterentur, quo teli genere atque animis hostibus pares videri possent, neque vi neque celeritate Anglis fuisse comparandos.'—P. 17. In 1554 Giacomo Soranzo, who had been ambassador at the court of Edw. VI., reports to the Venetian Senate, that the English army consists of archers, 'all the English being, as it were by nature, most expert bowmen, inasmuch as not only do they practise archery for their pleasure, but also to enable them to serve

ferre as Hierusalem ; as it shall appiere in the liues of Richarde the firste, and Edwarde the firste, kynges of Englande, who made seuerall iournayes to recouer that holy citie of Hierusalem in to the possession of christen men, and achieued them honorablye, the rather by the powar of this feate of shootynge.[a]

their King, so that they have often secured victory for the armies of England.'—*Cal. St. Pa.* (*Venetian*), vol. v. p. 548.

[a] The *Itinerarium Regis Ricardi*, which was formerly attributed to Geoffrey Vinsauf, but is now considered to have been written by Richard, Canon of the Holy Trinity in Aldgate, and formerly in the service of the Templars, contains the most complete account in existence of the Crusade in which Richard took part, and was clearly the work of an eye-witness. Archers are frequently mentioned, armed both with long bows and cross-bows. The King himself appears to have been as expert with the latter weapon as he was with the sword, and there is a graphic account of an incident which occurred during the siege of Acre, when a sort of duel took place between a Parthian archer and a Welshman, originating in the admiration of the latter's skill by his adversary, who challenged the crusader to mortal combat, the result being that the challenger was slain. The author of the *Itinerarium* bears frequent testimony to the value of the archers, and especially at the battle of Arsûf, Sept. 7, A.D. 1191, when, acting as rear-guard, they faced about and repelled the attack of the Turks. His description is as follows : 'O quàm necessarii fuerunt eâ die validissimi balistarii et sagittarii, satellites rigidissimi, qui concludentes extremitatem exercitûs, continuis pilorum jactibus, in quantum dabatur, Turcorum retundebant pertinaciam. Totâ quidem illâ die, quia Turci imminebant à tergo, apud eos versâ facie itinere præpostero potiùs viam carpendo quàm eundo proficiebant.'—*Chron. and Mem. of Rich. I.* vol. i. pp. 263, 264. The nationality, however, of the bowmen, except in the instance mentioned above, is not recorded. It is probable, however, that they were English or Normans, and there is a description of the disposition of the troops at the battle of Joppa, Aug. 5, A.D. 1192, which seems to anticipate the plan pursued by the English infantry in the present century, when the rear rank men in squares loaded the muskets of their front rank : ' Rex, armorum peritissimus, inter quoslibet duos sic se clypeis protegentes unum statuit balistarium, et alterum juxta ipsum, qui protensam expeditius jugiter aptaret balistam, ut videlicet unius esset officium balistam tendendi, et alterius jugiter pila jaciendi.'—*Ubi supra*, p. 416. The Editor has been unable to find any account of feats performed by archers in the Crusade of Edw. I. None such are mentioned by Matthew of Westminster. Maimbourg says that Edward arrived at Ptolemais in May, A.D. 1271, with only 300 *Knights*, English and French (*Hist. of the Crusades*, p. 402, ed. 1686). Marinus Sanutus, speaking of the same campaign, says : 'In ipso itinere Anglici, calore nimio, et intemperantiâ fructuum et mellis gravati nimis, in multitudine periere.'—*Lib. Secret. Fidel. Crucis*, p. 224, ed. 1611. Dr. Lingard says : ' With every exertion he could never collect more than seven thousand men under

The premisses considered, O what cause of reproche shall the decaye of archers be to us nowe liuyng? Ye what irrecuperable damage either to us or them in whose time nede of semblable defence shall happen? Whiche decaye,[a] though we all redy perceiue, feare, and lament, and for the restauryng therof cesse nat to make ordinances, good lawes, and statutes,[b]

his standard, a force too inconsiderable to venture far from the coast.'—*Hist. of Eng.* vol. ii. p. 505. The fact is our accounts of Edward's Crusade are singularly meagre, and we have nothing at all like the interesting memorial of the first Richard's expedition. Sir John Smythe says : ' I might also alledge, for the excellencie of Archers, the most wonderfull victorie wonne by King Richard the first in the holy land ; where, being Generall of the Christian armie, by the grace of God and wonderfull effect of his English Archers, he in a most famous battaile ouerthrewe that braue Saladin, Souldan of Egipt, with his notable milicia of Mamelucks (by many called Sarasins) and all the rest of his armie, which did consist of an innumerable number of horsemen and footmen, Turks and Arabians.' —*Discourses on Weapons,* p. 33, ed. 1590. Gibbon says that when Richard relieved Jaffa, ' sixty thousand Turks and Saracens fled before his arms. The discovery of his weakness provoked them to return in the morning ; and they found him carelessly encamped before the gates with only seventeen knights and three hundred archers.'—*Decline and Fall of Rom. Emp.* vol. vii. p. 265, ed. 1855.

[a] Harrison, in his *Description of England,* which was written in 1587, bemoans this sad fact. ' In times past,' he says, ' the cheefe force of England consisted in their long bowes. But now we haue in maner generallie giuen ouer that kind of artillerie, and for long bowes in deed doo practise to shoot compasse for our pastime: which kind of shooting can neuer yeeld anie smart stroke, nor beate downe our enemies, as our countrie men were woont to doo at euerie time of need. Certes the Frenchmen and Rutters (*i.e. Routiers* or foreign mercenaries, see *Hist. de la Milice Françoise,* tom. i. p. 104) deriding our new archerie in respect of their corslets, will not let in open skirmish, if any leisure serue, to turne up their tailes and crie, Shoot, English, and all bicause our strong shooting is decaied and laid in bed. But if some of our Englishmen nowe liued that serued King Edward the third in his warres with France, the breech of such a varlet should haue beene nailed to his bum with one arrow, and an other fethered in his bowels, before he should haue turned about to see who shot the first.'—P. 198.

[b] Even twenty years before the publication of *The Governour,* viz. in 1511, an act had been passed ' Concerning shooting in Longe Bowes,' the preamble of which asserted that ' Archerie and shotyng in long bowes is right litell used, but dayly mynessheth, decayth, and abateth more and more,' and the cause is stated to be ' that much partey of the comminalte and parell of the Realme, wherby of old tyme the grete nombre and substaunce of Archers hath growen and multiplied, be not of power nor abilite to bye theym longbowes of ewe to excersice shotyng

yet who effectuelly puttethe his hande to continual execution of the same lawes and prouisions? or beholdyng them dayly

in the same, and to susteyne the contynuall charge therof,' for, it is also alleged that 'by meanes and occasion of custumable usaige of Teynes Play, Bowles, Classhe, and other unlawfull games, prohibett by many good and beneficiall estatutes by auctorite of parliament in that behalf provided and made, grete impoverisshement hath ensued.' But towards the end of this reign the increased use of crossbows and handguns caused practise with the long bow to fall into still greater disuse, so that it was deemed necessary again to interfere and endeavour to revive the ancient exercise by legislation. Accordingly, in the 33rd year of the King's reign, A.D. 1541, two statutes directed to this object were passed, the first being entitled an 'Acte concerning Crossbows and Handguns,' and the second an 'Acte for mayntenance of artyllarie and debarringe of unlawful games.' In the preamble to the former it is stated that 'divers gentlemen, yomen and servingmen nowe of late have layde aparte the good and laudable exercise of the longebowe, whiche alwaye heretofore hathe bene the suertie, savegarde, and contynuall defence of this Realme of Englande, and an inestimable dread and terror to the enemyes of the same' (33 Hen. VIII. c. 6). Previously, however, to these statutes, viz. in 1514, an act (6 Hen. VIII. cap. 13) had been passed 'for avoidyng shoting in Crosbowes,' the preamble of which states that 'the King's subjects daily delite them selfes in shoting of Crosbowes, wherby shoting in long bowes is the lesse used, and diverse good estatutes for reformacion of the same have been made and had, and that notwithstanding, many and diverse, not regarding nor fering the penalties of the said estatutes, use daily to shote in Crosbowes and hand gonnes, wherby the King's dere and other Lords of this his Realme ar distroid, and shalbe daily more and more onlesse remedie therfore be provyded.' Lord Herbert of Cherbury makes the following comment upon this: 'Notwithstanding the use of *Caleevers* or Hand-guns (for muskets were not yet known), it was thought fit to continue the Bow. Wherein I cannot but commend the constancy, if not wisdom of those times; it being certain that when he that carries the *Caleever* goes unarm'd, the arrow will have the same effect within its distance that the bullet, and can again for one shot return two. Besides, as they used their Halberts with their Bow, they could fall to execution on the enemy with great advantage. I cannot deny yet but against the Pike they were of less force than the *Caleevers*. Therefore I believe the meaning of these times was, to command it as an exercise to the common people, and for the rest reserve it for those occasions when they might be of use. Howsoever, Hand-guns and Cross-bows were forbidden under certain penalties to all men that had less than 500 marks per annum.'—*Life of Henry VIII.* p. 23, ed. 1706. In another place the author last quoted puts into the mouths of some of those who spake at 'the council table' when the question of a war with France was discussed in 1511, the following arguments: 'What though with our 12,000 or 15,000 we have oft defeated their armies of 50,000 or 60,000? Stands it with reason of war to expect the like success still? Especially since the use of arms is changed,

broken, wynketh nat at the offendours? O mercifull god, howe longe shall we be mockers of our selfes? Howe longe shall we skorne at our one calamitie? whiche, bothe with the eien of our mynde, and also our bodily eien, we se dayly imminent, by neglectyng our publike weale, and contemnynge the due execution of lawes and ordinaunces. But I shall herof more speake in an other place; and retourne nowe to the seconde utilitie founde in shotyng in the longe bowe, whiche is killyng of deere, wilde foule, and other game, wherin is bothe profite and pleasure aboue any other artillery.

And verily I suppose that before crosse bowes and hand gunnes were brought into this realme, by the sleighte of our enemies,[a] to thentent to destroye the noble defence of archery, continuell use of shotynge in the longe bowe [b] made the feate

and for the Bow (proper for men of our strength) the Caleever begins to be generally received. Which, besides that it is a more costly weapon, requireth a long practice, and may be managed by the weaker sort.'—*Ubi supra*, p. 8. It appears that the price of a 'hand gun, with a bottle and mould to each,' was '9s. the piece' (Brewer, vol. i. p. 432), whilst in 1541 it was enacted that no bowyer should sell any bow 'of *Ewe*' for boys between the ages of eight and fourteen above the price of 12d., but bowyers were to have bows 'of ewe' of all prices from sixpence to twelve pence 'for youthe' (*i.e.* from seven to fourteen), and for youths between the ages of fourteen and twenty-one they were to provide bows of yew 'at reasonable prices.' It is obvious, however, that 'arms of precision' were gradually usurping the place of the once famous long bowe. 'On se servit beaucoup plus des Arbalêtes que des Arcs, parce que les flêches étoient lancées avec plus de force par l'Arbalête.'—*Hist. de la Milice Françoise*, tom. i. p. 309.

[a] Mr. Grose tells us that 'the first introduction of hand-guns into this kingdom was in the year 1471, when King Edward IV., landing at Ravenspurg, in Yorkshire, brought with him, among other forces, three hundred Flemings, armed with "Hange-gunnes."'—*Milit. Antiq.* vol. ii. p. 292, ed. 1812. M. Daniel says that the crossbow was used in France and England a *long time before* the reigns of Philip Augustus and Richard (1190 A.D.). 'Il avoit été aboli dans les deux Royaumes pendant plusieurs années qu'on observa le canon du second Concile de Latran (the 10th general council) et cet usage fut rétabli d'abord en Angleterre par Richard, qui fut imité en France par Philippe Auguste.'—*Hist. de la Milice Françoise*, tom. i. p. 309.

[b] Mr. Barrington, in his 'Essay on Archery,' in the 7th vol. of *Archæologia* says that the long bow was called the *English bow* in early statutes, but he attributes its introduction to Edw. I., 'who must have seen its superiority to the cross bow in the Crusades.' Mr. Roberts, in *The English Bowman*, has, however, shown

so perfecte and exacte amonge englisshe men, that they than as surely and soone killed suche game, whiche they listed to haue, as they now can do with the crosse bowe or gunne, and more expeditely, and with lasse labour they dyd it.[a] For beinge therin industrious, they kylled their game further from them (if they shotte a great strength) than they can with a crossebowe,[b] excepte it be of suche waighte, that the arme

that this is erroneous, and that the long bow was a weapon familiar to Englishmen nearly two centuries earlier. It is curious that neither Mr. Barrington nor Mr. Roberts (who styles the former's essay 'a very imperfect history of the English long bow') had apparently perused this chapter of *The Governour*, which contains so much that is interesting on this subject, and would have confirmed the view taken by the last-named writer, that 'the English archers of Richard I. used no other than the English long bow.' The conjunction of the words 'balistarii' and 'sagittarii' in the passage already quoted from the *Itinerarium Ric. I.* is sufficient to prove the presence of long-bow archers in the Crusade of the 12th century. Paulus Jovius, the Italian historian, and a contemporary of Sir Thos. Elyot, says: 'Apud Anglos in sagittis unica spes, et præcipua gloria crebris victoriarum proventibus parta, eas minimo digito crassiores, bicubitalesque, et hamato præfixas ferro, *ingentibus ligneis arcubus* intorquent, tantâ vi arteque, ut ad primos præsertim ictus squamosum thoracem aut loricam facile penetrent.'—*Descriptio Britanniæ*, fo. 16 b, ed. 1548. This latter fact indeed is corroborated by another Italian writer, Francesco Patrizi, who must not be confounded with his namesake, the Bishop of Gaëta, who says: 'Nelle saette degli Inglesi, che postavi un poco di cera alla sua punta, passava ogni fino corsaletto.'—*Paralleli Milit.* par. ii. lib. 2, p. 37, ed. 1594. Clement Edmonds says: 'In the times that our English nation carried a scourging hand in France, the matter between us and them touching Archery stood in such terms as gave England great advantage: for I have not heard of any Bow men at all amongst them; whereas our nation hath heretofore excelled all other, as well in number of Bow-men, as in excellent good shooting.'— *Cæsar's Commentaries translated*, p. 137, ed. 1695.

[a] Sir John Smythe calls the Long Bow 'our peculiar and singular weapon, wherein our people and nation, of a singular gift of God, and as it were by a naturall inclination, with good execution of lawes, came to be so perfect and excellent, without anie publique cost and charges either to King or realme.'—*Discourses on Weapons*, p. 27, ed. 1590.

[b] 'The excellency of the cross-bow was the great exactness of its shot, cross-bow men being much more certain of hitting their mark, than archers with the long bow; but, on the other hand, it would not carry to so great a distance, neither could it be so often discharged in the same time.'—Grose's *Milit. Antiq.* vol. ii. p. 290. M. Daniel, comparing the ancient weapons with the firearms of the 18th century, says: 'Les flêches portoient plus loin que nos fusils ne portent, et je pourrois apporter des témoignages d'anciens Auteurs, qui disent qu'elles alloient

shall repente the bearyng therof twent yeres after. More ouer in the longe bowe may be shotte m₀ arowes, and in lasse time, ne by the breakynge therof ensueth so moche harme as by the breakynge of the crossebowe. Besides that all tymes in bendynge, the crossebowe is in perile of breakyng.

But this suffiseth for the declaration of shootyng, wherby it is sufficiently proued that it incomparably excelleth all other exercise, passetyme, or solace.* And hereat I conclude

jusqu'à quatre, et jusqu'à six cent pas.'—*Hist. de la Milice*, tom. ii. p. 432, ed. 1724. Mr. Moseley, in his *Essay on Archery* (at p. 266, note), remarks that it by this is meant common military paces (each of two feet) the range mentioned = 400 yards. In *The Instructions for the Warres* of M. du Bellay, translated into English in 1589, it is said that 'although the Harquebusier may shoote further, notwithstanding the Archer and Crossebow man will kill a hundred or two hundred pases off, as well as the best Harquebusier.'—P. 25. According to the above computation the extreme range would = 133 yards, 1 foot. The range of a bow, according to Neade, who lived in the reign of Charles I. and endeavoured to revive the use of this ancient weapon of war, was from six to eighteen or twenty score yards. See the *Double-armed Man*, ed. 1625. Strutt says: 'How far the archers with the *long bow* could send an arrow, is not certain, but with the *crossbow* they would shoot forty rod, for in the *Dunstable Chronicle* we are told that Henry V. "came near to the city of Roan by forty rodes of lengthe, within shotte of quarrell."'—*Man. and Cust.* vol. ii. p. 44. Mr. Moseley says: 'The Cross-bow, as it is capable of being managed with greater accuracy than the Long-bow, has been in all times used in the chase, and even long after the construction of the musket was highly improved, the silent discharge of the Arbalest rendered it more valuable in the pursuit of timorous animals than any other weapon.'—*Essay on Archery*, p. 308, ed. 1792. This was obviously one e reasons why it was prohibited by statute in the 16th century. Mr. Froude says that from his own experience of modern archery he found a difficulty in believing that the range of archery was formerly 220 yards. But there is abundant evidence to show that this was not considered an impossibility. Shakspeare, speaking of a good archer, observes that 'he would clap in the clout at twelve score, and carry a forehand shaft a fourteen and fourteen and a half.'—*King Hen. IV.* Pt. II. act iii. sc. 2. Mr. Roberts records two extraordinary feats in the years 1795 and 1798. In the former year the secretary to the Turkish Ambassador shot an arrow with a Turkish bow 482 yards, and in the latter year the Sultan himself surpassed this by shooting an arrow (in the presence of Sir Robert Ainslie) to a distance which when measured was found to be 972 yards, 2 inches, and three-quarters.—*English Bowman*, p. 100, note.

* It was even recommended from the pulpits. Thus Latimer in one of his Lent sermons, preached before King Edw. VI. at Westminster, in 1549, said: 'Menne of Englande in tymes paste, when they woulde exercyse theym selues (for

X

to write of exercise, whiche apperteineth as well to princis and noble men, as to all other by their example, whiche determine to passe furth their liues in vertue and honestie. And hereafter, with the assistence of god, unto whom I rendre this myn account (for the talent I haue of hym receiued), I purpose to write of the principall and (as I mought say) the particuler studie and affaires of him, that by the prouidence of god, is called to the mooste difficulte cure of a publike weale.

Libri primi finis.

we must nedes haue some recreation—oure bodyes canne not endure wythoute some exercyse) they were wonte to goo a brode in the fyeldes a shootynge, but nowe is turned in to glossyng, gullyng, and whoring wythin the housse. The arte of shutynge hath ben in tymes past much estemed in this realme; it is a gyft of God that he hath gyuen us to excell all other nacions wyth all. It hath bene Goddes instrumente, whereby he hath gyuen us manye victories agaynste oure enemyes. But nowe we haue taken up horynge in tounes, in steede of shutyng in the fyeldes; a wonderous thynge that so excellente a gift of God shoulde be so lytle estemed. I desyer you, my lordes, euen as ye loue the honoure and glory of God and entende to remoue his indignacion, let there be sente fourthe some proclimacion—some sharp proclimacion—to the iustices of peace, for they do not their dutye. Iustices nowe be no iustices; ther be manye good actes made for thys matter already. Charge them upon theyr allegiaunce that this singular benefit of God maye be practised, and that it be not turned into bollying, glossyng, and whoryng wythin the townes, for they be negligente in executyng these lawes of shutyng. In my tyme, my poore father was as diligent to teach me to shote, as to learne anye other thynge, and so I thynke other menne dyd theyr children. He taught me how to drawe, how to laye my bodye in my bowe, and not to drawe wyth strength of armes, as other nacions do, but with strength of the bodye. I had my bowes bought me accordyng to my age and strength. As I encreased in them so my bowes were made bigger and bigger, for men shal neuer shot well excepte they be broughte up in it. It is a goodly art, a holsome kynde of exercise, and much commended in phisike. Marcilinus Sicinus, in hys boke *de Triplici Vita* (it is a greate while sins I red hym nowe), but I remembre he commendeth this kinde of exercise, and sayth that it wrestleth agaynst manye kyndes of diseases. In the reuerence of God let it be continued. Let a proclamation go furth, chargynge the justices of peace that they se suche Actes and statutes kept as were made for this purpose.'—*The Sixth Sermon*, p. 161.

END OF THE FIRST VOLUME.

APPENDICES.

APPENDIX A.

WILL OF SIR RICHARD ELYOT.

(See p. xxvi.)

IN the name of Almighty God, Amen. On the ix[th] day of Octobre, in the yere of our Lord God a thousande fyve hundred and twentye, I, Sir Richard Elyot, knyght, one of the Kinges Justices of his commen benche, beyng hole of body and of mynde, thanked be God, nevertheles servyng the uncerteyn houre of deth, and for that I may be the more redyer at the callyng of Almighty God of me from this present lyfe, I make this my last will concernynge my soule, body, goodes and catall, in forme following, revoking all other willes and testamentes made by me afore this sayd tyme concernyng the premisses or any parte thereof. ffirst I bequeth my soule to God the holy Trinitie, fader, sonne, and holy goost, and to the blessed Virgyn Mary, the moder of Crist Jesu, God and man, and Quene of hevyn, and to all saintes. And my body to be buried in the Cath. Church of Sarum, in the place there prepared for me and my wife, or elles in some other place after the discrecion of myn executours. Item I make myn executour of this my will, my sonne Thomas Elyot only, and my daughter Margery, wife of Robert Puttenham, Esquier, I will to be overseer of the same. Item I will, that after my dettes paide, and after the charges of myn exequies doon at myn enteryng and my moneth mynde and yeres mynde, be delivered to the reparacion of the said Cathedrall Church, xx[s]. And to every of the parishe Churches of Saint Thomas, Saint Edmond, and of Saint Martyns, of the Citie of New Sarum, to the reparacion of them, to be delivered to the handes of the Church Wardeyns of the said parishe Churches, vi[s] viii[d]. And to the reparacyon of the parishe Church of Saint Dunstone, in fflete streete, of London, iii[s] iv[d], to be delivered to the vicar of the same Church. And to the Church Wardeyns of the parishe Church of Longe Combe, in the countie of Oxon, for the reparacion therof, xiii[s] iv[d]. And to the provest and felowes of Lincoln College, in Oxon, for the reparacion of the Chauncell of the said Church of Long Combe, vi[s] viii[d]. And to every felowe of the said College there abydyng to pray for me, xii[d]. And to every ffelowe of Allsowlen College, in Oxon, xii^d. And to the Maister of the Churche of Temple, within Temple Barr at London, vi^s viii^d. And to the reparacion of the parishe Churche of Estshifford in Berks, xx^s. And to the parson of the same Churche every weke by one hole yere to pray for me, iv^d. Item I will that the prest executing the service at myn enteryng, moneth mynde, and yeres mynde, have at every of the same tymes for his labour and payne, xx^d. And every other of the same Churche where I shalbe buryed saying for me there placebo, dirige, and Masse, iv^d. And every clerk of the same Church where I shall be buried for every of the said tymes synging for me, iv^d. And every querester, ii^d. Item, I will that every of the places of the ffreres observauntes of Grenewich and Richemond, of the ffreres prechours, Mynours, Carmelites, and Austeyns in London, Oxford, Sarum, and ffisherton, have at my burying or moneth mynde to kepe dirige and Masse for me, iii^s iv^d. Item I will that every pour man that berith torches for me at my burying have a blak gowne of fryse or blak lynyng of brode cloth, ii yardes and iii quarters for a gowne and hode, of xvi^d le yarde or there aboute. And that every pour man and woman lying sike in their lodging, or bedride in the towne where I shall be buried or decesse, have delivered ii^d. And every other pour man and childe of the same have i^d, so that the nombre excede not two thousande. And yf pour people of other townes come to the doole to make up the nombre, than they to have as the other have. Item I will that myn enterynge, moneth mynde, and yeres mynde, be doon without any pompe or feste, and that noo Tombe be made upon my grave, but a flat stone with convenyent writing. Item I will that all my kynnesmen and women, and my nere alliances comyng to my burying or moneth mynde, by the desire of myn executour, have gownes or cotes, after the discretion of my executour, of blak cloth, and all my servauntes likewise. Item I will that the Abbesse of Shaftisbury and of Barking have every of theym one of my gilt spones, with these lettres R and E gravyn in their endes, to remembre me in their praiers, and to leve them to their successours. And every of their Mynchyns have iv^d and their prioresses viii^d to synge a dirige and a masse for me, and the prest that syngith the masse have vi^d. And that every Mynchyn in Amesbury and Wilton have iv^d, and their prioresses have viii^d, and the prest vi^d to synge ut supra. Item, I will that Alice Wymbourne have a gowne, a kirtell, ii smokke of Lakeram,^{a} hosis, and shois, and a white bonet and a kerchief, after the discrecion of my executour. Item I will that my daughter Elynour, Mynchyn of Shaftisbury, have ii sponys and a litell maser,^{b} and xx^s in money, and every

---

^{a} A cheap kind of linen.
^{b} A bowl or goblet. Nares is clearly wrong in saying that 'great magnitude seems always one property attributed to them.' *Glossary*, ed. 1822.

yere after as is provyded for hir by my wille of my landes. Item I will that my sonne, John Fetiplace the elder, Esquier, have the beddyng that I leve at Estshefford a yere after my decesse. And then I wille he have also the hangings of the Chambers there, and of the hall, and cusshyns, bordes, flormys, and chaiers there, shetes, napry there, not by me bequethed, brasse pottes and pannys, cawdrons, brochis,* spyttis, chaffers, and pewter vessell and other implementes of the Brewhouse then remaynyng at Shefford and not by me bequeathed, to be delivered after the said yere after my decesse to the said John Fetiplace, by the discrecion of my said executour. Item I will yf my said executour be disposed, and will sell any of my shepe remaynyng at Shefford or at Petwike, or any catall there beyng, then I will that as many as he will sell be solde to my said sonne, John Fetiplace, by paying for theym as other will geve, yf he will have the same shepe or catell. Provided alwey yf the same John or any persons for him interupt the possession of myn executour, or of any of his executours of the Mannour of Est Shefford with thappurtenaunces, by the space of oon yere after my decesse, except the mylle there, and the ferme of John Floode, or that the said John take from myn executour, or of any of his executours, any thinge of my goodes nat to him bequethed by this my wille, then I will that all my bequestes made to him be void. Item I will that after my decesse immediately [undecipherable] at Petwik, sevyntene score of ewes for the childre of my wife Elizabeth, late the wife of Richard Fetiplace, Esquier, according to oon Indenture therof made, or elles to be paid for every ewe, then at the tyme of my deth lacking thereof that nombre by myn executour or assign, xvi^d. And also the ferme of Petwik to be lefte to them according to the same Indenture. Item I will that every of my sonnes, John Fetiplace thelder, Edward Fetiplace, and John Fetiplace the younger, have a blak gowne cloth yf they be at myn enteryng or moneth mynde. And that every of my sonnes, Anthony and Thomas Fetiplace, have a blak gowne cloth yf they be at myn enteryng or moneth mynde. And at the day of their mariages every of theym to have xl^s, so that they interupt not the execution of my will nor trouble not myn executour. Item I will that my cosyn Agnes Brice, the doughter of Jamys Brice, have at the day of her mariage solempnysed x^{li}; and Jone Dodyngton have at the day of her marriage v^{li}; and Jone Godard have at the day of her mariage xl^s; and all other mayden servauntes beyng with me in service atte tyme of my decesse, have at the day of their mariage xx^s. Item I will that James Bryce have my gowne furred with ffichowe, and Richard Crouche have oon of my rydyng gownes and oon of my masters, and every of their wifes a gowne cloth. Item I will that my cosyn Margaret, somtyme wife of Richard Haukyns, have the lest of my

* The French word *broche* answers to our spit.

standyng gilt cuppes with the cover, she to leve hit after hir decesse to Jone hir daughter, wife of John Barowe, gentilman, of the countie of Gloucestre. And I will that the same Jone and hir husbonde have every of theym one gilt spone. Item I will that John Mychell, oderwise called Elyot, dwelling at Coker, in the countie of Somerset, have a gowne cloth, and his wife an other, and his sonne William, sumtyme my clerk, have a gown cloth and a gilt spone. Item I will that Henry Pauncefote, Charles Bulkley, David Brokeway, Thomas Mayre, and John Dyer, which have ben my clerkes, have every of them a gilt spone and a blak gowne cloth. Item I will that my servaunt Edward Harrison have oon of my litill masers, ii silver spones, and xx weders of my shepe, and oon kowe ; and every other not my clerk of my men servauntes beyng with me in household service atte tyme of my decesse, and have ben with me ii yeres, have for every yere that they have contynued in my service without departing, a weder of my shepe. Item I will that John Colpres, William White, and Thomas Tegan have every of theym a cote cloth, and every of their wifes a white petycote. Item I will that Margery my doughter, wife of Robert Puttenham, have ii lesse gilt saltes with a cover of the newe facion, ii standyng cuppis gilte with ii covers, ii litill gilt pottes for ale with ii covers, ii playn bolles of silver with a cover, ii nuttes garnysshed with silver and gilt, ii gilt sponys and vi silver sponys, and al my beddyng and naprye that I have at London in my chambre, except my ioyned presse, whiche I will Thomas Elyot have to the Temple, and there to leve it after his decesse, for there I had it. And I will that my said doughter after hir decesse leve all the said plate to hir childern. And yf she doo dye without childre, to my sonne Thomas Elyot, or to his childre. Item I will that my said daughter have the sparver [a] of my bedde at London, with the hanging of my chambre, except I will that my sonne Thomas Elyot have the border therof. And I will that my said doughter have my faire great prymer with silver claspe, and that my said sonne have my fair great sawter [b] written, and my prymer that I wrote myself, and my litell prymer that I occupie daily. And I will that my said doughter have all myn Englisshe bokes, and my said sonne my latyn bokes and frenche bokes. Item I will that my said doughter have delivered to her by my said executour or his executours whan she begynneth housholde, oon hundred of my best weders or xli[li] for them, ii oxen, iv bullokes, iii kyen, iii hogges or swyn, as she will desire. All my

---

[a] The canopy or tester of a bed.

' At home in silken *sparvers*, beds of down
We scant can rest, but still tosse up and down :
Here we can sleep, a saddle to our pillow
A hedge the curtaine, canopy a willow.'

Sir John Harington *Epig.* lib. iv. 6 ed. 1633.

[b] *I.e.* Psalter.

APPENDIX A. 313

other catell, horses, shepe, oxen, bullys, kyen, and swyn, all my plate money, and juelles not by me bequethed, I will my said sonne Thomas Elyott have, except I will that my doughter Margery have a cheyne of golde and a pair of beades of golde, which cheyne and bedes my wife Elizabeth desired me that my said doughter shoulde have. And I will that my said doughter, after hir decesse, leve all the said plate to hir childre, or yf they dye to my said sonne. Also I will that my said doughter have an ambling nag next the best of theym I have. Item I will that my said sonne have my ferme of Wynterslowe and all my shepe there. And I will that he have all my stuffe of housholde, naprye, vessell, beddyng in Sarum, London, Shifford, or elleswhere not by me bequeathed. Item I will that my sonnes wife have at libertie a brode gilt cupp with a cover and with a lowe foot, and that she have my best rynge of golde. Item I will myn executour bestowe amonge my pour servauntes or pour tenauntes, lynnen cloth of canvas and lokeram for shetes and smockes and shirtes after their discrecions, and blanket cloth for blankettes to the value of xl^s. Item I will Thomas Stopeham have one of my gownes furred with ffoynes and two silver sponys and one of my litill masers garnisshed with silver and gilt, and at his mariage x^{li}. Item, I will —— Ballard, the sonne and heire of Robert Ballard, Esquier, of Kent, and thre doughters of the same Robert whiche be maryed, or have be maried, have every of theym fyve poundes, and the doughter of the same Robert, being a mynchyn at Barking, in Essex, have xx^s, soe that they trouble not myn executour. And I will that all obligacions that I have in possession concernyng the said Robert be delivered to his said children. And yf they or any of theym wille sue at their cost for any duetie due their said fader, that then myn executours suffre the sute to be taken in their name to the use of the said childre. And I will that the casket with evidences of the londes in More lane or elleswhere be delivered to the next heire of the same Robert, or to their moder. Provided that if any of the said children trouble myn executours for the execution of the wille of their fader, to whom I was oon of the executours, than not they nor noon of theym to have any of the money by me before bequethed. Item I will that my doughter in lawe Elynour, doughter of Richard Fetiplace, Esquier, have after hir marriage celebrate fourty poundes to hir exhibicion yerely iii^{li} vi^s viii^d, till she be professed in religion. And at suche tyme as she shalbe professed to the said xl^{li} as moche as shalbe necessary in bokes or apparell to that entent. Provided always that yf she or any of her bredern or susters or any parsone for theym trouble myn executour and heire for any goodes or catalles that were their said faders, or of his moder late my wife, then this bequest made to hir and to all the other to be voide.

Ultima voluntas ejusdem Ricardi. This is the last wille of me

Richard Elyot, Knyght, oon of the Kynges Justices, concernyng my manours, landes, and tenementes, made the xiith day of Octobre, the xiith yere of the reigne of Kyng Henry the VIIIth. And be it knowen to al men, that all my manours, londes, and tenementes stande in feoffees handes, or in the handes of Recoverers, to the use of me and of myn heires, to the performaunce of my last wille. ffirst, I will that all my said manours, londes, and tenementes stande alwey still in my said feoffees and Recoverers handes, or in any other feoffees handes, to be made by theym or by their heires and the feoffmentes to be renewed as ofte as it may be perceyved by any of myn heires, or by any of my said feoffees or their heires, that the feoffees therof be decessed to the nombre of vi survivours of theym, they to make astate in fee to two other discrete persones, and forthwith to take astate ageyn to theym and to xii moo, wherof viii to be of the citie of Newe Sarum, suche as have ben Mayres of the same Citie, or be of the xxiv^{ti} Citezeins and likely to be Maires there, they to stonde seised and their heires to the use aforesaid. Item I will that my said feoffees and their heires and assignes after my decesse stande seased of the premisses to the use of my sonne Thomas Elyot, and of his heires males of his body commyng, and for defawte of such heires to the heires males of my body commyng, and for defaute of suche heires to all my doughters and to all the doughters of the said Thomas, and to the heires of their bodies commyng. And for defawt of suche heires I will that my Manour of Longcombe, and all my londes and tenementes in Longe Combe and Wotton, in the Countie of Oxon, remayn to my cosyn Thomas Fyndern, in the countie of Cambridge, lorde of the manor of Carleton, and to the heires males of his body comyng, and for defawte of such heires to the right heires of me the said Richard. Item I will that for defawt of suche heires as is aforesaid of me the said Richard and Thomas, and of our said doughters, that all my tenementes without Temple Barre of London, and in Staines, in the Countie of Middx, remayn to John Gilpurne, sonne of my suster Alice, and to the heires of his body comyng, and for defaute of suche heires to the heires of my said susters body comyng, and for defaute of such heires to Richard Crouche, sonne of my suster Johanne, sumtyme of the towne of Wyncalton, in the Countie of Somerset, and to the heires of his body comyng, and for defaute of suche issue to the right heires of me the said Richard, Thomas my sonne, and of our doughters as is aforesaid, to remayn to Thomas Somer my cosyn, son of Isabell, doughter of Kateryn, suster of my mother Johanne, doughters of John Bryce, otherwise called Basset, and to the heires males of his body begotten. And for defaute of suche heires of me the said Richard, and Thomas my sonne, and of our doughters as is aforesaid, remayn to James Brice, sonne of myn uncle John Brice, sonne of the said John Basset, sonne of Bryce Basset, my great grauntfader of my modersyde, and to the heires of the body of the same James begotten, and for defaute of suche heires to my right heires. And all my landes, tenementes, rentes, and services that I have in the counties of Wiltes, Southampton, and Dorset, except the said londes and tenementes intailled to the said James, and except the tenement and londes in Chalk, whiche I will that the profites therof be expended for my soule and my frendes soules and all cristen soules, as more largely apperith by an Indenture tripartite,* wherof the one parte remayneth with myn heire, an other parte in the Cathedrall Church at Sarum, and the thirde with the Maire and cominaltie of the Citie of New Sarum, for defawte of suche heires of me the said Richard, and of Thomas my sonne, and of our doughters, remayn to the said John Gilpurne and Richard Crouche, and to the heires of the bodyes of my said susters Johane and Alice, and to the heires of their bodies comyng. And for defawte of such heires, to John Michell, otherwise called Elyot of Coker, in the countie of Somerset, sonne of Philip, sonne of Michell Elyot, my grauntfader, and to the heires of his body comyng, and for defaute of suche issue to John Huet, of Tawnton, and to John Soper, sonnes of Alice daughter of Kateryn —— Lydford, suster of my fader Symon Elyot, and to the heires of their bodies begotten, and for defaute of suche heires to my right heires forever. Item I will that notwithstanding this intaill by this my wille made in fourme aforsaid, yf it fortune after my decesse that my sonne or any of myn heires of my body will eschaunge any of my said maners, landes, or tenementes, (except afore except) for any other mannors, londes, or tenementes of like value or better, with any persone, and leve the said manours, londes, and tenementes so exchaunged to my said heires or other accordyng to this my will, and to be intailled by will in forme aforesaid with the remayners by wille as is aforsaid, and stondyng in like feoffees handes still for the sure perfourmaunce therof, then it to be lefull to theym so to doo. Item I will that notwithstanding the said entailles and remayners afore declared, it be lefull to my said sonne and to every of the heires males of my body begotten after my decesse, to make a joyuntour to his wife of any of the premisses except as afore except for terme of his lyfe, to the yerely value of xx^{li}, in recompens of all other joyuntours and dowrie therof by her to be claymed or had, and also to make a will for terme of x yeres after his decesse of part of the premisses to the yerely value of xx^{li} for paymente of his dettes, mariage of his doughters, exibicion and avauncement of hys yong children not beyng his heire or heires. Item I will that my cosyn Alice Wymbourne have during hir lyfe the tenement that she dwellith in [in] Sarum, and yerely xiii^s iv^d of my heires as of my feoffees of the issues and profites of my

* See ante, p. xlv, *note* b.

said londes during hir lyfe. Item I will that my doughter Elynour, Mynchyn of Shaftisbury, have yerely of my said heire or feoffees during hir lyfe xiii˙ iv^d of the profites of my said londes.

Probatum fuit testamentum suprascripti defuncti coram Domino apud Lamehith xxvi die mensis Maii anno domini millimo quingentisimo xxii° juramento Thome Elyot executoris in hujusmodi testamento nominati ac approbatum et insumatum. Et commissa fuit administracio omnium et singulorum bonorum et debitorum dicti defuncti prefato executori de bene [et] fideliter administrando ac de pleno et fideli inventorio citra festum nativitatis Sancti Johannis Baptiste proximum futurum exhibendo, necnon de pleno et vero compoto reddendo ad Sancta Dei Evangelia in debitâ juris formâ jurato.[*]

[*] H.M. Court of Probate (Mainwaring fo. 24).

APPENDIX B.

(See p. xxviii.)

INQUISICIO indentata capta apud Ambrusbury in comitatu Wilts vicesimo die Aprilis anno regni Regis Henrici octavi sexto coram Willielmo Pownde Escaetore dicti domini Regis in comitatu predicto virtute officii sui per sacramentum Roberti Nicolas, &c. Qui dicunt super sacramentum suum quod per quendam actum in Parliamento domini Henrici nuper Regis Angliæ septimi, patris dicti domini Regis nunc, tento apud Westmonasterium septimo die Novembris anno regni dicti nuper Regis Henrici septimi primo inactatum et ordinatum fuit quòd Franciscus Lovell miles nuper vicecomes Lovell alias dictus Franciscus Lovell nuper vicecomes Lovell de altâ prodicione attinctus foresfecit dicto nuper Regi et heredibus suis omnia honores castra dominia maneria messuagia terras tenementa redditus reversiones servicia ac alia hereditamenta quecumque que idem Franciscus aut aliquis alius sive aliqui alii ad ejus usum habuit aut habuerunt dicto septimo die Novembris anno primo ejusdem nuper Regis aut unquam postea. Et ulterius Juratores dicunt quod dictus Franciscus fuit seisitus in dominico suo ut de feodo dicto septimo die Novembris anno primo ejusdem nuper Regis de et in manerio de Wanborough cum pertinentiis in dicto comitatu Wiltes ac de libertatibus subscriptis videlicet de letis visus franci plegii in Wanborough in eodem comitatu post festum Sancti Michaelis Archangeli et Pasche bis in anno annuatim tenendis cum omnibus eidem letis et visibus franci plegii pertinentibus ac (de) warrennis in dominicis ejusdem manerii et thesauris inventis in manerio et villâ predictâ ac de catallis felonum de se fugitivorum utlagatorum ac de Weaff et Straeff infra manerium predictum. Et quod manerium predictum et cetera premissa valent per annum in omnibus exitibus ultra reprisas xxxix [li] vi [s]. et viii [d]. Et ulterius iidem Juratores dicunt super sacramentum suum quod Johannes Cheyne miles jam defunctus omnia exitus et proficua manerii predicti cum pertinentiis a tempore attincture predicti Francisci usque xxx diem Maii anno regni nuper Regis Henrici septimi xiv° quo die prefatus Johannes Cheyne obiit percepit et habuit set quo titulo Juratores predicti penitus ignorant. Et quod Ricardus Elyot ad tunc serviens ad legem a dicto xxx[mo] die

Maii dicto anno xiv⁰ prefati nuper Regis omnia exitus et proficua manerii predicti cum pertinentiis usque quintum diem July anno dicti domini Regis nunc tercio ad usum domini Regis percepit et eidem nuper Regi et domino Regi nunc per manus Johannis Heyron unius Receptoris dicti nuper Regis et domini Regis nunc solvit. Et quod Edwardus Darelle miles a dicto quinto die July anno tercio dicti Regis nunc omnia exitus et proficua manerii predicti cum pertinentiis usque diem hujus Inquisicionis capte cepit et habuit.

In cujus rei, &c.[a]

---

[a] Excheq. Inquis. post mort. (Southampton and Wilts) 6 Hen. VIII. Wm. Pounde Esc. m. 2. P.R.O.

APPENDIX C.

(See p. xxxiii.)

IN *The Topographer and Genealogist*, Sir Richard Elyot's first wife Alice, is stated to have been the daughter of Sir Thomas Delamare, of Aldermaston, in Berks, and widow of Thomas Dabridgecourt, of Stratfield Say, who died October 10, 1495.[*] This fact was not brought to the notice of the Editor until the Life of Elyot was already in print. In Berry's *Hampshire Genealogies*, the same lady is said to have remarried *Nicholas* Elliott. If the former statement be correct, our author's birth must be postponed to a somewhat later date than we had assigned to it.

[*] Vol. i. p. 198.

APPENDIX D.

(See p. lviii.)

ProThome⎫
Elyot de ⎬
Con. ⎭

REX omnibus ad quos &c. salutem. Sciatis quòd cum nos per literas nostras patentes quarum data est vicesimo primo die Octobris anno regni nostri quarto dederimus et concesserimus dilecto nostro Ricardo Eden, clerico, officium clerici Consilii nostri habendum occupandum et exercendum dictum officium prefato Ricardo Eden per se aut ejus deputatum sive deputatos sufficientes durante vitâ suâ cum vadio et feodo quadraginta marcarum per annum eidem officio pertinenti cum omnibus aliis feodis commoditatibus et emolumentis predicto officio spectantibus sive pertinentibus prout in eisdem literis nostris patentibus plenius continetur. Et quia dictus Ricardus Eden diversis negociis suis implicitus non solum [non] possit commode operam suam impendere officio predicto sine imminenti jacturâ rerum suarum aut gravi ac periculosâ negligenciâ rerum (et) nostrorum negociorum officio predicto incumbentium, sed nec alium suo loco obeundum et exercendum officium predictum ex omni parte idoneum prout officium illud exigit et requirit deputare nedum invenire queat, ob quod dictus Ricardus cunctis consideracionibus eum moventibus predictas literas nostras patentes in Cancellariâ nostrâ in manus nostras reddidit cancellandas et ibidem jam cancellate existunt. Nos officium predictum nolentes esse vacuum debito ministerio quo minus cause in Consilio nostro in dies emergentes debite curentur exequantur et exerceantur ducti consideracionibus ante dictis nos impense moventibus de graciâ nostrâ speciali ac ex certâ scientiâ et mero motu [literis] nostris dedimus ac per presentes damus et concedimus dilecto nostro Thome Elyot, armigero, officium clerici nostri Consilii eundemque Thomam clericum Consilii nostri facimus ordinamus et constituimus per presentes habendum occupandum et exercendum dictum officium prefato Thome Elyot per se aut ejus deputatum sive deputatos suos sufficientes durante vitâ suâ cum vadio et feodo quadraginta marcarum per annum habendum et annuatim percipiendum ad festum sancti Michaelis Archangeli et festum Pasche per equales porciones de Thesauro nostro ad receptum Scaccarii nostri per manus Thesaurariorum et Camerariorum nostrorum pro tempore existentium necnon liberatam nostram de vesturâ nostrâ pro temporibus estatis et hiemis eidem officio debitam et consuetam prout Robertus Rydon, Johannes Baldiswell aut aliquis alius unquam habuit annuatim percipiendam ad magnam garderobam nostram per manus custodis ejusdem pro tempore existentis unà cum omnibus et omnimodis aliis feodis proficuis commoditatibus muneribus emolumentis et advantagiis eidem officio pertinentibus sive spectantibus in tam amplis modo et formâ prout prefatus Ricardus Eden aut Robertus Ridon aut aliquis alius sive aliqui alii dictum officium antehac exercens sive occupans exercentes sive occupantes habuit et percepit habuerunt et perceperunt. Eo quod expressa mentio, &c.

Teste Rege apud Westm.
Per ipsum Regem, &c.

The following memorandum appears on the margin of the roll :— Vacat irrotulamentum harum literarum patentium pro eo quod per consideracionem Curie Cancellarie litere ille adjudicate fuerunt nullius esse vigoris eo quod infrascriptus Ricardus Eden non sursum reddidit literas patentes sibi de officio infrascripto factas ad intencionem infrascriptam. Ideo istud irrotulamentum cancellatur et dampnatur.[a]

[a] Pat. Roll 19 Hen. VIII. pt. i. m. 11. P.R.O.

APPENDIX E.

(See p. clxxxi.)

INQUISICIONE indentatâ captâ apud Newemarket in comitatu predicto septimo die Septembris anno regni Henrici octavi dei gratiâ Anglie Francie et Hibernie Regis fidei defensoris et in terrâ ecclesie Anglicane et Hibernice supremi capitis tricesimo octavo coram Thoma Bowles, Armigero, Escaetore dicti domini Regis de comitatu predicto virtute brevis ejusdem domini Regis *de diem clausit extremum* post mortem Thome Eliott militis defuncti eidem Escaetori directi et huic Inquisicioni annexi per sacramentum Willielmi Ruse junioris, generosi, Willielmi Wyse, Johannis Caverell, Johannis Curde, Ricardi Simondes, Galfridii Thornebacke, Johannis Hasill, Willielmi Sterne, Thome Smithe, Willielmi Battell, Johannis Webbe, et Thome Hinton. Qui dicunt super sacramentum suum quod predictus dominus Henricus octavus dei gratiâ Anglie Francie et Hibernie Rex fidei defensor et in terrâ ecclesie Anglicane et Hibernice supremum caput fuit seisitus in dominico suo ut de feodo racione attincture Thome Crumwell nuper Comitis Essex de et in maneriis de Carleton et Willingham cum pertinentiis in dicto comitatu Cantebrigie ac de et in advocacionibus ecclesie parochialis de Carleton predicto cum capellâ de Willyngham eidem annexâ ac de advocacione ecclesie parochialis de Weston Colevyle in dicto comitatu Cantebrigie unà cum quâdam pensione duorum solidorum et sex denariorum annuatim percipiendâ de Rectore de Weston Colevyle predicti et successoribus suis et de aliâ pensione duorum solidorum annuatim percipiendâ de Rectore Ecclesie parochialis de Carleton predicti et successoribus suis in capellâ predictâ necnon de et in decimis et porcionibus decimarum vocatis Barbedors ac decimis et porcionibus decimarum in Weston Colevyle predicto ac eciam de et in viginti messuagiis quingentis acris terre quadraginta acris prati centum acris pasture ducentis acris bosci decem libris redditûs ac de diversis aliis proficuis et hereditamentis cum pertinentiis que fuerunt predicti Thome Crumwell in Carleton Brinkley, Carleton Barbedors, Weston Colevyle et Wyllingham in comitatu predicto prout per recordum inde plenius patet. Et predictus Dominus Rex sic inde seisitus existens per literas suas patentes gerentes datam quarto die Augusti anno regni sui tricesimo secundo pro

APPENDIX E.

diversis consideracionibus in eisdem litteris patentibus specificatis de gratiâ suâ speciali ac ex certâ scientiâ et mero motu suis dedit et concessit prefato Thome Elyott militi in dicto brevi nominato et domine Margarete uxori ejus predicta maneria de Carleton et Willyngham necnon advocaciones et jus patronatûs predicte ecclesie parochialis de Carleton cum predictâ capellâ de Willyngham et predicte ecclesie de Weston Colevyle in predicto comitatu Cantebrigie ac predictas decimas et porciones decimarum vocatas Barbedors ac decimas et porciones decimarum in Weston Colevyle predicto necnon omnia et singula premissa et hereditamenta sua quecunque cum suis pertinentiis situata jacentia et existentia in villis parochiis hamletis et campis de Carleton Brinkley, Carleton Barbedors, Weston Colevyle et Wyllingham predictis in comitatu predicto que fuerunt predicti nuper Comitis Essex ac que ad manus predicti domini Regis nunc devenerunt aut devenire debuerunt et que in manibus ejusdem domini Regis tunc fuerunt racione attincture aut forisfacture predicti nuperComitis Essex, habendum tenendum et gaudendum predicta maneria advocaciones decimas et porciones decimarum ac omnia et singula premissa prefato Thome Elyott et domine Margarete uxori ejus heredibus et assignis suis imperpetuum prout in eisdem litteris patentibus Juratoribus predictis super capcione hujus Inquisicionis in evidenciâ ostensis plenius continetur. Virtute quarum quidem litterarum patencium predictus Thomas Elyot et Margareta fuerunt conjunctim seisiti de et in predictis maneriis et ceteris omnibus et singulis premissis in dominico suo ut de feodo. Ipsisque sic inde seisitis existentibus prefatus Thomas Elyott obiit et prefata Margareta eundem Thomam supervixit et se tenuit intus in maneriis predictis et ceteris premissis cum pertinentiis et adhuc tenet et est inde seisita in dominico suo ut de feodo per jus accrescendi. Et dicunt eciam Juratores predicti quod predictus dominus Rex fuit seisitus in dominico suo ut de feodo de et in manerio de Histon Evesham cum suis membris et pertinentiis universis in Histon Evesham, Histon Deny, Hoggyngton, Impington, Ewton, Milton et Landebeche in dicto comitatu Cantebrigie ac de et in Rectoriis appropriatis de Histon Evesham predicto in dicto comitatu Cantebrigie unâ cum advocacione donacione et liberâ disposicione vicarie ecclesie parochialis de Histon Evesham predicto. Et idem dominus Rex sic inde seisitus existens per litteras suas patentes gerentes datam quinto die Decembris anno regni ejusdem domini Regis nunc tricesimo primo pro diversis consideracionibus in eisdem litteris patentibus specificatis ex gratiâ suâ speciali ac ex certâ scientiâ et mero motu suis dedit et concessit predicto Thome Eliott et Domine Margarete uxori ejus predictum manerium de Histon Evesham cum suis pertinentiis in Histon Evesham, Histon Deny, Hoggington, Impington, Ewton, Milton et Landebeche predictis in dicto comitatu Cantebrigie ac eciam predicta Rectoria appropriata de Histon Evesham predicto necnon advocacionem donacionem et jus patronatûs vicarie ecclesie parochialis de Histon Evesham predicto habendum tenendum et gaudendum predictum manerium de Histon Evesham cum suis pertinentiis necnon Rectoriam et advocacionem vicarie ecclesie de Histon Evesham predicto et cetera premissa prefato Thome Elyott et Domine Margarete uxori ejus et heredibus ipsius Thome Elyott prout per easdem litteras patentes Juratoribus predictis in evidenciâ similiter ostensas plenius patet. Quarum quidem litterarum patencium pretextu predictus Thomas Eliott et Margareta fuerunt seisiti de et in manerio predicto et ceteris premissis conjunctim sibi et heredibus ipsius Thome Elyott. Ipsisque sic inde existentibus seisitis predictus Thomas Elyott obiit et prefata Margareta eundem Thomam Eliott supervixit et se tenuit intus in predicto manerio de Histon Evesham et ceteris premissis et adhuc tenet et est inde seisita in dominico suo ut de libero tenemento per jus accrescendi. Et ulterius Juratores predicti super sacramentum suum predictum dicunt quod diu ante obitum predicti Thome Eliott quidam Johannes Rowe, serviens ad legem, Johannes Graynfeld et Edwardus Hasilwoode, armigeri, fuerunt seisiti de et in maneriis de Weston Colevyle, Moynes, et parva Carleton alias Loppams cum pertinentiis ac de et in viginti et quinque messuagiis sexcentis acris terre centum acris prati trescentis acris pasture quingentis acris bosci et sexaginta solidis redditûs et redditibus decem caponum duarum librarum piperis et duarum librarum cumini cum pertinentiis in Weston Colevyle, Carleton, West Wrattyng, Baburham, Balssham, et Wickham in dicto comitatu Cantebrigie ac de et in advocacione ecclesie de Weston Colevyle in dominico suo ut de feodo ad usum predicti Thome Eliott et heredum suorum et ad inde perimplendam ultimam voluntatem ipsius Thome Eliott. Ipsisque sic inde seisitis existentibus per quasdam indenturas inter Willielmum Pawlet, militem, Dominum Seynt John, pro nomine Willielmi Pawlet militis honorabilis hospicii domini Regis, ex unâ parte, et predictum Thomam Eliott ex alterâ parte confectas, quarum data est secundo die Januarii anno regni dicti domini Regis nunc vicesimo quinto dictus Thomas Eliott tam in consideracione augmentacionis joincture dicte Domine Margarete tunc uxoris ejusdem Thome quàm pro diversis aliis bonis consideracionibus ipsum Thomam tunc specialiter moventibus convenit et concessit per easdem Indenturas cum predicto Willielmo Pawlett quod idem Thomas faceret ac fieri causaret Roberto Norwiche, militi, Nicholao Carewe, militi, Egidio Alington, militi, Johanni Harcot, militi, Edwardo Knyghtley, servienti ad legem, Edmundo Marvyn, servienti ad legem, Rogero Chomley, servienti ad legem, Johanni Hynde, servienti ad legem, Johanni Pawlett, armigero, Thome Hutton, Willielmo Paris, Francisco Barentine et Roberto Southwell unum sufficientem et legittimum statum in lege in feodo simplice de et in predictis maneriis de Carleton, Weston Colevyle, ac de et in omnibus et singulis premissis cum pertinentiis in Carleton, Weston, Wyllingham, West Wrattyng, Baburham, Balssham et Wickham in dicto comitatu Cantebrigie ad usum predicti Thome Eliott et dicte domine Margarete uxoris ejus et heredum de corpore ipsius Thome Eliott legitime procreatorum et pro defectu talis exitus post mortem predictorum Thome Eliott et dicte domine Margarete ad usum heredum de corpore Ricardi Eliott, militis, patris predicti Thome Eliott, legittime procreatorum, et pro defectu talis exitus remanere inde rectis heredibus ipsius Thome Eliott in feodo simplice prout per easdem Indenturas Juratoribus predictis super capcione hujus Inquisicionis in evidenciâ similiter ostensas inter alia continetur. Et postea predictus Johannes Rowe et ceteri predicti Cofeoffatores sui ad specialem requisicionem predicti Thome Eliott per cartam suam gerentem datam quarto die Maii anno regni dicti domini Regis vicesimo sexto tradiderunt et demiserunt Johanni Alington et Nicholao Stutfeld, generosis, predicta maneria de Weston Colevile, Moynes, et parva Carleton ac cetera premissa cum pertinentiis in Weston, Carleton, West Wratting, Baburham, Balssham et Wickham habendum et tenendum predicta maneria et cetera premissa predictis Johanni Alington et Nicholao Stutfeld heredibus et assignis suis imperpetuum ad solummodo usum dicti Thome Eliott et heredum suorum imperpetuum prout per eandem cartam Juratoribus predictis in evidenciâ ostensam plenius patet. Pretextu cujus iidem Johannes Alington et Nicholaus Stutfeld fuerunt de predictis maneriis et ceteris premissis seisiti in dominico suo ut de feodo ad solummodo usum dicti Thome Eliott et heredum suorum imperpetuum. Ipsisque sic inde seisitis existentibus predictus Robertus Norwiche, Nicholaus Carewe, Egidius Alington, Johannes Harcot, Edwardus Knyghtley, Edmundus Mervyn, Rogerus Chamley, Johannes Hynde, Johannes Pawlet, Thomas Hutton, Willielmus Paris, Franciscus Barantine et Robertus Southwell, ex assensu et procuracione predicti Thome Eliott ac in complementum convencionum in predictâ Indenturâ specificatorum Termino Pasche anno regni domini Regis nunc vicesimo sexto per quoddam breve *de ingressu super disseisinam in le post* recuperaverunt omnia predicta maneria terras tenementa et cetera omnia premissa cum pertinentiis per nomina in recordo illo specificata versus predictos Johannem Alington et Nicholaum Stutfeld ipsis Johanne Alington et Nicholao tempore ejusdem recuperacionis de eisdem maneriis et ceteris premissis seisitis existentibus in dominico suo ut de feodo. Virtute cujus recuperacionis predicti Robertus Norwiche, Nicholaus Carewe, Egidius Alington, et alii recuperatores prenominati in predicta maneria et cetera premissa intraverunt et inde seisiti fuerunt in dominico suo ut de feodo ad usum predictorum Thome Eliott et dicte domine Margarete uxoris ejus et heredum de corpore ipsius Thome Eliott legittime procreatorum et pro defectu talis exitus ad usus supra dictos. Et sic fuerunt inde seisiti ad usus supradictos quousque in

Parliamento ten o anno vicesimo septimo dicti domini Regis nunc quoddam *Statutum de Usibus* fuit editum et ordinatum per quod quidem statutum predictus Thomas Eliott et Domina Margareta fuerunt in possessione dictorum maneriorum et ceterorum premissorum in loco usûs predicti et inde seisiti sibi et heredibus de corpore ipsius Thome legittime procreatis remanere inde secundum usus superius declaratos ipsisque Thoma Eliott et Domina Margareta inde de tali statu seisitis existentibus idem Thomas Eliott obiit et prefata Domina Margareta eundem Thomam supervixit et se tenuit intus in maneriis predictis et ceteris premissis cum pertinentiis et adhuc tenet et est inde seisita in dominico suo ut de libero tenemento per jus accrescendi. Et dicunt ulterius Juratores predicti super sacramentum suum predictum quod predictus Thomas Eliott obiit apud Carleton predictam in predicto comitatu Cantebrigie xxvi° die Marcii ultimo preterito sine heredibus de corpore suo legittime procreatis. Et quod Ricardus Puttenham, armiger, est consanguineus et proximus heres predicti Thome Eliott videlicet filius Margerie Puttenham sororis predicti Thome. Et quod predictus Ricardus Puttenham fuit tempore mortis dicti Thome Eliott plene etatis videlicet xxvi annorum et amplius. Et dicunt ulterius Juratores predicti quod predicta maneria de Carleton et Willingham et cetera premissa cum pertinentiis in Carleton Brinkley, Carleton Barbedors, Colevile, et Willingham tenentur de dicto domino Rege in capite per servicium iv[te] partis unius feodi militis pro omnibus aliis serviciis exaccionibus et demandis. Et valent per annum ultra reprisas xlviii[li] xviii[s]. Et quod predictum manerium de Histon Evesham et cetera premissa in Histon Evesham, Histon Deny, Hogginton, Impington, Ewton, Milton et Landebeche tenentur de predicto domino Rege in capite per servicium vicesime partis unius feodi militis ac per redditum quatuor librarum et sex solidorum ad Curiam ejusdem domini Regis Augmentacionum Corone sue singulis annis solvendum pro omnibus aliis redditibus serviciis et demandis quibuscumque. Et valent per annum ultra reprisas quadraginta libras et decem solidos. Et quod predictum manerium de Moynes tenetur de dicto domino Rege ut de honore suo Richemonde per fidelitatem et redditum sex solidorum et sex denariorum pro omnibus aliis redditibus serviciis et demandis. Et quod predicta maneria de Weston Colevile et parva Carleton ac advocaciones de Weston Colevile et cetera premissa in Weston Colevile, Carleton, West Wrattyng, Baburham, Balssham, Willingham, et Wickham tenentur de Episcopo Eliensi per fidelitatem tantùm pro omnibus aliis redditibus serviciis et demandis. Et quod predictum manerium ˚de Moynes et predicta maneria de Weston Colevyle et parva Carleton et cetera premissa in Weston Colevyle, Carleton, West Wrattyng, Baburham, Balssham, Willyngham, et Wickham valent per annum ultra reprisas sexaginta et decem libras. Et dicunt Juratores predicti quod predictus

APPENDIX E.

Thomas Elyott in dicto brevi nominatus nulla alia sive plura dominica maneria terras sive tenementa in dicto comitatu Cantebrigie die quo obiit tenuit de dicto domino Rege in capite ne aliquo alio modo nec de aliquo alio in dominico nec in servicio. In cujus rei testimonium uni parti hujus Inquisicionis penes predictum Escaetorem remanenti tam predictus Escaetor quàm predicti Juratores sigilla sua apposuerunt alteri vero parti penes predictos Juratores remanenti predictus Escaetor sigillum suum apposuit. Data apud Newemarket predictam die et anno supra dicto.[*]

[*] Chancery Inquis. post mortem 38 Hen. VIII. pt. 1, No. 16. P.R.O.

APPENDIX F.

THE Editor not having discovered the relation between Patrizi's work and *The Governour*, in time for the following passages to be inserted in their proper places, they are collected here in order that the reader may compare them with the corresponding passages in the text.

Page 40, note d.

'Nam cum victor Ilion ingrederetur, multa oculis et animo lustravit illectus Homericâ lectione et vetustissima quamplurima perquisivit: quod cernens quidam eum rogavit, *Velletne Paridis citharam cernere?* Tum comiter ridens respondit, *Eam nequaquam sibi cordi esse, sed Achillis citharam videre malle, quâ ille non Veneris illecebras, sed fortissimorum Ducum gesta et res inclytas canere consueverat.*'—*De Regno et Regis Instit.* lib. ii. tit. 8.

Page 42, note a.

'Philippus Macedonum Rex, (ut Plutarchus refert), cum accepisset filium suum suaviter ac scite aliquando cecinisse, placide illum objurgavit dicens: *Nonne te pudet quòd scienter ac pulchrè canere scias?* Satis enim regi putabat esse Philippus si canentibus aliis adesset, ubi ocium ei suppeteret, et certantibus inter se musicis spectatorem ac judicem se præberet. Artem vero illam profiteri humile quippiam et abjectum esse existimabat.'—*Ibid.* lib. ii. tit. 15.

Page 44, note a.

'M. quidem Vitruvius affirmat bellica omnia tormenta vel à Regibus, Ducibus, Imperatoribusve inventa extitisse: vel si qua ab aliis accepissent, fecisse ea longè meliora.'—*Ibid.* lib. ii. tit. 14.

Page 46, note b.

Cernebatur illic Alexander qui leonem adoriebatur, et juxta eum aderat Craterus inter canes et alios venatores. Expressit enim Lysippus simili-

APPENDIX F.

tudinem Alexandri et amicorum ejus adeò ut pene spirantes vivique esse viderentur.'—*Ibid.* lib. ii. tit. 1.

Page 47, note b.

'Simulacrum Jovis Olympii quod ex ebore fecerat Phidias Atheniensis, quo nihil præstantius in eo genere omnes ferè scriptores extitisse testantur, cum intueretur Pandenus pictor eximius, admiratione magnâ ductus artificem rogavit unde tam præclari operis exemplar accepisset? Tum Phidias ex tribus Homeri versibus ejusmodi imaginem delibasse respondit, qui sunt ad hanc fermè sententiam :

> Inde superciliis jam Jupiter annuit atris,
> Concussitque comam pulchro de vertice rector
> Æthereus, nutu et summum tremefecit Olympum.'
> —*Ibid.* lib. ii. tit. 4.

Page 59, notes b and c.

'Hos itaque Homeri libros tantâ aviditate edidicit Alexander, ut parvo tempore ad parem usque tanti præceptoris eruditionem prope accederet, eosque semper sub pulvino habebat, horasque aliquot per noctem somno sibi eripiebat, ut cum summo poetarum aliquamdiu vigilaret. . . . Utrasque Homeri rapsodias ei perdiscendas præbuit (*i.e.* Aristoteles), ut ex Iliade quidem corporis vires, superbamque in hostem iracundiam quandam sumeret : ex Odysseâ vero animi virtutes eliceret, versutias caliditatesque hominum cavere discereL'—*Ibid.* lib. iv. in procem.

Page 78, notes a and b.

'Alexandrum, quem ex virtute magnum nuncupaverunt, ut nonnulli scriptores perhibent, summâ diligentiâ scrutari solitum aiunt loca in quibus bellum esset gesturus, semperque eadem picta intueri voluisse, ut picturam illam legendo ea dignosceret quæ cavenda quæve adeunda essent. Romani etiam idem facere consueverant, et regiones in quibus pugnaturi essent, antequam bellum decernerent, pictas ostendere. Ingruente enim Gallico tumultu vel Sociali bello pictam præbebant Italiam.'— *Ibid.* lib. iii. tit. 14.

Page 174, note b.

'Epaminondas Thebanus vir fuit omni virtute præstantissimus, omnesque artes ac disciplinas calluit quæ ad summum quemque imperatorem pertinent. Is postquam adolevit palæstræ dare operam cœpit, non tam magnitudini virium inserviens quàm velocitati agilitatique corporis, illam quidem ad athletarum usum, hanc autem ad belli utilitatem existimans pertinere. Exercebatur igitur quotidie mane currendo desiliendoque, vesperi autem luctando, ut stans aliquando in armis hostem contra se stantem complecti locoque exturbare posset vel terræ illidere, sive fugientem saltu cursuve assequi.'—*Ibid.* lib. iii. tit. 3.

Page 175, *note* a.

'Piraticâ nam classe Ponticum mare aliquandiu infestaverat, et ubi segnitiem pelagi aut reflantes ventos cernebat, non sinebat socios ignaviâ torpere. Hinc Homerus Achillem ὠκυπόδα, hoc est velocem pedibus, sæpe appellat.'—*Ibid.* lib. iii. tit. 3.

Page 175, *note* b.

'Alexander Macedo præter cæteros æquales suos currendi celeritate præstitit; et quum aliquando rogaretur à familiari quodam suo num quid in stadio certare vellet Olympiaco, respondit: *Agerem id quidem quàm libentissimè si mihi certamen cum regibus esset, verùm si cum privatis decernerem iniqua admodum victoria esset.*'—*Ibid.* lib. iii. tit. 3.

Page 176, *note* b.

'Marius quum septimum iniret consulatum jamque maximâ esset senectute quotidie in campo cum adolescentibus exercebatur, agilitatemque corporis ad arma tractanda et ad equitandum in tantâ ætate (annum enim octogesimum agebat) omnibus ostendebat. Ad cujus rei spectaculum complures concurrebant, non tam exercitum visuri quàm vires ac robur grandævi consulis cum juvenibus congredientis.'—*Ibid.* lib. iii. tit. 3.

Page 177, *note* a.

'Campum Martium Romani, in quo juvenes exercerentur, juxta Tiberim elegerunt, in quem post gymnica certamina se mergerent, non modo ut pulverem sudoremve abluerent et à lassitudine aquæ beneficio recrearentur, verùm ut nandi quoque usum perdiscerent, cui non tantum equites peditesque consuescerent, sed etiam equi ipsi, qui longè aptius liberiusque flumina trajiciunt si natare consueverint, nec undarum vorticibus facilè cedunt nec terrentur aquarum impulsu. Multos enim in historiis legimus beneficio optimè nantis equi vitæ periculum evasisse, et ex contrario nandi imperitiâ complures parvâ etiam altitudine

APPENDIX F.

impetuve aquarum obrutos ac demersos. Nec mirandum id quidem est, ut primùm enim umbilico tenus abluuntur, vix gradum figere possunt vel rapaciore undâ vestigium subducente vel lubricis saxis fallentibus.'—*Ibid.* lib. iii. tit. 4.

Page 179, note a.

'Ju'ius Cæsar quum ad Alexandriam pugnans irruente hostium multitudine solus à suis in ponte destitutus impetum ulterius ferre non posset, et multis missilibus impeteretur, in mare se mersit, ac nando per ducentos passus ad proximam navem evasit, elatâ lævâ, ne libelli quos tenebat perfunderentur, paludamentum verò mordicùs trahens, ne hostis spolio illo potiretur, utque tutior aliquantulum à telis esset.'—*Ibid.* lib. iii. tit. 4.

Page 179, note b.

'Admirantur summopere historici virtutem ac robur Sertorii, eumque omnium bellatorum pugnacissimum fuisse affirmant et alterum Hannibalem à Celtiberis appellatum. Ejus prima militia sub Scipione fuit adversus Cimbros, qui in Galliam transierant, in quo bello quum infeliciter pugnatum esset Sertorius graviter vulneratus equum amisit et indutus thoracâ et scutum atque arma tenens Rhodanum fluvium rapacissimum, qui inter Rhetos Noricosque fluit, per adversos fluctus nando trajecit et non sine magnâ hostium admiratione ad suos pervenit.'—*Ibid.* lib. iii. tit. 4.

Page 180, note a.

'Quâ quidem (*i.e.* peritia) se carere iniquo animo ferebat Alexander. Et quum aliquando maximum flumen cum omni exercitu transmittere opus esset, paucos equitum ad tentandum vadum præmisit: cujus altitudo primum summa equorum pectora adæquabat, mox ut in medium alveum ventum est cervice tenus equi abluebantur, tum milites omnes pavore torpebant, et nemo audebat in fluvium se mergere. Hoc quum cerneret Alexander, *O me deterrimum*, inquit, *qui nunquam nare didicerim!* Deinde confestim rapto incumbens clypeo audacter trajecit. Cujus exemplum alii secuti, partim nando, partim equitibus hærendo, partim autem sublatis in verticem sarcinis, hastisque nitentes pedibus transmisere, adeò ut ex tanto exercitu nihil præter pauculas sarcinulas desideratum sit.'—*Ibid.* lib. iii. tit. 4.

Page 181, note a.

Quanto etiam usui fuerit nandi peritia in primo Punico bello ex hoc videri potest. Concitaverant Pœni classem remisque impellebant eam, ut à Romanâ classe per fugam evaderent. Hoc quum cernerent complures Romani juvenes cuncti se è transtris in altum præcipitant, et subitò adnantes magnâ vi hostiles naves in portum pellunt retrahuntque; et hoc pacto Imperatori suo Luctatio capiendas parvo cum labore præbuerunt.'—*Ibid.* lib. iii. tit. 4.

Page 183, *note* a.

'In Thebarum enim expugnatione quum graviter vulneratus esset, Alexandrum in alium equum transilire neutiquam est passus, sed dolorem contemnens fortiter in officio permansit.'—*Ibid.* lib. iii. tit. 2.

Page 186, *note* a.

'Equitandi ratio à teneris annis percipienda est, antequam corpus obdurescat, obstipumve fiat, dum nervi sine rigore sunt et membra facile quoscunque usus accipiunt.'—*Ibid.* lib. iii. tit. 2.

Page 190, *note* b.

'Alexander Macedo ubi ab acie et armis quies aliqua aderat assiduâ venatione oblectabatur. . . . Et illi quidem aliquando colluctatio fuit adversus maximum ferocissimumque leonem, quem post magnam difficilemque pugnam summis viribus tandem stravit. Forte tum aderat Spartanorum legatus, qui vehementer admiratus dixit: *Utinam, Rex inclyte, pro magno aliquo imperio cum leone tibi esset certamen!*'—*Ibid.* lib. iii. tit. 6; lib. ii. tit. 1.

Page 197, *note* b.

'Proinde hoc genus aucupii nequaquam priscis seculis notum fuisse arbitror, quum de eo nihil clarè nec Græcè nec Latinè scriptum invenerim. Plinius tamen refert in Thraciæ parte super Amphipolim homines atque accipitres societate quâdam aucupari, et illos ex harundinetis ac silvis aves excitare, accipitres autem supervolantes deprimere illas captas aves, deinde aucupes cum illis partiri. Quâ ex re suspicari possumus initium fortasse hujus aucupii à Thracibus manasse.'—*Ibid.* lib. iii. tit. 7.

INDEX

TO

THE FIRST VOLUME.

ABA

ABARROW, John, father-in-law to Sir T. Elyot, lxii
Abiron, the punishment of, 13
Achilles, excelled Agamemnon in prowess, 16; taught to play the harp by Chiron, 39; excelled in running, 175
Acumen, the meaning of the word, 169
Ad judices, the game called, 288
Æsop, his fables suitable for children, 56
Æthiopians, war-dances of the, 221
Agamemnon, chosen as their leader by the Greeks, 16; called by Homer "shepherd of the people," 16; Mr. Gladstone's remarks on this phrase, 16, *note* b
Agricola, Rodolph, of Groningen, 72, and *note* b
Alcibiades, the character of, 250; instructed by Socrates, 250
Alexander the Great, his desire to see the harp of Achilles, 40; his fight with the lion represented in bronze by Lysippus, 46; the remark of a Lacedæmonian on the combat, 190; his gratitude to Aristotle, 52, 107; taught by Aristotle to read Homer, 59; caused maps to be made of the countries through which he passed, 78; his character as described by Q. Curtius, 85; by Arrian, 85, *note* a; his ambition while yet a child, 175; his regret at not being

AQU

able to swim, 180; his horse Bucephalus, 182
Alexander, Bishop of Alexandria, cl
Alexander Severus. See *Severus*
Alyngton, Giles, on the same commission with Sir T. Elyot, in Cambridgeshire, lxi
Ambassadors, called Orators in the sixteenth century, 119
Ancients, the, advantages possessed by, over moderns as regards education, 32
Angels, hierarchy of, according to theologians, 4, 6
Angelus de Clavasio, a casuistical writer of the fifteenth century, his remarks on dice-play, 274, *note* a
Angliæ, De rebus memorabilibus, an unpublished work of Sir T. Elyot alluded to by Ascham, clxxiv
Antoninus, Marcus Aurelius, the favour he showed to his tutor Proculus, 52; surnamed the philosopher, 103
Antwerp, Stephen Vaughan, the English Resident at, in 1531, lxxv
Apicius, the school of, characteristics of, 24
Appleton, Sir John Fetiplace buried at, xlix
Apprentices, children bound, in the sixteenth century, 139, 163, 168
Aquinas, Thomas, the author of *De Regimine Principum*, lxiv; his division of the heavenly hierarchy, 4, *note* a

ARB

Arbeau, Thoinot, his *Orchesographie*, the only practical work on the subject of dancing in the sixteenth century, 203, *note*; his comparison of ancient with modern dances, 231, *note* a

Archers, feats performed by English, in other countries, 298, 299, and *notes*

Archery, advantages of, in the sixteenth century, from a military point of view, 297; comprehended under the term artillery, 297, *note* c; decay of, in England, 301; its utility for sporting purposes, 303

Aristippus, dialogue between Plato and, ci; school of, characteristics of, 24

Aristocracy, the form it took in Greece, 8; its disadvantages pointed out, 10

Aristophanes, the comedies of, to be substituted for Lucian as a lesson for children, 57; suitable for learning by heart, 57

Aristotle, his remarks on music, 42; letter of Philip of Macedon to, 51; gratitude of Alexander the Great to, 52, 107; taught Alexander to read Homer, 59; at what age the *Ethics* of, should be read, 92; character of the early translations of, 92; remarks of Ludovicus Vives on the translations of, 92, *note* a; his definition of prudence, 240

Art, a taste for, how to be cultivated, 48

Art of English Poesy, The, by Richard Puttenham, clxxxii

Artillery, archery comprehended in the word, 297, *note* c; the word, when first used, *ibid.*

Artists, foreign, employed in England, in the sixteenth century, 140

Arundel, the Earl of, in the Low Countries, clxxxv

— the castle of, legend concerning, 184

Ascham, Roger, contrasted with Sir T. Elyot by Hallam, lxxi; his reference to Elyot's *De rebus Angliæ memorabilibus*, clxxii; his letter to Sir W. Paget about the *Toxophilus*, clxxiii; his remarks on riding, 182, *note*; his conversation with Sir T. Elyot about

BAR

archery, 290, *note* a; his definition of the word artillery, 297, *note* c

Athenians, the, democratical form of government adopted by, 9; their treatment of their public men, 18

Athletics. See *Exercises*

Attalus, the invention of dice attributed to, 274

Augustine, Saint, his condemnation of dancing, 204, 209

— de Augustinis, physician to Wolsey, his letter to Cromwell about Elyot, lxxxi.; was in England about 1536, cxxvii.

Augustus, Octavius, the Emperor, Rome not free from faction until the time of, 20; read Cicero and Virgil to his children, 33; Vitruvius dedicated his work to, 44; wrote poetry, 69; never spoke without preparation, 76; his favourite expression, 245; reproached for playing at dice, 277

Avarice, of parents, a great impediment to education in the sixteenth century, 98, 113; Peacham's remarks upon, 113, *note* a; Lord Bolingbroke's remarks on, in connexion with the law, 142, *note*

BACCHUS, the pagan worship of, 210

Baker, Thomas, fellow of St. John's Coll. Camb., his bequest to the University, cxxv

Ball (a dance), origin of the word, 204, *note* b

Ballads, in vogue in the sixteenth century, 211; derivation of the word, 211, *note* a

Banquet of Sapience, The, Elyot's work called, cxv

Barbary, what Roman provinces included in the country called, 191; derivation of the word, 191, *note* a; state of, in the sixteenth century, 191, *note* a

Barcelona, Chas. V. sailed from, in May, 1535, cxx

Bargenette, the dance called, 230

Bartholomæus, of Lucca, completed the *De Regimine Principum*, lxiv

INDEX.

BAS

Base dances, Robert Coplande's rare book on the manner of dancing, 203, *note*, in vogue in the sixteenth century, 230
Basset, Sir John, of Umberleigh, civ
Beasts, wild, none in England in the sixteenth century, 192
Bees, an example of monarchical form of government, 12
Berghes, the Marquis de, a friend of Sir T. Elyot, xcv
Berners, Lord, Deputy of Calais, civ
Beroaldo, Philip, author of *De Optimo Statu*, lxiv
Berthelet, the printer of *The Governour*, lxix, xcviii, xcix, civ, cxi *note*, cxiv, cxv, cxlii., cxlv
Beselles, the family of, Sir T. Elyot connected with, xxi
— Elizabeth, married Richard Fetiplace, xli
— William, the owner of Besselsleigh, xlii
Bevis, Earl of Southampton, the legend of, 184
Boleyn, Anne, lxxi, lxxxiii, xcv, cxliv
Bologna, Dr. Hawkins and Cranmer at, lxxxv
Bolton, Edmund, his *Hypercritica*, clxxxiii
Bonner, Bishop, a letter from, to Cromwell in 1532, xcviii
Bow, cross, the decay of archery caused by the introduction into England of, 303 ; its disadvantages, 305
— long, the shooting with, commended, 290 ; its superiority to the cross-bow, 304
Bowling, the game of, used in the sixteenth century, 296 ; described by Markham, 296, *note* c
— alleys, mentioned, 296, *note* c
Boys, at what age they should be withdrawn from women, 35 ; should be taught music for recreation, 42 ; also painting and sculpture, 43 ; Latin and Greek, 50, 54 ; put to study law too young in the sixteenth century, 132 ; taken from school too soon, 163 ; athletic exercises recommended for, 170; should be taught to ride young, 185

CAN

Bradenham, in Buckinghamshire, the seat of Lord Windsor, clxxxii
Brawle, the figure called, in dancing, 242 ; meaning of the word, 242
Brian, Sir Francis, lxxi, lxxii
Bruerne, the abbot of, in Oxfordshire, lvi
Brussels, Sir T. Elyot ordered to remain at, lxxvii ; his account of his embassy there, lxxxvi
Bryskett, Ludovic, his *Discourse of Civil Life, &c.*, lxx
Bucephalus, Alexander's horse called, 182
Buckingham, the Duke of, the trial of, xliv, xlv
Budæus, author of *De l'Institution du Prince*, lxx ; also of *Commentarii Linguæ Græcæ*, cxxxvi, *note* c
Burford Priory, picture of Sir T. More at, xliii
Burghley, Lord, *The Arte of English Poesie* dedicated to, clxxxvii
Burnet, his *Hist. of the Reformation*, errors in, xcii
Butts, shooting at, practised in the sixteenth century, 291

CÆSAR, Julius, his *Commentaries* not to be read by boys, 86 ; but by princes and their councillors, 88 ; his character as an orator, 107 ; his feat of swimming, 179 ; his horse, 183 ; an example of industry, 251 ; his power of dictating three letters at once, 252 ; his discovery of leap year, 265 ; his diligence, 265
Calais, visit of Henry VIII. to, in 1532, lxxxv
Calepino, Ambroise, his *Dictionary*, cxxxvi
Cam, the river, undergraduates drowned in, in the sixteenth century, 176, *note*
Cambridge, borough of, Sir T. Elyot, M.P. for, clxvi
— Castle of, Commission of Gaol Delivery for, lxi
— University, Sir T. Elyot not a student at, xxxviii ; Cromwell, High Steward of, clxv
Camden, the antiquary, alludes to Sir T. Elyot, xxxvi
Canning, George, his power of dictating two despatches at once, 252, *note* a

CAR

Cards, children of noblemen taught to play at, in the sixteenth century, 34; may be used for purpose of instruction, 283
Carleton, in Cambridgeshire, xlvi, lxxxviii, xci, clxiv, clxviii, clxxix, clxxx
Carteleigh. See *Kirtling*
Carthaginians, naval battle of, with Romans, 180
Carving, in wood or stone, boys to be taught, 43
Castle of Health, The, Elyot's book called, civ, cvi, cxvi, cxlii
Catlage. See *Kirtling*
Cato, learned to dance in his old age, 222, *note* d; his remarks on idleness, 270 *note* a
Catullus, the amatory character of his poetry, 123
Chalk, Broad, in Wiltshire, Sir R. Elyot's estate at, xxxiv, xlv
Chaos, meaning of the word, 3
Chapuys, Ambassador of Chas. V. in England, lxxi; announces Sir T. Elyot's appointment to Chas. V., lxxi; gives an account of an interview with Sir T. Elyot, lxxxiii; alludes to Elyot in a letter, xcvii
Charford, North, in Hampshire, Sir T. Elyot's wife born at, lxii
Charger, the advantage of riding a, in battle, 182
Charlemagne, the Emperor, his learning, clxiv, III
Charles the Fifth, Emperor, born, 95 *note* d; Sir T. Elyot appointed envoy to, lxxi; his appointment announced to, by Chapuys, lxxi; the object of Elyot's mission to, lxxii; injured by a fall from his horse, lxxvii; letter from Chapuys to, lxxxiii; Sir T. Elyot makes himself agreeable to, lxxxiv; behaviour of, to Elyot, lxxxvii; another letter from Chapuys to, xcvii; his expedition to Tunis, cxvii; imparts the news of Sir T. More's death to Sir T. Elyot, cxviii; his letters to the Vicomte de Lombeke, cxix, cxxi; a letter of, cxxi; his history written by M. Henne, cxxiii; his cause of complaint against Francis I., cxxiv; *The Golden Book*, written for, by Guevara, cxlv; allu-

CLE

sion to, in *The Arte of English Poesie*, clxxxiv; the *Institutio Principis Christiani* written for, by Erasmus, 95, and *note* e
Chasseneux, Alexandre, a French writer on jurisprudence, clxi.
Chelrey, Sir Thomas de, xxxii
Chess, the game of, commended, 284; English book on the moralization of, 285; its scarcity, 285; some account of Caxton's *Game of Chess*, 285, *note*; the *Moralizatio Scaccarii* generally attributed to Pope Innocent III. shown to be really written by Johannes Gallensis, an Englishman, 287, *note*
Cheyne, Sir John, his connexion with the Manor of Wanborough, xxviii
Childhood, the age of, 70
Children, easily contract bad habits, 30; to be tempted, not forced, to learn, 32; should learn to speak Latin, 33; acquire bad habits of pronunciation, 35; ill-treatment of, by masters in the sixteenth century, 50 addicted to gambling, 136
Childrey, a village in Berkshire, xxxii; the families of Fetiplace and Fynderne connected with, xli
Chiron, the Centaur, taught Achilles to play the harp, 39
Chotin, M., his account of the expedition of Charles V. to Tunis, cxxiii
Christchurch, Convent of, in Norwich, dispute between, and Corporation, xliv
Cicero, his *Topica*, when to be read, 72; his *De Partitione Oratoriâ*, 73; his definition of history, 82; his *De Officiis*, 92; as an orator and pleader, 157; his character drawn by Tacitus, 157; his Verrine Orations, 158; his praise of the law of the Twelve Tables, 160
Circumspection, defined, 253
Claisshe, the game called, 295
Claudius, the Emperor, his encouragement of art, 43
Clement, Mr., a friend of Sir T. Elyot, cxviii
Clerk, a term of reproach in the sixteenth century, 99
Cleves, Anne of, received at Blackheath, cxliv

INDEX. 337

CLE

Cleves, William, Duke of, book dedicated to, by Sturm, lxx.
Cleyburgh, Dr., a Master in Chancery, lvii, lviii, cxxix
Cocles, Horatius, the story of, 178
Coker, a village in Somersetshire, the original seat of Sir T. Elyot's family, xxvii
Colonna, Ægidio, his treatise *De Regimine Principum*, lxiv
Columella, recommended as a study, 13
Combe, Long, the manor of, l; letters dated from, lv, cxxvii
Comedies, contain a picture of life, 124; the rise of, sketched by Vives, 124, *note* c; advantages to be derived from, 125
Common places, lawyers', 153
Commoners, in the city of London, who are called, 2
Compton, Sir William, on a commission of Oyer and Terminer, xliv
Confirmation, a term of rhetoric answering to the legal term Replication, 151; defined in Wilson's *Arte of Rhetorique*, 153, *note* a
Confutation, a term of rhetoric answering to the legal term Rejoinder, 151; defined in Wilson's *Arte of Rhetorique*, 153, *note* a
Constantine, the Emperor, learning of, 111
Cooks, how tested before being hired in the sixteenth century, 114; wages paid to, in the sixteenth century, 114
Cooper, C. H., Mr., his *Athenæ Cantabrigienses*, xxv, xxvi, xxxviii, lxi; his *Annals of Cambridge*, clxv
— Thomas, Bishop of Lincoln, edited and enlarged Sir T. Elyot's *Dictionary*, cxxxix
Cordax, the Greek dance called, 229
Cornwall, Sir Richard Elyot in commission of the peace for, xxxvi
Coranto, the dance called, 230, *note*
Corybantes, the dances of, in Phrygia, 213
Cosmography, a knowledge of, recommended, 77
Coudray, Peter, father of Lady Windsor and father-in-law of George Puttenham, clxxxii

CYP

Coursing, recommended as an exercise for ladies, 195
Courtney, Sir William, foreman of a jury, xliv
Cox, Leonard, his *Art of Rhetoric*, 119, *note* b
Cranmer, Thomas, accompanied Elyot to Ratisbon, lxxvii; consecrated Archbishop, xciv; succeeded as Ambassador by Hawkins, xciv, *note* b
Crassus, the Roman General, his ignorance of geography, 79
— Lucius Licinius, the Orator, 155
Creation, the, natural order observed in, 5
Cromwell, Thomas, letter from Sir T. Elyot to, liv; was in Oxfordshire in 1528, lv; letters from Vaughan to, about Elyot, lxxv; letter from Augustine to, about Elyot, lxxxi; letter from Elyot to, complaining of the losses sustained by him abroad, lxxxv; another letter to, on the same subject, lxxxix; Master of the King's jewels, xcvi; letter from Elyot to, xcvi; the *Dialogus Marforii et Pasquilli*, sent by Bonner from Rome to, xcviii; created Baron Cromwell, cvii; *The Castle of Health*, dedicated to, cvii, cxlii; accompanied by a letter to, cix; styled Treasurer of the King's jewels, cx; appointed Master of the Rolls, cxv; visits the monasteries, cxv; letter from Elyot to, asking for some assistance, cxvi; letter from Elyot to, respecting a Royal Proclamation, cxxv; appointed Lord Privy Seal, cxxix; letter from Elyot to, complaining of poverty, cxxix; Elyot's *Dictionary* presented to, cxxxix; accompanied by a Latin letter to, cxl; present at the reception of Anne of Cleves, cxliv; Sheriff of Cambridgeshire, clxv; High Steward of the University, clxv
Crusades, the, of Richard I. and Edward I., 300
Curetes, the dances of, 213
Cursor, Papirius, why so called, 176
Cyprian, Saint, Bishop of Carthage, his sermon translated by Sir T. Elyot, civ

Z

CYR

Cyrus, King of Persia, his ignorance of geography, 79; anecdote of, erroneously attributed by Elyot to Xerxes, 271 and *note*

DACRE, Lord, Warden of the Marches, lii
Dacres, Robert, succeeds Elyot as Clerk of Assize, lvi
Daliance, meaning of the word, 276
Dancing, the art of, imported from France, 202, *note* c; early works on 202, *note* c; condemned by the clergy, 203; by Saint Augustine, 204; by the Fathers, 204, *note* b; in vogue at Rome during the decline of the empire, 205 and *note* a; indecent fashion of, in the sixteenth century, 206 and *note* a; idolatrous pagan, 207; reason of Saint Augustine's objection to, 208; his objection did not extend to all, 209; recommended by Sir T. Elyot as an athletic exercise, 202, 212; and by Thoinot Arbeau for the same reason, 212, *note* b; the supposed origin of, 213; Proteus supposed to represent, 215; supposed to have been first introduced at Syracuse, 217; mentioned by Orpheus and Musæus, 217; how practised in India, 218; supposed to be imitated from the motion of the planets, 218; of David before the ark, 219; warlike, of the Lacedæmonians, 221; of the Æthiopians, 221; circular, as practised at Erdeven in Brittany, 221, *note* a; of the Greeks, 222; and Romans, 222; of the Salii, 223; pantomimic, at Rome in the time of Nero, 224; account of, by M. Baron, 224, *note* a; commended by Socrates, 228; various manners of, practised by the ancients, 228; in the author's own time, 230; comparison instituted by Arbeau between ancient and modern, 231, *note*; revival of, in Europe, 232, *note* a; represents matrimony, 233; by a concord of the masculine and feminine qualities, 237; the first figure in, called *honour*, 241; the second the *brawle*, 242; description of the

DIC

brawle in Sir John Davies's *Orchestra*, 243, *note*; the third called *singles*, 246; the figure called *reprinse*, 253; the *double*, 262
Darrell, Sir Edward, of Littlecote, xxviii, xlii
Dathan, the punishment of, 13
David, King, his delight in music, 39; his dancing before the ark, 219
Deer, red and fallow, hunting of, 193; hunted by Henry V., 193, *note* a; by Henry VIII, 193, *note* a; by Charles the Fifth, 193, *note* a; killing, by shooting or coursing not recommended, 196; shooting, with the long-bow, 303
Defence of Good Women, The, cxliii.
Delos, dancing in, 217
Demaus, Mr., his *Biography of Tyndale*, lxxvi
Demetrius, the Phalerian, his advice to Ptolemy, king of Egypt, 81
— the Cynic philosopher, 224
— King of Parthia, golden dice sent to, 278
Democracy, of the Athenians, 9; the disadvantages of, 11
Demodocus, the blind bard, 64
Demonicus, the oration to, when published, cvi; ought to be learned by heart, 75
Demosthenes, the orations of, 75
Denny, Antony, gentleman of the Privy Chamber, cxxxiv
Derbyshire, the family of Fynderne seated in, xlvi
Dice, children taught to play with, in the sixteenth century, 34, 105; playing, declared illegal, 105, and *note* a, 272 *note* a; found in Middle Temple Hall, 136, *note* a; a sign of idleness, 272; the evils accompanying, 273; supposed to have been invented by Lucifer, 273; or Attalus, 274; cheating with, how practised in the sixteenth century, 273, *note* a; condemned by theologians, 274, *note* a, 275, *note* a, 276, *note* a; the Emperor Octavius Augustus blamed for playing with, 277; story of the Lacedæmonians finding the Corinthians playing with, 277; Chaucer's version of the same story, 277, *note*

INDEX.   339

DIC

c; golden, sent to Demetrius, 278; Chaucer's version of this story, 278, *note* a; ruinous consequences of, in the sixteenth century, 280, and *note* a

Dictator, when elected by the Romans, 19; the temporary character of the office, 20

Dictionary, the first Latin-English, compiled by Elyot, cxxxix

Diogenes, the Cynic, a saying erroneously attributed to, 112, *note* b

Dionysius, king of Sicily, reduced to teach grammar while in exile, 34

— of Halicarnassus, his works, 81

Dioscorides, the works of, read by Sir T. Elyot, xxxix

Discretion, the meaning of the word, 267

Divines, mealy-mouthed, 281

Dixie, Wolstan, Lord Mayor of London, clxxxviii

Doctrinal of Princes, The, cv

Dodieu, Claude, le sieur de Vély, lxxviii, *note* b; cxxi, cxxii, cxxiii

Double, the figure called, in dancing, 262

Dowsing, William, the iconoclast, clxxix

Drawing, the various advantages of, 45

Dugdale, his error in the *Origines* respecting Sir R. Elyot, xxix

Dulverton, Sir Richard Elyot's estate at, xlii

Dumb-bells, exercise with, 171

Dyer, Sir James, married Sir T. Elyot's widow, clxxxi

EAST, one of the printers of *The Governour*, lxix

Ecclesiastes, the book of, recommended to be read, 94

Ecclesiasticus, the book of, recommended to be read, 94

Eden, Richard, Clerk to the Privy Council, li, lx

— Thomas, letters patent granted to, lx

Edgar, king, the government of, 23

Education of Children, The, Elyot's book called, cxlii

Election, a part of prudence, 263

Elements, the four, the order of, 4

ELY

Eliot, Sir John, said to be allied to Sir Thomas Elyot, lx

Eloquence, the definition of, 116; the language of the law devoid of, 134; forensic, unknown in England, 149, and 150, *note* a; of Q. Scævola, 155; of Cicero, 157

Elyot, Sir Richard, his pedigree, xxvii; practises at the bar, xxvii; holds the manor of Wanborough for the Crown, xxviii; a Commissioner for Wiltshire, xxix, Serjeant-at-law, xxix; Attorney-General to the Queen Consort, xxx; his marriage, xxxi, and App. C.; a trustee for Sir John Kingston's son, xxxii; issue of his marriage, xxxiv; his chambers in the Inns of Court, xxxiv; his estates in Wiltshire, xxxiv; his visit to the monastery of Ivy Church, xxxv; Justice of Assize, xxxvi; in the commission of the peace for Cornwall, xxxvi; death of his wife, xli; his second marriage to the widow of Richard Fetiplace, xli; in the commission of the peace for Berkshire, xlii; Judge of the Common Pleas, xlii; knighted, xliii; summoned to Parliament, xliii; one of the arbitrators in a Norwich case, xliv; the part he took in the trial of the Duke of Buckingham, xliv; goes the Western Circuit for the last time, xlv; his will, xlv, and App. A.; his grave unknown, xlv

Elyot, Sir Thomas, erroneously called Sir *John*, xx, *note* a; ignorance of writers respecting him, xxii; probable date of his birth, xxx; accompanies his father to Ivy Church, xxxv; the friends of his youth, xxxvii; studied neither at Cambridge nor Oxford, xxxviii; studies medical treatises, xxxix; his acquaintance with Linacre, xl; Clerk of Assize on the Western Circuit, xl; his salary, xl; inherits estates in Cambridgeshire, xlvi; involved in a law suit, xlvii; inherits estates in Oxfordshire, l; Clerk of the Privy Council, l; his duties, liii; his name mentioned in the statutes of the realm, liii; Sheriff of Oxfordshire

z 2

ELY

and Berkshire, liv; writes to Cromwell, liv; mentioned by John Knolles, lvi; resigns the Clerkship of Assize, lvi; his successor in that office, lvi; his salary as Clerk of the Privy Council withheld, lvii; his health injured, lvii; the patent of his office cancelled, lviii.; his services unacknowledged, lix; buys the wardship of Erasmus Pym, lix; supposed to be allied to Sir John Eliot's family, lx; knighted, lx; compelled to pay Sir W. Fynderne's executor, lx; in the Commission for Oxfordshire and Cambridgeshire, lxi; also in the Commission upon Wolsey, lxi; his marriage, lxii; publishes *The Governour*, lxii; his obligation to Patrizi, lxv; his desire to augment the English language, lxvi; his critics, lxvii; his object in writing *The Governour*, lxviii; his imitators, lxx; appointed Ambassador to Charles V., lxxi; his instructions, lxxii; ordered to arrest Tyndale, lxxv; goes to Tournai, lxxv; communicates with Stephen Vaughan, lxxv; goes to Ratisbon, lxxvii; his account of Worms, lxxvii; of Spire, lxxviii; of Nuremburg, lxxviii, lxxix; his friendship with Augustine, lxxxi; returns to England, lxxxii; has an interview with Chapuys, lxxxiii; ruinous expense of his embassy, lxxxiv; Sheriff of Cambridgeshire, lxxxv; letter to Cromwell, lxxxv; his salary as Ambassador, lxxxvii; letter to Cromwell, lxxxix; erroneously said to have been sent to Rome, xci; probable cause of the error, xci; payment made to him as Sheriff, xciii; letter to Sir John Hackett, xciv; and to Cromwell, xcvi; publishes *Pasquil*, xcviii; and *Of the Knowledge which maketh a Wise Man*, xcix; letter to Lady Lisle, cii; publishes a *Sermon of St. Cyprian* and *The Rules of a Christian Life*, civ; dedicates them to his step-sister Susan Kingstone, civ; publishes *The Doctrinal of Princes* and *The Castle of Health*, cv, cvi; presents a copy of the latter to Cromwell, cix; his

ELY

answer to his critics, cxi; publishes *The Banquet of Sapience*, cxv; a Commissioner to inspect monasteries, cxvi; letter to Cromwell, cxvi; absent from England at the time of More's execution, cxvii; hears the news from Charles V., cxviii; the probable cause of his absence from England, cxix; may have joined the African expedition, cxxiii; letter to Cromwell about the Royal Proclamation, cxxv; letter to Cromwell asking for some of the lands of suppressed monasteries, cxxix; the cause of his apparent neglect, cxxxii; his *Dictionary*, cxxxiv; receives assistance from the King, cxxxiv; his remarks on previous lexicographers, cxxxv; his Latin letter to Cromwell, cxl; publishes *The Education of Children*, cxlii; dedicates it to Margery Puttenham, cxliii; publishes *The Defence of Good Women*, cxliii; present at the reception of Anne of Cleves, cxliv; publishes *The Image of Governance*, cxlv; is denounced by Bale as an impostor, cxlv; and by Dr. Wotton, cxlvi; this charge examined, cxlvii; the authenticity of the work discussed by Dr. Hody, clviii; the real interest of the work to modern rea'ers, clxii; purchases an estate in Cambridgeshire, clxiv; author of *How one may take profit of his enemies*, clxv; M.P. for the borough of Cambridge, clxvi; a second time Sheriff of Cambridgeshire, clxvi; publishes *A Preservative against Death*, and dedicates it to Sir Edward North, clxvii; his reasons for writing it, clxviii; his work *De rebus Angliæ memorabilibus*, clxxii; inquiry whether this was ever published, clxxiii; credited with other works, clxxvi; his state of health, clxxvi; his death, clxxviii; buried at Carleton, clxix; his monument, clxxix; his grave unknown, clxxx; apathy of the inhabitants of Carleton with regard to his memory, clxxx; his intestacy, clxxx; re-marriage of his widow, clxxx; inquisition upon his death, clxxxi; his heir, clxxxi;

EMM

supposed allusion to, in *The Arte of English Poesie*, clxxxiv.

'Εμμέλεια, the Greek dance called, 229

Emperors, Roman, why called *Divi*, 49

Encolpius, *The Image of Governance* supposed to be a translation from the Greek text of, cxlvi

Encyclopædia, meaning of the word, 118

England, condition of, under the Saxons, 22

Enopliæ, Greek dances called, 230

Epaminondas, the learning of, 107; his athletic exercises, 174

Erasmus, his treatise *De duplici copiâ Verborum, &c.*, 73; the date of its publication, 74, *note* a; his *Institutio Principis Christiani*, commended by Elyot, 95; some account of this work, 95, *note* f

Euryalus, the story of, 64

Exercises, athletic, why necessary, 169; indoor, different kinds of, 171; wrestling, 173; running, 174; swimming, 176; fencing, 181; riding, 181; hunting, 186; coursing, 195; shooting, 196; hawking, 197; dancing, 203; archery, 290; tennis, 292; quoits, 295; foot-ball, 295; classhe, 296; bowling, 296

Experience, why necessary, 264

Ezekiel, the book of, forbidden by the Jews to be read by children, 130

F ABIUS, Q. Maximus, styled *Cunctator*, 255

Falconers, questions put to, on being hired, 114; wages paid to, in the sixteenth century, 114, *note* a

Falconry, the origin of, not known, 197; mentioned by Pliny, 197; by Aristotle, 198, *note*; by Ælian, 198, *note*; was probably introduced from India, 198, *note* a

Falcons, damage done by, in the sixteenth century, 200

Fawley South, the manor of, xxxii, xxxiii, xlii

Fees, paid to counsel in the sixteenth century, 150, *note* b

Fencing, a necessary accomplishment, 181

FRE

Ferdinand, brother of Charles V., lxxx *note* a

Ferrara, the condition of, in the sixteenth century, 22

Festus, Sextus Pompeius, the grammarian, cxxxv

Fetiplace, the family of, now extinct, xxi, xxxii, l

— Edmund, xlix

— Eleanor, cv

Fetiplace, Elizabeth, wife of Sir Richard Elyot xli, xlii, l

— John, xxxii, xli, xlviii, cv

— Richard, xxxii, xxxiii, xli, xlii

— Sir John, xlix

— Thomas, xlviii

— William, xxxii, xli

Field, Richard, printer of *The Arte of English Poesie*, clxxxiii

Findern, the village of, in Derbyshire, xxxi; flowers, legend respecting, xxxi

Fineux, Sir John, Chief Justice of the King's Bench, xl

Finlason, Mr., on the Roman law in Britain, 158, *note* e

Fisher, John, Bishop of Rochester, his death reported to Charles V., cxviii; his sermon prohibited by Royal Proclamation, cxxiv, cxxv; his sermon translated by Pace, cxxvi, cxxviii

Fitzwalter, Lord, son of the Earl of Sussex, lxx

Florence, condition of, in the sixteenth century, 21

Football, the game of, objections to, 295; observations of James I. on, 295, *note* b; how played in Cornwall, 295, *note* b; suppressed in Scotland by James II., 296, *note* a; M. Misson's remarks on, 296, *note* a

Forsyth, Mr., his quotation from *The Governour*, 150, *note* a

Foxhunting, as an exercise, 194; not mentioned in the *Book of St. Albans*, 194, *note* c; remarks on, in *The Country Farm*, and in Turberville's *Book of Hunting*, 194, *note* c

Francis I., his interview with Henry VIII., lxxxv; complaint made against, by Charles V., cxxiv, *note* a

French grammar, in the sixteenth century, 55; Palsgrave's, 55, *note* a

FRO

Frontinus, Julius, erroneously called Fronto, by Sir T. Elyot, 52, *note* d
Froude, Mr., his description of 'the English pale' in Ireland, 88 *note* b; his view of the national hatred of idleness, 139, *note* d
Fuller, author of *The Worthies of England*, xxii, cxxxix, cxliii, clxv
Fynderne, the family of, extinct, xxi, xxxii, xlvii
Fynderne, George, xlvii
— Thomas, xxxiii, xlvi
— Sir Thomas, xxx, xxxiii
— Sir William, xxx, xxxiii, xxxiv, xlvi, xlvii, lx, lxi

GALEN, the works of, studied by Sir T. Elyot, xxxix, clxxvi; Linacre's translation of, xl; forbids wine unmixed to be given to children, 97; recommends athletic exercises, 169; his *De Sanitate tuendâ*, 171; recommends wrestling as an exercise, 173; his remarks on various kinds of exercise, 289
Gallensis, Johannes, his remarks on dice-playing, 276, *note* d; shown to be the real author of a work attributed to Pope Innocent III., 287, *note*
Galliard, the dance called, 230 *note*
Gambling, in the sixteenth century, 136
Gardening, in the sixteenth century, 28, 129, 132
Genesis, the book of, forbidden by the Jews to be read by children, 130
Genoa, condition of, in the sixteenth century, 21
Gentlemen, the reasons for preferring, as magistrates &c., 27; learning supposed to be unfit for, 99, 168, *note* b
Geography, the study of, recommended, 77; of Strabo, 80; of Solinus, 80; of Mela, 81; of Dionysius, 81
Georgics, the, of Virgil, to be read by children, 13, 62
Germanicus, the Emperor, the learning of, 109
Germany, ancient, compared with modern, by Æneas Sylvius, 87, *note* d
Gibeah, the town of, called Gaba, 95, 219

HAL

Gleek, a game of cards, called, ci
Glosses, the, of the commentators upon the Civil Law, 146, and *note* a
Gnatho, one of the characters introduced in *Pasquil the plain*, xcix
Godfrey de Bouillon, elected King of Jerusalem, 102
Golden Book, The, written by Guevara, cxlv
Governess, a nursery, necessary for children, 29
Governors, inferior, called Magistrates, 25; why they are necessary, 26
Grammar, Greek and Latin, in the sixteenth century, 33; not to be made irksome to children, 55; French, 55
Grammarians, good, scarcity of, in the sixteenth century, 163; who ought not to be called, 164; described by Erasmus, 164 *note* b; and by Pace, 164 *note* b; Quintilian's definition of, 165
Granvelle, de, the Cardinal, cxxi
Granville, Sir Thomas, father of Lady Lisle, civ
Greek, why it should be learned before Latin, 54; grammars in the sixteenth century, 55; knowledge of, in England in the sixteenth century, 145
Greeks, the ancient, various forms of government amongst, 8; advantage as regards education possessed by, over modern nations, 32; their love of dancing, 222
Grevile, Sir William, a Judge of the Common Pleas, xlii
Guevara, Antonio de, his *Dial for Princes* or *The Golden Book*, cxlv
Guns, hand, introduction of, into England, 303

HACKETT, Sir John, English Ambassador in the Low Countries, xciv
Hadrian, the Emperor, his taste for the fine arts, 44; his learning, 108
Hales, Sir Christopher, Attorney-General, lxi
Hallam, Mr., his remarks on *The Governour*, lxviii, 50, *note* c
Halyabbas, an Arabian writer, studied by Sir T. Elyot, xxxix

INDEX. 343

HAR

Hardy, Richard, sold Sherfield to Richard Puttenham, clxxxi

Hare-hunting, with grey-hounds, 195

Harpocrates, one of the characters in *Pasquil*, xcix

Hawking. See *Falconry*

Haywood, Mr. John, a friend of Sir T. Elyot, cxviii

Henne, M., his history of the reign of Chas. V., cxxiii

Henry I., called Beauclerk, 99; his character drawn by the Abbé Suger, 99, *note* b; by Fabyan, 99, *note* c; by Matthew Paris, *ibid.*; by Ordericus Vitalis, *ibid.*; by William of Malmesbury, *ibid.*

Henry VII., a pattern of circumspection, 256; the troubles of his reign, 257; the character of his laws, 258; the estimation in which he was held by foreign princes, 259

Henry VIII., his opinion of *The Governour*, lxviii; his instructions to Sir T. Elyot, lxxii; his interview with Elyot on his return, lxxxiii; his visit to Calais, lxxxv; his instructions to his Ambassador at Rome, xcii; his *Introduction into Grammar*, cxii; his loan of books to Elyot when compiling his *Dictionary*, cxxxiv; his expedition to Boulogne, clxxiii; inherited his father's good qualities, 260; his character drawn by Fulwell, 260 *note* c; by Cardinal Pole, *ibid*; by Mr. Turner, 261, *note* a; by Mr. Froude, *ibid.*; his fondness for the game of tennis, 292, *note* a; a first-rate shot with the long bow, 297, *note* b.

Hermogenes, the Greek rhetorician, 72: his works published, 73, *note* a

Herodian, Sir T. Elyot acquainted with, clvii

Herriard, in Hampshire, the seat of P. Coudray, father of Lady Windsor, clxxxii

Hesiod, the poet, Sir T. Elyot's opinion of, 70

Hierarchy, the order of the heavenly, 4, *note* a

Hiero, story illustrating the tyranny of, 216; the introduction of the name, accounted for, 216, *note*

IOP

History, the study of, recommended, 81; Cicero's description of, 82; of Rome, by Livy to be read first, 82; superior to every other study, 91

Hobby, the hawk called, description of, 199 and *note* a

Hody, Dr. Humphrey, his criticism of *The Image of Governance*, clix

Homer, verses of, translated by Elyot, 47; the works of, Elyot's opinion of, 58; studied by Alexander the Great, 59; resemblance between Virgil and, 61; mention of dancing in, 217, 222

Honour, to whom it appertains, 6; the first step in dancing called, 241; of what it is composed, 242

Horace, Sir T. Elyot's opinion of, 68; verses of, translated by Elyot, 123

Hormus, the Greek dance called, 230

Horses, Virgil's accurate knowledge of, 63; use of, for war, 182

How One may take Profit of his Enemies, Elyot's book called, clxv

Hunting, the favourite amusement of the sixteenth century, 104; an imitation of war, 186; as practised by the Persians, 187; the Greeks, 189; and Romans, 191; of deer, 193; fox, 194; hare, 195

ICKNIELD STREET, in Wiltshire, the old Roman road called, xxxii

Idleness, children allowed to grow up in, in the sixteenth century, 115, 161; Sir T. Wilson's remarks on, 161, *note* b; what it is, 270; Northbrooke's *Treatise against*, 270, *note* c; dice-playing a mark of, 272

Image of Governance, The, cxlv–clxiv

India, hawking probably introduced from, 198, *note* a; the worship of the sun accompanied by dancing in, 218

Industry, what it is, 249; a word recently introduced into the language, 249; how used in the statutes of the realm, 249, *note* b

Infants, signs of intelligence in, 29; their minds, how corrupted, 30; precocity of, 30

Interludes, in English, 126

Iopas, the minstrel, 64

IRI

Irish, the, rude character of, in the sixteenth century, 88
Isocrates, Sir T. Elyot's opinion of, 74; his advice to Nicocles, 82
Issue, meaning of the word as used by pleaders, 154 *note* a
Ivy Church, near Salisbury, visit of Sir T. Elyot to the monastery of, xxxv

JEROBOAM, called Hieroboaz, 14; elected by nine out of ten tribes of Israel, 14
Jesus College, Cambridge, Sir T. Elyot erroneously said to have been educated at, xxiv, xxxviii
Jethro, the father-in-law of Moses, called Hietro, 14
Jews, governed by two kings, 14; under the Roman government, 15; what books of Scripture were prohibited by, 130
Johannicius, the *Introduction* of, read by Elyot, xxxix
John, King, his charter to the county of Devonshire when restored to its proper custody, 192, *note* a
Joshua, the successor of Moses, 14
Jourdain, M. Bréchillet, his account of the early translators of Aristotle, 92, *note* a
Judges, the book of, placed by Sir T. Elyot among the books prohibited by the Jews, 130, *note* a; old Roman game called playing at, 288
Justice, potters and tinkers not fit persons to administer, 7; liable to be disregarded by a democracy, 11; rulers of the Jews chosen for their excellence in, 14; subordinate officers necessary to assist the sovereign in the administration of, 25; Henry VII. advanced, 258

KINGS, government of the children of Israel by, 14; government of Romans by, 18
Kingstone, John, xxxii, xlii, cv
Kirtling, the manor of, in Cambridgeshire, clxviii
Knighthood and Battle, the Cotton MS.

LEG

called, discovered to be a metrical translation of Vegetius *De re militari*, 177, *note*
Knolles, John, mentions Elyot's appointment as clerk to the Privy Council, lvi
Knowledge which maketh a Wise Man, Of the, Elyot's work called, xcviii, xcix

LACEDÆMONIA, story of the embassy from, and the Corinthian gamblers, 277
Lactantius, Sir T. Elyot acquainted with the works of, 48
Laertius, Diogenes, his history of phiosophy, c, *note* a
Lampridius, quotations from, in *The Image of Governance*, clv, clvii
Language, only without learning, evil result of, 116; the English, poverty of, 129, 243, 245, 268
Latin, children to be taught to speak, 33, 54, 116
Law, the English Common, founded on reason, 134; the difficulty of studying, in the sixteenth century, 135; boys put to the study of, too early, in the sixteenth century, 132, 136; at what age study of, should commence, 141; derived from the best foreign laws, 144; Civil, study of, in England in the sixteenth century, 145; language of, barbarous, 134, 149; pleading, conforms to the ancient rules of rhetoric, 148, 151; capable of being brought to still greater conformity, 154; stile of the ancient writers on the Roman, 156; study of the ancient Greek and Roman, recommended, 161
Law-Latin, barbarous, in use in the sixteenth century, 134, 142, 149, 154, 160
Law-Students, given to gambling in the sixteenth century, 136, and *note* a; their studies made repugnant to, 138; the great number of, in the sixteenth century, 145
Lawyers, Sir T. Elyot's opinion of, from his own experience, 137; require to be well paid, 150
Legh, a writer of the sixteenth century,

INDEX.   345

LEL

his plagiarism from *The Governour* in his *Accidens of Armory*, 184, *note* a
Leland, the antiquary, his notice of Elyot, xxxv, clxxiv
Lenthall, William, Speaker of the Long Parliament, purchased Besselsleigh, l
Leonidas, tutor to Alexander the Great, 37; alluded to by Hincmar, a writer of the ninth century, 37, *note* b
— King of Sparta, his opinion of Tyrtæus the poet, 71
Library, Royal, of Henry VIII., cxxxiv
Lily, William, Headmaster of St. Paul's School, xxxvi
Limitors, certain friars called, 234
Linacre, the founder of the College of Physicians, his translation of Galen, xl, 171; notice of him by Paulus Jovius, 171, *note* a; and by Pace, *ibid.*
Lisle, Lady, letter from Sir T. Elyot to, cii
— Lord, Deputy of Calais, ciii
Lister, Sir Richard, Chief Baron of the Exchequer, lxi
Littlecote, the seat of Sir E. Darrell, xxviii, xlii
Livy, his history, should be read by boys before any other, 82; his third Decade, 89
Λογοδαιδάλοι, rhetoricians called, 120
Lombeke, the Vicomte de, Ambassador of Charles V. in France, cxix, cxxi
Lord, to swear like a, use of the phrase, 275
Lovell, Lord, the attainder of, xxviii
Luard, Rev. H. R., Registrary of Cambridge University, his evidence as to Elyot, xxxix
Lucan, his *Pharsalia*, why to be read, 69
Lucas, Thomas, a Commissioner for Cambridgeshire, lxi
Lucca, Bartholomæus of, his *De Regimine Principum*, lxiv
Lucian, his Dialogues, a selection from, to be read by boys, 57; but not the whole, 58
Lucifer, supposed to have invented dice-play, 273
Lucretia, the rape of, by Aruncius, 18, 34

MON

Lycon, the Grammarian, 50
Lycurgus, instituted war-dances, 221
Lysippus, his statue of Alexander the Great, 46

MACHABEES, their government of the Jews, 15
Magistrates, the word employed by Sir T. Elyot to denote inferior governors, 25
Malshanger, the seat of Sir W. Warham, clxxxii
Man, the qualities natural to, 236
Mansuetude, the word, previously unknown in the English language, 268
Maps, use of, recommended, 45; of Ptolemy, 77; of Alexander the Great, 78; of Italy, 78
Marforio, the statue called, at Rome, xcviii
Marius, the Roman Consul, athletic exercises of, 176
Marsh, Thomas, one of the printers of *The Governour*, lxix
Marston, Long, the manor of, clxxxi
Martial, Sir T. Elyot's opinion of, 128; metrical translation of some verses of, 128
Master of the Rolls, Dr. John Taylor. lvi; Cromwell, the first layman appointed, cxv
Maturity, the word, newly-coined, 243
May-games, 266, and *note* a
Meautys, John, Clerk to the Privy Council, li
Mela, Pomponius, his geographical works, 81
Meleager, his fight with the boar of Calydonia, 190
Messengers, the name not applied to ambassadors, 119
Messina, Charles V. at, cxvii
Michal, her contempt for David, 219
Mirandola, John Picus, Earl of, civ
Modesty, Cicero's definition of, 267; the word, not previously known in English, 268
Molembais, P. de Launay, seigneur de, xcv, and *note* d
Monarchy, the best form of government, 11; examples of in nature, 12
Montpellier, the University of, cxiii

MOO

Moots, legal, in the sixteenth century, Sir T. Elyot's description of, 148
More, Sir Thomas, his picture painted by Holbein, xliii ; Sir Thomas and Lady Elyot friends of, lxii ; his *Utopia*, lxviii, lxix ; the news of his death communicated to Sir T. Elyot by Charles V., cxvii, cxviii ; effect upon Elyot's career of his friendship for, cxxxii
Morisco, the country of Morocco called, in the sixteenth century, 191
Morris, Francis, of Coxwell, son-in-law of Richard Puttenham, clxxxii
Moses, a monarchical ruler, 13
Musæus, the poet, mentions dancing, 217
Music, a taste for, to be encouraged by a tutor, 38 ; but not to be indulged to excess, 41 ; miserable, of Nero, 41 ; the efficacy of, 214 ; remarks on by Ascham, 214, *note* a ; by Puttenham, *ibid.* ; by Peacham, *ibid.*

N APLES, question whether Sir T. Elyot was at, cxx ; the family of Poderico of, cxlix
Naturess, Dr., executor to Sir W. Fynderne, lx
Negligence, of parents, one of the causes of the decay of learning, 98, 115
Nero, the Emperor, the music of, 41 ; story of, and the pantomimist, 227
Nestor, Dionysius, the grammarian, cxxxv, and *note* d
— the Homeric hero, his advice to Agamemnon, 254
Newmarket, inquisition taken at, on the death of Sir T. Elyot, clxxxi, and App. E.
Nicholson, Dr., Bishop of Carlisle, his notice of Sir T. Elyot, clxxiv
Nobleman, a, exercises necessary for, 181
Nonius Marcellus, the grammarian, cxxxv
Norfolk, His Grace the Duke of, his letter about Bevis, 185, *note*
North, Sir Edward, Chancellor of the Court of Augmentations, clxvii ; M.P. for Cambridgeshire, clxviii

OXF

Northbrooke, a writer of the sixteenth century, his plagiarism from *The Governour*, 272 *note* a, 273, *note* b, 277 *note* a
Nuremburg, the city of, Sir T. Elyot's account of, lxxviii, lxxix
Nurse, a wet, qualities indispensable in, 29 ; dry, or governess also requisite, 29 ; should be careful to speak good English, 35

O CTAVIUS, Augustus, the Emperor, Rome not free from sedition until the time of, 20 ; his speeches always carefully prepared, 76 ; his use of the word *matura*, 245
Omitted, passages, in subsequent editions of *The Governour*, 27, 48, 49, 159, 160, 304, 305
Orators, Demosthenes and Cicero the most celebrated, 75 ; as defined by Cicero, 117 ; by Tacitus, 117 ; require a heap of all manner of learning, 118 ; ambassadors called, in the sixteenth century, 119
Order, consists in difference of degrees, 3 ; perceptible in the creation, 5 ; is absent, where all things are in common, 7
Oribasius, the works of, read by Sir T. Elyot, xxxix
Orpheus, mention of dancing in the poems of, 217
Ortus Vocabulorum, the work called, cxxxiii
Orwin, Thomas, licence granted to, to print *The Arte of English Poesie*, clxxxvii
Ovid, the *Metamorphosis* of, Sir T. Elyot's description of, 67 ; the *Fasti* of, 67 ; Sir T. Elyot's metrical translation of the *Rem. Amor.* (131-136), 128
Oxford, Sir T. Elyot erroneously stated to have been educated at, xxiii
— Castle, commission of gaol delivery for, lxi
Oxfordshire, Sir T. Elyot in commission of the peace for, l ; Sheriff of, liv ; Cromwell's visit to, lv

PAC

PACE, Richard, his translation of Fisher's sermon, cxxviii; his *De Fructu*, 164, *note* b; his opinion of grammarians, *ibid*; his letter to Colet, 168, *note* b; his opinion of Linacre, 172, *note*
Padua, the University of, cxiii
Paget, Sir William, letter from, to Cromwell, cx; Ascham's letter to, clxxiii
Painting, a taste for, should be encouraged in children, 43; its advantages, 46; Englishmen inferior in the art of, to foreigners, 140
Palermo, Jean de Carondelet, Archbishop of, xcv, and *note* a
Pandects, the, 156
Pandenus, the painter, his admiration of Phidias, 47
Parker, Richard, his *Sceletos Cantabrigiensis*, xxiv
Parma, the Duchess of, Regent of the Low Countries, clxxxv
Partridges, scarcity of, in England in the sixteenth century, 200
Pasquil the plain, Sir T. Elyot's work, xcviii
Pasquinade, origin of the term, xcviii
Patrizi, Francesco, Bishop of Gaieta, his *De Regno et Regis Institutione*, lxv; not to be confounded with the following, 304 *note*
—— the younger, his philosophical works, lxv, his remarks on English archers, 304, *note*
Paulet, Richard, husband of Lady Windsor, clxxxii
Peacham, Henry, his *Compleat Gentleman*, lxx; his plagiarism from *The Governour*, 181, *note* a
Peleus, the father of Achilles, 36
Perotti, Nicolas, his *Cornucopia*, cxxxv
Persia, the mode of hunting adopted in, 187
Pheasants, scarcity of, in England in the sixteenth century, 200
Phidias, the sculptor, his ivory statue of Jupiter, 47
Philip, King of Macedon, his early life, 36; his rebuke to his son Alexander, 42; his letter to Aristotle, 51; his wish that Alexander should be instructed by Aristotle, 106

POE

Philosophy, moral, at what age to be studied, 91; education incomplete without the study of, 131; what it teaches, 162
Physic, Sir T. Elyot studied works on xxxix, cxi; the study of, in England in the sixteenth century, cxi, 145
Physicians, indignant with Elyot for writing the *Castle of Health*, cxi; the College of, foundation of, 146, *note*
Picus, John, Earl of Mirandola, civ
Pins, a game played in the sixteenth century, 295
Pius II., Pope, otherwise called Æneas Sylvius, 87, *note* d; his comparison of ancient with modern Germany, *ibid.*; his *De liberorum educatione*, 124, *note* a
Planets, the motion of the, supposed to have suggested dancing, 218
Plato, the works of, when to be read, 93; his celebrated saying, 104; his account of the origin of society, 117; on poets and poetry, 122
Plautus, Sir T. Elyot's metrical translation of *Amphitruo*, iii, 2, 127
Playfellows, to be carefully chosen for children, 31
Playing, at dice, forbidden by law, 105; at judges, 288; at soldiers, 289, *note*
Pleading, law, nomenclature of English, in the sixteenth century, 151; Wilson's rules for, in his *Art of Rhetoric*, 152, *note* a; should be brought back to the ancient form used by the Romans, 154
Plebs, the Latin word, meaning of, 2
Pliny, mention of bees in, 13; of hawking, 197
Plutarch, a saying of, quoted by Sir T. Elyot in a letter, cxxxii; his *Lives*, 18
Pocock, Mr., assigns a wrong date to Elyot's instructions, lxxii; erroneously attributes a letter of Sir T. Elyot to Augustine de Augustinis, lxxxi, *note*
Poderico, the family of, at Naples, cxlix
Poets, contempt for, in England in the sixteenth century, 120; why called *Vates*, 122; ancient, false notion

POE

concerning, 123; how they should be read, 131
Poetry, the first philosophy, 121
Pointz, Sir Frances, his *Table of Cebes*, clxvi
Pollard, Lewis, serjeant-at-law, xxix; in the commission of the peace for Cornwall, xxxvi; knighted, xliii.
Pompey, his passion for hunting, 190
Pontano, Giovanni, his *De Principe*, lxiv
Poor, the, in what respect wiser than the rich, 168
Populus, the Latin word, meaning of, 2
Port, Sir John, of Etwall in Derbyshire, xlvii
— Elizabeth, wife of George Fynderne, xlvii
Portugal, King of, his illegitimate daughter, xlviii
— Lady Talbot born in, xlviii; Royal Arms of, xlix
Preachers, Mendicant, 235, and *note* a
Preservative against Death, A, the last book written by Elyot, clxvii
Prévost, Jean, brought Patrizi's work to Paris, lxv
Pricks, shooting at marks called, 291
Pride, false, of parents, a cause of the decay of learning, 99
Primero, a game of cards called, ci
Privy Council, how constituted *temp.* Henry VIII., li
Probus, Æmilius, the works of, 18
— Aurelius, the learning of, 110
Proclamation, Royal, of Henry VIII, with regard to seditious books, cxxiv
Proculus, tutor to M. Aurelius Antoninus, 52
Profit, the word, synonymous with weal, 1
Promptorium Parvulorum, the work called, cxxxiii
Proteus, supposed to symbolise dancing, 215
Proverbs, the, of Solomon, to be read, 94
Providence, the definition of, 246
Ptolemy, Philadelphus, ordered the Scriptures to be translated, clviii
— the maps of, 77; the advice given to, by Demetrius Phalareus, 82
Public weal, a, definition of, 1; divided by Sir T. Elyot into two branches, 24; contains a perfect harmony of degrees, 43
Puebla, Fernando de la, Elyot's correspondence with, lxxxiii
Puttenham, George, hitherto supposed to have written *The Arte of English Poesie*, clxxxii; the authorship attributed to him by Mr. Haslewood, clxxxiii; shown not to have been the author of that work, clxxxiv
— Richard, heir to Sir T. Elyot, clxxxi; purchases an estate at Sherfield, clxxxi; marries, clxxxii; travels on the continent, clxxxvi; obtains the royal pardon, clxxxvi; presumably the author of *The Arte of English Poesie*, clxxxvi; in prison, clxxxviii; ill-treated by the Master of Requests, clxxxviii; his will, clxxxviii
— Robert, marries Sir T. Elyot's sister, xxxiv
Pym, Erasmus, wardship of, Sir T. Elyot buys, lix
— John, impeached by Charles I., lix

QUO

QUINTILIAN, the third book of, recommended as a study, 73
Quoits, the game of, played in the sixteenth century, 295
Quotations from ancient authors—
Ælian, *Var. Hist.* (xiv. 22), 217
Aquinas, *Summ. Theolog.*, 4, 6
Aristotle, *Pol.* (iii. 11 [16]), 26; (vii. 15), 32; (viii. 2 [3]), 42
Augustan History, 52, 288
Augustine, Saint, 204, 208, 209
Aulus Gellius, *Noct. Att.* (iv. 19), 97; (ix. 3), 106; (x. 11), 244
Cicero, *De Invent.* (i. 8), 149; (ii. 15), 153
— *De Officiis*, (i. 29), 239, 288; (i. 31), 138; (i. 33), 260; (i. 40), 267; (i. 43), 240, 267
— *De Oratore* (i. 6), 118; (i. 12), 116; (i. 28), 155; (i. 39), 155; (i. 44), 161; (ii. 9), 82, 117
— *Tusc. Disp.* (i. 26), 122; (ii. 26), 84; (iii. 1), 29
Columella, *De Re Rust.* (xi. 1), 270
Curtius, Q. (i. 2), 37, 51, 175; (i. 3), 52, 107

QUO

Quotations from ancient authors—
Eutropius (viii. 5), 53; (viii. 7), 108
Galen, *De sanitate tuendâ*, 98, 170, 171, 173, 174
Hieronymus, Saint, *Comment. in Ezekiel*, 130
Homer, *Iliad* (i. 250), 255; (i. 528), 47; (ix. 186), 40; (ix. 300), 40; (ix. 534), 190; (xiii. 730), 222
— *Odyss.* (iii. 245), 255
Horace, *Epist.* (ii. 1), 123
Isocrates, *ad Nicocl.*, 82
John of Salisbury, *Polycraticus*, 277, 278
Justin, *Historia* (i. 3), 271; (xxxviii. 9), 278
Lactantius (iii. 12), 49
Laertius, Diogenes, 51, 112
Lucian, *De Saltatione*, 217, 218, 221, 222, 227, 228
Martial, *Epigram* (xii. 34), 128
Nepos, Cornelius, *Epaminondas*, 107, 174
Origen, Saint, *Cantic. Cantic.*, 130
Ovid, *Rem. Amor.*, 128, 270
Patrizi, *De Regno et Reg. Inst.*, Append. F.
Plato, *De Rep.* (v. 18), 104.
— *Phædr.* (51), 120
— *Apol.* (5), 265
Plautus, *Amphitruo*, 128
Pliny, *Nat. Hist.* (viii. 64), 183; (x. 10), 198
Plutarch, *Alexander* (4), 37; (5), 37; (8), 59, 107; (15), 40; (40), 190; (58), 180; (61) 183
— *Apophth. Reg. et Imp.*, 82
— *Cæsar* (49), 179 (59), 265
— *Cleomenes* (2), 71
— *De Alex. Virt.* (9), 175
— *De Solert. Animal.* (14), 183
— *Numa* (13), 222
— *Pericles* (1), 42
— *Pompeius* (12), 190
— *Poplicola* (16), 178
— *Sertorius* (3), 180; (13), 191
— *Theseus* (9), 189
— *Timoleon* (15), 34
Proverbs (xxviii. 19), 240
Quintilian (i. 1), 31, 32, 54; (i. 3), 51; (i. 4), 165; (ii. 3), 168; (ii. 5), 82; (iii. 1), 120; (iii. 6), 149; (viii. 2), 255; (x. 1), 131

RUF

Sallust, *Catilina* (1), 244
Strabo (viii. 6), 190; (x. 3), 213
Suetonius, *Julius* (64), 179.
— *Octavius* (64), 33; (71), 277; (84), 76; (85), 69
Tacitus, *de Oratoribus* (30), 118, 158
Terence, *Eunuch.*, 127
Valerius Maximus (iii. 2), 181
Vegetius, *de re Milit.* (i. 10), 177
Virgil, *Æn.* (i.), 64; (vi.) 65; (xii.) 65
Vitruvius, 44
Xenophon, *Cyropæd.* (i. 2), 189
— *Œconom.* (4), 271

RAMPANES, the manor of, in Berkshire, xxxii
Rapin, the historian, his error with respect to Sir T. Elyot, xci
Rasis, an Arabian writer, his works read by Sir T. Elyot, xxxix; referred to by Burton in his *Anatomy of Melancholy*, 284, *note* b; and by Dr. Hyde, *ibid.*
Raynsford, Mr., lxxxix, xci, ciii
Rebeck, the musical instrument called, 225
Rehoboam, called Roboaz, 14; the tyranny of, 14
Repetition, recommended for children as an exercise for memory, 57
Reprinse, the figure in dancing called, 253
Res, the Latin word, definition of, 1
Rhetoric, when to be taught, 72; what it is, 119; the formal divisions of, 149
Riding, a necessary exercise, 181; should be learned early, 185; at what age, according to Galen, 186, *note* a
Robert, Duke of Normandy, styled Curthose, 100; elected King of Jerusalem, 102; taken prisoner by Henry I, 103
Romans, governed by kings, 18; valued martial prowess, 177; delighted in dancing, 222; adopted Greek words into their language, 268
Rome, the history of, 83
Roper, William, his story about Elyot and Chas. V., cxviii
Rounds, the dances called, 230
Rovers, shooting at marks called, 291
Rufus, William, his death, 101

Running, as an athletic exercise, 174
Rutters, meaning of the word, 301, *note* a
Rydon, Robert, Clerk to the Privy Council, l
Rymer, his MSS. used by Bishop Burnet, xcii

SALERNO, the school of medicine at, cxi, *note*
Salii, the institution of the, 223
Salisbury, Sir Richard Elyot's estate near, xxxiv
Saluces, François, Marquis de, cxxi.
Sandoval, the Spanish historian, cxxiii
Sardanapalus, the story of, 271
Saul, chosen king, 14; his evil spirit, 39, 214
Savigny, Jean de, printed Patrizi's work, lxv
Saxons, England under the, 22
Scævola, Q., the Roman lawyer, 155
Scepeaux, François de, Maréchal de Vieilleville, clxxxvi
Schoolmasters, their cruelty in the sixteenth century, 50; their small salaries, 113; their ignorance, 163; their occupation despised, 166; the description of them given by Erasmus, 167, *note* a
Scipio, Africanus, his fondness for Xenophon, 84
Scotch, character of the, in the sixteenth century, 88
Seckford, Mr., Master of Requests, clxxxviii
Selden, his remarks on *The Image of Governance*, cli
Senate, of Rome, instituted by Romulus, 20
Sermons, in England, in the sixteenth century, 126
Sertorius, called by the Spaniards the second Hannibal, 179; his feat of swimming, 179; his love of hunting, 190
Severus, Alexander, the Emperor, a letter alleged to have been written by him to the Bishop of Alexandria, cl; his *Axiomata politica et ethica*, clxi; his tutor, 52; his learning, 110; confounded by Sir T. Elyot with Septimius Severus 288, *note* b

Shalm, the musical instrument called, 225
Shalstone, in Buckinghamshire, Sir T. Elyot's step-sister buried at, xxxiii
Shefford, East, the seat of the Fetiplace family, xli
Sherfield upon Loddon, estate of, purchased by Richard Puttenham, clxxxi
Silius Italicus, his *Punica*, recommended to be read, 69
Singles, the figure in dancing called, 246
Sirach, Jesus, quoted, 25
Sleep, what amount of, sufficient for children, 97
Socrates, his commendation of dancing, 228; called the wisest man in Greece, 265
Solinus, the geography of, 80
Solomon, the Proverbs of recommended to be read, 94
Speech, why given to man, 264
Sphere, treatises on the, 77
Spire, the city of, Sir T. Elyot's description of, lxxviii
Staughton, Great, Lady Elyot buried at, clxxxi
Star Chamber, clerk of the, his salary, li
Stonehenge, Sir T. Elyot's acquaintance with, xxxvi
Strabo, the Geography of, 80
Strype, the historian, his errors with respect to Sir T. Elyot, xci, cxxviii
Sturm, John, his *De educandis Principum liberis* compared with *The Governour*, lxx; his remarks on the Latin language, 67 *note*
Suger, the abbé, his character of Henry I., 99, *note* b
Swear, to, like a lord, use of the phrase, 275
Swimming, long neglected as an athletic exercise, 176; practised by the Romans, 177; by Cæsar, 179; by Sertorius, 179; Alexander the Great ignorant of, 180; advantages of, 181
Sylvius, Æneas. *See* Pius II., Pope

TABLES, the game called, in the sixteenth century, 282, and *note* b

TAC

Tacitus, the Emperor, learning of, 110
— the historian, his works, 90; his definition of an orator, 117
Talbot, Lady, married to Thomas Fetiplace, xlviii
Tarquinius, Superbus, his exile, 18, 20, 34, 178
Tayler, Dr. John, Master of the Rolls, lvi, cxv
Tennis, the game of, 292
Terence, the false notion with respect to, in the sixteenth century, 123; Sir T. Elyot's metrical translation of, 127
Tetrarchies, the form of government established by the Romans in Judea, 15
Theatre, the Roman, Elyot's description of, 41
Thebans, their aristocratical form of government, 9
Theodosius, the Emperor, learning of, 111
Theseus, his fight with Phera, 189
Throckmorton, Sir John, married Richard Puttenham's sister, clxxxi; his epitaph written by Richard Puttenham, clxxxiv
Tildisley, William, Librarian to Henry VIII., cxxxiv
Tillemont, M. de, alludes to *The Image of Governance*, clii
Time, ancient, Sir T. Elyot's definition of, 197
Titus, the Emperor, his taste for the fine arts, 43
Toppi, a Neapolitan writer, cxlix
Tortelius, the Italian grammarian, cxxxv, and *note* e
Tragedies, at what age to be read, 71
Trajan, the Emperor, said to have been the pupil of Plutarch, 53
Trallianus, Alexander, his works read by Elyot, xxxix
Translations, of foreign works, recommended by Elyot, 269
Treasurer of the king's jewels, Cromwell styled, cx
Tribunes, Roman, elected by the people, 19
Tunis, the expedition of Chas V. to, cxxiii

VIR

Turgions, the dances called, 230
Tutor, the qualities necessary for a, 36; Phœnix, to Achilles, 36; Leonidas, to Alexander the Great, 37; the duties of his office, 38; should not fatigue his pupil, 38; should encourage a taste for music, 42; Aristotle, to Alexander the Great, 52; Proculus, to M. Aurelius Antoninus, 52; Frontinus, to Alexander Severus, 52 *note* d; Plutarch, to Trajan, 53; should encourage athletic exercises, 171; Socrates, to Alcibiades, 250
Tyndale, William, Sir T. Elyot ordered to arrest, lxxv, lxxvii

ULYSSES, the subject of the Odyssey, 60
Understanding, man approaches most nearly to God in, 5; those who excel in, ought to be highest in authority, 6; the Latin equivalent of, 131
Uzza, called Oza, 95; the fate of, 95

VALERIUS Maximus, copied by Patrizi, lxiv
Valla, Laurentius, his *De Elegantiâ*, cxxxv, *note* f; his remarks on the Commentators on the civil law, 147, *note*
Vannes, Peter, Secretary to Henry VIII., cxxvii, cxxix
Varro, Marcus Terentius, the grammarian, cxxxv; his derivation of the word public, 2
Vaughan, Stephen, the English Resident at Antwerp, lxxv; his letters to Cromwell, lxxv, lxxvi
Vaulting, as an athletic exercise, 186
Vély, le Sieur de, Claude Dodieu, lxxviii, *note* b; cxxi, cxxii
Venice, condition of, in the sixteenth century, 22
Venus, the Pagan worship of, 210
Verres, the Orations of Cicero against, 158
Verses, boys to be taught to make, 68
Versifiers, who were called anciently, 120
Virgil, resemblance between, and

Homer, 61; the *Bucolics* and *Georgics* suitable for boys, 62; also the *Æneid*, 64; to be preferred before any other Latin author, 66

Vives, Ludovicus, recommends the compilation of a good Dictionary, cxxxiii, note a; tutor to Charles V. and the Princess Mary, daughter of Henry VIII., 92, note a; on elegiac poets, 124, note a; his sketch of the rise of comedy, 124, note c; on dancing, 206, note a

WAR-HORSE, advantage of riding a, in battle, 182; of Alexander the Great, 182; of Cæsar, 183; of Bevis Earl of Southampton, 184

Water, to lay in, a proverbial expression, 258

Weal, public. See *Public*

Weight, putting the, as an athletic exercise, 171

Weston Colville, the manor of, xlvi, lx

William Rufus, his death, 101

Willingham, the manor of, clxiv

Willis, Browne, his references to Elyot, xxvi, lx, clxvi

Wiltshire, Sir Richard Elyot's estates in, xxxiv

Winchcombe, family of, bought East Shefford, l

Windsor, Lady, wife of George Puttenham, clxxxii

Wolsey, Cardinal, an arbitrator between the Corporation of Norwich and the Monastery, xliii; hears the suit between the Fyndernes and Elyot, xlvii; appoints Thomas Elyot Clerk to the Privy Council, l; increases the jurisdiction of the Star Chamber, li; his attainder, lxi

Wolman, Dr., Dean of Wells, li, lii; assigned to hear causes of poor suitors, li

Women, coursing a good exercise for, 195

Woodstock, men of, summoned to London by Elyot, lvi

Worms, the city of, described by Sir T. Elyot, lxxvii

Wotton, Dr. William, his censure of *The Image of Governance*, cxlv–clxi

Wrestling, as an athletic exercise, 173

Wynkyn de Worde, printed a sermon of John Fisher, cxxv; his *Ortus Vocabulorum*, cxxxiii

XENOPHON, the Cyropædia of, Guevara's *Golden Book* resembles, cxlv; Sir T. Elyot's opinion of, 84; on hunting, 186

Xerxes, story related of, by mistake for Cyrus, 271 and note a

ZENOBIA, one of the characters introduced in *The Defence of Good Women*, cxliii

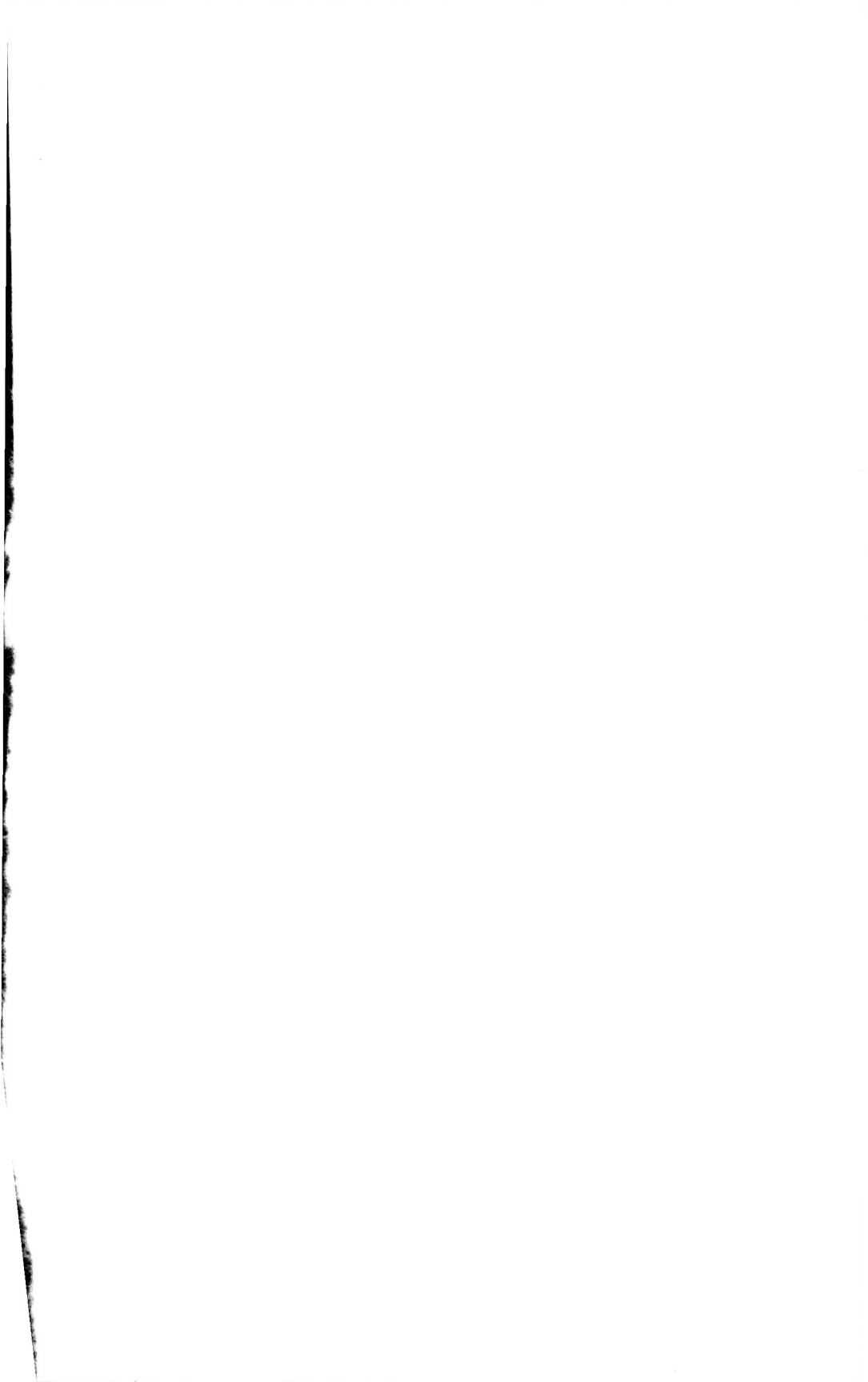